Dark Speech

THE MIDDLE AGES SERIES

Ruth Mazo Karras, Series Editor
Edward Peters, Founding Editor

A complete list of books in the series is available from the publisher.

Dark Speech

The Performance of Law in Early Ireland

ROBIN CHAPMAN STACEY

PENN

University of Pennsylvania Press

Philadelphia

Publication of this volume was aided by a grant from the Guggenheim Foundation.

10   9   8   7   6   5   4   3   2   1

Published by
University of Pennsylvania Press
Philadelphia, Pennsylvania 19104-4112

Library of Congress Cataloging-in-Publication Data

Stacey, Robin Chapman.
    Dark speech : the performance of law in early Ireland / Robin Chapman Stacey.
       p. cm. — (Middle Ages series)
    Includes bibliographical references and index.
    ISBN-13: 978-0-8122-3989-8 (cloth : alk. paper)
    ISBN-10: 0-8122-3989-X (cloth : alk. paper)
    1. Law—Ireland—History.   2. Law—Ireland—Language—History.   3. Sociological
jurisprudence.   4. Law, Medieval.   I. Title.   II. Series.

KDK156.S73   2007
349.41509—dc22

                                                                    2006050919

With love and gratitude to my family: Bob, Will, Anna, Dad, and Wes

And in sad tribute to the memory of two of the best: Patrick Wormald (1947–2004) and Professor Sir Rees Davies (1938–2005)

Contents

Ba dorcha didiu in labra ro labrasatar ind filid isin fuigiull-sin 7 nírba réill donaib flathaib in brethemnus ro-n-ucsat. "Is lasna firu-so a n-oenur a mbrethemnus 7 a n-éolus," oldat na flaithi. . . . "Ní tuicem-ni cétamus a rráidite." "Is menand," ol Conchobar, "biaid cuit do chách and-som óndíu; acht a n-as dúthaig doib-sium de, ní-s-ricfe. Gébaid cách a dréchta de."

Dark was the speech which the poets spoke in that case, and the judgement which they gave was not clear to the princes. "Their judgement and their understanding belong to these men alone," said the princes. . . . "Moreover, we do not understand what they say." "It is plain," said Conchobar: "henceforth everyone will have a share (in judging); except for what pertains properly to them therein, it will not fall to their lot. Each will take his own portions of it."

—"Pseudo-Historical Prologue to the *Senchas Már*" (text and translation by John Carey)

Introduction

It is often the case that the most important and unanswerable—and importantly unanswerable—questions are asked by those who know relatively little about the subject under discussion. Even the most naïve of queries from a community member in the back row can generate panic in an experienced lecturer possessed of a mastery of his subject, but not of its implications. And of course students are notoriously good at asking the sort of question which, if thought about at all honestly, could take days or even weeks to answer properly. So it is that this study also begins, for it too has its origins in one such confounded lecturer, and in one such unanswerable query. Some years ago, a student raised her hand in the middle of a lecture I was giving about the native Irish legal tradition and its relationship to the new dispensation prevailing in the island after the coming of Christianity. This was a subject I thought I knew relatively well, but her question was one that had never occurred to me, at least not in the terms in which she chose to phrase it. Why, she asked, would a literate jurist, working in a tradition that would ultimately produce the largest number of vernacular legal texts extant from anywhere in pre-twelfth-century Europe, choose in his own written lawbook to characterize the ecclesiastical legal tradition (but not his own) as *recht litre*, "written law?"[1]

The question was a good one, and on one level eminently answerable: the longevity and appeal of native oral lore, the impact of the Scriptures and other early Christian writings on a hitherto exclusively oral culture, the tremendous promise represented by the new technology of writing introduced to Ireland by Christian missionaries. On another level, however, it seemed considerably more difficult, and the longer I thought about it the less satisfied I became, both with the specific response I had given and with my general understanding of the nature of the legal and political world these texts were purporting to describe. It is one thing to know that oral legal procedures exist, and quite another to imagine how and why they might actually have worked. The jurist who so confidently distinguished his own tradition from that of *recht litre* did so not because he perceived writing to be unimportant, but because he believed the essence of his tradition to lie elsewhere, in the performance of law rather than in what was—or could ever be—written about it. The authority of the procedures with which he was familiar lay not in their sameness, in their ability to be captured in writing, but rather in their difference, in the potential for success or failure that existed every time a king proclaimed a verdict from a mound or a farmer intoned a contractual formula. Risk, not security, is the essence of performance, and performance, not inscription, was the essence of "the law" as our jurist knew it.

Performance has, to date, played a relatively minor role in our thinking about early medieval law and government.[2] Students of the judicial ordeal have long recognized the dramatic nature of the ritual with which they are concerned.[3] And other, no less theatrical productions have been detected as well in the insular and continental legal sources: the public perambulation of the boundaries of a contested estate, for example, or the throwing of earth on a person rendered liable for a kinsman's offense.[4] Indeed, scholars now remark quite openly on the performative element of early law, on the important role played by spectacle and show in the small, principally nonliterate cultures of the early Middle Ages.[5] But despite our acknowledgment of the theatrical character of early medieval justice, despite our increasing tendency as historians to make use of the terminology of the stage, we have yet to probe very deeply into the metaphor we employ. What does it mean to talk about law as theater, to speak about the "performance" of transactions as mundane as the sale of a pig, or as agonizing as the receiving of compensation for a dead kinsman? Historians have tended to use drama as a metaphor for legal rituals of this sort primarily in order to emphasize the publicity attendant on the affair. Attention has focused almost entirely on the issue of social memory, on the means by which imagery and symbol preserve in the collective consciousness of the nonliterate that which might otherwise be forgotten.[6] What will be argued in this book, however, is that the appeal to memory was but a single aspect of the role played by performance in early law. The power of legal performance, like that of other more easily recognized forms of verbal art, lay as much in its ability to create and to transform as to record.

And as with performance, so with speech and language generally.[7] Earlier generations of anthropologists sought to define the phenomenon of performance as precisely as possible, drawing boundaries around that which they thought did and did not constitute "performance" within the cultures they studied. Dell Hymes was particularly insistent that performance not become a "wastebasket," a formless category of action into which to dump everything we do not otherwise know how to characterize. He himself differentiated between *behavior* ("anything and everything that happens"), *conduct* ("behavior under the aegis of social norms"), and actual *performance*, which he argued constituted a subset of conduct in which those performing assume a "responsibility for presentation" to an audience or a tradition.[8] Richard Bauman refined Hymes's characterization somewhat, defining performance as "the assumption of responsibility to an au dience for a display of communicative skill,"[9] and pointing to the manner in which it "calls forth special attention to and heightened awareness of the act of expression and gives license to the audience to regard the act of expression and the performer with special intensity."[10] Another concept emerging as prominent in the literature was that of the frame—whether geographical, chronological, or ritual—within which performative actions often occurred and were interpreted by those who witnessed them.[11] Central to all of these constructs was an emphasis on the performer's deliberate shouldering of responsibility toward his tradition and his audience. As anyone who has ever actually put themselves forward in such a way will immediately recognize, performance is an inherently paradoxical venture, an occasion both of power and vulnerability, since a performer displaying his mastery of his art inevitably renders himself open to the assessment of others. "Did he perform poorly, did he perform well?" When the performance in view has legal as well as artistic implications, these are questions of more than passing interest.

The views advanced by Hymes and Bauman have greatly improved our understanding of the workings of performance within oral cultures, although the issues raised by their attempts to define and delimit the phenomenon are unlikely to be resolved any time soon.[12] It is possible to take a relatively narrow view of performance, defining it solely in terms of formal, framed procedures whose ritual aspect makes them easy to differentiate from more ordinary forms of social interaction. However, it is also possible to take a totally different view, defining performance more broadly, in a way that encompasses a wide variety of public demonstrations of status or affiliation, however brief and unpatterned. Traditionally, anthropologists have been as interested in the abstract as in the particular—that is, gleaning from the specific societies they study a sense of how their structures and traditions compare with those by which humans in other world cultures have historically organized themselves. In recent years, this emphasis on identifying what is "fixed" and "traditional" in society has waned somewhat. Culture tends now to be viewed as constructed and constantly evolving rather than as stable and immutable: for many scholars the challenge currently is to capture a sense of movement within the society they study rather than to establish boundaries around the practices by which in an earlier age that society might have been defined.[13] Even the most nuanced of anthropological works, however, continues to display an interest in categorizing and distinguishing like from unlike, not least because it is so difficult to engage in cross-cultural comparisons without to some degree reifying that which one seeks to compare. It was probably inevitable, for example, that Catherine Bell's excellent book on strategies of ritualization (of which great use is made in the present work) would be criticized for treating ritual as an "it" and falling thereby into errors she had objected to in others. It is difficult to write on a topic one cannot to some degree define.[14]

But while it is thus understandable that anthropologists should seek to delimit performance from other aspects of the cultures they observe, the historian's primary goal remains that of understanding the particular rather than identifying the abstract, a fact that permits—perhaps even mandates—a different approach. Having begun with performance, I quickly found that I could not end there. The more closely I contemplated those procedures standing out in the Irish sources as unquestionably "performative," the more apparent it became that in the particular culture in which I was interested, such events did not occur in isolation, but were rather part of a larger nexus of beliefs about language and the exercise of power. Indeed, the authority to which many of these procedures laid claim within the community was inconceivable outside the context of such beliefs, not least because the speech many of them envisaged resonated so deeply with authoritative words spoken (or written) elsewhere. Thus what had been a work about law and performance quickly became a book about the manner in which publicly enacted words and actions of all types—and their opposites, including silence—were used to construct legal and political relationships in a period in which traditional hierarchies were very much in flux. Such an overlapping of performance with speech and language generally is not unique to Ireland, although there are elements in early Irish culture that make it particularly difficult to separate one from the other (the political prominence of poets, for example). But while not unique to Ireland, it is certainly relevant to it: the more I read the more convinced I became that there was nothing to be gained by treating performance separately from the larger world of culture and language of which it was a part, and a great deal to be lost.

The connections between speech and performance are most visible in the scholarly fields devoted to their explication. Sociolinguistics as a discipline is closely linked to performance theory, a fact that should not surprise us. One seeks to understand the manner in which language structures and regulates social relations (and vice versa), while the other imagines the structuring of social relations through formalized events in which language often (though not inevitably) has a role to play. Ritualized events often involve speech that differs in various ways from the speech of ordinary everyday interaction, and that speech frequently draws upon or alludes to types of language significant in other contexts. Moreover, phenomena that are bread-and-butter issues to sociolinguists, such as situational language use, codeswitching, and the social differentiation of codes, are all elements potentially important to an understanding of performance, just as they are of the social and political structures of the culture within which that performance takes place. Especially important to a sense of the authority claimed by performance (as by public speech generally) is the sociolinguists' observation that, in many cultures, it is not only language per se, but the form and syntax of that language that matters. In other words, the power claimed for particular types of speech is in many instances directly related to the structures of which that speech is composed, just as the structures of which that speech is composed are directly related to the nature of the authority claimed for it. Hymes has commented on the manner in which all too frequently anthropologists rush through the form of the speech they are studying to get to its content, whereas linguists in a hurry to explicate its points of grammatical interest pay little attention to what the statement before them actually says. In many cultures, the power of speech cannot be easily separated from the nature of the language in which that speech is couched nor the venue in which it occurs: the best approach, he argues, is one that takes all such elements into account.[15]

This have I tried to do in what follows. In many ways, the idea that performative speech might be linked to power in early Irish society will not seem terribly new. It is a commonplace among Celticists to speak of the "power of the word"—to remark, for example, on the unusual language depicted in the sources as a hallmark of those with claims to otherworldly knowledge, or on the manner in which the powerful spoken genres of satire and praise exalted or diminished the standing of individuals in medieval Ireland and Wales.[16] But if this study thus seems to replicate trends in existing scholarship, it also departs from them in significant ways. Typically, the power of performance has been associated primarily with self-consciously religious or artistic contexts and individuals—druids, seers, poets, and the like—just as matters pertaining to language have generally been treated by literary specialists rather than by historians. Law and politics have not usually entered into the discussion, except in the form of comments on the political implications of satire or the historical links between jurists and poets.[17] The manner in which language structures legal relationships among persons living together within political communities has not been studied in detail, nor have the links between publicly enacted speech and performance as a more generalized phenomenon (for example, nonverbal as well as verbal performance). A particularly important aspect of this study is the relationship between politics and aesthetics. It is a central contention of this book that the production (and prevention) of verbal art was a key element in the structuring of legal and political hierarchies in early Ireland, both on the level of metaphor (how power was discussed) and of actualization (how power was acquired and exercised). Performance appears thus in this work not only as an object of study in its own right, but also as a lens through which to detect struggles for dominance otherwise obscured from view—a role it has hitherto played only rarely in existing scholarship.[18]

In short, what follows is less a study of the abstract phenomenon of performance than it is of the inner workings of one particular legal system, and less an inquiry into ritual per se than into the type of power ritual can effect. Although considerable attention is given to the sort of formal, framed performances on which the theorists are inclined most easily to agree, more than half the book focuses on the ways in which publicly executed speech of all kinds structures and defines the hierarchies within which people live. The first section of the book is devoted explicitly to performance per se, with Chapter 1 focusing on nonverbal performative events (or at least events that appear in the sources as nonverbal, which may of course be quite a different thing). With Chapter 2 we enter the specialized world of professional justice, and with it the elaborate rhetorical performances attributed to jurists and kings. The speaking of law was a matter of aesthetics as well as of office—indeed, what is implied in the texts is that the authority both of particular legal performances and of the men who produced them was in some sense linked to their aesthetic competence as performers, just as it was in the more obviously artistic venues of poetry and storytelling. Chapter 3 begins an exploration of beliefs about speech and language in early Irish society and, specifically, how both are depicted in the sources as actively shaping legal identities and relationships within the community (often in performance). Chapter 4 extends these observations by using the equation of speech and power to trace the tensions inherent in the restructuring of legal and judicial hierarchies in the wake of the advent of Latin European ideas about law and rule. With Chapter 5 we cross from the world of public speech to that of the written text by examining language which, in its very essence as language, comments on performative speech and its relationship to authority in a rapidly changing legal world. And the Conclusion departs from the lawbooks to argue that the perspectives revealed in the Irish sources can be helpful to understanding instances of performance documented elsewhere in medieval Europe.

A word must be said about the sources, and about the methodological presumptions on which this work is based. The focus of this study is early medieval Ireland, and the period under consideration the early Christian period, between the seventh and ninth centuries of the Common Era. From many points of view, Ireland is an ideal subject for such a study. Even apart from the impressive quantity of extant Latin literature— saints' lives, penitential and canonical collections, poetry, letters—there is a body of vernacular material unparalleled anywhere in the European west before the twelfth century. Most appealing is the literature, an irresistible corpus of tales running the gamut from the heartrendingly tragic, to the studiedly political, to the humorously obscene. The *Táin Bó Cúailnge* and attendant Ulster Cycle stories are merely the best known of this truly exceptional body of material. Recent translations have made many of the delightful tales centering around Finn and his band of heroes available at last to the general reader, although the numerous stories dealing with kings and peoples of the historical era are unfortunately still somewhat difficult of access.[19] Other vernacular genres exist as well, preserved in numbers unimagined by historians of other contemporary European cultures: genealogies, poetry, saints' lives, annals, and a full range of place-name tales.[20] All are testimony to the remarkably fruitful intersection of traditions and technologies occurring in the wake of the conversion of the island to Christianity. Whereas elsewhere in western Europe (apart from Wales, Scandinavia, and England), native literary traditions struggled only briefly before becoming engulfed by the tidal wave of Latin learning, in Ireland they not only survived but flourished under the new dispensation.

Prominent among these vernacular sources—not least by virtue of a reputation for inaccessibility—are the laws, available to scholars today in an edition that runs six single-spaced volumes without substantial notes, indices, or translations.[21] Their relative user-unfriendliness does not mitigate their importance. Unlike the law codes of the early English and continental realms, which at least made a pretense (and sometimes a great deal more than that) of being connected to the royal court, the Irish lawbooks emanated from a professional class of jurists, the earliest known anywhere in medieval Europe. More will be said later about these individuals and their work; suffice it to say at this point that the approach they took to the writing of law, while highly stylized and schematic, nonetheless betrays a keen awareness not only of the institutions themselves, but of the sociological underpinnings of those institutions. The tracts of which the lawbooks are composed are not records of legislation, but rather extended discussions of the structures and practices prominent in Irish society of the period: clientship, fosterage, social status, regulations concerning animal behavior, dues owed to and by the church, just to name a few. Some show signs of being structured around native patterns of learning—heptads, triads, and the like—whereas others testify to the tremendous impact of the church on both society as a whole and the legal tracts in which that society is described.[22] Historians differ in their assessment of the demonstrably "native" element in the extant legal corpus;[23] however, there can be little doubt that what remains to us today is the product of the joining of two great legal traditions, native and Christian, each with its own mythology, specialists, and sense of the past.

But how then can one hope to use legal sources of this nature—written, stylized, and largely descriptive in nature—to talk about something as immediate as performance? In continental or English tradition, historians would turn in such a situation to charters, trial records, or judicial transcripts to get as close as possible to the actual circumstances of particular cases. Sadly, as those familiar with the field already will know, such records do not exist in great numbers from pre-Norman Ireland.[24] Indeed, because the state of manuscript survival for Ireland is unusually poor, it is impossible even to determine whether what we are confronting here is an actual gap in the evidence or merely an accident of survival. Some historians have argued from the little that remains that a "Celtic" charter tradition embracing Scotland, Brittany, Ireland, and Wales once existed, even if only a tiny percentage of this tradition is extant today;[25] others have argued, by contrast, that the almost total absence of charter and diploma evidence from the period suggests that these genres never really gained enough popularity in Ireland to pass into general use.[26] The question is of more than passing interest, as the answer would likely reveal much about the manner in which the early Irish envisaged law and the legal process. Whatever the truth, it is unquestionable that our inability to resurrect the details of even a single "real-life" lawsuit poses a formidable obstacle to anyone wishing to resurrect the oral world within which disputes arose and were settled. The lawbooks can—and often do—describe the procedures by which legal cases were supposed to proceed from stage to stage in the course of their settlement. Regrettably, they do not tell us what actually happened in any one particular instance.

To say this is not to give up on any hope of understanding. It is true that a description of performance can never substitute for the reality of the thing itself. Musical notation can instruct a player in the mechanics of a song, but cannot capture the clarity of tones or exquisite lingering on notes that makes a performance memorable. Likewise in the legal setting, where an awkward gesture or infelicitous intonation of the voice might induce an audience otherwise predisposed to acquiesce in the claims being asserted to hesitate in their acceptance of them, or a judiciously timed snort undermine even the most tightly scripted of presentations. However, as Margaret Bent has demonstrated with respect to the more overtly performative world of medieval music, the reminder that performance was always for our subjects the primary referent can be valuable in itself.[27] This is particularly true of those aspects of medieval life that in modern culture are so far separated from one another as to suggest that there could never be substantial links between them. Politics and art, for example: when we speak of the "power of language," we mean usually to highlight the power of words to sway our emotions and fears. In the early medieval world with which we are concerned, by contrast, words exercised a power not dissimilar to that of the sword. These sources may not be everything we desire; they may not represent even to the remotest degree a satisfactory substitute for a recording or transcript of actual legal proceedings. For all their faults, however, they cannot help but reflect the quiet cultural presumptions on which the practices they describe were predicated, and this is valuable in itself.

Moreover, absence is not all there is. It is tempting for historians acquainted with the sources extant from other early medieval European cultures to describe the work of the Irish jurists in largely negative terms—in other words, in terms of what they did not leave us rather than what they did.[28] And it is certainly true that there are frustrations associated with working with lawbooks willing to discourse at length on the mechanics of distraint but obstinately opposed to mentioning even a single, historically verifiable cow. However, to focus only on what is missing does considerable disservice to what we have. It is true that what we write will inevitably be a history of ideas rather than of events; on the other hand, as Thomas Charles-Edwards points out, ideas about culture are no less real than are events themselves.[29] Indeed, as Philippe Buc has recently argued, the historicity even of seemingly well-attested occurrences may be more apparent than real: in a very real sense, we may *all* be writing a history of ideas, whether we realize it or not.[30] It is thus a working premise of this book that even the most stylized of descriptions opens a window onto the world that produced it. Irish historians may not be able to tell how a given procedure worked on a particular occasion, but they can recreate to a considerable extent the priorities and principles around which it was constructed. This is important, because it is precisely such an understanding of general principles that is so difficult to glean from the types of legal texts extant from other medieval European lands, where performative events tend either to be mentioned so briefly that one can no longer recreate the ideas that lay behind them, or else described in such transparently political ways that one cannot feel confident as to the accuracy of the account.

Some of the sources utilized in the following work present special challenges to the historian, and it is important to acknowledge those difficulties here at the outset. The closest we get to a description of how legal cases might actually proceed are texts that purport to reproduce, often verbatim, the words and gestures exchanged by parties in dispute. Some of these texts take the form of juristic citations of the formulas and verbal conventions appropriate to specific legal occasions. *Berrad Airechta*, for example, a tract on suretyship dating to c. 700, is actually constructed around a series of contractual formulas (supposedly) quoted word for word in the tract. Others belong more to the genre of fiction than of law per se: mythical accounts of lawsuits associated with pseudohistorical figures of the pre-Christian past. Often these accounts occur as individual scenes or episodes within a larger fictional narrative, although some exist as independent tales that would appear to have been deliberately composed in order to underscore the legal point being made. Obviously there are significant differences between these two types of "verbatim account," not least of which is the transparent artificiality of the fictional tales. On the other hand, there are important similarities as well. Even the tales occur almost always in legal contexts, either in actual law tracts or in collections that betray a considerable amount of legal knowledge on the part of their composers. Indeed, it is clear that a good proportion of these tales were actually used in the instruction of apprentice jurists, constituting such a standard item in the oral curriculum of the law schools that they could be referred to in shorthand form. Clearly, the presumption must have been that their general contours and characters would have been well known to all.[31] In fact, storytelling would seem to have an important educational technique for the Irish jurists generally. Law tracts of all traditions and regions made use of this tactic, drawing on characters from the literary realm like Finn, Cú Chulainn or Conchobar's jurist Sencha on the one hand, or characters from the Bible like Lucifer, Adam, or Cain and Abel on the other.[32]

Neither the formula summaries nor the tales can be regarded as uncomplicated sources with which to work. Insofar as they present their accounts as *ipsissima verba*, they are crucial to an understanding of the role played by language and performance in structuring and resolving legal disputes. Insofar as the principal characters in these texts are either exemplary or transparently fictionalized, however, they cannot be taken simply at face value. The words they report could have little or nothing to do with those spoken in the course of ordinary judicial proceedings—certainly it would be extremely unsafe to take them as representing anything even approaching a transcript of an actual legal case. On the other hand it would be equally unsafe to dismiss them, as both types of source would appear to be the work of specialists well versed in the language and procedures of the legal tradition. One must thus be very clear about the assumptions with which one approaches these texts and the questions one asks of them. It would be perfectly possible to argue, for example, that these are literary fabrications having little or nothing to do with the realm of the oral. In this case, sources of this kind would presumably be of limited value to historians interested in reconstructing the realities of an early Irish court. Alternatively, one could understand the language these sources report as broadly reflective of the language actually used in legal situations, a stance that would considerably broaden the possibilities inherent in such texts. Crucial to both of these interpretations is the issue of the manner in which these excerpts were composed and the purposes they were intended to serve. Can "word-for-word" accounts that make no pretense of being transcriptions be useful at all to historians working several centuries after they were composed?

These are complex questions on which scholars are likely honestly to disagree. In what follows below I have tried to grapple with these issues, realizing that not all are likely to be convinced by the conclusions to which I have come. My work makes no necessary presumption about the oral or written origins either of the tales themselves or of the language reported in them. The explosion of interest in the relationship between the spoken and the written word that followed on the pioneering work of Albert Lord and Milman Parry in the earlier part of the twentieth century profoundly reshaped our sense of the possibilities of the early medieval source material. Anglo-Saxon specialists were among the first to take up the challenge: passionate debates over the role played by "oral" formulas in the composition of the extant early English texts began in the 1950s and have raged furiously ever since.[33] Questions of a similar nature became in the 1970s a central theme in scholarship on early Irish literature as well;[34] most recently, Joseph Falaky Nagy's highly original examination of the manner in which medieval literati imagined the relationship between oral and written has taken the field to an entirely new conceptual level.[35] Much of the discussion in Celtic circles has centered on the archaic and oral (seeming) style of text known as *rosc* or *roscad*—a debate that is itself embedded in an ongoing and often bitter historiographical dispute between those who would emphasize the native element in our extant texts and those who would give the nod instead to Latin Christianity as the likely source for the forms and practices described in those texts.[36] Scholars who see Irish literature and law as having by definition originated in a Latin monastic milieu are likely to see *rosc* as literate in origin—both Johan Corthals and Kim McCone, for example, see *rosc* as a learned *Kunstprosa*, the literate product of a Latin-educated elite. Those less inclined to the monastic hypothesis are more open to the idea of an oral poetry memorialized in writing at a time subsequent to its composition. For these scholars, what remains to us is obviously *Kunst*; whether it is *Prosa* is another matter altogether.[37]

The debate over the origins of *rosc* is directly relevant to the issue of legal performance, for *rosc* is a style of language frequently associated with legal proceedings in the tales. The use of *rosc* is by no means confined to legal situations; it is the language also of prophecy, of supernatural insight, and of verbal contestation generally.[38] But it is definitely the language most closely associated with the spoken legal realm: judicial verdicts, for example, as well as the pleas of plaintiffs, are frequently depicted as having been couched in *rosc*. Happily, it is not the purpose of the present work to resolve the controversy over origins, and frankly it is difficult to see why all examples of *rosc* must have a single origin in any case. The fact that some passages can be shown to have originated in writing and to be contemporaneous with the prose by which they are surrounded has no necessary implications for the genre as a whole.[39] What is important for the purposes of this study is less the actual origins of such texts—whether they were composed orally or in writing, in other words—than the manner in which they were conceptualized in the sources that cite them. Almost always *rosc* is imagined as speech—instructional, admonitory, mysterious, mocking, prophetic, riddling, and even flirtatious, but largely oral in its conception and delivery.[40] This is particularly true of legal *rosc*. Even in the *Bretha Nemed* tracts, where rhetorical language is employed more generally than in any other legal texts, it is notable that the majority of *rosc* passages are phrased in a way as to indicate speech—either couched in the vocative or the first or second person,[41] or attributed explicitly to particular speakers.[42] One can thus speak in terms of *rosc* as a primarily oral style, as long as what one means by that is a type of language conceptualized as oral, regardless of whether it actually originated orally or in writing. In other words, the issue of how language is employed is separable from that of how it was composed: the fact that *rosc* existed as a literary style does not negate the fact that it was perceived by those who knew and composed it as being a type of language intimately associated with—indeed, deliberately evocative of—the oral realm.

To remark on the connection between *rosc* and the realm of the oral is not, of course, to demonstrate that the language attributed to mythical jurists in the tales has any necessary connection to how judicial exchanges would actually have proceeded in real life. It would be foolhardy to deny the possibility that what we are seeing here belongs more to the world of the imagination than to that of eighth-century Ireland. On the other hand, the consistent association with the oral, coupled with the fact that the legal tales in which *rosc* appears seem to have been authored by those with expertise in judicial affairs, make it difficult simply to dismiss this style as being nothing more than literary art bearing little relationship to the real-life world of the spoken word. When jurists in contact with ordinary legal arrangements in the localities wished to depict judicial statements in court, this was the language to which they turned. When they wished to instruct novices in the complexities of their craft, this was the language they chose to teach them. Unless we wish to believe that the jurists imagined the fictional cases they described in ways entirely different from the manner in which cases would actually proceed in the locality—and then taught those erroneous practices to persons entering their profession for reasons best known to themselves—we must take these accounts seriously.

Nor can we simply dismiss this style as a type of speech associated with the mythological past. Many *rosc* passages are attributed to characters imagined as having lived long before the coming of Christianity to the island—heroes like Cú Chulainn, for example, or kings like Conchobar and poets like Amairgen. However, there are clear indications in these sources that rhetorical speech was an aspect of contemporary legal life, and not merely a literary conceit designed to evoke a world now long gone.[43] *Rosc* may in certain circumstances evoke the past, but this is by no means a necessary association. All in all, seeing these accounts as literary fictions entirely divorced from reality seems by far the harder intellectual position to take—not least because the evidence taken together suggests that speech and language were crucial aspects of the negotiation of power relations generally in early Ireland, and not merely in legal venues.

This then is the most important methodological presumption on which this study is predicated: that even sources that do not allow one access to the language used in actual lawsuits still allow one to speak generally about the manner in which language was used in social and political contexts like law. This does not mean that we need to see the formulas and fictions cited by the jurists as reproducing the actual language used in any particular historical legal suit. What it does mean is that we need to consider seriously the possibility that these "verbatim" accounts reflect, in a general way, the linguistic character of legal events as they would normally have progressed. In other words, while these texts might not duplicate the words used by actual parties in dispute, they might well reproduce the nature of the lexicon upon which such parties would have drawn. While they might not reprise the syntax of any historically verifiable judge, they could easily duplicate the syntactical structures such a judge would have employed. And while they might not recapture the poetry of any particular judicial performance, they seem very likely to reflect the importance of law as a form of verbal art. Moreover, the remarkable consistency obtaining among these texts in terms not merely of language, but of the linguistic patterning of the occasions they describe—the alternation between plain and heightened speech, for example—suggests that we can also learn a lot from them about the manner in which the rhythm of the language itself contributed to establishing the authority of the event. Judges and litigants in these texts are not always—or even primarily—depicted as speaking in *rosc*. Heightened language tends to occur in particular sequences and situations, and only when the speech in question is regarded as especially privileged in its significance and authority. Again, this is evidence of great importance for those who would understand the performative dimension of early law. Just as the character of a musical piece is determined as much by the mathematical relationship existing between the notes of which it is composed as by the identity of those notes *tout court*, so also the evidence suggests that it was not only the words themselves, but how these words were put together, that mattered in legal affairs.

It is a given of our culture that whereas art and drama are by nature wild, imaginative, and risky, law is stolid, objective, and obscure. One has only to call to mind the popular stereotypes of the practitioners of each of these crafts to understand the ubiquity of the perception. Were an avant-garde artist to appear in a three-piece suit of tailored wool we would probably be surprised; were the justices of the Supreme Court of the United States to shed their robes in favor of Birkenstocks and sagging jeans, the shock might well be fatal. How accurate these stereotypes are for our own culture is best left to others to determine. What is unquestionably true is that such an opposition between art and politics, and between drama and law, does an injustice to the realities of life in the early Middle Ages. To use the term "drama" to describe the procedures by which order was achieved in early Ireland is not simply to employ a metaphor of convenience; it is, rather, to recognize the creative, fluid, and inherently risky nature of the event. Performances may transport the audience to unfamiliar settings and introduce them to characters previously unknown, but implicit in every such event is the very real possibility of failure—the chance that the audience will reject the proffered message and revert to a reality of its own choosing. It is this sense of daring and immediacy that the present study attempts to recapture, if only dimly, like a world glimpsed through the shadows that fall after the applause has finished and all have left the stage.

Chapter 1
The Play's the Thing

It can be difficult to escape our own preconceptions about what law is and how it works. So persuasive a model does our own legal system seem, so inherently "natural" its premises and foundation, that it is all too easy to find ourselves imaginatively bound by its central presumption that law derives its force from its existence as a text and its origins in the state. Recent work in legal anthropology is beginning to make us sensitive to other models; we now know more than we used to about the manner in which, for example, social and familial bonds functioned as ordering devices in communities in which institutions of lordship were inchoate or still developing.[1] The manipulation of cultural memory has also emerged as a key theme in new work on the subject.[2] To date, performance has played only a minor role in such discussions—in part because our evidence for it is so diffuse and difficult to contextualize, and in part because it is hard to know what to make of actions that, on their surface, appear so wondrously strange.[3] A clod of earth is thrown in the air, a withe is tied around the anvil of a smith: once having pointed to the obvious utility of such events as mnemonic devices, it is difficult to know what to say. And even in stressing the mnemonic aspects of such actions we may risk missing the point. For this is but a way of commenting on their apparent oddness, on the likelihood that such things would be remembered because they were inherently bizarre and set apart from the events of everyday life. But performative procedures, like other ritual events, did not exist outside the social matrix within which they took place; they gained meaning as much by what they echoed and alluded to as by what they sought to subvert.[4] Embeddedness as well as singularity was the source of their power.[5]

And it is precisely this embeddedness that has proved so difficult for historians working in the early medieval source material to reconstruct. There must have been a world of meaning in the grasping of a *festuca*, in the three long days that a plaintiff might wait publicly for his respondent to appear, likely even in the fact that King Alfred was washing his hands when one hapless suitor approached.[6] But our chances of tapping into this world from this distance seem disappointingly slim. We are outsiders to a system that relied for its efficacy on shared values and perceptions—values we no longer hold, perceptions we no longer comprehend. All too often we learn of performative procedures from the briefest of notices in a charter or law text: they appear as moments frozen in time, brilliant, seemingly solitary events whose relationship to the actions taking place around them is never clearly articulated. This has if anything heightened our sense of their inherent eccentricity. And yet without some way to assess their connection to the whole, we are likely to be quite lost in our attempts to interpret them. As Catherine Bell has argued, ritual is not an independent entity, it is a way of acting, and as such must be considered in the context of all other ways of being and doing.[7]

Performance was the unspoken assumption that lay behind all of the various procedures, partnerships, and *politesses* by which public order was defined in early Irish culture. Indeed, as will later be argued, there is evidence to suggest that law can reasonably be viewed as an actual performance tradition. To say this is not to imply that that which was "legal" was rigidly separated in Irish society from that which was not. Rather, procedures we would characterize as "legal" occurred and were interpreted within a broad tradition of public speech and action, one in which specialists and nonspecialists alike participated. There may seem a world of difference between the elaborate rhetorical performances of the jurists and the purposeful cattle driving of an aggrieved farmer, but in many ways the two are points on a single continuum of communicative display. As were indeed performances of an even less marked variety: the backdrop for the formal, framed procedures that most readily attract our attention was the ongoing performance of public and personal identity. In a society like this one, in which riches were not plentiful but status mattered very much, the continual acting out of social distinctions like class was not merely customary, but indispensable. Historians intent on understanding the necessity of display to the identification of rank could do worse than to contemplate a photograph published by Patrick Heraughty in his account of life on the tiny western island of Inishmurray before its evacuation in 1948. Kingship did not come to Inishmurray until sometime in the nineteenth century, and then largely as a result of the islanders finding themselves one night in a state of—in the words of those good Victorians Edith Somerville and Martin Ross—"not to say dhrunk, but in good fighting thrim."[8] But come it did, as an honorific institution at least. And in Heraughty's photograph, two fishermen sit side by side on a low wall: apart from the fact that one is slightly plumper and is smoking a pipe—and happens to be the reigning "king" of the island—there seems not a particle of difference between them.[9]

The display of status likely mattered more to medieval kings and nobles than it did to the inhabitants of Inishmurray, since examples of successful "identity performances" greet one at every turn in the Irish texts. The ostentatious exhibition of movable wealth is a constant theme in both the legal and the literary sources—the silver and gold articles worn by nobles or kings on festival days,[10] for example, or the precious brooch of the *aire déso,* "lord of vassalry," the gold and silver bridles of the *aire túiseo,*[11] "lord of precedence," and the elaborate costume of Étaín in the tale *Togail Bruidne Da Derga*.[12] Equally communicative were the different levels of clothing said to be accorded to young people in fosterage. The late commentary on *Cáin Íarraith*, the main tract on fosterage, goes into considerable detail on the subject of clothes, distinguishing between persons of various ranks according to a variety of different measures. Children of the freeman classes wore clothes that were dark or muted in color, whereas children of the noble classes had garments that were all or partially colored. Higher grades of nobles could expect new colored garments in every season; lower grades had to content themselves with new clothes on a more occasional basis. The sons of kings were to be dressed in a fashion far exceeding that accorded other children,[13] and gold and silver ornamentation was reserved for royalty and the very highest nobles in the territory.[14] This type of display was hardly unique to Ireland, of course: anyone familiar with medieval sumptuary legislation elsewhere in Europe would find all of this instantly recognizable.

Precious objects like gold and silver and lavish garments were rare, and often social rank was displayed through items of a rather more mundane character. One could, for example, write a very lengthy article on the social significance of food and public eating in early Irish society.[15] Recent work has made clear just how potent a symbol the consumption of food was in the ancient and medieval worlds; indeed, without some understanding of beliefs about food it would be impossible to make any sense at all of some of the most significant events in Christian history, like the Council of Jerusalem, or the sanctification of fasting, or the astonishing female saints about whom Caroline Bynum has written so compellingly.[16] Food mattered: who had it and who did not, who was given it and who gave it to others, who ate it, who refused it, and in whose company those actions were taken. One does not have to read very far into the sources to see how true this was for early Ireland as well. The "champion's portion" is a familiar topos in early Irish literature, as is the magical cauldron that provides automatically the cut of meat most appropriate to the status of the person it serves.[17] But the link between food and rank is more than a mere literary trope. *Uraicecht Becc* and *Críth Gablach*, two important tracts on status, define the grades they describe in large part by food, as does the clientship section of *Bretha Nemed Tóisech*—both the food that persons of those grades would pay to their lords in rent, and that which they and their retinues would consume or display themselves.[18] Food is also a dominant theme in the main tract on sick-maintenance, *Bretha Crólige*.[19] *Córus Béscnai* conceptualizes the mutual obligations of lord and client and of church and laity as "feasts," not least because food of various sorts (food-rent, hospitality, food given to pilgrims and the poor, the maintenance of criminals in sanctuary, and of course the holy "food" of baptism and communion) would have changed hands as a result.[20] And the principal tract on unfree clientship, *Cáin*

Aicillne, not only calculates the food-rent owed by various grades down to the last leek, but goes into such detail regarding the brewing of malt that one could follow the directions still today and come up with something reasonably potable.[21] Food preparation and consumption were even used as metaphors for essential concepts within the culture such as, for example, poetic inspiration,[22] or the taking on of lordship.[23]

It might be argued that passages like these functioned simply as picturesque illustrations of the amount of wealth associated with each rank and were not meant to imply a performative role for food. However, it is clear that at least in some cases the consumption of food had a deliberately public aspect to it. The public display of status-linked food is at least suggested by the vessels of milk and ale and the flitch of bacon that a freeman is said to have "in his house always" (*in[n]a thig do grés*).[24] And a public role for the consumption of food is surely implied by the numerous provisions detailing the foods and condiments to which persons of different ranks were entitled while on sick-maintentance visits. Fruits, garlic, celery, butter, ale, bacon—all were to be rationed out with mathematical precision according to the social standing of the injured person, with penalties to be paid if something due to a person because of his rank was lacking.[25] Similarly, judges appointed by the *túath* were entitled to a certain amount and quality of food in respect of their office: a legal poem on judicial refection declares that the offering of scrawny or cartilage-ridden meat to such officials is an act punishable by fines.[26] The fact that penalties were to be paid in both of these cases if the food provided proved unsatisfactory or inappropriate to the individual's status must imply the existence of some public assessment process, either before or during consumption. A brief passage in *Bretha Crólige* even suggests that in sick-maintenance cases, a particular "judge" was officially charged with ensuring that the food proffered matched the status of the individual who received it.[27] What we are seeing in such passages, I would argue, is not merely a description of the alimentary expectations of particular social classes, but the performance of social rank and legal indebtedness through the medium of public eating.

Status was also communicated by behavior and by the public exercise of specific prerogatives. Again, the basic principles here will be familiar to historians of medieval Europe generally. Rank was performed by where one sat in the royal hall,[28] the presence or absence of chained hostages in one's custody,[29] the retinue in or with which one traveled,[30] whether one was taught as a fosterling to ride,[31] whether one was taken away to be nursed,[32] one's ability to manipulate particular social codes,[33] and in numerous other ways. Sometimes official or exalted status was proclaimed through culturally specific rituals of deference, like the splendidly contrasting rising and kneeling by which Patrick is said by Muirchú to have been greeted upon his arrival at Tara.[34] Often, however, such recognition was communicated in a less self-consciously formal—though no less public—manner, as in the day's worth of reaping and plowing said to be owed by a people to its judge. It is nowhere indicated in the text how often this day's service might have been demanded. However, the passage in which it is discussed may imply that the judge received this labor on days he was actually sitting in judgment—in other words during the time he was performing the task for which it functioned as both compensation and symbol.[35] In any case it seems likely that its significance was as much performative as agricultural.

Social rank was not the only message that could be communicated by being and doing. A distinction very familiar to those who work in Irish and Welsh sources is that between status and honor. Thomas Charles-Edwards differentiates between the two thus:

Honour is opposed to shame: they are the publicly declared valuation put upon a person by those who know him. Honour and shame are not merely two opposing valuations, two opinions of a person generally held throughout his range of acquaintance; they must be publicly declared in some way or another. . . . Status, on the other hand, implies a hierarchy of social ranks within which individuals have their place. It implies systematic social differentiation using some general scheme of valuation according to occupation, wealth or whatever it may be.[36]

So tangible were these states of honor and shame that all free persons had an honor-price—an amount to which they were entitled in compensation in a case of injury or insult—as well as a wergild.[37] There were many ways in which a person's honorable or dishonorable state could be communicated to those around him or her. Some were verbal;[38] others centered primarily either on action or, frequently, on significant *inaction*—that is, inaction when action would usually be anticipated. A significant portion of Irish law is devoted to detailing the things that normally a person of a given rank would be expected to do that that person was not allowed to do because of his or her temporarily (or permanently) dishonorable condition. Dishonored kings or lords or women could not claim fines normally due to them;[39] impious churches or churchmen could not defend their rights to alms and donations;[40] persons who had been publicly proclaimed by their kindred were not entitled to normal maintenance and support;[41] unlawful lords and kindred heads could not exercise the jurisdiction they normally would be entitled to over family members and subordinates.[42] The usual understanding of such provisions is to see them as consequences for misbehavior, and there is obviously a great deal of truth to this view. However, we ought not to overlook the important role significant inactions of this sort played in publicly proclaiming to the community who was honorable and who was not. Honor and shame were not immediately transparent qualities, and they were susceptible to change without warning. Just as the wearing of a brooch or finely textured garment proclaimed the rank of individuals in society, just as the exercise of lordship displayed the fact of that lordship to all, so also did the nonperformance of prerogatives normally associated with a person's position bring his moral status into full public view.

Indeed, in the end it is perhaps the public-assessment aspect of such provisions that most clearly underscores their performative nature. For inactions of the sort referred to above were not merely ways of informing neighbors of a given state of affairs. Rather, they helped to bring that state of affairs into being by actively soliciting community collaboration in making the point they had to make. Community acquiescence would often have been necessary in order for the consequences enumerated above to take effect. People must agree that the behavior of a cleric or his church warrants a refusal to pay normal ecclesiastical dues; they must accept as a general consensus the labeling of a person as legally incompetent; they must recognize the ways in which a king or lord or kindred head has failed his subordinates in order to sanction the rejection of his authority. Their disapproval must be palpable, and it must be publicly marked. To characterize the restrictions placed on persons who fail in their obligations as mere penalties for misbehavior is to risk missing the dynamism of the event—the manner in which offender, victim, and community came together, or in some cases visibly did not come together—to display injustice.

The ongoing performance of identity, of status, and of moral standing was an essential element in how individuals in early Ireland ordered their lives and communities. But it was merely the backdrop against which the true legal dramas of the period were set, and it is time now to turn our attention to these more formalized procedures. As we have seen, performance theorists have long maintained the necessity of distinguishing between true performance and other aspects of human social exchange.[43] Bauman's emphasis on the "special intensity" with which an audience regards events he would label truly "performative" and Hymes's focus on the performer's responsibility to the tradition and audience within which his actions will be interpreted provide useful perspectives from which to view the early Irish material. For in Ireland also the distinction between full formal performance and the ongoing, considerably less structured display of identity at which we have been looking is an important one. Social order there was in large part vested in a number of ritualized procedures that would have to be regarded from any point of view as formal performances. Significantly, there is no indication in the texts that most of these procedures necessarily involved jurists or other recognized legal personnel, a fact that may imply that the performance itself was enough. It is at the workings of some of these spectacles that I wish to look in what follows.

Distraint

Formalized performances of the sort recognizable to theorists like Hymes and Bauman tended to cluster in early Ireland around moments of particular social danger. This is nowhere spelled out in the lawbooks as a conscious principle, but it is quite apparent in the distribution and content of the procedures themselves. What determined the formality of the procedure employed—the barriers it erected between itself and "ordinary" life—was less the specific nature of the original offense than the nature of the remedy by which redress was likely to be sought. Responses that replicated, and thus had the potential to inspire in turn, theft, the forcible occupation of land, or violence were precisely those most narrowly constrained by the boundaries of performance.[44] One of the most elaborate of these procedures—and possibly one of the most commonly employed as well—was that of distraint, the formal seizure of livestock or other property in order to satisfy a claim or force a defendant to come to law. Even by the elevated standards of the early Irish jurists, the rules governing distraint were exceptionally complex. This is in part because the process may have varied greatly from region to region, and because distraint as an institution was likely still evolving at the time the lawbooks were compiled. *Di Chetharshlicht Athgabála*, the principal text on the subject, appears to incorporate so many chronological layers that it could almost be regarded as an inadvertent history of the institution. Certainly the compiler was aware that changes had occurred over time in the procedures governing distraint, as he makes frequent reference to their origins and development in his work.[45] Moreover, the number of fictionalized characters and mythological events that he introduces into his tract is unusually large, a practice that is itself a likely indication of the relative novelty of much of what he has to say.[46]

The various procedures associated with distraint in early Ireland are fairly well understood at this point, thanks mainly to the work of three scholars, Honoré D'Arbois de Jubainville, Daniel Binchy, and, most recently, Fergus Kelly.[47] Binchy outlined what he perceived as the most important stages in the evolution of the procedure, and his account, though overly schematized, is still quite valuable. The earliest stage, he postulates, was that of unrestricted seizure of property by one person from another. Gradually certain limits were placed on the manner in which such seizures could be made: notice had to be given before the property was taken, and objects became subject to periods of delay before they were regarded as entirely forfeited to the claimant. By the time *Di Chetharshlicht Athgabála* was compiled in the eighth century, a complicated process known as *athgabál íar fut*, "distraint with a stay," had become (or at least was presented by the compiler as)[48] the standard procedure. Two other distraint rituals are also described in the tract. One was a procedure to be followed in cases where the person being distrained against was not the defendant himself, but a kinsman or guarantor (*inmlegon*)[49] acting on his behalf. The other, *tulathgabál*, "immediate distraint," involved fewer delays and thus stood as an intermediate stage between unrestrained seizure and full-blown *athgabál íar fut*. Binchy regarded this as an early phase in the evolution of *athgabál íar fut*, and there are certainly arguments to be made in support of this position. However, one should also keep in mind the possibility that *tulathgabál* represents another, contemporary but less formal (and possibly less lawyer-intensive) version of distraint known to the compiler.[50] The other major source on distraint in early Ireland, an Old Irish text only parts of which have as yet been edited and translated, seems to imply the existence of a variety of procedures in use at the time *Di Chetharshlicht Athgabála* was compiled.[51]

To characterize *athgabál íar fut* as "elaborate" is to understate the case considerably. The process began with the claimant giving a formal public notice (*apad, airfócre*) to the defendant that distraint was imminent; the length of this period of notice is defined in the text as five days if the person distrained is the actual defendant, and ten days if a kinsman or surety is being prosecuted in the defendant's place.[52] If no attention was paid to this notice, there next followed a period of "delay" (*anad*), during which time the object apparently remained in the defendant's possession. The length of this delay varied considerably: depending on the nature of the case or the gender of the participants (the two-day delays all involve women or women's handwork), the period of delay could last for one, two, three, or five days. Much of *Di Chetharshlicht Athgabála* is taken up by enumerating the various specific cases that fall under each category of delay, and there has been some discussion as to the rationales lying behind these categories, although no one has yet been able to identify a consistent principle governing their distribution.[53] Later commentaries assert that during this stage, the claimant was allowed to enter the defendant's land and segregate those animals liable to distraint from those which were not. A passage in *Berrad Airechta*, a law tract on personal suretyship dating to c. 700 C.E., suggests that a segregation of this sort might be done in certain situations. However, it is unclear whether this was a routine part of the distraint procedure at the time *Di Chetharshlicht Athgabála* was compiled.[54]

If the defendant had still made no move to answer the claim by the time the delay period had expired, the actual seizure (*tóchsal*, or *tobach*) of the property took place. According to the ninth-century glosses to the *Senchas Már* contained in H 3. 18, this had to be done in the early morning, before the animal (here presumably a cow, although sheep were also used as a milk source)[55] had been taken to the milking enclosure.[56] The animal(s) seized were then driven to a pound (*forus n-athgabála*) in the presence of witnesses.[57] Kinsmen of a defendant who were being distrained against on his behalf received a formal verbal notice (*fasc*) informing them of the place to which the animals had been taken. Binchy was of the view that this notice was a privilege granted only to those standing in for defendants and not to the offender himself, but one passage in the text seems to suggest that notice of this sort might have formed a normal part of the procedure.[58] After the animals had been seized, another delaying period, called *díthim*, literally "falling forfeit," or "lapsing," began, which probably lasted the same length of time as had the earlier delay period (*anad*) for that particular offense.[59] The H 3. 18 tract on distraint suggests that the animal might be moved at this point onto the green (*faithche*) of the claimant, his lawyer, or the *aire túise* (kindred representative); it would then fall forfeit after ten days if the offender had not met his obligation or offered a gage of his willingness to come to law by the end of this period.[60] Other tracts maintain that it was at the end of the period of lapsing that the actual forfeiture of the animals (*lobad*) began. This process took place over time, with five *séoit*'s worth of animals forfeit the first day, and three *séoit*'s worth every day thereafter.[61] Once forfeited, an animal could not be recovered, but the owner could ransom those cows not yet forfeited by meeting his obligations and compensating the claimant for his expenses in keeping the animals in the pound.

Many of the theatrical aspects of this process will doubtless be evident even to those unaccustomed to thinking in terms of a connection between performance and legal ritual.[62] The public execution of "scripted" actions, the directed use of gestures by which actors rendered tangible the relationship obtaining now between them—indeed, the fact of an audience itself, in that everything was done before witnesses—all underscore the importance of spectacle and display in matters of the law. Perhaps the most significant characteristic of the distraint procedure was the manner in which it constructed, for both participants and onlookers, a frame of reference within which its most dangerous aspects could be interpreted and contained. For the act of distraint was not transparently interpretable as a cultural practice. Without some guidance given bystanders as to how the actions taken were to be construed, it was likely to be misinterpreted. On one level, it was a display of the plaintiff's claim to ownership over the defendant's property; on another, it precisely recapitulated theft. Moreover, when cattle were the property seized, it recapitulated more than this. The *táin*, "cattle raid," was such a standard item in the vocabulary of lordly aggression in early Ireland that it is difficult to imagine that the forcible seizure of cattle by one neighbor from another would not carry overtones of threatened political subordination.[63] Indeed, although the word *áin* is probably the most common term used in the texts to describe the act of driving distrained animals from their owner's land, the word *táin* also occurs.[64] Implied within distraint were the serious offenses of theft and violent dispossession, and while this juxtaposition of lawful and unlawful may seem curious or even counterproductive, in fact it contributed to the effective functioning of the procedure by making the point quite clearly that those who did not observe law themselves had no right to its protection when they and their goods came under attack.

But if the potency of distraint lay to some degree in the manner in which it mimicked raiding and theft, so also did its threat. Violence too often begets violence, and if tempers are high the distinction between lawful and unlawful seizure may not be as evident as those concerned with the maintenance of social order would wish. Hence the care with which the jurists framed their procedure; hence also the numerous restrictions with which they hedged it about, detailing precisely which animals could and could not be taken and from where.[65] Anthropologists have identified many ways in which a performative frame can be constructed around an event.[66] Language as a framing device will be discussed in a later chapter; for now, it is sufficient to remark that the terminology of distraint probably itself functioned to some degree in this manner. The words used for the actual seizure of goods (*tóchsal* and *tobach*) were not generally used in contexts relating to theft, but carried within themselves implications of seizures done specifically in order to satisfy a legal claim.[67] Similarly, *athgabál*, "distraint," was usually (though not invariably)[68] distinguished from *gabál*, "seizing, conquest," although the significance of the preverb *ath-*, "second, repeated," in this context is still unclear.[69] And as we have seen, the more neutral term *áin*, "driving," was preferred to *táin*, "cattle raid."

Considerably more potent than these terminological distinctions, however, was the frame established by the movement of bodies in time and space.[70] The procedure made elaborate use of time: everything took place within the confines of an elaborate schedule to which participants were expected to adhere. There was a discernable beginning and a discernable endpoint to the process, and each stage between those two terminal points was itself strictly delimited in terms of time. Most—probably all—of these stages were initiated by explicit public action, and the beginning of one phase marked the end of the one that had preceded it. The *apad*, "notice," inaugurated both the procedure and the frame within which all subsequent events would occur. It is unclear precisely how the boundaries of the first delay period (*anad*) were indicated, although if as later sources suggest it was customary for the claimant to enter the defendant's land at the beginning of this stage to segregate the vulnerable animals from the rest, this would fulfill the function of notifying all that the period of *anad* had begun. The formal seizure of the animals marked the midpoint of the process and the beginning of the second period of delay (*díthim*). Again, it is unclear how the end of this stage would be indicated and the period of actual forfeiture (*lobad*) begun, but two different scenarios are offered in the texts for the forfeiture of the animals. In one, certain animals were forfeited every day—and would thus presumably have been removed from the enclosure by their new owner. In the other scenario, the beginning of the final forfeiture period was proclaimed by the physical removal of the animals to the green of the claimant or his representative. In each case, however, the passage from one stage to another, as from the beginning to the end of the frame itself, was measured in the daily rising and setting of the sun.

In addition to framing the procedure as a whole and marking the stages of its progression, time served several other important functions in urging the defendant to respond to the plaintiff's claims. It played a crucial role in helping to distinguish events happening within the frame from actions they might otherwise have resembled, most notably, of course, theft. The seizure of goods was not immediate, but gradual, with each new phase of the proceedings tempered by intervals of rest and negotiation—a clear attempt to defuse hostilities that might have been ignited by a more hurried or forceful confiscation. At the same time, the procedure was as inexorable as the march of time itself. Once begun, the movement of property from one person to another could only be stopped by an offer to come to law or by forfeiture—in short, by the rupture of the frame. The publicity attendant on all phases of the event ensured a mounting sense of pressure on the defendant as the claim moved through its various phases. And in the final stage, at least in the procedure outlined in *Di Chetharshlicht Athgabála*, the sense of urgency was heightened even more by the knowledge that the passing of each day brought further loss. Time moved slowly in the beginning to facilitate negotiation; it moved rapidly at the end to urge on the recalcitrant. It then stopped altogether, once the claim with which it was identified had expired.

Another important element in this procedure was its use of space. The slipping away of the animals from the possession of the defendant was dramatized by their gradual, but quite literal, distancing from his household. In the earliest stage, the animals remained in the possession of the defendant, and his lands remained free from outside intrusion. However, if the later commentators are right, on the expiration of this stage, an incursion was made onto his lands to segregate some animals from the rest. This event marked the first intrusion into the private space of the defendant: the intruder then withdrew, but the animals remained behind him enclosed and restrained. In other words, his space and his animals, while still his own, had been redefined as open and vulnerable to reordering from outside. When the delay period had itself expired, another entry was made on the lands of the offender and animals were physically taken from his possession into a neutral space, the pound. Sometimes this pound was located on the lands of the claimant, though it did not have to be.[71] No doubt, the closer the animals were to the claimant, the more pointed the message was likely to be; however, the true significance of the pound lay in its neutrality, in the symbolic access it afforded both claimant and defendant. The procedure outlined in H 3. 18 takes matters to their logical conclusion: in this version of the forfeiture process, the future passage of the animals from the possession of one man to another was dramatized by their removal from the pound to the green of the claimant or his representative—in other words, from a neutral space to one associated with the claimant.

Of course the hope was that things would never get this far. The defendant had the option at any point in the process to respond to the claim against him, and reconciliation rather than forfeiture was the true goal of the procedure. William Murphy has pointed out how so often in situations of conflict, authoritarian discourse or action masks a hidden, but highly significant, process of consensus building—a contrast he expresses in theatrical terms as the difference between that which takes place on- and offstage.[72] One of the striking things about the distraint process is how despite the harshness of what is actually being done (the seizure of property), considerable latitude is still given to the defendant. His chances for a negotiated settlement are spatially and chronologically drawn further and further out, only at the end falling finally from his grasp. Indeed, even in the actual seizing of the animals was an effort made to lessen the affront to his honor. For whereas part of the point of requiring the property to be taken in the early morning was presumably to ensure that the day's milk would benefit the claimant rather than the defendant,[73] there was an important spatial element here as well. Milking enclosures were usually located in the farmyard itself, close to the house.[74] Since the laws governing theft suggest that taking of property from the immediate vicinity of the house constituted the greatest offense to the honor of the victim, the seizure of an animal before it was brought into the enclosure was likely to have been perceived as less provocative than taking it from within his farmyard would have been.[75] The claimant's onstage actions spoke of dispossession and dishonor, but offstage room was made for consensus and the mutual saving of face.

But what then of the content of the drama taking place within this frame? Theorists have drawn our attention to the "emergent" and "strategic" qualities of rituals of this type, to the manner in which within a temporary dramatic setting, social roles and hierarchies can be transformed or realigned.[76] This was certainly true in Ireland, where neighbors, lords, and clients had by and large known one another since birth, and where landscapes were familiar and the succession of seasons unchanging. Procedures like distraint allowed, even commanded, the temporary reinterpretation of such constants. Local enclosures typically used for other purposes became the cattle pounds to which animals would be brought; seasons associated with plowing or reaping were broken up into artificial fragments as the claim progressed through its various stages. Persons standing in a particular relationship to others in the community took on new roles and personalities: neighbors became claimants or defendants, kinsmen and lords became guarantors and witnesses.

This is not, of course, to say that old identities and relationships were abandoned altogether. Certain people were not allowed to participate in distraint because of who they were outside the frame, for example; a son could not distrain against his father, while persons of particularly high or particularly low status were treated in another manner altogether when claims were lodged against them.[77] Similarly, a person's status or reputation affected whether his land could be used as a pound.[78] But the transformative nature of the frame is nonetheless evident. Hierarchies were created that did not necessarily correspond to those obtaining outside its bounds. Men of similar status could have the equality between them disrupted by the existence of a claim; persons of privilege could see their power over another diminished or redefined. The radically transformative potential of legal performance is perhaps most clearly visible in the rituals by which distraint was taken from the privileged (*nemed*) classes. In the case of a claim being brought against a craftsman or other professional, for example, the person seeking justice symbolically incapacitated the tools by which the professional pursued his craft—tying a withe around a smith's anvil or around the foot of a priest's altar, taking away the equipment of a doctor or the stave of a poet.[79] A professional who failed to respond to this summons before taking up his tools again could be distrained against in the ordinary way; in other words, his special status could be removed from him by the power of performance.

Equally telling is a procedure that has garnered particular attention in the wake of the dramatic hunger strikes undertaken by modern Irish prisoners in British jails. Fasting was a procedure used in medieval Ireland against persons of particularly high status, such as kings and high ecclesiastical officials.[80] In one version of the procedure, fasting is said to have been accompanied by a notice (*apad*) of the claim, although in *Di Chetharshlicht Athgabála* it seems itself to function as the preliminary notice that the taking of distraint is imminent.[81] In both cases, however, the idea seems to have been that a person would publicly not eat outside the house of the official against whom he wished to lodge a claim. The person fasted against was not allowed to eat until he had offered either a surety or a gage to guarantee that he would respond to the claim. If he ignored the claim, he lost all privileges normally due to a person of his status.[82] Binchy argued that the sanctions behind fasting and the incapacitating of a professional's tools lay originally within the realm of primitive magic and taboo. The claimant would fast to the death if necessary, and a high-status person who ignored his actions risked "pollution and . . . other quasi-magical consequences that might result from a death on one's premises."[83] By the ninth century, he claimed, the beliefs that had once made this practice so potent had waned, and fasting had become "a purely symbolical gesture . . . shorn of all its terrors."[84]

This may be true. However, it is notable that neither of the two main Old Irish tracts on distraint present fasting as an obsolete practice; rather, they seem to regard it as the most appropriate contemporary means of obtaining redress from an overwhelmingly powerful offender. Fasting remained a common theme in Irish secular and ecclesiastical literature throughout the pre-Norman period,[85] and it was still being reported in the annals as a real practice in the century the Normans actually arrived.[86] Perhaps then we need not resort to notions of primitive magic and taboo in attempting to make sense of the procedure. Indeed, its associations were likely to be and have remained multivalent throughout the period of its use. When practiced by clerics, as it would seem from the sources often to have been, fasting likely tapped into many of the same fears and beliefs visible in the high medieval ritual of the "humiliation of saints" discussed by Patrick Geary.[87] In the secular realm, fasting is easily comprehensible as a form of legal performance. Eating was, as we have seen already, a potent symbol in Irish culture. Moreover, munificence, hospitality, and the responsibility to care for and act justly toward inferiors were requisites of all forms of lordship, secular and ecclesiastical—as much a part of who a lord was and what he did as curing was for a doctor or saying Mass was for a priest. Partaking of food while another publicly went without was a display of social relations gone awry, of responsibilities left untended. It constituted a direct challenge to the obligations implicit in nobility and lordship—privileged identities which were in large part defined by the performance of such obligations. What one did not, one was not—and if one did not act like a lord, one had no real claim on the prerogatives associated with that rank. To eat in the face of the hunger of another was publicly to shirk that which made one what one was.

Performances that had the power to transform individuals and relationships had also the potential to reshape the society within which they were enacted. But this was clearly dangerous: alterations in social identity had in some manner to be contained lest anarchy ensue. Here the importance of the construction of a performative framework within which such transformations could take place is evident. Historians of social memory have demonstrated that rites of termination often recall, in order to repudiate, rituals of inception. Thus did Louis XVI's public trial and execution deliberately invoke the coronation the revolutionaries sought to contravene.[88] It may therefore be significant that each successive development within distraint looked back to what had come before. The final period of delay was predicted by the first; the actual forfeiture of the animals recalled their earlier removal from the defendant's custody. Performance was bounded at both ends, although this is not to say that events occurring within the dramatic frame had no impact on what went on outside. Indeed, the presumption that lies behind the framing of transactions is that in a small community no individual action is ever entirely discrete. Hostility may spill out beyond the boundaries to endanger the social fabric as a whole; the loss of a craftsman's status may eventually be actualized in the world outside the frame of symbolic distraint. But performance can function, if imperfectly, as a containing device, and it does, moreover, actively solicit the involvement of the community within which it occurs.[89] To give an audience a stake in a particular drama is to invite their participation in ensuring that the matter eventually reaches its desired end. Performance—by definition emergent and quixotic—can help paradoxically to script a stable outcome.

Tellach

Time, space, the movement of bodies within a conceptual frame: all were essential aspects of the manner in which distraint was effected and contained in early Ireland, and all were equally crucial to the procedures governing another dangerous flash point in this society, disputes over the ownership of land. The process by which a person registered a hereditary claim to land not then in his or her possession was called *tellach*, "entry." We are fortunate that the workings of this process have recently been discussed with great sensitivity and attention to symbolic detail by Charles-Edwards, since the main text on the subject, *Din Techtugud*, is particularly rhetorical and difficult.[90] Charles-Edwards reconstructs the outlines of the procedure as follows. Like distraint, *tellach* probably began with a preliminary notice (*aurfocrae*) to the person occupying the land that an entry was about to be made.[91] If the defendant showed no signs of conceding law by the tenth day following the *aurfocrae*, another notice (*apad*) was given; if the defendant was still recalcitrant, the claimant immediately made his first entry onto the land, crossing over the ancestral graves surrounding the estate with two horses in hand and accompanied by a single witness. He then withdrew and waited to see whether the occupant would agree to come to law. If the claim was conceded, the occupant gave a personal surety (*naidm*) on the fifteenth day that the claimant would be allowed to do a circuit (*immitecht*) around the land on the twentieth day, a display of ownership that Charles-Edwards compares to the medieval English custom of beating the bounds. The text does not say what form of guarantee would be offered in the case where the defendant contested the claim but agreed to come to law, although either a surety or a gage seems likely.

If the defendant remained obstinate, however, the claimant made his second entry on the twentieth day, this time with two witnesses and four horses—horses that he unyoked and allowed to graze before withdrawing. After this entry, if the claim was conceded, the surety was given on the twenty-fifth and the circuit around the land took place on the twenty-eighth. If no response was forthcoming, the claimant would then make his final entry on the thirtieth day with three witnesses and eight horses, which animals he publicly stabled and fed. This time judgment was immediate: if the occupant agreed to the demands of the claimant, the surety and the circuit took place that same day. However, if the defendant refused, the claimant now took possession by tending to his animals, kindling a fire on the hearth, and spending a night in the house. An interesting variant on this procedure was the form of *tellach* used by women, in which the periods of waiting and withdrawal were shorter, the animals ewes instead of horses, and the act of taking possession marked by the female claimant bringing onto the land in the final phase a kneading trough and a sieve.

Charles-Edwards's analysis of the process underscores many of the points made earlier with respect to distraint. He notes its highly dramatic nature, pointing to the bipartite nature of the ritual, the fact that the first two entries constitute ceremonies that display the claim, and the third a ceremony that displays the satisfaction of the claim.[92] The timing of the process was crucial to the ritualized pressure that was brought to bear on the occupant of the land: after each entry, he was given less and less time in which to decide to submit the claim to the decision of the judge, and in the final phase, judgment was immediate. As with distraint, the main goal was to force the occupant to agree to adjudication while allowing him not to lose face in the process: as Charles-Edwards remarks, "[t]he procedure begins by treating the defendant with tact, but it gradually becomes more peremptory."[93] Particularly interesting is the use of space: the focus shifts from the margins of the land where the grave markers are located, to the land itself, and finally to the house in the final stage, a progression that in the completed procedure unites "the ancient complex of house and land."[94] The prominence of time and space are likely to be old elements of the procedure, but Charles-Edwards argues that *tellach* was visibly evolving over time. The practice of allowing women to make legal entries onto land was likely a recent innovation in the law, as was the use of a preliminary notice in initiating the procedure. The latter Charles-Edwards sees as likely connected to the increasing intervention by judges in land claims and in the legal process as a whole.[95]

Our foray into *tellach* thus reveals a legal drama the contours and sanctions of which are very similar to what we saw earlier with respect to distraint: a highly framed procedure, with each phase clearly marked and delimited in time and space as is suitable for a sequence of events with such potentially serious repercussions for community order. It is also extremely predictive, in that each phase invokes another and constitutes in a sense a rehearsal for the final performance of taking possession. The horses predict their ultimate stabling and the farmwork that will be done with them; the kitchen utensils and the ewes predict the kindling of a fire on the hearth, the baking of bread, the making of cloth—in short, the resumption of normal domestic life. Only the breaking of the frame by the formal contesting or admitting of a claim can bring a halt to a process that otherwise leads inexorably to the surrender of the land—which must in the circumstances of a successful claim by the plaintiff be regarded as the normalization of relations within a kindred in need of reordering. It is no accident that the final resolution of the process both leads to and is symbolized by the creation of a productive household within the boundaries of the kindred's land: the family has been redrawn just as the land itself has been. The transformative potential of performance is nowhere more clearly visible than it is here.

Particularly striking in the *tellach* procedure is the omnipresence of boundaries: literal boundaries such as the grave mounds passed over by the claimant on his way into the enclosure, and symbolic boundaries such as the line between death and life he crosses as he goes.[96] The ten-day intervals in which the claim progresses—even the events following upon an occupant's concession of the claim—evoke the image of confines and limits. The giving of a *naidm*-surety was a highly bounded procedure, as will become evident in a subsequent chapter.[97] And *immitecht* literally means "going around"—in this case, presumably, the actual boundaries of the estate. In other words, even when the central path of the procedure was departed from, its entrances and exits were carefully monitored. This emphasis on boundaries is significant. Anthropologists have long disagreed on whether performative procedures reinforce or subvert the traditions they display, with some stressing the extent to which performance replicates and confirms preexisting cultural models,[98] and others emphasizing the potential inherent in "emergent" productions of this kind for norms to be undermined or questioned.[99] We cannot from this distance say anything about the physical gestures or tones that might have been used in practice to undermine or comment upon the process as it played out in real life. However, what is still visible is the manner in which the symbolic structure of *tellach* was designed to disguise and suppress the tensions that would necessarily have followed on a challenge to the kindred and an enforced redistribution of its land. For the images the process evokes are that of an intrusion ultimately absorbed, of relationships reordered and harmonized in the wake of probing from outside. The kindred closes in upon itself after the problem has been remedied; whole once more, its borders are restored as if nothing had happened. Dissent is folded into consensus. The symbolism of the process aims to save face for all—not only for the individual occupying the disputed land, but for the kindred as a whole, which is envisaged as standing intact at the end of the process as it had at the beginning, forever guarded by its dead.[100]

The existence of a performative frame was thus important to *tellach* in a variety of ways. Not only did it serve, as it did in distraint, to defuse the violence that might erupt in the course of an unpopular claim, it displayed the integrity of the kindred even in the face of a forced readjustment of their lands. It also, and crucially, provided onlookers with a context within which to interpret the actions of the claimant. Like distraint, *tellach* recapitulated an event that was both exceptional and everyday. Conjoined in distraint were the quotidian act of cattle driving and the threat of unlawful seizure; conjoined in *tellach* were the routine activities of every householder and the danger of the invasion of private land by outsiders. Each accomplished what it did in part by performing what was normal within a frame the very existence of which proclaimed the abnormality of the event. Without the witnesses, the ritual entry, the timing, the large number of horses (*Críth Gablach* posits two as the number a normal freeman would have on his farm),[101] it would not be easy to distinguish *tellach* from the actions of an average farming day. The ritualized activity of the claimant is embedded within, and makes sense only with reference to, the larger body of communal activity: it is the frame within which it occurs that make these actions privileged in their significance.[102] Ritual here both echoes and alludes to ordinary life; it also subverts it by, in this case, carving it up into artificial segments that call attention to the distance between what is lived and what is contrived.

The frame also provides a context within which to interpret the many different symbols at play in this procedure. Catherine Bell has termed ritualization a particularly "mute" form of activity, one that accomplishes its task "without bringing what it is doing across the threshold of discourse or systematic thinking."[103] She identifies as a common characteristic in the creation of a ritualized space the generation of oppositional symbols— binaries from within the shared culture that are deployed explicitly or implicitly within a ritual to order relations within it and, by extension, within the community for which it has meaning.[104] Such binaries are a visible and important part of the *tellach* procedure. The movement of the claimant and his animals across the borders of the land generates a series of contrasts that simultaneously structure and evoke the unity of the kindred that is the ultimate goal of the procedure: dead and alive, outside and inside, enclosed and free to roam, yoked and unyoked.[105] Indeed, as Bell suggests, contrasts of this sort can generate taxonomic associations of their own, associations which, though never articulated, are so powerful that they can evoke symbols otherwise unspecified. Thus does the articulated warmth of the hearth, when described in the context of the binaries mentioned above, imply the unstated existence of a colder world outside the kindred—a contrast particularly appropriate in a culture that uses physical warmth as a metaphor for filial piety and cold for its opposite.[106]

The nature of these symbols also contributes to another important aspect of ritualization, the manner in which it grounds what is done in cultural perceptions of the cosmic order, and hence in a source of authority believed to originate from outside the local community itself. The invocation of the binaries discussed above—death and life, settled and wild, hot and cold—have the effect of rooting *tellach* in recognized patterns of the Irish cultural universe.[107] Another striking example of this is the use of gender symbolism in the process.[108] Women's involvement in the claiming of land and in the *tellach* procedure as a whole was likely an innovation, as

Charles-Edwards has argued. But the manner in which they were integrated into the earlier all-male pattern of action is significant. Women were allowed only to claim a life interest in the land they sought to occupy, and even this was largely an exception to the normal rules governing female inheritance, which forbade the transmission of kindred land to women in most circumstances.[109] In the procedure outlined in *Din Techtugud*, the limitations on women's rights in this respect are articulated as symbols: the shorter intervals between entries mark their shorter tenure of the land, the ewes and baking implements underscore their centrality to the domestic sphere but also, by contrast with the horses of the man, their exclusion from the arable holdings of the kin. Translated into symbol, such restrictions appear as just part of how things are—an aspect of the order of the universe that mandates acceptance even in the face of doubt.[110] Another example of the grounding of controversial actions in the cosmic order is the prohibition against making an entry against a church across its burial mounds (*tellach cille tara fert*). The medieval church frequently supported its claims to permanent ownership of lands donated or bequeathed to it by asserting that it, unlike individuals and families, was ever living. Symbolically speaking, the church had no dead, and therefore no boundary between death and life for a claimant to cross.[111]

Sick-Maintenance

A third danger point in Irish society, along with the seizure of property and land, was violence, and here again performance played an important role in channeling potentially devastating personal tensions into an outcome acceptable to the community. Not all violence was unlawful in early Irish society: violence stemming from war,[112] dueling (a form of ordeal), self-defense, accident,[113] boys' games,[114] and other comparable encounters was regarded as inevitable and treated as justified in the sources. Certainly attempts were made to limit the impact of such interactions—the regulations governing the conduct of any deliberate act of violent encounter were numerous and strict. Duels, for example, were the subject of careful negotiation and arrangement between the parties before any blows were struck, and since their stated goal was to "illuminate falsehood" in a given dispute, the presumption in the law tracts at least was that the violence involved would often not be fatal.[115] Guarantors charged with the enforcement of a debt were allowed to use force to exact an overdue payment from a defendant, or even to imprison him; however, their actions were strictly tied to the terms and time limitations of the obligation in question.[116] One of the more interesting exemptions from normal penalties against violent behavior was that granted to a "first wife" in this polygynous society: violence inflicted by a first wife (*cétmuinter*) against a second wife (*adaltrach*) brought into the family by her husband was regarded as lawful as long as it did not result in her death. The glosses say that the exemption from penalties lasted only three days after the marriage, which would suggest the existence of a period of ritualized (or real) violence during which the affronted wife could act out her anger on a public stage.[117]

Lawful violence was not, of course, the most significant threat to social harmony, and several tracts describe an institution called "sick-maintenance" (*othrus*) through which victims of illegal violence received as partial compensation for their injury support and medical attention from the person who had wounded them.[118] The procedure is complex, and there are some contradictions in the extant sources. However, its basic stages are fairly clear: once a serious injury had been inflicted unlawfully on someone, the victim was given protection from further assault and then borne away from the "bloody soil" to a place of safety, either the house of a kin member of the offender, the offender's own house, or a recognized place of sanctuary.[119] Then either immediately or after a period of either nine or ten days (the texts differ on this issue),[120] a doctor was summoned to deliver a public verdict (*derosc*) on whether the victim was a candidate for sick-maintenance. The law tract *Bretha Crólige* exempts from nursing wounds that *na digaibh di mod na gnim na imtecht*, "do not take away from [the victim's] work or action or movement";[121] in other words, wounds had to be deemed serious, but not mortal. Another legal text, *Críth Gablach*, implies that a standing surety known as the *aitire* would have stepped in on the offender's behalf to take charge of the victim and guarantee his proper treatment, but it is not clear whether he would have intervened immediately after the injury or only once the doctor had determined that the victim was eligible for nursing.[122]

If the wound was judged mortal, the offender became liable for the heavy financial penalties associated with unlawful killing. However, if the victim was judged curable and eligible for *othrus*, he then made a formal demand for maintenance from the offender; anyone who refused a formal demand in the circumstances or who subsequently failed to provide the requisite nursing became immediately liable to fines. A passage in the law tract *Bretha Déin Chécht* suggests that the amount was equivalent to a cow for every night the victim was denied his proper due, and a cow is mentioned also in *Críth Gablach*.[123] The removal (*dingbáil*) of the injured party to the house where the nursing would take place was a strictly regulated affair. Before it took place, a formal contract (presumably involving sureties) was made as to the quality and terms of the nursing.[124] Gages were also exchanged between the parties. The victim received gages to ensure that he would be properly maintained, that a substitute would be supplied to his household to make up the work he would miss while he was away, and that he would himself be returned safely after the doctor judged him healed.[125] Each gage had its countergage, and although it is nowhere spelled out precisely what obligations the injured person undertook with respect to the offender, Binchy suggests (following later commentaries) that the victim guaranteed not to demand more in nursing than he was entitled to, that the substitute sent to his home to do his work would be safely returned, and that he himself would terminate his stay on sick-maintenance once the doctor had judged him ready to go home.[126] Once guarantees had been exchanged, the victim was formally removed to the house where he would be nursed: the removal itself was a highly public process, since accompanying the victim were his own lord, the *aitire*, and a person of sufficiently high status that his testimony as to the propriety of the removal would be accepted.[127] Since victims were normally attended by their retinues during a sick-maintenance stay, these persons would presumably also have formed part of the party.

Nursing could take place in a variety of locales. The choice of venue lay with the offender: he was even allowed to take the injured person into his own house for healing if despite his offense he was considered an *aire innraic*, an "honorable freeman," a designation referring presumably not merely to his reputation in the community, but to the nature of his relationship with the victim as well.[128] The important thing is that the nursing would take place in a house chosen by and thus likely associated with the offender; Binchy suggests that a house belonging to one of his kinsmen was most likely.[129] Once there, victims were entitled to various perquisites according to their rank. Offenders were required to provide certain foods in certain seasons, to provide meat and condiments[130] according to the status of the victim, and to maintain the retinue of the injured person as well.[131] Particularly lustful persons were even entitled to have women accompany them, presumably in the interests of satisfying all of the appetites that might conceivably arise during the period of their stay![132] Nor did the burden on the offender end there. Every nine days, the victim was entitled to have visitors who would pronounce on the course of his healing. These persons are said in the text to receive *fossugud*, "entertainment" from the offender, which means they must have been expected to take at least one public meal while there.[133] Sick-maintenance was terminated only once a physician had examined the patient and given his public verdict that the injury had healed enough for the victim to return home. However, if the wound had left permanent scars or disabilities, a further public appraisal process known as *iarmbrethemnas*, "after-judgment," determined how much the offender owed in compensation for the permanent nature of the injury.[134]

Sick-maintenance appears already to have been on its way out in at least some parts of Ireland by the time the majority of extant tracts were written. *Críth Gablach*, compiled around 700, refers to it as already a thing of the past, and as having been replaced by the payment of a status-linked fee that covered the injured person's food, missed work, and medical bills.[135] On the other hand, for the compiler of *Bretha Crólige*, a tract included in the eighth-century *Senchas Már* lawbook, *othrus* was still a living institution. And even the *Críth Gablach* compiler would appear to have still had access to a rhetorical text (oral or written) on the subject that he then reproduced in his own tract.[136] Elsewhere in the text he mentions a mother accompanying her son during nursing without any indication that this is an outmoded practice; presumably, if sick-maintenance was indeed obsolete in his region by the time he was composing his tract, it had not been long so.[137] Binchy suggested that the large number of exceptions mentioned in the major tract on sick-maintenance—people who, in other words, could not be borne away on sick-maintenance or were to be maintained by their own kindreds—was a sign of the institution's decline, which may well be true.[138] The exclusion of acid-tongued women (presumably on the grounds that their company would be too unpleasant) might seem to support this idea. However, most of those excluded from maintenance were persons of special status within the *túath*—kings, bishops, hospitallers, professionals like judges or poets for whom finding a substitute would be difficult, lunatics or others impossible to control.[139] Given how frequently these same persons were restricted (or excluded altogether) from participating in other legal activities within the kingdom, it may be that their exclusion should be seen less as signs of the inevitable decay of a particular institution than as instances of the type of identity performance discussed above.

Several of the performative aspects of the sick-maintenance procedure will be immediately apparent. It is the most tightly framed of any of the rituals examined to this point: initiated and terminated by specific, public verbal utterances (the proclamations of the physician, the oaths of the guarantor), the exchange and restoration of physical objects (gages) and the formal departure and return of bodies (the victim, his retinue, the lordly witnesses). The reasons for this have to do not only with interpretation—with the community's ability to discern the meaning of the comings and goings of which this procedure is composed—but with the violent nature of the offense and consequent likelihood of retaliation. Feud had a recognized place in early Irish culture: vengeance taken upon the slayers of a loved one is a normal presumption in Irish literature,[140] and *Cáin Aicillne* is quite explicit that vengeance is among the duties owed by a base client to a slain lord.[141] A specific officer, the *aire échta*, "lord of blood vengeance," was given special latitude and privileges in order to facilitate the pursuit of intertribal blood feuds.[142] The theme of the warrior who dishonors himself by living on after his lord has died does not have quite the literary resonance in Irish as it does in Anglo-Saxon, but it does occur as a motif in *Togail Bruidne Da Derga*, for example.[143] Indeed, in a version of the tale found in *Lebor na hUidhre* and attributed to a now lost manuscript, Conaire's destruction at the hostel is itself depicted as revenge for the destruction of the *síd*, "fairy mound," of Brí Léith by one of his ancestors.[144] But although feud was a recognized practice, its effects were as pernicious in Ireland as they were among Gregory of Tours' Franks. Every effort was made to prevent feuds from getting out of control: sick-maintenance both framed and displayed the compensation intended to dissuade the victim's kin from more violent forms of retaliation.

As with *tellach* and distraint, time and space played important roles in structuring and promoting the efficacy of sick-maintenance. Gages were usually pledged for specific intervals of time; the *aitire*-surety undertook his office for a period of service detailed in his oath.[145] The inherent unpredictability of the healing enterprise forbade the adherence to a strict time schedule of the sort by which the other procedures were regulated. Despite the lack of a fixed endpoint, however, time was not left to flow unchecked, but advanced in nine-day segments from the initial verdict of the doctor, punctuated by the visits of those who came to ensure that the cure was progressing as hoped. The sense of inevitable advance that was so crucial to *tellach* and distraint was thus a part of sick-maintenance as well, although the sense of urgency was perhaps somewhat less. Whereas the other procedures speeded up as the moment of actual forfeiture approached, sick-maintenance progressed at a steady pace until the cure had been completed. This differing use of time reflects fundamental differences in the nature of the procedures. Unlike *tellach* and distraint, which were performances of obligations unfulfilled (in other words, procedures designed to bring about agreements that did not yet exist), sick-maintenance displayed the satisfaction of a claim rather than its denial. Only in the case where a claim had been made and formally refused do we see the sense of mounting pressure associated with the use of time in the other two procedures: a cow every night until the offender comes to law.

But it is really the use of movement and of place that is most striking about this procedure. It is easy for Irish historians to overlook just how odd a practice sick-maintenance is. Other contemporary European legal systems certainly recognized the necessity to compensate a victim for his out-of-pocket expenses with respect to physician's fees and missed time at work. But normally this was done by the payment of a fee—in short, by a method comparable to the system that eventually replaced sick-maintenance in Ireland. The edict attributed to the Lombard king Rothari, for example, required the offender to be the one to find a physician to aid the wounded man, but there is no indication that the healing would take place anywhere other than the victim's home.[146] Sick-maintenance, on the other hand, centered on the removal of the injured party from his own space to one associated with the man responsible for his condition. Obviously there are practical reasons that might explain the transport of the injured person from his own house to that of another: provisioning a victim with food and herbs from one's farm is easier done in the vicinity of that farm than otherwise. However, in this instance as in *tellach* and distraint, movement was itself the message. Distraint marked the seizure of property from an offender by gradually removing it further and further from him; *tellach* marked the incorporation of a disappropriated heir into the kindred by bringing him further and further into the enclosure. Sick-maintenance began on the battlefield, moved into the home of the victim, and then deliberately moved out into the very heart of the offender's private space. His space was quite literally no longer entirely his own. Only upon the healing of the victim and his return to his own home were normal boundaries perceived as having been restored.

Moreover, the movement of the victim not only redefined the contours of space within the community, it reinscribed the nature of that space as well. The Irish sources are explicit on the need for silence in the house in which nursing was to take place: no games were to be played, no shouts were to be heard, no children were to be punished. The very animals themselves were silent. Particularly pointed are the numerous prohibitions against fighting in any form: *ni imesorgad mna na fir . . . ni imgonar . . . ni cuirter coin congail[e] . . . ni fertar scannail, ni curtar ilach na gair cocluiche,*[147] "neither women nor men exchange blows . . . there is no fighting . . . no dogs are set fighting . . . no brawls are made, no cry of victory is raised nor shout in playing games." Of the (roughly) fifteen conditions that *Bretha Crólige* details as being forbidden in a house where nursing is being undertaken, no less than ten have to do explicitly or implicitly with fighting.[148] A house of motion and noise became for the duration of the treatment period a house of silence and peace. Again, there were practical reasons for this: the raucous hubbub of every day life is not the atmosphere most conducive to healing. However, there was a symbolic message here as well. The prohibition against noise and disputation simultaneously invoked and repudiated the strife during which the injury occurred. Silence after battle was a performance of the lessening of tensions, the stilling of quarreling voices, the healing of old wounds between neighbors. As such, it helped to effect what it symbolized: sound itself could function as a guarantor of social order.

Other aspects of the movement of the victim into a space associated with the offender are equally striking. Embedded in sick-maintenance are references to a number of other types of significant motion in early Irish culture. In many ways, the movement of the victim paralleled his movement in ordinary life: he went on sick-maintenance accompanied by his normal retinue (*dám*), and in some cases by his wife as well. In this respect, his "visit" with the offender echoed usual Irish practices with respect to identity performance and to hospitality, where the rank of an individual was rendered instantly discernable by the nature and extent of his company and persons of substance required to tender hospitality to those who came.[149] But something more than an ordinary hospitality visit is being invoked here. For the number of persons the victim was allowed to entertain at the offender's expense every ninth day is explicitly said to be equal to *lin bis for fuiririud fiad[a],*[150] "the number [of persons] who are [normally] in his company on a banqueting visit." Banqueting visits were visits paid by lords to their clients as part of the collection of lordly renders: in other words, the victim is here projected into the role of a noble displaying his lordship over a person of lesser status. For the period of sick-maintenance, the offender, whatever his rank, was temporarily transformed into a "client" of his victim—a "clientship" witnessed and performed every ninth day of the cure.

Another interesting parallel invoked in this procedure is that of hostage-ship. When the injured person left the safety of his own home, he was obviously putting himself at risk by putting himself in the power of the man who wounded him. Both he and the substitute provided by the offender to the household of the victim for the purposes of making up his lost work were rendered vulnerable by their respective moves. The Irish were well aware of the potential for abuse and danger in this arrangement, which is why the exchange of persons was mutual, and why gages were given on both sides to ensure their safe return. *Bretha Crólige* states explicitly that one of the houses into which a victim could not be conveyed was one in which he felt threatened or endangered.[151] However, although the victim may thus appear to function typologically as a hostage in the procedure, in fact the symbolism is more complex than this.[152] Hostages were used in a variety of venues in early Irish society. Sometimes they symbolized subordination, and in such cases the giving of hostages was often one-sided only, from subordinate to superior, and the hostage not always treated very well. However, when *túatha* wished to emphasize the equality existing between them, or wished to enter into a treaty relationship with one another (known in Irish as *cairde*, a word that means, literally, "kinship"), the exchange of hostages was mutual. Moreover, hostages taken into captivity in circumstances in which a treaty had been contracted between *túatha* were treated quite honorably.[153] Sick-maintenance established a situation in which the exchange of "hostages" was mutual, but in which one (the injured person) was treated considerably more honorably than the other. An alliance is being forged, but in a way that makes it clear that the balance of power obtaining before the injury must first be reinstated. Like distraint and *tellach*, sick-maintenance enacts the balancing of debts and the restoration of peace by juxtaposing the exceptional (hostageship) with the activities of everyday life (lordship, clientship, hospitality, peaceful treaty relations).

Other interesting symbolic links appear in the various types of compensation said in *Bretha Déin Chécht* to be payable for specific types of injuries. Some of these compensatory payments would appear to have been owed in respect of the offense itself, while others represent additional fines that became payable upon a doctor's declaration that the injury had left a permanent blemish on the victim. In both cases, the determination of fines would appear to have been effected through a physician's public examination and pronouncement as to the seriousness of the wounds. In the former in-

stance, this would presumably have formed part of the doctor's initial verdict (*derosc*) on the injury—not least because the nature of the injury determined not only whether the victim was eligible for sick-maintenance, but
the percentage of the compensation the physician could expect to collect
as his fee as well.[154] The assessment of fines for permanent incapacity or
blemish was effected through a separate public process that took place at
the end of the healing period known as *íarmbrethemnas*, "after-judgment."[155]
One very important element common to both procedures, in addition to
their existence as public performances, was the symbolic use they made of
the body. Bell calls attention to how frequently strategies of ritualized activity are rooted in the body; indeed, it is "the interaction of the social body
within a symbolically constituted spatial and temporal environment" that
she sees as key to ritualization as a whole.[156] Bodies are central to sick-maintenance: from the initial bearing away of the injured person, to the various
examinations of his wounds by physician and friends, to his return across
the no longer bloodstained soil to his household at the end of the cure, the
body is the focus of the process.[157]

But it is not merely the physical body of the wounded person that is in
question. What Bell calls the "social body"—the body, that is, as it exists
within a particular social and political nexus—is very much to the fore in
sick-maintenance. Different concepts of "body" are superimposed upon
one another, both in the procedure itself and in the texts that describe it.
In the opening paragraphs of *Bretha Déin Chécht*, for example, the doctor is
said in his initial assessment of the injury to measure the size and depth of
the wounds he examines according to a standard consisting of cereal
grains. Not all grains are equal, however: superior overkings, bishops and
highly ranked poets were to be measured in grains of wheat, kings of more
than one *túath*, priests, and second-grade poets in grains of rye, the *aire déso*
and his equivalents within the ecclesiastical and poetic ranks in grains of
barley, and the *bóaire* (ordinary freeman) and his equivalents in oats. The
two lower ranks of freemen were assessed according to peas and beans respectively.[158] Binchy expressed some doubt about this as a practical
method of assessment, although he did make the point that it seems to reflect an accurate knowledge about the actual relative size of these various
grains.[159]

Binchy may be right in his reservations about the actual historicity of this
practice as a method of measurement. On the other hand, professional
fees are usually treated with deadly seriousness in the lawbooks, and numerous passages in the text make clear that the size of the physician's fee
is directly dependent on the size of the wound as measured in this manner.[160] Certainly if one does take the text at its word, as describing an actual performative event, the symbolic implications are powerful indeed.
For here, juxtaposed in one act, are the various "bodies" of which the cosmic order itself was perceived as being constructed: the body of the individ-

ual human male, the social body (comprising rank and the three orders of Irish society—secular, ecclesiastical, and poetic), and the natural body of the earth, represented by the grains and legumes used in the measurement process. Not merely the assessment of individual wounds (with their consequent fines), but the structure of society as a whole is presented as embedded in hierarchies of nature. The king's wounds, being measured in the smallest and most delicate of grains, received the largest compensation; the injuries of lesser freemen, being assessed by a much coarser standard, received far less. This was a procedure intended as much to display rank and consensus—and thereby discourage dissent—as to measure the physical wounds of one particular individual.

The social body is also very much to the fore in some of the more picturesque types of compensation outlined in the section of the tract pertaining to *iarmbrethemnas*. A lasting blemish to a "fair leg" is said, for example, to be compensated in part by the surrender of "choice imported horses" (*cumal cainchuisi formnaib ech nallmuiri*). This unusual currency obviously has a practical aspect to it—a person whose disability proved permanent might require horses in order to get around. However, the symbolic dimensions of the payment are also important. Not only would the horses serve in the community as an ongoing display of the fact and resolution of the injury, in them human, animal, and social are again juxtaposed.[161] Similarly, permanent blemishes on the literal face (*enech*) of a socially active individual were regarded as lasting wounds to his social and political face (*enech*) as well. Every time a blemished or permanently disabled man was forced to exhibit himself in his imperfect state in a political assembly, every time he was shamed by someone mocking his scar, the offender had to pay compensation for the blemish upon his face(s).[162] Just as boundaries are constantly evoked and reiterated throughout the *tellach* procedure, so also do bodies—human, political, natural—inform and structure sick-maintenance and its attendant procedures.

Not surprisingly, it is the body of the king that is most at issue. *Bretha Déin Chécht* says that a king's compensation for a broken bone varies according to whether he was injured "away from home" (*imuich*, literally, "out, outwards, outside"), or *ina thaig fein*, "in his own house." In the first instance, he is said to receive seven *cumals* worth of land—a very large amount, equivalent to the honor price of a tribal king; in the second, he was to be paid an amount equivalent to the value of his house with its goods (*ait[h]gin a treibe cona intr[e]ib*).[163] Binchy remarks on the oddness of such an assessment, since the injuries in question would both presumably have resulted from violent attacks upon the king's person and one would expect the penalties to be greater for an assault committed from within the household than for one committed outside the king's own residence.[164] His confusion is understandable, especially when one considers that theft from within someone's yard was considered more serious than theft from the lands outside of it, and that in any case an attack from within would likely involve treason.[165] If one views this compensation from the symbolic and performative point of view, however, it makes more sense. Honor is most publicly in play anytime the king travels outside his own boundaries. *Críth Gablach*, for example, makes clear that the retinues of public officials are larger when they are traveling on public errands than they are when they are going about their private business (*inna thúaith* versus *fo leith*).[166] Moreover, visible in this compensation are symbolic binaries of the sort that generate meaning within *tellach*: inside/outside (here the metaphorical *túath* rather than the king's residence per se),[167] house/land, civilization/nature, broken/whole. The king's body symbolizes the political body that is the *túath* itself: an attack upon it can be imagined as an assault upon the whole and, as such, more serious even than a fracture in the internal structure of the *túath*.[168] Hence also the fact that one compensation is paid in land and one in household goods: injured *túatha* are made whole through the acquisition and integration of additional territory, while wounds within the *túath* itself are healed through the reordering of the royal household that lies at its symbolic center.

The symbolic juxtaposition of the human and political bodies of the king may also help to explain a very odd form of compensation payment mentioned elsewhere in *Bretha Déin Chécht*. There a king is said to receive for a "one-grain" wound in the hollow of his temple an unfree man-at-arms with a breastplate (*fergnia daor hi soduin co luirig*) in compensation.[169] On its own this is very difficult to understand, since the other compensations mentioned are by and large assessed in the more standard currency of gold, silver, and farm animals. Binchy refers to this provision as "passing strange,"[170] and he is right to do so. If, however, the main point of this singular payment is less to compensate an individual king than to underscore the symbolic connection between himself and the *túatha* he is obligated to protect, then it becomes possible to speculate on possible meanings. The man-at-arms might symbolize the king as the "breastplate" of his people, that which stood between them and destruction. Alternatively, one might focus instead on the fact that the Irish word for "chief, lord" and "head" are one and the same (*cenn*), and the fact that the *fergnia* in question is protected only in his body. Leaderless *túatha*—*túatha* bereft of, or in this case, wounded in, their "head"—are in dire straits indeed. The evidence suggests that the Irish did not use helmets themselves. On the other hand, they must certainly have been aware of them, as the Anglo-Saxon aristocracy did make use of them; helmets could thus easily have been part of the Irish symbolic vocabulary. It seems unlikely that the insistence in the mythological literature that kings be physically perfect and that blemished kings resign their office was fully realized in the everyday politics of eighth-century Ireland.[171] However, it would not be at all unlikely to find such ideas enshrined in practices pertaining to kingship in this period; moreover, on a purely practical level, it is surely the case that if a king were ever to be forced to resign because of an injury, or he suffered an injury severe enough to prohibit him from ever resuming his office, his *túatha* would be left vulnerable and open to enslavement. Hence, perhaps, the significance of the *fergnia*—a public reminder of the consequences of a wound to the "head" that was both the human and political head of the *túatha* in question.[172]

The Giving of Gages

Distraint, *tellach*, and sick-maintenance were among the most elaborate and circumscribed of the legal procedures known in early Irish society, precisely because they centered on issues of such surpassing importance to it. But while they were unusual in some respects—their degree of formality, the blatant theatricality of the actions of which they were composed—they were not in the least unrepresentative of the way in which social order was generally assured in early Ireland. The sources are rich with allusions to a wide range of procedures and rituals that make similar use of time and space in their operations or that draw similarly on cultural perceptions and symbols in their functioning. It would be a mistake to see *tellach* and sick-maintenance as inherently different and set apart from the more ordinary legal business of the community, as procedures effective mainly because of their startling eccentricity and consequent mnemonic value. Similar presumptions are at work even in the most ubiquitous and unremarkable of legal transactions. An excellent example is the giving of gages.[173] Gages might be offered in a wide variety of circumstances. Persons gave gages to guarantee that they would come to law to answer a claim made against them,[174] or to indicate their willingness to conduct themselves honorably in future interactions;[175] they also gave them on behalf of others to assure third parties that obligations would be met.[176] Neighbors gave gages to one another to ensure that liabilities arising through accident or negligence would be taken care of, and kindred leaders gave gages to ensure that their dependents would behave properly with respect to king, church, and community professionals.[177] To judge from the number of times and contexts gages are mentioned in the sources, they must have been among the most common forms of legal interaction known in early Ireland.

Several aspects of gage giving will be familiar by this point, not least the manner in which this practice, like other more elaborate forms of legal ritual, restructured community perceptions of time and space. Space played an obvious role in the giving of gages, insofar as the item offered was usually either removed from the owner's possession entirely or put into the neutral space of a receptacle. Not all gages were surrendered physically to the claimant, although this was the usual practice: *Críth Gablach* alludes to the fact that a person offering a gage on behalf of his kindred could keep it in a receptacle (*cumtach*) that remained in his possession until such time as it was rendered forfeit by the actions of his kin-members.[178] And the principal law tract on the interest earned by gages, *Bretha im Fhuillema Gell,* itself cites as the type of gage that earns the smallest amount of interest a *gell forcsen*, "gage of overseeing," which remained in the hands of its owner with a "binding of fear behind its back" (*fonascc omna iarna chul*).[179] However, insofar as a person was not allowed to make use of the object while it was under pledge, even the *gell forcsen* must be considered to have been symbolically removed by the process to the neutral space between claimant and owner. If the defendant defaulted on his obligation, the gage would fall forfeit, thus being removed altogether into the possession of the claimant. In a case in which one person had offered a gage on behalf of another, the distancing of property from owner to claimant would be balanced by the return of that property (or its equivalent) together with the appropriate amount of interest from defendant to owner.

Gage giving redefined time within the community as well. Usually gages would be given to guarantee the performance of a specific obligation at or before a particular moment in time. Persons accused of violating the ordinance on Sunday observance, for example, would be expected to give a gage that judgment would be passed on their offenses on a specific day, which was also the case with respect to land claims being pursued by *tellach*.[180] Equally important was the role played by time in ensuring the redemption of gages given by a person on behalf of someone else. For such gages earned interest, and in most cases, that interest mounted over time. The general rule in *Bretha im Fhuillema Gell* would seem to be that interest or compensation for gages was payable in three intervals, the length of which varied but was usually ten days.[181] *Crith Gablach* speaks of the gage given by a kindred leader (*aire coisring*) on behalf of his kin lapsing over the course of a month, and of compensation for this lapsed gage mounting in three ten-day periods.[182] Some provisions underscored the urgency for the recalcitrant to come to law by speeding up the payment process over time much as was done in distraint and *tellach*, and in many cases the interest mounted as the time left to settle the obligation before forfeiture decreased. Status was a major factor in determining not only the amount of interest paid, but the length of time over which that interest accrued, with persons of higher status earning interest for longer periods of time than did those lesser in rank.[183] Objects had their own relationship with time: racing horses that earned ordinary interest during much of the year entailed the payment of the full honor-price of the owner if they were unavailable to him during *Lugnasad* or other gatherings in the *túath* where he might be expected to field a horse.[184] The fine was waived only if the owner was provided with a substitute horse for the occasion. However, not just any old horse would do: the substitute must be one *oiges a mamu*, "that fulfills its obligations"—in other words, that has a chance of winning the race![185]

As a public performance, gage giving displayed not only personal obligation, but personal identity as well. The main tract on gage giving, *Bretha im
Fhuillema Gell*, makes it clear that persons offered as gages items perceived
to be symbolically representative of themselves. Nobles and ordinary persons might pledge the garments that proclaimed who they were, fighters
might offer their arms or seamstresses their needles. Containers for valu-
ables (*iadach*, often translated "wallet" or "bag") had to be given with their
customary ornaments and contents in order to earn full interest.[186] This
was partly a matter of value, of course, but it was also more than this: containers of this sort were usually given by wealthy and high-status women,
and a great deal of the effectiveness of the gage derived from the ability of
others to recognize instantly whose honor was at stake in the affair. A wallet stripped of its distinguishing ornaments was an item shorn of its
identity—and hence also of its power. So intimate was the perceived link
between the giver and the object surrendered that what was appropriate
for one person to give in gage was not for another. Arms offered by hospitallers in gage, for example, earned no interest. It was not unlawful for a
hospitaller to give such a gage, but it was meaningless for, as Kelly points
out, the hospitaller was not properly a military figure.[187] In giving a gage,
one was giving oneself—sometimes quite literally, in that persons who
pledged objects crucial to their livelihood or identity within the tribe were
presumably unable to make use of them during the time they were under
pledge.[188]

For this reason, gages were also both rooted in and reproductive of gender and status hierarchies within the *túath*. *Bretha im Fhuillema Gell* begins
by focusing on the issue of women's gages specifically, listing among the
items "proper for women to give in pledge" needles, wallets, and garments
for women of the noble and skilled classes, and the young of cattle for the
wives of freemen.[189] Moreover, the tract also enumerates items *not* proper
for women to offer in gage—in other words, objects identified with men.
Only with her husband's permission, for example, might a woman give
cows, horses, gold, silver, copper, or iron in gage, and the fact that any interest that accrued on one of these gages went to him rather than to her
underscores the fact that from the jurists' point of view it was he, rather
than she, who was the true donor.[190] Ownership was obviously an important aspect of this restriction, but so too was identity. Women could not give
such gages because they would then be giving something other than themselves. Precisely the same link between personal identity and the giving of
objects is visible also in the pseudohistorical prologue to *Cáin Adamnáin*,
where the "suggested donations" to Iona include a white tunic with a black
border from every penitent spouse, a *screpul* of gold from every woman of
the chieftain class, a cloth of linen from every wife of a young lord, and
seven loaves of bread from every unfree woman.[191]

Community perceptions about status and rank were also embedded in the customs regulating the giving of gages. Only kings, high-ranking clerics, and lords were allowed to pledge items of gold.[192] Moreover, interest payments on items offered on behalf of another appear in most cases to have been determined less by the value of the object than by the status of the giver. Gages consisting of objects manufactured from silver, for example, earned three yearling heifers (*dairt*) in compensation if they were given by a lesser freeman, five if they were given by a freeman of *bóaire* rank, ten if they were given by a lord up to the highest of the nonroyal ranks, fifteen if they were given by lords even higher in status, and thirty if offered by kings.[193] Similarly, the rules with regards to the interest earned by gages given by hospitallers and their wives differed markedly from those pertaining to other types of person.[194] Even more interesting—and indicative of the manner in which gage giving both reflected and perpetuated symbolic connections within the *túath*—are those instances in which interest payments did *not* vary according to status. Cows were the primary medium through which lordship was exercised in early Ireland, and when these served as gages, freemen received less in interest than did persons of the noble ranks. Garments and silver objects were also items through which social rank was performed and exercised, and interest for these items also varied according to rank. Neither household utensils nor regular horses, however, carried the same implications of lordship and subordination, and when these were given in gage, interest was constant across the social classes.[195] Objects had a language of their own—one that derived from institutions and activities seemingly unrelated to the pledging of objects (lordship, clientship, farming) but which directly helped to shape the manner in which one person offered a gage to another.

The intimate link between giver and object makes clear that gage giving replicated other forms of legal constraint, most notably, of course, hostageship itself.[196] Indeed, there is a close semantic relationship between the terms for "gage" and for "hostage" in the Celtic languages.[197] When a king or noble was forced to attend a festival, a hosting, or a gathering of the *túath* without the elaborate garment that a person of his rank would normally be expected to wear, his honor was held as hostage to the obligation he guaranteed as surely as ever his body could have been—a point that is underscored by the fact that in such circumstances the owner's honor-price immediately became due from his recalcitrant principal. Indeed, given how frequently specific garments would have been worn and how widely they would likely have been recognized in such intimate social settings— given also the political connotations and associations they would likely have carried with them from encounter to encounter—the absence or loss of a particular garment might have had a significant impact upon the community.[198] It is surely not accidental that those suffering the forfeiture of a festival garment received new garments in return. Just as the absence of an anticipated garment displayed to all the existence of an obligation or alliance—and the fact that an individual's honor was very much on the line—so also did the subsequent wearing of clothing acquired in interest for a lapsed gage serve as a permanent reminder that a gage had been given, forfeited, and redeemed.[199] All parties were reclothed thereby in innocence and honor.

Context and Authority

It would be possible to multiply almost ad infinitum a discussion of the numerous ways in which the public, formal movement of persons and objects in time and space was used to structure social order in early Ireland. The lawbooks are literally saturated with references to performances, framed and unframed, within which the basic business of the community could be initiated, conducted, and then let go. Male heirs sharing hereditary land between them once the close kindred had become extinct, for example, entered onto a five-year process in which they publicly measured and redistributed the land on an annual basis before finally having each heir formally plant a symbolic housepost in the share assigned to him in the year before the division became final.[200] Similarly, the process by which an individual established a prescriptive right to land (*rudrad*) through long-term occupation also advanced in set intervals of time, each of which was marked by a public declaration of a particular sort (*déitiu, aititiu, comdeitiu,* "recognition," "acknowledgement," "joint recognition").[201] Rejecting such a claim to prescriptive right was likewise conveyed through the performance of culturally significant public gestures, including deliberately trespassing on the land in question, putting one's own cattle on it, forcibly removing cows belonging to the occupant, tearing up fences, ostentatious lamentation, or even urinating (*fual*).[202] The placing of children in fosterage sometimes involved the formal appointment of guarantors, but always included the public handing over of the child with the equipment and retinue appropriate to his or her status.[203] And of course there were numerous ecclesiastical rituals designed to secure particular legal goals, including oaths,[204] ordeals,[205] and ritual cursing. Particularly interesting was the practice of *celebrad,* "celebrating"—presumably of the Mass. The nature of this procedure is not well understood, but it seems to have been used both to make and to enforce agreements between individuals and groups; in the latter case at least, it seems to have functioned more or less as an ecclesiastical version of *troscad,* "fasting."[206]

None of these performances stood alone as isolated events; each gained meaning by reference to other procedures and practices within the community. Many obligations were, for example, undertaken by the creation of formal contracts through the giving of guarantors, a highly framed procedure that will be discussed in a later chapter. However, some of the most important social affiliations known to early Irish society—lordship, clientship, ongoing relationships with professionals—deliberately es-

chewed the formalities of the full-fledged oral contract. Instead of offering
guarantors to one another for specific, short-term obligations, persons in
these long-term relationships initiated their affiliations without reference
to any sort of fixed time frame. These "immunities" (*ruidlesa*), as they are
known to us from the sources, were initiated and conducted instead
through the public exchange of goods and services—sometimes at fixed
times of the year, as with lordly food-rent, sometimes whenever the occasion warranted, as with fees for professional service.

What is most interesting about these procedures, however, is the manner
in which they gained potency from the *contrast* between themselves and full
formal contracts. In other words, much of the point of handling particular
types of relationship in this manner was to emphasize the ongoing nature
of the social connections thereby established. By *not* exchanging guarantors or setting time limits on the relationship, individuals made just as
strong a statement about their intentions and about the type of affiliation
into which they were entering as they would have had they chosen to do
these things. The two procedures—immunities and contracts—cannot be
understood apart from one another. Each implicitly made reference to the
other; each needed the other to make a statement about itself.[207] To consider clearly ritual activities like contracts—or sick-maintenance, or *tellach*,
or distraint—separately from the context within which they were enacted is
to risk losing sight of what actually made them work.

But what then was the source and nature of the authority that procedures like *tellach* and sick-maintenance commanded? Such questions are
particularly pressing for a culture like that of early Ireland, in which the
state played as yet relatively little role in the making and enforcement of
law. Performance theorists have long disagreed on the origins of the authority of ritualized procedures. Hymes and Bauman stress the context in
which the performer acts and his relationship to the audience and tradition for which he is performing;[208] Barba focuses more on the physiology
of the performer himself, on how his body moves and on the response it
engenders in those watching.[209] Bloch points to the manner in which what
is done in performance reproduces what is traditional, what is known and
has already been done.[210] Sherzer and Bauman underscore the importance of the audience's assessment of the verbal artistry of the performer
and the aesthetic qualities of the performance as a whole.[211] And Kratz
picks up on the latter idea, arguing that the emotional impact of rituals is
an important element in establishing their authority.[212] There is, of course,
no real reason to choose between these various perspectives: apart from the
issue of physiological response, which we are simply no longer in a position
to judge, all of these would seem from the evidence to afford us some assistance in understanding the procedures described in the lawbooks.[213]

But in the end it is probably the emphasis on shared action and belief,
the embeddedness in community practice and perception that most clearly

stands out from the Irish sources, as key to the efficacy of legal ritual. An important legal story in manuscript H 3. 18 discussed by Charles-Edwards in his work on *tellach* tells of a man named Nin mac Magach who unwittingly unyokes his horses on land that had once belonged to his kindred. He himself had known nothing about the land and did not intend by his actions to lodge a claim, as he tells the occupant when the latter (in improbably obliging fashion) informs him of his right to the land. Intentional or not, the unyoking of the horses has its effect: Nin's claim stands, and is later supported by the king after the occupant unlawfully ejects the offending horses from his land. It is difficult to know how much credence to place in this story. The glosses of which it forms a part have been dated to the last half of the eighth century and are therefore likely later than *Din Techtugud* itself.[214] And its central claim, that a man might unwittingly loose his horses on land he is unaware belongs to him, seems difficult to believe, to say the least. Indeed, given its likely date of composition, it may be that the most telling aspect of the tale is the prominent role it assigns the king in making the ultimate decision as to the fate of Nin's inadvertent claim.[215]

To the extent that we can trust this tale, however, the story is revealing of some of the basic presumptions underlying the performance of legal ritual in early Ireland. Charles-Edwards points to the seemingly automatic nature of the ritual. *Tellach* appears here, he argues, as a type of "legal sacrament" that "effects what it signifies" without the need for any explicit verbal exchange or even intention on the part of the claimant: "the act has been performed and the claim has therefore been made."[216] However, the tale makes clear as well the fact that the context within which it was performed was essential to the efficacy of the act. Nin's own confusion about what he has done clearly demonstrates that the act of unyoking horses, while culturally resonant, was one susceptible to differing interpretations.[217] Without witnesses to give meaning to the event, without an audience to interpret its significance, it would have remained precisely what it was—a routine gesture among many other such gestures. The unyoking of horses merely poses a question that the community itself must answer: is this a significant action, and if so, what importance should be attached to it? *Tellach* thus does "effect what it signifies," but not by rote. It is a distinctly "Donatist" sacrament, one in which the status of the primary participant—or at least his identity and perceived standing within the community—is directly relevant to the procedure's efficacy. Had Nin not been who he was, had his connection with the land not been recognized by those in his "audience," he might have been interpreted as lost, or a trespasser, or merely what he thought himself to be, a traveler in need of rest.[218]

Symbols are not static; they can "mean" in many different ways. Furthermore, they draw their potency, as does legal performance as a whole, from the manner in which they resonate with, rather than stand apart from, everyday life.[219] The driving of cattle across a person's land can mean everything or nothing. Hearth and home and filial piety are potentially implicit in the lighting of every fire—but so also are lightning and arson and the clearing of brush. This is why the framing of actions that we see in the lawbooks is so important. A full understanding of what is taking place depends on the audience's recognizing that a performance is occurring and an act of interpretation is required. This is surely also the key to the transformative power of performance. Those moving within the frame are, in Schechner's words, "not themselves" insofar as they have been transformed into claimants or defendants and witnesses, and "not not themselves" insofar as they have not left their usual identities entirely behind. The audience's role in effecting this transformation is crucial. Contextualized words and gestures have the force attributed to them by those for whom they have meaning. Bauman has referred to a "heightened intensity of communicative interaction"[220] existing between performers and their audience that induces spectators to accord authority to the messages conveyed by that performance. Onlookers must assent to a craftsman's loss of competence and refuse to seek out his services should a claim be brought against him. Paradoxically, it is the fictional nature of the temporary world of the frame, and the familiar and yet altered—and familiarly altered—identities of its inhabitants, that most clearly urge the audience to reflect upon the implications of what they see.[221]

In his important book, *The Implications of Literacy: Written Language and Models of Interpretation in the Eleventh and Twelfth Centuries*, Brian Stock draws a contrast between the oral cultures of the early Middle Ages and the "textual communities" that developed in the wake of the spread of literacy in the eleventh and twelfth centuries. He characterizes the important changes taking place in this period in a variety of ways: from oral gestural to textual, interpretive, and factually oriented, from symbolic to hermeneutic, from independent object to reflecting subject.[222] The eleventh and twelfth centuries saw, he argues, a profound shift from the immediately apprehensible symbol to the advent of a complex, textually based hermeneutic requiring active reflection and meditation on the part of individuals and groups. In the wake of the changes sweeping Europe in these crucial centuries, the "archaic" symbolism and ritual of the early Middle Ages underwent a profound transformation: "Archaic ritualism needed no interpretation; the meaning arose from the acting out or performing of events. This sort of ritual was replaced by a complex set of interactions between members of groups which is in large part structured by texts, or, at the very least, by individuals' interpretations of them."[223] No longer was the emphasis placed on the transparent "physicality" of the symbolic object; the focus shifted instead to the "interpretation" of an item that was no longer merely an object but now "an object of thought."[224] Symbols now moved within a network of allusion and intertextual reference that mandated interpretation as a necessary "addendum to what is seen, heard, and performed."[225]

The Irish evidence suggests a more complex view of the role of symbol and performance in early medieval oral cultures.[226] Procedures like *tellach*, or sick-maintenance, or gage-giving moved within an intricate hermeneutic of perception and experience that required interpretation and reflection just as surely as did the propositions of the early heretical communities Stock discusses so perceptively. Objects were not uncontested and fixed, but complex and multivalent. Likewise ritual: implicit within each individual performance were not only the hundreds of performances of that same genre that had gone before, but the many other related practices and beliefs—personal and communal—that gave that genre its resonance within the community. Gage giving "worked" not only because objects changed hands but because it alluded to hostageship; distraint "worked" not only because animals were taken but because it simultaneously threatened and repudiated theft; immunities "worked" not only because goods and services were exchanged but they were not contracts and never would be. Moreover, the meaning of objects or actions could change even within a single transaction, bringing a whole new set of associations to bear on the event. Agility rather than transparency was the hallmark of the "language" of performance. If the horse given by a parent to the foster-father for use in teaching a son to ride was not returned with the boy at the end of fosterage, it was "reinterpreted" as the type of fief given by a noble to a client for which food renders were now due. A horse that had once "meant" alliance and affection now testified to lordship and obligation; not only had the meaning of the horse shifted significantly, the relationship between the two families had been profoundly altered as well.[227]

Too often we have understood legal performance as recording rather than doing or, if doing, then doing mindlessly without room for reflective thought. Indeed, performance has traditionally been considered by medievalists primarily as an alternative to more literate methods of inscription. And there is a certain truth to this view, although Rosamond McKitterick's recent studies of the Carolingian sources have complicated considerably our vision of the early Middle Ages as an essentially oral culture.[228] What the Irish evidence suggests, however, is that performance had a form and function in medieval society that writing did not possess. It created a frame of action within which identities and hierarchies could be both transformed—often in ways disruptive of social or familial norms—and contained. And it not only informed, but demanded, a response from those who witnessed it. It also, and crucially in this society where state institutions of enforcement were not highly developed, embodied and objectified social conflict in a way that displayed the tensions that lay behind the event, but resolved them in what participants were likely to understand as a straightforward performance of communal values and beliefs.[229] Distraint, for example, was at once a presentation of conflicts between individuals and a performance of the communal norms by which such conflicts could be resolved. In rooting the disputes it scrutinized and sought to heal in the natural and political order, performance enjoined social consensus in a way that allowed for change while acknowledging only continuity.

Perhaps this is part of the reason why some have argued that within such an otherwise literate legal culture, the charter never really caught on. Writing was not the opposite of oral performance, although like any other aspect of life, it could be integrated into it. Stock writes of the "odd hybrid of a 'dispositive' twig sown to a 'probative' text" in charters from Burgundy and the Midi, and of the "quasi-magical" aspect of the ceremony of *levatio cartae*, in which pen and parchment were placed on the land to be conveyed, there to be "impregnated with earthly forces" so as to turn the charter into a "symbolic replica of the ritual by which the exchange was solemnized."[230] But perhaps what we are seeing here is not magic, but the integration of a new set of objects and symbols—pen and parchment—into a cultural tradition of performance and audience interpretation. Certainly it is worth noting that performance retained its importance even within the more broadly literate communities of the later Middle Ages. Robert Bartlett's examination of the legal category of "mortal enmity" demonstrates, for example, that performance played a crucial role in regulating legal affairs even in the sophisticated cities of high medieval Spain. A man who wished to declare another his "mortal enemy"—a designation that freed both parties from many of the constraints normally imposed by public authorities on private feud—did so by formally striking a blow on his enemy's shield in the town square.[231] And Caroline Bynum's elegant essay on twelfth-century individualism leaves no doubt as to the importance of modeling and role-play to medieval conceptions of the self.[232] Individuals sought literally to transform themselves into that which they admired, and their assumption of these roles was both marked and engineered by something that looks rather like performance. Indeed, the more radical and threatening the transformation the more public and framed the ritual by which it was effected: pilgrims and crusaders took public vows, settled debts and outstanding obligations, and ostentatiously regarbed themselves in the distinctive attire of their new identities. The Irish material may offer us a way in which to understand the background and content of such rituals. For these people, as for the medieval Irish and their Germanic counterparts, whom we glimpse in the law codes breaking alder twigs over their heads and publicly kissing the posteriors of stolen dogs,[233] surely the play was "the thing."

Chapter 2

Jurists on Stage

In many ways, the linking of law to performance makes sense to us even today. Courtrooms are natural venues for the dramatic: the last-minute confession, the sudden appearance of an ace-in-the-hole witness, the shocking revelation that lays bare the truth. Equally dramatic are the formalized gestures, rhetorical posturing, and somber traditional language by which proceedings notable otherwise primarily for their tedium are imbued with interest and authority. Lawyers are actors as well as advisers, directors as well as repositories of legal expertise. Oral performance is a critical aspect of the judicial process, even in the cosmopolitan, text-oriented world of our own day. That having been said, it is still the case that for us drama and law are typically regarded as fundamentally separate realms of endeavor, characterized by different goals, methodologies, and ways of thinking about the world. Drama is generally an occasion of pleasure rather than duty: fictional where law is "real," emotional where law is dispassionate. Drama imagines, moves, persuades, and even titillates; law defines, decrees, commands, and enforces. One is a matter of aesthetics and art, the other a peculiarly "social" science.

What we have seen so far of the enactment of law in early Ireland suggests an entirely different point of view. There drama and law were intimately linked. Performance was the means by which legitimate claims were articulated and pursued, communities alerted to irregularities within their boundaries, and relationships among neighbors redefined in accordance with their obligations. Perhaps most radically, performance had the power to vest ordinary individuals with a competence they did not normally possess. And what was true of these ordinary individuals was even more true of the legal professionals who by the eighth century clustered thickly around kings and courts and parties in dispute. By the time the principal lawbooks of Ireland were compiled, many legal procedures would have been conducted in the presence of—and likely under the active supervision of—jurists and advocates trained specifically in the law.[1] For these men, performance was more than just a means of communication, it was an essential aspect of their craft—one that lay at the very heart both of their authority as professionals and of the efficacy of the proceedings over which they presided. Indeed, it is the central contention of this chapter that law constituted in early Ireland an actual performance tradition: a form of verbal art with close ties to other contemporary arts like poetry and storytelling, in which success was defined by aesthetic as well as more self-evidently "legal" considerations. Like other arts, it had its own rhetoric, stagecraft, and internalized mythology; like them as well, it functioned as entertainment in a world attuned to the pleasures of oral performance.

The links between performance and law are most immediately apparent in what the sources tell us about the history and origins of the legal profession. To historians accustomed to the mechanisms of justice elsewhere in medieval Europe, the very existence of professional jurists at such an early date may come as something of a surprise. Roman bureaucracy and legal experts lingered on for varying amounts of time in regions that had once formed part of the empire. However, with the exception of Ireland—and, possibly, of Wales, Scotland, and Scandinavia, depending on how far back in time we are entitled to read the extant medieval evidence—jurists trained specifically as professionals in the law are in western Europe largely a feature of the high Middle Ages.[2] The term "professional" is, of course, a vexed one, and our sources are too fragmentary to allow us to know what percentage of the graduates of the Irish legal schools would meet Paul Brand's definition of a professional as one who spends the majority of his time acting in a legal capacity and gains the largest part of his income from doing so.[3] However, it is clear from the Irish sources that judges appointed specifically by king or church and earning their income from the law existed already by the time the majority of tracts were composed in the seventh and eighth centuries. Most small kingdoms would have had a judge appointed to act on their behalf who, in return for deciding basic types of cases within the kingdom speedily and without further specific compensation, received special privileges, labor service, and payments of food.[4] Good food, too: the sources clearly imply the advisability of offering shapely, well-fashioned cuts.[5] Judges could also be appointed as private arbitrators by parties in dispute for cases pursued outside the setting of the court; in these cases they took a specific fee for their services from the parties involved.[6] Nor were judges the only professionals on the legal scene. Advocates were a well-established feature of the Irish legal landscape by the ninth century at least, and depending on the circumstances, earned anywhere from a sixth to a third of the amount in dispute for every case in which they acted.[7]

One can thus be reasonably comfortable in using the term "professional" to describe judges and advocates in early Ireland; however, it is difficult to get equally cozy with a single notion of the origins and nature of the juristic class itself. To say that such issues are matters of considerable dispute is to engage in significant understatement; indeed, the prudent avoid the issue altogether. Classical sources suggest that the preservation and enforcement of law was regarded by many early Celtic peoples as an aspect of pagan religious ceremonial. Caesar reports that druids acted as custodians of law and justice among the Gaulish tribes of the first century B.C.E., combining their religious and secular roles by barring those who failed to meet their legal obligations from public sacrifice.[8] The Gaul of Caesar's day is of course far removed from the Ireland of the lawbooks, but the connection between religion and law to which Caesar speaks may once have been true of Ireland as well. The early penitential text known as the "First Synod of St. Patrick" depicts druids of the early conversion period as presiding over the swearing of legal oaths, and it is not unreasonable to think that their legal activities might have extended beyond this.[9] Indeed, the text itself seems to imply that Christian and non-Christian systems of justice often found themselves in competition with one another. Christians seeking out secular courts in an attempt to gain compensation for injuries done to them are, according to the authors of the text, henceforth to be considered as strangers (*alienus*) to the church.[10] Doubtless this provision speaks primarily to the desire of Christian communities to set themselves apart from their pagan neighbors by retaining jurisdiction over their own. However, there is a clear implication here that in pagan circles also law and religion were commingled and that pagan ceremonial continued to play an important role in legal matters into the early conversion period. Certainly the concern with distinguishing Christian from pagan, and ecclesiastical courts from secular courts, is very marked in the text: one gets from it the impression of two rival judicial systems, each grounded in religion, going head to head.[11]

If ever pagan religion had played an important role in legal matters in Ireland as it had in Gaul, then the manner in which the Irish chose to conceptualize the origins and authority of their legal tradition had changed significantly by the time the lawbooks were composed. We hear nothing further about the involvement of pagan religious leaders in legal matters—instead, poets rather than druids come officially to the fore. Law is depicted as having been passed down orally by generations of poet-jurists before being committed to writing with the coming of the faith. Excerpts purporting to come from the traditional body of oral law known as *Féne-chas*, and couched either in verse or in rhetorical prose, are cited frequently in the tracts.[12] And a myth designed to highlight the essential compatibility of native and Christian tradition appears in many texts, including *Córus Béscnai* (a tract in the eighth-century compilation known as the *Senchas Már*)[13] and an eighth- or ninth-century text known as the "Pseudo-Historical Prologue to the *Senchas Már*." In it, a poet, Dubthach maccu Lugair, is depicted as exhibiting the pre-Christian legal tradition for Saint Patrick, who then orders that that part of it which accords with Christianity—most of it, as it happens—be written down and preserved.[14] So well-known did this myth become that allusions to it appear in a variety of sources, including the *Annals of Ulster*[15] and the law tract *Bretha Nemed*

Déidenach, where Dubthach and Patrick were alleged to have sanctified in a similar manner the rights of poets to use their powers of satire in cross-border disputes—a right that the text conceptualizes as a "regulation" (*cáin*) originally made by the kings and poets of Ireland in the "beginning of the world."[16]

Indeed, whatever the actual origins of the legal profession in Ireland, by the time of the lawbooks the idea that poets were the historical bearers of the tradition was ubiquitous throughout the legal corpus.[17] The genuine prologue to the *Senchas Már* puts the matter quite succinctly: *Senchas fer n-Erenn, cid conid-roiter? Comchuimne da sen, ti[n]dnacul cluaise di araili, dichetal filed, tormach o recht litre* . . . , "The [legal] tradition of the men of the Ireland, what has preserved it? [The] joint memory of a pair of ancients, [its] recounting from one ear to another, [the] chanting of poets, [its] augmentation by the law of the letter (scriptural law). . . ."[18] *Senchas*, the word used for "tradition" here, is the most common word employed in the Irish sources for traditional lore of all kinds—historical, genealogical, and literary. Its use in this context has the effect of situating the transmission of Ireland's legal lore in the context of the transmission of all other types of cultural material—a process in which poets (and other oral performers, like *senchaid*, "historians," and storytellers) were regarded as being directly involved.[19] The written lawbook thus becomes but one stage in a long historical tradition of legal transmission imagined as already far advanced at the time Christian notions of law and justice entered Ireland. Through its title, the "*Senchas Már*," literally "Great Tradition," the lawbook claims descent from a putatively unbroken chain of versified oral performances; through its reshaping in accordance with the precepts of Scripture, it claims permanency in written form and a place in biblical history.[20]

Ultimately, the association of law with poetry became such a given that an elaborate historical schema of transmission from poet to poet was worked out in the schools: an eleventh- or twelfth-century poem attributed to Gilla in Choimded Úa Cormaic that may have served as a set text for student jurists traces the history of law in Ireland back to the poet Amairgen.[21] The focus of this poem is quite discernibly on the pre-Christian period, but the story of Patrick and Dubthach is told here, and mention is made of another luminary, Cenn Fáelad, whose story represents an interesting twist on the general theme of poets and the law. The late but picturesque tale incorporated into the preface to the law tract *Bretha Étgid* tells how Cenn Fáelad, whose "brain of forgetting" was removed in the course of being treated for an injury, took advantage of his expanded memory and fortuitous proximity to three different schools—a school of monastic learning, a school of native law, and a school of poetry (*scol leigind 7 scol feinechais 7 scol filed*). He became a student at all three educational establishments simultaneously; whatever he learned orally by day, he was said to have turned into verse and written prose by night. Interestingly, although this tale clearly speaks to a close relationship between legal and poetic learning, it is notable that law is not characterized in this story as having actually been preserved in verse: Cenn Fáelad seems to have to turn the law he learns *into* poetry before writing it down.[22]

It is difficult to know precisely what to make of this alleged historical link between law and poetry (which, as will be argued in a subsequent chapter, matters more to some redactors than to others). Nor is it easy to assess the apparent evolution of druids to poets hinted at in these accounts. Law could have evolved as a specialist discipline out of either religion or poetry—and the differences between these fields may in any case not always have been particularly stark. Caesar describes the Gaulish druids as having transmitted their teachings in verse, and poets were commonly linked with prophecy and otherworldly insight in Irish literature.[23] Moreover, druidism was being actively suppressed in Ireland from at least the seventh century, and it does not seem unreasonable to imagine that many members of the druidic classes might have turned to poetry as a profession when the triumph of the church made it expedient for them to make alternative career plans. (The clergy may also have been an attractive option.) Law could have evolved as a profession at any point, and of course the process did not need to have happened everywhere in Ireland in the same way. Alternatively—or additionally—the jurists' insistence on the poets' custodianship of the law may reflect their own desire to downplay the unsavory pagan elements of their own tradition. By the time the myth of Patrick and Dubthach was current, close ties existed between the clerical and poetic classes. Poets were ancestors to be proud of; druids were not.

Whatever the actual origins of the juristic profession, one cannot help but be struck by the fact that law was conceptualized as having evolved as a discipline out of one (or both) of the two most important performance traditions of the day: religion and poetry. Moreover, the links with poetry were ongoing and institutionalized, at least in some regions of Ireland, with considerable overlap in some areas between the juridical and poetic professions during the period of the composition of the tracts. Poets are represented as participating in the *airecht*, "court" of the kingdom (or overkingdom) in the tract on that subject; indeed, the chief poet, or *suí cach bérlai ollaman*, "sage of every language with the rank of *ollam*," as he is called in the text, is depicted as presiding with king and bishop over the court.[24] A significant substratum of the extant legal corpus is written in verse and rhetorical prose,[25] and since it is likely on linguistic grounds that not all of this verse had a direct connection with ancient oral teaching,[26] the translation of law into verse must have been an ongoing process, just as it was in the genealogical, historical, and literary material (surely also the import of the story about Cenn Fáelad). A significant proportion of both of the primary *Bretha Nemed* tracts, for example, consists of versified or rhetorical instruction attributed to poets well known in Irish culture generally.[27]

Breatnach has argued that the highly rhetorical *Bretha Nemed Toísech* was composed in the mid-eighth century by three kinsmen of the Uí Búirecháin family, one a bishop, one a judge, and one a poet.[28] And Binchy suggested long ago that jurists originated as a professional class from within the poetic ranks, citing *Bretha Nemed* as an example of a school in which the two disciplines had not yet separated out from one another.[29] There is reason to believe that poets figured more heavily in some law school traditions than in others, a point that will be taken up later in more detail; however, the ubiquity of the association throughout the legal tradition suggests that the connection between law and poetry was either genuine or, at the very least, philosophically significant to jurists of the historical period.[30]

Poetry was not the only performance tradition linked to law by the time the lawbooks were composed. Both the juridical and poetic professions were in this period closely associated with the church. The precise nature of that connection remains a matter of vigorous controversy among historians. Jurists were clearly Christian by the period of tracts—that much is agreed. What is less certain is whether they were also, and inevitably, clerics. Clearly the ties were close. Donnchadh Ó Corráin has characterized the intellectuals of Ireland as a single, ecclesiastically educated, mandarin class,[31] and indeed much of the training undergone by members of the various professions would appear to have overlapped. Jurists and poets alike drew on biblical and canonistic texts, often translating ecclesiastical episodes into their own professional "vernaculars" in ways that reveal their command of Christian learning. Scholarship—both in ecclesiastical matters and in the intricacies of verse production—was (along with birth into the profession) what the aristocratic *filid* haughtily maintained separated true poets like themselves from the lower-class, dubiously Christian, order of bards.[32] The stylistic impact of Latin grammatical textbooks on the vernacular law tracts is undeniable.[33] And members of the secular learned orders seem deliberately to have modeled themselves on the regulations governing the lives of their ecclesiastical colleagues. Indeed, in their writings, they conceptualized jurists, poets, and historians as a new levitical class, with claims both to the privileges and the prescriptions of the special people of the Old Testament.[34]

Given such close connections, it is not surprising that many scholars have agreed with Ó Corráin in seeing the jurists who authored the law tracts as precisely the same class of men who penned the canonical and exegetical writings of the period. Breatnach has shown, for example, that while most early Irish law tracts are anonymous, the tract *Cáin Fhuithirbe* was drafted by a group of clerics (and one poet). In his view, this is typical of the written tradition in general: the "writing of the law," not merely *Cáin Fhuithirbe*, but of the vernacular legal corpus as a whole, took place "under the direction of the Church."[35] Whether *Cáin Fhuithirbe* is sufficiently representative of the law tract genre to bear this kind of weight is a matter for debate: its style and ecclesiastical emphasis differ notably from the majority of tracts in the *Senchas Már*, for example. But it is certainly true that when we first start getting evidence for the location of legal schools, in a ninth-century text known as the *Triads of Ireland*, the places named are all monasteries.[36] And the first judge (*sapiens 7 iudex optimus*) we hear of in the annals was Ailill mac Cormaic, the abbot of the monastery of Slane, who died in 802—Slane being one of the places named in the *Triads* as a center of legal learning.[37]

Of course, the fact that certain monasteries were functioning in this manner by the ninth century does not preclude the possibility of legal learning taking place as well in other venues. Kelly and Charles-Edwards have offered compelling evidence for the possible existence of lay jurists: individuals of aristocratic background and literate training who were not themselves clerics. As they point out, not every law tract seems to toe the ecclesiastical line, and there are clear differences in reasoning and argumentation between "secular" and canon law texts.[38] Charles-Edwards has recently outlined a context in which learning of the requisite sort might have been obtained by such men. Education in early Ireland was, he suggests, divided into two stages, the first focused on grammar and rhetoric, with some biblical training, and the second, more advanced, on exegesis. Not everyone progressed through both stages: some who "might enter the ranks of the learned," but who were not destined for a career in the church, might complete only the first part of the training. Movement across the professions was possible for those whose birth and training entitled them to membership in the learned orders, secular and ecclesiastical; however, the sources themselves are careful to distinguish among those professions.[39] The literati of early Ireland were, in other words, more of a "complex aristocracy" than a single mandarin class. As Charles-Edwards suggests, an educational trajectory of this sort would allow for the possibility of lay jurists while providing an explanation for the backgrounds and priorities visible in the writings left to us.

Such questions are unlikely to be definitively resolved any time soon. Perhaps that is just as well: controversy and disputation are good for the academic soul, if not always for the alimentary well-being of individual scholars. It is worth making the point that nothing compels us to assume absolute uniformity in training and outlook among the authors of the lawbooks and thus to expend our energies trying to prove them one thing or the other. Indeed, such a view flies right in the face of the divergences in style and perspective visible in the extant tracts.[40] Be that as it may, what matters most for the present argument is that both the clerical and the poetic professions—those traditions most closely associated with jurists and the law in the period of the tracts—were intimately familiar with the power of the word in performance. Entertainment and the public enactment of communal priorities and perceptions were the stock-in-trade of the practicing poet. Poets worked for individual lords, for *túatha*, even for churches.[41]

Performing is what they did. And while it has become somewhat of a cliché at this point to speak of the "drama of the Mass," the point is no less true for all that. Nothing could be more theatrical than the celebration of the Eucharist, more revealing of the manner in which ritual transforms mundane actions like drinking or eating into moments shot through with significance. One can easily imagine the emotional impact of the event on the farmers and fishermen who witnessed it: the dramatic setting within or beside a holy building; the strangely configured ornaments and costumes that marked out the occasion as unusual and, paradoxically, invoked the memory of "preformances"[42] gone before; the sudden switch in language, from Irish to Latin, with its concomitant rupture of any sense of the normal. And at center stage the priest, the performer, the man who, by playing the character of a holy man, actually became one, simultaneously reshaping himself and the community he served. One has only to contemplate the radiant beauty of the Ardagh chalice or the Derrynaflan paten to understand the role that spectacle played in riveting the gaze of the faithful on the events taking place before them.[43]

Going to Court

Given the centrality of performance to the poetic and clerical professions, it would be surprising not to find similar dynamics at work in the judicial sphere, and it is time now to turn from the question of origins and affiliations to what is known of the legal process itself. Regrettably, our knowledge of justice in early Ireland is not as full as we would like. We do have brief tracts or passages on lawyers, pleading procedure, and seating arrangements within the court, and these are very helpful. However, apart from a brief notice concerning the historical king Congal Cáech and a lone record preserved in the Book of Durrow describing the resolution of an early twelfth-century dispute,[44] little remains to connect us directly to the strained and querulous voices of an early Irish court. From the period of the lawbooks, we have no records of actual legal cases, no *notitiae* or *placita*,[45] no narrative diplomas or chatty chronicles purporting to cite verbatim the speeches of the participants. In their stead, we are offered figments of the literary imagination—elaborate judicial orations attributed to mythical jurists, legendary kings, poets from a fictitious past. Abbot Ailill and his kind may well have issued decisions on the cases brought before them, but we will never know their substance; about the judgments of Conchobar's legendary jurist Sencha,[46] however, we are infinitely better informed.

But how then ought we to approach this odd mixture of "fact" and fiction? Clearly tales about Sencha and his mythical colleagues do not constitute verbatim representations of what went on in any particular Irish court. Equally clearly, however, they are productions of men in contact with the legal process as it actually was. They may even embody bits of instruction (oral or written) from the lawschools: the pleading offered by Art in the *Immathchor nAilella 7 Airt*, for example, incorporates (or at least draws on) a provision in the Latin *Collectio Canonum Hibernensis*.[47] Some texts may even have served as set pieces to be memorized within the schools, although it is impossible to be sure about this. However, what matters most is what these tales have to tell us about the way in which persons intimately familiar with law in action perceived their system to work. These stories are constructions, certainly. Literary constructions, undoubtedly, and in a very real way fiction. But then so is *Críth Gablach*, perhaps the best known and most often discussed of the status tracts.[48] Unless those who created these texts departed utterly from what they knew in a general sense to be true, they are constructions of great value to us. The distinction we draw between literature and law is but a chasm of our own devising; what these "genres" share is at least as important as the points in which they diverge.[49] In approaching the law we must do what we do with every piece of literature we study: read it for the truths concealed within the mythical constructs of which the text in question is composed. For if we do not read between the lines we are missing much of what it has to say.[50]

Perhaps the place to begin is with the evidence of the more straightforward—or at least less overtly "literary"—of these sources, the accounts of court procedure and personnel that remain to us. The first and most fundamental point to be made is that when formal judicial proceedings are described in these texts, they almost universally involve performance. This is true in terms both of their setting and of the manner in which they are conducted. Venues for judgment varied according to the nature of the dispute being resolved. Settings could be formal or informal. Certain cases likely took place at the home of the judge appointed by the parties in dispute to arbitrate between their respective interests. An old quotation from a now lost legal text known as the *Aí Cermna* speaks of the "five roads that are ridden to the house of a judge" (the roads in question represent types of judicial plea rather than actual roads).[51] Examples of these types of cases may well have included the types of dispute listed in a ninth-century text on which judges are expected to provide judgments "without delay"—in other words, without having to await the summoning of the *airecht*, "court." Included in this group are disputes relating to land law, neighborhood regulations, or relations between kinsmen.[52] The symbolism of the judge's house as a venue for dispute resolution is evident: conflicts could be removed thereby from spaces associated with individual litigants and resituated in a venue that symbolically underscored the impartiality and the authority of the judge in the case.

In other instances, particularly those in which the burden of an obligation fell more on one party than the other, disputes or outstanding obligations would likely have been resolved at the home of one of the participants. The tract on suretyship, *Berrad Airechta*, speaks often of the *forus* of an obligation, a term which should probably be translated in this context as "place appointed for payment," but which also often has the technical meaning of the formal public proclamation by which a judicial dispute was resolved. When a debtor must compensate a guarantor who has been rendered liable on his behalf, for example, the *forus* assigned is the debtor's own house; the place of payment and the public declaration by which that payment is verified as having been made are thus collapsed into one.[53] Not surprisingly, considerable anxiety is displayed in the sources about the possibility that a person might evade justice by being nowhere to be found when the obligation fell due, and great stress is thus laid on the advisability of dealing only with those from within the community whose residence is known and fixed.[54] Locating the *forus* of an obligation in the home of a debtor dramatized both the existence of the debt and the implicit threat to home and personal status posed by an unfulfilled agreement. Since all aspects of the case would have been conducted before witnesses, it stands to reason that the presence of neighbors would serve to bring considerable pressure to bear on those who remained recalcitrant. Public movement into the debtor's private space transformed both home and hearth into a forum for community judgment.

Lawsuits pursued in the public forum—presumably cases involving prominent individuals, or long-standing disputes, or matters of some consequence—would have taken place in the formal *airecht*, or court, of the *túath* or region. *Airecht* is a word with two meanings: "court," but also (and probably primarily) the assembly of the region at which public business generally was conducted.[55] The relationship between these two meanings is not entirely clear, but the evidence seems to suggest that the latter was a frequent, though not perhaps a necessary, venue for the former. (Another word found in the sources that seems to have had a similar range of meanings—both "assembly, meeting" and "judicial affair, decision"—is *dál*.) It is not entirely clear what types of issues apart from law and judgment might arise at an *airecht* in this larger sense, although the formation of political alliances, the proclamation of legislative initiatives, and the festive aspects of kingship and rule—feasting and the racing of horses—seem a very good guess. In this sense, then, the *airecht* functioned both as a setting and a context for dispute resolution—the physical area within which such matters were pursued and resolved, and the imagined political space constituted by persons and issues of importance to the region. As the former, it served as a frame that signaled to onlookers the solemnity and public significance of the specific events taking place there; as the latter, it was a reminder of the stakes and interests involved.

Cases heard at the *airecht* seem usually to have been held outside in the open air.[56] However, the sources suggest that for onlookers the precinct of the court formed a special and particular place: once within its bounds, a context for interpretation and action was established that separated what occurred there from activities taking place outside. Physical features within the court may have varied from region to region. One ninth-century text describes judges as sitting with the king or abbot who employed them and expounding the law from a mound to those in the region charged with listening (*Dligid toircsin taulche dó*).[57] Regardless of such details, however, it is clear that within the enclosure also, close attention was paid to the structuring of space. Indeed, the main tract on the *airecht* describes not only the court itself, but also the relationships between those within it entirely in such terms. Function and rank were communicated by the placement and movement of persons within the enclosure. Judges sat at its very heart: all movement made during the pleading and evidence-gathering part of the session seems to have been toward or away from these men, who were clearly conceptualized as both the literal and symbolic center of the proceedings. In one direction only did the judges themselves—or at least their words—appear to move. Judicial verdicts reached by judges had actually to be proclaimed by the king, bishop, and chief poet who sat behind them at the back of the court. These dignitaries are termed in the text the "cliff . . . behind the courts" (*all bis iar gul na n-airechta*). Cliffs do not move, and they cannot be moved beyond. That is the point—they form the stable jurisdictional backdrop against which justice was to be enacted.[58] Presumably then judges would have gone to the king and other dignitaries to consult once the time for proclaiming the verdict had arrived. A ninth-century text on judges may be speaking to this process when it envisages the judge *airbert fri flaith, fri senad, fri aes cerda, coná toirceat a túaith i n-indlighe*, "expounding [the law of the case] to the lord, to the synod, to the men of art, lest they act unlawfully towards their kingdom."[59]

Also part of the literal and symbolic "body" of the *airecht* were those who might be called upon for their special knowledge of tradition of the community and its customs, and those whose presence in some way bolstered the authority of those presiding over it. "Custodians of tradition" (*senchaid*), subordinate kings, and hostages, were said in the tract on the *airecht* to be situated to one side, in the *taebairecht*, literally, "side court."[60] The question as to why the paying sureties known as *ráth*s are said in the text to be located both here in the "side court" and also in the *airecht fo leth*, or "court apart," is an interesting one. Kelly (following a point made by Charles-Edwards) suggested that the main difference between the *taebairecht* and the *airecht fo leth* lay in the fact that the former contained a wide range of public figures and the latter the personnel for a normal contract (witnesses, contractual guarantors). With respect to the public role of the *ráth*, this seems a likely suggestion. I have argued elsewhere that there was an attempt in the eighth century to bring "private" transactions like contracts under the aegis of court and king; it is certainly possible that in the grouping of contract personnel together within the court we have a reflection of this process.[61]

However, envisaging the physical layout of the court as in effect a symbolic "performance" of the functions of those within it may give us another way to understand the placement of these figures in the "court apart." Persons assigned to that space are explicitly defined in the text in terms of their function as "go[ing] with clear memories into the midst of the court"—in other words, as being primarily there to give testimony on the facts of the case before them.[62] Hence, I suggest, their location "apart" (*fo leth*) from the rest, and hence also the unusual manner in which their movement is circumscribed: they are the only persons in the court specifically said to remain seated until summoned. Their placement "apart," like the constraints upon their movement, constitutes a "performance" of the independence of their testimony and their impartiality as witnesses. From a purely practical point of view, it would also have helped to ensure this independence by physically separating those testifying from those who had a stake in what they said.

But it is in the manner in which cases were pleaded and decisions proclaimed that the performative aspects of the formal process of judgment are most visible.[63] Presenting a case before the *airecht* would appear to have been, by the eighth century at least, a reasonably elaborate process. The early recensions of *Cóic Conara Fugill* list five "paths" or procedural options that litigants together with their advocates can select depending on the nature of their case. One of these almost certainly entailed the performance of an ordeal,[64] the others the formal appointment of guarantors or the public giving of gages. Early Irish law knew several types of ordeal, including the drawing of lots, the immersion of the arm in boiling water, contact with heated metal, the fighting of duels, and the swallowing of sanctified water.[65] From what we can tell, all of these various procedures were "performative" processes by any reasonable definition of that word: set apart from ordinary life by virtue of the solemnity and theatrical nature of the proceedings themselves, solicitous of community involvement, and transformative in their impact on participants. Similarly, the giving of guarantors and of gages entailed a highly public exchange of formulas, gestures, and personally significant objects. I have suggested elsewhere that we are seeing in *Cóic Conara Fugill* an attempt to transfer legal matters previously handled outside the court (private contracts, for example) into a more demonstrably public sphere of jurisdiction.[66] Regardless of whether that suggestion is accurate, it is evident that the performance of these particular judicial rituals within the confines of a marked space like the *airecht* could only have heightened the drama and formality of the affair.

Later sources suggest that the pleading process itself either became in time—or perhaps already was in the period of the tracts, depending on whether we can read later evidence back into that era—quite elaborate. The late recension H (H 3.18) of *Cóic Conara Fugill* contains what appears to be a mnemonically constructed list outlining the eight stages in the progress of a lawsuit:

Ré ria toga,	[Establishing] a date before choosing [a procedural path],
toga ria n-arach,	choosing [a path] before [the giving of] security,
arach ria tagra,	security before pleading,
tagra ria fregra,	pleading before counterpleading,
fregra ria mbreth,	counterpleading before judgment,
breth ria forus,	judgment before [the] proclamation [of the verdict and its basis]
forus ria forba,	proclamation before concluding,
forba for conair,	concluding upon a [judicial] path,
conair for a .iiii.	one path in addition to four,
condat a .u.[67]	adds up to five.

A ninth-century text on advocates describes what is either the stage known as *toga* or else an additional stage in the proceedings. There an advocate receives his case from his client and presents at least a preliminary plea to the court within twenty-four hours before determining in consultation with the judge which procedure is most appropriate; at this point, he then binds his client to that procedure.[68] Both texts seem to presume that all stages of the litigation would have taken place in public, most (if not all) of them within the physical confines of the *airecht* itself.

By at least the ninth century, and perhaps even earlier, the presentation of pleas before the *airecht* would (or at least could) have been done by a professional class of advocates known as *aigneda* (sing. *aigne*). Binchy outlined what he saw as the major stages in the development of these men: from kindred leader or personal spokesman (*fethem*), to agent, to professional pleader, to the hierarchy of professional advocates visible in the latest stratum of the sources. Three types of advocates are mentioned in the ninth-century text on the subject: the *glasaigne*, "fettering advocate," the *aigne airechta*, "court advocate," and the *aigne fris-n-innle breith*, "advocate whom judgment encounters."[69] In Binchy's view, the function of this highest grade of advocate was to take over the presentation of the case from the *aigne airechta* once the proceedings had reached a certain stage. However, as Breatnach has pointed out, while it is clear that the *aigne airechta* could call upon the services of the *aigne fris-n-innle breith* if he wished, the evidence does not suggest that a collaboration of this sort was inevitable.[70] Indeed, it appears that this high-status advocate would most often become involved at the formal request of the *aigne airechta*. Likely it was the possibility of this sort of collaboration that gave the *aigne fris-n-innle breith* the delightful sobriquet by which he is known in other tracts—*coingeltaid,* "joint-grazer"—a name that seems to speak to his joining together with the *aigne airechta* to "graze" cooperatively off the injustice at issue and, of course, off the profits of the case as well.

It is difficult to know how seriously to take this idea of a hierarchy of advocates. *Uraicecht Becc* envisages a similar hierarchy for judges, and it is certainly possible that the ranking of advocates reflects a parallel professional structure.[71] However, to the degree that this hierarchy seems to imply a highly regimented profession divided into a series of distinctive ranks, it may overstate the case. Only the two highest grades of advocate appear, for example, to have been regarded as qualified to act as an advocate in court. The honor-price of the "fettering advocate" is said to be only five *séoit*—that of a normal Irish freeman—and his duties appear to have been limited to enforcing judgments issued by others. In other words, he seems to have been little more than an average freeman who possessed enough legal training to allow him to take distraint, gages, or guarantors in a lawful fashion on behalf of the court.[72] The second rank of advocate clearly did function as a spokesman for his client; indeed, he was obviously an official product of the schools, since his knowledge of the law is characterized by the titles of written legal tracts with which he was expected to be familiar.[73]

The third rank of advocate is in many ways the most intriguing. He is described as extremely high in status himself, and as acting on behalf of those of similar rank (*túath* leaders and judges and kings); indeed, unlike the other two classes of advocate, he is of sufficiently high standing that he can make decisions about the progression of the case without consulting the judge appointed to it. Also unlike the other two classes of advocate, he is never said explicitly to study with a legal professional (*fer bélrai*), although he has been instructed by someone to whom he owes *pietas* and the acknowledgement of authority.[74] He is described as being expert in all branches of native law except *tulbretha 7 ainches mbreithe*, "immediate judgments and perplexity of judgment." However, this is a fairly major exception, in that these two categories encompass some of the most basic disputes known to early Irish society, including land disputes, cases pertaining to neighborhood law or the law of the kindred, matters relevant to distraint, questions that must be resolved by ordeal, and the like.[75] In other words, there are large areas of the law with which this person appears to have been uninvolved. Clearly he was no ordinary advocate. But who then was he? From the text, one would conclude him to have been a person of significant legal training whose office required him to act on behalf of high-status persons in cases for which an ordinary advocate was insufficient. However, one must at least wonder whether we ought instead to see his activities as a reflex of lordly jurisdiction—perhaps an aristocratic intimate of a noble household (secular or ecclesiastical) whose main function was to intervene on behalf of his lord in cases of interest to him.[76] This would explain, among other things, why his mentor (presumably, in this scenario his lord) is not termed an expert specifically in law, and why the text feels a need to distinguish his actions explicitly from those of the *rechtaire*, or "steward."[77]

What the evidence suggests, then, is an elaborate, formal process of proclamations, pleas, counterpleas, and testimony done in the presence of secular and ecclesiastical lords with the assistance of professionals trained specifically in the law. These proceedings led in turn to a public declaration by the judge of the law relevant to the case and by the lord of his verdict. Presumably, the intervention of the guarantors whose function it was to enforce the decision in the case then followed. One need hardly emphasize the publicity attendant on the affair, especially if the event coincided with a public assembly of kingdom or region. However, what is most striking about the procedure from the point of view of performance are the parallels between its use of time and space and that which we have remarked on already with respect to distraint and sick-maintenance. The proceedings took place within a space already marked in community eyes by its association with the resolution of disputes—a space the interior of which was subdivided (and in the case of the mound from which the judge speaks, physically configured) in ways symbolic of the relationships enacted within it. Movement within this space was both determined by and expressive of the roles played by the various participants. And while our sources do not tell us much about the manner in which time entered into the structuring of these proceedings, it is clear that they progressed in recognized stages marked by formal verbal utterances. Certainly the provision about pleading within twenty-four hours of a case's being confided to the advocate suggests that in formal legal matters, as in the more informal affairs examined in Chapter 1, time was an important element.[78]

Law as Art

To judge from the sources, however, the single most important aspect of judicial performance was the language and presentational style in which pleadings and verdicts were couched. Here we return to the issues of law and literary representation broached earlier. Our only sources for what might actually have been said within an early Irish *airecht* are the legal tales that occur throughout the lawbooks in a variety of contexts. We are in the odd and uncomfortable position of having to talk about the role played by performative language in judicial proceedings without having any actual transcripts to draw upon. This is where the unanimity of the texts is so comforting. Simply put, when sources purport to describe a legal process presided over or argued by jurists, they present the proclamations they make in the course of the case as formal oral performances, set apart from the rest of the proceedings by virtue of their style and mode of presentation. And while it is true that most of these examples come from texts of the *Bretha Nemed* tradition, a fact that of necessity raises questions about differences in regional practice and perception, not all of the texts do belong to this tradition, as will become evident below.[79]

The tract on sports judgments, *Mellbretha* (not a *Bretha Nemed* text), is an excellent case in point. As reconstructed by Binchy, and persuasively re-translated by William Sayers,[80] the story is one in which Fuaimnech, the daughter of the mythical king Conn Cétchathach, constrains those in residence at Tara not to eat or drink until she should be paid compensation for her foster-sons, injured in some way during a "confrontation or encounter" (*imairac no comriachtain*) between boy-troops on the plain of Brega. The dispute is then submitted to a jurist, Bodainn, who delivers a judgment the text of which is partially preserved in the extant accounts. Binchy attributed the prose preface that precedes Bodainn's judgment to a later writer, which may well be true. However, the textual fragment discovered by William and Anne O'Sullivan shows that a prose introduction laying out the circumstances of the case once preceded Bodainn's judgment in the earlier version as well.[81] This is important mainly because when Bodainn does speak, he breaks from the prose in which the text has been couched to this point to speak in verse:

Labram la féith fírinne[82]	Let us speak with the art of truth
fordom cuibse cuirethar:	what conscience imposes upon me:
cia clessat for gabulchless	although they may excel in one branch of feats
asa línaib línchluiche,	from among the full complements of their manifold games,
slán fiach inge othrus	[they are] free of penalties save for sick-maintenance
co tecma gáir guasachta.	until a cry of danger supervenes.[83]

Once he has finished speaking, the text reverts to prose, albeit a marked form of prose that Sayers has suggested may reflect the mnemonic techniques of oral tradition.[84]

What is most important for our purposes is the obviously performative nature of the jurist's presentation. Unlike the prose that both precedes and follows it, the judge's statement is couched in verse—heptasyllabic meter with trisyllabic cadences—and is heavily alliterative, both within and between lines: *féith fírinne / fordom cuibse cuirethar / cia clessat for gabulchless*, and the like. The artful repetition of words and sounds enhances the aesthetic appeal of the piece: **cless**at, gabul**chless**, **lín**aib **lín**cluiche. In sum, the artistry of the language in which the statement is couched marks a clear departure from the rest of the event, while its reliance on poetic techniques common in the period places it firmly within the realm of oral performance. This is not of course to say that the poem was necessarily composed orally, or even composed with the expectation of its being performed out loud. It could easily be a literary product from start to finish. However, *within the context of the tale, it functions as performance:* its language and poetic form mark it out as a special declaration clearly set apart from the rest of the proceedings.

That a jurist familiar with the legal process of his day should conceptualize judgment in this way is surely significant, especially given the extent to which his observations are paralleled elsewhere in other sources. Precisely the same alternation of prose and rhetorical speech is visible in the legal tale of Fergus mac Léti attached to the tract *Dí Chetharshlicht Athgabála*, a text in the *Senchas Már* lawbook. Again the setting is the Ireland of Conn Cétchathach, although the issue in this instance is the slaying of Eochu Bélbuide in contravention to the protection offered him by Fergus mac Léti, king of the Ulaid. One of the murderers was a son born to Dorn, daughter of Buide mac Ainmirech, by an unnamed foreigner (*deorath*). Fergus demanded compensation for the insult done to him, and although in this instance no judge is named, the context and wording makes it clear that in the rhetorical paragraph that follows on the description of the crime, we have the verdict pronounced by the judge in the case (text from H 3.18):

is de rocett: Foglaid forn mac (?) dia duirnn; dia foghlaid a cin do tuathaib targuth echtrann dun a forus fil co breith; biru a bas ninn mad rachtid adrorastar, no aurnaidet a mathair a mifolta; nis fol forreth nach a finntiu foisither cach connli cin cinged hi cumalacht ceim conduiri fri saegalrith sir; no chotacermain id laim lecter co .iii. mara muircrecha, ar is frit forruich.[85]

Of this it has been sung: "An aggressor against us is a son to Dorn (?). If he (be) an aggressor in respect of an offence against the provisioning by peoples, he is a foreigner to us in respect of the dwelling place in which he is until judgment.[86] I adjudge his death for it if he be a legally competent person who can be secured, or let his mother sustain [responsibility for] his misdeeds. Assistance shall not support her nor shall her kindred's land protect her. Every competent person [takes responsibility for] her crime;[87] let her go into slavery, advancing into servitude for the long course of [his or her] life. Or I judge that she be left in your hand [to be set adrift] for [the distance of] three *muirchrecha*[88] out to sea, for it is against you that she has transgressed."[89]

There is much that is unclear about this passage, although its main gist would appear to be that Dorn is to suffer for the crime of her son unless he can be found and made to pay the penalty for it himself. What is most important from our point of view, however, is the fact that the language of this unnamed judge's decision, while not in strict verse, represents a radical departure from the plain prose in which the rest of the story is couched. It is the type of language known as *rosc*: highly alliterative, rhetorical in expression, and containing linguistic features characteristic of what has customarily been termed archaic Irish.[90] Moreover, it is said explicitly in the text to have been "sung" or "recited" (*ro-chét*, from *canaid*). Once again, the break between the judge's proclamation and the language of the rest of the tale seems designed to underscore the performative nature of the former.

The connection between performance and judgment is an important theme also in the complex of tales detailing the conflict between the legendary kings Mac Con of the Corco Loígde and Ailill Ólomm of the Deirgthene. Four of these tales, dating to the eighth and ninth centuries, have been edited together by Máirín Ó Daly; of these four, three detail instances of judgment or false judgment.[91] Undoubtedly the most striking of these passages is the rhetorical verdict attributed to King Lugaid Laígde in the early tale *Scéla Mosauluim*.[92] The case in question is presented as a particularly difficult legal problem originating in the north of Ireland and brought subsequently into Munster for solution, a somewhat surprising change in venue that ought probably to be seen in the context of the tale's claim that Lugaid was the son of a former king of Tara.[93] The plaintiff's plea asks Lugaid to decide how a son is to be brought into the inheritance of his father, and deliberately invokes the authority of *fír naicnith*, the "law of nature"—the law believed to have obtained in Ireland before the coming of Christianity to the island.[94] Although the plaintiff's remarks are too spare to allow us to understand much about the circumstances of the case, Lugaid's verdict makes clear that the issue is one having to do with when a woman's oath as to the paternity of her child is to be accepted:

Fris-gart Lugith: Fír mná baíthe sceo gaíthe dlomthair. [Is] sí con-oí con-beir, [is] sí ro fitir contaibir[95] *toil, [is] sí for-thoing firu con-legat corpu fri baíse búadrath, [is] sí . . . fri bás sóeraib sceo dóeraib. For-toing a clanna bas gáeth nad- a claind -cummasca fri fóentacha folma, ar is báeth nech con- fri robaíth -ruici.*[96]

Lugaid answered: "May the proof of a [sexually] foolish or [sexually] prudent woman be proclaimed. It is she who protects that which she brings forth; it is she who knows whether she gives her affection, it is she who over-swears[97] men who have intercourse [with her] because of the perturbation of lust;[98] it is she who . . . (omission?) against death with respect to free and base persons.[99] She[100] who is prudent, [and] who does not associate her children with destitute prostrate persons[101]—[she it is who] overswears [men in the matter of the paternity of] her children, for whoever associates with the very foolish is [her or himself] foolish."[102]

Once again, Lugaid's verdict is marked out from the rest of the proceedings by the clever rhetorical prose in which it is couched. As in the other instances we have seen, there is alliteration (*con-legat corpu fri baíse búadrath*), rhyme (*baíthe/gaíthe, sóeraib/dóeraib*), parallel phrasing (*is sí . . . is sí*), and syntactical constructions often associated with poetry, such as preposed genitives (*baíse búadrath*) and tmesis (*con- . . . -ruici*) Of particular note in this instance is the constant play on the prefix *con-*, "jointly," which seems deliberately designed to invoke the sexual coupling that lies at the heart of the legal problem in question (the play on *con-* is even more evident than might be immediately apparent, in that *-cummasca* is a prototonic form of the verb *con-mesca*).

Another fruitful source for instances of the portrayal of juristic speech are the legal tales that the evidence suggests may have played an important role in the oral curriculum of the *Bretha Nemed* school.[103] Were we reliant only on the *Bretha Nemed* composers for our knowledge of these stories, we would be hard pressed to reconstruct them in any detail, since the main *Bretha Nemed* tracts quote this speech without giving us any indication at all as to what the tales themselves were about. Fortunately, a later author, whose work has been preserved in manuscript H 3. 17 of Trinity College

Dublin (TCD 1336), took it upon himself to summarize the stories before they could be lost.[104] This author would appear to have been working directly from a text or texts of the *Bretha Nemed* tradition, as his usual tactic is to quote a line or two from an extended rhetorical passage in one of the tracts and then introduce his own work with *is e scel foraithmenadar hic*, "the story he refers to here is. . . ."[105] His main goal was clearly to provide a fictional context for these rhetorical passages, although of course it is possible that the tales with which he was familiar differed significantly from the stories as the *Bretha Nemed* compilers themselves knew them.[106] Indeed, he bemoans on one occasion the fact that many of the stories referred to in the text from which he was working are no longer widely known in his own day.[107]

Of the roughly fourteen tales summarized by him (in varying degrees of comprehensibility, it must be said), eight contextualize the excerpt in question as an instance of formal judicial speech.[108] In three of these stories, it is the king who speaks, acting either on his own or in conjunction with a jurist to reach a decision on a legal case; in two others, it is the jurist himself, and in three (possibly four) others, a poet or poets acting in a judicial capacity. In all of them, the pattern is the same: the body of the tale is couched in plain prose, while all instances of (what purports to be) verbatim judicial speech are phrased in a type of heavily rhetorical, alliterative language that in the context of the story marks out what is said as oral performance.

A representative example of this pattern is to be found in tale three,[109] in which untended pigs belonging to a man named Mugna attack and eat the son of Maine.[110] Maine then takes Mugna's pigs in distraint to force him to resolve the claim against him for the death of the boy, and puts them into a house where there is a calf also belonging to Mugna. Mugna's pigs eat the calf as well, and both Maine and Mugna then approach Conchobar's legendary jurist Sencha—Maine seeking reparation for the death of his son and Mugna seeking compensation for his calf. Sencha, interestingly hesitant in this case to give judgment on his own, approaches Conchobar and asks for his verdict, which Conchobar then gives (the excerpt is from *Bretha Nemed Tóisech*): *Maine main, maine anmain; maine maín día mac mór foguil ae, anmaín immairicc dalta dá deil*,[111] "Damages to Maine, damages against Maine.[112] Damages to Maine for his son—his lawsuit is a great injury [to him]. Damages against [Maine] in respect of the destruction poured out by his (Mugna's) pigs."[113] Sencha then inquires further whether Maine should be given the pigs of Mugna in compensation, but Conchobar replies in another rhetorical passage that whereas animals under the supervision of a suitable caretaker are not liable for homicide fines in respect of their first offense, animals not under supervision incur the full penalty. What is particularly interesting about this tale is that all judicial speech reported in it, including not only Conchobar's decision on the matter but also Sencha's initial approach to the king laying out the facts of the case, is couched in *rosc*. Alliteration is evident throughout—Sencha's initial approach to the king, for example, begins *ruchtaid ruib ringsid maine maic miandan*,[114] "grunting pigs (?) tore apart [the son of] Maine son of Miandan." Moreover, the lexicon drawn on in these utterances is highly poetic and obscure. *Ruchtaid ruib* is a good example in itself—there are easier and more mundane ways to say "pigs." And there is wordplay as well, such as the deliberate juxtaposition in Conchobar's first speech of the personal name Maine and the word *maín*, "wealth" with its negative *anmaín*, literally "un-wealth," but here translated "damages."

Another tale from H 3.17 illustrates the same phenomenon.[115] In this story, a servant (*gilla*) of the Ulster hero Conall Cernach gives another of Conchobar's warriors, Lóegaire Buadach, in pledge (*i rrathaiges*) for the repayment of a debt within ten days. The servant defaults on the obligation, and Lóegaire does not see him until a year later at Emain Macha. Spotting the servant walking between his master Conall and another Ulsterman, Amairgen, Lóegaire advances carrying a rod (*flesc*), perhaps as a sign of his intent to enforce his claim. The servant answers Lóegaire's challenge by promising to do right (*cert*) by him in the matter. However, his offer is rather forcefully refused: Lóegaire seizes the spear Amairgen is carrying, and without further preliminaries slays the servant with it. A brawl erupts, and the matter goes to Conchobar and Sencha for judgment. The text does not specify who precisely was involved either in the fight or the resulting legal case, but the situation would seem to pit Lóegaire against both Conall and Amairgen—the former in virtue of the victim's having been his servant, and the latter as a result of the misuse of his spear.

As usual, the tale cited in H 3. 17 quotes only the first line of Conchobar's verdict; however, what appears to be a fuller version occurs in *Bretha Nemed Déidenach* under the heading of *Conchabhar cecinit*, "Conchobar sang":

Co do gaibh nech ní ad-ella? Ernedh (no do beir) Aimirghin arm urdhorn. dorn im adrubhairt domigedh gan aimhles nuadh, oighfiach fair faobhar sgeo rinn. rinn rolais Laogaire. let a buaidh, let a ambuaidh. Aimhirgin arm urdhorn.[116]

How does one recover what one undertakes? Amairgen bestows (or: gives) a weapon from [his] fist. A fist that has brought it [the spear] into play. Estimate it [as being] without harm [being intended] by him. A full fine on him (Lóegaire) in respect of edge and spear-point: a spear-point that Lóegaire threw. With you[117] [is] the victory [in the lawsuit], with you is the defeat. Amairgen [bestows] a weapon from [his] fist.

Once again, Conchobar's decision in the case is marked by its style as separate from the rest of the text. It is alliterative both within and among lines (although linking alliteration is not entirely consistent): **Erned**

Aimirghin **arm urdh**orn / **d**orn / . . . **d**omigedh . . . sgeo **r**inn / **r**inn rolais
Laogaire / **l**et a buaidh / **l**et a ambuaidh / Aimhirgin **a**rm **u**rdhorn. It employs archaic and rhetorical terminology (*sceo; dorn* and *airdhorn* instead of
the more mundane *lám*); and it signals the completion of the verse by repeating a phrase used earlier in the passage (*Aimhirgin arm urdhorn*), a common feature of early Irish poetry. Moreover, in this case we have an instance
of ordinary speech to which to compare it. The exchange between Lóegaire and the servant just before the latter's death, while distinguished by
the use of legal terminology (for example, *cert*), does not share any of the
rhetorical features of Conchobar's utterance. His proclamation is conceptualized in the context of the tale as performative; their conversation is not.

Other H 3. 17 tales depict judicial speech in precisely the same manner.
In tale one, both Morann's verdict and Neire's plea are phrased in the
rhetorical style, whereas the plaintiff's request to Neire to take on his
case—a request that presumably occurred outside the confines of the judicial hearing itself—is phrased in plain prose.[118] Tale two is particularly interesting, for in this instance we have both a judgment and the correction
of that judgment. A case concerning injuries inflicted on a man by pigs who
themselves had been attacked by a dog is presented—in highly rhetorical
language—to Coirpre Lifechair for resolution. Coirpre's judgment, which
is alliterative, draws on a technical vocabulary, and features an example of
the "archaic" verbal construction known as tmesis, then follows: *Diubruiter*
cach cethra 'na .c.cinadh, cia rorr, cia forgabad fuilib sceo crechtuibh esorguin on
sceo uithir ar codocertsat-sin ro rind riam rarsad,[119] "every animal is forfeited in
respect of its first offense, though it may have killed, though it may attack
with wounds and lacerations, beating, blemish and sickness, for they adjudge those who have killed with a point (teeth, in this case?) before."[120]
However, Coirpre has in this instance made a mistake: his father, Cormac
mac Airt, a king famed in Irish tradition for his sense of justice, corrects
Coirpre's erroneous judgment in a rhetorical passage of his own, assigning
the blame in this instance to the dog.[121] In tales four and six from the collection edited by Dillon, the judges in question are poets instead of kings.
The text in tale four is too partial to allow us to make very much of it, although the words that remain certainly hint at a verdict phrased in poetic
language.[122] Tale six features a judgment made by divination (*imbas*) after
the death of the alleged offender.[123] Several of the gages listed here are
mythical objects associated with characters known elsewhere in early Irish
literature, and two of them recur later in H 3. 17 in tales ten and eleven.[124]
In tale seven, Sencha is again the judge, this time in a case involving a
woman carried off to some degree voluntarily by a servant (*druth*, "fool,")
of Conchobar's. As in the previous instances we have examined, Sencha's
judgment is phrased in *rosc*, a language that immediately marks it out as
performance: *Ceithri hoga i nnaithgin neillnide ar cach tresi na toirsed*

taieltaidh[125] *taidell,* "four maidens in compensation for [her] violation for every three days that Taidell should not come [back] to her house."[126]

Examples of this sort could be multiplied over and over from the law-books and related tales. Cormac's judgment on a disputed sword is prefaced by a statement in *rosc* that appears also in *Bretha Nemed Déidenach* assigned to the poet-jurist Neire.[127] Tuathal Techtmar, ancestor of the Connachta and Uí Néill, addresses Ulster judge Sencha mac Ailella in *rosc* during the course of a land dispute resolution.[128] And two particularly well-articulated examples are the pleas, counterpleas, and verdict cited in the legal tale of Ailill and Art,[129] and Dubthach's dramatic declaration in the "Pseudo-Historical Prologue to the *Senchas Már*," both of which will be discussed later in this book. Again, these are tales rather than records of actual judicial speech. On the other hand, their unanimity is striking. Moreover, the phenomenon we have noted in the mythological sources seems to be confirmed by nonliterary texts about judgment. Legal tracts describing the judging process often imply a marked difference between judicial speech and more ordinary genres of discourse. *Bretha Nemed* texts particularly stress the role played by maxims (*fásaige*) and the type of alliterative legal verse known as *roscad* (pl. *roscaid* or *roscada,* generally taken as synonymous with *rosc*) in establishing the authority of a judge's verdict, although they also make clear that *roscad* in the absence of a thorough knowledge of the law of nature is insufficient.[130] (Presumably, many of the fictional verdicts cited earlier would have been considered *roscada*.) Great emphasis is laid on grounding judgment *co n-ailcibh roscud 7 fasach 7 tesdemuin,*[131] "on the rocks of *roscad* and maxims and (scriptural) testimony." Obviously the fact that a judge's decision might be based upon such authorities does not necessarily mean that they would always have been cited orally in his verdict. On the other hand, sometimes they clearly were, as in the case of Lugaid Laígde's judgment above. One *Bretha Nemed* text advises prospective judges that

fírbreth berur fri fasach; fas cach nanfasach, arachta cach dicanta, dicanta cach diaruid, diaruid cach difasuid ar id fasuide bearda bretha imo neire.[132]

true judgment is given upon a maxim; everything not in accordance with a maxim is empty, everything that has been chanted away is to be bound, everything unbound is to be chanted away, everything not in accordance with maxims is unbound, for it is maxims which establish judgments, o my Neire.

"Chanting" in this context would seem to refer to the recitation of maxims in the course of the judgment referred to: the passage seems to envisage a clear link between the validity of the judgment and performative speech. Small wonder that judges are instructed explicitly *ba f[e]asach, ba findsrothach,*[133] "may you be knowledgeable, may you be fair-speaking." Other texts make precisely the same connection.[134]

Performance and Authority: Aesthetics

The point is clear and it is consistent: when jurists in contact with the legal process in early Ireland thought and wrote about formal judicial speech, they characterized it as oral performance. Moreover, the evidence suggests that law, like other contemporary performance traditions, had its own aesthetic standards, conventions and modes of behavior. This is evident not only in the rhetorical language and poetic form that the lawbooks suggest was characteristic of formal legal speech, but in the very precise instructions given in the tracts for how such speech should be performed. The short passages on court demeanor and pleading procedure extant in manuscript E 3. 3[135] and, in a slightly different form, in the wisdom text *Tecosca Cormaic*, are quite clear. Litigants and their advocates are to speak clearly and fluently, without hesitating or stumbling; they are also to speak at an appropriate volume, neither too loudly nor too softly. And they are instructed above all to avoid all indications of anger, from shouting or speaking violently, to using abusive language, to inciting the crowd on behalf of their case. Indeed, to judge from the number of prohibitions placed on pleading tactics that might suggest irritation or emotional involvement on the part of the pleader, a display of annoyance was one of the most serious transgressions an advocate could commit.[136] They were also to refrain from intruding themselves into the affair in the form of self-praise, although one of the H 3. 17 tales suggests that advocates acting on behalf of a plaintiff might present the case as though it were their very own, perhaps in order to render their plea more immediate and more urgent.[137] And of course they were expected to know and abide by the rules of the judicial game: any attempt to change pleas or depart from modes of address and proof recognized in the community brought censure.[138]

At first glance, prescriptions of this type might seem to speak merely to practicalities relating to the peaceful conduct of court business. The prohibition against speaking too softly, for example, could well reflect the physical size of the space in which the proceedings were taking place and the number of participants involved in it, as Kelly suggests.[139] However, a number of these admonitions cannot be explained in such a manner. Hesitation, stumbling, stiffness or slowness of speech, shouting or speaking in an overly loud tone: injunctions of this sort betray an interest not merely in practical issues associated with proper judicial conduct, but in the actual aesthetics of the presentation.[140] They are guidelines to performers as to the artistic expectations of the tradition within which they are acting—stage directions, in a sense, and yet also more in that they speak to standards within a tradition and not merely to matters of individual style. The idea that the speaking of law might be regarded as an aesthetic experience may seem somewhat far-fetched to modern eyes. However, it is one borne out time and again in the sources relating to legal speech. Particularly striking is a passage found in H 3. 17: *Ceatharda frisa cuibdither a mberla feine . . . dluithe coibce . . . comuaim n-aisneisin . . . cuimre labhartha . . . tucait mbinniusa,*[141] "Four things by which the legal language of the *Féni*[142] is rendered harmonious: compact, cohesive [construction][143] . . . the metrical joining together of recitation . . . brevity of speech . . . a foundation of melodious sound."[144] Two specific aspects of performative legal speech are highlighted here: the construction of the utterance itself in accordance with customary technical standards for compositions of this type, and the production of a piece that is harmonious to the ear. What is said must be concise, must refrain from the vice of prolixity—and the passage cites examples of tediously prolix speech in case there should be any doubt—and must be constructed in such a way as to please the ear of the listener. Descriptions like these clearly suggest that legal speech was considered by the Irish a form of verbal art and, as such, was to be assessed not merely on the basis of its legal content, but on the extent to which it fulfilled the aesthetic expectations of its genre.

Aesthetics and artistic technique come together again in the manner in which the tracts suggest that legal cases were to be constructed and enunciated. In the passage cited above from H 3. 17, *[t]ucait binniusa,* "a foundation of melodious sound," is glossed *.i. a foclaibh 7 [i] n-analibh,* "that is, in respect of words and breaths." The reference to "words" (*focal*) almost certainly speaks to diction and the art of effective word choice, both obviously related to the production of melodious sound. The mention of "breaths" (*anal*) is, however, even more interesting. A brief passage from H 3. 18 gives us a clue as to what is meant by this:

.i. i nanalaib . . . : fot naenanala do boaire 7 .u. focuil inti, a do do filid 7 .x. focail indtib, a tri do flaith 7 focal ar .xx.it indtib, a secht do eclais 7 nai focail .xl.at indtib[145]

that is, in respect of breaths . . . : the length of a single breath for a freeman and five words [are to be articulated] in it (the breath), two [breaths] for a poet and ten words [are to be articulated] in them, and three [breaths] for a lord and twenty-one words [are to be articulated] in them, and seven [breaths] for a church[man] and forty-nine words [are to be articulated] in them.

This principle of determining the number of inhalations to be taken during a performance according to status, and of enunciating five words per breath in cases pertaining to the freeman and poetic grades and seven words per breath for cases involving lords and clerics, is spelled out even more clearly in a short tract on "breaths" contained in Egerton 88, which in turn draws on *Bretha Nemed Toísech:*[146]

Mo nere nuallgnaith, diamba brithem, ni bera ai nad urscarttha, arabeir corus nae: ai flath[a], aie filed, ai feine; ai flatha fod teora nanala ar imtimcellugud (?) flath filed feine;[147] *ai filed nad feth comdire fri flaith, canar dib nanaluib, ar us treisi filethus feinechus; ai feine fod nanala cenmotha righbruigaid no rechtuire righ, ar dlige rechtuire foraei. . . . Co deich do focluibh feduir fir fonadma, ar ba deichtib donidnacht do daine dagrecht ro fir feine fuirmed.*[148]

My Neire accustomed to proclaiming, if you would be a judge, may you not judge a lawsuit that you do not "clean out," that proceeds in accordance with the regulation governing lawsuits: the suit of a lord, the suit of a poet, the suit of the Féni (free Irishmen). A suit of a lord: [it entails] the length of three breaths because of the mutual surrounding of lords, of poets and of the Féni. A suit of a poet who does not advance to equal honor-price to a lord, let it be sung in two breaths, for the status of poet is stronger than the status of the Féni. The suit of the Féni: [it entails] the length of one breath, except for a royal hospitaller or royal steward, for a steward is entitled to a superior [level of] lawsuit (literally an "oversuit"). . . . Up to ten words is the truth of the *fonaidm*[149] advanced, for it was in tens that the Good Law (e.g., the Mo*saic* law) was given to men, [the good law] by which the truth of the Féni was established.[150]

The intersection of artistry, technical skill, and politics could hardly be clearer than it is here. In these passages, speech itself becomes a vehicle for the performance of social rank and the assertion of legal rights. Persons of superior status are entitled to perform or have performed on their behalf (the text does not make clear which) longer and more complex judicial utterances. Particularly interesting are the last few sentences, which suggest that even a temporary elevation in social rank due to the holding of public office might reshape the distribution of authoritative speech within the community. Even more striking is the way in which the aesthetics of the performance both mirror and perpetuate the status distinctions envisaged in the tract. At issue here is poetic technique in all its aspects: not only the rhythm and construction of the piece but the clarity of the performer's enunciation as well. It is technically more difficult to articulate clearly seven words in a single inhalation of breath than it is to articulate five; presumably only accomplished performers would be capable of performing the former feat with any degree of success. It seems reasonable to infer that the more intricate the speech, the more artistically pleasing the performance was likely to be regarded as being. Law was art; the possibility that it served also as entertainment must be seriously considered.

Here we must pause to contemplate the link between law and other more obviously entertainment-oriented traditions like storytelling. The lawbooks testify to the existence of a common mythology among legal specialists—fictional characters and "settings" that serve as the backdrop for the early history of the law as the jurists understood (and constructed) it.[151] And individual tracts also make frequent use of fictional stories to illustrate the principles they outline, a practice that appears to be particularly common in cases where the custom in question was not of long standing.[152] Many characters and stories mentioned in the lawbooks seem to have had meaning largely within a specifically legal context—the female jurist Bríg, for example, who appears both in *Din Techtugud* and in *Di*

Chetharshlicht Athgabála, or the tales of Asal and of Cóicthe in that same tract.[153] Similarly, Morann and Neire Núallgnáith are most closely associated with law and texts of the wisdom tradition, although Neire may appear also in the poetic eulogy for St. Columba, the *Amra Choluim Chille*.[154] But whereas characters like these figure largely in the legal texts, others can be found elsewhere in Irish storytelling tradition, secular and ecclesiastical. References to characters associated with the Ulster Cycle, for example, are very common. The legendary Ulster king Conchobar features both in the H 3. 17 tales and in the tract on distraint, but is considerably more famous for his dealings with Cú Chulainn and his rule from Emain Macha.[155] Similarly, Conchobar's jurist Sencha was at least as well known for the *cráeb sídamail*, "peacemaking branch," with which he often attempted to calm the fractious Ulstermen as he was for being an authoritative judge.[156] Éogan mac Durthacht, one of the "bad guys" in the sad tale of Deirdre, is mentioned along with Amairgen, the father of another Ulster hero, Conall Cernach, in the law tract known as the *Heptads*.[157] And Conall Cernach himself finds himself at odds with his heroic counterpart Lóegaire Búadach not only in the delightful saga of *Fled Bricrenn* but in the *Bretha Nemed* legal tales as well.[158]

There are characters from the historical and pseudohistorical literature mentioned in the law tracts,[159] and also from the Finn Cycle.[160] And then of course there is the ecclesiastical storytelling tradition. Recent work on the law has made clear just how frequently the jurists drew on ecclesiastical tales and characters in their writings.[161] Patrick is famous as a character not only in hagiography, but in pseudohistorical and genealogical traditions as well. His poetic counterpart Dubthach features in the hagiographical literature of the day as the disappointed suitor of Saint Brigit in the ninth-century *Bethu Brigte*.[162] It is probably not necessary to remark that Judas Iscariot, Lucifer, and Adam, all of whom appear in the contract tract *Di Astud Chor*, also led full, if not exactly tranquil or rewarding, lives outside the lawbooks.[163] Indeed the relationship between the legal and literary traditions was clearly not limited to the scripting of brief tales about or allusions to famous literary personages. Neil McLeod has recently argued for a considerably more direct integration of the two with respect to the mythology surrounding Dian Cécht, physician of the mythical Túatha Dé Danann.[164] This is certainly the case with Patrick as well: Joseph Nagy has argued persuasively that the encounter between Patrick and Dubthach that is said to have resulted in the composition of the *Senchas Már* lawbook must be seen in the context of the many other instances of *immacallam*, "dialogue" between literate clerics and representatives of the pagan oral past occurring throughout the literary and hagiographical traditions.[165]

Tales and characters like these are of course known to us only from written sources, and we have no real way of knowing whether they would have featured also in the public performance of the law. Without records to tell us what jurists actually said and did, it is difficult to know what oral use they might have made of them. Certainly they played an important role in judicial instruction, which is itself depicted in many sources as a performative venture.[166] And legal schools may have varied in this respect: of the two principal lawbooks of medieval Ireland, *Bretha Nemed* seems more inclined to make extended use of fictional narratives and of characters known principally from other genres. However, it is at least worth noting that the texts on which we are dependent for our knowledge of poetry and storytelling likely also had their origins in the literate setting of the monastery, and yet most scholars simply presume that the characters and themes in these texts had a significant oral existence outside the boundaries of the ecclesiastical enclosure.[167] Given the role played by fiction in the written legal tradition—given also the jurists' own need to sway the audience to their point of view—it seems unlikely they would have failed to make use of such a valuable tool. Myth was clearly used by jurists in their written work to instruct and to validate particular approaches or institutions. It seems probable that in the oral setting, it was also used to entertain and persuade.

But was there then a link between the ability to entertain and the ability to persuade? Here we come at last to the issue of authority, and to the manner in which communities and individuals in dispute were induced to lend support to particular judicial proceedings. Of course it mattered fundamentally who proclaimed the verdict in question. Large swords have a tendency to be persuasive even in the absence of eloquent legal rhetoric, and to ignore the realities of power in situations of this nature would be foolhardy. If a king declared a case to be settled in a particular way and had the authority to back up his position, it was unlikely to be challenged. However, the role played by performance in early Irish dispute resolution must surely enrich our sense of how things might work in the absence of such coercion. The evidence presented thus far suggests that law in early Ireland was a form of verbal art, grounded as much in aesthetics—themselves status linked and hence not politically neutral—as in the imposition and enforcement of communal norms. This is a fact of more than ordinary importance to our understanding of early Irish law. For as we have seen, the art of the legal specialist did not exist in isolation from other genres of oral performance: as the sources make clear, legal art was embedded in a complex network of cultural and artistic traditions, secular and ecclesiastical. What jurists said and did in the course of their job resonated directly with practices and perceptions outside the judicial arena, most notably poetry, religion, and storytelling. And in those arts, it was the ability to perform effectively that gave authority to the event. Poems that display greater intricacy in their construction will garner more attention than poems that are loose or ill-formed; priests who speak forcefully will likely command more respect than those who mumble. The aesthetic quality of the event could determine the authority enjoyed both by the performance itself and by the specialist who enacted it.

Historians are not accustomed to thinking about aesthetics as a basis for political power, although this is a point that has been current in the anthropological literature for many years. Studies of the past three decades have underscored the extent to which in many world cultures verbal art is a crucial part of how society organizes itself and its values. Beliefs about language can themselves have an impact on how onlookers assess a given event. William Sayers's superb article on the dialogue between Cú Chulainn and his wife-to-be Emer highlights the intimacy perceived to exist between verbal eloquence on the one hand, and wisdom on the other. As he points out, *binne*, "eloquence, melodiousness," is actually equated with "truth" in one medieval Irish gloss.[168] One cannot help but wonder about the extent to which variations in the aesthetic impact of the individual performances associated with a given legal case might themselves have helped to determine its eventual outcome. As Corinne Kratz points out, the emotional impact of an individual performance is often a crucial element in establishing the affective power and transformative potential of the whole. Dramatic elements like staging or timing can profoundly affect the willingness of an audience to lend credence to the statements made during that event—as we ourselves know only too well from our own experience with the courtroom.[169]

It is impossible for us to judge the aesthetics of any particular performance at this distance. However, the sources do suggest that the longer and more elaborate a performance was, the more authoritative the audience for whom it was enacted would have considered it to be. Certainly there are indications that the link between eloquence and truth was believed to obtain in legal as well as social matters. Particularly interesting in this respect are texts that purport to describe false or erroneous judgments issued by kings. False judgment is, for example, a major motif in the complex of tales surrounding the rivalry between Mac Con and Ailill Ólomm.[170] *Cath Maige Mucrama* tells of a dispute that ensues when two foster-brothers, Éogan mac Ailella and Lugaid Mac Con, both lay claim to the same magical harper whom they pluck out of a tree. Ailill is asked to judge between their respective claims, whereupon it is revealed that although Lugaid had claimed the music first, Éogan had claimed the musician. Ailill subsequently awards the musician to Éogan, his own son, a biased and all-or-nothing outcome that the composer of the text clearly regards as unjust. The composer is not alone: Lugaid contests the verdict, and the matter has eventually to be settled on the battlefield, a socially destructive war that pits one foster-brother against another. What is most striking about Ailill's erroneous judgment, however—especially in the context of the other judgments we have examined so far—is the brief, truncated, and completely unrhetorical prose in which it is delivered: *"Is fír,"* or Ailill, *"la Éogan in fer,"*[171] "It is true," said Ailill, "Éogan gets the man." In this instance, the falseness of the judgment is not only revealed by the absence of eloquence, but to some degree effected by it as well: Ailill's language proves unable to persuade those in attendance of the justice of his position.

Similar presumptions about language and truth are visible also in the famous story of Cormac's correcting of the false judgment of Mac Con, a correction that results in the ousting of Mac Con from the kingship. This story is told twice in the collection, once in *Scéla Éogain*, where it is summarized rather than spelled out in detail, and once in *Cath Maige Mucrama* itself, which quotes the language both of the original judgment and of Cormac's challenge to it. In both passages, the legal issue is the same: sheep have eaten the woad crop of the queen, and Mac Con declares that the sheep are to be forfeited by their owner in compensation for the offense. Cormac, however, challenges this judgment, observing that the proper compensation in such a case is the shearing of the sheep in question, with the wool going to the queen, since both woad and wool will grow back in the future. Most interesting from our point of view is the language in which the proceedings take place:

Táncas i rréir Meic Con. "At-berim," or Mac Con, "na caírig ind." Ro boí Cormac 'na mac bic for dérgud inna farad. "Acc, a daeteac," orse, "ba córu lomrad na caírech i llomrad na glasne, ar ásfaid in glassen, ásfaid ind oland forsnaib caírib."[172]

[That case] came before Mac Con for decision. "I declare," said Mac Con, "the sheep [to be forfeited] for it." Cormac, a small boy, was beside him on the couch. "No, foster-father," he said, "the shearing of the sheep in return for the shearing of the woad would be more just, for the woad will grow and the wool will grow on the sheep."

Here again we see an unjust verdict delivered in plain, unornamented, and exceptionally brief language. Cormac's correction of Mac Con's decision, however, while not as heavily rhetorical as many of the statements we have seen (perhaps because he is a young boy at the time?), nonetheless employs a number of familiar techniques: parallel phrasing (**lomrad** *na caírech* i **llomrad** *na glasne;* **ásfaid** *in glassen,* **ásfaid** *ind oland*), alliteration (*córu/ caírech/caírib;* *ásfaid/ásfaid/oland*), and of course the metaphorical juxtaposition of shearing and growing. The complexity of his speech—and thus the aesthetic qualities and persuasiveness of his performance—trumps that of Mac Con hands down.

The connection between the quality of the legal case as performed and the authority subsequently accorded to that event recurs also in other sources of the period. In some, the connection is clear: *Bretha Nemed Toísech,* for example, speaks of lawsuits and prosecutions being ruined because of "very evident poetic faults."[173] In others, the connection is certainly implied, but is perhaps less clearcut than in the stories above. Cormac's correction of Coirpre's judgment about the rampaging pigs is an excellent example. Coirpre's judgment itself is definitely artistic speech, employing as it does many of the poetic techniques visible in other passages of this type. However, it is quite brief and—relatively speaking—intelligible, in that it says exactly what it means: "every animal is forfeited in respect of its first offense, though it may have killed, though it may attack with wounds and lacerations." Cormac's correction is twice as long, takes the form of the poetic structure known as a *dúnad*,[174] and is much more heavily ornamented than is Coirpre's speech. There is considerably more alliteration (***Cairpri clumar; baoth/breth/bidh; clitchuib/cund/coigertuibh; toich/tadhall/torbu/toiseaghar***), and more speech that is allusive or obscure. Indeed, the most straightforward clauses of the poem are the lines with which it opens, which are clearly intended as an insult to Coirpre himself: *Aill . . . mo cairpri clumar, mosber cach dochann baoth a breth, bidh iar tacruib clitchuib do cund coigertuibh,*[175] "Listen, my Coirpre of great fame, every incompetent person will soon give judgment; foolish is his judgment; let [this case] proceed after suits to a competent person for sheltering judgments."[176] In other words, while the contrast between the two proclamations is not as marked here as it is in some other cases, the manner in which they are constructed and presented seems nonetheless to presume an equation between the truth of the statement and the complexity of the language in which it is couched.

Performance and Authority: Prophecy

To this point, we have looked at authority from the point of view of the aesthetics of the performance. Another issue raised by the close connections between law and other verbal arts in Ireland is that of inspiration and the origins of specialist knowledge. Certain forms of verbal art—poetry in particular—are often conceptualized in early Irish literature as mantic endeavors, the secular counterpart to Christian prophecy, concerned with the proclamation of truths acquired partly or wholly from the otherworld. Recent scholarship tends not to stress the otherworldly elements of the poetic profession. Breatnach, in his editions of two critical texts on the subject, "The Caldron of Poesy" and *Uraicecht na Ríar*, for example, lays relatively little emphasis on the otherworldly, preferring to emphasize instead the rigorous training and ecclesiastical learning poets (*filid*) regarded as necessary to their work.[177] And McCone and others have also taken issue with the image of the pagan, otherworldly inspired poet, pointing to texts which associate the *filid* closely with the church, and which distinguish sharply between the learned order of *filid* on the one hand and the ignorant, pagan, lower-class bards and satirists with whom the *filid* obviously felt themselves to be in competition on the other.[178]

Breatnach and McCone developed their views in reaction to earlier scholarship in which poets tended to be depicted less as craftsmen than as visionary beings whose special insight was bound up with the performance of exotic pagan rituals.[179] Unquestionably, their work has been a useful corrective. We now have a new appreciation of the poet as artist and learned technician—the proud member of a hereditary profession that zealously guarded its privileges and access to lordly patronage. In particular, the matter of the close connections between the *filid* and the church has now been placed beyond all dispute. However, to dismiss altogether the idea that poetry was regarded also as a mantic endeavor is to fly in the face of a great deal of evidence, much of it contemporary with the law tracts themselves.[180] The link between poetry and prophecy is embedded in the ancient terminology of the profession: poets are, literally, "seers" from the etymological point of view.[181] Even learned and unquestionably ecclesiastically informed texts do not shun the otherworldly elements of the craft altogether. The "Caldron of Poesy," for example, may place most of its emphasis on technical training and hereditary status, but it also associates the acquisition of *imbas* ("poetic visionary insight") with sexual desire (often a focus for the otherworld in Irish tradition), magical hazels, and the *síd*, or "fairy mound."[182]

Recently, John Carey has struck a healthy balance between these two visions of the poetic profession, arguing convincingly that while later literati often deliberately exaggerated the otherworldly and pagan elements of the craft—sometimes in order to condemn them, sometimes in order to romanticize a past they no longer truly knew—evidence for an early belief in a divinatory aspect to the profession is none the less quite strong. What Carey calls "the prophetic faculty" of *imbas* is, as he remarks, attested as an aspect of poetic composition in at least three sources dating to the Old Irish period. Little is said in these texts to help us understand what precisely was meant by *imbas*. However, its connection with otherworldly inspiration and insight is clear. In Carey's words, it would be in his words "perverse to ignore or downplay" entirely the mantic aspects of the craft.[183] This is true not least because pre-Christian notions about the prophetic powers of poets were so easily amalgamated with ecclesiastical ideas about prophecy and divine inspiration. Indeed, the essential compatibility of poetic and religious prophecy is spelled out explicitly in "The Caldron of Poesy," which refers to *fáidi déodai 7 dóendai*, "divine and secular prophets" whose words are all *fásaige 7 bretha*, "maxims and judgments" and therefore to be taken seriously.[184]

Given the close ties perceived to exist between jurists on the one hand, and poets and churchmen on the other, it is not difficult to imagine that similar ideas about prophetic authority may have operated in the legal sphere as well. Just as poets were perceived to tap into otherworldly wisdom in their verse, so also do the sources suggest that jurists were regarded at least in some quarters as conveying through their verdicts a truth validated not merely by their knowledge of the law, but also by their access as verbal artists to otherworldly insight. The relationship between language and authority will be discussed in more detail in the following chapters; it is sufficient to note here that one of the outward signs of this truth appears to have been the artistry and obscurity of the language in which it was proclaimed.

Perhaps the clearest exposition of such ideas in early Irish legal literature is the remarkable eighth or ninth-century text known as the "Pseudo-Historical Prologue to the *Senchas Már*,"[185] a version of the myth of the encounter between Patrick and Dubthach to which allusion has already been made. According to the story, the pagan Irish desire to test Patrick and the Christian sense of justice and so choose one of their own to slay Patrick's charioteer in order to see what Patrick will do. Patrick is very angry—he often is in hagiographical literature, and his wrath never bodes well for those who cross him—but wisely selects an expert in native Irish law, the poet Dubthach maccu Lugair, to deliver a verdict in the case. After some preliminary expressions of doubt on the part of Dubthach as to his ability to resolve the dispute without angering Patrick in the process, Patrick tells him essentially to speak what he is inspired by God to speak. The poetic judgment that follows is set apart from the ordinary prose in which the rest of the tale is told by its being phrased in *rosc*: it displays exactly the same syntactical and stylistic features we have seen used in other texts for occasions of this kind. Indeed, in this case, the distinction between Dubthach's judgment and the rest of the proceedings is marked not only in the language he uses but in the manner in which that language appears in the manuscript itself. Harley 432, the only manuscript that cites the text of Dubthach's decision, presents the judgment in the large script reserved in Irish legal manuscripts for text regarded as "canonical." The rest of the story is written in the smaller text customarily used for gloss and commentary—and this despite the fact that Kim McCone has shown that the two are interdependent and likely contemporaneous compositions.[186]

There are several intriguing aspects to this text. Dubthach's judgment is clearly depicted in the tale as performance—indeed, in this instance the cosmos itself provides a dramatic setting for his proclamation by marking the start of the proceedings with an earthquake.[187] Perhaps most interesting, however, is that his judgment is conceptualized as being a prophetic utterance, inspired at once by God and by Dubthach's own poetic insight. The intersection of law, prophecy (pagan and Christian), and verbal art is here made very clear. Particularly striking is the way in which the text of the judgment itself juxtaposes native and Christian notions of authority in a manner designed to underscore the fundamental compatibility of each with the other. There can be no doubt as to its essential orientation: the text is overtly Christian in tenor and content throughout.[188] But the new dispensation is portrayed as building on rather than rejecting the past. The judgment speaks, for example, of the *fír Fíadat*, the "Lord's truth," a phrase that implicitly (and deliberately) invokes the native concept of the *fír flathemon*, the "truth of the ruler." This latter is a complicated concept, but at its heart lies the belief that the ruler is a sacral figure and the justice of his rule embedded in nature to such a degree that any deviation in his moral standing will directly affect the cosmic order. In origin the idea is almost certainly pre-Christian, although the enthusiasm with which such ideas were taken up and embraced by Carolingian kingship theorists among others shows that it was one that could easily be adapted to the new religious circumstances.[189] And indeed just such a breach in the cosmic order is alluded to a few stanzas later in the judgment, where Dubthach is depicted as avowing "by my cheeks, which pledge and dignity will not make blisteringly hot, that I have judged a sound judgment."[190] The reference to blistered cheeks speaks to the belief widely attested in Irish sources that a false judgment uttered by a judge or king would be revealed by an immediate alteration to the physical environment—in this case, the cheeks of the false judge blistering red-hot for shame. But perhaps the clearest expression of the idea that Christian and poetic prophetic faculties both contributed to Dubthach's perception and subsequent proclamation of the truth occurs in the climactic moments of the judgment, where he proclaims his actual decision with the words *[b]retha rechta dom-roíd i réir m'éicse*, "[t]he judgment of law that He has sent me in accordance with my poetic insight . . ."[191] Here God becomes the source of the poet's special prophetic powers.

None of this is to suggest, of course, that an actual knowledge of the law was regarded as unimportant, either for Dubthach himself or for his less mythical judicial colleagues. That, presumably, is what the law tracts are all about. There is nothing in the legal tracts to suggest that technical knowledge and prophetic insight were ever seen as anything but entirely compatible with one another, just as there is nothing in the treatises on poetry to suggest that technical skill and *imbas* were viewed as mutually inconsistent. Indeed, Dubthach's main function in the "Pseudo-Historical Prologue" is to serve as a knowledgeable representative of native tradition as a whole: this is why it is he who is later asked to summarize native law for Patrick in order that the latter might purge it of its unacceptable aspects and give it written form. To highlight the manner in which judgment and juristic speech could be conceptualized as partaking of native and Christian traditions regarding prophetic utterance is certainly not to downplay the more quotidian aspects of the juristic profession. And it is of course difficult to know just how seriously such ideas might have been taken in the world outside the schools. The point is rather to sharpen our sense of the broad spectrum of elements that gave law and lawyers their authority. Juristic performance was not the same as Christian prophecy, clearly. Nor was it synonymous with poetic performance, which had a much more explicitly entertainment aspect to it. But it overlapped with both of these traditions in ways that it is essential not to overlook.

The mantic aspects of the legal craft are underscored by yet another element of the laws, one that may throw light on further aspects of the juristic profession. As Maria Tymoczko has suggested in a characteristically insightful article, it was customary for medieval Irish poets to choose deliberately to disguise their own identities by speaking through the persona of an authoritative poet within the tradition rather than in their own voice. This practice of "poetic masking," as she calls it, was an important aspect of the craft. Through it, an artist rooted in place and time suppressed his own name and circumstances in order to assume the identity of a mythical or historical poet associated with particular emotions or experiences—love, loss, grieving for times long past.

A sign of a *traditional* poetic mask in early Irish or Welsh literature is evidence that a mythic, legendary, or heroic figure has been used over a considerable span of time as the vehicle for affective poetry associated with a limited but determinate range of feeling. Thus a traditional poetic mask can be distinguished on the one hand from the occasional use of a historical or legendary character for masking purposes and on the other hand from the speaking of poetry by a narrative-bound character. Oisín is a clear example of a traditional mask, since this figure is associated with a large body of poems with a similar thematic and affective range spanning a considerable period of time; the speaker of the poem "Aithbe damsa bés mora" may represent the second type, where a mythic character, Buí or the Caillech Bérri, is used effectively as a mask in a particular poem. Fedelm banfáith, who speaks the poem beginning "Atchíu fer find firfes cles" addressed to Medb in *Táin Bó Cúailgne* . . . is an example of the third type, whose poetry is primarily a narrative act within a specific tale.[192]

Masking was a way to distill an emotion or a point of view to its very essence: by restricting what the performer said to the range of sentiments associated with that character, it clarified and focused attentions on the message expressed. It authorized the voice of the individual poet by embedding it within a tradition authorized by long usage, and it simultaneously constricted and liberated that voice by freeing it from the dictates of time and place and social expectation. Because only those who understood the nature and purview of a mask could fully interpret its message, it also constituted a celebration of the values of the community within which it had been donned.[193] One particularly striking aspect of the mask was its links with the realm of the ecstatic, the mystical, the shamanic. As Tymoczko points out, poems of prophecy and mantic vision are often associated with masks in Celtic tradition.[194]

There are distinct hints in the lawbooks that poetic masking of this sort was a feature of the legal tradition as well. Indeed, a tradition of legal masking may even help to explain why sources with such a keen interest in verdicts proclaimed by kings and jurists of the mythical past seem to show so little regard for the decisions of their real-life equivalents. The period of the canonical legal texts is perhaps too short for us to identify truly "traditional" masks in the sense outlined by Tymoczko, and certainly in the legal sources there is a great deal of overlap between the three categories she discusses. Dubthach is of course himself a mask: the virtuous pagan whose encounter with Patrick is the occasion of so much prophetic verse.[195] Bodainn's judgment in *Mellbretha* would presumably be an example of the speaking of verse as an act constrained by narrative, and Conchobar's various declarations in H 3. 17 would seem to fall under the category of a (pseudo)historical figure being used as an occasional mask without any real consistency in the manner of message attributed to him. Sencha is an interesting case. Usually he is depicted as the very model of the wise and knowing judge. However, in *Din Techtugud* he proclaims an erroneous judgment pertaining to women's methods of claiming land that is then corrected by a female jurist Bríg (herself the standard judge for judgments on cases pertaining to women).[196] Even in this he displays consistency, however, in that he does not so much depart from his standard persona of experienced judge as function as an exemplar of the best in male judicial wisdom—and hence as a foil for Bríg's more authoritative judgment in a case concerning members of her own sex. Sencha's basic essence—wise male judge working in concert with a great king—remains the same, even when his function does not. Indeed, this is undoubtedly why the glossator identifies Bríg as his daughter. He is less a mask for the communication of particular ideas than an icon for a specific type of judgment: male, royal, official, informed both by knowledge and by experience.

The same could be said of characters in the wisdom and instructional literature such as Morann and Neire, who are constantly invoked throughout the *Bretha Nemed* material. The subjects these figures address vary tremendously, ranging from gages to poetic learning to neighborhood law and status. In that sense they—and legal masks generally—differ from figures like Oisín. Like Sencha, their consistency lies less in the expression of a particular range of emotional response or subject matter than in the invocation of a specific instructional venue—in this instance, the direct oral teachings of teacher and pupil within an ancient, and hence authoritative, tradition.[197] Phrases such as "my Neire Núallgnáth, if you would be a judge, you should judge . . . ," and "O wealthy, mighty Morann, tell me how . . . ," and "state O Neire, how . . ." introduce what purport to be conversations between teacher and disciple. Often in *Bretha Nemed* these exchanges seem a bit one-sided. Many are conceptualized as declarations on a particular subject addressed by Morann to Neire,[198] while some seem to be imagined either as questions posed by Neire which Morann then answers, or as exchanges in which Neire's purported question to Morann is so detailed that the answer is essentially given in the course of asking the question.[199] Sometimes the instruction is imagined as quite extended: the wisdom treatise *Audacht Morainn* ("Testament of Morann") purports to be a lengthy address to Neire which Neire is then himself told to communicate to King Feradach Find Fechtnach. In all of these texts, however, the characters of Morann and Neire are more or less fixed, both in relationship to one another and to the tradition they represent. Morann is the teacher and Neire the disciple or, in the case of one of the H 3. 17 tales, Morann is the judge and Neire the pleader.[200] They are both, however, wisdom figures, endowed both with technical knowledge and poetic insight: indeed, in one passage it is Neire himself who is appealed to. In another, it is he who is accredited with judgments on the status of various ranks of poets.[201]

Other figures function in similar fashion within the legal tradition: the famous poet Amairgen, for example, whose advice is sought in the *Bretha Nemed* material on the subject of poetic honor-price and prerogatives, and the poet Athairne, to whom is ascribed a passage on the topic of compensation due to poets.[202] Both of these figures differ from Morann and Neire in that their wisdom seems to be focused specifically on poetry rather than on law in general, as befits their characters as they are defined elsewhere in early Irish tradition. The role they play as masks within the legal tradition is, however, very similar.[203] Another instructional legal "couple" whose exchanges range broadly over various aspects of the law and who approach what one might term "masklike" status are the kings Cormac mac Airt and his son Coirpre Lifechair. An important wisdom tract, the *Tecosca Cormaic*, is purportedly addressed by Cormac to Coirpre. And the law tract *Bretha Étgid* begins with a tale about how Cormac was wounded and thus put out of the kingship of Tara. His son Coirpre then took over the kingship and caused a law tract—*Bretha Étgid* itself, naturally—to be composed consisting of his father's instructions to him on the subject of negligence and intent in cases of injury or death.[204] Other references to conversations between the two abound, including one on the taking of a woman by force,[205] and another on the making of unwise contracts.[206] More generally outside the law tracts, Cormac seems to have been especially known for his wisdom, and in that capacity, his correction of the erroneous judgments of others. One famous story, alluded to earlier in this chapter, tells of his supplanting of Lugaid Mac Con in the kingship of Tara by correcting the false judgment Mac Con had proclaimed regarding sheep trespassing on the woad crop of the queen. This is a literary and historical tale, part of Cormac's "heroic biography."[207] However, the parallels between it and the legal tale told in H 3. 17 about Cormac's correcting the false judgment of Coirpre regarding the aggressive pigs are striking. The H 3. 17 story never mentions the fable about the woad directly, nor the putative instructional relationship between Cormac and Coirpre. However, the fact that Mac Con is wrong and Cormac is right in their assessment of the case is implicit in the choice of characters themselves—an element of the poetic mask each represents.

We know nothing about the manner in which jurists might have made use of these masks. However, the narrative conventions of the lawbooks themselves, combined with the close links perceived to obtain between the juristic and poetic professions, raise the possibility that jurists of the Christian period chose to speak through the persona of one of their mythical professional brethren in rendering their decisions rather than under their own names—another reason, perhaps, why we know so little about real-life judges of the period. A jurist donning such a mask would take unto himself a special sort of authority—the wisdom of the past, the divinatory powers of the prophet, the vision of the artist. It is also striking that so many legal masks cluster around figures associated with the instructional tradition. The portrayal of legal education in this manner must raise questions about the traditions of transmission and instruction that lie behind the written tracts. If what has been argued above is correct—that law was viewed in many schools as a form of verbal art with strong conceptual and technical links to other performance traditions like poetry and prophecy—then one would expect these aspects of the profession to leave their traces in the extant sources. Perhaps masking was a part of the educational tradition as well, a method by which jurists subsumed their own identities into that of the tradition they represented and, in so doing, established a pattern for the relationship between themselves and their disciples that transcended both centuries and words.

Performance and Authority: Innovation

Another important issue to which the anthropological literature alerts us is the role performance can play in facilitating the process of social and political change in largely oral cultures. Performative events appeal to audiences on a variety of levels and summon onlookers to action in very specific ways. They have the potential to reshape a community from within far more dramatically than could a purely prescriptive pronouncement issued by an external authority. As a type of art, legal performance carries within itself the seeds both of stability and of fragmentation, of predictability and of risk.[208] Individual legal dramas inevitably take place against a reassuring backdrop of familiarity and long usage, with specific displays implicitly invoking in audience members memories of earlier judicial events. A judge's proclamation or a pleader's plea commanded attention in part because it was recognizable within the context of similar actions gone before. Its authority stemmed from its being both rooted in the present and capable of transcending it, grounded in the competence of the individual performer and yet intrinsic to the historical memory of the group. Indeed, it is this very ability to overlay the fragile tensions of the moment with the (seeming) stability of the past that is the great strength of performance as a regulator of social relations: participants act within a tradition they simultaneously help to construct.

And yet even the most tightly scripted of events has the potential to deviate from the norm. In theory at least, performance reacts only to the moment: that is why it is so immediate and so potent. Bell makes the point that the performance of ritual or other, seemingly predictable events is not merely the "dramatizing or enacting [of] prior conceptual entities."[209] It is, rather, the active and ongoing (re)formulation of belief. "Tradition" is composed of numerous individual "traditional" acts—any one of which may depart from what is expected radically to reshape the status quo. Such departures may be accidental; they may be personal, rooted in the performer's own desire to subvert or render humorous the sequence he enacts. But they may also be deliberate, the result of a conscious decision to implement social change. In this sense, as Carlson observes, performance functions frequently as "a site for the exploration of fresh and alternative structures and patterns of behavior."[210] Moreover, the artificiality of the event and its apparent focus on the individual can help to ease tensions arising from alterations of this sort. For as Kratz remarks, changes accomplished through performance often present themselves as developments within cultural categories or social orders rather than as major alterations to the fundamental structures they represent. Because performance by definition relates to individual cases, it has the potential to initiate serious social change in circumstances that retain the overall impression of historical and cultural continuity.[211]

Nowhere are these aspects of performance and power more visible than in the story of Dubthach and Patrick. At issue in this tale is a major cultural and jurisdictional shift, from paganism to Christianity, from the rule of Lóegaire and his druids to that of Patrick. The story is obviously fiction, and ought in no sense to be taken as a description of the actual chain of events by which Ireland became a Christian culture. What is interesting about it, however, is that when Irish literati wished to find a way to talk about this process of cultural transformation, and to portray it in a manner that emphasized collaboration and continuity rather than hostility and rupture, they chose performance. Here there is no question as to the gravity of the shift envisaged: the transfer of jurisdiction in legal affairs from one cultural and religious system to another. The focus, however, is on the individual case of the slaying of Patrick's charioteer, and on the "traditional" manner of its resolution (Dubthach's performance). Implicit in his verdict is the radical overhaul of the pagan system he represents and within which he performs. But in the immediacy of the moment, attention is concentrated on the individual case at hand, and on Dubthach himself, who is presented as nervous and uncertain as to what his prophetic insight is about to cause him to say. The change is dramatic, but obscured by the comforting sameness of the event; the threat is real, but lessened by the apparently limited scope of the proceedings. Of course, we cannot at this distance determine whether the dynamics visible in the "Pseudo-Historical Prologue" obtained as well in real life. However, it is suggestive that the jurists chose to portray things in this way. In their work, we may catch at least a glimpse of the functioning of performance within early Irish culture.

What the example of Dubthach and Patrick also makes clear is that for at least some of the jurists at whom we have looked in this chapter, both the process of justice and the essence of the legal tradition itself were realizable only in performance. It is no accident that when Patrick asks to be instructed in native law so that he can bring it into accord with the new Christian dispensation in the "Pseudo-Historical Prologue to the *Senchas Már,*" Dubthach is explicitly said to have to *perform* it for him:

Is ann ro herbad do Dubthach taisbénad breithemnusa 7 uile filidechta Érenn 7 nach rechta ro fallnasat la firu Érenn i recht aicnid 7 i recht fáide, i mbrethaib indse Érenn 7 i filedaib doaircechnatar donicfad bélra mbán mbiait .i. recht litre. . . . Ina bretha fíraicnid trá didiu ro labrastar in Spirut Naem tre ginu breithemon 7 filed fíreon fer nÉrenn ó congbad in insi-seo co cretem anall, dosairfen Dubthach uili do Pátraic.

Then it was entrusted to Dubthach to exhibit judgement, and all the poetry of Ireland, and every law which had held sway among the men of Ireland, in the law of nature and the law of the prophets, in the judgements of the island of Ireland and among the poets who had prophesied that the white language of the *Beati* would come, i.e. the law of scripture. . . . As for the judgements of true nature which the Holy Spirit uttered through the mouths of the righteous judges and poets of the men of Ireland, from the time when this island was settled until the coming of the faith: Dubthach revealed them all to Patrick.[212]

The word translated here by Carey as in the first instance "exhibit" and in the second "revealed," is the same: *do-aisféna,* literally, "shows, recites, exhibits, sets forth." In other words, Dubthach does not merely summarize the tradition he represents, or list its main tenets for Patrick's benefit. Instead, he is conceptualized as performing it, as communicating its essence through public enactment. And while on one level this speaks to the circumstances of the period in which he is supposed to have lived (when law does not yet exist in written form), on another it makes clear where the essence of the tradition is thought to reside. Just as Dubthach cannot simply state his judgment in the case of the slain charioteer but must perform it in order to give it legitimacy, so too he cannot simply summarize the law of the pre-Christian Irish for Patrick. Only by performing it can he bring it to life—in this case in order that it might be transformed through his performance by its ultimate merger with the law of the book.

Dubthach's reluctance to summarize what cannot in the end be contained within the confines of mere description returns us to what must surely be one of the most enduring mysteries of early Irish law. Ireland was without question one of the most literate and sophisticated cultures in western Europe in the Middle Ages, and the only one with a demonstrably early professional legal tradition. Its legal remains are, in the European context, almost unimaginably vast: some eighty tracts extant partially or in full in the vernacular, together with several important Latin legal texts as well. And yet side by side with these tracts and lawbooks there is the virtual absence of "pragmatic" legal sources: *placita*, charters, capitularies, dispute resolutions, and the like. There is a reason for this—there must be. It is inconceivable that in such a supremely literate culture records of this kind could not have been made had the literati wished to make them. It is, of course, possible that such texts did once exist but do so no longer. The Vikings were certainly not kind to the early Irish church and its manuscripts, although Ó Corráin among others has recently argued that their effects on the schools were not as dire as has customarily been assumed.[213] Wendy Davies has identified what she believes to be a distinctively "Celtic" form of Latin charter characteristic of Brittany, Ireland, and Wales in the early Middle Ages. Texts such as those attached Tírechán's Life of Patrick are, she argues, reflexes of this charter tradition and evidence of the existence of such material in an Irish context at one time.[214] And *Berrad Airechta*, among other texts, suggests the role that what it calls "godly old writing" (presumably charters) might play in the settlement of disputes.[215] Perhaps then the issue is one simply of extancy.

However, there are problems with simply writing off the matter in this way. The absence of a particular type of evidence from the historical record is always a tricky thing to interpret, especially when so few exemplars remain to prove the existence of the genre in the first place. One of the most striking aspects of the written material that remains to us from Ireland is, in Charles-Edwards's words, "how little of it is designed to do the jobs usually performed by the more utilitarian written documents in ancient, medieval, or later literate societies."[216] Moreover, in this instance other explanations present themselves. The purview of the written charter may have been much more limited than we have imagined. There are, for example, some indications in the laws that the manner in which an agreement ought to be confirmed was perceived to vary according to the status and profession of the individual involved. The *Senchas Már* law text on prescriptions, *Do Thuaslucud Rudradh*, identifies three different ways of establishing a prescriptive right (*deirbdílse*) to property: witnessing (literally *cluas* "hearing"), inspired poetry, and writing (for example, testamentary documents, charters, and the like). Witnessing it associates with the Féni, and poetry with poets; writing is reserved for clerics, specifically the monastic official known as the *comarba*, "heir."[217] A similar division is hinted at in *Berrad Airechta*, which lists five (but promises seven) things that prevent the dissolving of contracts: witnessing, immoveable (boundary) stones, guarantors, bequests, and "godly old writings" (*senscríband deoda*). Writing, in other words, appears in these texts to be exclusively associated with the church.[218] Perhaps we ought to be thinking of written instruments as having been perceived as appropriate mainly (and possibly only) for clerical officials, and that transactions and dispute resolutions in which laymen participated were simply presumed to be handled orally, without the necessary benefit of writing.

In many ways, such a link between literacy and the church would hardly be surprising. In England as elsewhere, the charter seems to have originated as a device for protecting ecclesiastical property. However, elsewhere in medieval Europe its use spread quickly first to royals, and then to laymen, as its value as a protective instrument became clear. What is odd about Ireland—at least if we are not being misled by the distribution of the evidence—is the church's lack of success in generalizing it as a genre, and (if this is not going too far) the apparently exclusively ecclesiastical context of the charter.[219] Performance offers us a way in which to understand this apparent failure. If justice was effected only in performance, it stands only to reason that charters could not simply replace native practice. Moreover, performance was *personal*: written instruments may have been associated with the clerical class not merely because literacy was particularly linked to the church, but because writing was viewed as both the unique personal possession and chief performative venue of the cleric, just as poetry was for the poet, or witnessing and participating in legal rituals like *tellach* was for the ordinary layman. For in the end, it is difficult to separate these processes from the individual performer, a figure simultaneously anonymous and universal. Small wonder that jurists coming from different schools were apparently able to ply their trade in different regions of Ireland without challenge. One did not have to be familiar with an individual performer in order to accord him the authority due the tradition he represented.

In this we see the true significance and scope of juristic performance in early Ireland most clearly. For dispute resolution is a form of political action: it establishes the authority of individuals and regimes, it restructures relationships within the community, it reaches out beyond the parties visibly in dispute to touch the lives of those who might not overtly appear to be involved. In a society like that of early Ireland, in which no centralized government existed to create and enforce the laws we today associate with the maintenance of social order, performance was essential. Within the physical space of the *airecht* (or comparable venue for judgment), the public performance of the law involved onlookers emotionally in the proceedings, established a context within they could interpret what they saw, and lent stature to the verdict and the jurist or king who proclaimed it. Within the infinitely less tangible space of the spiritual imagination, performance appeared as irrefutable proof of the divinatory and historical veracity of what had been decided. Irrefutable because, as Maurice Bloch points out, to communications of this sort, there is no easy way of saying "no."[220] It is paradoxical, and yet true, that something as conspicuously artificial as performance can serve to convince participants of the naturalness and inevitability of the truth it proclaims.[221] Events and decisions that are essentially political in nature—indeed, that may even be rooted in the very worst of human exclusionist tendencies—can be imaginatively transformed into schemes purporting to originate in an external, usually divine, source.[222] And at the heart of this process in Ireland was the jurist, a figure in whom technician and artist were conjoined. Like the beauty of a poem, the justice of his verdicts was grounded not only in his skill as a craftsman and his knowledge of the law, but in the prophetic faculties embedded in and revealed by his art.

Chapter 3
The Power of the Word

The political history of Ireland, a land of innumerable kings and intensely local identities, has proven incredibly difficult to write. There is nothing like a Charlemagne to help an anxious historian streamline a teeming mass of kings and kinglets into comprehensibility, and Ireland had nothing like a Charlemagne—at least not the centralizing, all-controlling, proto–European Union Charlemagne of the popular imagination.[1] Many excellent recent studies have successfully sidestepped the problem of "too many kings" by focusing less on individual rulers than on power in the various venues in which it was exercised—kingship, clientship, dynastic alliances, the church—and through such works, we have dramatically increased our understanding of early Irish society.[2] However, there is more still to be learned about the manner in which such entities actually functioned. For as our study of the jurists has already suggested, political life in Ireland did not revolve entirely around the exercise of power by military force. Behavior in local communities was regulated in large part by the everyday words and gestures of men and women: authority was embedded as much in the moment as in the bureaucratic machinations of distant rulers. To focus entirely on office-holding and institutionalized venues for power is to underestimate the power and paradoxical "permanence" of the ephemeral exchanges through which the early Irish expressed some of their most important political ideas. Marshall Sahlins has commented on the dangerous tendency of an earlier generation of anthropologists to contrast the prescriptive elements of a culture with its more performative aspects—and then to concentrate on the former in preference to the latter in the mistaken belief that they were the more stable of the two.[3] We as historians would do well to heed his lesson.

Over the past several years, cultural studies have come into their own as a legitimate part of the historian's agenda, although their impact has only relatively recently begun to make itself felt in the field of early medieval history. Old habits die hard, and of course the contrast between politics and poetics is enshrined even in the basic terminology of the historical profession. It is instructive, for example, to try to imagine what precisely the opposite of "pragmatic literacy" might be—and then to think about why it is that these two "types" of literacy are perceived as being such opposites.[4]

Historians of Ireland have in general been more attuned to the idea of a relationship between politics and performance than have other medieval European historians because of the unusual extent to which poetry and storytelling intruded upon the social landscape of that culture. An enormous amount has been written—mostly by literary scholars—about, for example, the power of poetry and its practitioners, the prevalence of *rosc* as an authoritative form of discourse, and the interplay between oral and written in early Irish narrative.[5] Particularly powerful genres of public speech—curse and satire foremost among them—have come in for scholarly attention,[6] and the complexities of the language of the lawbooks are much better understood now than they were a generation ago.[7] In general, scholars are well aware of the richness and diversity of language use in early Ireland, and in that sense, what follows in these pages is nothing very new.

On the other hand, to acknowledge the existence of powerful speech and speakers in a given society is not necessarily to argue that language—in the sense both of speech and of code—was a crucial and systematized element of political order within that society, and this is the case that will be put forward here. Even within the field of Irish studies, politics and aesthetics tend to be studied by scholars trained in different disciplines and regarded as essentially separate spheres of intellectual inquiry. Only with respect to poetry—which all too often is made to stand in for the arts as a whole with respect to issues of power—does one see much of an overlap. And even then there are limits. Poets and rulers appear in the scholarly literature as more or less self-contained figures who encounter one another primarily in the context of patronage. Unless one is paying, praising, or reviling the other, the two are not usually treated together.[8] And other types of performative traditions—storytelling and music, but also genealogies and law—figure for the most part either in scholarly discussions of art, or in discussions of politics, but not in both. And yet separating politics from art, and poetry from other genres of performative art (like law), conceals from view some of the most fundamental organizing principles of early Irish political life.

For nearly four decades, anthropologists and linguists have been writing about the ethnography of language use and the social significance of code. Some have focused on the formalized language of government and ritual;[9] others on the social and political implications of the entire range of a culture's linguistic repertoire.[10] One subject that has attracted particular attention is the phenomenon of "codeswitching": the shifting of dialect, language, or style in response to changing social situations or groupings.[11] One representatively suggestive study is Joel Sherzer's examination of the Kuna Indians of Panama and Colombia.[12] The linguistic system among the Kuna is stunningly intricate: Sherzer documents an elaborate continuum of situational language use, embracing codes ranging from colloquial and informal on the one hand, to exalted, fixed, and obscure on the other. Colloquial styles are accessible to and used by all, regardless of rank. Exalted or ritual speech styles, by contrast, are consciously restricted to—because expressive of—particular social contexts (for example, political, ritual) or roles (for example, chief, healing specialist). Within the realm of ritual speech alone, three distinct traditions exist, each possessing its own lexicon, phonology, and syntax. What we are seeing in the Kuna is a linguistic system in which social meaning is communicated not merely by words or intonation, but by the code speakers employ. Moreover, not only is society structured by language, language is itself shaped by the social uses to which it is put in Kuna society. Literally every aspect of the language, from sound patterns to grammar to vocabulary, is intimately tied to ways of, and social venues for, speaking. Women use different sounds and intonational patterns than do men; speech used in the context of ritual tends to add suffixes to verbs more frequently than does ordinary speech.[13] So entwined are society and speech that one simply cannot separate a study of the Kuna political and ritual system from a study of the language use through which it is both expressed and perpetuated.

Thus for the Kuna, as for many other cultures, politics and poetics are inseparable. To contemplate the one in the absence of the other robs each of the intensity and richness that makes it so fascinating. Moreover, it is actually poetics that are at issue, and not merely speech: Sherzer makes a point of stressing the manner in which the aesthetic properties of language and language use are directly linked to their social effectiveness.[14] What I wish to argue in the following is that a similar relationship between politics and poetics obtained in early Ireland, and that an understanding of the mechanisms of legal enforcement, the duties of kingship, or the prerogatives of aristocratic status can take us only so far in understanding the manner in which society was ordered. For the Irish also knew several different ways of speaking, and in Ireland too did language function as a form of cultural organization. Speech defined status: it displayed it, it asserted it, it even had the power to take it away. Similarly, language itself—oral and written—was used and altered situationally as a way of exercising jurisdiction over others and structuring relations between persons in society. This chapter will focus primarily on code and language use as a central ordering device on all levels of society, from the establishing of social hierarchies and identities to the structuring of individual legal events. The chapters that follow will take up the issue of speech as a venue for political competition and a vehicle through which to assert claims to lordship. It is my hope that tracing such connections will offer us a way in which to see politics at work on a number of different levels, across all social ranks and in a variety of contexts.

A word must be said first about the relationship between language and speech. Language communicates on many levels and in many different venues. Typically meaning is communicated by the ordinary use of words—by one person saying or writing something to another in an everyday sort of way and having that message be more or less understood. However, as we saw in the example of the Kuna, meaning can also reside in the nature of the language used, or in the choice to switch from one particular code to another in a given situation. This is true both of speech and of text: decisions as to code can be made orally and aimed primarily at an audience of onlookers; alternatively, they can be made within the context of a written text and aimed mainly at users of the book or manuscript in question (including those who are not literate but have a text read to them). Language can even convey meaning when the code in which the event is conducted is unintelligible to the audience in question. The code used in curing and magical ceremonies among the Kuna, for example, is demonstrably a language, in that it can be analyzed phoneme by phoneme in the way one might do with English or French. On the other hand, those witnessing these ceremonies, while capable of judging the performance on its aesthetic merits, will usually have no idea of what is actually being said. What they do understand is that the use of this particular style of language is a sign of the authority both of the speaker and of the ritual itself.[15]

It is when we enter the realm of the oral that we begin to need to consider the effects of speech and (usually though not inevitably) language simultaneously. Like language, speech conveys meaning in a variety of ways: by tone, by accompanying gesture, and by the code speakers choose to employ (for example, by the language they use). Also significant—and certainly relevant to the early Irish situation—are the restrictions that can be placed by a culture upon those who seek to engage in public speech. Not everyone is allowed to speak in all situations; not everyone's words are given the same degree of weight. Even in instances where the language employed in a particular situation is relatively unmarked by comparison with other possible codes within the lexicon of the speakers,[16] the fact of a person's being allowed to engage in (or even listen to) that speech can in itself convey a particular meaning about that person's social position or status. In the curing and magical ceremonies mentioned above, for example, the right to speak establishes the speaker as a rightful master of the ritual code, while the right to listen establishes the onlookers as members of the community served by the spirits being addressed. Those who are allowed neither to speak nor to hear are established by their incapacity as outsiders to the community. In what follows, an attempt will be made to examine both speech and language, although of course our knowledge of the former is necessarily indirect and it is not always possible to distinguish precisely between them.

Language, Status, and Identity

The early Irish not only made use of, but consciously recognized and accorded distinctive names to, different varieties of code. Calvert Watkins has described a basic bifurcation in the language, what he terms a difference between "the language of gods" and the "language of men," that is paralleled elsewhere in various Indo-European linguistic traditions.[17] The ordinary language of everyday life ("language of men") is referred to in different ways depending on the text. The most common term is *gnáthbérla*, "customary language," which appears both in the Middle Irish sections of the grammatical tract *Auraicept na nÉces* and in *Sanas Cormaic*.[18] As Watkins remarks, *gnáthbérla* is distinguished from other codes in that it is "unmarked" by its lexical or grammatical eccentricities, (apparent) age, or association with any particular ritual or professional context. It is the ordinary language of Ireland and, as such, presumably accessible to all.[19] In opposition to this generalized tongue then stand the various "marked" codes of the medieval period: *bérla Féne*, or "legal language" (literally, "the language of the Féni"), *bérla na filed*, or "the language of the poets," *bérla bán*, "white language," which is glossed in one text as *.i. inna canóine*, "of the Scriptures"—in other words, Latin.[20] The language of the poets is subdivided in the later parts of the *Auraicept* into *fásaige na filed*, "the maxims of the poets" and the *berla fortchide na filed*, "the obscure language of the poets," a division understood by Watkins to refer to lesser and greater degrees of rhetorical intricacy. In his view, "ordinary language" (*gnáthbérla*), "legal language" (*bérla Féne*), and "poetic language" (*bérla na filed*) exist on a similar continuum of linguistic complexity: legal language is "marked" with reference to ordinary Old Irish but "unmarked" with respect to the highly obscure forms of the poetic language.[21]

Watkins's sense of a linguistic continuum is confirmed by other early Irish sources, as we shall see later in this chapter. Moreover, his distinction between a "language of gods" and a "language of men" makes the important point that the Irish both recognized the existence of marked codes within the vernacular and distinguished among them on linguistic grounds. However, it is clear from other sources that within the broad categories outlined in the Middle Irish sections of the *Auraicept* there existed as well several subcategories of language that would have been recognizable to those making use of them. "Poetic language," for example, is a term that embraces several very different types of discourse, of which the two best known are rhyming syllabic poetry and *rosc/retoiric*.[22] The broad category of "legal language" can also be subdivided into a variety of ways of speaking, including *fásaige*, "maxims," *rosc(ad)*, "rhetorical verse or prose,"[23] ornamented language of the sort we shall examine later in this chapter with respect to *Berrad Airechta*, ordinary language, and Latin. Some of these may seem more like genres than like actual codes—maxims, *roscada*, rhyming poems—and of course there is an inevitable degree of overlap among them, especially with respect to technical vocabulary.[24] On the other hand, each fills the requirements of a code in various and important ways. Each is characterized by a lexicon, grammar, and syntax specific (though not necessarily unique)[25] to itself, and each communicates merely by the fact of being used something about the context and authority of both speaker and statement.[26]

Indeed, to regard these merely as genres is to risk underestimating the extent to which codes like these helped to regulate social identities and behavior in early Ireland. What stands out most clearly from even a brief survey of the literature is that code served both to mark the nature of a given event and to establish of the professional identity and authority of the person(s) presiding over it. This is of course most immediately apparent in the churchly realm, where the use of Latin automatically defined the occasion as ecclesiastical and established the speaker as a person with clerical training, if not actually a cleric himself. Poetic language is more difficult to pin down in this respect, in that it cannot be exclusively identified with any single context: poetry can be art, or prophecy, or satire, or praise, or law, or all of these at once. However, the choice to use a particular type of poetic language, especially in a context in which other types of language also occurred, must surely have been intended to communicate to the reader/listener something specific and important about what was being said.

Breatnach's recent discovery that *rosc*, the most arcane and elevated form of poetic discourse, was not (merely) an archaic form of the language as had previously been thought, but rather a true linguistic code, has marked a major advance in our ability to appreciate the symbolic significance of language. Indeed, Breatnach, McCone, and others have now identified several instances in which sources composed in the classical Old Irish period—some of them Latin and ecclesiastical in nature and origin—were deliberately translated into *rosc*.[27] Curiously, little has been written to this point about why anyone would have regarded such a project as worth undertaking in the first place: in general, the phenomenon is noted, described, and then passed over with little attempt at explanation. In fact, however, it is difficult to avoid the conclusion that the implications of *rosc*—social, political, artistic—were regarded as being sufficiently different from the implications of the code in which the excerpt had originally been composed as to make the act of translation worthwhile.

What those implications might have been has to date been outlined only in the most general way by scholars.[28] And of course the answer may vary from context to context, and from text to text. In the narrative literature, for example, *rosc* is often associated with dialogues taking place at moments of heightened tension within the story—especially dialogues that invoke or examine relations between male and female characters and, by extension, men and women in general.[29] The classic example of this is the conversation in the *Táin Bó Cúailnge* among Fergus, Ailill, and Medb about Medb's adultery with Fergus.[30] *Rosc* is also frequently used to invoke or signify prophetic or otherworldly knowledge, such as the discussions that result in the druid Cathbad's prediction of the birth of Deirdre in *Longes mac n-Uislenn*.[31] In the lawbooks, *rosc* is used in a variety of ways. It is the language of legal authority, as we have seen already with respect to the verdicts delivered by jurists or kings examined in the previous chapter—Bodainn, Fergus mac Léti, Sencha, Conchobor, and Dubthach—not least because of its connections with poetry and prophecy. It can also mark statements attributed to ancient mythological specialists within the tradition, such as Morainn and Neire in the *Bretha Nemed* texts, Laidcenn mac Ercaid in *Bretha Déin Chécht*, and Cenn Fáelad in *Bretha Nemed Toísech*.[32] Indeed, one of the implications of the use of *rosc* in a legal context would seem to be that the statement in question has the authority both of age and of oral custom. Breatnach's work clearly demonstrated that *rosc* did not have to be archaic or oral in terms of its actual date and venue of composition. However, in terms of the social and political expectations it generated in those for whom it was performed, the sources imply that *rosc* was indeed regarded as both "archaic" and "oral"—even when it was in actuality nothing of the kind.

Other types of legal code presumably invoked somewhat different frameworks of interpretation. Unlike *rosc*, which transcended genre and context, *fásaige*, "maxims," appear to have been restricted to the legal (or wisdom-literature) context and regarded as an expressly "legal" form of language, a point that will be taken up later in more detail.[33] The invocation of *fásaige* thus automatically defined an event as legal in nature, while establishing the speaker as a person with knowledge of the authoritative legal tradition to which reference was being made. Moreover, maxims differ significantly from *rosc* in explicitly avoiding the personal. Although collections of maxims can be (and often are) ascribed to named authors—not all of whom are mythological[34]—individual maxims themselves tend not to be identified with the opinions of any particular authoritative individual. Rather, they purport to originate in a generally accepted body of custom not circumscribed by its association with any one person or point of view. Indeed, it is in their implicit claim to objectivity that their value in a legal and judicial setting lies—a claim no less potent for being transparently fictional. Maxims can, after all, also be shaped to promote particular ends, even if their very impersonality makes them a particularly potent form of legal code. The unfairness of even the most blatantly partisan of verdicts can be cloaked by reference to a tradition that seems on the surface so removed from any type of self-interest.

One of the most interesting aspects of the link between these various legal codes and the frameworks of interpretation they set up in the minds of listeners is the manner in which their linguistic characteristics themselves underscore the message they aspire to communicate to their audience. *Rosc* is, quite simply, art: its lexicon is exotic and its syntax pointedly different from that of ordinary vernacular Irish.[35] And as art, it is inherently personal, its effectiveness dependent on the persuasiveness of the individual who performs it. This is why, I suggest, it is so frequently personalized as to speaker and context. It is *felt* as performance, and it is used to communicate the *idea* of performance even in cases where the excerpt itself originated in writing (as may often have been the case with the passages that appear in our sources). Maxims, by contrast, are defined by the enduring universality of their stylistic elements: their lexicon is rarely bizarre, though often technical; their grammar and syntax are simple and entirely predictable. Colin Ireland isolates in his edition of the maxims attributed to Flann Fína only three different syntactical patterns, none of which is in the least bit complicated, and notes that 75 percent of all maxims share a common alliterative pattern.[36] Even when prescribing behavior, maxim phrasing is both abstract and universal: *[s]cuirith dochiall deimnigthiu; dororben fosair firnadmen*,[37] "defective understanding dissolves confirmations; a [proper] foundation promotes true bindings"; *[i]dan cach ndíles, anidan cach n-indles;* "everything immune from claim is pure, everything actionable is impure";[38] *[d]liged coibche certugud, [d]ligid comaithches coímchloud,* "a contract (or bride price) merits adjustment, the law of neighborhood merits reciprocity."[39] In other words, the social import of these codes mirrors the manner of their composition, just as the manner of their composition mirrors their social import. What we are witnessing here is the phenomenon described for the Kuna by Sherzer—the manner in which language at once shapes and is in turn shaped by the social and political uses to which it is put.

Despite the apparent impersonality of the *fásaige*, there can be little question as to their value in establishing the authority of individuals who made use of them. Code functioned not only to identify the context within which an event took place, but to establish the professional identity of the person(s) presiding over that event. Clerical status was proved not merely by access to the relevant holy places and vessels, but by the ability to command the sacred code of Latin. Similarly, the recitation of a poem was a mark of the speaker's claim to identity as a poet and, thereby, to the prerogatives of poetic status. Judicial speech is particularly interesting. We have seen already how obscure or arcane performative language established the identity—and therefore authority—of individual jurists. However, the evidence suggests that code served not only to authorize individuals acting in a judicial capacity, but to distinguish among their powers and jurisdictional purviews as well. The type of language to which such persons had recourse in their legal decisions defined both their professional identity and the grounds on which they claimed the right to speak. According to the status tract *Uraicecht Becc*, poets, clerics, and lords drew upon different codes in making and proclaiming their legal decisions.[40] Poets are said to make (and/or proclaim) their decisions on the basis of *roscada*, clerics on the basis of Scriptures. Lords, by contrast, claim mastery over all three "languages": *roscada, fásaige* and Scriptures. The equation between language and lordship is nowhere more clear than it is here: in this text, rank is defined by language and language by rank.[41]

What was true of professionals appears to have been true also of members of the nobility in general. Speech and language functioned also as markers of personal and class identity. The literary sources suggest, for example, that nobility was asserted not merely through the display of wealth or clientage, but through the use of elevated or obscure discourse in particular social situations. Sayers's sensitive study of the rhetorical exchange between Cú Chulainn and Emer in the *Tochmarc Emire* shows men and women both engaging in a type of witty, arcane, and immensely sophisticated repartee that he argues marks its practitioners as participants in a shared aristocratic culture.[42] In their use of language as much as in what they actually say, Cú Chulainn and Emer identify themselves to one another as adherents to a common set of cultural norms and expectations. Emer here reveals herself as very much a part of the heroic tradition of which Cú Chulainn is the shining exemplar—in her choice of code, she summons him to actions befitting his social and personal identity and is in turn so summoned herself. Joanne Findon argues further that the artistry of Emer's speech—more elaborate and aesthetically complex than the speech of those with whom she sees herself in competition—allows her to exercise a control over her circumstances that she would not otherwise have."[43] It also projects her into a power structure from which she would otherwise have been excluded by virtue of her gender. Her mastery of the code of mastery, as it were, permits her an independent voice: in Findon's view, "women's words" could challenge the limits placed by a male warrior culture on female identity and initiative.[44]

It seems likely that it was not merely the nobility who were concerned with issues of status and speech, or for whom the judicious use of the voice was an empowering device. Unfortunately, the relentlessly aristocratic perspective of the extant sources means that we can say nothing about code among the lower social classes. We can imagine that dialect, accent, and diction must have been as revealing of social origins in early Ireland as they are in, for example, England or America today, but since we have no direct knowledge of the code(s) in use among ordinary Irish men and women of the period we have little to go on. If we cannot talk about code, however, we can talk about speech in general. The sources make clear that the apportioning of public speech in ways that acknowledged the prerogatives and limitations of individual ranks of person was one of the primary means by which status was conceptualized, defined, and performed. Speech acts play an important role in distinguishing among social ranks in the status tract *Críth Gablach*, for example. Side by side with wealth as an indicator of social rank in the text are the various forms of *insce*, "speech, public statement," to which individuals are said to be entitled. Every independent male grade is explicitly said to have the right to engage in restricted amounts of socially significant speech—acting as a witness or guarantor for instance—up to an amount equal to their honor-price but no more.[45]

Particularly interesting is the manner in which speech is limited or denied altogether to the dependent grades. Two ranks of juvenile males (*fer midboth*) are distinguished in the tract, for example, both of which enjoy fewer prerogatives than ordinary freeman grades because of their youth and limited property. The younger of these can act as an oathhelper only for very small amounts ranging from a needle to a heifer, and is apparently denied other forms of public speech.[46] The older of the two, by contrast, gives oath for a larger amount and appears to have the right to testify in a limited fashion in a public forum (presumably court). He is actually called in the text the *fer midboth conoí insci*, "who sustains speech," and while the nature of this speech is nowhere precisely defined, it is said to be "collected for him in three words for three days," and to be "sustained" by him without increase or diminution—qualifications that certainly make it sound as though testimony is at issue.[47]

The mention of the "three words" is intriguing: Binchy points to a passage elsewhere in the laws that suggests that the "three words" in question referred to the very few, very specific issues on which the testimony of a *fer midboth* would be accepted.[48] This is quite plausible: another term for "word" is *focal*, which can certainly have the meaning of "statement" in general.[49] And *Berrad Airechta* refers to the testimony of a guarantor as his *bríathar*, "word," glossed *aipert*, "saying" in the text.[50] However, the passage cited in the preceding chapter, in which different numbers of publicly presented words were accorded to the various social grades in line with their rank, suggests another, more literal, possibility as an explanation. In that passage, seven words per breath are associated with the lordly grades, and five words per breath with the freeman ranks; the according of "three words" to the dependent *fer midboth* seems on the face of it to fit well within this schema. Perhaps rather than suggesting something about the topics a *fer midboth* was entitled to address, the "three words" referred to here characterize the brevity, quality, and complexity of the oral presentation made by or on behalf of men of this rank. It is certainly worth noting that although the various status tracts vary considerably among themselves in their listing of the social grades and the honorprice to which each is entitled, an honor-price of five *séoit* is fairly standard for full freemen, three *séoit* for members of the dependent classes, and seven to ten *séoit* for the *aire déso*, the lowest of the noble ranks.[51] In other words, the words per breath granted an individual was the same as his honor-price and vice versa: speech quite literally mirrored rank.

Other texts are not as explicit in quantifying language use and its relationship to status, but the idea that speech is both a prerogative of rank and a means by which it is defined and asserted it is found throughout the legal and literary tradition. The legal concept of "overswearing," (*for-toing*) for example, in which the testimony of persons or institutions of higher rank automatically overcomes that of those lesser in rank, speaks to exactly this equation of power and public speech. *Críth Gablach* mentions the practice several times,[52] and overswearing forms part of the standard vernacular of ecclesiastical power relations as well. One of the claims advanced by the *Liber Angeli* on behalf of Armagh is that no other church of the Irish may draw lots to settle disputes with Armagh (a procedure adopted in cases where the parties involved were of equal status), and that indeed the ruler of Armagh automatically overswears the prelates of all other ecclesiastical establishments in Ireland.[53] And *Bretha Nemed Toísech* distinguishes between the "good" church that fulfills its spiritual obligations and the "evil" church that fails in its basic responsibilities. The former overswears others and is not itself oversworn (*[f]or-toing side for cách, ní for-tongar fuiri*), while the latter can be oversworn by any more "righteous" institution (*[n]í fortoing for fírén, for-toing fírén fuiri*).[54]

The right to engage in publicly recognized speech was thus one of the mechanisms by which lordship and social status were measured and displayed. Nor was this a phenomenon associated only with secular life: access to and restrictions on performative liturgical speech were crucial elements also in the establishment of the hierarchy of the early medieval church. Latin was the universal code of the church; however, even within this code clear distinctions were made as to who could say what. The Eucharistic Prayer was to be recited only by priests, for example, while only deacons could proclaim the Gospel—indeed these remain items of privileged speech still today in Catholic traditions. But more than just speaking was at issue: the right even to *hear* particular types of speech was an important component of power relations in this period. In the early Middle Ages, catechumens were generally dismissed from the Mass after the sermon and not even allowed to hear the recitation of the Creed and the Eucharistic Prayer, for example.[55] In Ireland specifically, the difference between speaking and hearing—and not speaking and not hearing—marked crucial distinctions within the Christian community. The *Liber Angeli* tells us that only bishops, priests, anchorites, and "other religious" (*caeteri relegiossi*) were allowed to offer "praises" (*laudes*) in the southern basilica of the church of Armagh; other orders, including virgins, penitents, and the married, merely listened to preaching in the northern district.[56] In other words, high-status clerics had the right both to speak and to hear in a privileged space, while church members lesser in rank were allowed to hear, but not to speak themselves. And of course these two categories imply the existence of yet a third: a group so distanced from God's word by virtue of their behavior (or, conceivably, their status) that they were excluded altogether from the speech by which that word was disseminated in the world.

Language and the Reshaping of Social Identities

The literary sources thus bear out the impression given in the law tracts that language use functioned in early Ireland as a marker of personal affiliation and identity. Indeed, Cú Chulainn's first "subtextual" question to the woman he is wooing—"Can you follow my speech?"[57]—points to precisely such an equation. Her comprehension of his obscure language, together with her own ability to respond in kind, establishes her in his eyes as a suitable candidate for his attentions. But both legal and literary sources suggest a more active role for language than that of merely describing or displaying a status that already exists. Even more common in the literature—likely because more replete with dramatic potential—is the situation in which language in use as speech actually constructs or reshapes status, usually through public praise or satire. Words could increase or diminish honor, if deployed in particular ways by particular individuals. As we have seen, honor meant everything in early Irish society; moreover, when a person was a member of the ruling classes, injuries to individual or familial honor could become matters of intense public concern. For while honor and status were not the same things, a person of high status who acted in a manner judged by others to be dishonorable risked losing the clients and supporters on whom his social rank in large part rested.[58]

Public praise and blame were crucial aspects of this social system in that they announced to the world the measure of a person's moral standing. If a man was prosperous and generous, his reputation and standing would be spread far and wide; if, by contrast, a man or lord was niggardly and sly, he could be held up to public ridicule and his support would melt away. Speech played a critical role in the process by which individuals were constructed and maintained as honorable or dishonorable, generous or mean. Several different kinds of speech are in question: random gossip was certainly not irrelevant to such matters, then as now. However, considerably more important to this process was deliberate public speech—speech performed specifically in order to characterize an individual in particular ways, whether for good or for ill. Some performers were perceived as inherently more powerful and authoritative than others. Especially potent were the words of poets: poetry composed and conducted in accordance with the complex regulations governing early Irish verse carried an authority that was both feared and respected by persons with stature to lose. For just as honor and dishonor were quantifiable entities in early Ireland, so also were praise and satire more than just terms by which one might characterize the way one person spoke of another. They were, rather, actual genres of formal poetic interaction—important in their own right as aesthetic genres and shapers of reputation in a world in which such mattered profoundly. Indeed, poetry was in a very real sense a staple of public lordship in medieval Ireland—an important feature of rule well into the post-Norman period.[59]

Medieval Ireland knew two main forms of social poetry: praise poetry and satire. The image of the bard ceaselessly praising his lord in hopes of reward was not merely a literary topos, but also an historical practice of great significance. Poets composed poems for their patrons that celebrated their deeds and generosity; in return, patrons rewarded the many poets who visited their court with a vigorous display of munificence. Nor were all poets itinerant. Properly trained products of the poetic schools were officially appointed by kings or *túatha* to serve the needs of court and community. Indeed, every *túath* was supposed to have a poet in its employ, and by the Middle Irish period, even the larger monasteries kept poets on their staff.[60] There were many reasons for which lords and communities might choose to keep poets as more or less permanent members of their establishments—for entertainment, for assistance in judicial matters, and likely for the exaction of dues as well. One of the main advantages must surely have been to ensure for their patrons a certain degree of consistency in the extent and content of the praise meted out. Nastiness could arise even in a long-term relationship, of course, but would presumably have been less common. Words are wonderfully ambiguous, and the dangers posed by itinerant or unaffiliated poets must have seemed particularly great. The law tract *Gúbretha Caratniad*, for example, expresses grave concern about disingenuous verse—poetry that pretends to be praise but deliberately falls so short that it actually constitutes satire.[61] And of course the primary fear voiced in the literature is that of versifying visitors who stay too long and eat too much: poets who eat their host out of house and home, confident that their ability to make or break his reputation will shield them from punishment for even the grossest of alimentary abuses.[62]

Certainly it is fear rather than gratitude or affection that comes across in the sources as the principal emotion generated by the presence of poets at court. The threat posed by the biting words of a satirist was both real and potent. So serious were the effects of public verbal ridicule believed to be that the Irish sources imagined it as actually causing traumatic physical injury to the person in question. The damage to the body reflected the disruption believed to be engendered in the human spirit and in nature by the performance of dishonorable acts. Searing blisters of shame were said to appear on the face and cheeks of the dishonored person: insofar as the Old Irish word for "face," *enech*, was also the word for "honor," persons whose *enech* had been reddened (*imdergad, grísad, enechrucce, ruidiud*) by such blemishes had thus quite literally "lost face" before their peers.[63] Praise poetry could remedy this situation. Persons who had been dishonored had to be cleansed of their shame as publicly as they had been afflicted with it, and praise poems, which normally served to establish or confirm a person's reputation, were the main means by which that could be accomplished. *Bretha Nemed Déidenach* expresses the idea in mythical terms: when the poet Athairne sought to placate the river Mourne, which had overflowed its bank in protest at an insult, he had to compose a laudatory verse in order to restore the river to its proper dimensions. The metaphor used is that of silver, tarnished by misuse, which recovers its sheen only once it is polished with the bristle of praise.[64] Similarly, the law tract *Gúbretha Caratniad* speaks in less fanciful terms of a king who has been satirized, but who holds on to his honor because the praise bestowed on him afterward outweighs the shame induced by the satire.[65]

Praise might therefore countermand the effects of satire in some circumstances. Overall, however, satire stands out very clearly from the legal and literary sources as a source of tremendous concern.[66] Satire—particularly unjustified satire—is a common theme in many Irish tales, where it usually appears as a form of verbal assault associated with the vengefulness of excessively greedy poets.[67] Legal sources tend to emphasize more official types of satire, such as the enforcement of cross-border claims, the levying of compensation in places "where the barbs of satire are answered and the barbs of weapons are not."[68] But not all satire was of such an official nature. There were many ways in which persons could bring dishonor upon another, not all of which were verbal. Mocking a person's physical person by word or gesture, or jeering or laughing at him, could all be construed as satire, as could alluding to a physical blemish by using one's own body to point out the area of disfigurement.[69] Even giving a person or entity an uncomplimentary nickname fell into the category of satire, especially if that epithet had the misfortune to stick. One source tells of a company visiting a certain church who were given a skimpy and unpalatable meal as their repast. Packing their bags hurriedly, they passed on to another, more gastronomically sympathetic venue—but not before bestowing on the offending church the name by which it was forever afterward known: *Ceall Chorrfesi*, the "Church of the Lousy Supper."[70]

Verbal ridicule posed the most serious threat, however, and the sources display considerable fear toward those who were regarded as masters of their tongues. Not all who satirized were members of the professional poetic elite. As has been mentioned already, serious concerns are expressed about lower-class, ill-educated, or female poets engaging in the practice, a point that will be taken up in more detail later in this book.[71] *Bretha Crólige*, for example, includes among its list of people who are not brought away on sick-maintenance but who are instead maintained by fee in their own homes a woman satirist (*be rinnuis*).[72] Similarly, the low-class satirists known as *cáinti* are listed together with druids and plunderers as men who receive only the maintenance fee due to the ordinary freeman, even if their status was actually higher than this.[73] But the fear of those who could wield words to ill effect is not limited to persons of this class. *Bretha Crólige* places similar restrictions on the sick-maintenance rights of the undoubtedly aristocratic and impeccably educated male *filid*. The text explains this by saying that the skills of such men are so specialized that they cannot be replaced in their job were they to go away on sick-maintenance; however, it is not too difficult to imagine that the fear of the verbal power they might bring to bear against their hosts also played a role in their exclusion from normal nursing practices.[74] A passage in *Bretha Nemed Déidenach* speaks to precisely this issue when it instructs contracting parties not to allow the person with whom they are dealing to use a poet, bard, or satirist (*éiges na bárd na cáinte*) as a guarantor for their half of the deal *ar ná rod aorad dligedh sgeo indlighedh ar as rechtaidh gach ae a theangaidh,*[75] "lest they satirize you lawfully or unlawfully, for each one is a master of his tongue." Other fears associated generally with poets of all ranks surface also in the sources, such as concerns about unjustified or illegal satire,[76] the practice of satirizing individuals after death (presumably because of its likely effects on future generations),[77] and the repeating of a satire composed in one region in a distant area of the country.[78]

Verbal satire took many forms, many of which are spelled out in a text edited by Howard Meroney in 1950 known as *Cis lir fodla aíre?*, "How many kinds of satire are there?"[79] The best analysis of this text, as of the subject in general, has been done by Liam Breatnach in two important articles.[80] Breatnach there outlines the three most important distinctions between the types of satire practiced in early Ireland: satire could be publicly or privately performed, it could take the form either of poetry or prose, and it could either identify the subject specifically, by name and locale, or refer to him or her in vague terms that left the question of identity up in the air.[81] A particularly valuable aspect of "*Cis lir fodla aíre?*" are the samples of satire included in the text, for these give a sense of the many different approaches satirists might employ. Some verses are very subtle, more in the nature of an innuendo than what we might think of as full-fledged ridicule. Others leave no room for doubt as to the satirist's point of view, being outright insults unsusceptible to any other interpretation.[82] Particularly amusing are the genres that mean the opposite of what they seem to say. *Tamall molta,* "a slight bit of praise," compliments the subject of what is putatively a praise poem in such pointedly modulated terms that insult cannot help but result.[83] And then there is its opposite, *tár molta,* "outrage of praise," or *ró molta,* "excessive praise," where the subject of the satirical verse is praised so extravagantly that the effect is one of derision rather than acclaim.[84]

But what then was the nature of the sanctions believed to lie behind satire? For at least one type of satire listed in the text might seem from its treatment in the sources to have had overtones of magic. The relationship between satire and magic is a vexed one: magic has played a prominent role in scholarship on the genre, as magical rituals are so often depicted as drawing for their efficacy on beliefs about the power of ritually charged language similar to those lying behind the Irish practice of satire.[85] Certainly there are examples of satires in the Irish material that look greatly like spells. *Sanas Cormaic* tells of a satirical poem composed by one Néide against his uncle Caíar, king of Connacht, which hardly seems satirical at all:

Maile, baire, gaire Caíar
cot-mbéotar celtrai catha Caíar
Caíar di-bá, Caíar di-rá—Caíar!
fo ró, fo mara, fo chara Caíar!

Evil, death, short life to Caíar,
spears of battle will have killed Caíar,
may Caíar die, may Caíar depart—Caíar!
Caíar under earth, under embankments, under stones![86]

Néide's verse wishing death on his uncle has an effect: Caíar immediately breaks out in blisters and flees into exile leaving the throne to his nephew. His actual death, however, is postponed for a year—and even then a belatedly repentant Néide who has come to find him in exile is killed along with him.[87] In sociolegal terms, the whole affair may have been viewed as having come out just about right. As Meroney points out, the person recording this story clearly regarded the outcome as just, an example of a death for a death, of "restitution in kind."[88] However, as magic *tout court*, it would seem on the face of it not to have been an unqualified success, at least not from Néide's point of view.

The type of satire that has most commonly been associated with magic is the *glám dícenn*, which is mentioned but not described in "*Cis lir fodla aíre?*" And in fact, Néide's poem is referred to in a later manuscript source (H 4. 22) as an example of a *glám dícenn*, although there is no particular reason to think that the author of this source had any real insight into the genre.[89] Néide's satire against Caíar takes the form of ordinary verse in the *Sanas Cormaic* version of the story; however, *glám dícenn* is described in later sources as an elaborate and undeniably magical ceremony in which poets chant satirical verse in a ritually significant place and time while stabbing a clay effigy of their victim with thorns from a whitethorn bush.[90] Meroney has termed this late account an "absurdity," arguing that it was the invention of an author who knew nothing about the actual nature of the *glám dícenn*.[91] Speaking strictly in textual terms, this may well be right. On the other hand, *Uraicecht na Ríar* is an early source, written by and for members of the poetic profession, and it too bears out the idea of a link between magic and at least some forms of satire. It does not use the phrase *glám dícenn* specifically (though it appears in the glosses), but it does list among the elements of which satire is constructed "magical wounding" (*congain comail*) and *corrguinecht*, which latter is explained in O'Davoren's Glossary (a sixteenth-century compilation, but one that contains a great deal of Old Irish material) as a ritual that involves standing on one foot, closing one eye, and putting one hand behind the back (?) while chanting the *glám dícenn*. It also speaks of satire being performed in what seem to be ritual places and times: in the shade of a particular type of tree, and in three periods over the course of a lunar month.[92]

It is difficult to know what to make of such references. A correlation between magic and satire would not be surprising in the least, given the manner in which poetic powers were often conceptualized in early Ireland. Nevertheless, the evidence clearly suggests that the two were not as a rule synonymous terms. None of the forms of satire described in "*Cis lir fodla aíre?*" involve spells, or even anything that looks like a spell: their sanction seems social rather than supernatural. And even *Uraicecht na Ríar*, the main early source for an association of satire and magic, implies a distinction between the two when it characterizes Néide's performance as *áer tri bricht*, "satire through a spell," as though the two were generally separate things.[93] In other words, even if the *glám dícenn* ought to be considered as a species of magic—which Meroney clearly doubts[94]—neither it nor *corrguinecht* ought to be allowed to stand in for the genre of satire as a whole. For the most part, satire "worked" because words really mattered—not (or not merely) in the way that magical incantations mattered, but because they projected onto a public stage the individual failings of those in the community who had not lived up to their responsibilities in life. They gave voice to public perceptions of right and wrong and, in so doing, helped to bring about the very disgrace they described.

It is significant that magic is not nearly as prominent a theme in the early texts as it becomes in later sources. Annalistic references to people being "rhymed to death," for example, come from the eleventh century and later, as do the references to the "rat rhyming" for which Ireland later became famous.[95] Carey has pointed to a tendency among later medieval authors to exaggerate the magical or pagan aspects of the poetic profession for their own political purposes. Practices or customs originally innocent of supernatural associations were often reimagined by later authors as exotic pagan rituals,[96] and the increasing prominence in the sources of *glám dícenn* and other apparently magical varieties of satire may well be a reflex of this same phenomenon. *Glám dícenn*, which Meroney has argued meant something like "permanent attack," but which contains the adjective *dícenn*, literally, "without a head" (or, in Meroney's less exotic translation, "endless"), may well have attracted such reinterpretation because of eerie nature of the images it summoned up. And although there is better evidence for *corrguinecht* as a magical practice, it is nonetheless conceivable that the ritual posture to which it alludes may have had a sociological (rather than inherently magical) significance that we no longer understand.[97]

Perhaps the best way to approach satire is not through magic, but rather through its similarity to other performative legal procedures like distraint; indeed, several passages make this comparison directly.[98] Regardless of the magical or religious sanctions believed to be implicit in the procedure, the emotional and psychological subtleties of the genre were significant. Most obvious is the manner in which satirists used time and increasing social pressure to force the subject of the satire to come to terms. Like distraint, satire was often performed over a period of some days, during which time the unfortunate target of the poet's wrath (or his kindred)[99] had the chance to respond to the claim being made against him. Not all such procedures appear to have constituted full-fledged satire in themselves: some poets stretched things out by not immediately identifying their target by name, but rather hinting that such disclosure would be forthcoming in a future poem were nothing done to satisfy the poet's claim. This too is like distraint, where the main purpose of the initial phases of the procedure was to hint at bad things to come rather than to cause them immediately to come about. One type of satire mentioned in "*Cis lir fodla aíre?*" is called *dallbach becthuinedhe*, "lightly-established innuendo." In this type, the satirist provides almost, but not quite, enough information to allow listeners to recognize the person or locale being chastised. One of the most famous (and humorous) of all Irish satires is even less specific in its degree of innuendo—but even it, in its explicit refusal to reveal the victim's name, implicitly threatens to do just that in a subsequent verse:

Atá bean as tír—ni h-abar a h-ainm;
maighidh esdi a delm amal cloich a tailm.

There is a woman from the country—I do not say her name;
Her fart breaks from her like a stone from a sling.[100]

The closest comparison to distraint, however, is the very formal genre of satire involving the recitation of (and hence often known as) a *trefocal*, "three words," a poem in which praise and criticism were mixed as a warning sign of the unambivalent vituperation soon to follow should the claim continue to be ignored. *Trefocal* involved staged waiting periods very similar to those envisaged for distraint—to which it is implicitly compared in *Bretha Nemed Tóisech*, which prohibits distraint to poets on the grounds that they should enforce their claims through their art and not through the seizing of cattle.[101] Breatnach has outlined the general contours of the *trefocal* procedure, which extended over thirty days:[102] a ten-day period of notice (*apad* or *fócrae*—the same words used for notice in procedures of distraint), a ten-day period during which the *trefocal* itself was recited, and another ten-day period during which gages offered would still be accepted. If the offender still refused to answer the claim of the poet at the end of these three stages, full satire would ensue and, according to some sources, various payments then became due from the offender. The staged aspect of this procedure is obvious. *Trefocal* depended for its efficacy on the artificial reshaping of community notions of time and space. Like distraint, it both drew upon nature and refashioned it: *Uraicecht na Ríar* speaks of the recitation of satirical verse in "the three periods in the circuit of the moon."[103] Like the other performative procedures we have examined to this point, this resculpting of local routine created a frame within which ordinary actions (poems of praise) were performed in an extraordinary manner (ambivalently, admixed with blame)—a combination which, like the frame itself, inevitably called the community's attention to their special significance.

Certain Middle Irish texts suggest that at least by a later period, the message communicated by the *trefocal* might often have taken written as well as spoken form. According to these texts, the end of the ten-day period of warning (or of the period of *trefocal*—the sources differ on this point), the satirizing poet was to take a rod shaped like a cross, and inscribe his intent to compose poetry "in the name of God" on the first arm, the name of the perceived offense on the second, the name of the offender on the third, and praise for him on the fourth. This rod was then set in the ground and became part of the performance. Indeed, it appears to have mirrored quite literally the verbal presentation that accompanied it. For the statements inscribed on the cross are surely the "three words" (*focal* can mean either "word" or "statement") to which the name *trefocal* itself refers.[104] Insofar as neither composition nor cross consisted entirely of praise nor entirely of satire, but instead constituted a combination of the two, they were termed *brecc*, "speckled," in the sources—a reference to the conceit found elsewhere that praise was white, and satire black, in color.[105] Our understanding of the function of the planting of the cross is necessarily dependent on knowing when in the process it would have taken place. If the cross was put into position at the beginning of the *trefocal* period, as some texts say, it would presumably have acted as a keying device, signaling the onset of performance and serving as a tangible version of the oral poem. If it was not planted until the end of this stage, it must have served both as a physical reminder of the words that had been spoken in that place, and as a sign that the period of pledging was underway. In either case, the juxtaposition of the poet's rod with the foremost symbol of the Christian church testifies eloquently to the various types of sanction implicit in the practice.

No example of a cross of this sort has survived, but remarkably, there is extant an actual example of a *trefocal* poem dating to the Old Irish period, "*A mo Comdhiu néll!*"[106] To remark that this is not a straightforward text is merely to comment on how skillfully, even gleefully, the poet has done his job of walking a fine artistic line—between insult and praise, and between certain and uncertain layers of meaning. In fact, Meroney does not even interpret the poem as a genuine *trefocal*, seeing it rather as "a comic dialogue, the allegory of a Poet's tentative conversion to Christ, when, scorned by the decadent great . . . and unpaid for a mundane ditty, he plans to entreat with hymns for heavenly gain." The people against whom the *trefocal* is perpetrated in the poem, the Fir Arddae, Meroney interprets allegorically, "as men of High Place," or "Blushing Heights . . . not least among whom is the Poet."[107] However, there is very little support in the text itself for the elaborately theological interpretation Meroney proposes. The name Fir Arddae is attested elsewhere in the literature, and there is no reason to regard them as mythical beings.[108]

Moreover, as Breatnach has pointed out, the poem mirrors so precisely the structure of the *trefocal* as described in the sources that there can be little doubt but that it is an actual example of the genre.[109] The *trefocal* proper is prefaced by invocations by the poet to the Lord (verse 1) and to *Cíall*, "Good Sense" or "Reason," (verse 11), requesting advice on the manner in which he ought to proceed in the face of the tremendous wrong he perceives the Fir Arddae to have done him (he had composed a poem for which they then refused to pay). Ought he to praise again those against whom he has a claim, even though their past track record would suggest that his verse was unlikely ever to be rewarded according to its due (verse 2)? Or ought he to proceed immediately to satire—clearly his own inclination—allowing the harshness of his words to lacerate their reputation within the community? Good Sense then weighs in on the matter, advising caution and warning the poet that turning so soon to satire may alienate others whose favor he might wish to enjoy in the future. Much better, Good Sense suggests (verses 24 and 26), would be a more moderate approach: the production of a composition that is only "half rough" (*lethamhnus*) and "without bad color" (*dodath*)—in other words, "speckled" rather than "black"—a poem that causes blushing (*grísadh*) but is not yet actual satire (*áer*).

And this is precisely what the poet proceeds to do, beginning with verse 33 and continuing through the final invocation to the Lord in verse 70. In best *trefocal* fashion, the poet first names the offenders in verse 35, describing the bountiful hospitality with which the Fir Arddae first welcomed his visit—a bit of praise that serves to emphasize the contrast between their initial reception of him and the inexplicably cruel disappointment he then goes on to describe. The offense is named specifically three separate times, in verses 44, 45, and 48, and the threat of satire then follows in a series of exclamations that have a frightening and almost incantatory aspect to them: *Gromfa, gromfa! Glámfa, glámfa! Áerfa, áerfa!*, "I will mock, I will mock! I will jeer! I will jeer! I will satirize! I will satirize!"[110] Because it is still at this point the poet's intention to warn the Fir Arddae rather than to satirize them formally, the harshness of his invective is then mitigated by a series of statements praising their liberality, high social standing and wealth (verses 61–68). Even here though he can not resist one last dig: one of the final verses emphasizes the contrast between their generous and noble appearance on the one hand, and their refusal to pay what is so clearly owed to him on the other (68).

The poem is thus very clearly a *trefocal* as that genre is described in the sources, and there is no reason to believe that either its targets or the events it describes are mythical. Meroney is right, however, in pointing to the complexity of the language and the technical skill displayed in the crafting of the poem. Puns and double entendres are numerous throughout the piece. The first line of this seventy-two-stanza poem, "*A mo Comdhiu néll!*" sets the tone for what follows. On one level, it is an address to God: "Oh, my Lord of the clouds!" And insofar as the *trefocal* cross also began[111] with an appeal to God, and "Lord of the clouds" is an appellation for the deity found elsewhere in the sources, the invocation seems reasonably straightforward.[112] However, as Meroney points out, the expression is actually quite ambiguous, and susceptible to other translations altogether.[113] The word used for "clouds" in the text is *nél*, which can also mean "mists" and hence figuratively, "obscurities" (Meroney's translation); the word used for "Lord," *coimdiu*, is related to *con-midethar*, "rules," but also "assesses, estimates." When read in this manner—"Oh, my master of obscurities," or "Oh, my assessor of obscurities"—the first line of the poem becomes a direct allusion both to the inherent ambivalence of the *trefocal* genre, in which nothing is stated outright but everything is implied, and to the poet's own mastery of his craft, which allows him to walk the very fine line between warning and satire.

Indeed, one of the very striking aspects of the poem is the manner in which the message communicated on the surface of the poem is underscored subtextually by the language employed by the poet. Lexical and rhythmic parallels between words and phrases are deliberately established in order to call attention to the magnitude of the threat posed to the Fir Arddae. In verse 2, for example, the final words in the second and fourth lines—which form a perfect rhyme with one another—are *glámaibh*, "with satires," and *dálaibh* "[in the] assemblies." It is difficult to see this as anything other than a reminder of both the venues in which a satire on the Fir Arddae might ultimately be performed and the widespread impact such a satire would have on their reputation. A similar point is made in verse 35, in which *áes an Arda*, the "people of Aird," is paired with *ní clú ladga*, "no slight renown,"—an obvious allusion to the state the Fir Arddae would find themselves in the wake of a formal satire by the poet. Verse 19 pairs (*conda*)-*áera*, a form of the verb "to satirize," with *sáera*, "free, noble"—a reminder of the social standing and prestige the Fir Arddae would no longer possess were the satire to proceed. And an even more subtle usage of these same words occurs in verse in 47, which links *áerfa, áerfa*, "I will satirize, I will satirize," with *gním not-sáerfa*, "a deed that will save you" (or "a deed that will ennoble you")—the deed in question being, of course, the act of finally rendering an adequate payment for the poet's artistic efforts. Verse 25 simultaneously evokes the nature of the threat, the means by which punishment will be effected, and the neglected poem itself in its linking of *dedhlaib dúaine*, "elements of [the] poem," with *ferb for grúaidhe*, "a blister [of shame] upon [the] cheeks." This same point is made again in verse 48, which uses alliteration to link *dígail*, "vengeance," with *díghna dúaine*, "reproach by means of (but also 'contempt of') a poem,"—and then pairs the latter by rhyme also with *gríbhdai grúaidhe*, "cheek talons."[114]

Trefocal poems thus work for many of the same reasons that distraint works: the carefully calculated timing of the procedure, which gives the offender the space he needs to do the "right" thing on his own, and the gradual heightening of tension between the parties and within the community, which increases the urgency on all sides for the dispute to be resolved. Both are highly public procedures, aimed as much at the community as at the offender—obviously with the hope of encouraging friends and neighbors to bring pressure to bear on the parties to work out a resolution to the dispute that will be satisfactory to them both. The dramatic parallels with distraint also are quite clear. Just as the gradual removal of a cow is both a statement of the offender's intent to pursue the claim and a preview of the dispossession to come, so also is the poet's display of his technical and creative gifts both a proof of his ability to ruin the offender's reputation and a foretaste of the satire through which that damage will be effected. The performance of a *trefocal* poem thus constitutes a form of distraint: against status and reputation rather than a herd, and accomplished through the manipulation of words rather than the wielding of a staff. The sanction is different, as are the precise means by which those sanctions are threatened. The psychology, however, is precisely the same.

Not just any words will effect the desired outcome, however. One of the crucial points underscored by the textual subtleties of the *trefocal* against the Fir Arddae is the importance of the connection between efficacy and aesthetic presentation. The recitation of a poem against an offender, like the performance of a verdict by a judge, is an artistic as well as a legal experience. The more artfully the poet displays his skill, the keener the threat. This is why the subtle innuendos fashioned from the rhyming and alliterative pairing of words and phrases are so important to the functioning of the poem: they are proof of the poet's mastery over words and, thereby, of the authority those words will carry if they come ultimately to be used against the Fir Arddae. An incompetent satire matters little—it is essential that the poet establish that he can carry out his threat in a manner to which others will pay attention. This equation of efficacy with artistic and technical ability is a point made frequently throughout the legal sources. At least one Middle Irish text suggests that metrical flaws in satirical verse can mitigate its effectiveness: committing one of the "twelve faults of poetry" (*ma do-rigni ni don da fubaib .x. aircitail*) results in a fine upon the poet and the postponement of his case.[115] And *Bretha Nemed* makes it clear that a poet's competence in satire and other legal matters is determined by his verse-making abilities, which in this text are in turn equated directly with the extent of his learning and professional training. Lower-class poets—those without the training deemed necessary by the authors of the text—simply cannot speak with the authority of their educated brethren, and their words matter correspondingly little in the social arena.[116] Art and power cannot be understood in isolation from one another.

One of the other striking aspects of the *trefocal* against the Fir Arddae is its forthrightly Christian perspective. The poem begins with an invocation to God (ambivalent as it may be) and ends with the poet's promise of repentance and plea for salvation. The next to last couplet refers to *inscib et-*

laib, "through pure (or 'sinless') speech," a turn of phrase that in context establishes an implicit contrast between the praising of God and the half praise/half satire of the *trefocal* itself. There is no reason to doubt that satire was itself a native genre; however, native and ecclesiastical ideas on the power of the word seem either to have overlapped or to have influenced one another over time as did, of course, the learned classes themselves. For satire was undoubtedly practiced by Christians: upper-class, ecclesiastically educated poets (*filid*) were fond of depicting lower-class satirists as pagan and therefore given to magic,[117] but they did this primarily in order to lay claim to the practice themselves. At least two of the verses cited in "*Cis lir fodla aíre?*" are attributed to clerics, and one of them is a poem by an abbot satirizing the literacy of a clerical colleague.[118] Clerical satire in particular derived its efficacy not only from the social pressure it brought to bear on the offender, but from the implicit threat of divine intervention were things not to be put right. Moreover, clerics were not restricted in their claims to making use of the devices of the secular poets: satire had direct procedural parallels in the ecclesiastical sphere. Functionally, it is very difficult to distinguish the satire of the *filid* from the maledictions of Christian clerics and saints, as Tomás Ó Cathasaigh has shown.[119] Certainly there are clear parallels between the satire procedure outlined in the poetic sources and the psalms of malediction about which Dan Wiley has recently written, where as part of a cursing ritual, a different psalm was recited every day against an offender for a period of twenty days in order to get him to come to law. As he points out, the parallels both with satire and with distraint are striking—and not at all coincidental.[120]

Speech and language both thus played an essential role in establishing and proclaiming rank in Irish society. Sometimes this was accomplished through restrictions on the type or amount of public speech accorded an individual; sometimes it was done through public speech acts (for example, praise or satire) directed at an individual. Poets exercised particular power because they knew how to wield words in ways that could either exalt or wound: certainly it is not accidental that the "measure of a man's worth" tended often to be equated with the liberality he had demonstrated toward the poets in residence at his court. In any case, though, words did not merely report status; they resculpted it. They were weapons of great power, able to condemn individuals to a lifetime of solitude or bring an end even to the most distinguished of reigns. Public speech was not a passive entity, capable merely of encapsulating or displaying distinctions of rank that drew their vigor from elsewhere. It was, rather, an active force, a weapon of social aggression and alliance, shaping as well as shaped by those engaging in it. Usually when we look to explain the workings of a given historical society, we look either to its rulers or to its mechanisms of governance. These are important aspects of culture, certainly, but focusing on them to exclusion of other factors risks missing the essential fluidity of the human interactions of which communal life is inevitably composed. The Irish example suggests a more complicated vision of social life, one in which performance and politics are not opposites, but rather inseparable elements of the functioning of culture.

Language and the Structuring of Obligation

To this point, we have looked at various ways in which language and public speech established, displayed, and reshaped notions of status and rank in Irish society. Another angle from which to approach the link between performance and power is to consider the role that language—translated into speech—played in defining and structuring personal and political relationships within the community. That we can aspire to do this at all is due to the survival of a remarkable text on the subject of contract that purports to quote the language actually used in the making of contractual obligations. Contract is not, perhaps, a topic destined to stir the soul of the modern reader, but it was a subject of tremendous significance to the early Irish, who relied on the strength of the contractual bond to confirm many of their most important social and political arrangements.[121] Long-term relationships like clientship, fosterage, and tutoring were generally not undertaken by the elaborate mechanisms and guarantors characteristic of the formal oral contract.[122] However, most other arrangements crucial to the ongoing prosperity of the community—loans, sales, exchanges, short-term labor agreements, and the like—were indeed confirmed in this manner. Reneging on such arrangements was considered a very serious offense, one that threatened dishonor to parties and disturbed the social balance of the community; contracts were therefore hedged about with a number of highly public, highly formal rituals designed to serve as safeguards against default.[123]

The publicly performed manipulation of language played an essential role in structuring these rituals. Normally we would know very little about the language used in early medieval legal dealings, since in Europe generally (and never in Ireland, as far as we know) it was not customary in this period to make detailed transcripts of such proceedings. However, *Berrad Airechta*, a legal text on the subject of suretyship dating to c. 700 C.E., preserves what purports to be a verbatim account of phrases spoken by contracting parties to mark the various stages of their agreement, from the undertaking of the original obligation to the eventual resolution of the debt.[124] Of course, as has already been remarked, historians have always to be wary of claims of verbatim reportage. The exchanges recorded in *Berrad Airechta* are presented as direct speech—ritualized discourse taking place between two contracting parties and their guarantors. However, while it is certainly possible that contracting parties in early Ireland would actually have recited the phrases cited in *Berrad Airechta* word for word, this is far from a necessary conclusion. Even apart from the issue of how and why such a transcript of such an event might have been made, the extreme localism of Irish life makes it unlikely that contracting parties would have made use of precisely the same words and phrases in every region of the island.

On the other hand, common sense alone would suggest that the phrasing in *Berrad Airechta* is unlikely simply to have been entirely made up, and indeed, other texts of the period imply that the language cited in *Berrad Airechta* does reproduce, in a general way, the actual linguistic dynamics of such an event. Very similar language appears, for example, in a brief passage on the acquisition of a sheep incorporated into a text on the desirable qualities of cows. This text is not itself a contract; however, one passage in it replicates the language of contract in its instructions to a would-be buyer as to how to negotiate the complexities governing the buying and selling of sheep. Buyers are told to "appoint sureties" (*aic maccu*), both to guarantee the health and appropriate appearance of the animals they wish to purchase and to ensure that their own payments are forthcoming at the established time and in the right amount. *[A]ic maccu* is a formula that features prominently in the *Berrad Airechta* exchanges,[125] and the sheep passage as a whole displays many of the same rhetorical features characteristic of the contractual rituals described in that tract, most notably, alliteration, parallelisms, and arcane diction.[126] In other words, significant similarities in phrasing, style, and structure link the exchanges cited in *Berrad Airechta* with what we know about contractual language from other contemporary (and unrelated) texts, and this suggests in turn that we may make use of this evidence in our study.

Contractual procedure itself was complex. Contracts were normally initiated by the would-be creditor, who recited to his debtor a list of the obligations to which the debtor was committing himself. Guarantors called *nadmen* (singular *naidm*), "binding-sureties," then repeated a shortened version of this statement to the debtor, who signaled his acceptance of the terms by means of a special formula—*aicdiu*, "I appoint *naidm*-sureties"— and by joining hands with creditor and *naidm*-surety both. The creditor then himself appointed *naidm*-sureties of his own to the debtor to guarantee that he would behave properly in receiving his payment. In most cases, a further paying-surety called the *ráth* was then given by the debtor to the creditor, also through the exchange of formulas and the giving of *naidm*-sureties; the debtor then appointed still more *naidm*-sureties to guarantee the *ráth* that all expenses incurred while serving as his guarantor would be met. *Naidm* and *ráth*-sureties thus functioned in tandem to ensure the re-payment of the debt: the role of *naidm*-sureties was to remember and enforce the details of the agreement, while the role of *ráth*-sureties was to pay the debt on the debtor's behalf if the latter defaulted. A "full-dress" Irish contract would therefore involve a minimum of eight *naidm*-sureties, two *ráth*-sureties, and a full complement of witnesses.

That we are here in the presence of formal legal performance cannot seriously be doubted. The parallels with distraint, *tellach*, and sick-maintenance are marked. The original exchange of formulas established the geographical and chronological parameters of the obligation, setting a time and place for the repayment of the debt. Repayment was to be effected at the creditor's house (or that of his agent), a literal moving of property from one place to another that enacted in dramatic terms the change of ownership involved.[127] Missed payments were countered by mounting interest charges that both alerted the community to the imminence of default and brought pressure to bear on the offender. And the symbolism of the affair itself underscored the necessity for repayment. Hand met hand in what was at once a symbol of the binding of the debt and a foreshadowing of its eventual collection. Just as in *tellach*, where the binary symbolism of the event generated a series of unspoken taxonomic associations, so also did the ritual of contract evoke the social promise and threat implicit in an agreement between neighbors: tight/loose, together/apart, whole/fragmented.[128] In other words, we have in contractual procedure all of the elements of legal performance discussed earlier in this work: the artificial manipulation of time and space, the complex symbolism of the exchange, the utterly transformative nature of the ritual itself.

What differentiates the procedure outlined in *Berrad Airechta* from the others examined earlier is the role played by language in the event. (As far as we can tell, that is: it is possible, and perhaps even likely, that distraint and *tellach* also involved the recitation of specific formulas or phrases of which no record today remains.)[129] Code, codeswitching (and, as we shall see, patterns of speech and silence) played an essential role in establishing and structuring relationships of legal obligation. Perhaps most obvious was the role language played in framing the event. Whereas in *tellach*, distraint, and sick-maintenance it was primarily action that initiated and sustained the frame—the crossing of boundaries, the enclosing of cows, the deliberate stabling of horses—in contract, it was speech that fulfilled these functions.[130] Words helped to bring an agreement into being, delineated the boundaries of that agreement, and structured the progress of events within it in a way that invited community intervention and support. Wordless verbal events quite likely also played a role in determining the structuring and outcome of such agreements. These are of course lost to us now today. Still, it is not difficult to imagine gestures, sounds, or particular modes of delivery serving to frame and identify a transaction, or sniggering and jeering and the emission of unedifying sounds being used to undermine or subvert it.

Drama comes in many forms. Curtains do not always rise or lower to signal the boundaries of performance. Over the past few decades, linguistic anthropologists have called our attention to the existence in many societies of certain "keying" or "cueing" devices: deliberate shifts in register or linguistic style that serve both to demarcate special events from ordinary occurrences taking place in the community and to define the nature of those events. Frequently these devices are linguistic or, more accurately, metalinguistic in nature—in other words, language that calls attention to itself as language and, thereby, to the speech act or performance of which it is a part.[131] Common devices include, but are certainly not limited to, parallelism or repetition, fixed phrases or formulas, archaic or otherwise distinctive phrasing, conscious appeals to tradition or the past. *Berrad Airechta* makes clear that linguistic keying devices of this sort figured heavily in Irish contractual procedure. The language employed by contracting parties was clearly a "marked" form of discourse—one which, though not as heavily saturated with metalinguistic elements as *rosc* or *Fénechas*, was likely to have differed substantially from ordinary speech. Within *Berrad Airechta* itself, the shift in code is marked by the passage from the tract's own description of the contractual ritual, which is written in what has been called the "plain" or "textbook" style of early Irish prose,[132] to the language of the agreement itself, in which the use of alliteration, parallelism, and technical vocabulary is very noticeable. This shift takes place within the format of the written text, but the clear implication here is that this written shift reproduces a change taking place within the realm of speech.

Undoubtedly the most important function served by the switch from ordinary speech to the marked speech of the contractual ritual was the construction of a performative frame of reference within which all subsequent actions were to be interpreted by the community for whom the ritual was enacted. Formulae like *aic maccu*, "appoint *mac*-sureties,"[133] or *gaib it laim*, "take in your hand," marked the boundaries of the dramatic frame within which the rest of the obligation took place. They also established the manner in which onlookers were to understand and react to the actions following on from these words. *Mac* or *naidm*-sureties were synonymous with contract; so also was the hand-in-hand binding procedure to which the *gaib it laim* formula spoke. Once these words were spoken, the audience knew broadly what to expect. The boundary between ordinary life and life within the contractual frame was underscored by the distinctly out of the ordinary style of the language in which the binding of the obligation on the debtor was effected:

Gaib fort laim fiach dam-sa dia laithiu airchiunn isind forus (ainscogeth) cen indscugud, cona indrucus 7 a inchusc, cona focal 7 a dilsi 7 a dilmaine. . . . Atdaime samlaid for forus 7 follus 7 fiadain. . . . gaib it laim samlaid cen eluth cen esngabail cin ailsith cin fuatach cin act cin airesc cen dorath cen dichell.[134]

Take on your hand that [this] debt [will be paid] to me by you on [such-and-such] a future day, in this place appointed for payment, unchanged [and] without alteration, with its full lawful worth and its [proper] appearance, with it having been tested, and its immunity from claim and freedom from dispute [guaranteed]. . . .

May you acknowledge also [your obligations] with respect to the place appointed for payment and [with respect to] clarification through witnesses. . . . Take in your hand likewise [that you will fulfill your obligations] without evasion, without defect, without negligence, without [forcible] removal, without stipulation, without condition, without difficulty, without neglect.

If indeed these phrases reproduce in a general way the usual language of contractual procedure as has been suggested, there are several metalinguistic techniques to which one can point as playing an important role in differentiating agreements of this sort from ordinary interaction within the community. Alliteration is quite a marked feature of this language. The two stressed words *fiach* and *focal* alliterate not only with one another and with the unstressed conjugated proposition *fort*, but with *forus, follus,* and *fiadain.* *[A]mscogeth* (*recte* **a**inscogeth) alliterates with *indscugud, indrucus, inchusc* and, later in the procedure, *élúth, esngabail, áilsith, ac[h]t,* and *airesc.* *[D]ílsi* alliterates not only with *dílmaine,* but with *dorath* and *díchell.* Another striking feature of the language is the prevalence of parallelisms—in other words, the underscoring of particularly important concepts through the use of terms that are synonymous or nearly so. *Ainscogeth* and *indscugud* ("unchanged" and "without alteration"), *dílsi* and *dílmaine* ("immunity from claim" and "freedom from dispute"), *ac[h]t* and *airesc* ("stipulation" and "condition"), and (in a more general sense) *dorath* and *dichell* ("difficulty" and "remissness") are all examples of such parallel phrases.

Language very similar to this appears in the *Táin,* when a precocious Cú Chulainn exchanges agreements of protection with the boy-troops of Emain Macha. The two principal verbs used in *Berrad Airechta* for the assumption and acceptance of an obligation appear also here: *geibid foraib, geib-siu* fort, "take on yourself" and *ataimem omm,* "I acknowledge it indeed."[135] *Berrad Airechta's* specific phrasing does not recur in the passage on the acquisition of sheep mentioned earlier;[136] however, that passage displays enough significant qualities in common with the *Berrad Airechta* material as to suggest that the metalinguistic features of the binding rituals reported in that text reflected more than just the literary pretensions of those who composed it. Most obvious is the introductory keying phrase *aic maccu,* and the characteristics of the language in which the sheep's desired attributes are described:

Aic maccu a cairaich slan noicc ninnraic sochraid solomrad . . . nip forfind no fo(ro)finn . . . nip ladrach, nip letheirlach . . . ropai uaitsiu a cairaich indraicso aes 7 coland 7 oland.

Invoke sureties for a healthy young proper well-shaped easily-sheared ewe . . . may she not be white-backed or white-bellied . . . may she not have defective hoofs, may she not have uneven tufts . . . may it (the payment) be given by you for this sheep, proper with regard to age and body and wool.[137]

The alliteration here is evident: *slan, sochraid* and *solomrad,* "well-shaped" and "easily-sheared," *forfind* and *fofinn,* "white-backed" and "white-bellied," *ladrach* and *letheirlach*, "with defective hoofs" and "with uneven tufts," *indraic* and *aes*, "proper" and "with respect to age." One additional aspect is the rhyming pair *coland*, "body," and *oland*, "wool," which is not paralleled directly in *Berrad Airechta*. And while there are fewer parallelisms—most of the characteristics outlined as desirable in the sheep are separable and would stand on their own to anyone who really knew sheep—the constant repetition of qualities creates a cadence to the passage similar to that of the *Berrad Airechta* passages.[138]

One feature characteristic of both the passage on sheep and the *Berrad Airechta* binding formulas is the recurrence of particular syntactical structures into which different words might be substituted as seemed suitable to the occasion. In *Berrad Airechta* it is the repetition of *cen*, "without," that sets the rhythm of the event (*cen foer cen anad cen imdegail . . . cen eluth cen esngabail, cen ailsith, cin fuatach*, and so on); in the text on sheep it is the use of *nip*, "may she [the sheep] not be, may she not have" (*nip toich, nip gungablach, nip congalfinnach, nip daintach, nip ancrad, nip ladrach, nip letheirlach*, and so on).[139] Either of these structures would have been easy for participants to build upon in imaginative ways, or in ways particularly suited to their own situation—an indication of the potential for creativity inherent in this procedure. It is worth noting that some of the phrases cited in *Berrad Airechta* may have been sufficiently well known and broadly used as to signal the involvement of guarantors on their own, even apart from their metalinguistic qualities. The expression *cen acht cen auresc cen doraith cen dichell*, "without stipulation, without condition, without difficulty, without neglect," is used also in two other contractual binding procedures described in that text—that by which the paying surety the *ráth* undertakes his duties, and that by which the debtor guarantees that he will compensate the *ráth* should the latter have to pay on his behalf.[140] *[C]en dichell, cin ailseth*, "without neglect, without negligence," and *cen acht, cen arusc, cen dorath cen dearmat cen dichell*, also occur in the speech by which the noncontractual hostage surety known as the *aitire* was bound. Moreover, the oath by which the *aitire* was bound to his duties contains additional synonymous or alliterative pairs that suggest that formulaic language of this sort was a feature not only of contractual ritual, but of transactions involving guarantors generally: *do nirt 7 do luth* ("your strength and your power"), *cen toghais cen toll, cen tobhach*[141] ("without fault, without force, without concealing anything"), *cen dearmat, cen dichell* ("without negligence," "without neglect").[142]

The manipulation of language was thus crucial to Irish contractual procedure. The switch in code, from ordinary conversation to a heightened and more specialized form of discourse, served both to alert the community as to the existence of a contractual arrangement between the parties and to create a performative frame within which all events related to the agreement would then proceed. Language served also to structure the obligation from within, marking the stages through which it progressed and proclaiming an end to the relationship once the demands of all parties to the agreement had been satisfied. Historians who study the process by which public memories are constructed and reconstructed over time have often made the point that reenactment—whether of a special ceremony or occasion, or of an important moment in time—often plays a crucial role in shaping the manner in which the history of the event is understood. Even in cases where the aim is less to reproduce a memory precisely than to re-fashion it in ways more conducive to the priorities of the present, societies often return to past precedent in their ceremonial reconsiderations of the occasion. This is why rites intended to alter or even to repudiate earlier events so often resemble that which they purport to negate. Thus do grad-uation ceremonies frequently reprise the garb and language of the rituals of matriculation.[143]

In Ireland, the public memory of an oral contract was constructed—and, if need be, reconstructed—in exactly the same manner. From the point of view of the language utilized by the parties to the agreement, every step along the way (at least that we can trace on the basis of present evidence) seems intentionally to have recalled the original binding procedure. The words used by the creditor in binding the debtor to his promise to compen-sate his paying surety in the case of default, for example, closely parallel those used (again by the creditor) in binding the debtor to the original ob-ligation:

Gaib fort laim fiach . . . isind forus a[i]nscogeth, cen indscugud . . . cin acht cin airesc cin dorath cin dichell.[144]

Take on your hand that [this] debt [will be paid] . . . in this place appointed for payment, unchanged [and] without alteration . . . without stipulation, without con-dition, without difficulty, without neglect. (Excerpted from the binding of the orig-inal debt by the creditor on the debtor)

Aicc macu . . . icfai a slan . . . a forus to thigi fadein ainscuigeth cen cumscuguth . . . cin acht cen auresc cen doraith cen dichell.[145]

Invoke sureties . . . that you will pay his compensation . . . its place appointed for payment is your own house, unchanged and without alteration . . . without stipula-tion, without condition, without difficulty, without neglect. (Excerpted from the binding of the *ráth*'s compensation on the debtor by the creditor)

The *cen acht cen airesc cen dorath cen dichell* formula appears again in the words by which the *ráth*'s suretyship was bound on him, which also have some lexical similarities to the original binding of the obligation.[146]

Similarly, the process by which the debt was resolved seems also to have deliberately invoked the terminology of the original binding procedure as a way of reminding onlookers of the terms of the earlier agreement before moving the contract on to its next stage. *Berrad Airechta* envisages several possible outcomes to the undertaking of a contractual obligation. First, all could proceed as planned, with both parties showing up at the proper place and time to fulfill their responsibilities. Unfortunately, the tract tells us very little about this process of normal, on-time repayment—perhaps because juristic intervention would not have been required in such cases. However, we are given the words spoken when one of the two parties—creditor or debtor—showed up at the time arranged for repayment to find that the other party was not there. In this case, the person who had appeared at the proper time and place recited a statement that precisely reiterated the substance of his own original undertaking. The debtor, for example, proclaimed himself ready to make payment in words closely duplicating the original promise he had given to the creditor:

fiach dleghar dim-se sunn indiu ag ondar sunn. . . . cona focal 7 a dilsi 7 a dilmaine . . .[147]

the debt that is due from me today, here it is . . . with its [quality] having been tested and its immunity from claim and its security from dispute [guaranteed]. . . . (Excerpted from the statement of the debtor who has appeared ready to pay the debt)

Gaib fort laim fiach dam-sa dia laithiu airchiunn . . . cona focal 7 a dilsi 7 a dilmaine . . .[148]

Take on your hand that [this] debt [will be paid] to me by you on [such-and-such] a future day . . . with its [quality] having been tested, and its immunity from claim and freedom from dispute [guaranteed]. . . . (Excerpted from the original binding of the obligation on the debtor)

This statement looked both backward and forward, in that it had the effect of reappointing *naidm*-sureties for the debt, while rewarding the debtor for his compliance by extending the obligation for another year's time.

Creditors who showed up to recover their debts from debtors who did not appear—presumably a more common occurrence—also made reference in their statements to the language they had earlier used in making the agreement: *Atrogath macu be coir airitin 7 dingbalae, sla[in] 7 frettechtae tairis,*[149] "I have appointed *mac*-sureties that I will behave correctly with respect to receiving and removing [the payment] and [with respect to a declaration of] freedom from loss and renunciation [of any further claims on the debtor]." *Berrad Airechta* does not give us the full wording of the promises made by the creditor during the original agreement; however, we infer that his original promises would have been made in these words from the fact that these are the very words used also by the debtor who comes to repay his obligation but finds his creditor missing. In such an instance, the debtor recapitulates not only the undertakings he himself had given during the original binding, he also acknowledges the obligations owed to him by the creditor—obligations to which the creditor had committed himself at the time of the binding of the debt: *acht ní fore tairic 7 dingbail, slan 7 fre-ittec 7 [f]resndal de . . . ,*[150] "except insofar as delivering and removing [the payment], [the declaration of] freedom from loss and the renunciation [of any further claim] and service may take its place (i.e., take the place of part of the debt payment). . . ."

Upon the formal proclamation of their willingness to collect the debt owed to them, creditors became thereby entitled to request payment from the paying surety, the *ráth*, appointed to them during the original binding of the debt. Once a *ráth* had paid the outstanding debt on behalf of the defaulting debtor, the debtor administered an oath to the creditor, requiring him to declare the obligation at an end: *toing do dia asnoebath cach dliguth. Toimmur deruth cach techta in huidib 7 airisnib . . . ,*[151] swear to God that it is an extinction [of the debt] according to each entitlement, that you have exacted [the debt] entirely, according to each propriety, in accordance with the [established] times and arrangements. . . . This language again returns us to the language of the original binding of the obligation, in that it closely recalls both the words by which the *ráth* had originally been bound to his duties, and those by which the debtor had been bound to compensate the *ráth*:

Aicc macu . . . digene fir firnde conut diba cach thechta . . .[152]

Invoke sureties . . . that you will act according to the truth of justice until it [the debt or the suretyship] is extinguished for you according to each propriety. . . . (Excerpted from the binding of his suretyship on the *ráth*)

Aicc macu . . . a forus to thigi fadein ainscuigeth . . . manach dibath ar brith na brei-them . . . ,[153]

Invoke sureties [for the payment of the proper compensation] . . . the place appointed for payment is your own house, unchanged . . . unless there be an extinction [of your debt] according to a judgment or a judge. . . . (Excerpted from the binding of the *ráth*'s compensation on the debtor)

Given the deliberateness with which *ráth* and debtor exacted a formal acknowledgement from the creditor to the effect that the debt had been paid and that the obligation was at an end, it seems likely that creditors and debtors who appeared on time to conclude their agreement in a manner commensurate with the terms of the original contract might also have performed similar such oaths.[154]

Language thus played a crucial role in establishing the fact of a contractual agreement within the community, in delineating the various stages of that agreement, and in terminating the arrangement once payment had been rendered. Because the relationship between the parties was understood to be constantly evolving, it was essential that the public memory of the event be every bit as fluid. The stages through which a given agreement might pass before its final resolution could not be foreseen, and it was necessary always to keep an eye both on the present and the past. A clear priority of the procedure was to make room for change while remaining within the original parameters established for the event. This is why the terminology associated with the various stages so often referred back to something done earlier within the frame, and why the language of termination echoed, but did not precisely recapitulate, the language of inception. The self-conscious establishment of boundaries around the event was also crucial, not least because of the potential for violence to spill out of the frame was so great. For as with the other procedures examined so far, one of the most striking—and dangerous—aspects of the contractual procedure was the manner in which familiar identities were reshaped within the boundaries of the event. Men who were neighbors, sons, brothers, and lords became creditors, debtors, and guarantors to one another; familiar places within the community were recast as places of payment, denial, or shame.

What contractual procedure reveals that distraint and *tellach* cannot is the role played by public speech in facilitating and maintaining such shifts in identity. A man who normally speaks like the farmer or fisherman he is takes on an entirely new aspect when he begins speaking in alliterative or formulaic phrases. People listen to him differently, assessing his actions in light not merely of who they know him to be, but also of the role they perceive him to be attempting to assume. Again, Schechner's characterization of ritualized persons as "not themselves" and yet "not not themselves" seems especially apt. Moreover, the change in language—from ordinary conversational code to the heightened discourse of contractual procedure—constitutes a deliberate summons to the community actively to intervene in perpetuating the public memory of those identities, and in ensuring that promises made while in the guise of those characters will be fulfilled within the boundaries of the frame.

But if language thus helped to temporarily reshape the identities of those participating in such agreements, it also helped to forestall the inherent violence potentially implicit in any agreement gone awry in a small community by creating a performative stage on which unjust or disruptive actions could take place in relative safety. For there was always the possibility that things would go wrong—that neighbor would cheat neighbor, for example, or one relative would take advantage of another. No matter how tightly framed the procedure, serious tensions will inevitably arise between those who live and work with one another on a daily basis, especially when property is involved. In such instances, language acted not only to separate, but to unite: in other words, it served not only to set people apart from their ordinary roles, thus minimizing the chance of hostilities spilling out over the boundaries of the frame, but also to bring people together by underscoring their existence as a community. The terminology of contract was sufficiently specific and odd that only those with inside status within a community would recognize its significance. Only those conversant with the traditions of the locality would recognize from the use of *aic maccu* or *gaib it laim* that the making of an oral contract was imminent, and only those in the know would be qualified to assess the linguistic validity of the event. Corinne Kratz makes the point that transformations effected through well-known social ceremonies are not changes in social or cultural categories per se, but rather changes made within such categories that have the effect of validating the system of which they are a part. An individual's status may be completely transformed by such a ceremony; however, the occasion itself is one that underscores the continuity and cohesiveness of the community within which it takes place.[155]

This is particularly true because it is the community itself that must grant authority to the transformation taking place in the course of such ceremonies. A rite must persuade in order to be effective. Codeswitching and the use of heightened language must surely have played a critical role in such calculations, convincing onlookers of the legitimacy of the arrangement and the seriousness of the participants. Terms like *aic maccu* would have acted to validate the procedure in much the same way that familiar terminology authorizes other contemporary performances. Modern audiences will, for example, accept as "genuine Shakespeare" even plays in which Romeo and Juliet are cast as members of rival biker gangs as long as the roars of the Hondas are punctuated by the dulcet rhythms of Elizabethan English. It is important to realize, however, that such language is not merely comfortable and authorizing, it is also needy and provocative. It demands a response from those who listen to it, simply because it is as odd as it is familiar. Victor Turner has commented on what he calls the "reflexivity" of formal social dramas like legal cases, by which he means the degree to which onlookers are invited not merely to witness events, but actively to reflect upon and evaluate the meaning and effectiveness of what they see. Often, this high degree of reflexivity is achieved through the use of "languages or metalanguages, verbal or nonverbal," which allow a ritual to rise above the mere recapitulation of events to a plane in which active scrutiny and intervention on the part of the audience are invited.[156] Only thus can onlookers give their consent to the message being communicated.

The evidence suggests that a high degree of reflexivity was implicit in early Irish contractual procedure, and that this reflexivity was achieved, in large part, by the deliberate use of stylized language. But reflexivity implies judgment, the ability to distinguish authentic from inauthentic—which in turn implies the existence of community standards by which such things could be measured. What gave the language spoken by participants its authority? Part of the answer must be its very familiarity, as we have seen—a familiarity that both celebrated and perpetuated the sense of community upon which it was predicated. However, this can be only part of the answer, for it explains nothing about why this particular type of language might

carry the weight it does. Here it is helpful to try to visualize words and actions in the context of the culture from which they emerge. Embedded in
the language of contractual procedure are quiet references to other forms
of authoritative speech in early Ireland, particularly juristic and poetic
speech. There are significant differences between the tongue used by the
contracting parties in *Berrad Airechta* and full-blown *rosc*—the former does
not, for example, employ or invent deliberately archaic grammatical forms
or structures, which is almost a signature characteristic of *rosc*. However,
they do share some very important elements in common, most notably alliteration, obscure synonyms or parallelisms, and odd syntax. Indeed, I sus-
pect that for those in the know, it would be impossible to hear the speech
used in contractual procedure without it on some level bringing to mind
the unquestionably authoritative language of *rosc*.

The language of *Berrad Airechta* would thus seem from the evidence to
have existed on a continuum of heightened language with *rosc* at one end
of the spectrum and ordinary unmarked conversational speech at the
other. This is not unusual: many world cultures that rely on language and
codeswitching to communicate sophisticated political and legal concepts
also display significant links among the various types of heightened language they employ.[157] Indeed, comparisons with other societies suggest
that in Ireland it may have been through listening to authentic poetic performances that ordinary persons learned to recognize and, ultimately, to
"compose" in the contractual genre.[158] The language of contract must have
evoked a wide range of cultural associations and responses in those who
heard or performed it, and drawn its authority from those associations. In
its connections with the poetic speech of the *filid*, it spoke to hierarchies of
learning and aristocratic status; in its predilection for obscure or ritual vocabulary, it made reference to magic and the power of the word; in its
adoption of structures and forms associated with oral composition, it deliberately evoked the oral past of traditional Irish law; in its resemblance to judicial maxims, it conjured up the authority of the jurist. To put the matter
into the terms of modern scholarship: if it is not genuinely *Kunst*,[159] it par-
took of same, if not a true *Hochsprache*,[160] a register of distinction nonetheless.

Such issues return us once again to the questions raised earlier about
politics and aesthetics. If it is right to see the language cited in *Berrad
Airechta* as essentially one version of the basic template—lexical, grammatical, phonological—upon which parties to contractual agreements
would have drawn, then this has important implications for the nature
of legal bargaining and, perhaps, for the role played by legal dealings in
community life and entertainment. Like all templates, the basic form of
the contractual procedure would have been subject to manipulation and
enhancement on a variety of counts. Parties might need to tailor their
words to fit the circumstances of their individual obligation; they might

choose to speak differently depending on the status of the participants or onlookers involved; or they might attempt to match in the complexity of their linguistic presentation the complexity of the arrangement they were attempting to establish. Another element that might well have come into play is art. It may seem odd to think of contractual procedure as a forum for art, but looking at the *Berrad Airechta* phrases one can imagine a wide variety of presentations, all of which follow the same general model, but differ enormously in their sophistication and artistry. Two of the passages on contract included in *Di Astud Chor*, for example, speak of agreements being bound *inscib ánaib airlabrae*,[161] "in glorious statements of speech." Here again the connection between poetry, politics, and law seems inescapable. What is most beautiful and most complex may also be most authoritative.

Berrad Airechta thus tells us quite a lot about the importance of both language and speech in establishing and validating legal obligations in early Ireland. One could certainly wish for more evidence of this kind; on the other hand, we are lucky to have as much as we have. It does suggest new ways of approaching some familiar texts in the legal corpus. One of the most amusing ditties from the laws is a poem about the loaning of a cart:

"*In esser dom to á?*"	"Will you lend me your cart?"
"*Tó, mani má mo á.*"	"I will, if my cart doesn't break."
"*Ara tairi mo á mó?*"	"Will my cart come back soon?"
"*Mani má to á, tó.*"	"If your cart doesn't break, it will."[162]

As Watkins suggests, the poem is an old one. It is presented in the text as a record of a conversation overheard between two farmers in Connacht, although it would be folly indeed to argue that this is what it actually represents. This poem is no more likely to derive from a truly agricultural context than the religious nature poems for which Ireland is so famous are likely to have originated in genuine leafy glades.[163] It is a clever joke, and a learned one, incorporating as it does the ancient and very rare word *á*, "cart," and punning with almost visible glee on words of similar aspect, such as *to* and *tó*, *mo* and *mó*. On the other hand, its general tenor and the love of wordplay it reveals may well speak to something real in early Irish culture: a celebration of language and linguistic difference that would not be entirely out of place even in the most vulgar of social venues. Perhaps reading this poem in the light of the manipulation of language that *Berrad Airechta* suggests was so much a part of contractual procedure might help us to understand why such a clever poem would be situated in such a seemingly improbable context.

In addition to *Berrad Airechta*, one other intricate example of the use of code as a communicative and structuring device in relationships of legal obligation has survived from the Old Irish period, a legal tale known as the *Immathchor nAilella 7 Airt*, the "Mutual Restitution between Ailill and Art."[164]

This text presents itself as a verbatim transcript of a lawsuit between two mythical figures: Ailill Ólomm, a legendary king of Munster, and Art mac Cuinn, the brother of Ailill's wife Sadb and son of the eponymous ancestor figure of Leth Cuinn, Conn Cétchathach. The issue at hand is whether Sadb, who has been repudiated by Ailill at a point prior in time to the events of the tale, has the right to share in the fosterage of the twins she had borne him before their separation. Her brother Art is the plaintiff in the case, having brought the suit on her behalf; Ailill speaks for himself. The judge to whom the case is submitted is clearly a prototypical figure: his name is Ollam, which simply means "expert, master," and was a term used both for chief poets and for judges of the highest rank. Ollam's verdict in the case may not strike modern readers as necessarily enlightened: he judges that Ailill has full rights to his children and that Sadb should be, from the point of view of the law, out of the picture. As the editor of the text Johan Corthals points out, the key to this baffling judgment lies probably in the medieval belief that only one child at a time could be begotten from a single man, and that twins therefore necessarily implied adultery.[165] Certainly the judge's final verdict leaves no doubt but that he perceived Sadb as the party in the wrong in this case.

The case presented in this text is admittedly much more of a fictional tale than a record of an actual lawsuit. On the other hand, it is also almost certainly the work of a practicing jurist or jurists, someone in touch with the realities of law as it was practiced inside and outside of the schools. Indeed, the tale reads like it might have been written in order to instruct apprentice lawyers in some of the subtleties of their new trade. As we have seen, storytelling apparently featured prominently in the educational circles of the *Bretha Nemed* school, for example, and this text shares a great many stylistic similarities with texts of that school.[166] Its characters are mythical; however, there is no reason to believe that the legal situation to which it speaks is equally so. As always, it is difficult to assess whether the language of the tract is generally authentic—the tale is clearly a literary production, the work of a well-read and intelligent author, and partakes therefore more of the written than the oral sphere. On the other hand, the manner in which it uses language and codeswitching is fully in keeping with what we had seen elsewhere in Irish legal literature, both respect to judges and their pronouncements, and with respect to language generally.

In this text, the contrast is less between plain and marked prose than it is between varieties of rhetorical speech, and the switching of codes involves not merely language, but poetic structure. As Corthals remarks, "The metres used in the *Immathchor* are a constituent part of its elevation of style, and the metrical fluctuation observed in our text is to be understood as a function of the course of the action."[167] The judge's invitation to the disputants to begin the case is couched in ordinary prose. As soon as it begins, however, there is a marked stylistic shift, with both the claimant's and the defendant's pleadings being phrased in the same kind of heavily alliterative, nonmetrical, language. Both pleading and counterpleading are further linked to one another through the frequent repetition of the prefix *com*, "joint," or "common": *comaltor*, "joint fosterage," *comtháirgetha*, "common provisioning," *combuithe*, "living jointly," *comlabartha*, "common conversation," *comléicther*, "is put out of" (Art); and *comberta comtárcithe*, "children of common provisioning," *cobligi*, "lying jointly together," *commámsa*, "common union" (Ailill).[168] Considering that this is a case about *comaltor*, "joint fosterage," the use of this particular prefix in the initial pleadings hardly seems accidental.

Art's response to Ailill's counter plea then closely reiterates Ailill's own phrasing:

Ailill: *It díllsae cétraga mná aurnadme, ar-nascatur comberta comtárcithe, cobligi, commámsa.*

Forfeited are the children of a woman bound by marriage, by which the offspring of common supply, common sleeping, common union is bound.[169]

Art: *Is fír éim at ndíllsa cétraga mná aurnad[me], ara-nascatar comberta cobligi, commámsa, comtárgetha . . .*

It is true that they are forfeited, the children of a woman bound by marriage, by which the offspring of common sleeping, common union, common supply are bound . . .[170]

In other words, all three of the initial pleadings (plea, counterplea, response) are linked together by virtue of the language in which they are couched. This has the effect not only of tying these statements to one another, but also of demarcating this part of the procedure from what follows.

The pleading phase of the proceedings ends when the judge announces that he will pass judgment in the case. Significantly, his statement is couched in a totally different meter—octosyllabic, with trisyllabic cadences—and does not draw on the lexicon of either disputant. It is heavily alliterative, and deliberately so, in that alliteration functions here as a linking device much as rhyme did in the *trefocal* on the Fir Arddae examined earlier. Words beginning with the sound of *s* (*soera*, "noble women," *seichletar*, "who are passed over," *sárigetar*, "that are outraged," *saluib*, "with filth") underscore the contrast between nobility and dishonor that the judge has decided at this point in the proceedings lies at the heart of the case; words beginning with *b* (*[b]iru-sa*, "I will give judgment," *breth*, "judgment," *co bráth bráthnigfus*, "that will remain forever") speak to the solemnity and permanence of the process of judgment itself. Ailill then delivers what proves to be the winning speech. Lexically (and to some degree syntactically) it recalls his earlier plea:

Mui mo . . . cétmuinter . . . mui a nnod-ail, mui a n-alar and.

To me belongs my . . . spouse . . . to me belongs that which she rears, to me belongs what is fostered in that place.[171] (Excerpted from Ailill's original plea)

Mui mo macc, mui mo ingen.

To me belongs my son, to me belongs my daughter.[172] (Excerpted from Ailill's subsequent speech)

(Other lexical similarities include *mná aurnadme,* "woman bound by marriage," in §3 and *fer fonadme,* "men bound as sureties," in §6; and *mo chain cétmuinter,* "my fair spouse," in §3 and *mo chaine céttmuintire,* "of my fair spouse," in §6).

Metrically, however, Ailill's speech is distinct from anything that has been said so far. And the judge then delivers his verdict in a speech that not only identifies Ailill's remarks as having been the deciding element in the case, but that echoes these remarks both metrically (both employ long lines with alliteration with trisyllabic cadence) and lexically:

fer fonadme, "of the enforcing sureties," *de tuathaib,* "from the peoples," *mo chiniuth,* "my children," *cen compert cinath,* "without offspring of sin," *a mmáthar muincoirche,* "their mother who makes wily contracts."[173] (Excerpted from Ailill's speech)

dagnadmannaib tuath, "by the peoples' good enforcing sureties," *cinaith,* "sin," *a chintiu,* "his children," *compert cinath,* "offspring of sin," *mná míchorchi,* "of the untrustworthy woman."[174] (Excerpted from the judge's speech)

As Corthals points out, the final bit of the judge's judgment, where he articulates the general maxim upon which his judgment (and all subsequent decisions of this kind) are founded, changes meter yet again.[175] In sum, the artistic manipulation of language functions in this tale not only to delineate the stages through which the case proceeds (pleas; judge's proclamation of his intent to give judgment; winning speech; judge's verdict), but to mark its internal affiliations as well. When the judge first speaks, he has not yet decided the case and the code he chooses differs from that adopted by either litigant; once he has decided the case, the language of his verdict mirrors Ailill's winning presentation.

The *Immathchor* is not, of course, a transcript of an actual legal case. Moreover, even when its contents can be shown to resonate with passages known from elsewhere, it is not always clear what that means. Corthals points out that one of the phrases put into the mouth of Art is very similar to a passage in the Latin canon law collection *Collectio Canonum Hibernensis,* a fact that he takes as a sign that the author of the *Immathchor* was here engaging in something of a literary jeu d'esprit.[176] But while Corthals's view is certainly plausible, it is equally possible to take this coincidence of expression as evidence that practicing canon and "secular" lawyers might both draw on similar phrases.[177] Nor, as we have seen, are the citations incorporated into *Berrad Airechta* likely to represent a verbatim transcript of contractual procedure. My point is not that most legal encounters pursued in the community would likely have followed such an intricate pattern, but rather that this is the role those conversant with legal practice in this culture imagined that language would play in framing and structuring legal events. It is not enough to track the doings of kings and armies in our search for social order in early Ireland; it is not enough to define nobility solely in terms of birth and personal display. Judicial institutions and personnel are only part of the story in this period and place. Language and speech defined and reshaped social identity; they structured and cemented relationships of obligation. If one seeks to divorce language from power, or to understand politics and aesthetics as unrelated (or even antithetical) to one another, one risks losing sight of the manner in which "government" actually worked. One must never underestimate the power of the word: spoken, performed or, as we shall see in the next chapter, even withheld.

Chapter 4

Voicing Over

To those who study such things, it can sometimes seem as though the revolutionary shift in personnel and priorities that took place in Ireland during the centuries following the early Christian missions was exceeded only by the lengths to which many Irish intellectuals went to pretend that nothing of earthshaking significance had actually occurred.[1] To judge from their work, apart from a few druids losing their jobs or having their heads bashed in by belligerent saints, and the odd pagan king suffering death, dispossession, or testicular decay as a punishment for appropriating property claimed by the church, the transition from pagan to Christian was relatively problem free. The native poetic orders merged without complaint into the new intelligentsia of the church, jurists discovered with delight that native and Christian laws coincided on almost every point (once a few crucial bits about the jurisdictional and fiscal prerogatives of the church had been added in), and in general, everyone got along with everyone else in a splendidly sunny manner. And of course there is some truth to this view. The spectacular fusion of native and Christian that was undoubtedly the greatest legacy of the conversion resulted in an explosion of vernacular and Latin literature unparalleled elsewhere in the medieval West. That we can today know anything at all about early Irish social and legal practice, or revel in the humor of tales like *Fled Bricrenn* or *Mesca Ulad*, is due entirely to this fruitful coming together of traditions.

However, it is simply not possible that sunniness and delight were all that there was. The changes in perspective were too dramatic, and the threat to established personnel too great, to pass without negative comment of any kind. Moreover, even apart from the introduction of new traditions and practitioners, there is reason to think that significant changes were also afoot within the native intellectual elites themselves. It has long been suspected, for example, that the emergence of jurists as a distinctive professional class was a relatively late development, not long preceding the composition of the lawbooks,[2] and it seems equally probable that the loudly Christian *filid* of the late seventh and eighth centuries had not themselves been always as separate from the pagan practitioners they decried as they preferred to imagine.[3] As Charles-Edwards has remarked, "The likelihood is that the final settlement expressed in these texts involved far more readjustments to the Irish learned orders than they would have liked to admit."[4] Unfortunately, readjustments of this sort will inevitably be difficult to trace in sources dedicated to proving the antiquity and historical authenticity of the status quo. The complicated negotiations, false starts, and dead ends that must have gone into the emergence of what are presented in the lawbooks as long-standing offices and institutions are largely occluded from view.

One approach that may help to restore some sense of movement to the largely static terms in which such matters are presented in the sources is to examine texts and events of the period through the lens of speech and performance. For so potent was the equation of speech with power in Irish society, so pervasive the belief that rank entailed the right to give voice on behalf of those of lesser status, that conflicts over rights to authoritative public speech became for the Irish both a means toward and a metaphor for the assertion of jurisdiction by one individual or group over another. We have already seen the equation between speech and power expressed in a variety of ways. Some sources associate particularly intricate forms of language with persons of high rank. Thus is the status of a Cú Chulainn or an Emer expressed and displayed by the deliberately elevated tone of their conversation, unintelligible to those not of similar social standing or education. Some sources instead take the route of linking high status to the right to give public testimony or speak on behalf of persons of lesser status. As we have seen, *Críth Gablach* asserts that one of the important distinctions between the two grades of *fer midboth* (or between any of the freeman grades, for that matter) was the extent to which each was granted the privilege of public speech. And persons or churches of higher status could "overswear" those inferior to them in rank, in essence "voicing over" their testimony so that it could not be heard.[5]

These few examples that we have examined already constitute, however, only the tip of a very large iceberg, one that is worth examining in greater detail. The perception that power and speech were closely linked is absolutely pervasive throughout the Irish sources, both literary and legal. One of the most striking passages of the "Pseudo-Historical Prologue to the *Senchas Már*," for example, refers to the ancients of Ireland apportioning a measure of rights to "lawsuit and speech to each man according to his rank" (*tomus n-aí 7 innsce do chách iarna miad*).[6] The compilation known as "The Alphabet of Cuigne mac Emoin" contains a number of different maxims that explicitly characterize lordship in terms of public speech: *cach flaith a forfuacra*, "to every lord his [rights of] proclaiming"; *cach toíseach co taisealbad*, "to every chieftain his [rights of] declaration"; and *geil-bríathrach cach flaitheamain*, "every lord is splendid in words."[7] Similar sentiments characterize the maxim collection attributed to Flann Fína (Aldfrith, king of Northumbria?): *ferr soithnge slóg*, "an eloquent person is better than an army"; *ad-cota miltengae breithemnas*, "eloquence produces judgment"; *tosach córae caínepert*, "fair-speech is the beginning of peace"; *ad-cota áine airlabrai*, "brilliance makes one a leader" (literally "fore-speaker"); *ad-cota flaith folabrad*, "lordship brings about grumbling" (literally "underspeaking").[8] Indeed, the connection between speech and power is evident even in the terminology of lordship itself. *Críth Gablach* describes the *aire coisring* as the *toísech 7 aurlabraid*, "the leader and spokesman" (again, literally "forespeaker") of his kindred,[9] while the name of another noble grade it discusses, the *aire forgill*, literally means "lord of superior testimony."[10] *Bretha Nemed Toísech* terms the proper judge as *fer laburta láin*, "a man of full speech,"[11] and later uses the terms *án-thengtaid*, "splendid spokesman" (literally, "brilliant tongued one"), and the *suithengtaid*, "eloquent tongued one," to characterize persons of high rank.[12] In fact, so established is the idea that lords are by definition people who speak eloquently in public venues that matters can even work the other way around as well: *roscad* (pl. *roscada*), a type of elevated, authoritative speech characteristic of the public performances of judges, poets, and kings is glossed in one text with *righ-scotha . . . na righ-innscida*, "kingly words, or kingly speech."[13]

The perception that lordship and public speech were intrinsically linked is not difficult to understand, given the ways in which lords were conjoined by their position to represent or, literally, "speak for" their clients in various legal and social venues. But there may be more to it even than this. The association between high rank and the use of particular types of language may also have a basis in patterns of linguistic usage that would help to explain its prominence in the literature. One of the enduring mysteries of the Old Irish language as it remains to us today is its apparent lack of regional or dialectal variation.[14] Often we can determine from internal references that a given text was composed in a particular region of the country: the *Bretha Nemed* lawbook has been localized in this manner to Munster, for example, and the *Senchas Már* to the northern midlands.[15] However, while there are certainly significant stylistic differences separating these two lawbooks, the language itself is remarkably consistent from one text to the other. And what is true of the lawbooks is true too of the tales, which it has also not proved possible to localize. Usually the remarkably uniform character of the Old Irish that remains extant to us today is taken as a sign of its importance as a literary language—the code of the literati and a important token of their intellectual authority. However, Charles-Edwards has recently suggested that standard Old Irish may also have been the language spoken by the secular aristocracy, and that lurking behind the widespread dissemination of standard Old Irish were the political and military successes of the Uí Néill and Éoganachta.[16] If this is true, then a widespread assumption that authoritative speech is intrinsically linked to worldly power would seem only natural.

The equation between lordship and public speech is, however, only one part of a whole. For implied in the speech of the dominant is the silence of those subordinate to them. To the elite, few things were as frightening as the unchecked speech of those who should be silent: *Bretha Crólige* excludes from all claims to sick-maintenance women whose speech it regards as dangerous to those with whom they might be billeted, including female satirists and those known in the community to be—not to put too fine a point on the matter—gossipy bitches.[17] If the lordly elite are portrayed as persons of eloquent diction whose status is in large part defined by their public performances, the voices of the impoverished and oppressed are, by contrast, widely conceptualized in the sources as stilled, dangerous, or even inhuman. *Bretha Nemed Tóisech* speaks of the *étengthaid aneolach*, "unlearned non-speaker," a person obviously imagined as the opposite of the more fortunately aristocratic *ánthengtaid*.[18] In some texts, persons of subordinate status are described as actually unable to speak—or, if physically capable of speech, nonetheless unable to prevent others from "voicing over" whatever they might say. One passage in *Bretha Nemed*, for example, characterizes the speech of low-class poets as less than human, "the croaking and cawing of petty stammering maws" (*graice coirne crais minguiti*).[19] And *Berrad Airechta* characterizes the legally incompetent—a group in which are included fools, imbeciles, lunatics, exiles, castaways and, most tellingly, wives—as those who "possess mouths behind their backs" (*[t]echtait beolu iarna cul*) because anything they say can be impugned by their legal guardians.[20] A temporary loss of status on the part of an individual could be expressed in similar terms. In the women's boasting contest detailed in *Fled Bricrenn*, Emer's superiority over Fedelm and Lendabair is underscored not merely by the complexity of the verse she performs, but by the sheer volume of what she has to say: her loquacity is such that the other women seem by comparison almost "silent."[21] Similarly, the men of Ulster are said both in the *Táin* and in *Mesca Ulad* to be prohibited in certain circumstances from speaking before the king, just as the king himself must remain silent before his druids speak.[22] Poets who are distrained against are enjoined not to perform publicly until the claim has been answered. Clergymen likewise are forbidden while under distraint to recite the Creed or the Lord's Prayer or to go to Mass. Like the poets, they too have been silenced and, in that silencing, have lost that which gives them rank.[23]

The equation of lordship with speech, and subordination with silence, is also a basic—if never directly articulated—presumption of many of the legal procedures examined in earlier chapters. As we have seen, the requirement outlined in the sick-maintenance tracts that absolute silence be maintained in the house in which the victim is being healed has normally been interpreted in terms of the demands of the healing process. The analysis offered earlier took a somewhat different tack, pointing to the manner in which the victim's intrusion into the offender's personal space caused a redefinition of that space to the detriment of the offender. Now it is possible to go even further in interpreting the symbolism of this event. If silence equals subordination, and speech—in this case, the festive sounds made by the victim and his guests during the mandatory hospitality sessions the offender was required to host—was for many a manner in which to claim superior standing in a relationship, then an important aspect of the enjoining of silence on one party by another was the assertion of authority over that person. The contrast between speech and silence would thus implicitly reinforce the message of the hospitality sessions which, as we have seen, were themselves expressions of lordship. It would be interesting to know whether similar alternations between speech and silence characterized other performative procedures like distraint. It may be significant that plaintiffs initiated the proceedings by giving verbal notice of their intentions; however, since it is impossible to say anything about what verbal exchanges might have followed thereafter, we cannot be sure how and whether defendants might have been invited to speak on their own behalf.

But it is probably in contractual procedure that the manner in which patterns of silence and speech acted to create or reinforce hierarchical relationships between parties becomes most strikingly apparent.[24] In each of the suretyship arrangements described in *Berrad Airechta*, it is the person setting the conditions of the suretyship who does all the talking. The creditor, for example, details to the debtor the parameters of his debt and asks him to appoint sureties to guarantee that he will fulfill these obligations;[25] later, in a separate arrangement, he outlines the debtor's obligation to compensate his paying surety in the case of default and asks him to appoint guarantors for that responsibility also.[26] Similarly, the person for whom the paying surety acts is the one to detail the surety's obligations and to ask him to appoint yet further guarantors to ensure compliance.[27] Some amount of speech was granted to the guarantors involved in the affair. After some of these exchanges at least, and perhaps after all of them, the *naidm*-sureties involved repeated a highly truncated version of the terms of the agreement, and asked the defendant whether he would indeed agree to appoint sureties.[28] However, the speech of the *naidm*-sureties was both secondary to, and largely derivative of, the speech of the person to whom the obligations were owed—a fact that underscores their intermediary status in the event.

But even these guarantors enjoy more authority than the person assuming the obligation. For only at this point, after the *naidm*-sureties have spoken and well into the procedure itself, does the person taking on the obligation finally speak. Even then, his is a speech the contents and terminology of which have been entirely dictated to him by those superior to him in the agreement—a one-word response that merely repeats in the first person the verb used by the *naidm*-sureties in their statement to him:

(*Naidm*-sureties): *In n-aicde i nogic na raithe teite aurut?*[29] "Do you appoint [us to guarantee] the complete payment of the *ráth*-surety who acts as surety on your behalf?"

(Debtor): *Aicdiu,*[30] "I appoint [*naidm*-sureties]."

Underlying the visible structure of the contractual process was thus an alternation between speech and silence that would have had great symbolic significance for the audience witnessing the proceedings. To give voice to the terms of the arrangement was to lay claim to authority over it; silence, by contrast, carried implications of subordination and hence underscored the indebtedness and (temporarily) diminished social standing of the individual taking on the obligation.[31]

Moreover, it is not merely silence that is at issue. For the person assuming the obligation does speak. However, what he says is completely dictated by and subsumed into what he has heard. Maurice Bloch has written at length about the manner in which what he calls "formalised language" can automatically call forth a particular and predictable response. Certain expressions must by tradition be followed by others equally well known; in Bloch's words, "speech act A can only be followed by speech act B."[32] In such circumstances, what is said in response to a statement of this sort does not represent the freely chosen word of the speaker, but an utterance coerced from him by the formalized language in which the "conversation" is taking place. Bloch sees such speech as a form of social control, a way of suppressing dissent and individual initiative. Often, as he points out, such statements presuppose not only a particular response but an entire way of political acting, one very much to the advantage of the existing status quo. To accept the terms set for one is to accept the right of the speaker to say them and, hence, his authority.[33] It is not difficult to see the relevance of such observations to the process outlined in *Berrad Airechta*. Contractual procedure was all about the revision of identities and obligations within the local community: for an audience sensitive to the symbolic significance of public speech, the patterning of sound and silence would have constituted a literal performance of the social and legal hierarchies created by the contract.

Speaking for Others

Bloch's perspective raises the important question of other possible applications of the association of speech with authority, particularly in the broader political realm, and here we return to the questions raised earlier in the chapter about the reshaping of the ruling classes in the wake of the arrival of Christianity. What I wish to argue in what follows is that the association between speech and power was so pervasive in Irish society that disputes over access to authoritative speech became for the elite a way to characterize and experience the jurisdictional conflicts that simply must have accompanied the assimilation of the new faith into the old regime. For the literati, imagining particular persons as speaking while others listened or were forced into silence was a way in which to express both the reality of power relationships and the tensions inherent in jurisdictional struggles. It is no coincidence that there are so many extant Irish texts depicting individuals attempting to limit or deny altogether rights to public speech to others. Kings, jurists, and poets are consistently the main characters peopling these stories, but the positions they occupy differ from text to text—a fact that is in itself an indication of the extent to which opinions varied on the roles each should play in the new order. Traditionally, these tales have been considered separately from one another, as have the political and social issues they appear to raise. When read against the backdrop of early Irish beliefs about speech and power, however, they shed light on the process by which the prerogatives of the native intellectual elite were redefined in the wake of Ireland's incorporation within the Christian European world.

Perhaps the most basic and ongoing concern demonstrated in the legal texts was the integration of native tradition within the new Christian dispensation. Often, as we have seen, this was done within a context designed to illustrate the essential compatibility of the two. In the eighth- or ninth-century "Pseudo-Historical Prologue to the Senchas Már," for example, when the poet Dubthach is summoned by Patrick to give judgment on the particularly contentious issue of how to punish the slayer of Patrick's servant, the text makes clear that native and Christian custom on this point are indeed reconcilable. Dubthach's poetic verdict on the case sets forth the legal issues involved, convincing all present that the transition from pagan to Christian Ireland can be negotiated in such a way as to respect native custom while acknowledging the ultimate superiority of the church. The tale communicates this essential compatibility through the issue of voice. For the words the audience hears in this verdict are not those of the poet Dubthach, the putative performer of the judgment, but of the Holy Spirit himself:

"Maith trá," ol Pátraic; "a ndobera Dia for erlabrai, ráid amin. Non vos estis qui loquimini, sed spiritus patris uestri qui loquitur in uobis," 7rl. Bennachais iarum Pátric a gin-sum 7 doluid rath in Spirta Naím fora erlabra co n-epert: INTÚD I NGEINTLECHT GNÍM OLC NÁD INDECHAR, 7rl.

"Well, then," said Patrick; "whatever God may give [you] to say, speak thus. *It is not you who speaks, but the spirit of your Father who speaks in you*," etc. Then Patrick blessed his mouth, and the grace of the Holy Spirit came upon his speech so that he said: "An evil deed which is not punished is a relapse into paganism," etc.[34]

Here Dubthach's physical voice is that which is heard by the audience; the words he pronounces, however, are not his own. God is depicted as the true speaker and therefore the chief authority in this performance, a point underscored by Patrick's switching of codes—from Irish to Latin, from oral to scriptural text—at the crucial moment in which he blesses Dubthach's mouth. Precisely the same idea occurs again in the following paragraph of the text, where it is claimed that the Holy Spirit had been speaking and prophesying through the mouths of the *breithemon 7 filed fíréon fer nÉrenn*, "righteous judges and poets of the men of Ireland,"[35] from the time the island was first settled, which is why so much of native law and justice coincides with that of the new Christian dispensation. The contrast in both instances is thus less between speech and silence than it is between a musical instrument and the performer who plays the instrument: the instrument makes the sound, but the power and originality of the presentation reside in the artist alone. The fact that the event is legitimized by an appeal not merely to native ideas about speech and power but to a scriptural quotation on the power of God's Word, demonstrates how proximate native and Christian ideas on this subject were (or could be made to look). It is itself testimony to the reconciliation of native and Christian—albeit under Christian authority—that is the main point of the tale.[36]

Some tales depict the relationship between native and Christian custom as more decidedly confrontational. The contrast between silence and authoritative speech plays a crucial role in the Middle Irish prologue attached to the historical *Cáin Adamnáin*, "Law of Adamnán," for example. In this prologue, the Irish saint Adamnán has to be tortured by his mother before he will agree to proclaim a new "law" protecting women from having to participate in battle. Kings of every province oppose these reforms since, according to the tale, it was customary for women to bear the burden of both domestic and martial labor. Not surprisingly, most men seemed content with this traditional arrangement—including initially both Adamnán and God, in that the angel who liberates Adamnán has essentially to be blackmailed into agreeing to do what he wants. (According to the text, freeing women from their obligations was a personal project of the Virgin Mary.) During the period of his torture, Adamnán is depicted as essentially mute. Not only is a stone placed in his mouth during much of the proceedings, he is later actually mocked by one of his overconfident (and soon to be regretful) royal enemies as *bodur amlabor*, "the deaf [and] dumb one."

Once Adamnán has emerged from his punishment, however, he becomes capable of speech once more and engages in an elaborate public performance, speaking the words and performing the sounds (the ringing of his clerical bell) that force the kings hostile to his reforms ultimately to give way. Significantly, the kings who had been so vocal in their opposition to him before he regained his speech never speak again.[37] The political issues implicit in this tale are more muted than they are in the "Pseudo-Historical Prologue," but they are no less real. The actual law to which the prologue was attached itself represented a tangible instance of secular and ecclesiastical cooperation, in that it was proclaimed and enforced by kings and prominent clerics working in concert. However, Adamnán is represented as having to prevail over the machinations of several evil secular officials in his quest to win protection for the innocent. Despite his earlier reluctance, the text leaves no doubt as to whom credit for this change in traditional custom is ultimately due. Heaven ordains it, and the kings who oppose it in the name of native custom are forced subsequently to fall silent and hearken to Adamnán's words.[38]

Similar themes are at work in two very interesting episodes from *Bethu Brigte*, the Old Irish life of St. Brigit, where power is displayed not merely by the alternation between speech and silence, but by the alternation between Irish (the language of native tradition) and Latin (the language of the church). In this text, Brigit lives as a child with her mother, who is the slave of a druid (*drui*)—albeit a druid whose own uncle is a Christian. At one point the druid and his uncle are in a house when they hear the girl Brigit—at that time a child too young to speak—murmuring in a low voice. The druid does not dare address her directly, but sends the uncle in to see what she is doing. On his first visit, the uncle also does not dare to speak, for he finds the girl praying. However, encouraged by the druid, he later returns and addresses her in Irish, asking her to "say something to him" (*epir ni frim, a ingen*). She does respond to him, but in Latin: *Meum erit hoc, meum erit hoc*, "This will be mine, this will be mine." The uncle is mystified by what she has said, and seeks illumination from the druid, who explains that she is predicting that she will possess the place they are in until the day of doom. In response to the uncle's dissatisfaction with the idea of the daughter of a slave controlling such valuable property, the druid confirms the truth of Brigit's prophecy in Latin, the language of the faith that will soon supplant his own: *Vere implebitur. Ipsius erit hic campus, licet exeat mecum ad Mumenenses*, "Truly will it be fulfilled. This plain shall be hers even though she go with me to Munster."[39]

In this episode, Brigit's current (and ultimate) authority, and therefore of the church she represents, are communicated both by her premature ability to speak, and by her ability to command the speech and language of others. The uncle—who although a Christian is not entirely sympathetic to her cause—is at first completely silenced by her voice (raised in prayer), and then trumped by it. On his second visit, he attempts to assert his control over her by ordering her to speak. Her response, however, makes clear his failure to control her voice: she predicts her eventual triumph in Latin, a holy, learned and implicitly aristocratic language that he does not know and cannot understand. The druid himself—a curiously supportive figure in the text, given the threat she and others like her pose to his job—is also silenced by the holy girl in that he does not dare address her directly when she is praying. He is, however, portrayed as understanding the language of her prophecy, and indeed confirming it, albeit in Latin—a shift in code that makes clear that it is in fact Brigit who has commandeered his speech rather than the other way around. Particularly potent are the oppositions generated in this episode: between youth and age, poverty and wealth, servile and noble status, Christian and pagan, Irish and Latin. On one level, these oppositions go to the very heart of the radical social doctrine implicit in Christianity, in which the weak displace the strong and the poor claim precedence over the wealthy. On another, they serve to highlight the contrast between speech and silence that is so crucial to this text. The voice of the powerful will be assumed by those who to this point have been the "unlearned non-speakers" of their culture: lordship and submission are what this episode is all about.

The second passage in *Bethu Brigte* in which language and speech are used to address issues of power focuses not on the transition from paganism to Christianity but on relations between the two great Christian centers of Armagh and Kildare.[40] In this story, Patrick and his company are at the royal center of Tailtiu trying to resolve a charge that has been lodged against bishop Brón, a member of Patrick's household. A woman claiming that she was seduced (or possibly even raped) by Brón when she came to him to take the veil, brings before Patrick a son that she is "returning" (*tathchor*, literally "putting back") to Brón in order to get his paternity recognized. Brigit is then seen approaching the assembly, and bishop Mel tells Patrick to call her aside, outside the gathering, because she will be able to find out the truth of the matter from God as long as she is not in Patrick's presence, "for she will not do miracles in the presence of holy Patrick." Brigit is taken aside where, in the presence of all the clerics present except Patrick, she addresses the woman, asking her to name the father of her baby. When the woman imputes the child to Brón, Brigit signs her face with the cross, whereupon her head and tongue swell up and she falls silent. Patrick then returns, and Brigit addresses the child in the presence of the entire assembly, asking it to name its father. The infant—in normal circumstances much too young for speech—answers in Latin that his mother was lying, that Brón is innocent, and that his real father is a lowly misshapen man sitting on the periphery of the assembly. The crowd is ready to punish the lying woman by death; Brigit, however, intervenes, stating that she should do penance instead. Once her penance is completed, the swelling disappears, leading all to glorify Brigit.[41]

There are many interesting aspects to this story, and not a few questions. The main point of the story is of course to highlight Brigit's power and the special connection to God from which it derives. She is able first to silence the lying woman by causing her tongue to swell, and then to make the infant speak, and speak in the language of the church. Brigit's ability to cause others either to speak or refrain from speaking underscores her authority not only over the situation and its principals, but over the truth—even hidden truths—as well. More interesting and complex is the relationship envisaged in this episode between Patrick, chief cleric of Armagh, and Brigit, patron of Kildare. On the surface, Patrick can be said to "frame"[42] the proceedings. The assembly is one in which he appears to have considerable power—indeed over which he may even be officiating—and his authority is such that Brigit is said to be much too awed to perform miracles in his presence. On the other hand, the patterns of speech and silence established in this text renders its message considerably more ambiguous. Patrick remains essentially silent throughout: when we first meet him, he is engaging in debate about the question of the infant's paternity and the charge lodged against Brón. That this has not proved a productive debate is made evident by the fact that no solution has yet been found; the problem remains *aneturgnaid*, "mysterious, unfamiliar, obscure."[43] It is Mel, bishop of southern Tethbae, who sees Brigit approaching and tells Patrick what to do, and it is Brigit who resolves the issue, freeing one of Patrick's own household in the process. Even when he returns to watch the miracle of the child, Patrick never speaks. The voices we hear all belong to Brigit.

Even the issue of Brigit's deferential reluctance to perform miracles in Patrick's presence is more complicated than it appears. For in fact she *does* perform a miracle in his presence. Patrick is there when the child speaks; he is absent only during Brigit's initial questioning of the woman and the subsequent swelling that renders her mute. Moreover, although Brigit is said to have been taken outside the gathering (*for leith asin dáil*)[44] in order to address the mother, the miracle of the child is explicitly said to have been performed in the presence of that same assembly (*fiad aes na dála[e]*).[45] When Patrick goes to watch her address the child, he goes *to her in* the assembly (*du-tet Patraic cuca ind uair-sin in forum magnum*,[46] with accusative of motion) where he then stands, not speaking, throughout the rest of her performance. Either the text has gotten the sequence of events wrong and failed to mention that Brigit returned to the assembly after addressing the woman, or the assembly has in effect gone to her, along with the clerics of Patrick's household and, eventually, Patrick himself. Where Brigit is *becomes* the assembly; where Patrick is becomes an empty silent place from which he is motivated ultimately to move. Adding further resonance to the symbolism here is the fact that we know from the *Airecht* tract that there was a section in the court known as the *airecht fo leth*, "the court apart," in which sureties and witnesses sat, neither approaching nor being approached, until the time came for them to go into the center of the court to offer their testimony.[47] Brigit is also taken *for leth* (an expression which, like *fo leth*, means "apart, aside") in the assembly—the difference is that the "court" in question comes to her to hear testimony that she herself extracts from another. The periphery becomes the center; the witness becomes the central figure in the proceedings. Brigit's "act of deference" to Patrick is in fact the occasion of his (relative) marginalization.[48]

Kings and Jurists

The language of speech and silence was thus used both to illustrate the fundamental compatibility of pagan past and Christian present—by force if necessary—and to establish the ultimate jurisdiction of Christianity and its officials in cases where disputes arose. The evidence suggests, however, that similar power struggles and negotiations, also conceptualized as conflicts over control of authoritative speech, accompanied the development of other political entities during this period. Another issue of particular importance was the question of who properly ought to exercise jurisdiction over legal and judicial affairs. Even a very quick read-through of the writings that remain is enough to make the point that a variety of different individuals had once claimed—and were for the most part still claiming in the period of the law tracts—the right to intervene in or supervise legal proceedings. In addition to poets, we must count kings, jurists, and clerics among those asserting some right to authority in law on the grounds either of tradition, political power, or morality.[49] Druids are mentioned in a sixth-century text known as the "First Synod of St. Patrick" as supervising oaths given by inhabitants of the community.[50] And several texts suggest that rendering decisions on disputes arising within their particular crafts community was one of the prerogatives and responsibilities of master craftsmen.[51]

Negotiating (or in many cases renegotiating) the jurisdictional boundaries between these various entities in the wake of the conversion must have been a complicated matter. The silencing of the druids is a matter of historical fact, accomplished probably by the early ninth century at least, although we cannot today reconstruct the details of the manner in which it occurred. Establishing the relationships among the others, however, must have been an ongoing, and indeed, open-ended process of claim and counterclaim. For Ireland posed unique challenges to Christians entering the island: a tradition of local and essentially nonbureaucratic kingship, the existence of an entrenched class of specialists claiming authority over matters pertaining to the law, and the unusually prominent political role accorded poets and other masters of the language. Incoming clerics faced in Ireland an obstacle they had not faced elsewhere in quite the same manner—the need to develop a vision of Christian kingship and law that respected the traditional claims of other established groups within the culture. Elsewhere in Europe, kings played (or had been taught by incoming missionaries to play) an essential role in lawmaking and the administration of justice and, therefore, in the consolidation of the legal position of the church. In Ireland, however, kings were not alone in exercising significant political power, and the task of reconciling their needs with the traditional prerogatives of other powerful groups was therefore far from simple.

One specific relationship that emerges from the sources as having been particularly delicate to negotiate was that between king and jurist. This is an issue on which modern scholarly thinking has changed substantially in the past several years. Until only fairly recently, historians tended to believe that Irish kings played no substantial role in the administration of justice. The reasons for this belief are complex. It is of course true that Irish kingship appears to have been considerably less bureaucratic than its heavily Romanized Germanic equivalent, and in what became a highly influential series of lectures, legal scholar Daniel Binchy argued for a vision of Irish kingship as largely sacral and symbolic in character.[52] Binchy's view has since been revised in important ways in recent scholarship, but its appeal has been enduring. For while he himself was far from being a romantic, his ideas on Irish kingship proved quite appealing to those steeped in popular cultural and ethnic stereotypes regarding the "Irish character." Celtic princes hedged about with sacred taboos and mysterious rituals seemed just the thing for a people so inherently creative that they could not be reined in by the mundane constraints of "ordinary" law and government.[53] No serious scholar espoused this view, of course. However, what one might call its scholarly equivalent—a presumption of Irish "otherness," and of an unbridgeable cultural gulf separating Ireland from her medieval European neighbors, particularly in the matter of kingship and governance—dominated both Irish and European historical writing for many years.[54]

In fact, as we now realize, kings *are* mentioned frequently in the lawbooks as presiding over judicial proceedings—sometimes alone, and sometimes together with a judge.[55] Moreover, there has long been evidence available to suggest that in Ireland as elsewhere in medieval Europe, legal jurisdiction was a key element of lordship. Scholars have known about the existence of *cáin*-legislation (issued under joint royal and clerical sponsorship) since the most famous one, *Cáin Adamnáin*, was first edited in 1905.[56] Moreover, our appreciation for the hardheadedness of Irish kingship has expanded exponentially in recent years. It now seems fairly clear that kings knew what they were doing before the Vikings (and the church) arrived to show them the advantages of strategic brutality. Like other European rulers, they murdered their opponents, collected dues, used clerical appointments to their personal advantage, and generally did what it took to assert their control over individuals and communities subordinate to them. It is true that their powers differed from those of other contemporary European rulers in significant ways; historians who equate sophistication in rule with the existence of extensive royal legislation and muniments, for example, are destined for disappointment. However, as Charles-Edwards has remarked, "the impression of weak kingship may derive from looking in the wrong places for evidence of strength."[57] From the point of view of the extant sources, and most particularly the evidence of the lawbooks, the perception of royal disengagement from legal and judicial matters is decidedly at odds with the sources.

To say this, however, is not to suggest that royal involvement in judicial affairs was comprehensive, or unquestioned, or resistant to change over time. It is possible, even likely, that kingship as it existed in the period of the lawbooks was not the same as kingship as it had historically been exercised.[58] We will likely never know the degree to which kings exercised jurisdiction over judicial affairs in the pre-Christian period. Indeed, we cannot know the extent to which the jurists themselves constituted a discernable class in this early era. By the time we first meet them in the sources, they are already claiming a considerable degree of authority in legal transactions, a situation unique in western Europe at this time. Moreover, the lawbooks from which they work appear to have been the product of professional legal schools rather than royal chanceries—indeed, they do not to have been associated in any way with any historically verifiable ruler, again something that sets them apart from most (though not all) legal collections of the day.[59] On the other hand, authority over law and the administration of it are two separable spheres of endeavor. One can remember that which one does not administer, and it is possible, as Binchy has suggested, that the emergence of a juristic class with responsibilities for legal adjudication as well as preservation was a relatively new phenomenon in the age of the lawbooks. We will likely never know for certain.

Regardless, it does seem a fairly safe bet that the king's role in law and justice was undergoing significant change in the period of the tracts. Wherever the church entered into the pagan regions of early medieval Europe, it sought out strong kings to spread its message and ensure the consolidation of ecclesiastical prerogatives and personnel. This is why the exaltation of the office of king became such an important plank in the program of postmissionary generations. Bede and Gregory of Tours are but two of the authors making substantial contributions to kingship theory in this period. As early European penitential texts clearly attest, jurisdiction over legal matters was an important part of that program as well.[60] Indeed, the *cáin* itself may well be an ecclesiastical innovation—something suggested to kings by ecclesiastics interested in building up the royal office, in other words, rather than a native genre later appropriated for clerical use.[61] They seem certainly to view themselves as literate in nature in origin: as Breatnach has observed, it is a particular feature of *cáin* texts to constantly make reference back to themselves as texts—something that native legal writings do not do.[62] Historically speaking, then, it may well be that in Ireland royal involvement in legislation and justice was relatively limited in the pre-Christian period; if so, however, the king's role looks to have been changing substantially in the period of the lawbooks, presumably under ecclesiastical influence.

Evidence of such developments and of the readjustments they inspired within the native intellectual elite is reflected in variety of texts centering on the issue of authoritative speech. In an excellent article published in 1988, Marilyn Gerriets assembled considerable evidence from the law tracts to show that kings did participate in judicial decision making in early Ireland, an argument that is now generally accepted.[63] One of the texts on which she drew in that article was the legal tract *Gúbretha Caratniad*, "False Judgments of Caratnia," an admittedly rather odd text in which the famous—and mythical—jurist Caratnia pronounces a series of what appear to be false judgments on a variety of legal issues to the eponymous royal ancestor of Leth Cuinn, Conn Cétchathach. Every time Caratnia announces a decision, Conn asserts that his judgment contravenes an established principle of early Irish law (which it does). However, Caratnia then reveals to Conn the exceptional circumstances that in this case render his "false" judgment appropriate.[64] For Gerriets, the cooperation displayed in the tract between Caratnia the jurist and Conn Cétchathach the powerful progenitor of the North mirrors what she saw as the normal working relationship between kings and judges in early Ireland. Kings were expected to have some general knowledge of the law and were certainly involved in the judicial process. However, they were as a rule much too busy making war on their neighbors to acquire the specialized knowledge of law that real justice required, and thus employed juristic specialists like Caratnia as their agents. In her view, the relationship between Caratnia and Conn is representative of the historical tie between kings and jurists.

Gerriets's rereading of this text is both astute and persuasive: royal and juristic cooperation is indeed what the tract is about. However, there may be more to it than that. The relationship between king and jurist may be considerably more ambivalent and dynamic than has previously been realized. Both the brief foretale that introduces the tract and the unusual nature of the conversations taking place within it suggest that the relationship between king and jurist is being actively constructed rather than merely described. Perhaps the most mysterious section of the *Gúbretha* is the part that has received least attention, the short, curious tale with which the tract begins:

Gúbretha Caratniad Tesct[h]i in so. Do Dáil Chuinn dó. Brithem Cuind Cétchathaig. Robo mor immad a innmais. Ro-tescsat a muinter 7 fo-rácabsat iarum. Do-chuaid la Cond dia thig 7 ro-íccad. Ba baglach, intan no-labrad [i] sochaide; ba fírbrithem immurgu 7 ba airgech, intan búid i n-uathad intí Caratnia. Nach breth do-beirthe co Conn, fos-cerdded Conn cuci sum. Fo-chomairced Conn dó: "Cisi breth rucais?"[65]

These are the false judgments of Caratnia the "Cut Up One." [He was] of Dál Cuinn. [He was] the judge of Conn Cétchathach. The jealousy over his wealth had become great. His household had cut him up and had left him afterward. He had come with Conn to his house and had been healed. That man, Caratnia, used to judge incorrectly when he spoke before a multitude; he was a true judge however, and he was astute, when he was alone. Any judgment that was brought to Conn, Conn would put it to him. Conn used to ask him: "What judgment have you given"?

To my knowledge, no one has yet attempted an interpretation of this story: Gerriets cites it without explanation as an example of the collaboration between king and judge, while Thurneysen is fairly obviously at a loss.[66] The mystery is of course why the jurist's own intimates should attack him in such a manner: There seems at first glance nothing to explain such violence, and nothing to link the substance of the tale with the legal tract it introduces. Even the glossator is mystified: he rejects the oddness of the tale all together and glosses *tesct[h]i*, "cut, cut up," with *tinscantaid* (*.i. foglamma*), "a beginner (that is, with respect to learning)," and *ro-tescsat*, "had cut," with *ro-tréicset*, "had abandoned," thereby inventing a scenario in which Caratnia's pupils abandoned him as a teacher out of jealousy at his accomplishments.[67]

A return to the issue of the relationship between king and jurist gives us a way in which to think about this problem. It is unclear from the text whether Caratnia had been a practicing jurist before the attack, although that is certainly implied: the tale reads most naturally as an explanation of how Caratnia came to be in Conn's employ, but we are not told how exactly he had accumulated his wealth. What is stated clearly, however, is that it is members of his own household, people who would normally have been expected to support and benefit from his prosperity, who are the ones to turn against him. This might suggest that Caratnia had been keeping his fortune to himself rather than using it for the public or familial good; alternatively, it might imply injustice on the part of his family. In either case, it is only once Caratnia is integrated within the royal household and his talents turned to the service of the king that peace is restored. The tale read in this way functions as a moral object lesson about the dangers of private enterprise and the social benefits of cooperation between king and judge. Indeed, if Caratnia had been a judge before entering Conn's employ, it may be that private *juristic* enterprise is what is specifically at issue. Judges working on their own are a potential threat to social order; judges working for and through kings, on the other hand, bring prosperity to all.

There is another way to read this tale, however, one that would suggest quite a different subtext to the relationship between king and judge. Caratnia's epithet, *tescthe*, the "cut or cut-up one,"[68] is peculiar, to say the least. There would appear to be little doubt about the word's derivation: *tescthe* is the past participle of *do-esc*,[69] and the verb is in fact actually used in the story to describe the nature of the violence inflicted on the jurist by his household (*ro-tescsat*). Both Thurneysen and Gerriets translate the verb as "attacked" or "wounded" (*verwundet*), although only Thurneysen tackles the puzzle of the epithet, suggesting rather despairingly that it might have become confused with an original *tesctha*, "*des Schneidens*," and refer to the acuity of Caratnia's judicial decisions.[70]

Translations like these, which implicitly minimize the weirdness of the encounter, are certainly plausible; they may even be right. Along these lines, one could also read *do-esc* as "cut off" in the sense of Caratnia being "cut off" by his kindred; *iccaid* would then presumably be translated as "saves" rather than "heals" (though from what Caratnia is being "saved" is unclear to me).[71] However, given the odd nature of the restrictions attached to Caratnia's knowledge later in the tale, it may be that we ought not to try so hard to soften the strangeness of the event. If one retains the usual meaning of the verb—to "cut, hack off, sever," or even "kill"—one has then a story of a man cut up, mutilated, or perhaps even killed by his household, abandoned, taken into a house by a king, cured, and then either instated or reinstated within the community as a wisdom-bearing figure. In short, this tale may be casting Caratnia into the role made famous by scholars Nora Chadwick, Joseph Nagy, Patrick Ford, and Daniel Melia:[72] the shaman, a figure whose violent removal from human society, initiated by an attack made upon him, propels him over and across the "boundaries between worlds"[73] into the liminal realm with which otherworldly knowledge was so frequently associated in Irish tradition. Upon his reintegration into society—symbolized here by healing at the hands of the king, society's ultimate representative—Caratnia is established as a conduit through which otherworldly wisdom is rendered accessible to human society. Like many such figures, he still bears the physical scars of his experiences: even upon his return from the otherworld, he is *tescthe:* "cut up, mutilated."[74]

On such a reading, Caratnia would appear to be conceptualized in the tale not as a mere functionary or agent of the king, but as one whose wisdom transcends ordinary human knowledge in that it stems from the otherworld. He mediates between the oppositions by which the human and, significantly, the royal intellect is bounded. Indeed, oppositions similar to those found in other shamanic Irish tales feature also in Caratnia: household/wilderness, injured/well, deformed/intact, and perhaps even dead/alive. Even the fact that the attack upon Caratnia is initiated by members of his own household has possible parallels in the *Cáin Adamnáin* prologue, where that good saint's tortures are devised and implemented by his own mother, and in the tale of Amairgen, who in the course of his initiation is symbolically "slain" out of jealousy by the man who later becomes his foster-father and instructor in the poetic arts, Athairne.[75] There may even be an echo here of Christ, executed at the instigation of his own people, who returns from death in order to bring God's wisdom and grace to an ignorant populace.[76]

The case for reading the tale in this manner is strengthened by the nature of the conversations by which Caratnia's knowledge is communicated to the king. The format of these conversations, which form the body of the law tract proper, is evident from the following examples:

"Rucus tathcreic cundartha iar n-adaig." "Ba gó," ar Cond, "nod-birt." "Deithbir dam sa," ol Caratnia, "ar ba argat do-celt a ainme."

"I judged [in favor of] overturning a transaction after a night," [said Caratnia]. "What you judged was false," said Conn. "It was proper[77] for me [to judge thus]," said Caratnia, "for it [concerned] silver that concealed its flaws."[78]

"Rucus ráith ar macc mbeoathar." "Ba gó." "Ba deithbir, ar ba creic cétmuintire 7 fochraic tíre."

"I judged [in favor of the validity of] a suretyship [given] on behalf of a son of a living father." "[What you judged] was false," [said Conn]. "It was proper [for me to judge thus," said Caratnia], "for [the suretyship in question] concerned the purchase of a wife and payment for land."[79]

"Rucus dílse cuir mbél cen folaid." "Ba gó." "[Ba] deithbir, cach socho[i]nn a saithiud."

"I judged [in favor of] the immunity from legal claim of an oral contract without [corresponding] considerations [having been exchanged]." "[What you judged] was false," [said Conn]. "[It was] proper [for me to judge thus," said Caratnia, "for] to every competent person [belongs the consequences of] his having allowed himself to be cheated."[80]

The pattern here is clear and consistent: the king's attempts to correct Caratnia's seemingly false judgments, while grounded in a surface knowledge of the law, must bow to the superior knowledge of his jurist.

Oddly, no one has yet commented on the genre to which these conversations belong. There cannot be much doubt on that subject, however: they are riddles,[81] exhibiting all of the characteristics of what anthropologists call the "paradox" riddle, a puzzle the solution to which requires that two mutually contradictory things be true simultaneously—in this case, that a judicial verdict be true and false at the same time.[82] That riddles should form part of an educational text of this sort is not surprising. Like the other extant Irish legal tracts, the *Gúbretha Caratniad* was likely composed at least in part to serve educational purposes within the schools, and the cognitive element of riddles makes them ideal instructional tools.[83] In the case of Caratnia specifically, the educational element is very much to the fore: both halves of the riddle often have something of the status of proverbs within the legal tradition, and students learn thereby the exceptions to rules as well as the rules themselves.[84]

But riddles are much more than useful educational tools. As Joan Radner has demonstrated, the genre itself is used frequently, in Irish and in other world traditions, to underscore the limitations of human knowledge and categorizing techniques. "[R]iddling," she writes, "reminds people of the unknown, of the limitations of what they regard as sensible and logical, of the inadequacy of their understanding." They are "manipulations of the power of knowledge," that implicitly render ambiguous or paradoxical that which might otherwise seem to be predictable and secure.[85] Strictly speaking, there is nothing mysterious or even particularly complex about what Caratnia tells the king. However, the manner in which he conveys it itself communicates a vision of Caratnia's wisdom as transcending ordinary human categories like true or false, right or wrong. Significantly, Caratnia never denies the king's charge that his judgments are "false"—he merely specifies the circumstances that in this instance render the falsehood true. His judgments are false, but they are also true. He embraces the paradox, and thus rises above its limitations.

Caratnia's riddling discourse thus underscores the mysterious and other-worldly nature of his knowledge. Moreover, the nature of his conversation links him to other wisdom-bearing figures in Irish tradition. Like Amairgen or the spirit in the tale of Senchán Torpéist,[86] Caratnia also enters on his public career by speaking in riddles—a parallel that may lend credence to the shamanic reading of the tale. The king, by contrast, is incapable of re-solving the puzzles posed to him; he sees nothing but the obvious without Caratnia's aid. This is significant, for as the anthropological literature on riddles makes clear, the relationship of riddler to the person addressed is one of superior to dependent. Riddles function, in almost every culture in which they appear, as a means by which one person lays claim to power over another. And while Conn may pose the initiatory questions in this text, the riddler is clearly Caratnia: the poor plodding king gets it wrong every time. However, while the king cannot recognize a truthful judgment when he hears one, at least he can proclaim it. In this we see the true complexity of the text. For Caratnia cannot speak what he knows: his insight deserts him in a crowd. In order for his mysterious knowledge to be rendered cultur-ally useful, the king must extract it from him and articulate it on his behalf. Each is necessary to the other and to human society as a whole. Justice de-pends on the king giving voice to a truth that only his jurist can discern.

Here we return to the issue of the relationship between king and jurist with which we began. For Gerriets, whose interest lay in demonstrating royal involvement in judicial affairs, the relationship between Caratnia and Conn typified the normal working partnership between king and jurist, an association that she reads back into the pagan past. In her view, while Chris-tianity might well have strengthened the king's judicial role, it did not sub-stantially alter it.[87] However, when read alongside of other Irish writings on performative public speech, *Gúbretha Caratniad* suggests a degree of dy-namism in the relationship that Gerriets's model overlooks. As we have seen, kings may have participated in judgment, but even in the period of the tracts, they did not have a monopoly upon it. Jurists, poets, clerics, and others within the community appear in the tracts as a normal part of the dispute-resolution process, and often they seem to be functioning outside the presence of the king. However, the consolidation of justice under royal authority was a priority for kings and their advisers everywhere in Europe in this period, and the same must have been true as well for Ireland. The difference was that there existed in Ireland what did not exist elsewhere: an entrenched juristic class, conscious of its standing and privileges.

Gúbretha Caratniad seems to me a window on the process by which the boundaries between king and jurist were negotiated. In its depiction of ju-ristic wisdom as otherworldly it upholds the prerogatives and traditional stature of that class. It is no accident that in the private conversations between the two it is the jurist who gives voice to the complexities of the law and the king who is reduced to brief, formulaic statements of incomprehension. However, in its insistence on the promulgation of judicial verdicts by kings, *Gúbretha Caratniad* also brings Irish practice into line with the Christian European ideal. Indeed, in its reserving to kings the performative aspects of justice, the text seems to discourage private juristic enterprise altogether: certainly the king's presence appears here as not merely appropriate, but actually necessary, to the realization of true justice. In this, we mark the true significance of the format of the text. Riddles often tend to cluster around moments of personal and political transition, channeling potential conflicts into relatively harmless venues, and illustrating that opposing viewpoints can be profitably reconciled. Caratnia and Conn cooperate as well as they do because neither is capable of speaking the whole truth on his own: like the two halves of a riddle, king and jurist must be joined together in order to be fully understood.

Nor is *Gúbretha Caratniad* alone in reflecting on such issues. The relationship between king and jurist figures prominently in many texts. Most resemble *Gúbretha Caratniad* in envisaging significant collaboration between the two. *Críth Gablach*, for example, pictures the judge as part of the normal entourage of the king.[88] However, the balance of power between these figures can be characterized very differently, depending on the perspective of the author. Often the relationship is conceptualized as favoring the king. One passage from the *Triads of Ireland*, for example, remarks that *ni tabair labrai acht do chetru .i. fer cerda fri haír 7 molad, fer coimhni cuimnech fri haisnéis 7 scélugud, brethem fri bretha, sencha fri senchas,*[89] "[a king] does not grant speech except to four men: a man of art,[90] for [dispensing] satire and praise, a historian with a good memory, for recounting and narration; a judge for judgments; [and] a storyteller, for [recounting] traditional lore." In this passage, lordship is expressed directly in terms of the power to allow or prevent others from engaging in publicly significant speech.[91] Judges are depicted as necessary—they must speak in order to give voice to the judgments rendered in the court. However, they are distinctly under the royal thumb (as are poets): there is no sense here in which royal prerogatives are compromised by the existence of another authority in the court.

A similar balance of power seems to be envisaged in many of the various tales associated with the *Bretha Nemed* lawbook. In several of these stories, kings are envisaged as pronouncing judgment entirely on their own, without the assistance of a legal specialist. In one, Coirpre Lifechair as king delivers a verdict—albeit one later corrected by his equally royal father Cormac mac Airt—on the case of a man attacked by pigs being chased by the hounds of another. There is no indication of the involvement of a jurist.[92] In another instance, a prosecution over the violation of a guarantee and the killing of a servant is referred to the king Conchobar and to his jurist Sencha. The two consult together, but it is Conchobar who performs the verdict, a scenario that exactly parallels the relationship envisaged in *Gúbretha Caratniad* between Caratnia and Conn.[93] Perhaps the most overtly royalist of the tales is one that tells of a lawsuit that arises concerning the ferocious (and regrettably unattended) pigs of a man named Mugna. The plaintiff, Maine, goes to Sencha seeking justice for his son, who has been devoured by the pigs in question. However, Sencha very distinctly passes the buck to his royal boss. According to one version of the tale, *[l]otar i fuigell sencha; luid-side d'fochmarc a brithe co concubhar co nerbert fris: "ruchtaig ruib .r.,*"[94] "they went to obtain the judgment of Sencha; that one (Sencha) went to ask Conchobor for his judgment, and [Sencha] said to him: '*ruchtaig ruib .r*' " (thereupon follows Sencha's rhetoricized summary of what has happened). Conchobar then answers Sencha with his (equally poetic) judgment (*Maine main* and so on). In the B.M. Nero A 7 version of the tale, after the king's initial decision in this case, Sencha asks him to elaborate still further on what is to be done, a query that Conchobar answers with yet another rhetorical pronouncement.[95] In other words, in both versions of this tale, Sencha's role in this case is to pose questions to Conchobar that he alone appears able to answer. The contrast with Caratnia and Conn is very marked.

Other texts seem to envisage a more proactive role for jurists in such matters. In the tract on the *airecht* ("court") edited by Fergus Kelly, for example, judges (*brithemain*) sit in the center court in order to set forth the relevant law to the court (*do-aisféna*); kings, bishops, and the chief poetic legal expert sit by contrast in the "back court" in order to pronounce judgment (*breth*). Both events seem to be imagined as speech acts, and both are regarded as part of the official "promulgation" (*forus*) of the verdict. Even in this text, however, the activities of the back court seem clearly take precedence over the pronouncements from the center, in that its occupants are depicted as the ultimate authority against which everything else comes to rest.[96] Very different is the view of the judge in the two texts on judges edited by Breatnach. In one, an important prerogative owed to a publicly appointed judge is that all others in the court listen in silence to his exposition of the law (*étsecht a airberta*).[97] The second text is even more explicit. Here one of a judge's primary responsibilities and privileges is said to be *airbert fri flaith, fri senad, fri aes cerda, coná toirceat a túaith i n-indlighe,* "expounding law to the lord, to the synod, [and] to men of art (poets), so that they not act unlawfully towards their kingdom."[98] Breatnach translates *fri* here as "with," making the exposition of the law an event conducted jointly by king, bishop, poet, and judge. However, *fri* usually carries connotations of "to," or "against," and given the clear implication that these lords would lapse into injustice without careful supervision by a judge, I think the above more true to the sense of the occasion. In other words, the contrast here is on the knowledgeable speech of the jurist and the consequent silence of the high-ranking rulers around him. Given the symbolic implications of the contrast between speech and silence—lordship on the one hand, subordination on the other—the partiality of the passage is striking.

The evidence thus suggests that it would be a mistake for us to regard he relationship between king and jurist as it appears in the lawbooks as a fixed and unchanging connection of long standing. Revealed in the various conceptualizations of the relationship between the two is tremendous uncertainty as to the boundaries of their relative responsibilities. What we are witnessing in tales like that of Conn and Caratnia are attempts to work out the contours of their spheres of jurisdiction. In most imaginings of the relationship, only one person gives voice to the authoritative verdict, while the other is relegated to a more consultative role. Given the ubiquity in early Ireland of public speech as both the means to and a metaphor for the assertion of jurisdiction, such a division of responsibilities is significant. For embedded in it are traces of the issues and conflicts that lay at the heart of the process by which the boundaries of this essential relationship were eventually worked out. Reflected in these tales are attempts by kings to enhance the authority of their office by limiting the possibilities for private juristic enterprise and attempts by jurists to maintain their hold on the discipline by subtly questioning the depth of the king's knowledge of legal issues. Opinions clearly varied as to who should be the public "voice" of the law. Nor are such issues limited strictly to legal texts: the famous "hierarchy of speaking" said in the *Táin Bó Cúailnge* to obtain among the Ulstermen of Conchobar's day seems likely to relate to precisely these same issues.[99]

However, just as significant as the divisions visible in these sources is the evident concern with cooperation. In most characterizations of the relationship, both parties are portrayed as necessary to its success, an indication of the fact that the claims of both king and jurist were too well established to be ignored. Kings could not be left out of the equation altogether in a country newly open to European ideas about the Christian obligations of rulership. Ambitious rulers—and the annals make clear that a large number of kings fell enthusiastically into this category—simply could not afford to neglect the prerogatives and financial rewards accruing to those in a position to intervene in judicial affairs. It is regrettable that so little charter evidence survives from Ireland; charters surviving from other contemporary European cultures leave little doubt as to the keen interest displayed by rulers in the settlement of disputes, and it would be surprising were Irish kings to be very different in this respect. And yet equally strong was the tradition that guardianship of the law was rightfully vested in the hands of a specialist class—be they poets, druids, or jurists. Even the most royalist of texts reserves a prominent role for the jurist, and while this is perhaps in part a reflection of the authorship of the extant texts, it is striking nonetheless. The emergence of a juristic class separate from the poetic and pagan religious orders may have been, as Binchy and others have suggested, a relatively recent development. However, the notion that there existed a learned class charged with custodianship of the law was clearly one of long standing: only in such a manner can we understand the survival of this class and its prerogatives into the historical period.

Poetic Voices

Relations between king and jurist were but one important element of the renegotiation of jurisdictional and professional boundaries that characterized the assimilation of the church into native Irish society. Another crucial series of struggles and compromises centered around the position of poets in Ireland's newly Christian culture. Some of these struggles would seem to have occurred within the poetic orders themselves. By at least the late seventh century, the *filid* of Ireland appear in the sources as a distinctive and highly visible professional class. Aristocratic, highly educated, and ardently devoted to advancing the interests of their kind, they represent themselves as charter members of the intellectual and social elite of the island. Especially striking are their ties to the church, which seem almost self-consciously intimate. They acknowledge their pagan past, of course, but prefer to emphasize stories like that of Dubthach, in which a *fili* is the first to profess his reverence for the newly arrived Saint Patrick. By the seventh and eighth centuries, when the majority of our sources were penned, many *filid* were either monastically educated themselves or relatives of persons in high standing in clerical circles. As Breatnach has argued, *Bretha Nemed Toísech* was, for example, composed by three kinsmen of the Uí Búirecháin family, a bishop, a judge, and a poet.[100] In the eighth century, the poetic grades came to be conceptualized as numbering seven, in deliberate imitation of clerical ranks,[101] and some tracts of the same period maintained that poets were subject to the same marital and ethical restrictions as clerics, following Old Testament admonitions on the behavior of the Levitical classes.[102]

It is important to realize, however, that both the history and the position of the poetic orders were more complex than they were often presented as having been. For although the *filid* were unquestionably the cream of the poetic crop, they were not the only versifiers making the rounds in Ireland in those days. Several tracts speak to the existence of a complex order of bards by the late seventh century. Indeed, it is likely that, despite the protestations of the *filid* to the contrary, their emergence from within the ranks of the bards as the elite of the poetic order was a development that did not long predate the composition of the main tracts about them.[103] Other types of versifiers are testified to also in the sources, many of them very rude fellows indeed: satirists, jesters, purveyors of doggerel, and other entertainers besides. There are even various types of female performers mentioned. The evidence for female poets generally is scanty and ambiguous at best, although the existence of female satirists at least seems fairly certain.[104] We have already seen references to them in the tracts on sick-maintenance, and the legal tale of Fergus mac Léti features a bondsmaid (a former aristocrat) named Dorn who uses satire to exact her revenge on the king who mistreated her.[105] Several terms exist in the literature for women who engaged in satirical or criticizing talk (*birach briathar, ben rindas, bancháinte, canait scél, rindele, banbhard*), and it seems altogether likely that satire, whether formal or informal, may have been an important genre of female speech.[106]

To remark that the reaction of the *filid* to these people was less than favorable is to engage in serious understatement. They were, after all, in direct competition with them for power, patronage, and generally speaking, the resources with which to carry on. Poets traveling from one part of the country to another were entirely dependent on the generosity of the lords to whom they came. Those remaining in place were more stable from many points of view, but in the end equally vulnerable to a ruler's whims. As we have seen, poets were often appointed to fill official posts within the *túath*, and while the evidence suggests that poets acted as officials of the *túath* as a whole in the Old Irish period, becoming appointees of the king himself only in the Middle Irish period, it is still not difficult to imagine that a ruler's favor was key to the successful retention of the poet's office. While acting in an official capacity, they could be asked to fulfill certain tasks within a locality or local ruler's hall, a lucrative position indeed, and they played an important role in the adjudication of disputes, both within and without the community.[107] Often poets working on behalf of a king or tribe could be called upon, for example, to enforce cross-border claims "where the barbs of satire are answered and the barbs of weapons are not."[108] Poets could also be appointed by high-ranking clergymen or by individual monasteries to serve their needs.[109] Small wonder, then, that poets were as competitive as they were with versifiers of lesser status. While the artistry of a professionally trained *fili* was no doubt considerably greater than that of a local, self-educated performer, that difference might not always have been appreciated by the local populace and its ruler. Indeed, one *Bretha Nemed* text suggests that bards also might be adopted by individual *túaths*, and makes clear that many of noble and even royal status practiced the bardic arts.[110]

Competition for patronage with others of the versifying class was but one of the fears of the professional poetic order, however. The *filid* were very concerned to prove their Christian credentials, a point on which they clearly perceived themselves as highly vulnerable. For although poetry was easier to assimilate within the newly Christian dispensation of the island than was druidism, it seems quite likely that paganism had been an important part of the past of the poetic art. Given the manner in which poetic inspiration was conceptualized in the postconversion era, for example, it seems a good bet that pagan beliefs—if not in fact actual pagan rituals—had earlier been viewed as playing more than a passing role in the creative and intuitive process. Carey has documented a tendency among later literati to exaggerate the magical and prophetic side of poetic profession in its early years. However, as he has also shown, there is evidence for a divinatory aspect to the practice of poetry in several early sources.[111] Moreover, certain poetic practices like satire could easily be construed as un-Christian (at least when practiced against clerics instead of by them). Belief in a divinatory power separate from that of God's, or in the ability of the magical power of the word (as opposed to the Word) to reshape the natural order, could be viewed as posing a substantial threat to the authority of the church. Hence the eagerness of the *filid* to establish their Christian credentials by affiliating their order to the hierarchy of the church: only in such a way could they escape the dubious past of their profession.

Both in terms of their history and their contemporary actions, therefore, the *filid* were vulnerable, and they knew it. The heavy emphasis on Christianity that had become by the late seventh century such a crucial part of the manner in which the *filid* defined themselves likely gained considerable urgency from a perceived necessity to repudiate a pagan past with which they had once been intimately associated. Such anxieties were only made worse by the fact that many versifiers of the non-*filid* classes had apparently not yet rejected the pagan aspects of their profession as thoroughly as the church would have preferred. Often in the tracts, satirists (*cáinti*) and lower level poets (the *oblaire*, for example) were lumped together with that most recalcitrant of offenders against the Christian order, the druid. Satirists particularly were frequently depicted as traveling with outlaw bands known as *fianna*, indulging themselves in violence, mayhem, and the wildest forms of pagan worship.[112] The anxieties of the *filid* that they not be tainted with the same brush seem very understandable.

What we cannot know, of course, is whether these charges were true. Intimate connections with paganism and druidry became a charge leveled deliberately by the *filid* at their lower-class competitors in an effort to assert their moral superiority and consequent professional dominance. The extent to which low status poets and satirists might actually have been involved with brigandage and paganism is uncertain; what is absolutely clear, however, are the lengths to which the *filid* went to portray them as such. Self-definition as well as competition for patronage was at issue. Stressing their ideological distance from the pagan past and the impeccable nature of their contemporary ecclesiastical connections was one of the ways in which the *filid* of the late seventh and eighth centuries were able to emerge as a discernable class from among the bards and other lesser breeds of poet with whom they had previously been joined. Unlike even the most high-status of bards, *filid* were men of inherited rank, whose fathers and grandfathers before them had also been poets and to whom the art therefore came naturally.[113] They were not only Christian, but extensively educated in ecclesiastical as well as native culture. A proper poetic education provided students with the skills necessary to integrate native and Christian traditions into a seamless whole. Recent studies have made clear the extent to which the *filid* immersed themselves in Latin learning and the monastic culture of the day: the absolute pinnacle of poetic achievement could thus only be reached by those expert in both ecclesiastical and native lore.

Constructing positive images of themselves was one element of the process of self-definition; denigrating their rivals was another. For if this was how the *filid* saw themselves, their competitors they imagined as fellows of little education, little breeding, and a transparently laughable level of poetic skill. Source after source emanating from aristocratic poetic circles stresses the ignorance, barbarism, and all-around bad character of the lesser poetic breeds. The lower-class satirists known as *cáinti* came in for particular grief. One of the most delightful tales of the period, *Cath Maige Tuired*, is structured in part around a contrast between the socially productive art of the *fili*, whose talents enrich the community he serves, and the destructive carping of the *cáinte*, who cares only for himself. As McCone has shown, this contrast, pursued to such effect in *Cath Maige Tuired*, became a important theme in Irish literature generally.[114] Several law tracts, for example, *Bretha Crólige* foremost among them, consciously restrict the rights and prerogatives of the *cáinte* and the *oblaire*, another lower grade of poet. Accusations of paganism fit suspiciously well within such an agenda.

These struggles within the poetic profession give us an important glimpse of some of the strategies that lay behind the reshaping of at least one element of the native intellectual elite. Scholars have long been aware of these attempts by the *filid* to establish their authority vis-à-vis their poetic rivals; what has not been generally recognized, however, is the significant role played in this process by Irish perceptions of the relationship between speech and power. For the *filid* as for their competition, performance was both the basic means to and the primary expression of power: patronage and jurisdiction were acquired by publicly "giving voice." Passages celebrating the purity and power of the properly trained poetic voice appear throughout the literature. Thus are the elite of the poetic profession characterized in "The Caldron of Poesy" as men *condat fásaige bretha a mbríathar; condat desimrecht do cach cobrai*, "[whose] words are maxims and judgments and they are an example for all speech."[115] Another passage in the same text embraces a different implication for silence in its description of the properly trained judge, but maintains the importance of the ability to give voice to the authority of the individual: he should be a *fer taóe co taisccide, fer laburta láin*,[116] "a man of silence with regards to [the] safeguarding [of secrets or information], a man of full speech."

And yet speech alone, in the absence of technical knowledge and a thorough grounding in Christian tradition, does not carry authority.[117] Just as the exaltation of the learned voice served as a means by which the *filid* advanced their claims, so also did the silencing or demeaning of the voices of those they considered to be lesser poets become an important tactic for *filid* looking to consolidate their own positions. A rhetorical passage in *Bretha Nemed Tóisech* draws on the symbolic contrast between speech and silence in its comments on ignoble persons who seek to intrude themselves into judicial processes in which they do not belong: *atainegatt suitheangaidh, fodosuidhither said, doscan fili, aristuasise ile, nosberuid roscca . . . ,*[118] "wise-tongued ones impel them, sages sustain them, a *fili* gets the better of them in song (literally: sings them away), many listen to them, rhetorical maxims judge them. . . ." We have already seen the speech of the lowly *longbard* characterized as more animal than human in *Bretha Nemed Tóisech.*[119] Other *Bretha Nemed* passages deride the effectiveness of the speech of the poetic subgrades like the *drisiuc,* the *taman,* the *oblaire,* and the *dul,* making the point that the voices of those whose learning is not sufficient to allow them to compose complex verse can be safely ignored. In one text, the performance of members of the poetic subgrades when enforcing a particular obligation or debt from an offender is portrayed as legally ineffectual: *do-fuasluice laid laogha, ni toipgither tresa tamun,* "a *láid* (a type of poem) releases calves [as distraint], the onslaughts of *taman*'s do not levy (anything)."[120] Another passage remarks derisorily that the *drisiuc* levies only up to the value of three balls of wool with his performance.[121] As we have seen already, "manifest metrical faults" of the sort one might anticipate from unlearned poets are termed elsewhere in *Bretha Nemed Tóisech* "the ruin of a suit, the destruction of a prosecution."[122] Another text portrays them as chatterers of little significance or skill whose efforts do not even earn them honor-price.[123] And in yet another poem, the metaphor of the mead-hall becomes the mechanism for distinguishing between those who are inside participating orally in the culture of the hall and those who, like the *drisiuc* and the *dul* are stationed where they are separated from the crowd and can neither speak nor hear effectively.[124]

Misuse of the poetic voice also appears as an important concern.[125] Several texts seem almost to presume that poets of the lesser orders will abuse the power of their voice by engaging in unlawful or unjust satire, and seek to limit their opportunities for performance accordingly. One text remarks that the privileges of the *drisiuc* relate directly to the legitimacy of his behavior as a performer, a reservation not mentioned for the higher grades and one that in itself expresses the composer's skepticism as to the *drisiuc*'s innate capacity for distinguishing appropriate from inappropriate.[126] *Uraicecht na Ríar* describes the *taman* as someone who *canaid tres for cách,* "assaults everyone with his recitations," and one of the glosses to the *oblaire* contained in this same tract cites a poem found elsewhere (where it is also associated with poets of low rank) which shows the poet viciously threatening a woman's honor if he is not given food immediately.[127] Also manifest in the sources is a fear of the dangers of ignorance: *Ni herba bretha a mbeolu anfeich*,[128] "do not entrust judgments to the mouths of those lacking in knowledge," admonishes one passage. By contrast, the upper grades of poet are defined in several texts in large part by their *idnae*, "purity"—a state of being that both reflects and derives from their learning, social and sexual behavior, and noble birth. The tracts leave no doubt but that the lawful and efficacious use of the poetic voice is inextricably linked to the learning and moral purity associated only with members of the *fili* order.[129] Of course, as has been remarked already, the urgency of the prescriptions placed on the speech of the poetic subgrades itself gives the lie to the *filid's* claims as to their ineffectualness. One does not bother to deride or prohibit what does not matter: clearly the impact of these rival poets was greater than the *filid* preferred to admit.

The consolidation of the poetic hierarchy to the advantage of the *filid* was one aspect of the debates swirling around and within the poetic orders in this period. Equally important were the struggles taking place between the *filid* and authority figures outside the poetic orders—struggles not dissimilar to the conflicts we have already seen between king and jurist. Poets were controversial individuals generally—indeed, many of the tales told about them at the time suggest that some thought that poets, like druids, should be removed from society altogether. For despite the claims of the *filid* themselves to be among the most upstanding of public citizens, others viewed them as inherently disruptive figures. Apart from druids, outlaws, and other scalawags, there is no other group as denigrated and feared, no other company as frequently mocked and banned. One of the most famous stories told about the early (historical) saint Columba, for example, was his (mythical) intervention at the (historical) convention of Druim Cet to save the poets of Ireland from banishment. Earlier historians tended to read this tale quite literally, and to take the banning of the poets as an actual historical event. Scholars now read the story as a tale fabricated to enhance the saintly legend of Columba: to construct him as a wonder worker and, as Joseph Nagy has shown, a negotiator between the worlds of oral and literate.[130] But a story does not have to be historically accurate in order to be historically true: one can hardly imagine more eloquent testimony to the very real suspicions engendered by a group so dangerously powerful that they could only be neutralized by their physical removal from society.

The containment of the poets of Ireland seems to have become a popular theme in Ireland in late Old Irish and Middle Irish literature. Poets serve as a symbol of greediness and the abuse of hospitality; they are depicted as inspiring awe, but also tremendous fear. Much like nature itself, they are characterized as a force with the potential either to heal or to destroy, over which ordinary persons have almost no control.[131] But while many of these tales center on the alimentary excesses of poets on tour, a significant number of them focus on the issue of their speech and its role in the judicial process in Ireland. The very obscurity of the language in which their verdicts are delivered seems itself to pose a threat to the settled life of the community. When operations fundamental to the stability of ordinary living pass into the hands of a class of men unable or unwilling to speak in ways that others can understand, chaos is inevitably the result. Stories of this sort ought not to be overlooked or assimilated without comment into the other types of antipoet tales of the day. For these tales, centered as they are on the issue of authoritative public speech, speak directly to the jurisdictional struggles taking place in this period.

Undoubtedly the premier tale of this sort in the legal manuscripts is the "Pseudo-Historical Prologue to the *Senchas Már*," which itself follows directly from the earlier tale known as the "Colloquy of the Two Sages."[132] After the native poet Dubthach has, with Patrick's blessing, proclaimed his judgment in the case of Patrick's slain charioteer, the men of Ireland decide that they want Dubthach and Patrick to reform Ireland's laws in light of the island's conversion to Christianity. Dubthach performs Irish legal tradition in its entirety for Patrick, and all present come happily to the realization that the Holy Spirit had been speaking through the mouths of the righteous men of Ireland for quite some time:

Ar in Spirut Naem ro labrastar 7 doaircechain tria ginu na fer fíréon ceta-rabatar i n-inis Érenn amail donaircechain tria ginu inna prímfáide 7 inna n-uasalaithre i recht petarlaice. . . . Ina bretha fíraicnid trá didiu ro labrastar in Spirut Naem tre ginu breithemon 7 filed fíréon fer nÉrenn ó congbad in insi-seo co cretem anall, dosairfen Dubthach uili do Pátraic.

For the Holy Spirit spoke and prophesied through the mouths of the righteous men who were first in the island of Ireland, as He prophesied through the mouths of the chief prophets and patriarchs in the law of the Old Testament. . . . As for the judgements of true nature which the Holy Spirit uttered through the mouths of the righteous judges and poets of the men of Ireland, from the time when this island was settled until the coming of the faith: Dubthach revealed them all to Patrick.[133]

Dubthach's performance suggests that, with the exception of only a few matters, the most important of which have to do with making provisions for the church and ensuring its proper dues, traditional law accords completely with the new dispensation of the church. A commission of nine men is established to record this new law, comprised of three kings, three bishops, and three poetic or legal specialists—a grouping that underscores the main point of the passage, which is the reconciliation between native and Christian laws.

At this point in the story, there then occur three paragraphs that outline the past that has just been replaced by the new dispensation engineered by Patrick and Dubthach. They are worth quoting in their entirety:

9. *Co tánic Pátraic trá, ní tabairthe erlabra acht do t[h]riur: fer comcni cumnech fri ais-néis 7 scélugud, fer cerda fri molad 7 aír, brithem fri brithemnas a roscadaib 7 fásaigib. Ó thánic Pátraic immurgu, is fo mámmus atá cach erlabra donaib í-seo do fiur in bérlai báin .i. inna canóine.*

10. *Ón uair ro-n-uc Amorgein Glúngel cét breith i Ére, roba la fileda a n-oenur brethem-nus cosin Imacallaim in Dá Thuaruth i nEmain Mache .i. Ferc[h]ertne 7 Néde maic Adna ima t[h]ugain suad baí oc Adna mac Uithir. Ba dorcha didiu in labra ro labrasatar ind filid isin fuigiull-sin 7 nírba réill donaib flathaib in brethemnus ro-n-ucsat. "Is lasna firu-so a n-oenur a mbrethemnus 7 a n-éolus," oldat na flaithi. "Is dongaba dó dorime leo. Ní tuicem-ni cétamus a rráidite." "Is menand," ol Conchobar, "biaid cuit do chách and-som óndíu; acht a n-as dúthaig doib-sium de, ní-s-ricfe. Gébaid cách a dréchta de."*

11. *Doallad didiu breithemnus ar filedaib acht a ndúthaig de 7 ro gab cách de feraib Érenn a drécht den brithemnus amail ro gabsat Bretha Echach maic Luchta 7 Bretha Fachtnai maic Senchath 7 Gúbretha Caratniath Teiscthi 7 Bretha Moraind 7 Bretha Éogain maic Durthacht 7 Bretha Doet Nemthine 7 Bretha Bríge Ambue 7 Bretha Dén Chécht ó legaib, ce ro bátar-side i tús. Isin aimsir-sin domídetar maithi fer nÉrenn tomus n-aí 7 innsce do chách iarna miad, amail ro gabsat isnaib Brethaib Nemed 7rl.*

9. Until Patrick came, (authority in) speaking was only granted to three men: the historian with a good memory for explanation and narration; the man of art for praise and satire; the judge for giving judgements with *roscada* and maxims. After Patrick's coming, however, all of these (kinds of authoritative) speech are subject to the possessor of the white language, i.e. of the scriptures.

10. From the time when Amairgen Glúngel gave the first judgement in Ireland, judgement was in the hands of the poets alone until the "Colloquy of the Two Sages" in Emain Macha, i.e., (the colloquy) of Ferchertne and Néde mac Adna con-cerning the sage's mantle which had belonged to Adna mac Uithir. Dark was the speech which the poets spoke in that case, and the judgement which they gave was not clear to the princes. "The judgement and their understanding belong to these men alone," said the princes . . . "Moreover, we do not understand what they say." "It is plain," said Conchobar: "henceforth everyone will have a share (in judging) except for what pertains properly to them therein, it will not fall to their lot. Each will take his own portions of it."

11. So poets were deprived on the power to judge, save for what pertained prop-erly to them; and each of the men of Ireland took his own portion of judgement. Such are the Judgements of Eochu mac Luchta, and the Judgements of Fachtna mac Senchad, and the False Judgements of Caratnia Teiscthe, and the Judgements of Morann, and the Judgements of Éogan mac Durthacht, and the Judgements of Doet Nemthine, and the Judgements of Bríg Ambue, and the Judgements of Dian Cécht concerning physicians (although those were given first). At that time the no-bles of Ireland adjudged the measure of lawsuit and speech to each man according to his rank, as they are reckoned in the *Bretha Nemed*, etc.[134]

These passages confirm what we have already seen in the other excerpts we have examined from this text, namely that access to public speech is both the central theme and metaphor of the "Pseudo-Historical Prologue." Every jurisdictional dispute to which the text alludes is phrased in terms of access to authoritative speech; conversely, every issue of disputed speech speaks directly to a conflict of jurisdictions. Because poets cannot speak in ways that others understand, they are "silenced" while other speakers take their place.

Moreover, at issue is not merely speech, but language itself. One of the most striking aspects of these passages is their use of the term *bélrae* (later *bérla*), literally, "language," to mean "legal tradition." In the passage above, it is the written law of the Scriptures that is meant—the "white language" of the church to which all other tongues must henceforth be subject. But ecclesiastical legal tradition is not the only law conceptualized in this manner. Sources outside the "Pseudo-Historical Prologue" make it clear that the normal Old Irish word for "native legal tradition" was *bérla Féne,* "the language of the Féni." *Uraicecht Becc,* for example, distinguishes three ranks in the hierarchy of jurists. The first is the crafts judge, whose competence is characterized in terms of the craftsmen and goods over whom and which he is perceived to have jurisdiction. The others, however, are described in terms of the legal "languages" they have mastered: the *breithem berla Feni 7 filidiacta,* the "judge of the language of the *Féni* and of poetry," and the *breithem tri mberla,* "judge of three languages," who is the highest of all, having expertise in canon law as well as poetry and native law.[135] The tract on the *airecht* ("court") refers to three ultimate authorities who are the foundation on which all justice rests: the king, the bishop, and the *sai gacha berlai ollamand,* "the expert in every legal language with the rank of master" (probably the chief poet).[136] And the *Heptads* refer to the fee collected by a judge for his services the *lóg mbérlai,* literally, the "payment for language."[137]

Thus for the early Irish, law was language, and even more significantly, language was law, in the sense that it both differentiated the legal from the nonlegal and established the credibility of those claiming jurisdiction in legal matters. As we have seen, legal transactions and specialists derived their authority from the public performance of a style of language that served in itself as a sign of their knowledge. It was language rather the prospect of intervention by state authorities that made Ireland's law a "national" law despite the absence of a centralized government, and language rather than office that encouraged communities in dispute to consent to abide by judgments rendered by jurists from outside the locality. And while other European traditions might seem to express a similar link between law and language in terms like *veredictum, dit, sententia,* and the like, in fact there is a crucial difference. The European terms refer to judgment and the proclamation of judicial decisions; the Irish to law and the legal tradition itself. This is why the "Pseudo-Historical Prologue" can treat the performance of rhetorical speech as synonymous with the native legal tradition as a whole: Dubthach is an expert not merely in tradition, but in the composition and performance of the authoritative speech by which that tradition is invoked, encapsulated, and recognized. We need to take the characterization of Irish legal tradition as the *bérla Féne* seriously.

Like all good origin legends, the tale of Dubthach and Patrick constitutes an attempt to provide historical validation for relationships obtaining at the time the tale was composed. The basic point is clear: the newly acquired dominance of the church over all legal matters, native and ecclesiastical, and the acquiescence of the traditional learned orders of Ireland to this arrangement. Whereas before the coming of Patrick, certain men—the poet ("man of art"), the judge, and the historian—are said to have enjoyed authority in speech because of their recognized expertise in their individual disciplines, afterwards all speak only by permission of the church. The (written and spoken) language of Scripture and European culture has superseded all other previously independent speech. But while cultural accommodation is the main point of the story, the attention paid in the text to more distant elements of the ancient Irish legal past suggest that is it not the only one. One of the other major themes of the tale is the inappropriateness of poetic involvement in the judicial process. For whereas the taking over of what had previously constituted authoritative speech on the island by the church is depicted as following on from what was in essence an ordeal—Patrick's sidestepping of the trap laid for him by his divinely sanctioned appropriation of Dubthach's voice—the arrangement obtaining immediately before Patrick's arrival is presented as the result of a correction of an abusive situation. The dangerous arrogance and incomprehensibility of the poetic orders are depicted as having earlier posed a clear threat to the stability of society, one remedied by the direct intervention of a legendary king. When Conchobar removes jurisdiction in judicial affairs from the "men of art" on the grounds that their "dark" rhetorical speech is completely incomprehensible to the lords (*flaithi*) responsible for public order, he is imagined as acting in the interests of the community: saving the men of Ireland from the chaos engendered by men whose speech can neither be contained nor understood.

This casting of blame is significant, for in it we see a reflex of contemporary tensions surrounding the claims of poets to participate in legal affairs and the administration of justice. Again, this is an origin legend, a projection onto the past of the opinions of the contemporary composer as to how things ought to be. In this tale, there can be no question as to the author's sympathies. Boundaries are drawn very tightly between appropriate and inappropriate spheres of poetic endeavor. Henceforth, poets will no longer enjoy the right to interfere in the judicial affairs of those who are not members of their order, but will exercise jurisdiction only over what pertains uniquely to them. What precisely is encompassed in their purview is nowhere spelled out precisely in this text. However, a later version of the story appended as a commentary to the "Introduction to the *Senchas Már*" defines it as *genelaige fer nerenn 7 aisti cach airchetaill 7 duili sluinnti 7 duile feda 7 scelugud co laidib . . . ET brethemnus firon a corus a cerde . . . ,*[138] "the genealogies of the men of Ireland, and the meter of every poem and the works on names and the works on letters and storytelling with lays . . . and true judgment in the propriety of their art." In this version of the tale, the issue is not the role of poets in dispensing justice, but rather the process by which they came to give up the pagan practices that had characterized their art in the preconversion period. Accordingly, the tone of the text is quite conciliatory—indeed, Patrick explicitly commands that poets continue to enjoy precisely the same honors and accolades now as they had when their powers were broader.[139] However, in the "Pseudo-Historical Prologue," where the issue is one of contemporary jurisdictional superiority rather than the long-ago vanquishing of a no longer powerful faith, the tone is very different. The impression left in this text is not that of the co-operative reordering of society but rather that of a powerful political order rightfully deprived of its jurisdictional prerogatives because of its own malfeasance.

Into whose hands, then, do these important prerogatives fall? This question is more difficult than it appears, not least because it is not currently possible to identify all of the persons named in the text as having taken over from the poetic orders in matters of justice. Of the individuals cited, one is unknown (Doet Nemthine), two are kings (Eochu mac Luchta and Éogan mac Durthacht), four are jurists (Fachtna mac Senchad, Caratnia Teiscthe, Morann, and Bríg Ambue), and one is a mythical physician (Dian Cécht).[140] Three of these persons are associated with extant tracts (Caratnia, Morann, and Dian Cécht), although only one (*Bretha Déin Chécht*) was incorporated into the *Senchas Már* to which the "Pseudo-Historical Prologue" was ultimately appended.[141] Significantly, with the single exception of Dian Cécht the physician—who is explicitly located in the mythological past—all of the persons named are either kings themselves, or jurists, many of whom we know from other texts in the tradition to have cooperated with kings. Caratnia worked with Conn Cétchathach, as we have seen, while Morann is supposed to have compiled his *Audacht Morainn* (itself a tract on kingship) for Feradach Find Fechtnach.[142] And while Bríg herself is not explicitly associated with a particular king, she is depicted in the tracts as having intervened in or corrected judgments issued by Sencha, Conchobar's legendary judge.[143] None of them is, as far as we know, a poet.[144] This portion of the "Pseudo-Historical Prologue" returns us, in other words, to ideas not dissimilar to what we saw earlier in the *Gúbretha Caratniad*. The ensuring of justice is not a matter for poets whose principal qualification consists of their mastery over a tongue none can understand. It is, rather, the business of kings working in close collaboration with jurists trained in the law—the product of royal authority, and simultaneously a prerogative and a benefit of well-counseled lordship.

The composer's eagerness to prioritize kings and jurists over poets is also why it is Conchobar the king who, in conjunction with his nobles, decides the matter. The king appears in this text as the rightful dispenser of speech: his judgment does not silence the poets altogether, but imposes significant limitations on what they can say and do. Henceforth their speech is to be strictly confined to matters directly affecting their own profession; the king, by contrast, emerges as a speaker of unlimited range. After the coming of Patrick, his is no longer the ultimate power, of course—the main point of the "Pseudo-Historical Prologue" remains the subjection of all to the church. Certainly the contrast between this text's version of the three experts offered in this text and that offered in the *Triads* is quite striking. For whereas the "Pseudo-Historical Prologue" says nothing of how authority in speech was conferred upon these three experts, in the *Triads*, the issue of royal jurisdiction is rendered quite explicit.[145] One might infer that for the author of the "Pseudo-Historical Prologue" also these three experts had earlier spoken only by the permission of the king, but all the text actually says is that after the coming of Patrick, all speakers are now subject to the speech of those who know a language others (including kings) do not—in other words, Latin. The emphasis of the "Pseudo-Historical Prologue" is clearly on strong royal power, exercised according to the will and discretion of the church—a partnership imagined as having been prepared for in the pre-Christian period by Conchobar's farsighted removal of the poets whose improper use of language posed such a threat to the realization of justice.[146]

The idea of the king as the master or distributor of authoritative speech returns us to *Uraicecht Becc*, a text on personal status usually associated with the *Bretha Nemed* tradition we have looked at earlier in this work.[147] The text opens with some important observations about justice among the Irish:

Cid i naragar brethemnas berla fene. Ni [anse]. I fir et dliged 7 aicned. Consuiter fir for ros-gadhaibh 7 fasaidibh 7 teistemhnaibh 7 firaibh. Consuiter dliged for coraibh bel 7 aititen. Co[n]suiter aignen for logaid co corus. Consuiter fir 7 dliged imaille for nemedh. Nach breit nad asdaiter nach ae, nis fil i ndeoch etir. Nach breith egalsa dochuisin, is for fir 7 dliged 7 screptra consuiter. Breth filedh im[murgu]: forosgadhaibh consuiter. Breath flatha im[murgu] consuiter foraibh uili: foroscadaibh, et fasaigib, testemnaibh firaib.[148]

In what is judgment bound in Irish legal tradition? Not difficult. In truth and entitlement and nature. Truth is established on the basis of *roscada* and maxims and true testimonies.[149] Entitlement is established on the basis of oral contracts and acknowledgment. Nature is established on the basis of [the] remission [of obligations] and proper arrangements.[150] Truth and entitlement together are established through dignitaries (*nemed*). Any judgment that is not grounded in one of these is not valid at all. Any judgment of the church that exists, it is established on the basis of truth and entitlement and Scripture. [The] judgment of a poet, moreover, is established on the basis of *roscada*. The judgment of a ruler, moreover, is established on the basis of them all: on *roscada*, and precedents, and true testimonies.

This is a complicated paragraph, not least because our understanding of the range of meanings for the legal terms used in it is at best incomplete. "Truth" and "entitlement" have often been seen as distinct procedural "paths" followed by jurists in court, but this is far from certain. In some texts "truth" seems primarily to refer to the types of cases likely to be settled by ordeal, and in others to oath or personal attestation.[151] However, other texts do not usually associate "truth" in these senses with *roscad*, legal precedent, or testimony, as is done here. "Entitlement" is linked to oral contracts in the text on contract, *Berrad Airechta*, as well as here in *Uraicecht Becc*, so its usage seems more consistent.[152] "Nature," however, is not usually identified with any specific type of procedural approach but is rather the term used throughout the tradition to distinguish native law before the coming of the church from its postconversion successor. Moreover, the text seems to conflate the types of proof that might be offered in a particular dispute (ordeal, oath, testimony) with the textual (including oral) precedents in which judges might ground their decisions (*roscad*, *fásaige*, Scripture).

Perhaps the most interesting aspect of the text is its desire to associate particular types of proof or precedent with the type and purview of the judge in question. All judgments are established through persons of the privileged (*nemed*) classes, formally defined in a passage following shortly after this one in the text as poets, churchmen, and rulers.[153] Whenever poets act in a judging capacity, their judgments are to be based on *roscada*, legal principles or precedents couched in rhetorical poetic language. By contrast, when churchmen participate in the judicial process, their judgments are to be grounded in "truth" (here the reference may well be to oaths or ordeals), "entitlement" (for example, the existence or absence of an oral contract governing the relationship being judged) and Scripture (the application of biblical precedent to the situation they are called upon to decide). Most telling is what is said about judgments issued by rulers. For their judgments are explicitly said to embrace all of the various authorities that might be offered as proof or rationale in Irish law, oral and written. In other words, the authority of the king encompasses not only the oral tradition on which the authoritative speech of poets is based (as well as the various different forms of oral proof that parties in dispute might choose to offer), but the written tradition of the church as well. The king is, in other words, the master of all languages: poetic, evidentiary, and scriptural—even if this mastery consists largely of his listening to the "speakers" under his authority.

The perspective of the compiler of *Uraicecht Becc* thus differs somewhat from that expressed in several of the other texts we have examined. Unlike the compiler of the "Pseudo-Historical Prologue," for example, the composer of *Uraicecht Becc* sees poets as quite properly involved in the process of judgment—and it is worth noting that nothing is said here about poets limiting themselves only to cases involving their own order.[154] Moreover, in *Uraicecht Becc* it is the king rather than the church who subsumes all other legal "languages," including Scripture. In practice this may well have meant that the king was to be advised in his judgments by those possessing direct knowledge of the "texts" in which he grounds his decision. Indeed, it may be that we should understand *Uraicecht Becc*'s ultimate goal as being to portray poets as not merely an appropriate element of royal justice, but as a necessary one.[155] Nonetheless, for the compiler of this text, it is clearly the king who is in charge—the king who combines in his own person the oral and written resources of the legal system as a whole. Again, the contrast with the "Pseudo-Historical Prologue," in which poets are silenced and kings cringe at the awesome splendor of Patrick, whose power is so great that he can literally appropriate the voice of the entire Irish legal tradition to that point, is striking.

Nor is the "Pseudo-Historical Prologue" the only text to construct the relationship between king, jurist, church, and poet in a way that itself suggests that the extent to which the relationship among these various authorities was still very much in the process of being worked out at the time the lawbooks were being composed. *Uraicecht Becc*'s king may be the ultimate master of all languages, oral and written; for the composer of the *Gúbretha Caratniad*, however, king and jurist are linked in a symbiotic relationship that prevents one from speaking sensibly without the assistance of the other. In the Nero A. 7 *Bretha Nemed* tale, Sencha the jurist can only give voice to questions about the tradition in which he is himself a supposed expert. For the author of this tale it is the king, Conchobar, who apparently is the only one able to discern and perform the solutions to the problems by which Sencha is so baffled. Completely opposite to this picture is the situation implied in the texts on judges edited by Breatnach, where the judge standing alone lectures a silent court. Without his counsel, publicly performed and silently assimilated, not only clerics and poets but kings as well would likely conduct themselves illegally with respect to the people they were supposed to protect.

In fact, what these various texts have most visibly in common is their use of speech and silence as a means by which to express the uncertain boundaries of authority obtaining among these offices in the centuries following the conversion. If public performance was key to the assertion and realization of political and professional jurisdiction in early Ireland, then equally important was its opposite, the muting or appropriation of competing voices. Speech was the vehicle through which power was both constructed and exercised: silence, the burden borne by those who did not prevail. This is a contrast of great inherent significance for those who would understand Irish political writing, for it constitutes the "language" in which a great deal of Irish kingship theory was inscribed. Historians of other European cultures will look in vain for an Irish equivalent to Bede or a Hibernian parallel to the vigorous lawmaking activities of the Carolingians. What we are witnessing in these legal tales, however, is equally significant: the attempts of a body of literati to sculpt an image of what it meant to be a Christian king in a culture in which jurisdiction did not traditionally reside only—or perhaps even principally—in the royal office. Texts like the *Gúbretha Caratniad* and the "Pseudo-Historical Prologue" are a window on the translation of Roman and ecclesiastical notions of lordship into a native vernacular of peculiar potency. That in the process their composers have left for us a record of their own hard-fought efforts to establish the boundaries of their own voices as professionals is yet one more indication of the changes wrought in Ireland by the advent of a troublesome new faith.

Chapter 5
Voices Within the Law

To this point, language and performance have appeared as relatively stable and unchanging phenomena in this study, as ways of being and doing characteristic of all parts of Ireland throughout our period. That this should be so is due in large part to our sources, which tend to minimize or disguise evidence of regional variation or change over time. Also a factor, however, are long-standing professional assumptions about the nature of the legal tradition itself. It has long been common in the field of early Irish law to speak as though what was true about one text or school was necessarily true about others as well. Scholars have tended to emphasize the remarkably "national" aspect of the vernacular legal tradition—the extent to which jurists from one region in Ireland seem to have been expected to be able to function in another, the absence of dialectal divergence in the extant tracts, the relative lack of evidence for substantial variation in regional custom.[1] Indeed, the entire debate between nativists and antinativists regarding the nature and clerical content of the lawbooks has been to this point silently predicated on such ideas. To demonstrate the origins or authorship of one text is to demonstrate the origins of them all—or at least such has been the implication. Breatnach's conclusion from his study of *Cáin Fhuithirbe* that the redaction not just of that particular text but of "the vernacular laws in general" was "under the direction of the church" is a key case in point.[2]

It is certainly true that there are striking similarities among the extant tracts, not least because texts composed in one school seem frequently to have made their way to others. Quotations from or references to other tracts are common across the legal corpus. *Di Astud Chor* cites provisions both from the genuine "Introduction" to the *Senchas Már* and from *Berrad Airechta*;[3] *Berrad Airechta* quotes phrases found also in *Bretha Nemed Tóisech*;[4] *Bretha Crólige* makes use of a maxim found also in *Bretha im Fhuillema Gell*;[5] *Bretha Déin Chécht* shares one with *Di Gnímaib Gíall*.[6] Examples of similar citations back and forth among tracts are legion.[7] On the other hand, despite the connections to which such citations attest, difference is clearly also reflected in the sources that remain to us. Even a cursory glance at the extant tracts suggests the extent to which schools varied in their priorities, curriculum, and approaches to instruction.

And yet scholars have tended to focus less on such differences than on what Kelly calls the "essential unity" of the tradition as a whole.[8] The reasons for this are many and varied. Early interpretations, particularly those associated with the Indo-Europeanist approach, saw the law in more or less teleological terms. Binchy commented long ago, for example, on the unusual importance accorded poetry in texts produced by the *Bretha Nemed* school.[9] He concluded on the basis of the rhetorical style in which most of the tracts associated with this tradition had been written that the school in which they had been produced was one in which "*filidecht* [the craft of poetry] *still* included law and 'history' as well as poetry," and in which "poetry and jurisprudence were *still* undifferentiated" (emphasis mine).[10] In other words, the gap between the school in which the *Bretha Nemed* tracts had been produced and other contemporary law schools was for Binchy a matter of institutions at different stages of development. *Bretha Nemed* was a school in which law had not *yet* separated out from poetry as it was ultimately destined to do and had already done in other regions of the country. *Bretha Nemed* jurists might have been a bit behind the times, but in Binchy's view the anticipated trajectory of development of their tradition was the same as it was elsewhere in Ireland.

Of course it is not merely the teleological instincts of historians that have contributed to the impression of homogeneity within the legal tradition. Also tempting us in the direction of downplaying the differences among the extant tracts are considerations of historical methodology. When sources are as scarce and reliable information as relatively thin on the ground as they are for the cultures of the early medieval west, historians quite naturally tend to read passages in one text in light of seemingly related passages in another. This may in turn lead them to intuit affiliations and draw conclusions that are not necessarily warranted by the evidence in question. For example, as will be argued later in this chapter, the fact that one tract attributes an archaic (looking) citation to *Fénechas*, "native oral law," does not mean that all archaic (looking) passages in the lawbooks ought necessarily to be similarly attributed. Nor does it suggest that *Fénechas* as a concept was conceptualized everywhere in the legal tradition in precisely the same way. What is true about *Fénechas* is surely true also about other fundamental aspects of the native legal tradition: its origins both as profession and as discipline, for example, or its traditions of staffing and personnel, or its vision of the authority upon which procedures and provisions were perceived to rest. Knowing how to contextualize information gleaned from disparate texts is difficult to do in the best of circumstances; when evidence is so limited, the temptation to generalize is especially great.

Thus it is that it is only in the past few years that other perspectives have begun to emerge. At the forefront of such studies has been Thomas Charles-Edwards, who argues that the diversity we know to have obtained both in clerical education and in Irish church life as a whole makes a single origin and outlook for the laws unlikely. In his view, there are visible differences between the perspectives of native secular lawyers and their colleagues on the ecclesiastical side of the fence.[11] Common sense alone would suggest that regardless of one's stand on the likelihood of a specifically "secular" legal profession, Charles-Edwards is surely right in underscoring the diversity and fluidity of the legal tradition. The advent of the church introduced into Ireland completely new ways of thinking about law—radically different perceptions about its sources, authority, and manner of presentation, novel thoughts about who should be in charge.[12] Moreover, even apart from the impact of the church per se, traditional notions of native custom and personnel seem almost certain to have been influenced by ideas about law and government entering Ireland from England and the continent. Questions about the relative authority of king and jurist is likely one such example; another is the increasing tendency in eighth- and ninth-century Ireland toward legislative pronouncements by church and king in a manner reminiscent of proclamations elsewhere in Europe. The peculiarly Irish features of Irish *cáin*-law should not obscure its general resemblance to the synodal pronouncements and capitulary-style legislation of early Frankish and Anglo-Saxon kings.[13] Surely it is not too fanciful to connect the increasing popularity (if not the advent altogether) of royal lawmaking with the arrival in Ireland of Roman and European models of kingship and justice.

And of course regional politics also must surely have had an impact on diversity within the legal tradition. Law schools were located in different parts of Ireland and were therefore of necessity immersed in the political realities of their particular locale. As far as we can tell, the school that produced the *Senchas Már* was located somewhere in the northern midlands, while the *Bretha Nemed* texts seem to have originated in Munster. *Críth Gablach* may be associated with Meath or south Ulster, while the ninth-century collection known as the *Triads of Ireland* names the monastic houses of Cork, Cloyne, and Slane as centers of *bérlae Féne*, *Fénechas*, and *brithemnas* respectively.[14] The role played by these schools in training persons destined to serve as judges and royal advisers seems likely to have inspired competition between schools, if not regions, for positions and prestige. At the very least the tracts ought not to be regarded as though they had been produced in a political or professional vacuum.[15] Moreover, even apart from politics per se, there is geography to be reckoned with. Ireland was in this period a sparsely populated, heavily regionalized island in which boundaries were constructed as much by impassable bogs and brakes as by political lines drawn by rulers. Given such variables, it is difficult to see how things could be everywhere the same.

Now, it is important not to go overboard in stressing differences among our extant tracts. The uniformity of language and anticipated application that characterizes the early Irish legal tradition *is* truly remarkable, if also truly relative, and it is at least as important to note that tracts and schools found it useful to share back and forth as it is to remark upon the ways in which their perspectives differ from one another. My point here is not that the apparent "sameness" of the legal tradition from region to region is untrue or uninteresting but, rather, that variations among tracts might repay further exploration. Certainly our understanding of the "fault lines" along which early Irish law schools tended to divide is superficial at best. The notion of a possible divide between "secular" and "ecclesiastical" law has been current in the literature for quite some time,[16] although in the wake of work done by Breatnach, McCone, and Ó Corráin, many scholars have now come to reject this idea in favor of a view that sees the laws always and inevitably as the work of clerics. At the very least, it would be fair to say that any consensus on this point that might once have obtained has now been ruptured. Another potential "fault line" is the dispute between the *Romani* and the *Hibernenses* parties within the early Irish church, which has been taken by some scholars as linked in some way to the laws. Almost always this has been considered from the point of view of the canons rather than of the vernacular lawbooks. Kathleen Hughes, for example, argued that members of the "Irish party" within the church appeared considerably more interested in and conversant with vernacular legal procedure than did their *Romani* counterparts.[17] On the other hand, collaboration is usually a two-way street, so it is not unreasonable to imagine that *Hibernenses* clerics might have had an impact on law texts emanating from a school or schools with which they had become affiliated.

Language and performance offer us additional ways in which to examine this issue of "fault lines" within the early Irish legal tradition. Linguistic style is perhaps the most obvious difference separating the tracts. Some rely heavily on rhetorical language or obscure, seemingly archaic syntax; others say what they have to say in a relatively straightforward prose that leaves little to the imagination. Some deliberately call attention to changes in style when they occur, identifying rhetorical passages as direct speech, or attributing it to named performers within the tradition. Others explicitly do not, but leave the boundaries between styles unmarked and uncommented on, as though trying either to disguise them, or to underscore the extent to which they ought not to matter. The importance of performance too varies from tract to tract. This is true not merely with respect to performance in the present—performative language and gestures serving to authorize particular laws or verdicts and the jurists who give them, in other words—but to performance as imagined in the past as well. Tracts differ significantly among themselves in terms of how they represent the oral-performative past and its relationship to the present. For some jurists, past and present are not easily separable; for others, the question is much less clear. Some see law in the past as if from a great distance, across the all-important barrier of conversion, an undertaking at once important to and yet inferior to that in which they perceive themselves currently to be involved. Others take a different approach, drawing the past into the present in ways that emphasize the extent to which one depends upon the other and cannot easily be separated from it. None of these points of view can be proven "wrong" about the history of the law, and none can be proven "right." Presumably, each individual vision of the past was in some sense "right" for the school that concocted it. What is most striking, and what remains constant from school to school and from tract to tract, is the extent to which language and performance emerge as one of the most important "dialects" in which conversations about competition and alliance were conducted.

An Age of Law

Historians have long recognized that the period following the eleventh-century rediscovery of Roman law in the west was a particularly fertile time for legal thought. Virtually every major western European monarchy produced at least one important lawbook in this era; these same centuries also saw the emergence of a system of professionalized justice in many lands.[18] Arguably as important for the history of medieval law, however, were the legal developments of an earlier age. In the wake of the collapse of Roman imperial authority in the course of the fifth century, Germanic cultures struggled to internalize and adapt the instruments of imperial rule for their own political purposes. Law was an important part of this process. Inspired—and probably often authored—by the now frequently clerical descendants of the former Roman ruling classes, written legal compilations began to appear in great numbers. Most revered were the great legal monuments of Late Antiquity—the "Breviary" of Alaric, Theodoric's "Edict," the Justinianic corpus itself. But other works quickly appeared on the political scene: first the Franks, Burgundians, Anglo-Saxons, and Visigoths, and then later, under Carolingian auspices, the Lombards, Bavarians, Frisians, Thuringians, and Saxons all produced law codes of their own.

Nor were codes the only manner of legal expression in this era. Other legal genres survive in great numbers, most notably charters, writs, *placita*, and the legislative (at least in appearance) capitularies.[19] The jury is still out on the extent to which written law actually played a role in the realization of justice in the localities.[20] What is certain, however, is that texts of this sort played a key role in the transformation of the Roman world, both by giving theoretical definition to notions of rule that were still very much in flux, and by providing kings a forum in which to render tangible their authority. And as for secular law and royal power, so also for canon law and ecclesiastical authority: Thomas Noble has argued that the period from 500 to 800 was as productive an era for canon law as the west would see until the great reforms of the eleventh century.[21]

It is difficult to define with certainty the degree to which legal developments in Ireland in this period were predicated upon those occurring elsewhere in Europe. Because the Romans never occupied Ireland, written law in Ireland was necessarily less the product of the encounter between native and Roman than between native and Christian. On the other hand, given the extent to which the church (in Ireland as elsewhere) drew on Roman ideas about governance and rule in constructing its own polity, what we are witnessing in Ireland ought probably still to be considered part of the same European-wide phenomenon. Indeed, the connection may be even more direct than this. The Irish were surely aware of the codification of the "laws" of various peoples in England and on the continent; they may well have seen themselves as participating also in that trend. There were intellectual and economic contacts back and forth between Ireland and a number of European countries in this period, and it is difficult to imagine that ideas about law would not have traveled along these same routes.[22]

Nor was vernacular law the only venue in which Irish and European legal traditions helped to shape one another. As Charles-Edwards has pointed out, it is in Ireland that we first see anything approaching a true system of canon law—a system that, as far as we can tell, originated in Ireland and moved eastward into Wales and thence onto the continent, rather than the other way around.[23] Certainly it is striking how, even apart from the possibility of direct imitation back and forth, written law came to play in both places such an important role in addressing the questions of ethnic and political identity that so troubled rulers of the period. For despite the obvious differences separating Ireland from lands once subject to Roman control, many of the questions raised by developments in this era were the same. The passage from strictly local identities to allegiances more regional—and ultimately, provincial and even "national"—in nature was a venture fraught with difficulty; so too was the task of establishing the proper relationship and boundaries between the "tribe of the church" and the "tribe" per se. In Ireland as elsewhere, law was one of the venues in which ideas about political and professional identity were first articulated and explored.[24]

Whatever the precise nature of the connection between legal developments in Ireland and events elsewhere, it is the case that the heyday of Irish legal writing (seventh through ninth centuries) overlapped to a considerable degree with the high point of English and continental legal activity (sixth through ninth and tenth centuries). It is difficult to say at what point law first began to be committed to writing in Ireland, as recent work on "Archaic Irish" has considerably undermined our confidence in our ability to identify with precision the dates of the earliest legal texts. We can be reasonably confident, however, that law had begun to find its way into written form at least by the middle of the seventh century, if not earlier. There are a few vernacular texts that seem likely on linguistic grounds to date to the era before 700 (at least until proven otherwise), including the oldest stratum of *Cóic Conara Fugill*, and poems on neighborhood law and on *tellach*.[25]

Other tracts can be dated to the period around 700, like *Berrad Airechta* and *Críth Gablach*; still others date to later in the eighth or even later centuries (for example, *Cró 7 Díbad*). Nor are the vernacular texts our only possible source for provisions of native law. Michael Richter has suggested that the earliest texts in which native legal ideas are to be found are actually the "Irish synod" provisions of the Latin canonical collection known as the *Collectio Canonum Hibernensis*, which provisions he dates to the period post 640.[26] One might add to this the fact that some noncanonical texts which themselves date to around 700 purport to quote extensively from an earlier oral law known as *Fénechas*, "the custom of the *Féni*."[27]

It is in the first half of the eighth century, side by side with the ongoing composition of individual legal tracts, that we first begin to see the production of larger collections of texts in law schools in the south and midlands of Ireland.[28] These collections are often referred to—not always very precisely—in modern scholarly parlance as "lawbooks." In fact, only one of these compilations, the *Senchas Már*, can be shown to represent a deliberately assembled collection of tracts (most separately authored and provenanced) that was meant to be experienced as a single lawbook. The Latin *Collectio Canonum Hibernensis* also appears to have been an intentional compilation, but of citations and exempla pertaining to specific moral and legal topics rather than of independent tracts. An even looser collection is the *Bretha Nemed* family of texts, all of which are believed to have emanated from a single school, but which were never as far as we can tell deliberately joined together in the manner of the *Senchas Már*.

Of these three compilations, possibly the earliest of the three—and certainly the odd man out in terms of language—is the *Hibernensis*, a Latin and forthrightly ecclesiastical text extant today in two recensions, A and B, which was likely compiled between 716 and 747.[29] Significant differences exist between the two recensions, and scholars have argued for decades over which recension is the older of the two. One may represent a revision or variant version of the other, or both might either have drawn on, or have been drawn upon, by a third, no longer extant, text.[30] Unusually for a text as early as the *Hibernensis*, we know the names of at least two of the men believed to have been involved in its compilation: Ruben of Dairinis (a monastery on the Blackwater River in Munster), who died in 725, and Cú Chuimne of Iona, who died in 747. Sadly, it has so far not proved possible to isolate with any degree of certainty the contributions made by each compiler, although significant work has been done in the past few years on the various sources upon which these men drew. The latest author cited in A is Theodore of Canterbury (obit 690), and the latest in B Adamnán of Iona (obit 704), a fact that has fueled a variety of hypotheses about the relationship between the recensions and their authors.[31] The problem is a difficult one, not least because of the significant distances (political as well as geographical) separating Dairinis from Iona.[32]

Of particular interest with respect to the *Hibernensis* is its approach and what that approach implies about the purpose(s) for which it was composed. At its most basic level, the *Hibernensis* represents a compilation of authoritative ecclesiastical passages arranged according to topic; indeed, Thomas O'Loughlin has argued that its true originality as a church law collection lies here, in its topical rather than chronological layout.[33] Biblical authorities are cited extensively, as are the writings of early church fathers such as Jerome, Origen, Augustine, and others, and Luned Mair Davies has recently demonstrated the importance of Gregory the Great's writings to the collection.[34] It is not always clear as to whether these authors are being cited directly or, rather, indirectly through collections of *excerpta* in which quotations from these authors were reproduced, although it is evident that in some cases at least, the compilers had access to numerous manuscripts of the texts in question.[35] The *Hibernensis* also quotes frequently from early continental (primarily Visigothic and Frankish) church councils—more extensively, indeed, than any other extant Hiberno-Latin text.[36] Sometimes it looks as though compilers may be working from their memories of what they had read rather than from the original text itself: for whatever reason, verbatim reproduction of the texts cited would not appear to have been a strong priority.

Of greatest interest to Irish historians are its quotations from synodal councils within the early Irish church. In the text these councils are identified either as the *Synodus Hibernensis*, "the Irish synod," or the *Synodus Romana*, "the Roman synod" or, occasionally, just *Synodus*. Scholars have long been aware of competing "Roman" and "Irish" parties within the church, and the *Hibernensis* has generally been taken as reflecting the existence of such divisions.[37] However, the most divisive bone of contention between the Irish and Roman synods was undoubtedly the dating of Easter, and this no longer appears to be an issue in the *Hibernensis*. Moreover, the text cites freely from both synods—sometimes even in the same chapter, as in Book XVIII, where the Roman synod is cited in support of the practice of burying people in their family burial ground, and the Irish in support of burying men in the church in which they have served as monks.[38] Bart Jaski has argued on the basis of this evidence that the dispute between "Roman" and "Irish" parties had at the very least "lost its edge" by the time the text was compiled, and this seems very likely to be right.[39] Indeed, one might perhaps go farther than this to speculate whether the compilers of the *Hibernensis* might have consciously been attempting to demonstrate the essential unity of Irish ecclesiastical tradition by placing statements from both synods side by side—just as Alfred was later to do in England, attaching the written laws of his Kentish and Anglian predecessors to his own code in an effort to establish its "national" character.[40]

Perhaps the most vexed question regarding the *Hibernensis* has been the function(s) its compilers intended it to serve. That some at the time regarded it as a *florilegium,* or reference work of quotations for use in preaching, seems fairly well established.[41] That it served not merely to bring together but also to investigate the theoretical underpinnings of church law on a variety of important moral issues is also clear.[42] What is still a matter of considerable debate is its relationship—intended or unintended—with native law. Legal historians are generally agreed that the *Hibernensis* was likely a product "of the same spurt of compilatory activity" as produced the vernacular law tracts.[43] To say this is not, however, to specify what the relationship among these tracts might have been. At the heart of the matter is the nature and extent of the jurisdiction to which the *Hibernensis* was attempting to lay claim. The text unquestionably embraces both secular and ecclesiastical topics, a fact that immediately renders the problem of its intended audience crucial. Was the *Hibernensis* a "canon law collection" or "manual on morality" meant to be used primarily in communities of clerics?[44] Or was it reflective of other types of divisions, a "blueprint for . . . Christian living" aimed at Christians living within a still largely "alien" society?[45] Might it have functioned as a resource for high-ranking ecclesiastics with monastic tenants and a lay population (presumably associated with church estates) under their authority, as Jaski suggests?[46] Or was its intended audience broader than this? Was it in fact a "major law book," a "juridical source [covering] not only spiritual but also ecclesiastical and social activity," as Luned Davies has argued?[47] And if the latter, might its purview have been perceived as extending to communities not under direct ecclesiastical jurisdiction?[48]

Complicating such matters considerably is the fact that even if we knew how those who compiled it intended to be used, we would be only marginally enlightened. A source constructed by its compilers to serve one purpose could easily come to be used or perceived in a different way altogether outside its original compositional context.[49] This is true both for those who might reasonably be expected to benefit and for those on whose authority it might be perceived as infringing. A text originally intended only for use in a monastic context, for example, could easily come to be regarded as threatening to native lawyers concerned with losing jurisdiction over populations hitherto entirely under their control if its reputation were to spread beyond the confines of the monastic estate in question. Similarly, ecclesiastical judges called upon to give judgment or to advise kings on difficult legal cases might well be tempted to consult what looked like an authoritative compendium of written church law, even if the book in question had never been intended originally to serve that purpose. In other words, even if one assumes that the original compilers of the *Hibernensis* intended to "complement" native law rather than supplant it—an assumption far from proven, in my view—it is still entirely possible that those charged with preserving native tradition might perceive the situation altogether differently and react according to those perceptions.[50]

It is in this context that one must consider the composition of two of the other important "lawbooks" of the day, the *Senchas Már* and the group of texts emanating from the *Bretha Nemed* school. The *Senchas Már* is easily the most extensive and sophisticated project of its kind known from Ireland in this period—indeed, it is arguably the most impressive legal undertaking in the west since the compilation of the Justinianic corpus. No complete copy of the lawbook has survived intact, but Breatnach has been able to reconstruct its contents quite plausibly, both from the tracts that do survive and from commentaries and glossaries containing excerpts from *Senchas Már* texts, often in what seems to have been their original order.[51] As reconstructed by Breatnach, the lawbook contained forty-seven or forty-eight independent tracts, many of them quite lengthy, on a comprehensively wide range of legal topics. It had a formal introduction, possibly written by the compiler himself,[52] and was at some point in time divided into thirds, probably in the Old Irish period.[53] Contiguity within the lawbook and similarities in phrasing have suggested to scholars over the years that certain tracts either had the same author (for example, *Bechbretha* and *Coibnes Uisci Thairidne* on the one hand, and *Cáin Iarraith*, *Cáin Sóerraith*, *Cáin Aicillne*, and *Cáin Lánamna* on the other) or emanated from within the same legal school (for example, *Bechbretha*, *Coibnes Uisci Thairidne*, and *Bretha im Fhuillema Gell*). Breatnach has recently pointed to phrasing similarities in noncontiguous tracts as well,[54] a fact that could be interpreted in a variety of ways: as casting doubt on the criteria on the basis of which joint authorship has usually been suggested or, alternatively, as raising other possibilities altogether, such as aggressive editorial intervention on the part of the compiler.

Given the comprehensive nature of the *Senchas Már*, it can hardly be doubted that the lawbook as originally compiled was intended to serve as a primary—arguably even *the* primary—compendium of native Irish custom and legal practice. It would be difficult to imagine an issue covered elsewhere in the legal corpus that the *Senchas Már* does not address (or at least did not address, since many of the tracts are extant now only in excerpts). Clientship, fosterage, status, contractual obligations, animal law, water rights, pledges, distraint, the relationship between church and laity, marriage and divorce, injury law, suretyship, laws pertaining to the manufacture of crafts and the maintenance of the forest, healing and physicians' fees—all these and more are covered. Like all Irish legal texts, it focuses more directly on relations between individuals and groups rather than on criminal law, although it does contain a tract on theft and two tracts (*Bretha Crólige* and *Slicht Othrusa*) on sick-maintenance, a practice usually associated with the unlawful wounding of one individual by another.

Everything points to its having been a carefully considered and well-thought-out compilation. Some degree of overlap among tracts is inevitable in a collection of this size, but what is in many ways most striking is how *rarely* topics are duplicated from tract to tract. We know, for example, that there were a number of status tracts in existence at the time the *Senchas Már* was compiled: *Uraicecht Becc, Críth Gablach,* and *Míadslechta,* to name only those still extant today. The *Senchas Már,* however, contains only one—different again from the other three and now extant only in fragments. If the *Senchas Már* compiler did have access to more than one tract on this subject, in other words, he did not choose to incorporate them all into his lawbook. What is true of status seems from the list of the titles of the tracts included in the lawbook to have been true of other legal topics as well. The compiler's aim seems to have been to include one representative tract on every legal subject that occurred to him as important rather than to collect any and all written material he could find on a given topic. This in turn seems to confirm the suggestion ventured earlier, that the compiler intended that his work serve as not merely *a* resource for information about native Irish law, but as *the* resource superceding all others.

Very different from the *Senchas Már* are the texts attributed to the *Bretha Nemed* law school, generally thought to have been located in Munster. Binchy was the first to postulate the existence of this school.[55] His argument was based on the similarities in perspective and style displayed by certain extant tracts, one of which actually opens with what may well have been the title by which it was most commonly known: *Bretha Nemed* or *Córus Bretha Nemed,* "The Proper Arrangement of *Bretha Nemed*" ("Judgments Concerning Privileged Persons").[56] Later commentators and glossary compilers ascribed passages from other texts as well to something they knew as *Bretha Nemed;* this led Binchy to suggest that "the name *Bretha Nemed* was used to cover a whole series of tracts which were originally associated with a particular school."[57] Many of these cited passages were to be found in a very difficult text printed by Gwynn in *Ériu* under the title of "An Old-Irish Tract on the Privileges and Responsibilities of Poets," and Binchy then identified this text also as a *Bretha Nemed* tract on this basis.[58] Today *Córus Bretha Nemed* and the Gwynn text are known under the titles given them by later scribes: *Bretha Nemed Toísech,* the "first *Bretha Nemed,*" and *Bretha Nemed Déidenach,* the "last *Bretha Nemed,*" respectively. Breatnach has argued that *Bretha Nemed Toísech,* by far the better organized of the two, was composed between 721 and 742 in Munster by a bishop, a poet, and a judge, all three kinsmen to one another.[59] Other tracts ascribed by Binchy to the *Bretha Nemed* school include the tract on status known as *Uraicecht Becc,* the oldest recensions of *Cóic Conara Fugill* on procedure, *Bretha Étgid* on accidental injury and death, the wisdom text *Audacht Morainn,* and possibly other aphoristic texts as well, such as *Findsruth Fíthail* and the *Aibidil Luigne maic Éremóin.*[60] Breatnach has since proposed that the tract on poets, *Uraicecht na Ríar,* was also associated with the school and was intended to constitute a "primer" or "introduction" to *Bretha Nemed.*[61]

By and large these ascriptions have either been accepted outright or repeated by modern scholars.[62] However, the criteria Binchy used to identify texts associated with the *Bretha Nemed* school are troublesomely broad and ought probably at this point to be revisited. Stylistic considerations rank very high on the list. Both *Bretha Nemed Toísech* and *Bretha Nemed Déidenach*, the two "certain" *Bretha Nemed* texts, are written in large part in a highly rhetorical, ostentatiously obscure style that makes use of many constructions associated with "Archaic Irish": alliteration, tmesis, Bergin's Law, preposed genitives, absence of the conjunction *ocus* ("and"), and the like.[63] Other important criteria articulated by Binchy include a Munster provenance, a preoccupation with "men of art" (particularly poets, but craftsmen as well), and an understanding of the term *nemed* that encompasses unfree as well as free and noble persons.[64] Kelly's analysis of *Audacht Morainn* added as possible (but not necessary) characteristics citations or close lexical parallels back and forth among tracts associated with the school, and the appearance of particular characters like Neire and Morann, both of whom are referred to frequently in *Bretha Nemed Toísech* and *Bretha Nemed Déidenach*.[65] Breatnach has also pointed to the extent to which the glosses and commentary of certain legal tracts draw on *Bretha Nemed* texts as a possible sign.[66]

By these standards, a strong case can and has been made for *Audacht Morainn*'s association with the *Bretha Nemed* school. *Audacht Morainn* displays the same style as the two "certain" *Bretha Nemed* tracts, makes use of expressions, syntactical structures, and legal personalities found in those tracts, and has a demonstrable interest in the *nemed* classes, which it also conceptualizes as including unfree persons.[67] *Bretha Étgid* is a clear possibility. The text, glosses, and commentaries cite or allude to passages in *Bretha Nemed Toísech* on a couple of occasions,[68] and certain subjects covered in the *Bretha Nemed* texts (for example, animal offenses) are discussed also in *Bretha Étgid*. Moreover, the pseudohistorical tale that opens the tract identifies the tract with Cormac, his son Coirpre, and Cenn Fáelad, characters who appear also in *Bretha Nemed* texts.[69] *Findsruth Fíthail* is stylistically very similar to *Bretha Nemed*; indeed, the former's characteristic interrogatory *co bér breith*, "how shall I give judgment?" occurs also in *Bretha Nemed Déidenach*.[70] Fíthal is, moreover, cited as a source of wisdom and judgment in this same *Bretha Nemed* text.[71]

Other texts raise issues of language versus content. *Uraicecht Becc* displays a keen interest in the *nemed* classes, and both the tract itself and its glosses cite extensively from *Bretha Nemed* texts.[72] However, the tract is written in a plain prose style entirely out of keeping with the rhetorical language associated with the school. If it does derive from the same school that produced the main *Bretha Nemed* tracts (and most historians would probably agree that this is likely), it must have been intended to function as a primer for beginning students, as Breatnach has suggested for *Uraicecht na Ríar*, also written primarily in textbook prose.[73] *Aibidil Luigne maic Éremóin* raises other difficult issues. It is certainly true that some of the maxims it contains are highly reminiscent of maxims found in *Bretha Nemed* texts.[74] On the other hand, the correspondences are not exact, and as maxims are among the most fluid and difficult to provenance texts in the entire legal corpus, there is no necessary reason to connect them with *Bretha Nemed* per se.[75] The RE recensions of *Cóic Conara Fugill* are very difficult to make a case for. The stylistic similarities are fairly superficial, there are no direct verbal correspondences of the sort visible with *Audacht Morainn*, craftsmen are not a particular concern, neither Morann nor Neire appear, and there are no direct citations from *Bretha Nemed* texts. The main argument in favor of such an affiliation would appear to be the similarity between the categories of judgment articulated in *Cóic Conara Fugill* and those mentioned in other (presumably) *Bretha Nemed* texts, like *Uraicecht Becc*. Since the overlap with *Uraicecht Becc* is not exact, and since its association with the *Bretha Nemed* school is far from certain in any case, this would seem a poor foundation on which to rely. Unless one wishes to argue that all rhetorical texts are by definition to be attributed to the *Bretha Nemed* school—and that would be a risky argument to make—there is little basis on which to affiliate the early *Cóic Conara Fugill* recensions to that school. *Fénechas*-style language is certainly a hallmark of *Bretha Nemed*, but there is no reason to think that it was unique to it—not least because language of this sort appears in some *Senchas Már* texts as well.[76]

Judging by the criteria established by Binchy and others, there are other texts also that have at least as good a claim as do the above to be associated with the *Bretha Nemed* school but have not yet figured in these discussions. Embedded in the tract on suretyship, *Berrad Airechta*, for example, is a brief tract on witnessing known as *Córus Fíadnaise*.[77] That *Córus Fíadnaise* was originally an independent text is evident both from the style, which follows very much along typical *Bretha Nemed* lines (the rest of *Berrad Airechta* consists primarily of plain prose, oral formulae, or maxims), and from the fact of its having been given a separate title. It is unclear whether the title was original to the composition itself or supplied by the *Berrad Airechta* compiler; all in all, the evidence probably points more toward the latter, in that the etymological gloss that follows immediately upon the title is almost certainly the work of the compiler, and there are clear parallels between this title and gloss and the title and gloss given by the compiler to the following section of the tract, *Córus Aitire*.[78] *Córus Fíadnaise* has a plausible claim to association with the *Bretha Nemed* school. Stylistically, it is linked in both general and specific ways to the main *Bretha Nemed* tracts: generally, in its syntax, rhetorical nature, and intensive use of interrogatives (particularly *codu*, "where is/does"),[79] and specifically, in its citation of two phrases that also occur in *Bretha Nemed Toísech*.[80] It shows no particular interest in the *nemed* classes, but suretyship and contract are also demonstrated interests of the school,[81] so a link with *Bretha Nemed* would seem a real possibility.

However—and this more than anything demonstrates the difficulties of assigning particular works to this law school—while *Córus Fíadnaise* itself does not show much interest in the craftsman classes, *Berrad Airechta* itself, apart from *Córus Fíadnaise*, does.[82] Ought *Berrad Airechta* as a whole then to be ascribed to the *Bretha Nemed* school? Probably not—but the fact that the question even occurs itself suggests that our current criteria for inclusion raise at least as many questions as they answer. At the very least, it is unclear how many of our current standards a text has to meet in order for its ascription to the school to be considered plausible. Nor has the importance of those particular standards, as compared to others by which the school might be defined, been established with any degree of certainty. For example, the discussion to date has downplayed what would likely appear to most readers to be the most important characteristic of the two certain *Bretha Nemed* texts—their clear and abiding preoccupation with the rights and prerogatives of poets. Obviously Binchy's comments about *Bretha Nemed* as a "poetico-legal" school speak to this aspect of the question; however, to date the centrality of this aspect of the texts has been obscured by virtue of its having been treated as one of a number of possible characteristics rather than as a (or the) primary consideration. For poets are clearly the dominant theme of both texts. *Bretha Nemed Déidenach* is entirely taken up with this subject, and while *Bretha Nemed Toísech* is more complex, it is still the case that two of its three sections are centered on issues pertaining to poets and poet-judges. A similar focus is visible in *Uraicecht na Ríar* and, to a lesser degree, *Uraicecht Becc* and *Audacht Morainn*, although the basic conceit of the latter is that it is the king, not the poet/craftsman, who is urged to make judgments regarding crafts and manufactured articles.[83]

Moreover, with respect to *Bretha Nemed Toísech* particularly, there is the issue of Christianity, which is also an absolutely central theme in this tract. Breatnach has shown that *Bretha Nemed Toísech* draws heavily on Latin canonical sources (most notably the *Hibernensis* itself) in its composition, as is suitable for a text that was the product of a collaboration between members of the ecclesiastical, poetic, and judicial professions. In fact, as will be argued later in this chapter, one of its central points is that poets (and other craftsmen) should judge their own, just as clerics do.[84] Its preoccupation with poetic purity (defined in patently Christian terms) and learning also speaks very clearly to the importance of ecclesiastical elements to this text.[85] By contrast, Fergus Kelly has argued that the earliest stratum of *Audacht Morainn* appears to be pre-Christian; as he points out, this is something of an obstacle to our understanding of the environment from which *Audacht Morainn* and *Bretha Nemed Toísech* might each have emerged.[86]

In short, we need probably to entertain a wider variety of explanations regarding the identification of texts as deriving from the *Bretha Nemed* school than we have done hitherto. It is possible that all of these texts are to be ascribed to a single school, but if so, some would seem either to date to different periods or to speak to different priorities, as reflected in the extent to which Christianity figures in their thematic makeup. What seems equally possible—and in some cases more likely—is that what we have here are texts emanating from different schools that have either had access to *Bretha Nemed* manuscripts (hence the citations), or else reflect similar assumptions about the jurisdictional prerogatives of poets and craftsmen because they derive from the same region of the island (Munster). This might help us to situate texts like the important status tract *Míadslechta*, for example, which has surprisingly not yet featured in any detailed way in discussions of the *Bretha Nemed* school. As Breatnach notes, *Míadslechta* appears "textually independent" of *Bretha Nemed*,[87] and large portions of it are written in normal textbook style. On the other hand, it is extremely interested in poets and men of learning, and it quotes extensively the *rosc* judgments of poet-jurists like Morann, Cenn Fáelad, and Cormac, figures who also appear in the certain *Bretha Nemed* tracts. Moreover, its Christian connections are clear. At one point it cites Solomon as an authority, quoting a passage from Proverbs in Latin in its discussion of satire and praise;[88] near the end of the tract there is a discussion of clerics in which one of the Irish canons is paraphrased.[89] In other words, *Míadslechta* displays several of the characteristics typically associated with the certain *Bretha Nemed* texts—even though it never quotes or cites directly to them. In the discussion that follows, I take an interest in the *nemed* classes, and particularly in poets, as an essential distinguishing characteristic of the school, and thus draw mainly upon the two certain *Bretha Nemed* tracts, *Uraicecht na Ríar*, *Audacht Morainn*, and *Uraicecht Becc*. Clearly, however, there is room for further work on this school.

Fault Lines

One important question raised by the existence of these schools and the texts they produced is that of their relationship to each other and to the legal and political worlds of which they were individually a part. As has already been mentioned, we have only a vague understanding of the "fault lines" along which schools tended to divide. To the extent that scholars have addressed the question directly, they have usually sought to correlate differences visible in the law tracts with divisions known from elsewhere in Irish society: *Hibernenses* versus *Romani*, native versus Latin, secular versus ecclesiastical. To this one ought probably to add differences of a more political or geographical nature: Munster versus the north and midlands, supporters versus opponents of Armagh. To approach the tracts in this way makes a great deal of sense; issues of this kind ought properly to enter into the discussion at some point, as indeed they will later in this chapter. However, what all of these approaches have in common is the desire to situate differences within the legal tradition first and foremost outside that tradition: the desire to explain visible variations among the tracts primarily with reference to the broader sphere of national and religious politics. What I wish to consider here is the possibility that the divisions we see in the extant tracts have their origins as much in divergent perspectives within the profession as they do in more widely recognized political rivalries.

Examining the issue through the lens of language and performance offers us the chance to step outside the usual ways of understanding the problem and gain new insights into the tradition as a whole. As has already been observed, there are striking differences among the tracts and lawbooks in terms of the style of language in which each is written. The *Hibernensis* is written in Latin, a fact that immediately sets it apart from other contemporary Irish legal compilations.[90] *Críth Gablach* and *Berrad Airechta* are written primarily in standard Old Irish plain and textbook prose of the eighth century,[91] though both (particularly *Berrad Airechta*) also quote frequently from (what purports to be) the traditional oral law known as *Fénechas*; as one might expect, those passages attributed to *Fénechas* tend to display linguistic features characteristic of earlier stages of the language. Plain and textbook styles of prose are also very much the norm in the majority of *Senchas Már* tracts; the two certain *Bretha Nemed* texts, by contrast, are written in a combination of plain and textbook prose on the one hand, and an almost aggressively archaizing, deliberately obscure form of rhetorical Irish that is very difficult to interpret on the other. Indeed, between them these two texts contain more *rosc*-style passages than any other extant tract or lawbook in the tradition. A few rhetorical passages of this sort occur as well in certain *Senchas Már* tracts. However, they are extremely rare, generally much briefer and less flamboyant than the *Bretha Nemed* material, and marginalized within the context of the lawbook as a whole.

It is the argument of this chapter that just as language played a major role in establishing and validating the social and political hierarchies described earlier in this book, so also did it function within the legal sphere to promote the priorities and perspectives of the law schools in which the tracts were written. The observations made above about the language of these texts are, of course, merely generalizations. The linguistic reality of our extant texts is far more complex than can be communicated in such a quick overview. Very few tracts are absolutely consistent stylistically: in most instances, language style can and does vary significantly even within the confines of a single text or compilation. Moreover, it is not always easy to identify linguistic breaks when they occur, nor even to categorize the various styles of language employed in a way that will yield meaningful results. Few could fail to notice a shift from textbook prose to *Fénechas*, given the latter's unusual lexical, syntactical, and grammatical structures.[92] However, many changes in style are infinitely more subtle: a quiet increase in the number of older linguistic forms (for example, the sudden appearance of the preverbal particles "*to*"or "*di*" for later "*do*"), or a brief display of alliteration or exotic vocabulary. Usually these shifts in style last no more than a paragraph or two; often they are confined to a single sentence only. Frequently, what might appear to be a shift in style is actually first and foremost a shift in genre, like when a text changes from plain prose to maxims, or from textbook prose to poetry. Alliteration and parallel adjectival and nominal structures noticeably increase in *Cáin Aicillne*, for example, when the composer turns from his previous topic to tackle the issue of the mutual responsibilities of kindred members, because that latter discussion is largely constructed around a series of maxims.[93]

But if the observations made above regarding style are generalizations, they are nonetheless important. Language matters: the style adopted by a compiler reveals a great deal both about his priorities in writing, and his sense of the tradition within which he is working. So too does the manner in which he chooses (or does not choose) to incorporate language visibly older or different from his own into his work. As has already been remarked, virtually every tract and lawbook in the tradition "mixes" styles to one degree or another. However, not all demarcate the boundaries between these styles or codes in the same manner or to the same degree. Some compilers explicitly signal such changes by ascribing the passages in question to authorities outside their own written work; others pass over them without comment or acknowledgment. To date, differences in the treatment of older or more rhetorical material have typically been taken as reflecting the relative age of the materials included in a given tract or compilation. And in the early stages of early Irish legal historiography, older (looking) material was deemed to be of greater interest than was the text in which it was embedded. Scholars like Binchy saw themselves as excavators whose job it was to sift through the more recent and, it was to be inferred, less interesting and "authentic" layers in the search for the valuable artifacts that might lie buried at the core.[94]

However, as our sense of the relationship between linguistic style and age of composition has changed, so too have our ideas about what makes a particular text important. For most historians today, the goal is less the recovery of the archaic in a given text than an understanding of it as a production integral to itself. Even the most random-appearing compilation of old and new offers a chance of reconstructing the principles and attitudes according to which it was composed; even authors compiling their texts from material already extant in the tradition are likely to put them together in a manner coincident with their own perspectives and priorities. Their work might be careful and deliberate, or it might be hurried or even careless. Not every stylistic shift or archaic passage will be one to which we can attach significance. It is, however, their work, and thus potentially a window on the circumstances in which it was produced. The decisions compilers make about how they present their material, old and new, can reveal a great deal about their purposes for writing, and about the nature of the authority on which they believed their work to rest. The texts before us vary tremendously in the way that they describe the legal past and present: it is from their differences even more than from their similarities that we will learn the most about the jurists who produced them.

What Is *Fénechas* Anyway?

We begin with the *Senchas Már*, the greatest legal production of the age. In order to understand the principles according to which it was constructed, however, it is necessary for comparative purposes to look first at two other prose tracts of roughly the same period that did not form part of the *Senchas Már*, *Críth Gablach* and *Berrad Airechta*. Both have the unusual distinction of being relatively well known even to Celticists not working primarily on early Irish law. *Críth Gablach* was one of the early editions published in the Medieval and Modern Irish Series put out by the Dublin Institute for Advanced Studies and has therefore been used by large numbers of Old Irish learners.[95] *Berrad Airechta* was brilliantly edited and discussed by Thurneysen in 1928 as part of his monumental study of suretyship; a modern English translation was done in 1986 and is still widely available.[96] Due in part to their relative accessibility, these texts have been unusually important in shaping current ideas about the making of the written law; indeed, so influential have they been that they have come in a very real sense to function as paradigms for the making of written law as a whole. For while both are written primarily in plain and textbook prose, both validate their descriptions of contemporary custom and institutions by reference to quotations from what they explicitly identify as *Fénechas*, the archaic, memorized oral lore of the early Irish legal tradition. This reliance on *Fénechas* is usually now taken as characteristic of the legal tradition as a whole. Compilers of the written law tracts inevitably drew not only on their knowledge of contemporary custom, but on *Fénechas*, the oral learning by which native law had been preserved through the ages. So pervasive is this view of the laws, indeed, that the general tendency is to assume that any citation or passage that looks "old" is likely an instance of *Fénechas* even when it is not explicitly identified as such.[97]

And this may well be true. On the other hand, it is also the case that *Fénechas* is a slippery term, one that is at once ubiquitous in the secondary literature on Old Irish law, and yet difficult to define with any degree of precision. For scholars who cut their legal baby teeth on Binchy's edition of *Críth Gablach*—not to mention those whose experience with early Irish law might have begun and ended with that volume—the standard definition is the one Binchy provided in his glossary to that text: "the traditional body of native custom . . . preserved by oral tradition in the law schools."[98] Kelly defined the word in much the same way in his *Guide to Early Irish Law*—"the law of the *Féni*, customary or traditional law"—and while at first glance, Kelly's definition seems more ambivalent on the issue of the oral aspects of the law, his work taken as a whole suggests that he imagines *Fénechas* in terms fairly similar to Binchy's.[99] A modest trundle through the lawbooks and related sources (triads, annals, *dindsenchas*) reveals other shades of meaning to the word. Often *Fénechas* functions as a generic term for "native law" as distinguished from other types of legal dispensation, such as canon law or *cáin* regulation.[100] Perhaps the most unusual usage in the lawbooks occurs in the tract *Din Techtugud*, where *Fénechas* means something like "a legal settlement having been reached"—presumably a reflection of the close relationship perceived to obtain between law having been proclaimed and law having been done.[101]

Considerably more is known now about the complexities of authenticating "orally" transmitted law than it was when Binchy first compiled his glossary, but his definition of the term remains standard still today. This is partly a reflection of Binchy's stature within the field, but partly also an acknowledgment of the fact that this is how the compiler of *Críth Gablach* himself seems to use and understand the word. Twice in his text the compiler cites what purport to be ancient oral customs of the *Féni*, introducing them with the phrase *ara-cain Fénechas*, "as the *Fénechas* sings it."[102] In both cases, the quotations cited display lexical and syntactical characteristics typically associated with *rosc* or *Fénechas*-style material: second-person instructional style, Bergin's Law, tmesis, and alliteration. One purports to give further information about the grade of *fer fothlai*, a rank in between that of the ordinary freeman and that of the lord, stating that "it is of this grade that the *Fénechas* sings."[103] The other appears to be the first sentence of what was likely a longer instructional piece on the subject couched in rhetorical style. Interestingly, while the text attributes the quotation in question to traditional oral law, it makes internal reference to what is presumably a political gathering or court in which matters pertaining to rank were made known: *Ara fesser gráda Féne fri mes [n-]airechta[e] adrímter*, "that you may know the grades of the *Féni*—they are enumerated according to [the] judgment of [the] court."[104] This may be intended merely to allude to the performative venue in which a jurist might be expected to enact his knowledge. On the other hand, the phrasing clearly suggests that this sentence refers to the source, rather than the venue of performance, of the law. The irony is patent: in presupposing active intervention by a court in the shaping of the law, this passage from *Fénechas* seems to contradict the idealized image of a body of custom passed on orally and unchanged from one generation to the next.[105]

Berrad Airechta follows much the same practice as *Críth Gablach*—indeed, the two tracts may even have originated in the same school.[106] Several passages, some of them quite lengthy, are ascribed to *Fénechas*; the fact that the *Berrad Airechta* compiler intended these citations to be read as excerpts from ancient oral tradition is evident both from the verb "sings" in the phrase he used to introduce them, and in their archaic-looking style and language. There are six such mentions in *Berrad Airechta*, all of them interestingly different in nature. Of these six, one omits the promised quotation altogether.[107] Another on fostering practices reads very much like what one would expect traditional oral teaching to look like, although the quotation as we have it cannot represent the original oral phrasing, since a correction or gloss has become entirely embedded within it (*ma fasaith suide no osath*): "Let him return the boy with his goods . . . with his goods is [the fosterling] adjudged until the end of fosterage. For the payment of a person who is not benefited from it is not swallowed up."[108] Two other quotations ascribed to *Fénechas* occur in the (probably) originally independent *Córus Fíadnaise* and reproduce passages or sayings from the (written) *Bretha Nemed* tracts.[109] Either the sources of "traditional oral law" are more complex than we have previously realized, even for the *Berrad Airechta* compiler, or it is a characteristic of (at least some) texts to accord the status of *Fénechas* to the two main tracts from this school.[110]

The only quotations from *Fénechas* that seem visibly performative in nature are a series of maxims, some in verse form, which occur at the end of the tract.[111] A variety of lexical, phonological, and alliterative links bind these maxims to one another in a manner that seems designed both to facilitate memorization and to be aesthetically pleasing—perhaps because they were intended to be appreciated primarily in performance.

Ni hois mana urnais.	Thou shouldst not lend if thou dost not bind,
Arna tois na tartais	for thou shouldst not swear what thou hast not given.
Ni midither na coimditer.	One does not judge something over which one has no control.
Tofet tomus mesu;	Estimation precedes judgments.
Ni forngartaigh na fuisethar senchas;	He who does not acknowledge tradition is no supervisor.
Ni senchae na forngair naill;	He who does not supervise an oath is not a guardian of tradition.
Ni noill cin cogrann;	It is not an oath without the casting of lots;
Ni cogrann cin compersana	It is not lot-casting without persons equal in status.

There is considerable wordplay here: the connections between *senchas* and *senchae* and *forngartaigh* and *forngair* are fairly obvious even to those who do not know the language. Those who have studied Old Irish will recognize also that *midither, coimditer, tomus,* and *mesu* all derive ultimately from the same stem.

Of course, in the wake of work by Breatnach and others on the archaic style in Irish we can no longer be certain about whether phrases of this sort actually are what they purport to be.[112] Indeed, given the embedded gloss, the reference to a political assembly at which laws might be enunciated, and the citations to written tracts, some doubt must exist as to whether even in these two tracts, the meaning of *Fénechas* is as simple and clear cut as we have often taken it to be. However, both the style and the manner of presentation of *Fénechas* passages in these tracts leaves no doubt as to how we are supposed to understand them: as citations from an ancient and, it is to be inferred, relatively stable body of tradition passed on from one generation to the next by chanting poet-jurists. As it happens, Charles-Edwards had recognized already by 1980 that these two tracts might be unusual in their usage of the term. In a footnote to his review of Binchy's *Corpus*, he voiced his suspicion that *Críth Gablach*'s use of the term *Fénechas* to mean "traditional oral law" might be characteristic of only a few tracts in the tradition.[113] But since he then went on in his review to adopt the word *Fénechas* as an umbrella term for any and all instances of ancient and seemingly orally derived material occurring in the lawbooks, whether explicitly identified as excerpts from *Fénechas* or not in the texts in which they occurred, the overall effect of his work was to confirm, rather than call into question, the picture of the law communicated in *Críth Gablach*. For him, the problem was largely one of terminology—what jurists called the early material they were quoting—rather than of agenda or perspective. The basic facts were still the same: at the heart of the written legal tradition lay an identifiable and quotable body of early law known to many, if not to all, jurists as *Fénechas*.[114]

All of which may well be true. My purpose in this chapter is not to challenge the traditional understanding of the term, nor to speculate as to whether what is cited to *Fénechas* in the law tracts might actually derive from ancient oral tradition. Instead I would like to rephrase the question and ask why jurists might choose to present their material(s) in the manner they do, for this has a great deal to teach us about the ways in which different schools and compilers conceptualized the tradition within which they were working. For Charles-Edwards was right: *Críth Gablach* and *Berrad Airechta*'s usage of the word *Fénechas* to mean "traditional oral law" is not representative of the legal tradition as a whole. In the main *Bretha Nemed* texts, for example, *Fénechas* is used at least once and possibly twice to refer to plain prose passages that are manifestly nonarchaic—nonoral, in other words—in style.[115] In one of these instances, the word may even refer to *Críth Gablach* itself: *Gradh flaithemuin co ngraduib feine cotacerta crich* (sic) *gablach a fenechus*, "The lordly rank together with the grades of the *Féni*: *Críth Gablach* declares them in *Fénechas*."[116] A similar usage is visible in the tract on poets *Uraicecht na Ríar*, which Breatnach has argued is to be assigned to the *Bretha Nemed* school. *Uraicecht na Ríar* ascribes three quotations to *Fénechas*. One quotation is couched in relatively plain prose—a style of language that forms a striking contrast to the quotation in *rosc* that follows immediately afterwards, which is not attributed to *Fénechas*, but rather to the mythical poet Neire.[117] The other two quotations are both in *rosc*, but can be shown to come from written legal tracts—indeed, from the main *Bretha Nemed* tracts themselves.[118]

For some compilers, then, the term *Fénechas* appears to have had no necessary implications either of antiquity or of oral origins. Jurists from different schools understood and used the term in very different ways.

Considering how central a term like *Fénechas* was likely to be within the legal tradition as a whole, this variation is interesting in itself. However, the evidence strongly suggests that there is more at stake here than mere differences in usage. For the *Críth Gablach* and *Berrad Airechta* compilers are unusual not merely in their understanding of the term, but in their decision to cite *Fénechas* in their lawbooks in the first place. The vast majority of Irish legal tracts never explicitly cite—indeed most never even mention—*Fénechas* at all. Foremost among this group is the *Senchas Már*. In all of the forty-eight[119] tracts extant partially or in toto that Breatnach has identified as having belonged to this massive lawbook, I have found only one explicit ascription to *Fénechas*—and that in a tract, *Córus Aithni*, which Kelly did *not* assign to the *Senchas Már*, and Breatnach himself appears doubtful about.[120] In fact, so consistently does the *Senchas Már* avoid the practice of citing to *Fénechas* that *Córus Aithni*'s inclusion within the *Senchas Már* is an issue that ought probably to be revisited.[121] Of course, it must be recognized that many *Senchas Már* tracts are extant only in fragments, and that it is possible that this picture might change were more evidence to be forthcoming. For the present, however, the absence of such references seems both deliberate and compelling.

This is not, of course, to say that the *Senchas Már* avoids all old or "oral" looking law—by which is meant phrases or maxims written in what Charles-Edwards defined as "*Fénechas*" style. As was remarked earlier, while the majority of the lawbook by far is composed in plain or textbook prose, older-looking material does occur. The tract on land claims, for example, *Din Techtugud*, is primarily comprised of archaic-looking poetry. However—and significantly—when material of this kind *is* incorporated into *Senchas Már* tracts, it is never ascribed to *Fénechas*. Very occasionally it is attributed to named poets within the tradition, as in the rhetorical section of the tract on physicians' fees, *Bretha Déin Checht*.[122] Much more frequently, however, old-(looking) law is simply incorporated silently into the plain prose material around it without any acknowledgment of a change in register or style. In the plain prose tract *Bretha Crólige*, for example, several stanzas of *Fénechas*-style material are tacked on at the very end of the main body of the text; the break in style is palpable, and yet is never explicitly acknowledged.[123] Similarly, *Di Astud Chirt 7 Dligid*, *Córus Béscnai*, *Cáin Aicillne* and other *Senchas Már* texts cite without comment runs of alliterative maxims, often in verse form, of a sort that in *Berrad Airechta* are ascribed by name to *Fénechas*.[124] In other words, the boundaries between linguistic styles are, in this lawbook, rarely commented upon or explained as they are in the tracts in which *Fénechas* plays a prominent role.

To observe such differences is not, of course, to prove that they matter. However, I would argue that the practice of citing or not citing *Fénechas*, of acknowledging or not acknowledging apparent variations in style or the age of material used, reveals a great deal about that compiler's ideas about the nature of, and authority within, the legal tradition he represents. In citing *Fénechas*, the compilers of *Críth Gablach* and *Berrad Airechta* are seeking to authorize their lawbooks by appeal to something that lies outside of their own written work: an ancient, identifiable, and quotable body of oral tradition. For these jurists, law composed in the present is validated by, and therefore by implication grounded in, a past, which, while implicitly coincident with the present, is nonetheless separable from it. It is a past parts of which can be communicated to succeeding generations of jurists—of all the extant tracts, *Berrad Airechta* seems to reflect most closely the processes and priorities of an oral legal curriculum from around 700 C.E.[125] But it is a past the authority of which resides in its stark refusal to be rooted in a particular time and place, in the mystery that surrounds the context in which the laws associated with it were originally composed and used. Most significantly it is a past which, like all pasts, is accessible now only in excerpts—the very brevity of which imply the existence in days gone by of a broader and potentially no longer fully recoverable body of wisdom.

Indeed, it may even be a deliberately manufactured past. As John Koch points out to me, the word *Fénechas* has not undergone syncope and therefore cannot be linguistically very early. It may even be a construction deliberately modeled on the more familiar (and syncopated) term *senchas*, "tradition, history, tales about the past." Later glossators sought sometimes to explain *senchas* as having derived from *Fénechas* by the substitution of one initial consonant for another, a line of development consistent with a view of the legal tradition that perceived the *Senchas Már* ultimately to have replaced the earlier oral law.[126] However, it is conceivable that the opposite may be nearer to the truth: perhaps *Fénechas* was a term coined on the model of *senchas* by jurists looking to underscore the particular connection of their law both to ancient oral tradition and to the political people the *Féni*. Of course, the *Senchas Már* as a compilation is almost certainly later than both *Críth Gablach* and *Berrad Airechta* and cannot, therefore, itself have been the model in question; the referent here would have to be *senchas* with a small "s" rather than the lawbook we know today as the *Senchas Már*. In any case, legal texts tend to draw either on *Fénechas*, or on *senchas*, but not on both in their characterizations of the authority of the legal tradition, a fact that may speak to real differences in how the schools that produced these texts perceived the nature and authority of that tradition.

For the tracts of the *Senchas Már* stand in stark contrast to *Berrad Airechta* and *Críth Gablach*. Whereas the latter appeal directly to the past in their invocation of *Fénechas*, *Senchas Már* tracts speak instead in the present tense, of how things are done *la Féniu*, "among the *Féni*." *La Féniu* is not, of course, an expression unique to the *Senchas Már*. On the other hand, it is used in that lawbook with a frequency that leaves no doubt as to its significance to the broader agenda of the work. It occurs at least once in more than half of the tracts of the *Senchas Már;* six tracts use it ten or more times, and three tracts more than twenty times apiece.[127] Indeed, the incidence is so high and so striking that one must presume either a high degree of authorial collaboration in the production of the lawbook or, at the very least, considerable editorial intervention at the stage at which its constituent tracts were brought together. But what is most remarkable about this phrase, and what most distinguishes it from the *Fénechas* references of *Críth Gablach* and *Berrad Airechta,* is its focus on the present. In the *Senchas Már,* even old-looking material is presented not as the orally transmitted customs of an ancient and authoritative past, but as the living, breathing traditions of a contemporaneous people.

Moreover, the *Senchas Már* makes no appeal to any body of legal tradition outside itself. The genuine introduction to the lawbook lays it all out quite clearly: native tradition, preserved for generations by the ear-to-ear chantings of poets, has been increased and strengthened by the advent of the church with its technology of literacy.[128] The pertinent changes have been made; the laws most necessary for the efficient functioning of society have been identified and put down in writing. That the laws in question are the laws of the *Senchas Már* is made absolutely clear in the introduction. Appropriate gradations of status were unknown "until the *Senchas Már* came." "It is in the *Senchas Már*" that the proper equivalences among king and clergy and poets have been laid out, that the four great *cáin* regulations of status and lordship and fosterage have been established, that oral contracts have been defined, that confusion has been prevented in the entire world.[129] It is difficult to resist the impression that with this lawbook, the canon has closed—at least in the eyes of the *Senchas Már* compilers and those they manage to persuade. The chantings of poets have, if not ceased, then at least been enclosed within the medium of script. It may not be accidental that the tracts of the *Senchas Már* differ significantly from other lawbooks of the period in referring primarily to poets as historical, as opposed to contemporary, figures on the legal scene, and that the two *Senchas Már* tracts that contain a greater percentage of *Fénechas*-style material than any others in the lawbook introduce or conclude this material with plain prose introductions and conclusions of standard *Senchas Már* style.[130] For this particular compiler, the truths of the past have been absorbed into a new, more modern version of the law, one that is authoritative on its own without envisaging further reference to any older body of native law—one that is the *Senchas Már* itself.

The *Senchas Már's* emphasis on the legal present, and on itself as a—or, more accurately, *the*—source of legal authority, is underscored by its treatment of the historical and mythological personalities to which it makes reference, and by the nature and venue of the performances ascribed to them. The use of the past to talk about the present is more or less ubiquitous throughout the early Irish legal and literary corpus. Almost all early

Irish texts, from poems to saints' lives to annals, make some appeal to pseudohistorical characters and events;[131] like all such texts, the *Senchas Már* has ways of talking about the past and its inhabitants that are particular to itself. In general, *Senchas Már* tracts make less use of fictional characters than do tracts associated with the *Bretha Nemed* school, for example, which may well be deliberate—yet another indication of the "presentist" orientation of the lawbook. It is certainly noticeable that when characters from the past do appear in this lawbook, they tend by and large to cluster around certain tracts, most notably *Din Techtugud* and *Di Chetharshlicht Athgabála*.[132] Most interesting of all, however, are those characters whose names seem to underscore the authority of particular written tracts within the *Senchas Már* itself. Many of those whose presence can be inferred in the lawbook are mythological craftsmen who have given their names to tracts focusing on the subject of their particular art: *Bretha Déin Chécht*, *Bretha Crédine*, *Bretha Goibnenn*, *Bretha Luchtaine*, and the like. Two are jurists, Sencha and Bríg, and it may not be coincidental that they, unlike the others, appear in more than one tract of this particular lawbook. Sencha is the judge of Ulster's legendary king Conchobar, and is thus a famous figure in his own right. What may be more pertinent to his appearance in this context, however, is the fact that his name is related to *senchas*, as in *Senchas Már*—in other words, his very name serves to reinforce the authority of the lawbook in which he appears. Bríg (whose name means "high status, privilege") is a female judge whose sole role in the texts in which she appears (*Din Techtugud* and *Di Chetharshlicht Athgabála*) is to deliver herself of authoritative verdicts regarding women's legal issues. In one gloss, she is identified as *ingen Sencha*, the "daughter of Sencha," and is thus almost certainly a doublet of her famous father—and, through him, of the lawbook with which he shares his name.[133]

The most important exception to this (relative) reluctance to use fictional characters is St. Patrick, whose revision of native law Breatnach has identified as a "recurrent theme" in the *Senchas Már*.[134] In fact the matter could be phrased more forcefully even than Breatnach has done, for Patrick is essential to this lawbook. Not only do the vast majority of Patrician references in the legal tradition as a whole occur in the *Senchas Már*, his story is told or alluded to in all three parts of this tripartite compilation: in five tracts for certain, likely eight, and possibly even more, given the incomplete state in which many of the tracts have been preserved.[135] Indeed, Patrick appears so frequently that his presence in this lawbook simply must be deliberate, a way in which to underscore themes central to the compiler. Even more striking than the number of times Patrick appears is the thematic consistency of the stories told about him. Despite his identity as a historical figure, in his appearances in the *Senchas Már*, he is as much a creature of the present as of the past. Almost always he appears as someone whose intervention has shaped the law into what it is today, in its written form, the *Senchas Már*. The legend of Patrick's encounter with Dubthach and his role in the initial writing down of native Irish law is told or alluded to constantly throughout the lawbook.[136] That the *Senchas Már* is to be regarded as the ultimate end result of this initial collaborative event is clearly implied in the original introduction to the lawbook, which roots the production of written law in the reconciliation of native oral custom with written Christian doctrine.[137] Whether the *Senchas Már* is supposed to be viewed as the actual product of the encounter, or simply as the end result of a process set in motion by that encounter, is unclear. What is certain—stated directly, in fact—is that the world was disordered and unregulated "before the *Senchas Már* came."[138]

Patrick's other appearances in the lawbook reinforce this sense of his story serving as an origin legend not merely for law in general, but for the *Senchas Már* specifically. Many of his reported actions either relate directly to particular tracts within the lawbook, or anticipate provisions described therein. With Patrick's advent, for example, the mutual obligations of church and people are said to have been clarified—that is *Córus Béscnai* in a nutshell.[139] It is Patrick who is alleged to have determined the regulations pertaining to hostage-suretyship laid out in *Bésgnae Ráithe*,[140] and Patrick who is envisaged as having corrected the property abuses detailed in *Do Astud Chirt 7 Dligid*.[141] Patrick establishes the fines for theft laid out in *Bretha im Gatta*,[142] and leaves unaltered the regulations regarding dogs preserved today in *Bretha for Conshlechtaib*.[143] In other words, Patrick's actions are imagined entirely within the context of the tracts that record them—tracts of the *Senchas Már* itself. He may be a figure of the past, but for the compiler his true significance lies very much in the legal present.

Bretha Nemed

That this focus on the text at hand is both deliberate and significant becomes immediately apparent when the *Senchas Már* is put side by side with other legal productions of the period. The principal *Bretha Nemed* tracts, particularly *Bretha Nemed Tóisech* and *Bretha Nemed Déidenach*,[144] manifest a sense of authority that is very different from that displayed by *Berrad Airechta*, *Críth Gablach* and other contemporary texts. As we have seen, the two principal *Bretha Nemed* tracts contain a great deal of rhetorical and archaic (looking) language. However, they make only infrequent appeal to *Fénechas*, and even when they do cite it their sense of its likely nature and origin differs significantly from that characteristic of *Berrad Airechta* and *Críth Gablach*.[145] Passages ascribed to *Fénechas* in texts traditionally assigned to the *Bretha Nemed* school, where they can be identified, either reproduce passages from written tracts (one could almost make the argument that for the *Uraicecht na Ríar* compiler, *Bretha Nemed Tóisech* and *Bretha Nemed Déidenach* <u>are</u> *Fénechas*), or are written in plain or textbook style (for example, nonoral, nonarchaic). In other words, whatever the reality behind the composition of these "*Fénechas*" passages, they do not appear to have been regarded by compilers of the *Bretha Nemed* school as necessarily oral or antique in origin. Perhaps this is why that on at least some of these occasions, the verb used to introduce the quotation is the less evocative *as-beir* or *dicit*, "says," rather than *ar-cain*, "sings."[146] Indeed, the *Bretha Nemed Tóisech* compiler seems to make such a distinction when he differentiates between *Fénechas* as "related" (*co-tacerta*) in unornamented prose in *Críth Gablach* and *Fénechas* as "sung" (*aruscan*) in verse by the poet Athairne.[147]

Fénechas, understood in its traditional sense, thus does not seem to have played much of a role in establishing the authority of the *Bretha Nemed* tracts in the way that it so clearly does in *Berrad Airechta* and *Críth Gablach*. Nor is the *Bretha Nemed* sense of authority any more coincident with that displayed in the *Senchas Már*. Patrick, so central a figure in the *Senchas Már*, appears only once in the two main *Bretha Nemed* tracts, and then only in a story that has clearly been modeled on the myth related in the *Senchas Már*.[148] Here, instead of validating the native legal tradition and overseeing its translation into written Christian form as he does in the *Senchas Már*, Patrick—acting again in concert with Dubthach, and in the reign of Lóegaire mac Néill—is depicted as the sanctifier and renewer of a *Cáin Einech*, "Law of Honor," promulgated by the kings and poets of Ireland at "the beginning of the world." The purpose of this "law" is apparently to confirm the rights—and perhaps even the obligation—of poets to act in enforcing claims across mutually hostile borders (*idir chríochaibh imdergaibh*) in instances where no previous alliance, or treaty, or legal understanding exists to regulate cross-boundary disputes.[149] In other words, the focus here is not the authority of a particular lawbook, nor even the reconciliation of native and Christian custom generally. Rather, the intent is to underscore the political and legal prerogatives of a social group the members of which appear primarily in *Bretha Nemed* tracts as *contemporary* as well as historical figures—poets. The use of the word *cáin* in this context is quite interesting. Normally *cánai* were promulgated and enforced by kings and clerics working together in collaboration to achieve a moral or charitable end—the relief of famine, for example, or ensuring the sanctity of Sunday, or arranging for the protection of women or other entities vulnerable to violence.[150] In choosing the word "*cáin*" to characterize the mythical "legislation" described here, the composer is projecting poets into a political and moral position normally occupied by the church—as we shall see, an important theme in *Bretha Nemed* tracts generally.

Indeed, *Bretha Nemed's* sense of the past and its relationship to the present differs significantly from that of other contemporary legal compilations.[151] Instead of citing Patrick or *Fénechas* as authorities, *Bretha Nemed* authors (purport to) quote instead from mythical poets of the pre-Christian era. Much of *Bretha Nemed Déidenach* consists of what are presented as verbatim poetic recitations from various poetic authorities, including Athairne, Neire, Morann, Nin, Senchán Torpéist, and some poetically inclined kings (speaking usually in their judicial capacity), such as Cormac and Conchobar.[152] Additional poets and kings are referred to by name or invoked as authorities on particular subjects or events—Amairgen, Roighin, Ferchertne, and Áed Sláne, for example.[153] And many passages are introduced simply with *as de asbeir an file*, "it is regarding this that the poet says."[154] What is true of *Bretha Nemed Déidenach* is true as well of *Bretha Nemed Toísech*: most of this tract also consists of self-contained poetic proclamations (often with a *dúnad* structure, where the last line echoes or repeats the first) addressed either by Morann to Neire or Neire to Morann. *Uraicecht na Ríar*, which is written largely in plain/textbook prose, contains only a few such citations, but they are also to poets of a bygone era,[155] and the basic conceit of *Audacht Morainn*, "The Testament of Morann," is that the text represents oral instructions sent by Morann to Neire so that he might advise King Feradach Find Fechtnach in the fundamentals of royal comportment. It is worth noting also that while many (and, in the case of *Bretha Nemed Déidenach*, most) of the topics addressed in these poems relate to poets or poetry, some of them do not. To Nin is attributed a long address on suretyship, for example, while Cormac speaks rhetorically about accomplices to the commission of a crime and Conchobar about intentional wounding.[156]

Interestingly, while poets are nearly ubiquitous throughout the *Bretha Nemed* tradition, there are clear differences among the various tracts as to who is cited and why. Athairne is the character most frequently cited in *Bretha Nemed Déidenach*, which is, as the title given it by Gwynn suggests, an "Old-Irish Tract on the Privileges and Responsibilities of Poets." It is not overall a terribly well-organized treatise, but rather a hodgepodge of reflections, sayings, and stories on subjects pertaining to poetry and poets. There is a clear theme to the tract as a whole, however: the boundlessness of poetic power and the rewards due to those who command it. Subjects covered include the metrical accomplishments of the various poetic ranks and the unchallengeability of gifts given to them, their relations with other *nemed* classes, and their rights to honor-price, protection, and privileges within the community. Not surprisingly, satire is a principal theme—in fact the text begins with the poet Athairne cursing the river Modarn (Mourne) for having overflowed its bounds. Danger and reward are constantly invoked,[157] and (as may have been the case in real life) the line between gifts given voluntarily and gifts compelled by the threat of satire is never sharply drawn. Poets are hailed among other things for their "wondrous knowledge" (*eolus iongnadh*)[158] of how to compose poetry that skates along the knife edge separating muted or excessive praise from outright satire (*áor go ndath molta 7 moladh go ndath náoire*).[159] And in one series of poems, entitled *Ail[iu] tighe tre filidecht*, "I request houses through the practice of po-

etry," a mythical poet makes a list of rhetorical demands of an unseen patron that range from the houses of the title to plentiful portions of sweet-
tasting ale and water.[160] Gwynn expresses surprise that it should be
Athairne, the powerful and obnoxiously greedy satirist of early Irish tradition, who serves in this tract as the primary representative of the poetic
order, but the tract's emphasis on the power of and rewards due the poetic
voice makes him an entirely appropriate choice.[161]

Bretha Nemed Toísech also has a great deal to say about poets but focuses on
an entirely different aspect of their life and craft. In this text, education is
an important theme, as is the inherently superior knowledge held by members of a particular craft or *nemed* group about their individual professions.
As has already been mentioned, it has been argued that *Bretha Nemed Toísech*
is a tripartite text, each section of which was written by a member of a different *nemed* group—a cleric, a poet, and a judge.[162] Each third focuses on
issues pertinent to the group of which its author was a member, although
the third part on judges clearly presumes that the categories of poet and
judge will frequently and naturally overlap. What is most interesting about
this tract is that all three sections situate what they have to say in the context
of the schoolroom. Part one, on the church, quotes only one person, Cenn
Fáelad mac Ailella, who is said in the Annals of Ulster to have died in 679.[163]
Cenn Fáelad is indeed a historical figure, but his importance in Irish legal
tradition stems more from the mythology that later evolved around his having become a student at three schools simultaneously—one a school of poetry and native law, one of monastic learning, and one of *Fénechas*.[164] His
presence in the part of the tract that deals with the church is itself a statement about the compatibility of ecclesiastical with native learning—a compatibility that lies at the heart of the structure, authorship, and imagery of
the text itself.[165]

The other two sections of *Bretha Nemed Toísech* are similar to *Bretha Nemed
Déidenach* in having largely been structured around (purported) quotations
from various authoritative poetic and legal figures. As with the first part of
the text, however, education is very much to the fore. Part two envisages a
pupil (presumably Neire) calling on Morann for instruction.[166] Part three
is the opposite. There it is the Morann the teacher who speaks to his largely
silent pupil: *Mo Nere Nuallgnaid, diamba brithem, ba fírbreithech; as misi morand
fírbreithech,*[167] "My Neire accustomed to proclaiming, if you would be a
judge, be true-judging: it is I, true-judging Morann." The rhetorical structure and linking alliteration characteristic of some of these passages may
suggest that they were composed in such a way as to facilitate memorization.[168] It is possible that what we have here are compositions the memorization of which formed a significant part of the oral curriculum within
the *Bretha Nemed* school—perhaps instructor and pupil even assumed the
"poetic masks" of Morann and Neire when performing these and similar
passages for those in attendance.[169] Indeed, as was suggested earlier, if per-

formances of this sort did constitute a significant learning technique within the school, this might be why the *Bretha Nemed* tracts make so much greater use of fictional characters and tales than do other legal texts of the period. It would be interesting to know whether the difference in perspectives visible in these two sections of the tract (for example, pupil invoking instructor/instructor addressing pupil) reflects real differences in approach within the disciplines of poetry and law. It is certainly of interest that the style of the jurists' section of the tract is no less rhetorical than that aimed at poets: in this school jurists as well as poets must learn poetic techniques if they are to succeed at their craft.

Texts of the *Bretha Nemed* school seem thus to localize authority within their tradition in a manner different from that adopted by compilations produced in other legal schools of the period: specifically, in the rhetorical performances of mythical poets and jurists rather than in the wisdom of *Fénechas* or the doings of St. Patrick. That this constitutes a deliberate strategy on the part of the *Bretha Nemed* redactors designed to underscore the main themes and priorities of their work cannot be doubted. As might be expected from the title of the two principal tracts and, through them, of the school from which they emerged, the *nemed* classes (chief among them poets and jurists) are the primary focus of these texts. *Audacht Morainn* counts craftsmen and crafts among the attributes of the tribe that the king must be competent to assess,[170] and the two "primers," *Uraicecht Becc* and *Uraicecht na Ríar*, detail the ranks of *nemed*s (in the case of *Uraicecht na Ríar*, poets specifically), outlining their qualifications and entitlements within the community. How these classes are to be defined varies somewhat from text to text. It is a general characteristic of *Bretha Nemed* texts to include low-status persons among the *nemed* classes, although the texts are equally explicit that the acquisition of numerous skills will lead to greater enfranchisement.[171] With respect to noble *nemed* persons, there are some discrepancies. Part three of *Bretha Nemed Toísech* counts three noble *nemed*s, church[man], lord, and poet, while part one counts four—church[man], lord, poet, and *ecnae*, or ecclesiastical scholar.[172] *Bretha Nemed Déidenach* also adopts the latter stance,[173] although logic would suggest that the threesome is the earlier schema.[174]

But it is not simply with the task of defining the *nemed* ranks that these redactors are preoccupied. A primary purpose of parts two and three of *Bretha Nemed Toísech* particularly is to lay claim to very specific prerogatives on behalf of the *nemed* classes, most particularly poets. Chief among these are claims to jurisdictional authority over the art or craft in question. Part two on poets puts the matter quite clearly: *cach nimidh a riar, cach dan a dliged . . . oscer cach a ceird araile*,[175] "to every *nemed* [belongs] his authority (*riar*), to every art its entitlement (*dliged*) . . . everyone is ignorant in the craft of another." Even more explicit is a passage from part three of that same text:

Mo nere nuallngnaidh, diamba brithemh, berur gach ndan do reir a suadh fadeisin, ar us cinmota saí cach dana rosuiged (?) bretha 7 brithemuin la [Féniu], ar us sain eolus cach dana condad sain a mbretha 7 a mbrithemuin, ar ni bera for ae ancesa, ainb cach a ceird aroile, arfoilge fodluim fircerda . . . oscar cach a ceird ar.ii.[176]

My Neire accustomed to proclaiming, if you would be a judge, let every art be judged under the authority (*ríar*) of its own expert, for judgments and judges have been established together with the expert of every art, since the knowledge of every art is separate, so that their judgments and their judges be separate, for you[177] ought not to pass judgment on cases where you are ignorant.[178] Ignorant is everyone in the craft of another; learning underlies true craftsmen;[179] an outsider is everyone in the craft of another.

Of special interest here is the use of the term *ríar*, "rule, stipulation, authority," for while it can carry the general meaning of "demand" or "wish," its normal meaning in legal contexts is "authority, jurisdiction" in the sense that a lord has jurisdiction over his clients, or an abbot over his monks.[180] In this context, the reference would appear from the passage cited above to be a judicial one—a claim that members of the *nemed* classes ought not to be subject to judicial decisions from external authorities, at least with respect to controversies arising concerning their craft. That specialists charged with rendering judgment on matters pertaining to their profession existed is made clear in *Uraicecht Becc*, which speaks both of a judge whose expertise is centered on *filidecht*, "poetry,"[181] and a "craftsman judge" whose judicial purview includes the "valuation and measuring and fashioning and remuneration of every product."[182]

The precise nature of the privileges being asserted in these passages is unclear. At the very least, *Bretha Nemed Toísech*, and perhaps other *Bretha Nemed* texts as well, would appear to be laying claim to immunity for the *nemed* classes from traditional hierarchies of judgment within the community regarding professional matters—in other words, the right to exercise jurisdiction, including legal jurisdiction, over themselves as a profession. Presumably such authority was imagined as usually being exercised in conjunction with, rather than at the expense of, the ruler of the community. *Audacht Morainn*, for example, envisages a collaborative relationship obtaining between Neire and his king: King Feradach is imagined as the one ultimately responsible for judgments passed on crafts and craftsmen, but Neire is clearly the one advising him.[183] And even those passages most assertive of clerical independence (as we shall see, the likely model for *Bretha Nemed*'s claims) envisage the king being involved in cases pertaining to clerics.[184] It is uncertain whether the prerogatives asserted here were conceptualized as extending beyond strictly professional matters to encompass any and all legal cases in which poets, jurists, and craftsmen might be involved, regardless of whether the issues implicit in these disputes were professional in nature. This was certainly the claim made in some quarters with respect to the "ultimate" *nemed*, the church. Even ordinary members of the Christian community were instructed to stay away from legal dealings with pagans in the "First Synod of St. Patrick," as we have seen. And a chapter heading in the *Hibernensis* is entitled *De eo, quod non judicandi sunt clerici a laicis, sed laici a clericis judicandi sunt,* "Regarding this, that clerics are not to be judged by laics, but laics are to be judged by clerics."[185]

Whether the privileges claimed for the poetic classes obtained in reality as well as in theory is, of course, another question altogether. Certainly *Bretha Nemed* authors were not afraid to stake out positions that others at the time would have regarded as extreme. Ó Corráin, Breatnach, and Breen have pointed already to what they call "the extravagant claims made for church law" in *Bretha Nemed Toísech* particularly. Church lawsuits (*ai ecalsa*) there are characterized as a *muir tar glasa,*[186] "a sea [flowing] across streams"—in other words, a force that cannot be contravened by the petty legal claims brought by men of the world. Such a radical vision of ecclesiastical privilege must surely have been a position with which many in that period would have disagreed.[187] It is certainly possible that what we are seeing in the *Bretha Nemed* passages on poetic jurisdiction is a reflection of actual historical privileges traditionally enjoyed by the *nemed* of Munster. On the other hand, given also that there are few hints of such autonomy to be found elsewhere in lawbooks emanating from other schools, the idea that *nemed*s of all social backgrounds ought to exercise authority over their own might have been one the redactors of *Bretha Nemed* were trying to effect rather than describe.

In any case, the manner in which these prerogatives are asserted in the *Bretha Nemed* texts make it likely that whatever their relationship to "real life," they are at heart intellectualized constructions of poetic privilege modeled on the example of the church.[188] The patterning of secular ranks or privileges after those of the church is a well-known practice among the jurists. *Críth Gablach,* to cite just one example, states outright that it is by analogy with the grades of the church that the grades of the laity have been established.[189] And the maxim *cach nemed a ríar,* "to every *nemed* belongs his authority," which is used in *Bretha Nemed* to justify jurisdictional independence for poets and craftsmen, occurs also in the *Senchas Már* tract on church-community relations, *Córus Béscnai.* In *Córus Béscnai* the context is clearly ecclesiastical: the phrase occurs in a paragraph designed to make the point that only churches that maintain the proper control over their members and remain "innocent" of misdeeds are entitled to their proper dues.[190] Of course, it is difficult to determine the original referent of a maxim like this—in other words, to infer from these two sources what the original point of the maxim might have been. The possibility that the *Bretha Nemed* authors have here appropriated a maxim usually used with respect to the church for the benefit of the poets whose cause they were advocating remains a strong one, but cannot ultimately be proved.

This possibility is strengthened, however, by a phenomenon to which Ó

Corráin, Breatnach, and Breen have recently drawn attention. As they have shown, imagining clerics in Old Testament terms as Levites, with all the special judicial prerogatives pertaining thereunto, became something of a topos among certain canonists and ecclesiastically educated legal scholars in Ireland.[191] Such privileges were originally claimed only for the church. However, in *Uraicecht na Ríar* (a *Bretha Nemed* text), they were extended to poets in imitation of the clerical model. Since freedom from outside jurisdiction was one of the qualities associated with the Levites by the canonists, it seems likely that the extension of jurisdictional independence to poets that we see in the *Bretha Nemed* tracts ought to be understood as yet another aspect of the canonists' construction of churchmen and, from there, other noble *nemed*s in the Levite vein. There is some question as to how widespread such perceptions would have been. Ó Corráin, Breatnach, and Breen suggest that the "clericalization" of the poetic class obtained generally "in Irish thinking." In fact, however, *Uraicecht na Ríar* is the only unambiguous evidence they cite for such an equation,[192] and given how well this idea meshes with the main themes of the *Bretha Nemed* tracts, the notion of poets as Levites may have been less of a general perception than a construction associated specifically with the *Bretha Nemed* school.

In fact, the evidence suggests that these Levitical parallels were probably a crucial element in the case the *Bretha Nemed* authors were making on behalf of poets and other *nemed*s in their work. The Levite classes as defined in the Old Testament included both judges and Temple performers; as Ó Corráin, Breatnach, and Breen have suggested, the latter have often been interpreted as prophets and could thus easily have been affiliated to the *filid* in the minds of Irish intellectuals.[193] The desire to construct poets and other noble *nemed*s as Levites likely also helps to explain other aspects of the *Bretha Nemed* redactors' characterization of these groups. Purity was, of course, a general concern throughout the church. Numerous sources across the legal spectrum make clear that the special prerogatives of churches were widely viewed in Ireland as being contingent on their moral character. Churches that did not maintain their proper "purity" (*idnae*) and "innocence" (*enncae*) lost thereby the privileges and exemptions to which they would normally have been entitled. This point is made over and over again in part one of *Bretha Nemed Toísech* on the church,[194] and in fact is a view found outside texts of the *Bretha Nemed* school as well. *Berrad Airechta*, for example, holds that alms and offerings and fees made to the church or its clergy are valid only if the institution and individuals concerned are morally free from fault.[195]

Assuming that the *Bretha Nemed* redactors were indeed modeling their vision of the proper prerogatives of the *nemed* class on the example of the church, it is not surprising to find purity as a major theme in those texts as well. However, given the Levites' connections both with ritual purity and with the teaching of the law, the reference was almost certainly more pointed than that. Two of the central themes in the *Bretha Nemed* texts are the purity and innocence of the *nemed* classes and their relationship to learning. *Uraicecht na Ríar* speaks of the poet who "illuminates nobility" not only through the extent of his mastery of the poetic craft and his poetic heritage, but "through his purity" (*tria idnai*) as well. This purity it defines in various ways, all of which would have been recognizable to those charged with assessing the purity of a priest and his church, including abstaining from the commission of crimes and the observance of religiously grounded restrictions on sexual activity.[196] Nor are noble poets the only persons of *nemed* status depicted as being subject to such requirements. *Uraicecht Becc*'s answer to the question of what gives honor-price to members of the *daernemed* ("base" or "unfree" *nemed*) classes is *airilliud 7 inrucus 7 idna*,[197] "merit and integrity and purity."

The purity of the *nemed* classes is an important theme in *Uraicecht na Ríar* and *Uraicecht Becc*, but it is really in the two principal *Bretha Nemed* tracts that the significance and implications of this idea are most clearly articulated. *Bretha Nemed Déidenach* lists purity, integrity, and modesty (*go niodhna, go niondracus, go bfele*) as elements that ennoble poets.[198] In the "estimation judgments" attributed later in the text to Morann, in which are listed the qualities according to which a variety of products and individuals (for example, iron, gold, garments, young girls, wood, horses) are to be measured, poets are said to be judged according to *ar a nionnracus 7 a ndruine, a niodhna*,[199] "their integrity, their skill, and their purity." Innocence (*enncus*) is clearly in this tract a desideratum even for bards, normally regarded as less accomplished and honorable members of the poetic profession.[200] In *Bretha Nemed Toísech* also the purity of the *nemed* classes is depicted as being essential both to their effectiveness and to any privileges to which they might lay claim. Part one on the church has already been discussed—the purity and appropriate behavior of the clergy is one of the central points of the piece.[201] Equally interesting, however, is part three on judges, which begins by stressing the behavioral requirements of the office—a resistance to bribes, and a commitment to judge according to truth as it can best be determined.[202] In this text, *nemed* status is inextricably interlinked with purity and honorable behavior—in fact, the tract contains a minitreatise on the importance of purity, learning, and proper poetic training that leaves no doubt as to the importance of ethical behavior: *dligthech cach nemed, nemed gach nidhan . . . Nibi nemedh nab tre cach aon indruic*,[203] "every *nemed* is lawful, every pure one is a *nemed . . .* he who is not honorable in every matter is not a *nemed*." Purity is even said to be one of the grounds on which payment for each poetic rank is determined, along with education and quality artistic production;[204] as in *Uraicecht na Ríar*, purity is defined here in a manner that seems intended to project poets (and presumably members of the *nemed* class generally) into the position of Levites. Thus is it said to be the "purity of marital relationship, purity of hand, purity of mouth, and the purity of learning that cleanses the impurity of every [type of] poetic composition."[205]

The connection visible in this last quotation between purity and learning is of particular interest, in that it speaks to another major theme of the *Bretha Nemed* texts, the key importance of education to *nemed* status and privileges, especially that gained by apprenticeship and/or attendance at a professional course of study. An obvious manifestation of this theme is the sheer number of times terms related to learning appear in these tracts: *eólas*, "knowledge," *fis*, "knowledge, information," *féth*, "knowledge, technical skill," *foglaimm*, "learning," *frithgnam*, "course of study." The contrast between those who are trained and knowledgeable in a given art, and those who are not (*oscar*, "unskilled, ignorant," *ainb*, "ignorant," *ainbfeith*, "unskilled," *aineolach*, "ignorant") is a point returned to time and again in all *Bretha Nemed* tracts.[206] In *Uraicecht na Ríar*, poetic rank is said to be decided not only by the poems composed and performed, but also by the course of study undertaken.[207] *Uraicecht Becc* makes it clear that literate learning (*legend*) automatically entails franchise.[208] And all three parts of *Bretha Nemed Toísech* equate advancing in the various professions to which the tract is devoted—church, poetry, and judgeship—with increased attendance at study and the acquisition of new skills. Bishops are distinguished from lower ecclesiastical ranks by virtue of having had forty years' exposure to *bélrae bán*, the "fair language" of the church.[209] Among poets, the percentage of honor-price due the different levels of poet is determined in part by the percentage of the artistic corpus they are determined to have mastered through study.[210] Judges too are expected through training to gain mastery over the law in all its aspects.[211] The links between the poet-jurists who are the main focus of the last two sections of the tract and other members of the *nemed* classes is made clear by a passage in which poets are actually portrayed as craftsmen—artists who work with knowledge in the way that a goldsmith might work with gold or a builder with tools.[212]

What is also clear from these texts is that learning and purity were viewed as necessary concomitants of one another. It is the "purity of learning" that cleanses the stains from flawed poetic compositions—stains that are by definition as much moral as they are artistic.[213] Impure persons (*anidan*) are depicted as inherently ignorant and unsound in judgment; their intellectual and moral flaws defile what is true and just, like blood upon a fresh white cloth or bitter tastes among the sweet.[214] Advancing in learning is not merely an intellectual achievement, it is a moral triumph, one with dramatic consequences for the proper order of society.[215] Breatnach has suggested that in an earlier period, high-status *filid* were not as separate from bards as they would later become. *Filid* looking to exalt their position and prerogatives modeled themselves on the ranks of the church, using scholarship as a basis on which to distinguish themselves from their less aristocratic and educated poetic colleagues.[216] This scholarship was in large part ecclesiastical in nature: poets learned to compose works in traditional meters the content of which often reflected the latest in Latin ecclesiastical writings.[217] Just as clerics advanced in spiritual rank and prestige as they advanced in learning, so also did poets—hence the link between purity and learning, art and rank.

Industrious scholarship, impeccable heritage, morally correct deportment—and of course artistic ability—all, according to *Bretha Nemed Tóisech*, were necessary elements of high *nemed* status, and all were mutually referential and sustaining. This sense of poets as learned artists engaged in a complex balancing act, a joining together of the elements perceived to be crucial to their art, is captured even in the lexicon drawn on by the tract's redactor. One of the most intriguing and oft repeated terms in the text is the word *ellach*, the verbal noun of *in-loing*, which also appears in conjugated form. Usually (and accurately) *ellach* is translated "poem, poetic composition," and *in-loing* as "compose," as in "he composes poetry."[218] However, the literal meaning of these words has to do with "joining" or "uniting together," and it is difficult to resist the sense that in many cases the text seems to be speaking not merely to the "joining together" of the elements of a poem, but to the uniting of something much broader: the technical skills and education that make poetic production possible, the familial legacy of craftsmanship that authorizes the performer and his product, and the moral and religious experience of the poet. *Ellach* used in this expanded sense thus constitutes an intentional play on words, a way of speaking about the production of artistic language by exploiting levels within that language.

Ellach, used in a sense that seems to supersede the strictly technical aspects of poetic composition, appears time and again in different venues.[219] Most striking is a passage from *Bretha Nemed Tóisech*'s "minitreatise" on learning and purity:

> *ni fogluim nad ellaing, nid ellaing nad ellaincc nath. . . . cach foghluim fogluim co hellach, ar us nemid cach fili iar nelluch arabeir for idnai. . . . anbobracht gac fili cin ellach, dall cach grad can idna., anidan cach fili arabeir can fogluim no cin fotha, fotha filed fogluim, fogluim filed firellach firidna.*[220]

He who does not compose (*ellaing*) does not learn, he who does not compose (*ellaincc*) a *nath*-poem[221] does not compose (*ellaing*). . . . Learning coupled with [the] joining together (*ellach*) [of the elements of poetry] is every [true] learning, for each poet who proceeds on the basis of purity in accordance with *ellach* is a *nemed*. . . . Every poet without *ellach* is [like] a person wasting away from disease, every grade without purity is blind, every poet who pleads without learning or without foundation is impure, learning [constitutes] the foundation of poets, true composing (*firellach*) [and] true purity[222] [constitute] the learning of poets.

In this context, it is significant also that the phrase *ni neme nad elluing, ni elluing nad elluing nath*, "he is no *nemed* who does not compose, he who does not compose a *nath*-poem does not compose," also occurs earlier in the tract in connection with passages repudiating the efficacy of verses composed by unskilled or imperfectly educated poets.[223] Phrases like these speak not merely to the lexical and syntactical weightiness of a poem, but to the balance of elements of morality, skill, learning, and heritage, from which true art derives.[224]

And it is here that we return to the issue of language, which for the *Bretha Nemed* redactors constitutes both a subject for discussion and a means of communication about that subject. As we have seen, one of the primary goals of the authors of these texts is to exalt the *nemed* classes by highlighting both the special jurisdictional privileges to which they ought to be entitled, and the moral and educational qualities from which those privileges were believed to derive. Since the art with which these authors are most concerned is poetry (including judicial poetry), it is not surprising that they make their case not merely through argumentation, but through a deliberate display of the power of a poet's most precious artistic resource, language. It is no accident that the language of these texts is as rich, complex, and elaborately obscure as it is, for the two main *Bretha Nemed* tracts are first and foremost showpieces for the poetic art they are attempting to exalt. Nor is it incidental to the larger purposes of their authors that rhetorical performances—whether by the poet-jurists of the past or by the redactors of the present—constitute the backbone of both texts. Even subjects as mundane as the fiefs taken by clients or the rules governing suretyship can become poetic occasions: at once a chance to educate future jurists in the language of the law, and a celebration of the power of poetry when performed by persons of the appropriate moral and artistic background.

But if highlighting the privileges due those who can manipulate this resource is one goal of these texts, another is ensuring that all those who lay claim to the benefits of *nemed* status are actually entitled to it. The strength of language as a foundation for power is also its great weakness: even those without proper training in the tradition can learn to speak in ways that to nonprofessionals may imply a moral and technical background that the speakers in question do not have. Distinguishing properly trained poets from "pretenders" was a serious concern in early Ireland, as is evident from a practice referred to in many sources whereby a person with some degree of poetic training (usually a *drisiuc*) would meet incoming poets at the borders for the purpose of assessing the "correctness" of their meters before allowing them to advance further into the territory.[225] As we have seen, the sources suggest considerable tension both within and without the poetic profession about its standing and prerogatives. Outsiders were often hostile to the broad powers claimed by poets in politics, society, and law; within the profession, educated *filid* found themselves threatened by the low-status or only partially educated versifiers they perceived to be seeking their jobs.

The previous chapter detailed how frequently in Irish literature generally metaphors of speech and silence were used to separate "deserving" *filid* from their ignorant and ignoble competitors. In fact, although enough evidence exists to suggest that the contrast between speaking and not speaking was used generally throughout early Irish tradition as a way of talking about power and its absence, most of the evidence with respect to poets specifically comes from *Bretha Nemed* texts. Clearly the threat posed by illborn, undereducated, or even dubiously Christian poets and jurists was one taken particularly seriously in this school.

Indeed, it is impossible to overestimate the centrality of the theme of appropriate versus inappropriate speakers in these texts, since the point is made over and over again in a variety of ways. Both of the principal *Bretha Nemed* tracts issue warnings about uneducated would-be jurists: *Ní erba bretha i mbeolaibh ainbféth. Ar nád aoí éttrocht tre aineolus neble*,[226] "May you not entrust judgments into the mouths of the ignorant, for a lawsuit is not [rendered] brilliant[227] through the ignorance of shameless persons." Sometimes humor is used to mock those not qualified to speak. The perils attendant upon the speech of the ignorant are brilliantly illustrated in *Bretha Nemed Tóisech*, for example, through a speech put into the mouth of one Dub mac Da Dochunn, "Dimwit son of Two Twits." In a difficult poem rife with imagery pertaining to speech and silence, Dub mourns the fact that the legal complaints of people like himself are routinely "sung away" by (properly trained) judges.[228] Nor is the use of wordplay underscoring the inherent superiority of the learned restricted to the prerogatives of poets and jurists. To those accustomed to thinking of all grades of the church as exalted persons, *Bretha Nemed Tóisech*'s injunction *Aill nad amrae recht dorsaid duim sceo glantaid*, "hear that the doorkeeper of a church is not a wondrous person, nor [lit. and] the exorcist," may come as something of a surprise. However, the rationale for this seemingly gratuitous insult becomes apparent in the second half of this same passage, where listeners are advised to accord particular respect to the bishop in accordance with his years of training in the "white language" of the law. This respect is characterized in the text as *scoth nádbi drochduini drécht*, "speech that is not the portion of an evil person"—again, a play on words designed to underscore the link between status and learning, since *drécht*, "portion," also means "poem." In other words, the contempt displayed in the rest of *Bretha Nemed Tóisech* for unlearned and ill-spoken poets and jurists is here extended to the clergy, causing the lower grades of doorkeeper and exorcist to be portrayed in an unflattering light.[229]

One very interesting by-product of *Bretha Nemed*'s concern with the speech of the ignorant are its reflections on *roscada* as a source of authority, an issue we have not seen taken up before in other contemporary tracts. The relationship between *roscada* and *fásaige*, "maxims," is one that has inspired a modest amount of discussion among modern scholars. As Kelly remarks, the two terms often occur together; the main difference he notes is that the term *fásach* is found mainly in legal contexts, whereas *roscad* is found in a wide variety of literature, legal and nonlegal.[230] *Bretha Nemed Toísech* complicates this picture considerably. On the one hand, *Bretha Nemed* redactors clearly value *roscada* as an important ingredient in the presentation and acceptance of a poetic judgment. Both *Uraicecht Becc* and *Bretha Nemed Toísech* speak of judgments consolidated *co nailcibh roscud 7 fasach 7 tesdemuin*,[231] "on the 'rocks' of *roscad[a]* and maxim[s] and testimony," and *Bretha Nemed Toísech* makes it clear that the judgments even of learned judges are "empty" if they be not couched in *roscada*.[232] Dub mac Da Dochunn's complaint speaks of *roscada* as one in a long list of things that undercut legal cases brought by twits like himself,[233] and one of the historical poets cited as an authority by *Bretha Nemed Déidenach*, Roighin, has the sobriquet *Rosgadhach*, "proficient in *roscada*."[234] Much of *Bretha Nemed* itself is written in *roscada*, and it seems likely that part of the reason for this lies in its value as a model for students attempting to learn the language in which they will be expected to perform.

On the other hand, *Bretha Nemed Toísech* also makes it clear that *roscada* uttered by persons who do not possess a full knowledge (*eólas*) of the tradition as a whole are insufficient to ensure a just judgment:

Ni lor eolus isnahaoib roscaduib manib maith a ngaos aicnid; is de adber an fili: id lia cesta canoine, it lia dorcha duil. Ni randa roscad, randad fir forragad taman teiscleimnec trebnairecht,[235] *ni airgither anbretha i riguib roceduil roclaid aicned ilclandach ae in athceduil. Ni rosca na roceduil randus fir do cach; is ferr aiccned ilclandach asi (sic, for asa) mbuaidh brethaib.*

Knowledge of the aforementioned *roscada* is not sufficient, unless [a judge] be competent in the wisdom of nature; concerning this the poet says: problems are more numerous than the canon law, obscurities are more numerous than what is laid down in the law. *Roscada* (alone) do not make the apportioning of truth: gleaning *taman*'s[236] oppress the chiefs of a court. Splendid judgements are not bound in the bindings of chanting. Prolific nature can undermine the suit consisting of repetition. It is neither *roscad* nor chanting which apportion truth to all. Better is prolific nature out of which judgements are triumphantly delivered . . .[237]

This is a difficult passage. Much has been written concerning "natural" law, which has resonance both in native and Christian tradition but here seems to refer generally to "native" law without specific regard to particular antecedents or affiliations.[238] One of the key issues in this passage, as Breatnach has pointed out, is the distinction between those who have merely memorized *roscada* (*athceduil*, literally "repeated song") that they then seek to apply to any situation regardless of fit, and those whose training has been sufficiently deep as to allow them to compose in the genre. When low-ranking poets like *taman*s attempt to insert themselves into judicial processes for which they are intellectually and artistically unprepared it stands only to reason that disaster will result.[239] In other words, it is not enough merely to be able to ape the sounds of the poetic language. One must have the ability to "compose" in the language of the law, by which is meant not merely a composition in words, but a "composition" in adjudication as well: the ability to resolve disputes for which no obvious precedent exists in native law. That native law is here being imagined in its textual form is suggested both by comparison with canon law (where the referent is also textual) and by the use of the word *dúil*, "codex." In other words, an effective judicial "performance" entails both a knowledge of the written law and the skill to turn it into poetry.

The redactors of *Bretha Nemed Toísech* are thus walking something of a fine line between their desire to endorse *roscad* as a necessary component of the performance of law and their concern with ensuring that the *roscada* of ignorant and unqualified versifiers not be accepted as authoritative. Their answer to this dilemma, as always, is knowledge—knowledge of "the law of nature" and, as other texts make clear, knowledge of the substance of Irish law as expressed in learned genres (oral and written), especially *fásaige*, "maxims," or "precedents." Usually, we as have seen, the terms *roscada* and *fásaige* have been taken as being essentially equal in terms of authority. However, the authors of *Bretha Nemed Toísech* are clearly able to envisage situations in which legal performances appear persuasive but are not in fact grounded in any real knowledge of the legal tradition (for example, Dub's, and those outlined above with respect to *roscada*). Whereas *roscada* on their own can be insufficient to guarantee a just outcome in the absence of professional training, the same does not appear to be true of *fásaige* in this text. Rather, *fásaige*—likely often incorporated into *roscada* in performance—are depicted as evidence of professional knowledge and thus critical to the ensuring of justice: "true judgment is given upon a *fásach*; everything not in accordance with a *fásach* is empty . . . everything not in accordance with *fásaige* is [considered] unbound, for it is *fásaige* that establish judgments, o my Neire."[240]

One of the clearest indications of the distinction *Bretha Nemed Toísech* redactors are drawing between *roscada* and *fásaige* is the frequent association of *fásaige*—but not *roscada*—with *forus*. *Forus* is a crucial term in both of the main *Bretha Nemed* tracts, as in the early Irish legal tradition generally, although its pointed association with *fásach* may be mainly a feature of *Bretha Nemed Toísech*. It is a fascinating word, and one that gives us great insight into the extent to which law and performance were linked in this culture. Literally *forus* means "foundation, basis, that which is stable" and from there "legal provision" or "principle," as in the principle underlying a law or legal declaration.[241] However, *forus* clearly also has a geographical and performative as well as an ethical component. In *Berrad Airechta*, it is the term used to describe both the place and the occasion on which contractual agreements would be fulfilled or renegotiated.[242] In both *Cáin Adamnáin* and the Annals of Ulster in regard to *Cáin Phátraic*, *forus* appears to integrate a complex series of actions and events: the enactment of the *cáin* itself, the provisions of which that *cáin* is composed, and the principles underlying those provisions.[243] Often it is translated "promulgation" for this very reason: *forus* recapitulates the authority resident in the moment and place in which law is performed by those who are morally, intellectually, and artistically qualified to perform it.

Not surprisingly, then, *forus* is often found in conjunction with words linked to speaking or to the performance of spoken genres, particularly in a judicial setting.[244] *Bretha Nemed Déidenach*, for example, speaks of establishing entitlement in a case *for forus firinnsge*,[245] "on the basis of the *forus* of true-speech." Morann is said to have brought forth "brilliant legal verse as a *forus*" in his case against the ill-fated Dub mac Da Dochunn, which verse Dub tries then to refute.[246] And Neire is instructed "*ba f[e]asach ba findsrothach, ba forus, ba firbrethach*,[247] "may you be knowledgeable, may you be fair-speaking, may you be as a *forus*, may you be true-judging." Since *forus* as a term embraces both the moment of decision and the principles on which that decision is based, it is thus of particular interest to find it linked as frequently as it is to *fásach* in *Bretha Nemed Tóisech*:

Mo nere nuallgnaid, diamba brithum, nis bera gan fis cin forus cin fásach. . . . Rob amne romeser resiu romeser breth fort: ni be cin fis, ni be cin forus, ni be cin fotha, ni be cin fonaidm.[248]

My Neire accustomed-to-proclaiming, if you would be a judge, may you not render judgment without knowledge, without *forus*, without a maxim (*fásach*). . . . May it be thus that you judge before a judgment be judged against you: may you not be without wisdom, may you not be without *forus*, may you not be without foundation, may you not be without security.

A similar point is made in another text, one that envisages judgment progressing in stages much as we saw earlier with satire and distraint: *dia nomuide nuithear firbrethuibh forus filed, firbreth berur fri fasach*, "on the ninth day the *forus* of poets is made known in true judgments; true-judgment is given in relationship to a *fásach*."[249]

It is thus not coincidental that *fásach* and *forus* are joined together as much as they are in this text, nor that *roscada* and *forus* are not conjoined in the same way. A knowledge of *roscada* alone is not enough to effect a true *forus*; only if the speaker is one entitled to speak by virtue of knowledge acquired in the schools—a knowledge of *fásaige*, in other words—can a just resolution be effected. Whether the association made by the *Bretha Nemed Tóisech* redactor between *fásach* and learning can be generalized throughout the legal tradition is unclear. A frequent gloss on *fásach* is *fis ogh*, "pure knowledge," whereas the gloss on *forus* is *fír fhis*, "true knowledge."[250] Glosses of this sort may testify to the perception of a connection between *fásach, forus* and knowledge as acquired in the schools that is wider than the confines of our texts alone. On the other hand, the connections drawn here suit the purposes of the *Bretha Nemed* redactor so clearly that it is difficult to be sure. In any case, the conjunction of these two terms highlights the extent to which the statement of law in authoritative form, whether as *fásaige* or *roscada* or both, was equated with the oral performance of the legal decision stemming from that law. Indeed, *Bretha Nemed Toísech* certainly suggests that while *fásaige* constituted the foundation with respect to which a verdict would be given, those *fásaige* might often be turned into poetic form for public presentation.[251] Principle and the performance of principle are intrinsically linked: the *roscada* and *fásaige* in which justice is grounded according to *Uraicecht Becc* constitute both the grounds on which kings and judges make their decisions and the oral genres through which they prove the "rightness" of their verdicts.[252]

The preoccupations of the *Bretha Nemed* redactors were thus very different from those who compiled the *Senchas Már*. Indeed, in many ways, the two seem often not even to be speaking the same "language"—from the point of view of agenda no less than of linguistic style. Members of the *nemed* classes, most particularly poets and poet-jurists, are *the* issue for the redactors of *Bretha Nemed*. The "primer" texts of *Uraicecht Becc* and *Uraicecht na Ríar* outline the basic privileges, dues, and entitlements associated with each *nemed* rank in a plain prose appropriate for those just beginning their course of study. However, it is in the two main *Bretha Nemed* tracts that we get a real sense of the priorities of the school itself. In these texts, especially *Bretha Nemed Toísech*, elaborate and linguistically intricate arguments are made regarding the *nemed*: their Christian affiliations, their intellectual and moral status, and the jurisdictional prerogatives to which their special status entitles them. Medium and message are the same: the learned language in which they are in large part written is at once the foundation of poetic power and a precious resource to be safeguarded at all costs. In contrast with the redactors of the *Senchas Már*, for whom the lawbook itself is the referent and the present rather than the past the major authorizer of contemporary custom, *Bretha Nemed* authors ground their assertions not in their own text, but in the very moment of performance, past and present. Sometimes these performances are instructional, as is Morann's advice to Neire; sometimes they are judicial, as are the verdicts rendered by poets of the past; and sometimes they are agenda driven, as is the language of the tracts itself. Always, however, they seek like all good performances to entice their audience into a particular way of seeing, to bring them to the realization that it is here, in the trained poetic voice—gifted, learned, and Christian to its very core—that true authority resides.

Old School Ties

What we have seen so far suggests a picture of legal schooling in Ireland very different from the one proposed by Binchy so many years ago.

Rather than thinking in teleological terms of inevitable stages of development through which all Irish schools might be expected to pass, it seems more profitable instead to inquire into differences (and similarities) in their agendas, personnel, and outlook. Regardless of whether law did develop historically as a profession out of poetry, as even the pseudohistory of the *Senchas Már* suggests, it is clear that the role of poets and poetry in the contemporary legal setting was not the priority for the *Senchas Már* compilers that it was for their *Bretha Nemed* colleagues. Nor, frankly (and presumably not coincidentally) was performance, at least not the elaborate verbal performances we have seen to this point, a fact that must raise the question of whether the association this book has sought to trace between performance and law was true for all regions of Ireland. The question is relatively easy to answer for nonverbal performances of the sort detailed in Chapter 1, since procedures of that kind are ubiquitous throughout the legal corpus. Distraint, sick-maintenance, gages, and *tellach* are all major topics in the *Senchas Már* lawbook—indeed, it is from tracts in that lawbook that we know most of what we know on those subjects.[253] Gages are discussed as well in *Bretha Nemed Tóisech*, as are distraint, suretyship, and fief payments.[254] And *Bretha Nemed Déidenach* contains a lengthy excursus on suretyship that incorporates, among other things, a payment schedule for the compensation of a compromised guarantor.[255] Instances of nonverbal performance are equally visible in the Latin *Collectio Canonum Hibernensis*: the time schedule for paying a contractual debt, for example, or the temporal limitations on a lord's ability to contravene a gift.[256] Performative procedures of this sort are referred to especially frequently in passages attributed to the *Synodus Hibernensis*, but they are by no means limited to them. Provisions tracing their origins to non-Irish synod sources include, for example, burial as a performance of church allegiance, public fasting or almsgiving, the offering of testimony in legal cases, and oathtaking.[257]

Verbal performances of the sort described in Chapter 2 are another matter altogether (realizing, of course, that any of the nonverbal performances referred to above might have had a verbal component that has left no trace in the extant written records). The vast majority of the rhetorical "judgments" that are our best source of information on this subject come from texts of or affiliated with the *Bretha Nemed* tradition. Of the cases cited in Chapter 2 above, for example, only two can be associated with the *Senchas Már*: the tale of Fergus mac Léti, incorporated into two manuscripts of *Di Chetharshlicht Athgabála*, and the "Pseudo-Historical Prologue to the *Senchas Már*." Even these are not without their difficulties. With respect to the tale of Fergus mac Léti, it is difficult to be certain about its links to the lawbook as a whole; for its part, the "Pseudo-Historical Prologue" is likely a ninth-century composition, a century later than the *Senchas Már*, and thus added onto it at a date subsequent to its original compilation.[258] Both of the *Sen-*

chas Már tracts on wounding and sick-maintenance contain rhetorical passages that might be construed in this way; however, both read more like oral instructions from teacher to pupil than judgments.[259] By contrast, both of the principal *Bretha Nemed* texts frequently report "verbatim" judgments by kings and jurists—indeed, the stories to which these verdicts relate would seem to have formed a crucial part of the oral curriculum in the *Bretha Nemed* school.[260] So striking are these differences, in fact, that one must at least consider the possibility that the type of rhetorical performance described in Chapter 2 was a regional phenomenon associated uniquely with Munster.

Such possibilities cannot be entirely discounted. *Scéla Mosauluim*, from whence comes one of the examples of judicial speech cited earlier, is a Munster text;[261] the same might be true of the *Immathchor nAilella 7 Airt*, considering that it is Ailill Ólomm, ancestor of the Munster Éoganachta federation, who prevails in the case over Art, the ancestor figure of Leth Cuinn.[262] Judicial speech in *rosc*-style also occurs in the tale known as *Esnada Tige Buchet*, the main protagonists of which hail from Leinster.[263] And it may be significant that the *Triads of Ireland* characterize two southern monasteries, Cloyne and Cork, as the centers of *Fénechas Érenn* and *Bérlae Féne Érenn* respectively, since both of these terms are associated in many texts with rhetorical or otherwise heightened language. By contrast, the midlands monastery of Slane is characterized in the *Triads* as the center of *Brithemnas Érenn*, "the Judgment of Ireland," and *brithemnas* is a term with no necessary link to the rhetorical language at all.[264] Why Munster might be different is difficult to say, although politics might have something to do with it. One of the striking differences between the *Bretha Nemed* and *Senchas Már* texts is the extent to which, in the former, the titles "judge" and "poet" seem to be synonymous in the contemporary context. It is an historical fact that Munster's polity was considerably more fragmented than was that of the north and midlands; certainly, the Éoganachta federation was broader and more diffuse than was that of the Uí Néill. Perhaps in these political circumstances poets enjoyed more jurisdictional independence and were able to act more frequently in judicial capacities, both within and outside their own communities (and profession).[265]

Against this possibility are texts that do not, as far as we know, hail from Munster and yet hint at the importance of performative speech. *Din Techtugud*, a *Senchas Már* tract, contains several rhetorical statements of law that might be construed in this manner, as do *Di Chetharshlicht Athgabála*, *Bretha Crólige*, and *Bretha Déin Chécht*.[266] Many of these passages are couched as instruction rather than as verdicts per se, but that is true also of *Bretha Nemed*. In any case, it is difficult to know how frequently the categories of instruction and verdicts might have overlapped. Rhetoricized "advice" from teacher to pupil on a matter of principle might easily have found its way into a verdict, as Kelly has suggested.[267] Likewise with *fásaige*, another recognizably judicial genre that could well have found its way into rhetoricized speech at the time of the proclamation of a verdict.[268] *Senchas Már* tracts cite *fásaige* often, sometimes identifying the passage in question explicitly as a *fásach*, and sometimes prefacing it with *is de atá*, "it is of this [situation] that it is said . . ."[269] Equally telling are the many offhand references to legal speech, speakers, or *roscada* that occur in *Senchas Már* tracts. *Do Thuaslucud Rudrad* mentions offerings *i mbelu uasalnemed*,[270] "in the mouths of high-dignitaries." And *Di Chetharshlicht Athgabála* speaks of the participation of a *suíthengthaid*, "expert speaker," in the taking of distraint; this same passage also mentions speaking in *rosc* as part of the procedure.[271] Many of the distraint stages described in this text are preceded by formal pronouncements; it seems reasonable to imagine that these might customarily have taken rhetorical form. Outside the *Senchas Már*, there is also evidence for verbal performance in what is, as far as we know, a non-Munster context in *Berrad Airechta*'s contractual formulas.[272] And even those texts that seem to support the idea of Munster as a special case may be more ambiguous than they appear. *Esnada Tige Buchet*, for example, has a strong Uí Néill as well as Leinster component; as its geographical axis is clearly centered in and around Kells, in the territories historically contested by the Laigin and southern Uí Néill, this might in the end argue for a midlands, rather than a Munster, referent for the tale.

The evidence thus, while slim, seems to go against rather than for an interpretation of rhetorical judicial speech as an essentially regional phenomenon. *Roscada* are more prevalent in *Bretha Nemed* texts than they are in tracts of the *Senchas Már* because they were important to the argument the *Bretha Nemed* redactors were trying to make, not because rhetorical speech was irrelevant to the judicial practice of the north and midlands. To say this is, however, merely to push the argument back a step, since the issue of why these lawbooks might differ so profoundly from one another remains still to be answered. Variations in regional political structure (Munster versus the north) might play a role, as has already been suggested. The particular perspectives and interests of the redactors who composed these tracts ought also not to be overlooked as an explanation, at least not for *Bretha Nemed Toísech*. From this distance, it is difficult to determine whether the Uí Búirecháin kindred to whom this tract is ascribed might have been unusual in claiming a bishop, a poet, and a judge within its ranks. Breatnach and others have taken this as typical of the collaboration between church and jurist that lies behind the production of the extant tracts, and perhaps this is true.[273] Regardless, however, it is still the case that the tract reflects even in its very structure the background of the three individuals who produced it. Moreover, what is truly striking about *Bretha Nemed Toísech* and the *Bretha Nemed* texts in general is less their interest in ecclesiastical matters than the role they envisage for poets: not merely their historical role, as per the *Senchas Már*, but their relations with the church and their assertions of the right to be involved in (contemporary) legal dealings.

Another possible explanation of the differences among these various lawbooks is politics within and among the legal schools themselves. The texts at which we have been looking are roughly contemporaneous with one another. Might the schools that produced them have been aware of, or perhaps even responding to, one another? Might they even have seen themselves as rivals? About the relationship between the *Senchas Már* and *Bretha Nemed* schools it is difficult to speak with any certainty. The texts produced by these schools differ so much from one another that the primary impression one gains from reading them is that of entities engaged in conversations taking place largely separate from one another. Their language is different, their methods are different, their interests and priorities are different. The only real evidence to suggest that one might be in some sense responding to the other occurs in the final paragraphs of the "Pseudo-Historical Prologue to the *Senchas Már*," where the substance of the law articulated in *Bretha Nemed* is said to have originated in the days before the arrival of Patrick and the subsequent promulgation of the *Senchas Már*.[274] Since the gist of the text is that the *Senchas Már* is now to be considered the ultimate statement of Irish custom, this statement would seem to relegate *Bretha Nemed* to the status of an older and now less authoritative tract. However, the "Pseudo-Historical Prologue" dates either to the late eighth or early ninth century, and was only affixed to the original lawbook in a complicated sequence of events that has been reconstructed by John Carey.[275] In other words, it cannot be considered evidence contemporary with the compilation of the *Senchas Már* for the compilers' attitudes toward the Munster school.

It is the relationship of the two vernacular lawbooks to the Latin *Hibernensis* that is the most interesting and, evidence suggests, the most charged. Once again there are clear differences in this respect between texts of the *Bretha Nemed* tradition and the tracts that comprise the *Senchas Már*. As Breatnach has shown, the redactors of *Bretha Nemed Toísech* drew on a text or texts of the *Hibernensis*, probably in its Munster version.[276] Some excerpts they translated into plain prose and some into *rosc*—clearly for these compilers, the Latin compilation was as much resource as competitor. Indeed, the joint authorship of this tract practically ensured that its perspective would be, at the very least, sympathetic to the concerns of the canonists. Mention has already been made of *Uraicecht na Ríar*'s (and, it has been argued, *Bretha Nemed Toísech*'s) adoption of the canonical idea of poets as Levites. The emphasis on purity and literate learning in both main *Bretha Nemed* tracts seems very likely to be an expression of this same idea; at the very least, it suggests a redactor sympathetic to a clericalized image of the poetic classes. Indeed, if it is correct to suggest that the redactors of *Bretha Nemed Toísech* were attempting to claim jurisdictional privileges for the *nemed* classes parallel to those enjoyed by the church, then it would be surprising to see them not exploit the parallels between the church and its law on the one hand, and the *nemed* classes and theirs on the other.

Of course there are important differences also between the *Bretha Nemed* tracts and the *Hibernensis*. The latter is a self-consciously text-based tradition, the former less clearly so. The latter relies on exegesis in its legal reasoning, the former on the application of categories of law to cases that arise.[277] On the other hand, *Bretha Nemed* redactors root the validity of their statements both in the "sayings" (broadly conceived) of particularly authoritative individuals, and in well-known stories within their tradition, just as *the Hibernensis* does. Whereas the *Hibernensis* cites Augustine or Isidore, *Bretha Nemed* cites Morann and Neire; whereas the *Hibernensis* turns to the story of Rahab the harlot to illustrate particular points,[278] *Bretha Nemed* uses the tales of its own tradition to bolster what it has to say. The issue of whether the *Bretha Nemed* tales were intended to function in anything like the same way the stories in the *Hibernensis* do is a complicated one. As Charles-Edwards points out, the use of authorities is not a common feature in early Irish vernacular law, although the practice is not unknown; the possibility thus remains that the *Bretha Nemed* lawyers thought what they were doing at least looked something like what they were seeing in their ecclesiastical model.[279] Most law tract authors must have progressed some distance through the ecclesiastical educational curriculum. Some, however, made it further than others. The *Bretha Nemed* redactors seem, on the whole, closer to their canon lawyer colleagues—or at least interested in portraying themselves this way—than do others of the period.[280]

The *Senchas Már*'s relationship to the canonical tradition in general and to the *Hibernensis* in particular is much more difficult to pin down. It is possible that the *Senchas Már* tract *Bretha im Gatta* drew upon the *Hibernensis* in its construction.[281] On the other hand, *Bretha im Gatta* is quite possibly the most ecclesiastically aware tract in the entire *Senchas Már* collection and therefore (arguably) atypical of the compilation as a whole. Ó Corráin, Breatnach, and Breen have argued for a close relationship also between *Córus Béscnai* and various Latin texts including the *Hibernensis*—indeed, the extent of Latin influence on this tract is in their view so great that they believe *Córus Béscnai* has "as much a right to be called a canonistic text as any of the Hiberno-Latin texts that have been called *canones* for a millennium or more."[282] However, their view is grounded in their general belief that the authors of all of the major lawbooks, Latin and vernacular, were members of a single, ecclesiastically educated "mandarin" class of Christian intellectuals and not all would agree with this premise.

Charles-Edwards has argued that *Córus Béscnai*'s depiction of relations between the church and its lay population as both mutual and contractual betrays a secular native point of view that is inherently different from the ecclesiastical stance on such matters.[283] While he agrees that the influence of Latin learning on the *Senchas Már* has been considerable—and in terms of grammatical training specifically, visibly greater on the *Senchas Már* than on the *Hibernensis* itself—he also makes the point that there are many ways in which secular lawyers could have gained access to the learning of the church without either being clerics themselves or having totally subsumed the interests and priorities of their profession into those of the church:[284] "whatever their background, the authors of the tracts claimed an authority to instruct by virtue of their expertise in a law which they rightly perceived as native and secular, even though it could and did borrow from a different law. This ecclesiastical law, in its turn, had no doubt that it should be contrasted with secular law, and its learned men with secular learned men."[285]

The question is thus a difficult one, and has not been rendered any easier by the black-or-white terms in which it is so often discussed. Almost invariably the focus has been on the background and training of the jurists who authored the tracts. Some argue that all legal literati of the period were by definition "ecclesiastical" in position and outlook, some that the evident variety in the nature and orientation of the extant texts means that it is still possible to distinguish "secular" from "ecclesiastical" lawyers in our sources. What makes this all so difficult is that in a culture in which even the compiler of the *Senchas Már* had likely "progressed a long way through a Latin curriculum of which exegesis was the culmination,"[286] the terms "secular" and "ecclesiastical" are inherently problematic. By the time the lawbooks are written, "native secular law" contains much that is Christian and grounded in exegesis; as is evident even from the (genuine) prologue to the *Senchas Már*, these provisions too have come to be regarded by the jurists writing them down as contemporary "native law." Certainly there must have been differences in the extent to which jurists were involved in the life of the church. Some lived and worked in monasteries, whereas others likely did not. Some were committed to articulating in their work the priorities and prerogatives of the church, whereas others were more concerned with the regulation of ordinary agricultural life in the community. But all were Christian, and many were ecclesiastically trained, even if they proceeded then to use this training to produce tracts that appear to modern scholars "secular" in nature. Indeed, this last is a modern characterization of the jurists' work, and probably not one that they themselves would necessarily have shared.

Perhaps it might be profitable to rephrase the question in terms of jurisdiction rather than of personnel, and in terms of struggles between specific institutional entities rather than of abstractions like "secular" and "ecclesiastical." For in a system in which at least some members of the church claimed the right to judge their own, "secular" and "ecclesiastical" will indeed have meaning as terms of jurisdiction, at the very least. In the Middle Ages (as arguably still today), conflicts of jurisdiction would most often arise and ultimately be resolved in the context of specific disputes over particular personal or institutional prerogatives; disputes of this nature could easily be sufficiently complex in nature as to transcend easy characterization in abstract terms. Literate, ecclesiastically educated lawyers in a school in which native law (by this point regarded as inherently Christian) was taught could easily come into conflict with literate, ecclesiastically educated lawyers in a monastic school over, for example, rights to jurisdiction over the lay tenants of a local monastic estate, or the position of judge within a given *túath*, or the securing of pupils at their school, or the right to adjudicate disputes arising from bequests made to an nearby church, or the right to preserve and interpret law for kings in the region. None of these conflicts can be easily characterized as "secular" or "ecclesiastical" in the sense of pitting inherently clerical against inherently lay interests—and yet in all one can see representatives of "the church" coming into conflict with representatives of "the laity." Of course, the church may well have tried in specific situations to articulate their claims in terms of abstract rights to ultimate jurisdiction. Something of the nature of the argument—as of the threat—can be inferred from the title of the *Hibernensis* chapter on judgment, which makes clear that at least some in Ireland at the time were claiming that while clerics could not be judged by the laity, the laity could be judged by the clergy. If Charles-Edwards is right that "native" lawyers were indeed "looking over their shoulders" more frequently at their ecclesiastical colleagues than those colleagues did at them, perhaps this is why.[287]

But is there then evidence of disputes arising over jurisdictional issues of this sort? Unfortunately, the type of sources that might reveal the existence of such conflicts—charters and court records, most notably—do not tend to survive from early Ireland. We are therefore dependent on indirect evidence, and here we return to the question of the relationship between the *Senchas Már* and the *Hibernensis*. One of the possibilities that has been raised in the scholarship on these two lawbooks is whether the *Senchas Már* (generally thought to be the later of the two) might have been compiled directly in response to the *Hibernensis*.[288] One might indeed go even further to wonder whether it might have been actually modeled on it. For the *Senchas Már* is unlike any other Irish legal text in terms both of the comprehensiveness of its coverage of legal issues and its self-consciousness as a text. Of course, it is impossible to know at this distance how Irish law might have been structured before it was put into writing—to know, specifically, whether the genre of the tractate reproduces a particular oral genre of which we no longer have any trace. What is most unusual about the *Senchas Már*, however, is the manner in which it joins tractate to tractate to produce a compilation that implicitly claims the right to regulate a wide range of issues—matters as diverse, for example, as marital and filial relationships, suretyship, gages, and the transgressions of bees and dogs. The *Hibernensis* too brings together into one compilation authoritative pronouncements

on a wide range of subjects, topically arranged. In fact, and possibly significantly, the *Hibernensis* covers *all* of the subjects mentioned above with respect to the *Senchas Már* (most of which have the appearance of "secular"
issues) and more.[289] The possibility that it might have appeared as something of a threat to the *Senchas Már* redactors does not seem all that far-
fetched.

That the compilation of the *Senchas Már* might have been stimulated by
a desire to imitate, and perhaps even compete with, the *Hibernensis* becomes even more likely upon close examination of the contents of the
Latin lawbook. One of the most striking features of the *Hibernensis* is its tendency to appropriate provisions and personalities likely to have originated
in "native" tradition. Patrick, a figure who is, as we know, central to the vernacular tradition represented in the *Senchas Már*, is reinterpreted by the authors of the *Hibernensis* as a canonical lawgiver.[290] Similarly, provisions that
almost certainly have their origins in "native" law, such as those on legal in-
competence, or on Irish forms of personal surety, are ascribed in the *Hibernensis* to synodal or Latin ecclesiastical sources. Thus the passage on legal
incompetents is attributed to the "Irish Synod,"[291] while the paragraph on
suretyship—which actually even contains a word, *rata*, borrowed *into* Latin
from Irish—is said to be the work of Augustine![292] Sometimes the direction
of borrowing is not entirely clear. *Hibernensis* XXI.6 defines three bases on
which judgment can be rendered—nature, analogy and Scripture. As those
familiar with the vernacular lawbooks will recognize immediately, both nature and analogy are concepts of great importance to "native" tradition: in
fact, if one were to add *fásach* and *roscad* to the mix, the *Hibernensis* passage
would overlap precisely with a comparable set of provisions from the late
recension of *Cóic Conara Fugill*.[293] However, while it is unclear whether
these categories of judgment are native or ecclesiastical in origin, what is
clear is that the provision on "nature" is, despite the latter's important reflexes in native law, attributed in the *Hibernensis* to Augustine.[294]

What is true of individual provisions is true also of the whole. Proclamations emanating from synods held within Ireland are joined in the *Hibernensis* to quotations from the Bible, established fathers of the church, and
continental synods, allowing the redactors to lay claim not only to the authorship of specific provisions of native law, but to the acts of lawmaking
and legal interpretation themselves. In the chapter on marriage, for example, a subject on which we know native and Latin law originally disagreed,[295] not only does the Latin view prevail, but provisions on
continence and on adultery attributed to synods held within Ireland are
placed side by side with passages ascribed to Augustine, Jerome, Isidore,
Moses, Origen, Paul, and Gaulish synods held in Narbonne and in Arles.[296]
The effect is both to underscore the historical authority of ecclesiastical
views on marriage by erasing native traditions on this subject, and to appropriate even those reforms that did originate in Ireland for the Latin

church. All books of law are in some sense books about the past: here the *Hibernensis* jurists quite literally rewrite the history of the law in Ireland in a way designed to reconstitute that law as part of a larger European legal tradition. If one imagines for a moment the likely reactions to such a claim on the part of the redactors of the *Senchas Már*—jurists who viewed themselves as responsible for preserving and proclaiming the ("native," and now also viewed as inherently Christian) law taught in their schools, jurists whose jobs depended on their jurisdiction over that law—one can imagine the rub. Regardless of the reasons for which the *Hibernensis* might originally have been compiled, it is not hard to see how it could have been a source of concern as well as inspiration.

If this is right, however, it is significant that when the *Senchas Már* jurists imagine themselves and their tradition, they speak not in terms of an opposition between "secular" and "ecclesiastical," but of the law of the Féni, and of themselves as purveyors of a vernacular and firmly Christian tradition newly encapsulated in written form, the roots of which stretch back into the pre-Christian past. For these jurists, it always, always, comes back to the *Senchas Már* itself, and it is their emphasis on that text that is perhaps the clearest indicator of their priorities and concerns. The opposition between native and clerical views of marriage, for example—surely one of the areas in which the divergence between the two traditions was most stark— is not depicted in the *Senchas Már* in terms of "secular" versus "ecclesiastical" practice. Indeed, the authors of *Bretha Crólige* rationalize native practices in this respect by reference to Old Testament polygyny and the customs of the "chosen [people] of God." For these jurists, the gap is not religious in nature, it is regional and cultural. The recognition of multiple unions is done in accordance with *bescnu inse [É]renn*, "the custom of the island of Ireland"; moreover, "native" views on marriage are still evolving. The law of the *Senchas Már* is still a living law: as *Bretha Crólige* makes clear, the possibility of abandoning polygyny for monogamy is a matter of contemporary dispute among experts in (native) Irish law (*ar ata forcosnam la Fene cia de as techta*). Nothing is said about a conflict in religious values, for this is not a conflict between "secular" and "ecclesiastical." Irish law is Christian law, and since Christian history provides two different models; it is, in the words of the redactor of the tract, "not easier to condemn [polygyny] than to praise it."[297] To the extent, then, that we must have a vocabulary with which to characterize the differences among these traditions, we could do worse than to adopt that used by the redactors themselves. "Secular" versus "ecclesiastical" does not adequately capture how these jurists understood their work, while "native" versus "clerical" both makes no acknowledgment of the clerical training many "native" lawyers would have received and implies a historically based resistance to change that is at odds with the adaptive qualities of Irish law. The best metaphor, as the jurists clearly saw, was language: a living, breathing organism whose powerful

roots in the past did not preclude the ability to grow and to change in response to events of the future. *Bérla Féne* could be opposed to the "white
language of the Beatitudes" much as Irish was opposed to the biblical languages of history in the contemporary grammatical tract *Auraicept na nÉces*:
with respect, but also without apology or concession.

In the end then, the evidence that we have, inadequate as it is, suggests
that the "fault lines" along which these texts divided might have been
grounded more in the ambitions of the men and schools that produced
these tracts than in abstract notions of "secular" versus "ecclesiastical."
The *Bretha Nemed* redactors seem more interested in claiming for the poetic classes the privileges enjoyed by the church than in distinguishing
themselves too starkly from their ecclesiastical brethren. The *Senchas Már*
jurists, by contrast, are keenly aware of the potential threat posed by texts
like the *Hibernensis* and are anxious to protect their position as guardians
of a fluidly "traditional" legal language. Further hints as to priorities and
affiliations that might lie behind these schools and their work survive in
other venues. Charles-Edwards has argued, for example, that the *Hibernensis* takes an anti-Armagh stance with respect to issues of ecclesiastical organization.[298] By contrast, the *Senchas Már* centers its origin legend on the
figure of Patrick, the (putative) founder of Armagh, and then regularly re-
inforces this link throughout the lawbook. The association between Armagh and the Uí Néill is almost automatic among early Irish historians, as
indeed it was for authors of the period itself, like Muirchú and Tírechán:
where Patrick appears, the Uí Néill are rarely far behind. A compilation
the size of the *Senchas Már* implies a considerable degree of organization
on the part of those who compiled and redacted it. It also presupposes
that the originating jurists had the requisite wealth, ability to travel and, if
necessary, means to coerce other schools into giving up for copying their
precious tracts and treatises. Some of the *Senchas Már* tractates might have
been composed or commissioned specifically for the purpose (particularly
those ascribed to a single author); if so, this too implies wealth on the part
of the commissioning school. In short, a production like the *Senchas Már*
seems easiest to imagine taking shape in the context of the sort of patronage that Armagh and/or the Uí Néill could have provided—just as the mo-
tives for which it was created seem easiest to imagine arising out of a desire
to increase the reputation and and dominance of the school(s) that produced it.

Law was well known in the early Middle Ages as a means of defining and
extending power, and it would be interesting to know whether the patronage we are hypothesizing might have been aspired to by the *Senchas Már* jurists was ever fully realized. Neither specific historical kings, nor particular
royal lines, are mentioned in the lawbook, and while Patrick plays a big role
in it, Armagh itself does not, at least not by name. The frequent references
to the Féni make clear the *Senchas Már*'s intentions with respect to legal

matters in the north and midlands; it would be interesting to know whether anything further was intended with respect to Ulster and Leinster. The hope may have been that law might play an important role in symbolically unifying the disparate territories brought under the rule of Armagh and the Uí Néill as it so clearly did (or was intended to do) for Charlemagne and the Carolingians. Again, it is difficult to know, and even more uncertain how and whether such claims might have translated into jurisdictional superiority in particular legal cases. The most one can say is that ideas of this sort would certainly provide a motive and context for a compilation of the sort the *Senchas Már* represents.

None of this is to deny the essential "harmony of spirit" that both Hughes and others believe obtained between native and ecclesiastical law.[299] Clearly the two traditions borrowed extensively from one another, a fact that of necessity implies some degree of contact between them. On the other hand, the differences among them in terms of reasoning and approach,[300] coupled with the very different priorities that each espouse, ought not to be overlooked. The fact that the written legal tradition as we know it today took shape in a general atmosphere of collaboration and give-and-take has little bearing on jurisdictional rivalries that might arise among individual schools (whether native or Latin) over patronage and prestige. And if it is right to think of jurists compiling the *Senchas Már* with an eye toward potential competitors—the authors of the *Hibernensis*, perhaps linked to Iona and thus in competition with Armagh—then the question of "secular" versus "ecclesiastical" must be reconsidered from a different angle. Law in Ireland might well have been a "national" law in the sense of obtaining in some degree across the island. However, the schools producing these tracts would seem to have had different priorities, agendas, and ways of thinking about the sources and legitimacy of law. Some redactors looked to authorities outside of themselves—*Fénechas* in the case of *Críth Gablach* and *Berrad Airechta*, the rhetoric of the poets of the mythological past in the case of *Bretha Nemed*. Others, by contrast, preferred to establish their own work as authorities—perhaps in reaction to other schools and texts with which they perceived themselves to be in competition. Ironically, what they all had in common is what to the modern reader most clearly divides them: the extent to which the language in which they composed their texts reflected their own historically situated claims and aspirations. For these jurists and the schools from which they came, the power of the vernacular was a key aspect of the vernacular of power.

The Dangers of Performance

It is important not to get so enmeshed in the intricacies of the written law-books that one forgets the broader oral world in which the jurists who composed them actually lived. What may have mattered most to the manner in which legal events and relationships were experienced on the ground was the unremittingly local nature of the place. Still today communities can be quite isolated from one another; in the Middle Ages, getting from one place to another, especially in harsh weather, would have been a difficult and time-consuming venture, even when the distances traversed were not physically very great. Small wonder then that forests, bogs, and wasteland loom so large in the medieval Irish imagination. Sources of the period display an agonizing awareness of the difference between "inside" and "outside" the realm of settled life, between the safety and warmth of the familiar and the cold, mysterious dark of the hills beyond. That this divide was conceptualized as social and legal as well as geographical in nature is evident also from the literature. The nakedness of the slave woman squatting shivering outside the enclosure awaiting the summons of her master in the *Cáin Adamnáin* prologue is a nakedness of the social as well as the physical being.[1] This is not, of course, to say that movement—broadly conceived, among identities and regions—was impossible in the medieval period. Rather it is to urge us to think deeply about the extreme intimacy that characterized life in this culture, and about how and why practices of the sort described in this study might have come into being.

What has emerged from this study is the centrality of performance: the notion of law as a gestural and verbal art, practiced to varying degrees by individual litigants and the jurists and kings who presided over their disputes. As previous scholars have remarked, such appeals to the senses are easily understood in terms of social memory. One remembers best that which distracts, astonishes, or physically hurts.[2] The sources suggest that there was more to it simply than mnemonics, however. Performance helped to distinguish everyday actions from those charged with special significance; it imparted to particular persons an authority which others did not have and which even that individual might possess only in specific contexts. It caused people to listen in certain ways, and to interpret actions susceptible of more than one meaning in a manner commensurate with the occasion. And it reimagined familiar places and identities in ways that allowed litigants to dramatize the changing relationship between them. A simple clasp of hands or change in code, from mundane to ornamented speech, could separate that which had been from that which now was. Simply put, performance was a way in which to render that which was intensely familiar, altered—however temporarily—into something apart from, but not necessarily other than, itself. Its prominence in the sources invites us to think about the challenges of accommodating the fluidity of human relationships within a local environment that changes slowly, if at all.

Paradoxically, performance seems also to have facilitated the movement of powerful persons across the boundaries and identities within which they and others were normally contained. Poets traveled, jurists traveled; warring kings and would-be lords moved from place to place seeking to expand their dominion. Something apart from sheer brute force must have allowed such men authority within the regions to which they came, must have induced communities to accord importance to what they said and did. For while swords are persuasive, the most critical weapon—for poets and jurists at least, and perhaps for rulers as well—would have been their ability to perform within recognized authoritative parameters. Poets had to demonstrate a knowledge of the appropriate meters and rhetorical structures before being allowed into a territory. Similarly, the professional expertise of jurists previously unknown within the locality was likely manifested as much in their way of speaking the law as much as in their apparent familiarity with it. Indeed, given the way in which the exercise of kingly power is portrayed in the sources that remain to us, perhaps we ought to imagine such considerations as relevant even to the consolidation of lordly rule. Winning power is one thing, but exercising it is another: if indeed an idiom of lordship obtained broadly throughout the island, the use of such a "code" would allow for radical changes in rule without kings and their agents seeming to transgress against existing structures of authority. Nor are secular rulers alone the only ones at issue. Surely it is not too far-fetched to imagine that anxieties of this kind might lie behind the translation of Latin ecclesiastical texts into *rosc*?

Particularly fascinating is the manner in which these vernaculars of power would seem to have overlapped. *Rosc* implied learning, status, authority and social standing not merely for poets, but for jurists and kings acting in their judicial role, a juxtaposition that suggests that the ability to command this difficult code evoked for the listener not only aristocratic birth or specialist training, but the darker realms of prophecy, wisdom, and otherworldly insight. Similar associations would appear to have clung—if at a distance—to the language of ordinary contractual litigants as well, at least to the extent that their "code" alluded to the authoritative language of the jurists. Of course, language is a slender peg on which to hang issues of great weight. Not all who are articulate are learned; not all who compose poetry enjoy the confidence of the otherworld. It is no accident that the sources betray such intense concern with the possibility that those whose background and education did not entitle them to speak would nonetheless attempt to do so. In a world in which power was vested in the word as orally performed, the fear of unauthorized but persuasive speech must have been tremendous. No surprise, then, that the ability to speak—for oneself and over others—would be so zealously guarded.

It is in fears of this kind that we perceive most clearly the extreme vulnerability of such moments. Politics and aesthetics were intimately conjoined. Kings, jurists, and litigants performed their statements within established structures and lexicons. Within those parameters, however, creativity and artistic innovation would seem to have been greatly prized; a particularly intricate or moving formulation might go a long way toward persuading an audience of the incontrovertibility of a given political "truth." Of course, aesthetic standards themselves were anything but status neutral. For the early Irish, art was deeply embedded in considerations of power and social status. That which was most beautiful was that which was most learned, most aristocratic, most authoritative—just as that which was most learned, aristocratic, and authoritative was also that which was most beautiful. The artistic intricacy of a lawsuit brought by or on behalf of a particular individual was expected to reflect directly upon his social standing and rank. Other the other hand, even the most exalted of performers can never be entirely certain whether his claims to mastery—whether over lawsuit, province, or professional discipline—will be accepted until the audience indicates its approval. Performance is in this sense the most dangerous business of all: not merely a distraction, but an occasion of unparalleled artistic and political exposure.

Such a Theatrical People

One of the obvious questions raised by this study is whether any of what we have seen in the Irish material helps us at all in understanding events and relationships elsewhere in medieval Europe. Popular stereotypes of the Irish as unusually artistic and verbally adept are an article of faith for many modern-day travelers to the Emerald Isle—indeed, when I have spoken about this project in public the most common reaction to my arguments is how quintessentially Irish it all seems to be. "Such a *theatrical* people," one listener sighed, as I finished a brief account of my argument, "has there ever been anyone like them for the blarney, I wonder?" Now embedded in this seemingly offhand comment was a very serious question, as I recognized later thinking back over the exchange. Not because of any ethnic predisposition to loquacity on the part of the Irish, but because, truth be told, there were social and political structures in place in Ireland that simply did not exist elsewhere. One would be hard-pressed to find contemporary European parallels for the prominence accorded poets and satirists in Irish culture, for example, or for the existence of a professional legal class at such an early period. Roman and urban structures that served as power bases for rulers elsewhere in Europe did not exist in the same way in Ireland, and it could easily be argued that the Irish were therefore more reliant on oral-performative ways of exercising lordship than were their European counterparts. If the prominence accorded performance in Irish political and legal affairs was unusual within the general European context, then the lessons of this study might in the end prove difficult to generalize.

The evidence suggests, however, that performance and the manipulation of register or code were not phenomena unique to Ireland. Indeed, historians are well aware that the public performance of obligation, reconciliation, and even of emotion was an important feature of medieval political life generally.[3] On the other hand, what has been called "performance" in this book has traditionally been discussed by specialists in non-Celtic subjects almost exclusively in association with, or actually under the rubric of, "ritual."[4] Only rarely do the words "drama," "theatre," or "performance" appear in the indices to books on events that might be viewed in this way; entries for the term "ritual," on the other hand, are usually quite full.[5] Even works that might at first appear to be exceptions in fact serve primarily to prove the rule. Clifford Geertz's work on what he calls the "theatre state" is of course the classic discussion of political performance; his true focus, however, is the means by which "theatre" simultaneously models and, then, remodels society through the process of ritual.[6] Andrée Courtemanche's recent essay on fourteenth-century Manosquin trials is structured according to what she calls a "theatrical analogy," with subsections of the article being devoted to "plot," "protagonists," and the like. However, for her it is ritual, not drama, which stands at the center of her study. Drama is but an analogy through which to understand the "ritualistic transformation" at the heart of the events she is analyzing; it is ritual rather than performance that "gives meaning to a performative act, allowing us to place it within the culture that produced it."[7] Patrick Geary's excellent work on the reimagining of the oral in early medieval written records calls openly for more attention to be paid to the phenomenon of oral performance. But Geary also is concerned with ritual, and with finding ways to bridge the gap between, on the one hand, the "ritualised performance" of procedures like oath taking and boundary demarcation and, on the other, the written texts through which those "rituals" are ultimately revocalized within the community (in performance).[8]

What is true of Courtemanche and Geary is generally true also of other scholars for whom "theatre" and "drama" are active metaphors. Even Fredric Cheyette, who displays great sensitivity to the performative aspects of the Languedocian charters with which he works, interprets his texts in terms both of ritual and of magic, invoking as he does on the one hand, the liturgy, and on the other, ancient Babylonian incantations.[9] That ritual rather than performance should have been so much the focus of scholarly enquiry is to a certain degree inevitable. As is evident even from the first chapter of this work, the most overtly "performative" procedures recorded in our sources are precisely those to which most of us would normally apply the term "ritual." Moreover, the attention traditionally paid to ritual has clearly paid off. What might broadly be termed "ritual studies" has emerged as one of the most fruitful and theoretically sophisticated medieval historical subfields in recent years—so fruitful, indeed, that there has recently been something of an historiographical backlash against the very concept. In his new book, *The Dangers of Ritual: Between Early Medieval Texts and Social Scientific Theory*, Philippe Buc rejects even the most thoughtful and nuanced usage of the term. As he argues, "[l]ike 'feudalism,' ritual carries within itself too much baggage to be conducive to clear thinking, at least as far as my own is concerned."[10] Buc is far from the first historian to have detailed the limitations of "ritual" as a theoretical concept; indeed, as Geoffrey Koziol pointed out in his review of Buc's work, few who have written on the subject have done so without significant methodological soul-searching of their own.[11] But he is surely one of the most emphatic, and the questions he raises are as pertinent to those who would talk about performance as they are to those concerned entirely with ritual per se.

Among the many important challenges Buc raises to the use of "ritual" as a category for historical analysis, one stands out as particularly relevant to the present study—specifically, the presumptions attendant on the nature and reification of the category itself.[12] Buc sees "ritual" as a category constructed entirely by social science theorists that obscures, rather than clarifies, the manner in which medieval persons themselves would have understood what they were doing. When scholars use social science theories of ritual to explain "how a ritual means"[13] they are explicating a category they have themselves invented, one that would be absolutely foreign to those participating in the event. One ordeal is not like another, and ordeals ought not in any case to be tossed into a pot with oaths, coronation ceremonies, knightings, and advents and analyzed as though they were one and the same thing. Worse yet, the widespread (in Buc's view) notion that what we identify as ritual tends always toward consensus and order is embedded, he argues, in the intellectual history of the idea itself. In his opinion, it is a fundamental misunderstanding both of the nature of the event, and of the sources themselves, to imagine stability as the inevitable outcome—or even necessarily the goal—of such procedures. Contemporaries were "starkly aware that danger inhered in ceremonies" and regarded them as anything but "seamless icon[s] of order."[14] The "meaning" of a ritual lay not in its patterned progression toward a predetermined end, but in the agenda of those who wrote about it: it was they who decided how best to construct it, as "good ritual" or "bad."[15]

Historians will (and ought to) devise their own personal responses to the challenges Buc raises. It seems unlikely for a variety of reasons that the term "ritual" will be banished from scholarly discourse any time soon. Extreme nominalism of the sort Buc evinces has the virtue of always being "right," in the sense that any category will disintegrate if pushed on hard enough. On the other hand, it is also remarkably unhelpful, in terms both of understanding what we see in our sources, and articulating our ideas about it afterwards.[16] Categories like "ritual" are by their very nature constructed—the question is really where one wishes to draw the line. Moreover, the idea that one ought not to attempt to analyze a given medieval culture on the basis of categories derived from outside that culture —in other words, that one ought to eschew entirely analytical tools developed in the modern rather than medieval setting—is one that merits scrutiny. It stands only to reason that criteria regarded by one era as important and constitutive might be perceived quite differently by another, and such shifts in perspective can bring great insight. Has not our understanding of medieval politics (in the broadest possible sense of that term) been immeasurably enriched by modern scholarship on gender, on space, on the nature and ramifications of textuality itself?

Of course Buc is correct to warn against the tendency to reify the category of "ritual" (and thus, by extension, performance) to such an extent that it becomes impossible to look past the general to the specific. Theutberga's queenly ordeal is likely to be quite different in nature and importance from that of a local village woman charged with adultery,[17] and if we adduce the two as evidence that all ordeals operate in the same manner or lead inevitably to consensus, we are likely to miss a very important boat.[18] On the other hand, the perils of ignoring altogether the procedural, linguistic, and spiritual similarities linking these events are equally high. To do this is to give up any chance of understanding why contemporaries might have chosen to bother with such a ceremony, what they hoped to gain from it, and how a person accused might ultimately have come to be regarded by others as having been exonerated by it. The fact that Theutberga's particular ritual had a "negative" outcome from the point of view of those who staged it and attempted unsuccessfully to control its outcome it does not in the least vitiate the potential—much less the intent—of ceremonies of this sort to succeed. Structure, (attempted) containment, and the appeal to the transcendent are common responses to extreme political danger. The fact that danger cannot always be averted negates neither the attempt, nor the conviction that a formalized structure of the sort represented by what we call "ritual" may represent for participants their best chance to secure a desired outcome.

This excursus into the pros and cons of ritual studies might seem unnecessarily long. And yet Buc's challenges are important, for they apply to performance as well, and not merely because performance has traditionally been discussed in association with ritual. For performance is, like ritual, also a modern and constructed social science category, one that can be difficult to define with any degree of precision. This is evident even from the wide variety of cultural practices and phenomena that have made their way into this present study, from the making of oral contracts and the proclaiming of satirical verse, to cattle driving, the recitation of *Fénechas*, and the silencing of unauthorized voices. Presumably, not all would even consent to the existence of a category called "performance"—some might regard such a thing as artificial or forced. On the other hand, without it we might never perceive elements that I would argue lay at the very heart of medieval Irish culture and politics: the hierarchies created by speech and silence, the link between aesthetics and authority, the power of the body in motion before an audience attuned to the significance of its movements. The category may be a modern one, but it is no less "true" to the period for all that. It is not that we know better than people living at the time, but rather that we know differently.

All of which returns us to ritual, and to the relationship between ritual and performance. Buc is right to suggest that ritual is as much a perception as it is an entity—as of course are other important historical abstractions, like "court," or "army," or even "legume."[19] He is also correct in pointing to the ways in which our understanding of the word "ritual" has tended subtly to shape the questions we put to our sources. The "ritual" quality of an event resides not merely in its actual structure, but in its structure as interpreted by those who write or speak about it subsequently. Ritual is in this sense as much a mode of analysis as it is an object of analytical exploration. Modern historians choose to employ the word "ritual" when they wish to highlight particular aspects of an institution or event: its staged and formalized structure, its repetition over time, its potential political or spiritual import (what we might call "transcendence"). Many events are deliberately structured in such a way as to embody these qualities, and it is on such easily recognized occasions that scholars have most often focused their attention: coronation ceremonies, civic advents, ordeals, the liturgy. Others, however, are more deliberately in need of construction by those looking on. The principal difference between routine and ritual, for example, is transcendence, a quality that can be bestowed by participants on even the most mundane of activities, like a father's daily nap, or regular attendance at the games of a much-loved baseball team.[20]

For medievalists, "ritual" has historically been a way in which to talk about events that take place more than once, display a particular patterned structure, and seem in their manipulation of time, symbol, and space designed to lead to a particular and transcendent outcome or consensus. To say this is not to assume that rituals are always the same or tend always toward the same goal. Indeed, most good historical writing on the subject (and much of it has been very good indeed) acknowledges not only the possibility but the near certainty that the meaning of rituals might be coopted, contended over, undermined, or simply change over time.[21] With due deference to Buc, there is in the scholarly literature a widespread awareness of difference. However, most scholars asked to consider the semantic associations of the term "ritual" would certainly turn to words of a very particular sort: "formal," "stylized," "scripted," "solemn," "profound," or even "empty"—"empty," that is, of a meaning defined by implicit reference to previous such occasions. With ritual, the structure of the event is always in view: to acknowledge that some rituals "fail" is not in any way to undermine the anticipation of stability and consensus implicit in the succession of acts of which that event is composed. Indeed, for those who wish to decenter the status quo, disrupting or appropriating the rituals through which that status quo is asserted and displayed might seem the surest possible route to success.

Now consider the semantic range of the word "performance," for it is utterly different. Performances are "sparkling," "witty," "new," "fresh," "spontaneous," "probing," "dangerous," and even "radical." Their goal is not (as is often said of ritual) to "stabilize," "order" or "repress," but rather to "enchant," "illuminate," "challenge," "destabilize," and "entertain."[22] Of course, any ritual can also do all these things and more. What is at issue here is not a hard and fast distinction between the ontological realities of the two categories, but rather the analytical approach we choose to take to the event before us: the ways in which we choose to characterize and contextualize it, the types of questions we put to it, the aspects of its makeup that we choose to highlight or suppress. When we use the word "ritual," we silently (and perhaps often subconsciously) communicate to our readers not only something "real" about the event itself, but also about how we believe its authority ought to be understood and interpreted. When we choose the word "performance" instead, we are pointing to something entirely different—*even if we are talking about precisely the same event.* With this subtle shift in wording, we are asking readers to contemplate not the patterned, formal, and ceremonial nature of the occasion before them, but rather its uniqueness, its fluidity, its spontaneity, its existence in and for the moment.

Thus while it is understandable that performance and ritual should historically have been considered together, it is important to realize that they are not the same thing, considered either as entities or as modes of analysis. Performance ought not to be considered as a sidebar, or reduced simply to "what happens" in the context of a ritual. Indeed, performance can happen outside of ritual altogether: at least some of the exchanges discussed in this book would appear to have taken place outside any formalized "ritual" structure (legal instruction, for example, or the switching of codes within personal conversations). Moreover, many "ritualized" procedures may have derived their authority within the community as much from their aesthetic qualities as performed—unique by definition—as from the extent to which they resembled previous such occasions in their structure. Performance is, in Gregory Nagy's terms, the quintessential venue for *mouvance*, the ongoing process of composing and recomposing before knowledgeable audiences. As such, "change" (artistic variation) is "esthetically proper" to performative events in a way that it would likely not be to a coronation, for example, or to a legal proceeding that anticipated or required the word-for-word recitation of particular phrases or formulae.[23]

Performance thus offers us something beyond what we can learn by studying ritual alone, both as a category of historical analysis, and as a lens through which to examine historical artifacts and cultures. It focuses our attention on different aspects of what is taking place: the staging, the language, the interaction among the actors and with the audience, the abilities (or lack thereof) of those onstage. It reminds us of the essential artifice of the event, of its peculiar status as an occasion both in and out of time, of the temporary nature of the roles assumed by the players and wide-ranging nature of the relationships it posits. Most of all, it reminds us what happens when an audience is gripped by the artistry of an occasion, or when an actor speaks with authority the language associated with the role he is playing. It roots the effectiveness of an event not merely in its formalized structure or in the stages through which it passes, but rather in its freshness, in the new light it casts on familiar symbols and identities within the culture, and in its insistence on the creative reinterpretation rather than rote recitation of what is known. By its very nature, then, performance is edgy and uncertain—prone to experimentation, novelty, and danger. It is difficult to imagine telling a person about to embark on a ritual to "break a leg"—even though it is painfully clear from the sources that good luck is precisely what some of the poor devils embarking on some of the rituals described in our sources could have used.[24] With performance, however, the expression seems quite natural, because the risks of failure are so very high.

In its emphasis on danger, a focus on performance both fills a gap in the existing literature on public events, and opens our eyes to elements of particular occasions (ritual and nonritual in nature) that otherwise risk becoming obscured or misinterpreted. When we as scholars wish to consider difference as well as sameness, when we wish to understand the peril in which individuals placed themselves by choosing to enact procedures that might, when considered as ritual, appear predictable and routine, we might find it valuable to place performance alongside ritual as an interpretative approach. Likewise when we wish to turn our attention to the language of a given event, to the manner in which shifts in register or code are deliberately deployed to establish the authority of one actor over another or allow an individual to lay claim to a particular identity or status. Even when we are talking about cultures far removed in place and time from the Ireland of the jurists, an attention to the performative aspects of a given event can sensitize us to aspects of medieval political life that have previously escaped our notice. For as we will see in what follows, "theatricality" in the social and political arena was not a quality restricted to the Hibernian realms.

The Art of the Oath

Sometime around the middle of the twelfth century, Bernard of Durban, scion of a prominent castellan family in what is now the south of France, took an oath of loyalty to Ermengard, viscountess of Narbonne. Relations between the two parties were choppy at best; on the other hand, as Cheyette, the most recent historian of these events, has noted, the oath taken by Bernard was poetry itself. Literally, even: Cheyette is able to scan the lines of the oath as it has come down to us as though it were song. As he remarks, "We are here in the presence not of legal contract but of verbal music whose rhymes and rhythms were calculated to plant the text deep in the memory of those who spoke and forcefully remind all who participated of the many occasions on which they had heard it before. We are in the presence of liturgy."[25] And in truth, Bernard's oath was not exceptional in the world in which he lived. People *had* heard it before. Oaths of this sort survive in their hundreds from medieval Occitania and Catalonia, often in conjunction with the written agreements (*convenientiae*) they guaranteed, the phrasing of which seems often to have overlapped significantly with that of the oath itself.[26]

Cheyette's perceptive exposition of the oath as performance links what might ordinarily be taken as a routine and rather commonplace profession of allegiance to the world of the spirit and the imagination. It is "music," "word magic," the negative phrasing of which ("I will not deceive," "I will not take") in Cheyette's words "darkly mirror[s] by antithesis the 'true faith' that lies at the liturgy's heart."[27] Observations like these bring us close to the emotional heart of the occasion. However, what we have learned from the early Irish evidence offers us the opportunity to build upon these insights and suggest new ways of looking at some of the oddities that typically characterized such events. For the Occitan and Catalan oaths have some peculiar features that have long proved a mystery to scholars.[28] They are frequently (though not always) undated, a practice unusual in this particular historical context. Participants typically identify themselves by reference to their mothers rather than their fathers, as would be the normal practice in most sources from this place and time. The language of the oath frequently switches back and forth between Latin and the vernacular,[29] and while it is possible to discern general patterns in these changes, they are such as to raise questions rather than answer them. Only rarely are substantives put in the vernacular—although certain words appear with regularity. Above all it is verbs, especially certain verbs, which in Zimmerman's words, define "la respiration du texte," and "l'ossature du serment."[30]

One does not have to read very far in the sources to observe these peculiarities for oneself. A good example is this oath, taken from the cartulary of the counts of Barcelona known as the *Liber Feudorum Maior* (vernacular terms and phrases are highlighted in bold):

*Ego, Arnallus Gozfredi, qui fui filius Adalaidis, de ista hora in antea fidelis ero tibi, Guirardo comite, qui fuisti filius Stephania, comitissa, sine fraude et . . . sine **engan**, sicut homo debet esse suo seniori cui manibus se comendat. Et de ista hora in antea ego, predictus Arnallus, **non dezebre te**, prephatum Guirardum, de tua vita neque . . . de tuos castellos, sed adiutor ero tibi . . . sine tuo **engan**, contra cunctos homines vel feminas, qui tibi auferre voluerit vel voluerint; et de tuo adiutorio **no m vedarei ne te n engannarei ne a comonir no me n vedarei per quantas vegades lo m manaras o me n comoniras** per te ipsum aut per tuos missos vel missum; et de ipso castello de Rechesen potestatem **no te n vedarei per quantas vegades me n demanaras** per te aut per tuos nuncios aut per tuum nuncium. Et sicut superius scriptum est, **si t o farei et t o atendrei** tibi, Guirardo iam dicto, et Agneti, coniunx tua et Gaufredo, filio eius . . . sine **engan**.*[31]

I, Arnau Jofre, who was the son of Adalaida, from this hour forward will be faithful to you, Guerau count, who was the son of Estefania, countess, without fraud and . . . without **deceit**, as a man ought to be to his superior to whom he commends himself by his hands. And from this hour forward **I**, the aforesaid Arnau, **will not cheat you**, the aforesaid Guerau, of your life or . . . of your castles, but I will be a supporter to you . . . without **deceiving** you, against all men or women who might wish (singular form) or wish (plural form) to take [them] away from you. And with respect to your support, **I will not refuse [it] nor will I deceive you with respect to it nor will I refuse to be warned however many times you will command it to me or warn me concerning it** either you yourself or through your messengers or messenger; and regarding that castle of Requesens, **I will not refuse you** control **of it however many times you will ask me regarding it** either in person or through your servants or servant. And as it is written above, **I will do it with respect to you and I will maintain it with respect to you**, the previously mentioned Guerau, and for Agnès, your wife and for Jofre, her son . . . without **deceit**.

There are several observations to be made about this text. First, it displays the qualities noted by previous scholars as characteristic of such oaths: the maternal identification, the negative phrasing, the lack of a fixed date, the mixed language. It has other peculiarities as well, features that in fact recur from oath to oath in this (and other) cartularies. Perhaps most remarkable to the modern eye is its phrasing—not just repetitive or formulaic or given to parallelisms, but almost obsessively so, with its attentiveness to niceties like singular or plural (the dual forms of "wish," for example, or "messengers or messenger"), and masculine or feminine (the would-be attackers). There is the meticulous repetition of names, as though anticipating the possibility that other Gueraus might suddenly surface to claim ownership of the service and loyalty proffered were it not specified to which Guerau the agreement was to pertain. And finally there is the admixture of oral and written: the oral form of the oath itself, coupled with what has been "written above."[32]

Other fascinating features of this oath become noticeable once it is compared to others in the same cartulary. As has been said, many oaths of the period contain the same admixture of Latin and the vernacular. However, when they are looked at side by side with one another, it becomes obvious that for all the similarities, the pattern is never exactly the same. The sentiment expressed above in general terms by the phrase *non dezebre te . . . de tuos castellos* is, for example, frequently articulated elsewhere using the verb *enganare* and, more precisely, by another phrase, *no l tel tolre ne te n tolre,* "nor take it (that is, the castle) from you nor take from you anything from it."[33] *Engan,* "deceit," can appear as either a noun or a verb and assumes different grammatical forms from text to text.[34] Similarly, many (but not all) oaths end with an expression involving different forms of the (already more or less synonymous) verbs *tenre* and *atendre.* All mean approximately the same thing; however, all are phrased slightly differently:

> *si o tenre et o atendre ego,* "thus I will keep it and maintain it (that is, the oath of loyalty)";

> *vos o tenrei et vos o atendrei totum ad te,* "I will keep it with respect to you and maintain it entirely with respect to you";

> *si t o farei et t o atendrei tibi,* "thus I will do it with respect to you and maintain it with respect to you";

> *sic faciam et attendam et teneam ego,* "thus I will do and keep and hold to";

> *si t o tenre et si t o atendre per directam fidem,* "thus I will keep it with respect to you and maintain it with respect to you through [an oath of] true faith" (possibly "unmediated fidelity");

> *t o atendrei et o atendrei sine forifacto,* "I will maintain it with respect to you and maintain it without forfeit."[35]

The variety is almost endless—even though the sentiments expressed are very similar. It is to be noted that one of the above phrases (and part of another) is in Latin, despite the fact that the oath from which is comes is written in a mixture of Latin and Catalan. This is typical throughout the corpus. Terms or phrases that recur across many oaths will appear sometimes in Latin, and sometimes in the vernacular (for example, *per nuncios,* "by messengers," versus *per . . . missagges*).[36]

Perhaps most noticeable to the modern eye are the lengthy and clearly intentionally rhetorical strings of verbs and verbal forms found in some (though not all) of the oaths in this cartulary. An oath made by William Bernard in 1084 is a particularly nice example: *no l te tolre ne te n tolre ne non te n enganare ne te n dezebre no l te vedare ne te n vedare ne no te n enganare ne ara nec in antea . . . ,*[37] "nor take it (the castle of Villanova) from you, nor take anything from you from it, nor deceive you regarding it, nor betray you regarding it, nor refuse you, nor refuse you regarding it, nor deceive you regarding it, either now or in the future . . ." Usually rhetorical runs of this sort center, as they do here, on verbs, and again, there is almost infinite variety in the manner in which they are combined. Sometimes, however, other parts of speech are in question, such as in the agreement cited by Cheyette with which we began, where there is a string of different persons and numbers of pronouns joined together by the single preposition *ab: ab aquel ne ab aquella ne ab aquels ne ab aquellas,* "with him or with her or with them (masculine) or with them (feminine)."[38] Other rhetorical devices employed in these oaths include alliteration (*honoribus quem hodie habes; contra cunctos; voluerit vel voluerint . . . vedarei . . . vedarei . . . vegades; manaras . . . missos vel missu; sicut superius scriptum est*);[39] assonance (*manaras . . . cominiras . . . demanaras*);[40] parallelisms (*oppido vel castella vel forteda; lo m querras vel me demanaras*);[41] chiasmus (*nec homo nec femina, nec femina nec homo*);[42] and generalized wordplay, both in Latin and in the vernacular.[43]

In short, what we see in the Catalan material parallels very closely what we saw earlier in the Irish contractual texts. Each oath or promissory statement is fundamentally different, and yet each is also fundamentally the same. Metalinguistic features like parallelisms and repetitions abound; codeswitching (from Latin to Catalan/Occitan and back again in the one case, and from unmarked to marked Old Irish in the other) is a prominent aspect of the occasion. The intensely negative phrasing of the Languedocian oaths is not precisely paralleled in the Irish. On the other hand, the obsessively repetitive, relentlessly specific aspect of the phrasing—the sense that the intent is to anticipate (and thereby eliminate) absolutely every possible circumstance that could arise to disrupt an agreement—is indeed a feature of both traditions.[44] Cheyette takes the tendency to put everything always in the negative ("I swear that I will not do such-and-such") as evidence of a "crabbed and mean-spirited society, filled with suspicion if not paranoia,"[45] and he may be right. If so, however, it is a paranoia shared by both cultures. At the very least, one can infer that both societies were familiar with—and hence anxious to guard against—the tradition of the equivocal oath, where the object sworn to by one party is not what the other party understood it to be, usually because the phrasing used was insufficiently precise (for example, "I said I would not attack your castle, but I did not guarantee anything with respect to your fortress," or "I said I had not allied myself to Gerard, but the Gerard about whom I was speaking was not the Gerard you thought I meant").[46]

So what might the Irish evidence have to suggest to us about the Languedocian oaths? Cheyette's insistence on their poetic and ritual qualities points the way for us in many important respects. Many of the features that have seemed so puzzling to scholars make considerably more sense if one

contemplates the event they describe from the point of view of performance. Both the missing date and the maternal identification can be understood in this way. Just as in Irish contractual ritual, persons entering into
the type of relationship created by these oaths were taking on new roles
within the social and political world they customarily inhabited. This new
relationship was to be created and experienced, however, in a time and
place set apart from the one in which they normally lived. It thus could not
be located in a "real" time and place even though it was indisputably bound
to both; rather, it existed simultaneously both in the religious space created
by the invocation of the deity, and in the performative space created by the
language and gestures attendant on the event. In the world outside the performative frame, men who were grown, independent, political actors would
not typically self-identify as children did, according to their mothers.
Within the frame, however, for the purposes of the oath, the men involved
had no fathers or paternal kindred, even if their biological fathers were still
alive at the time of the agreement (as was likely frequently the case).
Hélène Débax has recently argued that both parties to the oath conceptualized it as creating a new family, one in which the lord stepped in as "spiritual father" to his "spiritual" son and vassal.[47] This is surely right: men
divested themselves of their usual identities and relationships within the
performative frame in order to perform their own social and political
rebirth.

Even more compelling as evidence of performance is the issue of language. As Bernard's oath suggests, the alternating of codes or registers in
the course of creating legal and political relationships was not a phenomenon restricted to the Ireland of the jurists. What makes the texts from
Languedoc so interesting, and differentiates them from the oaths of earlier
centuries, to which they are clearly related,[48] is the presence of the vernacular.[49] Outside of the Irish context, mixed language sources of this sort are
relatively rare from the early Middle Ages, the closest parallels being the
vernacular boundary clauses and curses often appended to Latin charters
from early England or Francia, the texts of the vernacular oaths taken at
Strasbourg in 842 recorded in the (Latin) chronicle of Nithard, and the
few "intentionally vernacular Italian" sentences occurring in four tenth-
century charters.[50] Codeswitching between registers is more common.
Koziol speaks, for example, of a "rhetoric of petition and grace" and other
"ceremonial styles of speech" visible within Latin charters from eleventh-
and twelfth-century France.[51] The mélange of actual languages characteristic of the Languedocian oaths is, however, both unusual and valuable, not
least because they vary so markedly one from the other.

Of course, one cannot simply presume that the oaths as they survive to
us directly reflect the reality of the oral events they purport to describe.
Generally speaking, however, historians of medieval Languedoc have
tended to presume a reasonably direct relationship between written text

and oral oath, not least because it is difficult otherwise to explain the alternation between codes and use of the vernacular. Élisabeth Magnou-Nortier thus speaks of a *style oral* in the texts with which she is concerned.[52] Clovis Brunel, working with Provençal sources, more or less assumes that the words on the page reflect those spoken at the time, recorded so as to be preserved for posterity without significant distortion.[53] Michel Zimmermann makes the interesting suggestion that the alternation of Catalan and Latin in the oaths signals a responsive reading of the text of the agreement wherein the words kept in the vernacular represent those actually said by the oath taker.[54] And other authors are quite nuanced in their views, acknowledging the difficulties of linking the written sources to the oral event they purport to describe, and choosing instead to emphasize the extent to which written and oral were inseparable aspects of the ritual by which agreements were made and property transferred.[55]

The problem is a difficult one. Many of the oaths imagine the oath taker swearing to hold to the agreement *sicut superius* (or *supra*) *scriptum est,* "as it has been written above," which could be taken as evidence either that the oath (or *convenientia* to which it referred) was already in existence at the time the oath taker was speaking, or that a scribe was present at the agreement jotting down precisely what had been said.[56] If the former is the case, we must allow for the possibility of redaction by the scribe; if the latter, scribal intervention may be less of an issue. Perhaps the best we can do is to note with Kosto what this implies about the proximity of oral and written in the performance of such oaths. At the very least, the two events, performance and inscription of performance, are not so starkly separated that one is an unreliable guide to the other. The oath might be, as Geary suggests, a "fictional character" created by a scribe reimagining an oral event.[57] On the other hand, if so, it is an exceptionally knowledgeable scribe, one who seems to have been present at the time of the arrangement. In other words, the fact that these oaths differ from one another as much as they do matters, for what it suggests is that we have in these texts is something proximate either to the specific oral event in question, or to the nature of such events in general. Often the term "formulaic" is used in regard to such texts because of their similarities in phrasing,[58] but in fact it is their differences, rather than their similarities, that should strike us most forcefully. We are dealing here with something much more than just the random deployment of formulaic phrases—something very like *mouvance.* As Gregory Nagy observes, it is often "the degree of multiformity in the textual tradition that leads to the conclusion that an oral tradition is at work backstage."[59]

Imagining these oaths in performance (even if scribally redacted performance) takes us deep into the heart of what they are and how they might have functioned. Scholars have tended to link the change in codes, from Latin to Catalan (or Occitan) and back again, to the oral ceremony itself. As we have seen, Zimmermann postulates that the vernacular words might represent those actually spoken by the oath taker. Cheyette takes another tack, imagining the scribe "copying the oath on little slips of parchment, a text he knows so well that he cannot keep his mind on whether the words are Latin or vernacular . . . All conspired to impress deep seriousness on the moment: the company, the visible permanence of the oath being inscribed in ink . . . the magic of the rhythmic words."[60] Such a scenario is certainly possible. On the other hand, it is difficult to imagine how the language of an oath can be simultaneously "formulaic" and forgettable. Nor is it easy to understand why scribes might forget themselves in such regularized patterns: why when they "slip" from one code to another, it is almost always with respect to verbs, and why when they enter upon phrases in the oath that recur from one event to the other (for example, the *tenre atendre* clauses), they do not repeat them in precisely the same way. If these phrases are truly "formulaic," one would expect more consistency; if they are truly products of a wandering scribal mind, one would expect less regularity in the way in which they are presented.

The example afforded by the Irish evidence offers us another way in which to interpret these peculiarities. What we are seeing here, I would argue, are important and intentionally artistic aspects of the oral performative event (whether recorded verbatim or reimagined by the scribe). In performance, the change in code, from Latin to Catalan or Occitan and back again, underscored the most prominent aspects of the obligation, for participant and audience alike. A change in code inevitably calls attention to itself and, thereby, to that which it is intended to represent. Surely it is not accidental that the words most often highlighted in this way are the verbs, for they are both the heart of the agreement and the focus for anxieties. Equally important is the issue of language as art. It is tempting simply to gloss over the parallelisms and repetitions, or to see them either as meaningless redundancies or as indications of advanced legal paranoia. However, as both Kosto and Débax have pointed out, the essence of an oath is its individual nature: it binds only those taking and receiving it.[61] And while these oaths are very similar, they are also very different. Some are considerably more rhetorical than others: the words ebb and flow as if with practiced skill. Some, however, are more mundane, and show relatively little imagination in their phrasing. Nothing is more individual—and more universal—than art, and it is art, I suggest, that we are witnessing in these oaths. Art defines the personality of the agreement as surely as it engages the participation of the audience before which it is enacted.

There is also the issue of memory. Cheyette situates the musical elements of the oath largely in the realm of social memory: the rhythms of what is said inculcate themselves and the agreement into the memory of the participants, reminding them not only of the terms, but of previous occasions that have gone before.[62] His comments give us valuable insight into the mnemonic aspects of the procedure, but the issue may be even more complex than this. For as Mary Carruthers has demonstrated, memory in medieval thought was coincident not with rote recitation, but with creativity. Learning to repeat by heart was only the first step in a complex series of lessons designed to take one to a deeper level of understanding the essence of that which had been learned. One learned to repeat in order to learn how creatively to vary, for it was in the composition of tradition, rather than in its unimaginative reproduction, that true "memory" was believed to lie.[63] Just as Irish litigants and other authoritative speakers appear to have innovated within the parameters of the language traditionally associated with their occasion (contracts, the giving of verdicts), so too, I suggest, did the Languedocian speakers whose voices we are hearing in these texts—at whatever remove—reform and reshape the matter before them. Like all "traditional" speakers, they performed within the confines of their tradition. Like all artists, however, they looked to say what they had to say in new and different ways, in ways that would involve their audience while persuading it also of the legitimacy of the act. A role assumed by an actor will be accepted by those in attendance much more readily if the performance has been good: artistic language, carefully crafted and deployed, persuades more effectively than does the mindless recitation of a script.

The suggestions proffered above may not account for all of the extant oaths. Certainly it is important not to forget the technical and legal aspects of these agreements in our quest to understand their more aesthetic elements. On the other hand, as recent work has made clear, it would be a mistake to try to distinguish too sharply between the strictly political and the purely aesthetic in this instance. Languedoc was, as was Ireland, a culture of political performance. As Martin Aurell has demonstrated, political poetry played a critical role in the aristocratic struggles and comital politics of the twelfth and thirteenth centuries.[64] Poets were crucial figures at court, whether as established residents or wandering players. Jongleurs and troubadours commented freely on the merits and demerits of the nobles who patronized them, and even seemingly apolitical genres like the *pastourelle* could be used to voice criticisms of unsatisfactory rulers.[65] Indeed, so important were poets both to the maintenance and exercise of power, and to noble identity itself, that Aurell links the professionalization of the poetic discipline to the increasing self-confidence of comital power after 1220.[66] Moreover, the verse forms and language used by these artists directly reflected the political structures upon which they commented. The "explosion of private wars" of the early thirteenth century is chronicled in a series of *tensons*, a form of dialogue poem that recapitulates in verse form the back-and-forth nature of the conflicts it describes.[67] Language too mirrored the political relationships of the day. Poetic discourse was an authoritative discourse—the language not only of love and romantic fidelity, but of lordship, fidelity, and the keeping of one's word. Through this language, fidelity itself was, in Cheyette's words, transmuted "into a passion."[68] When the Comtessa de Dia sings of a personal betrayal by her lover, she sings also of the betrayal of the noble ideals of the class to which both belong.[69]

And it is in this last that we see the true context of the oaths with which we began. For as in Ireland, where many of the authoritative poetic speakers of the period were members of the educated classes, so also in Languedoc was the ability to speak artistically—and hence authoritatively—linked to noble status and to the world of the court. Nobles—among them the very highest nobility of the age—were both patrons and subjects of the troubadours. The involvement of Henry the Young King and of his brother Richard Lionheart in the patronage of the troubadours is well known as is, of course, that of Eleanor of Aquitaine herself. But aristocratic participation in the culture of performance was not restricted to the act of patronage. Nobles were troubadours and trobairitz themselves. William IX of Aquitaine is merely the earliest and most famous of the aristocratic poets of the age: indeed, before the professionalization of the art in the decades following 1220, many troubadours came from the petty nobility, and some from even higher classes. Aurell traces the biography of the poet Gui de Cavaillon, for example, expert poet and warrior, who after years of faithful service rose through the ranks to become the right hand man of the Count of Toulouse.[70] Guy's career illustrates the inseparability of art and politics in this period, when the language of love was coincident with the language of power, and when the ability to speak beautifully was viewed as intrinsically linked to the character of the ruler.[71]

In such a setting, the rhetorical aspects of these oaths take on a new and potentially darker significance. What ought we to imagine when we read an oath heavy with poetic figures and language? On one level, the speaker of such an oath may aspire merely to entertain or intrigue his audience so as better to impress upon them the terms of the agreement. On another, however, he may intend something more—the quiet assertion of a level of courtliness and authority vis-à-vis his new lord to which not all would automatically consent, for example, or a display of artistic competence designed to underscore his own qualities of mind while implicitly challenging those of his respondent. Or perhaps the reverse is the case. Given the frequently intimate connection between written *convenientia* and oath, perhaps one should imagine a situation akin to that of the Irish, where the speech of the inferior party might be appropriated by a person claiming superiority over him. In one of the early *convenientiae* cited by Kosto, for example, (what purport to be) the words spoken by the oath taker in the course of confirming the agreement are recapitulated in third person "objective" form and hedged about with the penalties that will ensue if the agreement should be violated. If one imagines the public reading of the written *convenientia* as part of the ceremony by which the agreement was effected, as Kosto suggests, the effect might well be that of the lord's appropriating or "voicing over" the original words of the juror.[72] And what of those oaths that are not terribly rhetorical, that appear more heavily reliant on formulas or, at the very least, less imaginatively phrased? Do such oaths reflect merely the competency of the performer? Or might we imagine a situation in which relatively mundane phrasing was used to express a certain lack of enthusiasm or sincerity on the part of the juror (either in reality or as reconstructed by the scribe recording the event)?

Language can be beautiful, engaging, compelling, or entrancing. But it can also be disruptive, subordinating, or undermined in performance through the manipulation of gesture or tone. An oath that on the surface reads to us as straightforward and sincere might in context appear mocking and corrupt; an oath that seems to us suspicious and distrustful because of the repetitive nature of its phrasing might in context be taken as a moving tribute to the courtly nature of those it honored. From this distance it is difficult to tell, not least because the essence of performance is its individual nature and immunity to generalization. The important point is that performance too constitutes a language, a way of speaking, a means of addressing the complex realities of the situation in which it takes place. Contemplating an event through the lens of performance does not take the place of appreciating it as ritual (where appropriate); both approaches offer ways to analyze events in the past. But the two are not synonymous. Ritual always entails performance if realized in real life, but the reverse is not necessarily true. Moreover, analyzing an event as performance focuses attention specifically on the ways in which interpretations of paradigmatic structures (the "script") differ from event to event rather than on how they remain the same. There can thus be few presumptions about the likely outcome. As in any situation in which aesthetic risks are being taken, there is always the possibility that things might go dreadfully, horribly, wrong. If anything, it is the potential for instability and failure, rather than for consensus, that is built into the concept of performance.

The Dangers of Performance

As we have seen, medieval Languedoc was, like Ireland, a peculiarly performance-oriented culture. Historians might therefore question whether the perspectives developed in the course of this book could prove useful in analyzing events in even those societies in which poets and troubadours did not actively participate in the politics of the period. Doubts of this kind return us to the early medieval period and, specifically, to the late Carolingian era. Perhaps the most famous instance of codeswitching in the early continental sources are the oaths taken at Strasbourg in 842 by two of the warring sons of Louis the Pious, Louis the German and Charles the Bald. At the time, Louis and Charles were each feeling threatened by the ambitions of a third brother, the emperor Lothar, against whom they had fought the important battle of Fontenoy the preceding fall. Louis and Charles had carried the day at Fontenoy, but Lothar was still quite powerful, and each brother feared that the other would defect to Lothar's cause, taking his supporters with him. The oaths taken at Strasbourg were thus designed to secure the alliance between Charles and Louis and to commit their respective followers, also by oath, to force their kings to keep faith with one another and refrain from entering into separate treaty arrangements with Lothar. As the historian Nithard, to whom we owe our knowledge of the event, describes the scene, the two kings began with some preliminary statements detailing Lothar's past treacheries; each then proceeded to take an oath of mutual support to the other. Significantly, each king swore his oath in the language of his brother: Louis, a native German speaker, spoke his oath in Romance, an early form of French, while Charles, whose first language was Romance, spoke his in Frankish, an early form of German. After the kings had finished speaking, their followers then followed with oaths of their own in which they promised to hold their lords to the promises each had made. Significantly, the oath taken by the supporters of each king was taken in those supporters' own native vernacular—only the kings, in other words, spoke in languages other than the one native to themselves.

What has made the oaths of Strasbourg so famous is the fact that Nithard included in his account what purports to be a verbatim transcript of the vernacular oaths in question. Those interested in the emergence of the early vernaculars, and particularly in the evolution of Latin into the various Romance tongues, have thus found these citations from *lingua romana et teudisca* extraordinarily important. Earlier scholarship on the oaths tended simply to presume that Nithard's account faithfully reproduced what had actually been said. From this, historians drew a variety of broad conclusions about the nature and evolution of languages within the Frankish empire: that by 842, Latin was no longer intelligible to the majority of people living in the empire, that Romance had by this point separated off from Latin and was well on its way to becoming French (and Spanish and Italian, and so on), and that the linguistic divisions within the empire must have been such that the kings could no longer assume that German nobles would understand Romance or that Romance speakers would understand German.[73]

Rosamond McKitterick subsequently challenged the idea that the words reported by Nithard might exactly reproduce those actually spoken by Louis and Charles, arguing (much as Buc does for his texts) that what we are reading here is Nithard's own construction of the event, and that Nithard was in essence merely "giving literary form to what was an extempore promise."[74] McKitterick and historian Janet Nelson also stressed the ideological aspects of Nithard's account and, specifically, the manner in which he used language to underscore his political agenda. As McKitterick has observed, both vernaculars are embedded in an otherwise Latin text.

By uniting all three languages of the empire in this way, Nithard is able simultaneously to call attention to divisions within the empire and present the alliance between Louis and Charles as a way in which to cement the "unity and coherence" of the whole.[75] Nelson points to Nithard's desire to persuade Charles's followers of the divine judgment implicit in the victory of Fontenoy and his sense of the importance of the settlement negotiated between Louis and Charles. For Nithard, she argues, unity is the most important royal priority, and it is this that accounts for the remarkable prominence accorded the oaths of Strasbourg in his history. He wants both to underscore the necessity of *fraternitas* among the brothers and hence within the empire, and to counter any propaganda coming from Lothar regarding the frankly deceitful manner in which Louis and Charles had won their victory at Fontenoy. His use of the vernaculars thus functions to highlight "the collective nature of these commitments" and to underscore the unity of the *populus Christianus.*[76]

Concerns about Nithard's agenda and the extent to which it might have colored his depiction of the events at Strasbourg, if substantiated, would make it difficult to treat his account as a straightforward reporting of what actually took place. However, recent scholarship has seen the pendulum swing back in the direction of according credence to Nithard's version of the oath. In a very important article, Ruth Schmidt-Wiegand has pointed to the written chancellery models lying behind the Romance oath taken by Louis, although those ascribed to the aristocratic followers of each king are, she argues, closer to normal speech.[77] Kosto also stresses the extent to which the words purportedly spoken at Strasbourg are grounded in the scribal traditions of the court.[78] Such a patterning of oral oaths on formal chancellery models suggests that the language may have been worked out ahead of time in negotiations between the participants. If so, what Nithard is reporting may have been carefully crafted speech the authenticity of which he was unlikely to get wrong, since its the legal authority was grounded in its proximity to courtly models. Indeed, the Annals of Fulda make clear that at least on one other occasion when the brothers exchanged oaths with one another (in 876), the text of their oath (sworn in *lingua theutonica*), was actually distributed to various important locales within the kingdom, there to be preserved against revision or loss.[79] Might Nithard actually have been working from such a text, distributed in conjunction with the swearing of the oaths of Strasbourg?[80]

The evidence thus suggests that we may indeed take Nithard's account of the words spoken at Strasbourg seriously—and it is worth noting that even those who have doubts are willing to concede at least some links between events as they occurred and events as they were reported.[81] Moreover, no one has as yet called into question the basic structures of the occasion, and it is these that allow—even encourage—us to analyze it as an instance of political performance. In fact, it is interesting that so little attention has yet been paid to these structures—or even, curiously, to what the kings actually are depicted as saying, except from the linguistic point of view. Many historians elide the phases through which the event progressed, as though they made little difference to the meaning of the affair. Nelson, for example, seems to confound the preliminary declarations made by the kings with the oaths themselves, implying as she does that even at this preliminary stage of the occasion, the kings switched languages.[82] McKitterick also does not distinguish between the declarations and the oaths: she makes a point of reminding her readers that each king spoke in the vernacular of the other, but she nowhere distinguishes those phases of the proceedings of which this was true and those of which it was not.

In fact, Nithard's account makes it clear that whereas the oaths themselves were sworn by Charles and Louis in the language of the other, the preliminary statements were made by each king in his own native language:

Lodhuvicus autem, quia major natu, prior exorsus sic coepit . . . Cumque Karolus haec eadem verba romana lingua perorasset, Lodhuvicus, quoniam major natu erat, prior haec deinde se servaturum testatus est . . .[83]

"Louis, however, who was the elder, thus began to speak first . . ." (*Here follows the text of the preliminary declaration regarding Lothar.*) "And when Charles had spoken these same words in the Romance language, Louis, who was the elder, then swore first to observe the following . . ." (*Here follows the text of the oaths.*)

From this it is evident that the oaths themselves constituted a unique performative space marked out from the declarations that preceded them by a sharp break in language. Just as in Irish contractual law, the switching of codes would seem to have served in performance both to alert the audience to the boundaries of the space carved out by the oath, and to focus their attention on what was happening within that space. It began when each king abandoned his native tongue and temporarily assumed the linguistic identity of his brother; it ended when each king reverted to his own political identity by resuming his customary language.

Significantly, only the oaths of the kings are marked out in this way: their supporters swore their oaths in their own native languages. In earlier scholarship, this was usually taken as an indication that each king needed to change languages in order to make sure that what he said would be comprehensible to the followers of his brother—the implication being that whereas the kings would naturally understand both languages, ordinary nobles might not. Such a conclusion is difficult to assess, as we know so little about the linguistic state of the nobility in this period. Regardless of whether the switching of codes has anything to tell us about language and the nobility, however, it tells us a great deal about kingship. Within the performative space, each king temporarily became in effect, a resident of the lands of the other, swearing his oath to his fellow countrymen in the lan-

guage in which they lived and worked and fought. The identities of the supporters, by contrast, were limited both within and without the performative
space of the oath: kings could transcend the linguistic and cultural boundaries of the empire, but ordinary men could not. What makes the switching of codes particularly potent as a symbol is that this linguistic
manipulation was being deployed against Lothar, the Emperor whose lands
literally straddled the physical divide between German east and Romance
west. Together, Louis and Charles implicitly laid claim through their performance not merely to dual identities, but to the unity of the empire itself.

And in fact, matters may be more complicated even than this implies.
For an analysis of the performative aspects of these events cannot help but
return our attention to language, and to the words reportedly spoken by
each man. Usually when the oaths of Strasbourg are quoted or discussed,
only one translation is provided for both oaths—the implication being, of
course, that what Louis said in Romance was precisely the same as what
Charles said in German. Fairly typical is this translation from Loyn and Percival's *The Reign of Charlemagne*:

For the love of God and for our Christian people and for our common safety I shall
from this day forth assist this my brother Charles/Louis with all the wisdom and
strength that God may give me, in the bringing of aid and in all other matters in
which a man should rightly assist his brother, provided he does the same for me,
and I will not willingly enter into any agreement with Lothar which may be harmful to this my brother Charles/Louis.[84]

Bernhard Scholz's *Carolingian Chronicles* translates the two oaths separately, but in such a way that each oath precisely repeats the phrasing of the
other (the only exception being that of the names of the parties involved):

For the love of God and for our Christian people's salvation and our own, from this
day on, as far as God grants knowledge and power to me, I shall treat my brother
with regard to aid and everything else as a man should rightfully treat his brother,
on condition that he do the same to me. And I shall not enter into any dealings with
Lothair which might with my consent injure this my brother Charles.

For the love of God and for our Christian people's salvation and our own, from this
day on, as far as God grants knowledge and power to me, I shall treat my brother
with regard to aid and everything else as a man should rightfully treat his brother,
on condition that he do the same to me. And I shall not enter into any dealings with
Lothair which might with my consent injure this my brother Louis.[85]

Other scholars who have discussed (but not translated) the oaths, like Nelson and McKitterick, also imply that the translations (from German to Romance) are sufficiently exact that each king swears to precisely the same
thing his brother had done.

However, this is not in fact true. For while Louis in his oath to Charles
declares that he will "assist this my brother Charles . . . as a man should

rightly assist his brother" (*si salvarai eo cist meon fradre Karlo . . . si cum om per dreit son fradra salvar dist*) and not enter "willingly into any agreement with Lothar which may be harmful to this my brother Charles" (*et ab Ludher nul plaid nunquam prindrai, qui meon vol, cist meon fradre Karle in damno sit*), Charles does not actually return the favor. He swears to the same terms, but omits all mention of Louis's name, committing himself to "assist this my brother in the manner a man ought rightly assist his brother" (*so haldih thesan minan bruodher, soso man mit rehtu sinan bruher scal*), and to "not enter willingly into an agreement with Lothar that might injure him" (*indi mit Ludheren in nohheiniu thing ne gegango the, minan uuillon, imo ce scadhen uuerdhen*). Charles's failure to mention Louis's name is extremely significant, since of course Lothar is also a brother to Charles: the wording of Charles's oath leaves it entirely unspecified which brother he will help.

What we have here, I would suggest, is an equivocal oath—one in which what is sworn to is technically "true," but morally very cloudy, in that it is intentionally constructed in a manner designed to allow Charles as oathtaker to maneuver himself out of the spirit of his promise even while he continues to observe the letter. Nor do the oaths of Charles's supporters compromise their lord's position in any way. They swear that they will not help Charles against Louis if Charles fails to keep his oath. However, since Charles's oath was only to "help his brother," this leaves plenty of room for him and his followers later to argue that he has in fact observed this promise should he later decide to throw his lot in with Lothar. The fraud is surely deliberate: Louis mentions Charles's name twice in his oath, and Charles omits Louis's name both times. The demonstrative pronoun "this" may appear to designate Louis, but this is not a necessary conclusion: indeed, in the words "this my brother" we may catch a glimpse of how a disingenuous wave of a hand or a gesture into the air can serve in performance to undermine the words actually spoken.[86] In this we see clearly the "dangers of performance": the moment at which what seems to be staid and patterned and predictable turns menacing and dark. The performative codeswitching that was intended to underscore the unity of the two brothers and of the empire they aspired to share was in this instance the occasion for trickery and deceit.[87]

The oaths of Strasbourg are a salutary reminder that surprises can lurk even within the most seemingly "ritualistic" of events. Contemplating an event through the lens of performance opens our eyes not merely to the ways in which similar occasions have proceeded in the past, but to the manner in which words and gestures and symbols come together at a particular moment in time to construct a relationship both between the parties themselves, and between them and their audience. What matters is not merely what previous experience suggests will be said and done but what actually takes place. The focus is less on the "script" of the "drama" than on what is done with that script, less on sameness and pattern than on fresh interpretation and departures from what the audience expects. The focus is also, and inevitably, on language, for rhetorical language and the manipulation of code are frequent (though not necessary) elements of political and legal performance. So too, one must imagine, is trickery and deceit, the darker side of linguistic power.

It is difficult to say whether other early medieval cultures viewed language and performance in similar ways. We know very little about the manner in which the artistic deployment of particular linguistic styles and codes served in this period to define or enhance political relationships. Robert Bjork's perceptive study of the Anglo-Saxon poem *Beowulf* is certainly suggestive, in that it underscores the manner in which the speech attributed by the poet to his principal characters reveals the state of the society they inhabit. There is speech that is orderly and controlled, and speech that portends chaos and confusion. The formalized speech of Hrothgar and Beowulf in the court of Heorot give way to the dangerously emotional ramblings of Unferth and the barely comprehensible cries of Wiglaf at his lord's death. Society's progression from one state to another can be traced through the state of its language.[88] And while few would argue that the speech reported in *Beowulf* represents that of your average Anglo-Saxon in the street, the connections drawn in the poem between language and social order may not be so easy to dismiss. It may be that what the Irish sources imply about linguistic art as both the guardian of the status quo and the means by which it can be challenged extended beyond the boundaries of the Irish Sea. Certainly the example of the Occitan and Catalan charters suggests that for other medieval cultures also, language and performance were key elements of power.

This then is the gift that the Irish evidence has to offer those who would look beyond the visible structures and institutions in which political relationships were vested in the early Middle Ages to the cultural understandings by which those structures and institutions were sustained. The work of the jurists affords us the opportunity to see how words uttered publicly in performance can function to establish identities, assert hierarchies, engage audiences, and transform social roles. It shows us art engaged in the service of memory, entertainment identified as a venue for power, and performance linked to ritual but not always synonymous with it. But it also requires us to perceive those who construct the scenes on which our understanding depends for the "speakers" they are. For it is well to keep in mind that gifts of language are notoriously treacherous, and that if this is a gift, it is one in the fullest Germanic sense of the word, embracing both the bitter and the sweet.[89] Power is derived and exercised not merely through speech, but through the ability to construct the speech of others. In the Irish lawbooks, the worlds of the constructor and the constructed overlap. Dark speech is powerful speech, for implied within its tangled skeins is the silence of those who have been denied a voice. And as everyone knows, the speech of lawyers can be exceedingly dark indeed.

Abbreviations

AM	*Audacht Morainn*. Ed. Fergus Kelly. Dublin: DIAS, 1976.
BA	*Berrad Airechta*. (See *Bürgschaft*.)
BB	*Bechbretha: An Old Irish Law-tract on Bee-Keeping*. Ed. T.M. Charles-Edwards and Fergus Kelly. Early Irish Law Series, vol. 1. Dublin: DIAS, 1983.
BDC	*Bretha Déin Chécht*. Ed. D. A. Binchy. *Ériu* 20 (1966): 1–66.
BFG	*Bretha im Fhuillema Gell*
BN	*Bretha Nemed*
BND	*Bretha Nemed Déidenach*
BNT	*Bretha Nemed Toísech*
Br. Crólige	*Bretha Crólige*. Ed. D. A. Binchy. *Ériu* 12 (1934): 1–77.
Bürgschaft	*Die Bürgschaft im irischen Recht*. Ed. R. Thurneysen. *Abhandlungen der preussischen Akademie der Wissenschaften* 2, Phil.-Hist. Klasse, Jahrgang 1928. Berlin: Verlag der preussischen Akademie der Wissenschaften, 1928.
C. Adam.	*Cáin Adamnáin: An Old-Irish Treatise on the Law of Adamnán*. Ed. Kuno Meyer. *Anecdota Oxoniensia*, Medieval and Modern Series 12. Oxford: Clarendon Press, 1905.
C. Aicillne	*Cáin Aicillne*. Ed. R. Thurneysen. In "Aus dem irischen Recht I. [I. Das Unfrei-Lehen]." *ZCP* 14 (1923): 336–94.
CB	*Córus Béscnai*
CI	*Cáin Íarraith*
CCF	*Cóic Conara Fugill: Die fünf Wege zum Urteil*. Ed. R. Thurneysen. *Abhandlungen der preussischen Akademie der Wissenschaften* 7, Phil.-Hist. Klasse, Jahrgang 1925. Berlin: Verlag der preussischen Akademie der Wissenschaften, 1926.
CCH	*Collectio Canonum Hibernensis*. (See *IK*.)
CD	*Cáin Domnaig*. Ed. Vernam Hull. *Ériu* 20 (1966): 151–77.
CG	*Críth Gablach*, ed. D. A. Binchy. Mediaeval and Modern Irish Series, vol. 11. Dublin: DIAS, 1941; reprinted, 1979. References are to line unless otherwise noted.
CIH	*Corpus Iuris Hibernici*. Ed. D. A. Binchy. 6 vols. Dublin: DIAS, 1978. References are to page.line unless otherwise noted.

CLP	*Celtic Law Papers Introductory to Welsh Medieval Law and Government: Studies Presented to the International Commission for the History of Representative and Parliamentary Institutions* 42. Ed. Dafydd Jenkins. Brussels: Les Éditions de la Librairie Encyclopédique, 1973.
CMCS	*Cambridge/Cambrian Medieval Celtic Studies*
CS	*Cáin Sóerraith.* Ed. R. Thurneysen. In "Aus dem irischen Recht II. [2. Das Frei-Lehen]." *ZCP* 15 (1925): 238–60.
CU	*Coibnes Uisci Thairidne.* Ed. D. A. Binchy. *Ériu* 17 (1955): 52–85.
DAC	*Di Astud Chor.* (See *EICL.*)
DIAS	Dublin Institute for Advanced Studies
DIL	Royal Irish Academy, *(Contributions to A) Dictionary of the Irish Language.* Dublin: Royal Irish Academy, 1913–76; compact edition, 1983.
DT	*Din Techtugud*
EICL	*Early Irish Contract Law.* Ed. Neil NcLeod. Sydney: Centre for Celtic Studies, University of Sydney, 1992.
GC	*Gúbretha Caratniad.* Ed. R. Thurneysen. In "Aus dem irischen Recht III. [4. Die falschen Urteilssprüche Caratnia's]." *ZCP* 15 (1925): 302–70.
GEIL	*A Guide to Early Irish Law,* by Fergus Kelly. Early Irish Law Series, vol. 3. Dublin: DIAS, 1988.
GOI	*A Grammar of Old Irish,* by R. Thurneysen. Translated from the German by D. A. Binchy and O. Bergin. Dublin: DIAS, 1946; reprinted, 1975.
IK	*Die irische Kanonensammlung.* Ed. H. Wasserschleben. Leipzig: Verlag Bernhard Tauchnitz, 1885.
MGH	*Monumenta Germaniae Historica*
PRIA	*Proceedings of the Royal Irish Academy*
RC	*Revue Celtique*
SEIL	*Studies in Early Irish Law.* Ed. R. Thurneysen, D. A. Binchy, and others. Dublin: Royal Irish Academy, 1936.
TRHS	*Transactions of the Royal Historical Society*
UB	*Uraicecht Becc*
UR	*Uraicecht na Ríar: The Poetic Grades in Early Irish Law.* Ed. Liam Breatnach. Early Irish Law Series, vol. 2. Dublin: DIAS, 1987.
ZCP	*Zeitschrift für celtische Philologie*

Notes

Introduction

1. E.g., in *CB*: CIH 527.16–17 and see *DIL* p. 436, cols. 167–68 for further references.

2. The issue is usually discussed under the rubric of "ritual" rather than of "performance," on which see further the conclusion to this volume. Valuable studies include Althoff, *Spielregeln*; Schmidt-Wiegand, "Gebärdensprache"; Koziol, *Begging Pardon and Favor*; Fichtenau, *Living in the Tenth Century*; Brown, *Unjust Seizure*, 135–38.

3. Peter Brown and Paul Hyams stress the manner in which the drama of the ordeal served to focus community anxieties about the accused: Brown, "Society and the Supernatural"; and Hyams, "Trial by Ordeal." Robert Bartlett takes a different approach in *Trial by Fire and Water*.

4. Davies and Fouracre, *Settlement of Disputes*, 29, 34, 39, 200–201, 271, for example.

5. Particularly influential in shaping our view of the early period—in some cases despite their focus on the high and late Middle Ages—have been the following: Stock, *Implications of Literacy*; Clanchy, *From Memory to Written Record*; Carruthers, *Book of Memory*; and Carruthers, *Craft of Thought*. The ongoing importance of oral communication is a central theme in many of Michael Richter's works, most notably *Formation of the Medieval West* and *Studies in Medieval Language and Culture*. More culturally specific studies include Patterson, "Honour and Shame"; Jaffee, *Torah in the Mouth*; Geertz, *Negara*; Humphreys, "Social Relations on Stage"; Harris, *Ancient Literacy*; Pierce, "'She Is Trouble'"; and Lesses, "Adjuration."

6. See Conclusion below, and McKitterick, *Carolingians and the Written Word*, 33–37; Davies and Fouracre, *Settlement of Disputes*, 167, 219, 226; Connerton, *How Societies Remember*; Fentress and Wickham, *Social Memory*; Geary, *Phantoms of Remembrance*; Kosto, *Making Agreements*; and Hen and Innes, *Uses of the Past*.

7. The progenitor of modern studies on speech and the social environment is J. L. Austin, whose *How to Do Things with Words* has become a classic. The connection between performative language and gesture has been explored recently by Schmitt in *La raison des gestes*.

8. Hymes, "Breakthrough into Performance," 13–20, quotes on p. 18.

9. Bauman, *Story, Performance, and Event*, 3.

10. Bauman, *Verbal Art as Performance*, 11.

11. On the concept of the frame, see Goffman, *Frame Analysis*; Goffman, "Facework"; Bauman, *Verbal Art as Performance*, 11; Bateson, *Ecology of Mind*.

12. Bauman and Briggs, "Poetics and Performance"; MacAloon, *Rite, Drama, Festival*; Bell, *Ritual Theory*; Schechner, *Between Theater and Anthropology*. A useful survey is Carlson's *Performance*.

13. To witness, the title of Kratz's book: *Affecting Performance*. A classic discussion is Geertz's "Blurred Genres."

14. See Conclusion, below, and Smith, Review of *Ritual Theory, Ritual Practice*, by Catherine Bell; Buc, *Dangers of Ritual*.

15. Hymes, "Contribution of Folklore," 43.

16. Watkins, "Language of Gods"; Ford, "The Blind"; Nagy, *Wisdom of the Outlaw*; Carey, "Obscure Styles"; and see references in note 34 below and, on satire, discussion below in Chapter 3.

17. An exception is Nagy's discussion of the "Pseudo-Historical Prologue to the *Senchas Már*" in his *Conversing with Angels*.

18. Scott makes a similar argument about gender in her influential essay "Gender: A Useful Category of Historical Analysis."

19. The classic of the Fenian genre is the *Acallam na Senórach*, newly translated and in paperback by Dooley and Roe as *Tales of the Elders of Ireland*; the king tales are partially available in *Silva Gadelica*. Nagy's *Wisdom of the Outlaw* is an indispensable study.

20. Hughes's *Early Christian Ireland* is a good, if now somewhat dated, survey.

21. *CIH*.

22. *Críth Gablach* testifies to the importance of the seven-grade hierarchy of the clergy to native thinking about hierarchy in the secular realm, for example.

23. See discussion below in Chapter 2.

24. The closest parallels are the "leading cases" of Irish tradition, such as the story of Congal Cáech's blinding by a bee, which Kelly and Charles-Edwards have suggested may reflect the circumstances of actual case: *BB* §31–35 (pp. 68–73), and see *GEIL*, 238–40.

25. Davies, "Latin Charter-Tradition."

26. Stevenson, "Literacy in Ireland," 32–35.

27. Bent, "Musical Stanzas." I am grateful to Dr. Bent for making this piece available to me in advance of publication.

28. Stacey, *Road to Judgment*, 13–15; *GEIL*, 238–40. A useful alternative to this manner of characterizing the sources can be found in Charles-Edwards, *Kinship*, 3–12.

29. Charles-Edwards, *Kinship*, 4.

30. Buc, *Dangers of Ritual*, 8–12, 248–51, particularly.

31. See discussion below in Chapter 2 and Breatnach, *Companion*, 349–50.

32. See Stacey, "Law and Literature."

33. Key names in this debate include Francis Magoun, Stanley Greenfield, Donald Fry, Jeff Opland, Ruth Finnegan, and John Miles Foley. A useful survey of the field of oral-formulaic theory as it had developed up to that point is Foley's *Theory of Oral Composition*.

34. Melia, "Parallel Versions"; Melia, "Remarks"; Ó Coileáin, "Oral or Literary"; Nagy, *Wisdom of the Outlaw*; Nagy, "Orality"; Nagy, "Oral Life"; Nagy, "Representations of Oral Tradition"; Nagy, "Sword as Audacht"; and Nagy, "Oral Tradition."

35. Nagy, *Conversing with Angels*.

36. See discussion below in Chapter 2.

37. McCone, "Frage der Register"; Corthals, "Frage des mündlichen oder schriftlichen Ursprungs der Sagenroscada"; Tristram, "Frage der roscada"; Tristram, *Metrik und Medienwechsel/Metrics and Media*; McCone, *Pagan Past and Christian Present*, 39–46; Corthals, "The *Retoiric* in *Aided Conchobuir*"; Corthals, "Early Irish Retoirics"; Carey, "Obscure Styles"; Carey, "The Rhetoric of *Echtrae Chonlai*"; Mac Cana,

"On the Use of the Term *retoiric*"; Cecile O'Rahilly, "Five Notes"; Melia, "Further Speculation."

38. Carey, "Obscure Styles."

39. A point implicit also in the work of Corthals, who stresses the manner in which *rosc* evolves over time from its sixth-century origins: "Early Irish *Retoirics*," 36.

40. See *rosc* excerpts cited in the works referred to above in note 37, for example, and on legal *rosc*, see discussion below in Chapters 2 and 5.

41. For example, *CIH* 1113.19–27; 1119.28–32.

42. For example, *CIH* 1116.29; 1119.7, 17; 1122.3; 1130.38.

43. *Rosc* is explicitly characterized in many legal texts as an element in contemporary judicial proceedings. According to the eighth-century status tract *Uraicecht Becc*, judgments rendered by lords are to be grounded in *roscada* and maxims (another type of heightened speech) as well as in more traditional forms of proof and proclamation: *CIH* 635.32–636.1, and see also 634.26 on the role of *roscada* in the procedural path known as *fir*, "truth," and discussion below in Chapter 5.

Chapter 1

1. A small sampling of the many excellent studies that have appeared in recent years would include Leyser, *Rule and Conflict*; Davies and Fouracre, *Settlement of Disputes*; White, *Gifts to Saints*; Rosenwein, *Rhinoceros Bound*; Rosenwein, *Neighbor of Saint Peter*; Wendy Davies, *Small Worlds*; McKitterick, *Uses of Literacy*; Stacey, *Road to Judgment*; Davies and Fouracre, *Property and Power*; Miller, *Bloodtaking and Peacemaking*.

2. Geary, *Phantoms of Remembrance*; Fentress and Wickham, *Social Memory*; Hen and Innes, *Uses of the Past*.

3. Performance has to date been discussed largely in terms of ritual, on which see Conclusion below. An exception that incorporates evidence from medieval law is the culturally comprehensive survey by Hibbitts, "Coming to Our Senses."

4. Bell, *Ritual Theory*, 220.

5. This point is made also by Koziol in his *Begging Pardon and Favor*, 289–324 especially, and in his review of Buc's book, "The Dangers of Polemic," 385–87.

6. The dispute between Chrotcharius and Amalbert is described in a record of a royal judgment given at Valenciennes in February of 692 or 693: text in Davies and Fouracre, *Settlement of Disputes*, 244–45, with translation on pp. 28–29. The King Alfred incident comes from the famous letter about the estate at Fonthill: English translation in *Select English Historical Documents*, §18.

7. Bell, *Ritual Theory*, 219–20.

8. Somerville and Ross, *Experiences of an Irish R.M.* and *Further Experiences*.

9. Heraughty, *Inishmurray*, 59, with photograph on p. 70.

10. *CIH* 467.34–35; 468.28–30; 469.7–11, 19–23 (*BFG*), for example.

11. *CG* 346 (and 345 on his silver bridle); 407.

12. *Togail Bruidne Da Derga*, lines 2–44.

13. *CIH* 1762.5, 14, 18 (*CI*); and *CIH* 592.9–10 = *Bürgschaft*, §12 (p. 8), where one of the measurements of proper fostering is said to be the manner in which the child is clothed (*BA*). An English translation of the latter text is available in Stacey, "*Berrad Airechta*," 210–33.

14. *CIH* 1759.11–36 (*CI* with glosses and commentary).

15. The best treatment of food and food production in early Ireland is Kelly's *Farming*, 316–59.

16. Bynum, *Holy Feast and Holy Fast*.

17. Perhaps the locus classicus for the champion's cut is the tale *Scéla Mucce Meic Dathó*. The magical cauldron is to be found in *Scél na Fír Flatha, Echtra Cormaic i Tir Tairngiri ocus Ceart Claidib Cormaic*, 187–88. Kelly points to two similar passages in the law tracts: Kelly, *Farming*, 358; *CIH* 349.36–350.5 and 880.17–26.

18. For example, *CG* 44–45, 148–50, 331–34, 380–82; *CIH* 1597.9–1599.42; 1610.40–1611.5 (*UB*); *CIH* 2231.9–36 (*BNT*).

19. *Br. Crólige*, §9 (pp. 10–11); §§21–22 (pp. 18–19); §§25–28 (p. 20–25); §§45–50 (pp. 36–41); §51 (pp. 40–43); §56 (pp. 44–45).

20. *CIH* 524.18–529.26 (*CB*).

21. *C. Aicillne*, §8 (pp. 347–48) for the brewing process. See also Binchy, "Brewing," 3–6.

22. "The Caldron of Poesy," and see Nagy, *Wisdom of the Outlaw*, for the complex myths surrounding Finn's acquisition of his special wisdom.

23. *CIH* 2231.39–2232.5; 2232.9–17 (*BNT*).

24. *CG* 184.

25. *Br. Crólige*, §§21–22 (pp. 18–19); §§24–28 (pp. 18–25); §§45–50 (pp. 36–41); §56 (pp. 44–45); §58 (p. 47).

26. *long brond is ae feichighthi . . . dlegait a mait munramair. CIH* 1268.20–26. This poem precedes a prose passage on the prerogatives of judges which has been edited and translated by Breatnach in "Lawyers in Early Ireland," 1–13, with passage on p. 8.

27. *Br. Crólige*, §31 (pp. 24–27) mentions a *brithem eola(i) i mbiadaib*, "a judge knowledgeable about refections." The glossator identifies this person with the leech, who can speak to what foods might be best for an injured person to avoid. However, given the heavy emphasis placed in the tract on the quantity and quality of the food provided the injured person and his retinue, it seems possible that the person referred to is precisely what he is termed in the tract—an expert in the [public] assessment of food-related obligations.

28. *CG* 577–97, for example.

29. *CIH* 219.5–6 (*Recholl Breth*); and 2231.40–2232.2 (*BNT*), where a person who held such hostages is listed as one of three kinds of lords.

30. *CG* 204, 299, 349, 366, 454–55, 466; *Br. Crólige*, §§26–29 (pp. 22–25), for example.

31. *CIH* 1761.3, 1762.21 (*CI*) and cf. *BA: CIH* 591.36–37 = *Bürgschaft*, §10 (p. 7). Compare the curriculum of sons and daughters of the lower classes as outlined in the later commentaries: *CIH* 1760.21–22.

32. *Br. Crólige*, §8 (pp. 10–11); §12 (pp. 10–13); §§16–17 (pp. 14–15); §§32–35 (pp. 26–28); §§43–44 (pp. 34–35); §54 (pp. 42–45). Examples of persons not taken away for nursing included those who were too powerful (king, bishop, hospitaller, pilgrim of God, poet, judge), too dangerous or unpleasant (women satirists, bitchy women, lunatics), too incompetent (fools), or who were not thought to have lived up to their legal obligations.

33. Sayers, "Concepts of Eloquence," and Ó Cathasaigh, "Rhetoric of *Fingal Rónáin*," are particularly sensitive studies of language use in early Irish tales.

34. Muirchú's life of Patrick, which dates to the seventh century: *Patrician Texts in the Book of Armagh*, I 17 (16)–I 19 (18), pp. 88–93; and see *CG* 604–6.

35. Breatnach, "Lawyers in Early Ireland," 8–9.

36. Charles-Edwards, "Honour and Status," 123–24.

37. The system is outlined in *GEIL*, 7–12.

38. Charles-Edwards, "Honour and Status," 135–40. To this one might add the formal "proclaiming" of kinsmen or dependents who had acted unlawfully with respect to their obligations, which almost certainly involved some sort of formal verbal notice—e.g., the "cold son" of *BA: CIH* 593.27–28 = *Bürgschaft*, §36 (p. 11).

39. *CIH* 14.34–15.16 (*Heptads*).

40. *CIH* 591.25–27 = *Bürgschaft*, §6 (p. 7) (*BA*).

41. *CIH* 593.27–29 = *Bürgschaft*, §36 (p. 11) (*BA*).

42. *GC*, §23 (pp. 331–32); *C. Aicillne*, §35 (p. 373). For contracts, including those between lords and clients, see Stacey, *Road to Judgment*, 56–70, 80–81.

43. See discussion in the introduction above. Goffman was one of the first to raise this question: *Presentation of Self; Frame Analysis*; and "Facework."

44. *CIH* 213.27–29 identifies illegal distraint, illegal *tellach*, and illegal dueling as offenses that judges and tribes must take particular care to control (*DT*).

45. *CIH* 413.29–415.9; and see the number of mytho-historical tales incorporated into the tract such as, for example, *CIH* 352.26–31; 353.26–355.33 ("Saga of Fergus mac Léti"); *CIH* 356.5ff.; 377.24–28; 380.14–22; 406.26–407.2. On the tract itself, see Breatnach, *Companion*, 286–87.

46. McLeod, "Concept of Law," 360; and "Saga of Fergus mac Léti," 48.

47. D'Arbois de Jubainville, *Études*; Binchy, "Distraint"; and Binchy, "Text on the Forms of Distraint"; *GEIL*, 177–86; and Kelly, *Farming*, 170–73, 521–32. For the description that follows, I draw primarily on Binchy's and Kelly's work except where otherwise noted.

48. The admonitions of the compiler regarding the necessity for a *suithengthaid*, "eloquent speaker"—e.g., a professional advocate—are suggestive (*CIH* 358.1–4, with a list of people forbidden from taking distraint on 358.15–359.29, and lists of other constraints imposed on the taking of distraint in the *Heptads*: *CIH* 36.23–40.24). Binchy suggests that advocates originally developed in order to "steer the claimant through the shoals and quicksands of the law of distraint" (Binchy, "*Féchem, Fethem, Aigne*," 25–26). I have suggested that perhaps "these shoals and quicksands themselves originated in the desire of jurists to be the ones to guide claimants through them" (Stacey, *Road to Judgment*, 139–40).

49. On this term, see *GEIL*, 179–80.

50. Binchy, "Distraint," 51–61; *GEIL*, 179.

51. *CIH* 896.9–901.13. *CIH* 891.19–41 (on the *aigne*) was edited and translated by Breatnach in "Lawyers in Early Ireland," 10–12; *CIH* 897.29–898.33 was edited and translated by Binchy, "Text on the Forms of Distraint"; *CIH* 897.10–29 was edited and translated by Kelly, in *Farming*, 521–32.

52. *CIH* 414.28–30.

53. See discussions in Binchy, "Distraint," 35–45; and D'Arbois De Jubainville, *Études sur le droit celtique*, 1:257–68.

54. *Bürgschaft*, §46 (p. 14). As Binchy points out, the *BA* situation appears to be a special one: "Distraint," 35–36.

55. Kelly, *Farming*, 73, 323–30, and see note to *laulgach* on p. 526.

56. *CIH* 897.1–3 (H 3. 18 glosses to the *Senchas Már*, on which see Breatnach, *Companion*, 338–46).

57. *CIH* 900.17–18.

58. Binchy, "Distraint in Irish Law," 46–47, but see CIH 409.17–19, where the four parts of the procedure are: "seizure after the evasion of law, security [of the items taken] after seizure, notice after security, and awaiting law in the proper place with proper mutual pledging in the time of law."

59. An argument in favor of the *anad* and the *díthim* being the same amount of time might be that the word *anad* is actually used of the period commonly called *díthim* (possibly in the more general sense of "staying") in the H 3. 18 tract on distraint: *CIH* 900.17–19.

60. *CIH* 900.19–21; the text indicates a divergence in opinion among the jurists as to exactly where the distrained animal had to be taken before the forfeiture period began.

61. *CIH* 362.21–23. On *séoit* and units of monetary value generally, see *GEIL*, 112–16. The most common equation for a *sét* is one heifer or half a milk cow: Charles-Edwards, *Kinship*, 478–85.

62. The relationship between ritual and theater is a complicated one, and has been subject to much discussion in the anthropological and theoretical literature. Among the most valuable treatments of the topic are Turner, *Ritual Process*; Turner, *Drama, Fields and Metaphors*; Turner, *From Ritual to Theatre*; MacAloon, *Rite, Drama*; Schechner, "Performance and the Social Sciences"; and Schechner, *Between Theater and Anthropology*. Carlson provides a good overview and bibliography in his *Performance*, 13–33.

63. Ó Riain, "The *crech ríg*"; Lucas, *Cattle*, 146–48. The *táin* was one of the recognized genres of medieval Irish storytelling: Mac Cana, *Learned Tales*, 73, 79–80.

64. For *áin* see, for example, *CIH* 40.20–21 (*Heptads*); for *táin*, see *CIH* 417.11 (*Di Chetharshlicht Athgabála*). The terms *áin* and *táin* are used together to describe a specific type of legal offense whereby one person drives his cattle over another's land without permission: *CIH* 205.15 (*Br. Comaithchesa*).

65. Kelly in *Farming*, 521–32, and see discussion below on restrictions on the types of pounds the claimant could use.

66. Crucial works in the development of the idea of the social frame include Bateson, *Ecology of Mind*; Goffman, *Frame Analysis*; and Bauman, *Verbal Art*.

67. *Tobach* is the verbal noun of *do-boing*, "levies," a verb used usually to indicate the taking of something believed to be owed to someone in tribute or in respect of a legal obligation (*DIL*, p. 227, cols. 215–16 and pp. 593–94, cols. 198–99). *Tóchsal* is the verbal noun of *do-fochsla*, and is usually used in the context specifically of distraint *DIL*, p. 233, col. 270, and p. 602, col. 266). The verb itself is used in *Críth Gablach* to refer to the taking of hostages by a king, but again this is in the context of something taken to enforce adherence to legal or political obligations: *húaire do-foxla ilgíallu*, "because he takes numerous hostages" (*CG* 460).

68. E.g., *CIH* 352.26 (though see note 352.30, where the two terms occur side by side). In *CIH* 359.34, the process has been carried out incorrectly and is therefore subject to legal penalties.

69. *Athgabál* is a Common Celtic term: Binchy, "Distraint," 27–30. *Di Chetharshlicht Athgabála* uses the verb *gaibid*, "take, seize" (of which *gabál* is the verbal noun) either to indicate distraint taken unlawfully (e.g., *CIH* 358.15–16, 359.29, 363.23–24), or else in conjunction with *athgabál* to indicate that the action has been legally carried out (e.g., *CIH* 358.1–4, 409.1–2, 409.13–14, 410.6–8).

70. Bell, *Ritual Theory*, 109–10.

71. *GEIL*, 178.

72. William Murphy, "Appearance of Consensus," 25–32.

73. And to link the onset of a new stage with the dawning of a new day.

74. Kelly, *Farming*, 40.

75. At least with respect to the theft of bees: *BB*, §§50–53 (pp. 84–87). Other texts make it clear that the place from which the item is taken is crucial to the perception of the seriousness of the offense: *CG* 217–19; *GEIL*, 147–48; *BB*, 161–64.

76. Bauman, *Verbal Art*, 37–45; Bell, *Ritual Theory*, 82–92; Handelman, *Models and Mirrors*, 23–41, 76–81.

77. *CIH* 37.6–7; 358.15–16; 359.29; 363.23–28; and see below on fasting and on distraining against a member of the professional classes.

78. Certain places were prohibited altogether from serving as pounds, including the houses of particularly high status people within the *túath* (hospitaller, *deorad Dé*, king, bishop), the houses of untrustworthy persons (thieves, low-class satirists, persons who evaded their legal obligations), and the grounds of a noble monastery (*cathuir uasal-nemid*): *CIH* 37.1; 40.20–24 (*Heptads*); 900.12–17 (unedited tract on distraint).

79. Binchy, "Text on the Forms of Distraint," §§5–9 (pp. 78–81).

80. *CIH* 36.23–37.8; 37.26–33 (*Heptads*). The primary sources on this procedure are 1) the text edited by Binchy in "Text on the Forms of Distraint," and 2) a section of *Di Chetharshlicht Athgabála* (*CIH* 365.5–367.7) that has been edited, translated, and discussed by Thurneysen in "Aus dem irischen Recht I," 260–75. See also Binchy, "Distraint," 34–35; and *GEIL*, pp. 182–83.

81. Binchy, "Text on the Forms of Distraint," §§8–9 (pp. 78–81); *CIH* 365.5–20.

82. *CIH* 366.1.

83. Binchy, "Distraint," 34. See also Binchy, "Text on the Forms of Distraint," 76. And see his remarks on the antiquity of the practice in "Irish History and Irish Law," esp. vol. 15, pp. 24–26.

84. Binchy, "Distraint," 35.

85. The most famous example is Patrick's fast against God as reported in the *Tripartite Life*, but there are many others. For examples, see F. N. Robinson, "Notes."

86. *Annals of Inisfallen*, ed. MacAirt, year 1108 (pp. 266–67), where Macc Fir Choctha huí Domnaill maic Diarmata is said to have died after having been fasted against by the community of Senán. For another example late in the pre-Norman period, see 1031 (pp. 198–99).

87. Geary, "Humiliation of Saints." An interestingly parallel practice are the "psalms of malediction" studied by Wiley in his "Maledictory Psalms." I am grateful to Dr. Wiley for allowing me to see this work in advance of publication.

88. Connerton, *How Societies Remember*, 7–10.

89. Boyer, *Tradition as Truth*, 82–85; Handelman, *Models and Mirrors*, 30–41.

90. *Din Techtugud* can be found at *CIH* 205.22–213.37. My description follows the account given by Charles-Edwards in *Kinship*, 259–73. Other discussions include *GEIL*, 186–89 and Kelly, *Early Irish Farming*, 432–33. An interestingly parallel procedure is the Welsh *dadannudd*, on which see Charles-Edwards, *Kinship*, 274–303. Breatnach discusses the tract itself in *Companion*, 292.

91. Or so it is implied in the H 3.18 text.

92. Charles-Edwards, *Kinship*, 259–61, 265, 272–73.

93. Charles-Edwards, *Kinship*, 261, 269–70, and, on women, 266–67.

94. Charles-Edwards, *Kinship*, 261.

95. Charles-Edwards, *Kinship*, 270, 272.

96. Some interesting work has been done on the subject of boundaries in early Irish literature: Ó Riain, "Boundary Association"; Sjöblom, "Threshold."

97. See below, and Stacey, *Road to Judgment*, 27–54.

98. E.g., Schechner, *Between Theater and Anthropology*; MacAloon, "Cultural Performances"; Turner, *Ritual Process* (although his *From Ritual to Theatre* envisages more room for creativity in such matters); Bloch, *Political Language*.

99. E.g., Bauman, *Verbal Art*; Kratz, *Affecting Performance*; Mikhail Bakhtin, *Rabelais*.

100. On the role of the dead in guarding the kindred's land and refusing an outsider whose right is not legitimate, see Charles-Edwards, *Kinship*, 261–65.

101. *CG* 158.

102. Bell, *Ritual Theory*, 218–20.

103. Bell, *Ritual Theory*, 93 and 222.

104. For the theoretical orientation of what follows in this paragraph, see Bell, *Ritual Theory*, 99–104, 108–17.

105. On the significance of unyoking as a symbol, see Charles-Edwards, *Kinship*, 265.

106. The Irish word for "pious, filial," is *gor*, "warm." *Goire* (from *gor*) is the word used to describe the legal obligation of children to support their parents in old age: *DIL*, p. 367, cols. 130–31 and p. 368, cols. 136–37. The opposite of a dutiful son is

the *mac huar*, "cold son" (who also appears in other texts as the *mac ingor*, "unwarm son"), mentioned in *BA* (*CIH* 593.27–28 = *Bürgschaft*, §36 [p. 11]).

107. Bell, *Ritual Theory*, 109–10 and 222.

108. Kratz stresses the importance of gender symbolism in the construction of power in her work on Okiek women: *Affecting Performance*, 49–53 particularly.

109. Charles-Edwards, *Kinship*, 82–84.

110. Charles-Edwards notes how hard the compiler works to establish the existence and legitimacy of the procedure—a fact that may itself suggest some degree of unhappiness with it: *Kinship*, 268.

111. *CIH* 23.26; 24.2 (*Heptads*).

112. *CIH* 31.19–32.1 gives this and other examples; see also 7.9–9.19 (both are from the *Heptads*).

113. *Bretha Étgid* focuses on such occurrences; in general, the rule seems to be that no liability for inadvertent injury is incurred unless genuine negligence was involved (*CIH* 250.1–337.36, and see discussion in *GEIL*, 149–51).

114. "*Mellbretha*," Sayers, "Games."

115. *CIH* 52.17–35. The ordeal aspect of the duel is made very clear in the phrasing: *Tait .uii. fiadnaise forosnat gae cach re*, "there are seven witnesses which illuminate falsehood [in] every duel." Dueling is discussed by *GEIL*, 211–13; there is a famous description of a judicial duel in Tírechán's *vita* of Patrick, *Patrician Texts in the Book of Armagh*, §32 (pp. 148–49).

116. *CIH* 7.9; 9.5 (*Heptads*); 239.37 (*Do Fastad Cirt 7 Dligid*); and see discussion of the enforcement process in Stacey, *Road to Judgment*, 34–43.

117. *CIH* 7.29–30, with gloss on 8.15–17, which also says that after three days, she had a further month in which she paid only half the normal penalties. CIH 8.9–10 gives the *cétmuinter* the right to kill her rival up to the end of three nights, with the penalty falling to half after that (*Heptads* and glosses to same).

118. The main discussions of sick-maintenance are Binchy, "Sick-Maintenance"; Binchy's introduction to his edition of *BDC* (pp. 1–20); and *GEIL*, 129–33. The principal tracts on the subject are *Br. Crólige*, *BDC* (both discussed by Breatnach in *Companion*, 303), and passages edited and translated by Binchy in his article on "Sick-Maintenance," 80–90.

119. *CG* 53–54 speaks of the victim being taken *tar fót crúach i n-ardnemed di[a] díte*, "across the bloody soil into a noble sanctuary for his protection." See also *Br. Crólige*, §21 (pp. 18–19) on the bearing away of clerics, and discussions by Binchy, "Sick-Maintenance," 105–6, and by Kelly in *GEIL*, 130–31.

120. See Binchy's discussion in his "Sick-Maintenance," 97–102.

121. *Br. Crólige*, §42 (pp. 34–35).

122. *CG* 52–62. This interpretation departs from that offered by Binchy in his account; for this interpretation of the nature of the *aitire*'s office, see Stacey, *Road to Judgment*, 87–98.

123. *BDC* §23 (pp. 36–37); *CG* 53. *Br. Crólige* §18 sets the penalty at one-third of the appropriate *díre*, "honor-price," although the cow is mentioned in the glosses.

124. *Br. Crólige*, §55 (pp. 44–45). Usually oral contracts of this sort involved *naidm* and *ráth* sureties, and a *ráth* is indeed mentioned in *CG* 59, alongside of the *aitire* sureties. However, it is also possible that the *aitire* would have continued to act on behalf of the offender throughout the process. *BA* conceptualizes the *ráth* as a form of *aitire*, which might explain *Críth Gablach*'s use of both terms without having to assume that both types of sureties would necessarily have been involved. Alternatively, this may simply be a reflection of differing regional customs. For a discussion of these types of guarantors, see Stacey, *Road to Judgment*, 27–54 and 82–111; for the *ráth* as a form of *aitire*, see *CIH* 597.4–6 and 597.30–599.17.

125. *Br. Crólige,* §60 (pp. 46–49), but compare with this the obligations outlined in *CG* 54–57, where the offender promises to provide a suitable environment for nursing, a doctor to care for the injured person until it is no longer necessary, and to guarantee the safety of the party who removes the victim to the place where he will be nursed.

126. Binchy, "Sick-Maintenance," 103–5.

127. *Br. Crólige,* §59 (pp. 46–47). The passage is highly rhetorical; for the identification of the *fiu-flaith fuissiten i feine fresndul,* "the worthy lord of acknowledgement (?) for attendance according to Irish law(?)," with the *aitire,* see Stacey, *Road to Judgment,* 275, n. 64. Binchy's interpretation can be found in "Sick-Maintenance," 105.

128. *Br. Crólige,* §23 (pp. 18–19), which exempts from consideration venues perceived as too dirty, noisy, or emotionally disruptive for healing to take place.

129. Binchy, "Sick-Maintenance," 105–6. *CG* 57 speaks of the victim being conveyed to the *forus túaithe,* "appointed place of the *túath,*" which MacNeill took as a reference to a public infirmary. It is worth noting, however, that *forus* is the term used generally in the law tracts to mean the place where a designated legal event—the repayment of a debt, for example—would take place. See discussion below in Chapter 5.

130. *Br. Crólige,* §22 (pp. 18–19); §§24–28 (pp. 18–25); §§45–50 (pp. 36–41); §56 (pp. 44–45).

131. *Br. Crólige,* §26 (pp. 22–23); §36 (pp. 28–29); §48 (pp. 38–39); §50 (pp. 40–41). Depending on rank, some retainers were maintained at a proportion of what their masters received: §28 (pp. 24–25).

132. *Br. Crólige,* §29 (pp. 24–25), although cf. §8 (pp. 10–11), where such persons are said to be nursed by their kin.

133. *Br. Crólige,* §62 (pp. 50–51).

134. *BDC* §§29–37 (pp. 39–48); and see also Binchy's discussion in *BDC,* 15–19.

135. *CG* 47–51.

136. *CG* 52–57, and see notes 47–63 on p. 26.

137. *CG* 488–89. Lines 480–88 may also refer to the institution; however, since they speak only of the *folog* due to the persons discussed, this is not a necessary conclusion, since *folog* is also the word used to describe the physician's fee that replaced formal *othrus,* as *CG* 47–48 shows.

138. Binchy, "Sick-Maintenance," 117–28; *GEIL,* 133.

139. *Br. Crólige,* §12 (pp. 10–11), §32 (pp. 26–27); *CIH* 53.6–21 (*Heptads*).

140. E.g., Conchobar's revenge on Noísiu in *Longes mac nUislenn* and Fergus's subsequent actions in that tale; Cú Chulainn's own death at the hands of the sons of Calatín; and the long-standing feud between Finn and the sons of Morna. In ecclesiastical literature, see for example, Carney, *Poems of Blathmac,* §130 (p. 45) and §114 (p. 39).

141. *C. Aicillne,* §24 (p. 364).

142. *CG* 358–67, with note on pp. 70–72; McLeod, "Status and Currency," 46–50.

143. *Togail Bruidne Da Derga,* lines 1519–26.

144. "*Slicht Libair Dromma Snechta inso,*" 244–45, lines 8014–19. The textual and manuscript history of the story is very complex; see Ó Concheanainn, "Notes on *Togail Bruidne Da Derga.*"

145. *CIH* 597.6–7, 16–18 = *Bürgschaft,* §65 (pp. 22–23).

146. *Gesetze der Langobarden,* Rothair's Edict, §128; for other examples, see Rothair's Edict §§78–79, 82–84, 87, 89, 101–3, 110–12, and the like.

147. *Br. Crólige,* §61 (pp. 48–49), and see also §23 (pp. 18–19).

148. Including games (a medieval form of training for war) and the beating of hides.

149. See notes to *dám, bés tige* and *bíathad* on *CG* pp. 75–77 and 82.

150. *Br. Crólige*, §62 (pp. 50–51).

151. *Br. Crólige*, §23 (pp. 18–19).

152. There are other interesting echoes here as well. The primary tract on hostageship, *Di Gnímaib Gíall Gaibter*, says that the compensation owed by a defaulting person to a hostage who has gone surety on his behalf is a cow for every night he is constrained to spend the night away from home. Similarly, *BDC* stipulates a cow for every night a victim is denied a (legitimate) right to nursing, and does so in words that exactly parallel those used in the hostageship tract. Given the distinctive phrasing, we seem likely to be dealing here either with an old formula, or with an explicit textual reference from one *Senchas Már* tract to another: compare *CIH* 1756.21 (*Di Gnímaib Gíall Gaibter*) with *BDC* §23 (pp. 36–37). The implications are intriguing. The injured person kept by the injustice of the offender apart from a house he has a right to occupy (a house of healing) is symbolically juxtaposed with the hostage kept apart by the injustice of his principal from a house he has a right to occupy (his own). Again it would appear that at least in those cases in which healing took place at the offender's house, this house was conceptualized as having been temporarily "reassigned" to the injured person during the period of *othrus*.

153. Stacey, *Road to Judgment*, 82–111.

154. *BDC*, §§3–4 (pp. 24–26); §§7–8 (pp. 26–27); §§16–20 (pp. 32–35).

155. See discussion by Binchy, *BDC*, 15–19.

156. Bell, *Ritual Theory*, 93. In addition to Bell's own chapter on "The Ritual Body," on pp. 94–117 of her book, see Benthall and Polhemus, *Body as a Medium of Expression*; and Feher, *Fragments*, volume three of which includes an exhaustive annotated bibliography and topical index.

157. Body symbolism and metaphor played a prominent role in Irish political discourse, so it is not surprising that they should figure also in law. Examples include *enech*, "face/honor"; *cenn*, "head/lord"; *memar*, "limb/"subordinate, dependent" (e.g., *CIH* 592.35 from *BA*); and *corp*, "body," which can mean both the literal body of an individual and the collective body of the kindred or *túath*.

158. *BDC*, §2 (pp. 22–23), and see §§5–8 (pp. 26–27), §§11–16 (pp. 28–33).

159. With wheat being the smallest: *BDC*, 9–10, 48–51. On the relative importance of the cereals in question in early Irish life, see Kelly, *Farming*, 219–28.

160. Not least because they were themselves penned by professionals dependent on fees of a similar nature.

161. *BDC*, §30 (pp. 40–41).

162. *BDC*, §31 (pp. 40–41).

163. *BDC*, §22 (pp. 36–37).

164. *BDC*, 57–58.

165. *BB*, §52–53, and see discussion above.

166. *CG* 379; 392–93; 454–55.

167. It should be noted that *i taig* is a common idiom for "inside," and is frequently used in opposition to *immach*: *DIL*, p. 581, col. 97. House and land are an important binary in the *tellach* procedure as well: see discussion above.

168. Fergus mac Léti's disfigurement at the hands of the sea monster (*muirdris*) seems to have little direct impact on his tribe, but it does lead to his being mocked by a person of low status. It is possible that an attack by a monster might be viewed somewhat differently from an attack by a real person: "Saga of Fergus mac Léti," §§6–8 (pp. 42–44).

169. *BDC*, §6 (pp. 26–27). The glossators take this as referring to a provincial king or even to the king of Ireland. Paragraph 5 speaks to the situation of a king of many tribes, and it may be that paragraph 6 does as well.

170. *BDC*, 13, and see notes on p. 55. *BDC* §12 (pp. 28–29) shows that a wound

to the temple was considered more serious than other types of wounds to the face, including injuries to the cheeks.

171. Fergus mac Léti being the exception in this respect.

172. Similar symbolic concerns may be visible in the later provision requiring an attacker to seek out three "foreign herbs" to treat a wound in the face of the king (*BDC*, §9 [pp. 26–27]). Might the foreign origin of the herbs speak to his position as an intertribal king?

173. The most valuable primary source on gages is *BFG*, which has not yet been edited or translated. Helpful secondary accounts include Binchy's note to *gell* in *CG*, pp. 94–95; and *GEIL*, 164–67.

174. E.g., in secular law as a result of distraint or *tellach*, on which see discussion above. In ecclesiastical law, gages were offered to answer charges that a person had violated a *cáin*: *C. Adam.*, §48 (pp. 26–27); *Cáin Domnaig*, §§3–6 (pp. 164–67); *CIH* 523.5–8 (*CB*). For other examples such as, for example, gages to guarantee court appearances, see *CIH* 2223.8–12 (*BNT*).

175. E.g., with respect to bees: *BB*, §§1–3 (pp. 50–51).

176. The cases handled in *BFG* are of this kind, since these were the only instances in which interest would have been paid: *CIH* 462.19–477.30.

177. *CG* 277–94.

178. *CG* 293–94.

179. *CIH* 46.19–21 (*BFG*).

180. *Cáin Domnaig*, §§4–5 (pp. 164–67); on *tellach*, see discussion above.

181. As outlined in the tale of Mugdorn, for example: *CIH* 467.36–39. See also *CIH* 469.19–23, but compare with this 469.7–8, where payment in made in three three-day periods (*BFG*).

182. *CG* 280–94.

183. E.g., *CIH* 470.23–25, 470.31–33 (*BFG*); 34.5–6, and 33.30–35.16 (*Heptads*).

184. *Lugnasad* was an especially crucial time of year, as it is then that the "Fair of Tailtiu," over which the king of Tara presided, seems to have been held.

185. *CIH* 471.22–25 (*BFG*).

186. *CIH* 464.9–12; 465.7–10 (*BFG*).

187. *CIH* 476.27–30; *GEIL*, 36. Others who earn no interest for gages of arms are poets and men who have sworn not to carry arms.

188. A skilled needlewoman, for example, who gave her needle, or a champion who surrendered his arms. This is presumably the reason for the extremely high interest afforded the needlewoman: *CIH* 464.1–3 (*BFG*).

189. *CIH* 463.28–465.31; quote is on 463.30 (*BFG*).

190. *CIH* 464.27–29 (*BFG*).

191. *C. Adam.*, §24 (pp. 12–15). On this text, see various works by Ní Dhonnchadha: "*Caillech* and Other Terms"; "Guarantor List"; "*Lex Innocentium*." Another helpful work is Melia's "Law and the Shaman Saint."

192. *CIH* 467.34–35 (*BFG*).

193. *CIH* 468.14–25 (*BFG*). See *CG* 77–78 on the *bóaire* and generally on status and rank, *GEIL*, 17–67.

194. *CIH* 465.21–23, 470.2–9 (*BFG*).

195. Compare *CIH* 470.2–33 on cows with 471.18–20 on cart horses and 471.22–25 on racing horses (*BFG*). This is not to say that horses were irrelevant to the display of status, of course—simply that they had different symbolic implications from cows. For household utensils, see *CIH* 472.1–4, and note that luxury objects are explicitly status linked in their treatment: 472.6–9.

196. Insofar as objects offered were rendered temporarily unavailable to their owners, gage giving also echoed the special kind of distraint used against the pro-

fessional classes. The main difference between them was that one was offered voluntarily and the other was not—which is, of course, what separates distraint from pledging as a whole.

197. See Kelly's note 55 on p. 164 of *GEIL*.

198. On the social and political implications of clothing, see essays by Charles-Edwards and by Stacey in Charles-Edwards, Owen, and Russell, *Welsh King and His Court*, 319–46.

199. *CIH* 469.7–11 and 469.19–23, and compare the half honor-price due freemen in such circumstances on 469.29–32. For silver ornaments, see 468.23–30 (*BFG*).

200. *CIH* 1034.3–11 (version H of *CCF*). And see the speculation in *DIL* regarding the practices that might lie behind the *flesc láma: DIL* p. 310, col. 164. I owe this reference to Dennis King.

201. *CIH* 574.1–4. There were "great" and "small" *rudrad* periods, some lasting years, and some months or even days: see above, and also *CIH* 748.31–749.26 (*Do taithmech rudartha budesta*).

202. All of which had to be performed "in the presence of honorable [witnesses]": *CIH* 749.27–38 and 756.8–11 (*Do taithmech rudartha budesta*, on which see Breatnach, *Companion*, 32–33).

203. See discussion above, and *GEIL*, 86–91.

204. Oath swearing was not, of course, solely a Christian practice: one of the provisions in the (probably) sixth-century "First Synod of Saint Patrick" proscribes penance for Christians who swear "before a druid as pagans do": *Irish Penitentials*, §14 (pp. 56–57). A commonplace in the literary sources is swearing by the elements or by tribal gods: Stacey, *Road to Judgment*, 200–203; *GEIL*, 198–202.

205. For differing views on the nature of the ordeal, see Bartlett, *Trial by Fire and Water*; Hyams, "Trial by Ordeal"; Brown, "Society and the Supernatural." None of these fine pieces treat Irish ordeals in any detail, on which the best discussion is *GEIL*, 209–11. The lengthiest primary source account of Irish ordeal practices (though late and mythological) is to be found in *Echtra Cormaic*: Stokes, "Irish Ordeals." Lot casting was a common way of settling disputes of various sorts. See *GEIL*, 208–9 and, for lots cast to decide disputed successions, *IK* §XXV.2 (p. 76), and §XXXVII.1a (p. 131); *CIH* 1289.7–9.

206. For discussion and references, see Stacey, *Road to Judgment*, 218–19.

207. Stacey, *Road to Judgment*, 73–80; Stacey, "Ties That Bind." For the theoretical background here, see Bell, *Ritual Theory*, 220.

208. Hymes, "Breakthrough into Performance"; Bauman, *Verbal Art*, 43; Bauman and Briggs, "Poetics and Performance," 70.

209. Barba, "Introduction," in Barba and Savarese, *Secret Art*.

210. Bloch, "Introduction," in Bloch, *Political Language*, 1–28.

211. Sherzer, *Kuna Ways*, 57–63, 191–92; Bauman, *Verbal Art*, 11.

212. Kratz, *Affecting Performance*, 17–18. Kratz herself lays the most stress on what she calls "contextual recreation" and "semiotic movement" in understanding the fluidity and transformative nature of ritual: pp. 39–41.

213. The role of tradition in establishing the parameters of all of the processes we have examined is unquestionable, and Kratz's observations on the affective power of performance is highly pertinent both to *othrus*, where the injuries of the victim must surely have evoked a powerful emotional response in those witnessing his conveyance to the place of healing, and to fosterage, where children parted from their parents and entered upon another life.

214. Breatnach, *Companion*, 338–46. The story can be found in *CIH* 907.36–908.6.

215. Kingship was changing dramatically in Ireland between the seventh and ninth centuries: Byrne, *Rise of the Uí Néill*; Byrne, "Tribes and Tribalism"; Charles-Edwards,

"Celtic Kinship Terms"; Ó Corráin, "Nationality and Kingship." On kingship and law, see Gerriets, "King as Judge"; and Stacey, *Road to Judgment*, 110–12, 135–36.

An interesting possibility is that Nin may be the same mythological sage to whom an important part of *Din Techtugud*, the main tract on *tellach*, is ascribed—indeed the H 3. 18 tale itself appears as a gloss upon that tract (*CIH* 907.36, citing to the first line of the tract). The gloss to the prose passage in *Din Techtugud* identifies the speaker of *CIH* 210.12–35 as Nin (210.15).

216. Charles-Edwards, *Kinship*, 265 and, for characterization of *tellach* as a "legal sacrament," see 259. The story as it stands does not include any reference to a ritualized verbal exchange. On the other hand, it would be unwise to conclude from this tale that such would not have been necessary. It is worth noting that verbal exchanges of a formulaic kind are reported "verbatim" in the instructions to Doidin that follow the story of Seithir told later in the manuscript: *CIH* 909.32–36.

217. As Charles-Edwards points out, the unyoking of horses occurs also in *Fingal Rónáin* as a metaphor for the asserting of rights to territory: *Kinship*, 265; and *Fingal Rónáin*, 10, lines 235–36.

218. An interesting contrast with this is the riddling dialogue between Cú Chulainn and Emer in *Tochmarc Emire*, which makes use of a number of geographical and military commonplaces which, in context, become explicit sexual references. There the performance is entirely private, intended in part to demonstrate to each the suitability of the other as a mate, and in part also to disguise their intentions from any broader audience. See Sayers, "Concepts of Eloquence."

219. This is not to say merely that symbols are multivalent, although they are. Rather it is to point to the many different cultural "schemes of action" in which they are incorporated, and the varying roles they play in different social contexts: Kratz (here enlarging on Bourdieu), *Affecting Performance*, 30–35.

220. Bauman, *Verbal Art*, 43; Bauman and Briggs, "Poetics and Performance," 70.

221. All of Schechner's works are relevant to this discussion: *Between Theater* and *Essays on Performance* particularly. See also Carlson, *Performance*, 53–55.

222. Stock, *Implications of Literacy*, 472, 252, and 531, respectively.

223. Stock, *Implications of Literacy*, 91.

224. Stock, *Implications of Literacy*, 254.

225. Stock, *Implications of Literacy*, 266.

226. A point made as well in a somewhat different context by Buc in *Dangers of Ritual*, 246.

227. *CIH* 591.35–37 = *Bürgschaft*, §10 (pp. 7–8).

228. McKitterick, *Carolingians and the Written Word* and McKitterick, *Uses of Literacy*.

229. Bell, *Ritual Theory*, 169–223.

230. Stock, *Implications of Literacy*, 48.

231. Robert Bartlett, "Mortal Enmities: The Legal Aspect of Hostility in the Middle Ages," lecture presented to a symposium on "Courts, Customs and Canons: Law in the Middle Ages," held at the University of Victoria on February 15–16, 1990. The paper was made available to me by the kindness of the author, to whom I am very grateful.

232. Bynum, "Did the Twelfth Century Discover the Individual?"

233. *L. Sal.*, §1 (P. 60); *L. Burg.*, §97, respectively.

Chapter 2

1. Binchy, "*Féchem, Fethem, Aigne*," 25–26, and see Stacey, *Road to Judgment*, 139–40.

2. The best account of the rise of the legal profession in a region of western Eu-

rope is Brand's *Origins*. See also Clanchy, *Memory to Written Record*, 248–51, 272–78; and Brundage, "Medieval Advocate's Profession."

3. Brand, *Origins*, 50.

4. References to tribal judges include *Br. Crólige*, §33 (pp. 26–29); *CD*, §§1 and 3 (pp. 162–65). On judicial responsibilities towards their kingdoms, see Breatnach, "Lawyers," 7–10.

5. *CIH* 1268.20–26.

6. Defined as a twelfth of the amount at issue in *CIH* 24.22–27.

7. Kelly, *GEIL*, 51–57, 242–63; Breatnach, "Lawyers," 10–13 on fees particularly; Binchy, "*Féchem, Fethem, Aigne*."

8. Caesar, *Gallic War*, §VI.13–14 (pp. 126–27).

9. *Irish Penitentials*, §14 (pp. 56–57).

10. *Irish Penitentials*, §21 (pp. 56–57).

11. The enforcement strategy adopted within the church to compel offenders to meet their obligations was excommunication—the Christian equivalent to the exclusion from public sacrifice: *Irish Penitentials*, §§14, 19, 20, and 21 (pp. 56–57), particularly. On the possible link between paganism and secular law, see the unpublished paper by Charles-Edwards on "Early Irish Law," particularly 18–23, 28–33, and 37. I am grateful to Professor Charles-Edwards for allowing me to see this manuscript.

12. E.g., *CG* 21–22; 461–65; *CIH* 599.16–23 = *Bürgschaft*, §§79–80 (*BA*). As will be argued later, law school practices seem to vary in this respect.

13. On which see Breatnach, "Original Extent"; and Breatnach, *Companion*, 268–314.

14. *CIH* 527.14–529.5; Carey, "Pseudo-Historical Prologue," 11–13. See further on this text Binchy, "Pseudo-Historical Prologue"; Carey, "Two Laws"; McCone, "Dubthach maccu Lugair"; and Nagy, *Conversing with Angels*, 89–91, 199–208.

15. *AU* for 438, pp. 40–41, quite obviously a later insertion.

16. *CIH* 1111.12–22.

17. On the manner in which the law is portrayed in legal memory, see Chapter 5 below, and Stacey, "Law and Memory."

18. *CIH* 344.24, 346.5–347.7 = Thurneysen, "Irischen Recht IV," 175, with notes on pp. 177–78.

19. A useful discussion of "purposeful storytelling" and the role of the *fili* in such matters is Mac Cana, *Learned Tales*, especially 1–32.

20. Similar themes with respect specifically to the law on distraint are sounded as well in the *Senchas Már* tract on that subject: *CIH* 396.4–5.

21. P. Smith, "Aimirgein"; and see Breatnach, "Canon Law," 439–42. The TCD 1336 (H 3.17) version of the "Pseudo-Historical Prologue to the *Senchas Már*" inserts into its account a long enumeration of the just pre-Christian jurists who were purported to have anticipated the reconciliation of the two laws: *CIH* 1653.16–1655.26.

22. *CIH* 250.33–251.3, where it is part of a longer preface attributing the majority of the tract to Cormac mac Airt's advice to his son Coirpre after the latter succeeded his mutilated father as king (*CIH* 250.1–24). On *Bretha Éitgid*, see Breatnach, *Companion*, 176–82. On Cenn Fáelad, see Mac Cana, "Three Languages"; and Breatnach, *Companion*, 368–69.

23. Ford, "The Blind, the Dumb"; Ford, *Celtic Poets*, xv–xxxi; Nagy, *Wisdom of the Outlaw*, 17–40.

24. Kelly, "Court Procedure," §2 (p. 85), with notes on pp. 90–91; *GEIL*, 47–49. On the *ollam*, see *UR*, 90–94.

25. Charles-Edwards, "*Corpus Iuris Hibernici*," 146–56 especially.

26. Breatnach, "Canon Law."

27. *BNT* in *CIH* 2211.1–2232.37 and (partial) in Breatnach, "First Third"; *BND* in *CIH* 1111.1–1132.40 (and note also 1133.1–1138.37). The text was printed with notes, but no translation, in Gwynn, "Privileges and Responsibilities of Poets." Breatnach's *UR* provides editions and translations of excerpts from both works; see also his discussion in *Companion* 184–91.

28. Breatnach, "Canon Law," 441–52.

29. Binchy, "*Bretha Nemed*"; and Binchy, "*Uraicecht Becc.*" See also Breatnach, *Companion*, 184–91.

30. *GEIL*, 47–49, and see discussion below in Chapter 5.

31. Ó Corráin, "Nationality and Kingship," 19.

32. *UR*, 85–100; Breatnach, "Caldron of Poesy." And see also, on lower-class bards and satirists, McCone, *Pagan Past*, 220–26; McCone, "Two Ditties"; and *GEIL*, 49–51.

33. Charles-Edwards, "*Corpus Iuris Hibernici*," 147–51; Charles-Edwards, "Context and Uses," 74–75.

34. Ó Corráin, Breatnach, and Breen, "Laws of the Irish," 384–412. Poets and laymen were also imagined as forming seven grades in imitation of the seven grades of the church: *UR*, 81–100.

35. Breatnach, "Ecclesiastical Element," 42–48, 52; and see also Breatnach, *Companion*, 212–18; and Breatnach, "Lawyers," 3–5. Other key works include Ó Corráin, "Nationality and Kingship"; Ó Corráin, "Irish Law and Canon Law"; Ó Corráin, "Early Irish Churches"; Breatnach "Canon Law"; Ó Corráin, Breatnach, and Breen, "Laws of the Irish"; McCone, "Dubthach maccu Lugair"; McCone, *Pagan Past and Christian Present*, 84–106; and Gerriets, "Theft, Penitentials."

36. *Triads of Ireland*, §§12, 16, and 21, and see Ó Corráin, "Nationality and Kingship," 13–16.

37. *AU* for 802, pp. 256–57. Breatnach lists the historical authors or jurists referred to in the tracts in *Companion*, 368–70.

38. *GEIL*, 232–38; *BB*, pp. 36–38; Charles-Edwards, "*Corpus Iuris Hibernici*," 156–62; Charles-Edwards, "Early Irish Law," 23–37; Charles-Edwards, *Gaelic Lawyer*; Charles-Edwards, "Construction." For a dissenting view on *Bechbretha*, see McCone, "Text and Authorship."

39. Charles-Edwards, "Context and Uses," 64–75, with quote on p. 74.

40. Charles-Edwards, "Context and Uses"; see also discussion in Chapter 5 below.

41. *UR*, 89–94.

42. MacAloon, *Rite, Drama*, 9.

43. On the liturgical rites of the church, see Warren, *Liturgy and Ritual*; Jones, Wainwright and Yarnold, *Study of Liturgy*; Jungmann, *Roman Rite*.

44. *BB* §§30–35 (pp. 68–73) for Congal Cáech; the Book of Durrow dispute is discussed by Sharpe in his "Dispute Settlement," 170–74.

45. A helpful glossary of such terms is provided on pp. 269–76 of Davies and Fouracre, *Settlement of Disputes*.

46. The name itself means "custodian of tradition." Hollo has recently discussed the figure of Sencha in ''Do my bidding.'' I am very grateful to Dr. Hollo for allowing me to see her work in advance of publication.

47. Corthals, "Affiliation of Children," §2 (p. 107, with translation on p. 109), and notes on p. 113.

48. A text hailed recently by a prominent historian as one of the few "outstanding pieces of social analysis" extant from early medieval Europe: Charles-Edwards, "*Críth Gablach*," 53.

49. A division now being probed by scholars of modern law: Schaller, *Vision of American Law*; Ward, *Law and Literature*; Ledwon, *Law and Literature*; and Green, *Crisis of Truth*.

50. One of the signs of the vitality of early Irish legal studies is the plethora of divergent approaches visible in the secondary literature. Two very different—though by no means mutually exclusive—approaches to the subject of contract can be found in Stacey, *Road to Judgment*; and *EICL*. Two recent takes on the subject of kinship are Charles-Edwards, *Kinship*; and Patterson, *Cattle-Lords*. An excellent example of how to read the law tracts in a manner that recognizes their inherent complexities is Charles-Edwards, "*Críth Gablach*."

51. *CCF*, §27 (p. 25); Breatnach, *Companion*, 162–63.

52. Breatnach, "Lawyers," 9–10.

53. *CIH* 598.23 = *Bürgschaft*, §74c (p. 27). For other references to the *forus* of the debt see, for example, *CIH* 594.24 = *Bürgschaft*, §44 (p. 13); 595.9 = *Bürgschaft*, §51a (p. 15).

54. The guarantor appointed to secure a debt in *BA* must, for example, himself give sureties to guarantee that he is, among other things, a "surety of rest"—in other words, of permanent residence. Criminal matters were particularly difficult in this respect. The inability to find and punish the true transgressor may be the issue in the tale of Fergus mac Léti incorporated into the tract on distraint, for example: "Saga of Fergus mac Léti," §2 (p. 37).

55. *DIL* (Compact Edition), p. 25, col. 195; see also *CG*, p. 73.

56. Sharpe, "Dispute and Settlement," in *Settlement of Disputes*, 186; Kelly, "Court Procedure," 81–82. Important work has been done recently on the manner in which structures of royal rule are visible in the archaeological record: see, for example, Bhreathnach, *Kingship and Landscape*.

57. Breatnach, "Lawyers," 8.

58. Kelly, "Court Procedure," 80–81; §§2, 6 (pp. 85–87).

59. Breatnach, "Lawyers," 9. Breatnach's translation emphasizes cooperation obtaining between judge and dignitaries: "expounding law with a lord." Usually *ar-beir fri* has overtones of opposition, however, and given the clause on preventing illegality, I have retained something of this meaning here.

60. Kelly, "Court Procedure," §3 (p. 85).

61. Stacey, *Road to Judgment*, pp. 130–40.

62. This as opposed to people like the *senchaid* mentioned in the text, whose testimony would not be to the facts of a specific case, but to long-established customs of the region: Kelly, "Court Procedure," §5 (pp. 86–87). These include witnesses generally, as well as those privy to the facts of individual obligations (the contractual guarantors mentioned in the text).

63. Recent attempts to grapple with the highly schematized sources on this issue include Kelly, "Court Procedure"; and Sharpe, "Dispute Settlement," 169–89.

64. Stacey, *Road to Judgment*, 117–19. On *CCF* itself, see Breatnach, *Companion*, 233–34.

65. *GEIL*, 208–13; Bartlett, *Fire and Water*, 5–6, 48; Stokes, "Irish Ordeals," 183–229. Recent studies of the ordeal take different positions on its intrinsic nature and its place within the community: Brown, "Society and the Supernatural"; Bartlett, *Fire and Water*; Hyams, "Trial by Ordeal."

66. For discussion and references, see Stacey, *Road to Judgment*, 112–40.

67. *CCF* recension H, §16 (p. 30) = *CIH* 1029.21–23. Thurneysen prints this in normal paragraph form, but I have reproduced the excerpt as a list in order to make clear its structure. Other information on aspects of the pleading process can be found in the late miscellanies in 23 Q 6: *CIH* 1146.21–1151.3.

68. Breatnach, "Lawyers," 10–11, identifying *astad airbertai* as collapsing two of the stages outlined in *Cóic Conara Fugill*: the selecting of the proper procedural approach and the giving of security.

69. Unless otherwise noted, all references to this text are to Breatnach's edition in "Lawyers," 11–12.

70. Binchy, "*Féchem, Fethem, Aigne*"; see also Breatnach, "Lawyers," 10–13, notes 42 and 48 particularly.

71. *CIH* 1613.38–1614.33, and see discussion in Stacey, *Road to Judgment*, 125–40.

72. Sureties to guarantee the appearance of a litigant in court or to guarantee that a defendant will come to law seems the correct translation in this context of *aitire* (see discussion in Stacey, *Road to Judgment*, 82–111, and cf. Breatnach's translation in "Lawyers," 10).

73. *Aignis lais uile 7 nascairecht 7 berrad 7 comaidhches 7 cáin lánomhnai 7 maccslechtai*, where the last four named are all names of written tracts: text in Breatnach, "Lawyers," 11.

74. *do fiur forid-cain*, "to the man who instructs him," as opposed to *fer bélrai las ndéne*, "the legal expert with whom he does [it—e.g., the law]."

75. In the text edited by Breatnach in "Lawyers," 9, they are termed *díanbretha*, "swift judgments." Similarly, "extremely difficult legal cases" (*aincessa mara*), are defined in *Cóic Conara Fugill* as matters that must be resolved through the ordeal: *CCF*, §3 (p. 16), and see discussion in Stacey, *Road to Judgment*, 117–19.

76. Perhaps to be identified with the *aire ard* or the *aire forgill* of *Críth Gablach* (on which see *CG* pp. 69–72). Such a relationship might explain why this type of advocate is said to owe not just the acknowledgment of his authority (*recht*) but also *goire*, "filial *pietas*," to the "man who instructs him." Normally this type of *pietas* was owed only to family members. However, political relationships in Ireland were often conceptualized as kindred bonds (the term for political alliance, "*cairde*" means "kinship"); indeed, this is a basic premise in the genealogies, for example. If the "man who instructs him" were his lord, this would make sense. Of the two other ranks of advocate, the lowest owes nothing but money to the legal expert with whom he studies: this is clearly envisaged as a one-time exchange of goods for services rendered. The second level of advocate owes *recht* ("authority") to the legal expert with whom he studies—in other words, theirs is envisaged as an ongoing relationship, one that transcends the boundaries of the school in which the instruction occurred. But only the third level of advocate is said to owe *goire*.

77. This is my understanding of the phrase *acht gníma rachtairi*. Another possible way to read this phrase is to see the *aigne fris-n-innle breith* as the *rechtaire*; in this case the meaning of the clause would presumably be that he was entitled or expected to act on behalf of his lord in everything except matters pertaining to his own past and present deeds as *rechtaire*.

78. In *DT*, as we have seen, a time for judgment was built into the ritual itself, and this is true also of the ecclesiastical *Cáin Domnaig*, the "Law of Sunday": "*Cáin Domnaig*," §§3–5 (pp. 164–67). Cf. also *CIH* 2222.34–36.

79. See discussion in Chapter 5 below, and *CIH* 358.2, an excerpt from the *Senchas Már* tract on distraint that underscores the importance of lawyers who are *suithengthaid*, "eloquent in speech."

80. Extant texts are to be found in *CIH* 1589.1–48 and 1338.5–1341.7 (following Breatnach, *Companion*, 263–64); and see also A. and W. O'Sullivan, "Legal Fragment." The most important studies are Binchy, "*Mellbretha*"; and Sayers, "Games."

81. *CIH* 1589.1–19, assuming that the speaker referred to in line is Bodainn, and that this is where the actual text of the verdict begins.

82. *féith fírinne* is an (appropriately) ambiguous expression, in that *féith* here could represent any number of different words: "tranquility" or "hereditary vein," as Binchy notes ("*Mellbretha*," 149, note e). Other possible translations include "skill," or even "breeze, blowing," since in Irish tradition breath is often linked to

poetic inspiration. Indeed, the birth of the art of poetry itself was said to have been heralded by a tremendous gust of wind: Radner, "Men Will Die," 172–78 especially.

83. Text from "*Mellbretha*," 148–49; the translation mainly follows that suggested by Sayers in "Games," 111.

84. Sayers, "Games," 112, 117–18.

85. *CIH* 882.11–16 (in the Old-Irish glosses to H 3. 18) = "Saga of Fergus mac Léti," §2 (p. 37 and partial translation on pp. 39–40).

86. Here following Corthals' proposed emendation of *dia* to *dia[m]* and his translation of much of the first clause of the sentence. He takes *forus* in the second clause to mean "principle," translating "because of the principle underlying the judgement": Corthals, "Affiliation of Children," pp. 119–20. This is certainly a possible translation. However, *forus* is a complicated term, with meanings ranging from the actual place appointed for the resolution of a dispute, to the principles according to which the dispute is settled, to the proclamation by which the matter is brought to a close. The issue here, as Binchy points out, is that while normally the kindred of an outsider son would be liable for his offense, in this instance that defense seems to be specifically precluded. This suggests either that Dorn's son's offense was deemed so heinous that he was not allowed to make compensation for the offense before judgment ("he is alien to us in respect of a settlement which is [offered] before judgment") or that his outsider status raises a concern about whether he can be located in time for judgment. The latter seems to me to be implied by "if he be a competent person who can be secured," and I have so translated it here.

87. Reading *cach conn li[a] cin*. I owe this suggestion to Thomas Charles-Edwards, for whose assistance I am very grateful.

88. A certain distance out to sea, in some texts defined as the distance from which a white shield on shore can still be seen: Byrne, "Setting Adrift"; and *GEIL*, 219–21.

89. As Binchy points out, this *rosc* is very corrupt and any translation is therefore likely to be uncertain. I follow Binchy's partial translation in many particulars here, although I have attempted to provide translations for phrases he left untranslated. The opening phrases are of special difficulty: *mac* is the reading proposed by Binchy, and it gives good sense in the passage; however, it is textually uncertain. *Dia duirnn* is quite difficult: I have translated it as though reading *do* for *dia*; alternatively, one could perhaps understand *dia* to contain a possessive pronoun referring to the unnamed foreigner: "[the] son [born] to his Dorn." However, one would not expect Dorn as a feminine name to be declined in this way, and one must thus consider the possibility that this is the masculine o-stem *dorn*, "fist, hand," which would give us something like "an aggressor against us is the son from his fist." In subsequent phrases, I read *rechtaid* for *rachtid*, and take *connli* as a subjunctive form of *condáili*.

90. "Archaic" syntactical features in this selection include tmesis (*nacha . . . foisither*) and the construction commented on by Corthals ("Affiliation of Children," 120) and described by Wagner in "Syntactical Feature" (*do tuathaib targuth*). For *rosc*, see Breatnach, "Canon Law," 452–53.

91. *Cath Maige Mucrama*. See comments on the dating of this text on pp. 18–36; Ó Daly identifies false judgment as one of the frequently recurring motifs: p. 17.

92. *Cath Maige Mucrama*, pp. 76–77.

93. *Cath Maige Mucrama*, "*Scéla Mosauluim*," §§4–6 (pp. 76–77).

94. *Fir naicnith*, "the law of nature," or "truth of nature," is a complex term, and is used here in an unusual way. Normally the term is used to contrast the native and "natural" law of the Irish with the law of the church, and its implications in such tales are generally positive, the intent being to stress the extent to which native Irish custom is "naturally" consonant with Christian values. However, in this plea the "law

of nature" appears to describe statements regarding the case rather than the law by which it is to be decided, and the king-judge is explicitly invited to "hear" *fir naicnith* rather than declare it. Presumably the implication is that the plaintiff's position accurately reflects the priorities of *fir naicnith* in a way that the defendant's statement will not. See *Cath Maige Mucrama*, p. 132, for references to a slightly different version of this plea.

95. The suggested emendation here reads *doa taibir toil*, but both manuscripts clearly have *co: contaibir toil* and *co tabair toil*; moreover, *con* is clearly intended to resonate with *con-oí* and *con-beir*, and I have therefore retained it here. Presumably it is intended to be a form of *con-to-beir*, "jointly gives."

96. I am here citing the normalized text as suggested in note 562f., p. 132, of *Cath Maige Mucrama*, "*Scéla Mosauluim*,"§6 (pp. 76–77). Another version of this text is to be found in *BNT: CIH* 2232.33–37. I am greatly indebted to the translated provided by Ó Daly, even though I have emended it slightly.

97. In other words, her testimony given on oath as to the paternity of the child overcomes theirs.

98. Literally, "who join bodies for the sake of. . . ."

99. Both texts read the same here, and yet something seems to be missing. Another possibility might be to read (with *Scéla Mosauluim*) . . . *fri baíse búad. Ráth si fri bás sóeraib sceo dóeraib* . . . "because of the triumph of lust. A guarantor she is against death with respect to free and unfree persons"—the woman is to act as a surety for her children's being legitimate even if the man in question has died, given that a case of this sort might well be taking place when an inheritance is being settled after a death.

100. Or "he," if the lenition that would normally indicate the third person masculine possessive pronoun *a* is simply not shown here. The maxim that closes this paragraph occurs frequently in contexts having to do with inheritance issues that arise when a man has had a child by a prostitute or promiscuous woman: e.g., *CIH* 1298.23–28, where this passage is cited and the subject taken by the glossator to be the man (*gach fer*); and see also 2230.1–2, where the neutral *nech* is the stated subject. I gratefully acknowledge Dennis King's assistance with this difficult passage.

101. Ó Daly takes this as a reference to the children of prostitutes: p. 77, which may well be right. On the face of it, however, if the referent is the woman (on which see previous note), the passage seems to be forbidding her to associate her children with prostitutes themselves. In any case, the main point presumably is to prevent women who associate with prostitutes (and might therefore be presumed to partake of their lifestyle) from swearing paternity on anyone.

102. Ó Daly (correctly, in my view) takes the opposition established in this passage between "foolish" and "prudent" (*báeth* and *gáeth* respectively) to refer to the sexual history of the woman in question—e.g., "promiscuous" versus "sexually prudent." On the other hand, because *báeth* and *gáeth* are also terms used frequently in the lawbooks to designate mentally or legally incompetent individuals, I have kept the translation neutral—e.g., "foolish" instead of "promiscuous"—in order to invoke both senses of these words. A mentally incompetent woman would presumably also not be able to swear paternity on someone.

103. Dated linguistically by Breatnach, *Companion*, 349–50.

104. *CIH* 2112.29–2118.2. Manuscript H 4. 22 contains two of these same stories (*CIH* 1560.32–1561.13 and 1561.14–23). The tales from H 3. 17 were published and translated by Dillon in "Stories from the Law Tracts," and I follow his numbering in my discussion of them. Some go back to an Old Irish original, while some seem to have been Middle Irish in date: Breatnach, *Companion*, 349–50. However, it is worth pointing out that many of these Middle Irish tales are being cited in eighth-century

Bretha Nemed tracts, so if the versions known to the H 3 .17 compiler resemble at all those from which the *Bretha Nemed* composers were working, the stories themselves may still be quite old.

105. E.g., *CIH* 2112.29; 2113.6, 16; 2115.38; 2117.36.

106. Differing versions of the tales would seem to be suggested by CIH 2229.5–10—at least assuming that *fomnach* is intended as a personal name.

107. *CIH* 2116.33–34.

108. There are tales in which the speech reported probably ought also to be regarded as formal judicial speech (or at least speech affiliated to it), but in which the circumstances of its utterance are not made clear. These examples include tale eight, in which Lugaid Lámfhada's speech—which at least represents his decision as kindred leader as to the affiliation of a son seeking affiliation with the kindred, and may represent also his plea before Sencha—is phrased in the rhetorical style (*CIH* 2115.15–37, and see 1560.32ff.). Particularly interesting is tale nine, in which all significant speech reported is in the rhetorical style, including the druid's warning as to the infidelity of Finn's wife and the satirical judgments made by the severed head of the druid (*CIH* 2115.38–2116.27; and see 1139.10ff., 1298.28ff., and 2230.3ff.). The full text of the druid's accusation (made in writing on a rod given by him to Finn) incorporates several proverbs repeated elsewhere in the lawbooks, including in tale twelve in H 3. 17: *Cuailli feda i foillim nairgit. Aith i fochlucht mac mna druithe dluthar i niarfine ucht acht mad iarna choir comadas comraiter is druthlaech la feiniu foircthe,* "A wooden stake in a fence of silver, deadly nightshade in the midst of [edible] water-parsnip: [this is] the son of a cuckolding woman that is pressed to the bosom of the 'after-kindred.' Except if it be according to suitable propriety that he be brought [into the kindred?], he is [regarded as] a cuckold among the learned *Féni*" (on *comraiter,* see *DIL* p. 154, col. 501, *cotrirther*). In the context of the tale, this represents the druid's "judgment" on the situation.

109. Tale three goes back to an Old Irish original: Breatnach, *Companion,* 349–50.

110. *CIH* 2113.16–25; the *Bretha Nemed* version of this tale, which consists mainly of the speeches made by Conchobar and Sencha without any great amount of background explanation, can be found on 2217.24–35.

111. *CIH* 2217.29–30.

112. I am following Dillon's phrasing here.

113. Taking *immairicc* here as "conflict, defeat," and hence "destruction," rather than *imm-airicc,* "suits, is appropriate to," and *dalta* as a participial form of *dáilid,* "distributes, pours out," and hence "conflict poured out to his pigs." Another possible reading would be to take *dalta* for *daltai,* "fosterling, ward," and read "the destruction of the ward of the two pigs." The ward in question would presumably be the calf, who is conceptualized as being in the care of the pigs that destroy him. In favor of this reading is the fact that the H 3. 17 tale refers to the calf as the *mac da bo,* the "son of two cows" (2113.20).

114. *CIH* 2217.26: either something would appear to have been misplaced or omitted in this sentence, or the two narrators are working with different versions of the story, since it is Maine's son, not Maine himself, who was killed by the pigs. The translation of *ruchtaid* (elsewhere *ruchtaig*) *ruib* is tentative. *Ruchtach* is an animal that emits a *rucht,* or a harsh sound of some sort; there is also a noun *rucht,* meaning "pig." *Ruib* is unknown, although Fergus Kelly kindly suggests to me that one might take it as the genitive singular of *rob,* "animal." The DIL suggests reading *duibh* for *ruib* in *Tromdhám Guaire. DIL* p. 513, col. 113, but the intentionally alliterative nature of the phrase seems to argue against that. Another possibility (less likely than Kelly's given the need to emend) involves reading *rubib,* dative plural of *rubae,* "wounding, killing": "grunting [pigs] with woundings tore apart."

115. The H 3. 17 tale itself has been dated to the Middle Irish period by Breatnach (*Companion*, 349–50). However, the excerpt from *Bretha Nemed Deidenach* (which seems to correspond fairly well with the tale in terms of content and attribution) is Old Irish.

116. *CIH* 1116.29–33. My translation is based on reading *no do beir* as an interlinear gloss on *ernedh* (the parentheses are mine); *ad-gella* for *ad-ella*; *im ad-rubhairt* as a perfective form of *imm-beir* with masculine infix; *domiged* (for *do-mided?*) as an imperative form for *do-midethar*, here retaining the *do* in order to alliterate with *dorn* (alternatively, it could be the second plural present tense of that same verb); and *ro-lá* for *rolais* (as it stands, second person singular). This part of *BND* makes frequent reference to tales and characters associated with the legal and pseudohistorical (literary) traditions.

117. Taking *let* as the preposition *la* with the second singular suffixed pronoun. Another possibility is to read *leth*, "half" or "partial." The referent here is probably Lóegaire, although a case could be made for Amairgen as well. In the end, both win and lose: Lóegaire by virtue of having avenged his earlier mistreatment, and yet incurring fines for the killing; Amairgen by virtue of having had his spear misused, and yet having also had that offense punished.

118. *CIH* 2112.29–39; 2216.25–2217.7. Both Morann and Neire are mythical jurists famed in early Irish tradition as legal specialists. One early legal text—really a *speculum principum*—is attributed to Morann and addressed by him to his foster-son Neire: *Audacht Morainn*.

119. *CIH* 2217.12–13, and cf. 2113.10–13.

120. Reading *for-gaba* for *forgabad*; and taking *rarsad* as a possible misreading of a double *r* in the subjunctive of *oirgid: -orrat*.

121. *CIH* 2113.6–15; 2217.8–23. This relates to tale two, the original of which goes back to the Old Irish period: Breatnach, *Companion*, 349–50.

122. *Cia rodaerad-som riam. Collud cochta Cernodon*, "Though he have been satirized before, [it is] a defilement of beauty (?) to Cernodon." "Beauty" is the translation suggested by Dillon; according to the *DIL*, the meaning of *cochta* is uncertain. The tale can be found in *CIH* 2113.26–2114.4 and 1134.6–25; it goes back to an Old Irish original: Breatnach, *Companion*, 349.

123. *CIH* 2114.25–38, where the poet's judgment begins with a line that in B.M. Nero A 7 is embedded in a larger unit (marked as a unit by the repetition of the appearance of the line *ni na daim inad* at the beginning and end of the passage); 2223.24–33, which is itself part of an extended discussion on gages: 2223.18–40. This tale is Middle Irish in date: Breatnach, *Companion*, 350.

124. Compare *CIH* 2223.34–35 with 2116.28–41. These latter are not actually tales, but explanations intended to serve as the background for tales the compiler of H 3. 17 then did not relate—possibly because he did not know them, as he remarks: *as mor do scelaib fil sund 7 is liach gan a fis*, "there are many stories here and it is a pity that they are not known" (*CIH* 2116.33–34; translation is Dillon's: "Stories from the Law Tracts," 61). Breatnach argues that it is not possible to decide on a date for tale eleven, but that tale ten is Middle Irish in language: Breatnach, *Companion*, 350.

125. Sic, for *dia taigh*, as in *CIH* 2229.9? Tale seven is Middle Irish in language: Breatnach, *Companion*, 350.

126. *CIH* 2114.39–2115.14; 2229.5–10.

127. Stokes, "Irish Ordeals," 201–2, with note on p. 228; Gwynn, "Privileges and Responsibilities," note to p. 34.13, on p. 226.

128. *CIH* 877.10–28.

129. *Immathchor.* In this text, the formal pleas offered to the judge are also

couched in poetic language, as they are as well in several of the stories incorporated into TCD 1336: e.g., at *CIH* 2112.29–35, 2113.6–15.

130. *CIH* 2222.17–18, and see note 64–66 in *UR*, p. 132.

131. *CIH* 2221.15–16, and compare *UB* 1592.8–21, where the judgment of the church is said to be grounded in Scripture and truth, the judgment of poets in *roscada,* and the judgment of lords (*breath flatha*) in them all: legal verse, maxims, and scriptural evidence. See also the phrase quoted both in the "Pseudo-Historical Prologue to the *Senchas Már*" and the related tale *Comthoth Lóegairi: brithem fri brithemnas a roscadaib 7 fásaigib,* "[the] judge for judgment based on *roscads* and maxims" (Carey, "Pseudo-Historical Prologue," §8 (p. 12), and Best and Bergin, *Lebor na Huidre,* 294, lines 9790–91.)

132. *CIH* 2222.36–38. The translation is uncertain, since *dicanta* can be construed either as the negative of *canaid,* "sings, chants," meaning "not chanted," or as being from *do-cain,* "sings, recites," and hence meaning "chanted." Reading it as a negative would yield a translation something like this: "everything that has not been chanted is to be bound (e.g., by some other means), everything not bound is not chanted." It is also possible that the authors of the tract were playing with the ambiguous meaning of the prefix *di-:* "everything chanted is [regarded] as bound, everything unbound has not been chanted." However, the basic point—that the chanting of maxims is linked to the legal validity of an action—remains intact regardless of the way in which one reads the phrase.

133. *CIH* 2228.35.

134. E.g., *CIH* 2222.9; and see below for a discussion of 2222.9–33. Another word that appears in this context is *árosc,* "saying, maxim, proverb," which in the context of the H 3. 17 tales seems to be regarded as a speech act: *ardarasc isbeir frit,* "a noble saying I say to you" (*CIH* 2216.27). See also 2227.20.

Similarly, the terms *airbert* and *frithbert* employed in the ninth-century texts on judging and pleading ought probably also to be considered as referring to formal judicial speech acts. The relevant passages are as follows (all translations from Breatnach, "Lawyers," 8–12): 1) *Dligid . . . étsecht a airberta,* "He is entitled [to demand] listening in silence to his exposition of law"; 2) *Caide ord breitheman do túaith . . . ? . . . breath 7 astad airberta 7 airbert aoí iarna hastad. . . . Is di foltaib breitheman . . . airbert fri flaith, fri senad, fri aes cerda, coná toirceat a túaith i n-indlighe,* "What is the duty of a judge to the kingdom . . . ? . . . judging, and determining [the correct method of] procedure, and proceeding with the case after it has been determined . . . Among the duties of a judge . . . expounding law with a lord, with a synod, with men of art, lest they act illegally towards their kingdom"; 3) *lethtrian ar frithbert,* "one-sixth for opposing," *lethtrian ar airbert,* "one sixth for acting in court"; 4) *cin astad n-airberta,* "without determining [the correct method of] procedure." In order to render these passages comprehensible to modern readers, Breatnach has here had to translate *airbert* differently almost every time it occurs. This is a helpful strategy for the reader, but may obscure its true nature as a speech act—the literal "putting before" the court by judge or pleader a case or the law relevant to that case. Sentence one might thus refer to judge's exposition of the law in a particular case. Sentences two and three might refer in the first instance to the binding (*astad*) of the particular type of oral approach envisaged—the manner in which the pleader plans to put the case before the judge, in other words—whereas the judge's *airbert* to king and synod would be a reference to his oral proclamation to (or with) them of the law in the case. The latter seems to be its sense in certain other passages where the active verb is used, such as a short passage in H 3. 18 that purports to record a conversation between Cormac mac Airt and his *dorsaid,* "doorkeeper, porter," on the subject of judges for neighborhood law. In the course of this conversation, Cormac makes reference to a *brithim ard arberta breith fir fiad rig 7 tuath*, "a noble judge who proclaims judgement in the presence of king and tribe" (*CIH* 573.18–19). *Frithbert* in the ninth-century texts obviously refers to this advocate's role as an enforcer for the court. However, since he is already said to receive a third for *tobach*, "levying"; might *frithbert* then refer to a speech act of opposition performed either in the court or as the first step in the process of collecting the amount owed?

135. Significantly, these passages in E 3. 3 are preceded by *UR* on the poetic grades and followed by a short passage from *BND* on voice (partially translated by Carey in "Vernacular Irish Learning"). One version of this text has been recently edited and translated by Ireland in his *Wisdom*, Appendix 2, 169–73.

136. The issue of anger appears also in the Latin canons: *IK*, XXI.15 (and see XXI.14, citing Isidore).

137. *CIH* 2112.32–33.

138. *CIH* 2341.8–2342.15, especially the "sixteen signs of bad pleading" on 2342.1–6. See also *Instructions*, §§22–25 (pp. 40–43). Injunctions against pleadings being too loud or too soft occur also in *CCF*: *CIH* 2200.3–10 = *CCF* §2 (p. 15).

139. Kelly, "Court Procedure," 81.

140. Corthals argues that such provisions are "ultimately based . . . on antique theory of judicial rhetoric," which is reflected also in the works of Isidore and Alcuin: "Affiliation of Children," 101 and note 28, pp. 101–2.

141. *CIH* 2069.30–35 (the whole passage extends to line 42).

142. *Bérla* or *bélrae Féne* is the term used throughout the lawbooks for the secular (e.g., non–canon law) legal tradition, and another possible translation of this sentence would be "through which the legal tradition is rendered harmonious." Its literal meaning, however, is "the language of the Féni"—in other words, the speech by and through which that tradition is realized. See discussion below in Chapter 3.

143. Literally: "compactness of cohesion."

144. *Tucait* literally means "cause, reason"; elsewhere the phrase reads *ar tucait binniusa*, "for the sake of euphony," here: *Auraicept na nÉces*, 634.

145. *CIH* 856.5–7.

146. *CIH* 1288.1–32, especially 1288.1–4.

147. This reading is uncertain. One would expect something more along the lines of *do filedaib 7 feinib*, "the surrounding of lords by poets and freemen," or even the third person form of the verb with accusative plural forms of the relevant nouns: "because lords surround (in the sense of encompassing, or taking care of) poets and freemen."

148. *CIH* 2225.12–16; 2225.26–27 = 1288.7–12, 1288.23–24. Part of this passage (*Go deich do foclaib*) is glossed in *CIH* 662.11–14 with a passage that replicates those cited above on the number of breaths and words appropriate to each rank.

149. Literally, "man of binding." Presumably this refers to a person during the time he is serving as a guarantor.

150. It is difficult to know whether the provision on the *fir fonadma* was inspired by, or is merely being justified in accordance with, the model of Moses and the Ten Commandments. Presumably the provision on the seven words per breath for the lordly and ecclesiastical grades is modeled on the seven grades of the church (which also provided the model according to which the secular grades are distinguished).

151. Breatnach has an extensive discussion of mythical authors mentioned in the tracts in *Companion*, 361–68. I have discussed the issue in more general terms in "Law and Literature."

152. Charles-Edwards, *Kinship*, p. 268.

153. For Bríg, see *CIH* 209.22–23; 407.1. A gloss in *DT* identifies Bríg as Sencha's daughter: 209.24. For Asal and Cóicthe, see *CIH* 352.26–31, with gloss on 352.32–353.1, and 406.26–407.2, where Cóicthe is identified by the author with Bríg herself.

154. This identification is likely, but not certain: see Kelly's note 9 to Neire in *AM*, §2 (p. 24).

155. See discussion above and *CIH* 406.26–407.2, for example. Many of the best known Ulster Cycle tales have been translated by Gantz in *Irish Myths*.

156. As in *Loinges mac n-Uislenn*, 43, lines 9–11; or in *Mesca Ulad*, 118–20, where Sencha intervenes several times to prevent bloodshed among the Ulstermen, once shaking his "peacemaking branch." Sencha appears frequently in the H 3. 17 tales (on which see discussion and references above), but he also shows up in two *Senchas Már* texts, *DT* and *Di Chetharshlicht Athgabála* (*CIH* 209.12–23 and 406.26–407.2, respectively). Hollo has recently examined the legal and literary aspects of Sencha, pointing to important differences between the two traditions in their characterization of him and arguing that the Sencha of the tales is not a judge, but an *aurlabraid*, a person who speaks on behalf of another: Hollo, "Do my bidding." She argues that these differences suggest a serious division within the intellectual professions, legal and literary. However, jurists frequently invented stories and characters to underscore the legal points they intended to make, and I am not convinced that discrepancies of this sort require us to imagine jurists and storytellers occupying different cultural worlds: Stacey, "Law and Literature."

157. *CIH* 63.7–11; and see the previous note for references to *Loinges mac n-Uislenn*.

158. The legal tale can be found *CIH* 2117.23–35.

159. Aengus son or grandson of Fiacha Fobrecc, for example: *CIH* 2114.25–27.

160. E.g., *CIH* 2115.38–2116.27, which constitutes one of the most fully developed of the legal tales.

161. Ó Corráin, "Irish Vernacular Law"; Ó Corráin, Breatnach, and Breen, "Laws of the Irish"; McCone, *Pagan Past*, 84–106.

162. *Bethu Brigte*, §14 (pp. 4–5), with translation on p. 23, and discussion of the date of composition on xxv–xxvii. Another version of the encounter between Patrick and Dubthach appears in Muirchú's seventh-century life of Patrick: *Patrician Texts*, 93, I 19. Hughes has argued that the *Vita Tripartita* of Patrick was "intended for preaching to the public on the three days of Patrick's festival": Hughes, *Early Christian Ireland*, 241.

163. *EICL* §§4, 13, 14 (pp. 128–29, 138–39, 140–41). *CIH* 682.1–10 tells the story of Cain and Abel in terms of Irish principles of injury and compensation, and then goes on in lines 10–15 to tell the brief tale of Ambia, daughter of Cain, a mermaid-like creature who was said to have given birth to twenty-two offspring at once.

164. McLeod, "Not-So-Exotic Law." I am grateful to Professor McLeod for making this piece available to me in advance of publication.

165. Nagy, *Conversing with Angels*, 200–8.

166. This would appear to be the essential premise behind the many dialogues between teacher and student found in the *BN* texts, e.g., *UR* §11 (pp. 48–49).

167. There has been a great deal of discussion about the origins of individual tales and of the written literary tradition as a whole, and about the relationship of that written tradition to oral storytelling: Mallory and Stockman, *Ulidia*; Mallory, *Aspects of the Táin*; Aitchison, *Armagh*; McCone, *Pagan Past*; Tranter and Tristam, *Early Irish Literature*; Mac Cana, *Learned Tales*; Nagy, *Conversing with Angels*.

168. Sayers, "Concepts of Eloquence," 133, 142–43.

169. Kratz, *Affecting Performance*, 17–18.

170. *Cath Maige Mucrama*, 17.

171. *Cath Maige Mucrama*, §9 (pp. 40–41).

172. *Cath Maige Mucrama*, §63 (pp. 58–59), and compare "*Scéla Éogain*," §§17–18 (pp. 70–71).

173. *CIH* 2224.27.

174. In which a poem begins and ends with the same (or deliberately reminiscent) word or phrase.

175. *CIH* 2217.14–17.

176. Or: "after sheltering lawsuits to a competent person for judgments." *Clitchuib*, "sheltering" should modify *tacruib*, "lawsuits" given its position in the sentence; on the other hand, it is bound by alliteration to *coigertuibh*, and abnormal word order is a hallmark of this type of artistic speech. Moreover, Cormac's judgment will shelter the pigs from forfeiture.

177. *UR*, where Breatnach also edits and translates several other short pieces pertaining to the subject; and Breatnach, "Caldron."

178. This is a major theme in McCone's book *Pagan Past*. See also McCone, "Two Ditties"; Sharpe, "Hiberno-Latin *laicus*"; and Cathasaigh, "Curse and Satire."

179. A key text for this point of view is the eerie description offered in the ninth-century *Sanas Cormaic* of the ritual by which the *filid* obtained their otherworldly enlightenment (*imbas forosnai*, "[the] knowledge that illuminates"): by first chewing on a piece of raw pig, dog, or cat meat, chanting over it in a pagan ritual, and then entering a dream state in which the future is revealed to them: *Sanas Cormaic*, §756. There would appear to be connections with Welsh tradition, where poetry was also viewed as a mantic endeavor. Traditions surrounding the otherworldly wisdom of the outlaw hero Finn, who when faced with a quandary would chew on his thumb to attain the knowledge he needed—thus eating raw, taboo meat in a manner not dissimilar to the ritual outlined in *Sanas Cormaic*—fixed the image of the visionary poet firmly in the scholarly imagination.

180. I have found the following works particularly helpful: Watkins, "Indo-European Metrics"; Nagy, *Wisdom*; Nagy, "Liminality"; Nagy, "Wisdom of the *Geilt*"; Radner, "Men Will Die"; Ford, *Poetry of Llywarch*, 5–11; Ford, "The Blind, the Dumb"; Bloomfield and Dunn, *Role of the Poet*, 35–41, 43–48, and 120–49 especially. I have also benefited from Dr. Shannon McRae's unpublished dissertation, "'A Dream of Purely Burning': Myth, Gender and Modernism" (Ph.D. dissertation, University of Washington, 1999). I am grateful to the author for allowing me to see this work in advance of publication.

181. Watkins, "Indo-European Metrics," 213–17; *Poetry of Llywarch Hen*, 5–11.

182. "The Caldron of Poesy," §11 (pp. 66–67).

183. Carey, "Three Things," 57–58, and see also more generally pp. 41–58. Carey explores this theme of romanticizing the pagan past in the prose literature in his paper on "Uses of Tradition" in *Ulidia*, 77–84.

184. Breatnach, "Caldron of Poesy," §12 (pp. 68–69).

185. For what follows, I have benefited considerably from Nagy's *Conversing with Angels*, pp. 200–8.

186. Text of the judgment edited and translated by McCone in "Dubthach maccu Lugair," 29–30 and 5–8, respectively; for his conclusion on the interdependency of the two sections, see 2–3, 17–18.

187. Carey, "Pseudo-Historical Prologue," §3 (p. 11), and see the fuller version cited by McCone on p. 6 of "Dubthach maccu Lugair."

188. The text of the judgment is edited and discussed by McCone in "Dubthach maccu Lugair," 28–35; the translation can be found on pp. 6–10 of that same piece.

189. McCone, "Dubthach maccu Lugair," §viii (p. 29). *AM* is one of our chief

sources of knowledge about the *fír flathemon*: §§12–28 (pp. 7–11) and discussion on xiv–xix. As Kelly has argued, in its earliest form *AM* "seems devoid of Christian elements" and thus unlikely to be the work of a cleric: *GEIL*, 236, and see his discussion of its contribution to our knowledge of conditions in pre-Christian Ireland in *AM*, xiii–xix.

190. Text and translation by McCone, "Dubthach maccu Lugair," §xi (pp. 7 and 29).

191. McCone, "Dubthach maccu Lugair," §xviii (pp. 8 and 30).

192. Tymoczko, "Poetry of Masks," 195–96. See also Tymoczko, "Inversions"; and Tymoczko, "Metonymics."

193. Tymoczko, "Poetry of Masks," 192–96.

194. Tymoczko, "Poetry of Masks," 199, 206–7.

195. He plays a similar role in certain hagiographical tales pertaining to Brigit. In *Bethu Brigte*, for example, he seeks to become her husband. In an effort to escape his suit—and, most pressingly, the insistence of her relatives that she make this prosperous match—she puts out her eye. Dubthach then releases her. In the circumstances, this might not appear an entirely selfless gesture; however, he accompanies his action with a gift of land to her and the church, and urges her to take the veil: *Bethu Brigte*, §§14–16 (pp. 4–5 and 23–24).

196. See, in addition to her encounter with Sencha, her role in the "Kinship Poem" edited by Charles-Edwards in *Kinship*, 516–19. Another interesting characterization of Sencha can be found in tale three of H 3.17, where he appears as hesitant and uncertain compared to Conchobar himself. His hesitation here is curious: it may relate to jurisdictional disputes between kings and jurists that will be discussed later in this work, or it may reflect Sencha's portrayal within the legal tradition as somewhat "inept": Hollo, "Do My Bidding."

197. They also serve to invoke the *BN* approach to law itself, which matter will be discussed later in this work.

198. Examples include *CIH* 2221.8–11, 2221.12–16, 2225.12–25, and the like. In 2231.37–2232.23 it is unclear whether the question *co direnar raith righ* is interjected by Neire or is a rhetorical question asked by Morann in the course of his statement.

199. Examples of this form include *UR*, pp. 28–33, 33–36, 36–39, 41–42; *CIH* 2220.26–29, 2220.30–38, 2221.1–7, and the like. I see no easy way of determining who the speaker is supposed to be in these cases. The obvious way to read these passages would be as questions posed to Morann by his student that he (Morann) then proceeds to answer. However, most of these passages seem to end by returning to the "O Morann" invocation with which the passage began, so one must either presume that Neire is imagined as still speaking (and hence having answered his own question), or that he hails Morann's wisdom once the latter has answered by repeating his name. Sometimes Morann himself asks a question and then answers it without Neire saying a word: e.g., 2222.34–38; sometimes Neire poses the question with "O wealthy mighty Morann" and someone (Morann?) then ends his answer with the "O my Neire" formula: 2232.24–32.

200. *CIH* 2112.29–35.

201. *UR*, 49–50 and 54–57, respectively. In the first, it is unclear whether the person addressing him is Morann testing his knowledge, or someone seeking the wisdom Neire himself can provide.

202. *UR*, 20–28 and 48–49, for example. See also the ascription to Athairne in *UR*, 44.

203. Amairgen was known as the chief poet of Conchobar's court. A helpful discussion of Amairgen's entrance into the poetic profession) is Ford's "The Blind, the Dumb."

204. The preface to the tract imagines the instructions of Cormac being integrated together with the wisdom gained by Cenn Fáelad at his three schools—and distinguishes the contributions of each according to turn of phrase: *CIH* 250.1–251.3. McLeod has translated excerpts from *Bretha Étgid* in his *Bloodshed and Compensation*, made available to me by the kind offices of the author, to whom I am very grateful. See also Breatnach, *Companion*, 176–82.

205. *CIH* 573.5–9. Shortly after this in the manuscript another conversation is recorded, this time between Cormac and Bríathrach, identified as the *dorsaid*, "doorkeeper," of Cormac, on the subject of what judge would be best to consult in matters regarding neighborhood law: 573.17–29. Once again, Cormac is the instructor.

206. *EICL* §37 (pp. 170–71). In §28 (pp. 160–61) of that text, the situations are—most unusually—reversed, in that the instructor is identified in the gloss as Coirpre and the invocation names Cormac as the person to whom he is speaking.

207. The best treatment of Cormac mac Airt in his various manifestations is Ó Cathasaigh's *Heroic Biography*. One version of the story about the sheep can be found there, 122–23, lines 85–110. For discussion of Cormac's judgment as an instance of the "Act of Truth," see 62–68. The tale *Echtra Cormaic i Tír Tairngiri* shows Cormac in a similar light, as performing an "Act of Truth": Stokes, "Irish Ordeals," 183–229.

208. MacAloon sums up a generation of work on such matters when he speaks of there being no performance without "preformance"—but then goes on to emphasize the risks inherent even in the most customary of events: *Rite, Drama*, 9.

209. Bell, *Ritual Theory*, 38.

210. Carlson, *Performance*, 15.

211. Kratz, *Affecting Performance*, 16–17.

212. Text and translation are Carey's: "Pseudo-Historical Prologue," §7 (pp. 12 and 18).

213. Ó Corráin, "Ireland, Wales," 94–97. An earlier statement of this view is Lucas, "Irish Norse Relations." Also relevant are Ó Corráin, "High-kings, Vikings"; and Smyth, *Scandinavian York*. A very helpful collection on issues relating to the Vikings in Ireland is Clarke, Ní Mhaonaigh, and Ó Floinn, *Ireland and Scandinavia*. Dumville has recently decried the tendency toward what he calls "cuddly Vikings" in his review of Ó Cróinín's *Early Medieval Ireland, 400–1200*, 29.

214. Davies, "Latin Charter-Tradition."

215. *senscriband deóda*: *Bürgschaft*, §62 (p. 21), and see also §81 (pp. 30–31).

216. Charles-Edwards, "Context and Uses," 62.

217. *CIH* 245.1–3; 244.23–25, and see Etchingham's discussion of this passage with respect to the church's policy on the property of its *manaig* (the specific example given in the text for the use of writing): *Church Organisation*, 451.

218. *CIH* 596.29–30=*Bürgschaft* §62 (p. 21).

219. Stevenson, "Beginnings of Literacy"; and Stevenson, "Literacy in Ireland," 30.

220. Bloch, *Political Language*, 9.

221. Myerhoff, *Number Our Days*, 86.

222. Bell, *Ritual Theory*, 109–10.

Chapter 3

1. The popular image of Charlemagne and his successors has recently come under fire in various scholarly accounts of the Carolingian period: Sullivan, "Carolingian Age"; and, most recently, Nelson, "Presidential Address."

2. For example, Ó Corráin, "Nationality and Kingship"; Herbert, *Iona; GEIL;* Bitel, *Isle;* Charles-Edwards, *Kinship;* Ó Cróinín, *Ireland;* Etchingham, *Church Organisation;* Charles-Edwards, *Early Christian Ireland.*

3. Sahlins, *Islands,* xi–xiii, and see the corrective qualification offered by Carlson in *Performance,* 30.

4. "Pragmatic literacy" is a term widely used to indicate literacy exercised in the service of bureaucratic or administrative objectives. The widespread currency of this expression is evident from its frequent appearance in book indexes (e.g., McKitterick, *Uses of Literacy,* 340). Some scholars show evidence of discomfort with the term. Katherine Forsyth carefully distinguishes between "literary" and "administrative" literacy in her essay in Pryce's *Literacy*—although such is the influence of the expression that the reference to her discussion in the index reads "literacy: pragmatic uses of" (pp. 42 and 293).

5. Relevant studies include: Ford, "The Blind, The Dumb"; Sayers, "Concepts of Eloquence"; McCone, *Pagan Past;* "Caldron of Poesy"; *UR;* Nagy, *Wisdom;* Nagy, *Conversing with Angels;* Stevenson, "Beginning of Literacy"; Stevenson, "Literacy in Ireland"; Ó Cathasaigh, "Rhetoric of *Fingal Rónáin*"; Corthals, "The *retoiric*"; Bloomfield and Dunn, *Role of the Poet;* Tranter and Tristram, *Early Irish Literature: Media and Communication;* Breatnach, "Zur Frage der *roscada*"; Stevenson, "Literacy and Orality"; Richter, *Formation;* Richter, *Studies,* 186–227; and studies by Edel and Smith in Ní Chatháin and Richter, *Ireland and Europe: Texts and Transmission.*

6. Ó Cathasaigh, "Curse and Satire"; Breatnach, "An Aoir"; Breatnach, "On Satire"; Meroney, "Studies in Early Irish Satire I. and II."; Ó Cathasaigh, "Curse and Satire"; O'Leary, "Jeers and Judgments"; and Robinson, "Satirists and Enchanters"; Stacey, "Satire."

7. Breatnach, "Canon Law"; Mac Cana, "Three Languages"; Charles-Edwards, "*Corpus Iuris Hibernici.*"

8. Ó Cróinín is concerned largely with poetry as a cultural phenomenon (*Early Medieval Ireland,* 192–93 and 214–22), and Charles-Edwards with the issue of social status and analogies between hierarchies (*Early Christian Ireland,* 125–36, and see remarks about druids and *filid* on pp. 197–99).

9. E.g., Bloch's *Political Language.*

10. E.g., Kratz's *Affecting Performance* and Sherzer's *Kuna Ways.* Among the most helpful of the theoretical works on the ethnography of language use are, in addition to the works listed above: Schechner, *Essays;* Bauman and Sherzer, *Explorations;* Ben-Amos and Goldstein, *Folklore;* Gumperz and Hymes, *Directions in Sociolinguistics;* Hymes, "Ethnography of Speaking"; Hymes, "Models"; Ardener, *Social Anthropology;* Bauman and Paredes, *Toward New Perspectives;* Bauman, *Verbal Art;* Turner, *Dramas, Fields;* MacAloon, *Rite, Drama;* Connerton, *How Societies Remember;* Handelman, *Models and Mirrors;* Bell, *Ritual Theory;* Bauman and Briggs, "Poetics and Performance"; Hymes, *Ethnography, Linguistics;* and Carlson, *Performance.* Ancient historians have done a lot of valuable work in this area already. Among the best of recent works are G. Nagy's *Poetry as Performance;* Martin's *Language of Heroes;* and Anhalt, *Solon the Singer.* Regrettably, this study appeared too late to take advantage of Habinek's *Roman Song.*

11. Heller, *Codeswitching;* Myers-Scotton, *Codes and Consequences;* Gibbons, *Code-Mixing and Code.*

12. Sherzer, *Kuna Ways.*

13. Sherzer, *Kuna Ways,* 47–48.

14. Sherzer, *Kuna Ways,* 191.

15. Sherzer, *Kuna Ways,* 128–38.

16. In other words, differentiated by syntactical, lexical, grammatical, or phono-

logical characteristics from the other types of language in use in that particular context. See discussion below.

17. Watkins, "Language of Gods."

18. *Auraicept na nÉces*, 1336; *Sanas Cormaic (YBL)*, 972. For *bérla Féne* as the term used for ordinary language, see *Auraceipt*, 1302. These texts and the *Auraicept*'s differentiation between various codes of Irish are discussed by Watkins, "Language of Men," 11–16.

19. Watkins, "Language of Men," 11–16; and see Carey, "Obscure Styles."

20. For *bérla Féne*, see *CIH* 1613.38–1614.32 (*UB*) and cf. 24.22; *Auraicept*, 1302–36. References and discussion can be found in *GEIL*, 48, 52–53, 193, 242, 260. For the tripartite division of codes and types of legal expertise, see *CIH* 1613.38–1614.32 (*UB*); and cf. 602.9; and for *bérla bán*, see "Pseudo-Historical Prologue," §9 (pp. 12–13). *Bérla na filed* is termed *berla . . . filidiacta* in *UB*: *CIH* 1614.20. *Bérla Féinechuis* appears for *bérla Féne* in a sixteenth-century obituary: *GEIL*, 260. The best discussions are, in addition to *GEIL*, Watkins, "Language of Men," 11–16; and Mac Cana, "Three Languages."

21. Watkins, "Language of Men," 14–16.

22. Breatnach defines *rosc* by comparison to prose and rhyming syllabic verse, noting that "the simplest definition of *rosc* is that it is neither of the other two" (Breatnach, "Canon Law and Secular Law," 452; and Breatnach, *Companion*, 370).

23. Breatnach, "Canon Law"; Breatnach, *Companion*, 370–71; and Charles-Edwards, "*Corpus Iuris Hibernici*," which differentiates between *Fénechas* (the ancient legal language embracing both maxims and *rosc*), "plain prose" and "textbook prose." Primary sources include: *CIH* 1040.37–39 (*CCF*); 1592.12–20 (*UB*); 2221.12, 16, 2222.9, 15–19, 31–38 (*BNT*); "Pseudo-Historical Prologue," §9 (pp. 12–13); *EICL*, §11 (pp. 136–37) and passim; *GEIL*, 195–97. On the use of Latin in the vernacular laws, see Ó Corráin, Breatnach and Breen, "Laws of the Irish," and Bracken, "Latin Passages."

24. Legal maxims, for example, are frequently worked into blocks of poetry or prose: 1) *dith naee, dith nadgaire* (*CIH* 596.24, cf. 2224.27); 2) *tresiu cach fir fonaidm/ferr fir fonaidm* (*EICL*, §§46 and 51 [pp. 180–81 and 184–85]), with which cf. Corthals, "*Immathchor*," §6 (p. 108); *EICL*, §24 (pp. 152–53); and *Aibidil Cuigni maic hEmoin*, §33. The word *roscada* is used at least once to describe what elsewhere are called maxims—e.g., the alternative title for the text known otherwise as the *Bríathra Flainn Fína*: *Roscada Flainn Fína*: Ireland (*Old Irish Wisdom*, 25–28). The archaic-(seeming) language referred to in several tracts by the name *Fénechas* seems to have embraced a variety of genres, including maxims, instructions from teacher to pupil, and passages in *rosc*. Indeed, the import of the term *Fénechas* varies significantly from tract to tract: see discussion below in Chapter 5.

25. Breatnach argues that *rosc* and rhyming syllabic poetry exist on a continuum with one another: Breatnach, "Zur Frage," 203–4; and his "Poets and Poetry," 70–74.

26. For maxims, see Ireland's *Old Irish Wisdom*, 10–12; for *rosc*, see Breatnach, "Canon Law," 452. For rhyming syllabic poetry, see *Medieval Irish Lyrics*, vii–xx; *Irish Syllabic Poetry*, 1–20; Watkins, "Indo-European Metrics"; and Breatnach, "Poets and Poetry."

27. Breatnach, "Canon Law"; McCone, "Dubthach maccu Lugair"; McCone, *Pagan Past*.

28. An exception is Carey, "Obscure Styles."

29. Dillon, "Archaism"; Findon, *A Woman's Words*, 70–71; and articles by McCone, Mac Cana, and Corthals in Tranter and Tristam, *Early Irish Literature*.

30. O'Rahilly, *Táin Bó Cúailnge, Recension I*, lines 1068–1146.

31. *Longes mac n-Uislenn*, ed. Hull, lines 14–49.

32. For Morann and Neire, see Chapter 2 above; *BDC*, §§25ff. (pp. 36–37ff.); Breatnach, "First Third," §§8ff., with discussion on p. 5. Breatnach argues that only §8 is to be attributed to Cenn Fáelad, which strikes me as a possible, but not a necessary conclusion. Nor does the ecclesiastical origin of §§12 and 22 seem a real barrier, since Cenn Fáelad's poem exists as a composition attributable to him regardless of where he got his material. In *BA*, passages in rhetorical alliterative style are attributed to *Fénechas*, there understood to mean "ancient oral law": *Bürgschaft*, §§59–61 (pp. 19–21) = *CIH* 596.8–29 (*BA*).

33. See below in Chapter 5, and *GEIL*, 196–97.

34. Ireland concludes that while the contents of the collection attributed to Flann Fína suggest the plausibility of an actual historical link between king and text, the language of the text as preserved makes it very difficult to be sure: Ireland, *Old Irish Wisdom*, 55–56. Dumville expresses his reservations about the identification of Flann Fína with Aldfrith, king of Northumbria, in "Two Troublesome Abbots."

35. Breatnach outlines the subcategories of *rosc* and some of its grammatical and syntactical characteristics in "Canon Law," 452–53.

36. *Old Irish Wisdom*, 10–12.

37. *CIH* 599.18 = *Bürgschaft*, §79 (p. 30) (*BA*).

38. *EICL* §41 (pp. 174–75).

39. *Old Irish Wisdom*, §§3.25 and 3.29 (pp. 72–73).

40. The passage ascribes certain genres within the law to specific social ranks. Kelly provides a potential link between these bodies of knowledge and the oral realm by speculating that judges might have quoted from them in the public proclamation of their verdicts: *GEIL*, 196.

41. *CIH* 1592.8–20. Nicholas Aitchison suggests that poets composed *roscada* in order to establish their credentials as high-status professionals: Aitchison, "Heroic Image," 98.

42. Sayers, "Concepts of Eloquence."

43. Findon, *Woman's Words*, 23–56, and see her portrayal of Emer's speech and point of view in her "Emer Versus Cú Chulainn." The educational angle to this exchange is an interesting one: as Sayers remarks, the tale suggests "a degree of parity between well-born men and women in expectations of their competence in the arts of speech" (Sayers, "Concepts of Eloquence," 138). The mechanisms by which women may have been educated in the elocutionary arts are unclear. Charles-Edwards documents extensive links between the male aristocracy and the learned elite in early Ireland, but the extent to which women could have participated in those arrangements is uncertain: Charles-Edwards, "Context and Uses." Also relevant to this issue is Clancy's "Women Poets."

44. Findon, *Woman's Words*, 46–56, 70–83.

45. E.g., *CG* 206–8; 261–65; 295–96, and so on.

46. *CG* 23–24. For this interpretation of *imm-toing*, see *CG*, pp. 99–100 under *luge*. I infer that other forms of public speech are denied to this status of individual from the fact that he is distinguished from the older *fer midboth* in (by implication) *not* "sustaining speech." Because the second *fer midboth* who does "sustain speech" is mentioned as neither adding to nor subtracting from this "speech," we must infer that it is to testimony that *insce* here refers.

47. *CG* 39–41.

48. *CG*, pp. 25–26, note to line 40.

49. As in the *trefocal* of the poet, on which see discussion below.

50. *CIH* 594.8 = *Bürgschaft*, §40 (p. 12).

51. *Uraicecht Becc* comes perhaps the closest to this schema, assigning a yearling

heifer to the *fer midboth*, but three *séoit* to the still obviously junior "second free-man"; five *séoit* are accorded the normal freeman, and seven to the *aire déso*: *CIH* 1597.9, 1610.40, 1611.17. *Críth Gablach* itself assigns three *séoit* to the junior freeman known as the *ócaire*; five-six *séoit* to the two ranks of normal freemen (*bóaire febsa* and the *mruigfer*); and ten *séoit* to the *aire déso*: *CG* 119–20; 160–61; 206–8; 347–48. On the *sét* as a unit of value, see *CG*, pp.105–6; *GEIL*, 114–16; and, most comprehensively, Charles-Edwards, *Kinship*, 478–85. A different point of view is advanced by McLeod, "Status and Currency."

52. *CG* 206–8; 261–65; 295–96; and on the practice of overswearing, see *GEIL*, 199–200.

53. The *Liber Angeli* in Bieler, *Patrician Texts*, 184–91, especially pp. 188–89.

54. Breatnach, "First Third," §§4 and 7 (pp. 10–11).

55. Yarnold, "Fourth and Fifth Centuries," in Jones, Wainwright, and Yarnold, *Study of Liturgy*, 95–110; Jungmann, *Mass*, vol. II, 90–97; and Warren, *Liturgy and Ritual*. I am grateful to Father William Rich for helpful conversations on this issue.

56. *Liber Angeli*, in Bieler, *Patrician Texts*, 186–87.

57. Sayers, "Concepts of Eloquence," 137.

58. *Críth Gablach* makes it clear that whereas the honor-price of a freeman accrued to him because of his possession of cattle, the honor-price of a noble derived from the number of clients in his retinue: *CG* 328–31.

59. This is evident from the importance of bardic poetry to Simms's study *From Kings to Warlords*, particularly her discussion of the poems as evidence for political life on pp. 4–6. The best discussions of poets and satire are all by Breatnach: *UR*; "On Satire"; and "An Aoir." See also Stacey, "On Satire."

60. *UR*, 89–94.

61. *CIH* 2199.23–24 and 2192.20–21 = *GC* §51 (p. 366) and §4 (p. 309) respectively.

62. One of the best of these stories is *Tromdám Guaire*, "Guaire's Greedy Guests," on which see Ó Coileáin, "Making of *Tromdám Guaire*." An excellent collection of translated tales on the virtues and excesses of poets is Ford's *Celtic Poets*, which includes *Tromdám Guaire*.

63. The distinction between Old Irish *ferb*, "blister [raised by satire or shame]" and Old Irish *ferb*, "word" (from Latin *verbum*) is not always clear in the sources—and not merely because the two words were both feminine a-stems. There is an interesting juxtaposition here with another cultural tradition that held that blisters of shame appeared also on the faces of kings or jurists who had uttered falsehood: see discussion in Meroney, "Studies in Early Irish Satire II.," 218–26.

64. *CIH* 1111.1–11. *Críth Gablach* plays on the face metaphor, saying that three things are needed to cleanse a face of the "filth" of satire: a pumice stone (public confession of the deed and a promise not to do it again); water (compensation to the person or persons injured); and a towel (penance): *CG* 302–13.

65. *CIH* 2199.23–24 = *GC* §51 (p. 366). *BNT* shows awareness of the fact that satire is likely to spread further than is praise, but still sees the latter as the only real compensation for the former: *CIH* 2219.25–26.

66. Some of what follows is taken from Stacey, "Satire." I am grateful to ABC-CLIO and to general editor John Koch for allowing me to reprint material from that volume. For the best discussions of satire, see note 59 above.

67. Literary sources on satire are numerous. Tales dealing directly or indirectly with the practice include: *Tochmarc Luaine ocus Aided Athairne, Imthecht na Tromdáime (Tromdám Guaire), Echtra Fergusa maic Léti, Cath Maige Tuired, Immacallam in Dá Thúarad, Aided Con Culainn*, the tale of Néide and Caíar incorporated into *Sanas Cormaic*, and the *Táin Bó Cúailnge*.

68. *CIH* 1592.26–39, and see also 1111.28, "spear-points of shame." For discussion and additional references, see Breatnach's "Addenda and Corrigenda to 'The Caldron of Poesy' " (text originally edited in *Ériu*).

69. *CIH* 1134.33–34 and Breatnach, "An Aoir," 11 and note 1 on p. 19; *CIH* 29.17–30.21; 1123.22–24; *BDC*, §31 (pp. 40–41); Binchy, "Saga," §§7–8 (pp. 38–39).

70. Meroney, "Studies in Early Irish Satire," §3 (p. 201), with translation on p. 204.

71. See discussion below in Chapter 4.

72. *Br. Crólige*, §32 (pp. 26–27).

73. *Br. Crólige*, §51 (pp. 40–41): this provision speaks to the enormous hostility demonstrated toward the *cainte* by the ranks of the ecclesiastically trained *filid*, on which rivalry see Chapter 4 below.

74. *Br. Crólige*, §12 (pp. 10–13).

75. *CIH* 1122.11–12.

76. *CIH* 15.14–15; 547.21–22; 1114.19–20; 1122.11–12; 1123.22–24; for example. Publicizing a physical blemish is mentioned as an example of unlawful satire: 30.8; and *BDC*, §31 (pp. 40–41).

77. *CIH* 117.30–118.13; 390.4–5 and 2124.23–24, for example.

78. *CIH* 30.8–9, and see 117.30–118.13 and 971.34–972.3.

79. Meroney, "Studies in Early Irish Satire."

80. Breatnach, "An Aoir"; and "On Satire." The discussion that follows is heavily indebted to both studies. Another important recent discussion is Wiley's "Maledictory Psalms," especially pp. 268–69.

81. Breatnach, "An Aoir," 12.

82. Meroney, "Studies in Early Irish Satire I.," §14 (p. 202), with translation on p. 206.

83. Meroney, "Studies in Early Irish Satire I.," §13 (p. 202), with translation on p. 205.

84. Meroney, "Studies in Early Irish Satire I.," §11 (p. 202), with translation on p. 205; §16 (p. 203), with translation on p. 206.

85. Robinson, "Satirists and Enchanters"; Elliott, *Power of Satire.*

86. Edition and translation by Breatnach from *UR* §23 (pp. 114–15, with discussion of other versions on p. 137).

87. The text of the story is given and discussed by Meroney in "Studies in Early Irish Satire II.," 212–15, and see alternative translation and discussion offered by Breatnach in *UR*, §23 (pp. 114–15), with notes on 137.

88. Meroney, "Studies in Early Irish Satire II.," 214–15, and see excerpt cited on 212–13.

89. This passage is printed and translated by Meroney, "Studies in Early Irish Satire II.," 212–13.

90. *CIH* 1564.27–1565.19; *UR* §24 (p. 114), glosses 5–7 especially. See the more elaborate version of this ceremony in *Mittelirische Verslehren III*, §155, and the discussion of both in *UR*, 140. Also valuable is Meroney, "Studies in Early Irish Satire II.," on the genre as a whole, and on its putatively magical elements.

91. Meroney, "Studies in Early Irish Satire II.," 218.

92. *UR* §24 (pp. 114–15), with notes and discussion on p. 140; *CIH* 1480.12. On the three periods, see discussion below.

93. *UR* §23 (pp. 114–15). See Breatnach's discussion in "An Aoir," 14, where he concludes that the *glám dicenn* was the only species of satire thought capable of causing death.

94. Meroney, "Studies in Early Irish Satire II.," 215–18.

95. *GEIL*, 43–44; Robinson, "Satirists and Enchanters," 95–97; Randolph, "Rat Satires."

96. Carey, "Three Things."

97. A symbol, perhaps, of the plight of an individual ostracized from the society in which he lives, who becomes thereby like unto a person with one eye, one hand, and one foot? A helpful discussion with references in the literature to *corrguinecht* is Scowcroft, "Abstract Narrative," especially 142, note 78; and see also Nagy, *Conversing with Angels*, 182–83; and *UR*, 140 and references there.

98. Breatnach makes this point in *UR*, 139; "An Aoir," 138–39; and "On Satire," 25–26. See, for example, *CIH* 884.1–3; 2226.31–34. Several sources make it clear that poets often enforced cross-border claims in certain cases—presumably one of the official duties the poet of a *túath* would perform for his people: *CIH* 1111.19–21.

99. Satire could be performed against members of the offender's kindred or lord in cases where the offender himself proved impervious to its sting: Breatnach, "On Satire," 27–30.

100. Meroney, "Studies in Early Irish Satire I.," §8 (pp. 201–2, with a translation on p. 205). The translation given here closely follows that offered by Lehmann in *Early Irish Verse*, §61 (p. 64).

101. Breatnach's "On Satire" collects a number of Old Irish references to the *trefocal*. See also *CIH* 2226.31–33.

102. *UR*, 138–39; Breatnach, "An Aoir," 17–19; see also Meroney, "Studies in Early Irish Satire III." *Trefocal* is alluded to frequently in Old Irish sources (e.g., *CIH* 2226.31–37) but the procedure itself is spelled out most fully in Middle Irish texts: *CIH* 2095.20–23; 2119.9–33; 956.38–957.4; and see further references in Meroney, "Studies in Early Irish Satire III."

103. *Cuairt escai*: text and translation from *UR*, §24 (pp. 114–15).

104. *UR*, 139; Breatnach, "An Aoir," 17–19. Cormac's Glossary defines them as two words of praise following after the "blushing" brought about by the third, a word of satire: Corm. Y 1228.

105. *Auraicept na nÉces* 5244, and "Caldron of Poesy," 79.

106. Also edited and translated by Meroney in "Studies in Early Irish Satire III."

107. Meroney, "Studies in Early Irish Satire III.," 59, with discussion on pp. 59–95.

108. Hogan, *Onomasticon Goedelicum*, 422, "*fir árda.*"

109. Breatnach, "An Aoir," 18–19. All references in the following discussion relate to the verse numbers established in Meroney's edition, 96–101, unless otherwise indicated.

110. Verse §47. Meroney's translation catches the rhythm and rhyme of the original: "I will sneer, I will sneer! I will fleer, I will fleer! I will jeer, I will jeer!": "Studies in Early Irish Satire III.," 106 (§48), which speaks of the "three griffin's claws" that scratch the cheek—a metaphor for honor.

111. And ended, in the sense that the beginning of a cross in which one is proceeding in a circular manner is also the ending. The *trefocal* poem on the Fir Arddae also begins and ends with an invocation to God.

112. *DIL* 476, col. 26.

113. Meroney, "Studies in Early Irish Satire III.," 60–61, note 5, where he suggests "compensator of obscurities."

114. That this technique was common in satirical poems is suggested by poems in the *Cis lir fodla aíre?* collection, e.g., *Mag Lacha/trathfa/flatha* and *cúl/clotha/clacha* in §3 of Meroney, "Studies in Early Irish Satire I." Another distinguishing feature of the language of the *trefocal* poem on the Fir Arddae—and a reminder of the parallels between satire and distraint—is its widespread use of legal language. The *aicned*, "nature," mentioned as opposing the sager counsel of Good Sense in verses 45, 48, 49 is, for example, at once a reference to the poet's own tempestuous nature, which urges him to proceed to full satire without delay, and to the "law of nature"

believed by the Irish to have held sway in that country before the arrival of Christianity. Technical legal terms appearing elsewhere in the poem include *díre n-ainech*, "honor-price"; *fócra*, "[legal] summons" (§24); *díbad*, "legacy" (§65); *dál*, "legal case, assembly" (often used in a double sense of "dispensing food and drink, displaying hospitality") in verses §§3, 9,13, 23, 30, 32, 37, 43, 44, 46, 49, 51, 53, 59, 60, 63; *gíall*, "hostage" (§47); *árosc*, "stipulation, saying" (§26); *cintach*, "offender" (§§29, 35); *conair cert*, "the path of right" (one of the five types of pleas recognized in Irish law —§31); and *cáin n-enech*, the "Law of Honor," which is mentioned also in *Bretha Nemed* (§29).

115. *CIH* 2119.9–13; Meroney, "Studies in Early Irish Satire III.," 122–30.

116. *UR*, 22–23, lines 58–66, with translation on p. 24.

117. See discussion below in Chapter 4.

118. Meroney, "Studies in Early Irish Satire I.," §§3 and 11 (pp. 201–2), with translations on 204–5. Ceallach mac Cumasgaigh, to whom the poem in §11 is attributed, is called the abbot of Fobar in his obit at *AU* 867/868.

119. Ó Cathasaigh, "Curse and Satire"; and see Geary, "Humiliation of Saints," and Little, *Benedictine Maledictions*, for continental parallels.

120. Wiley, "Maledictory Psalms," esp. 268–71. I have also benefited greatly from the author's unpublished Ph.D. thesis chapter entitled "Psalms of Malediction," and would here like to express my gratitude to Dr. Wiley for making his work available to me in advance of publication. The practice is referred to also in *Cáin Adamnáin*, where Adamnán is said to have established a ritual order of cursing (*ordd n-escoine*) that involved the recitation of certain psalms every day for twenty days: *C. Adam.*, §32 (p. 22).

121. On Irish contract, see *EICL*; Stacey, *Road to Judgment*, 27–54; and *GEIL*, 158–63.

122. Stacey, "Ties That Bind."

123. *CIH* 350.26–27; *EICL*, §34 (pp. 166–67).

124. As a tract, *BA* is both composite and complex. In addition to the contractual exchanges that lie at the heart of the text, there are also citations to the (putatively) oral teaching known as *Fénechas*, on which see below. Of particular interest are the number of aphorisms scattered throughout the text that are clearly regarded as "traditional" in the sense of being familiar quotations within the legal tradition, but which are not explicitly attributed to *Fénechas*: e.g., *CIH* 592.22, 26, 36, and 39 = *Bürgschaft*, §§21, 22, 24, 25 (p. 9). There is also an extended prose discussion of the *naidm* (*CIH* 592.22–594.37 = *Bürgschaft*, §§21–48 [pp. 9–15]); a series of poetic aphorisms on the subject of buying and selling, many (all?) of which are cited to *Fénechas* (*CIH* 599.16–38 = *Bürgschaft*, §§79–84 [pp. 30–32]); and a probably originally separate tract on witnessing, the Irish of which looks considerably older than that of the main body of the tract (*CIH* 596.3–597.3 = *Bürgschaft*, §§58–63 [pp. 19–22]).

The contractual formulas themselves occur in two sections of the tract: 1) a section on the *fechemain*, "contracting parties" where we get the language for the binding of the debt and for its eventual collection: *CIH* 595.2–596.2 = *Bürgschaft*, §§51–57 (pp. 15–18); and 2) a section on various forms of guarantor, including the paying surety known as the *ráth* where we get the language for the binding of the *ráth* to his duties and the guaranteeing of his eventual compensation should he be required to make payment on behalf of the debtor: *CIH* 598.16–599.14 = *Bürgschaft*, §§74–77 (pp. 26–29). Some guarantee of the general authenticity of the language may be implied by the fact that the formulas differ in the specific obligations they require from each person to the agreement, and that the language of contractual obligation differs significantly from that used for (largely) noncontractual arrangements like the hostage-surety known as the *aitire*. See further Stacey, *Road to Judgment*, 31–32 and 27–54 on making of contracts.

125. *CIH* 598.16, 19, 22, 26, 31, 35, 38; and 599.4, 10, for example.

126. This text has been edited and translated by Kelly in his *Early Irish Farming*, 506–20. Rhetorical language is found throughout this brief tract, especially in paragraphs 1–4, and in another text edited by Kelly on the qualities of horses (*Farming*, 555–59). The context of both texts is the same—e.g., the purchase/sale by contract of an animal of the appropriate qualities—although the first text is phrased as instructions to a would-be buyer, and the second as the answer to a rhetorical question asked by a judge, "*Co ber breith um techta eich?*" ("How should I give judgment about the proper qualities of a horse?").

127. *CIH* 595.4 = *Bürgschaft*, §51a (p. 15).

128. Bell, *Ritual Theory*, 101–4.

129. This is made more likely by the fact that distraint and *tellach* both were initiated by formal proclamations of intent: the *apad*, "warning notice."

130. Action was important also, of course, most notably the grasping of hands.

131. See, for example, Babcock, "Story in the Story: Metanarration in Folk Narrative," in Bauman, *Verbal Art*, 61–79.

132. Charles-Edwards, "*Corpus Iuris Hibernici*," 145–55.

133. *Mac(c)* is an earlier term for the *naidm*-surety, probably abandoned because of the potential for confusion with *mac*, "son": see Stacey, *Road to Judgment*, 19 and references cited there.

134. *CIH* 595.2–14 = *Bürgschaft*, §51a–c (p. 15).

135. O'Rahilly, *Táin Bó Cúalnge from the Book of Leinster*, lines 800–813 (pp. 22–23).

136. This passage occurs at the very end of a short tract on the qualities (desirable and undesirable) of cows. The passage that immediately precedes the section on sheep has also to do with cows and is written in a relatively plain prose style. However, the tract as a whole is mainly written in the second-person instructional (and highly rhetorical) style often associated with the *BN* school—a style in which alliteration and parallelisms play a significant role. Kelly edits another similar short text on horses later in his book (*Farming*, pp. 555–59)—this one explicitly phrased as instruction to apprentice jurists who find themselves having to rule on the qualities of animals in the process of changing hands from one owner to another. Like the sheep passage, the tract on horses shares some qualities in common with the contractual language of *BA* (alliteration, parallel constructions, and rhetorical phrasing), although it does not use the *aic maccu* or *gaib it laim* formula. The similarities are suggestive: if we can presume—as seems not unreasonable—that jurists acting as advocates might often have given advice to contracting parties as to what qualities they might stipulate in the animals they bought and sold, then these passages give us an indication as to how the more general expressions found in *BA* could be tailored to fit the circumstances of a particular obligation.

137. Edited and translated by Kelly, *Farming*, §§7–8 (pp. 507–8).

138. One factor may the technical animal husbandry–related vocabulary employed, which is much more extensive in the case of the sheep and horse texts than it is in the case of the generic contract envisaged in *BA*.

139. Such structures are a characteristic also of the court speech of the Chamula people of Mexico: Gossen, "Chamula Genres of Verbal Behavior," in Bauman and Paredes, *Toward New Perspectives*, 154.

140. *CIH* 599.10–11 = *Bürgschaft*, §76e (p. 28) and *CIH* 598.26 = *Bürgschaft*, §74d (p. 27), respectively.

141. The *aitire's* binding oath is to be found on *CIH* 597.6–25 = *Bürgschaft*, §65 (pp. 22–24).

142. Since we know the phrasing of the *aitire*'s oath also from *BA*, it could be argued that these similarities are the result of the same author's having written both the section on the *aitire* and the section on contractual binding. However, it is equally likely that the author is merely here reproducing formulas in common use for both kinds of suretyship relationship. In any case, the general characteristics of this language—the alliteration, the use of parallelisms and synonymous pairs—are unlikely to be his invention.

143. Connerton, *How Societies Remember*, 7–10; Bell, *Ritual Theory*, 106–10, 120–30; Carlson, *Performance*, 15, 24–25; Turner, "Liminality and the Performative Genres," in MacAloon, *Rite, Drama*, 24–26.

144. *CIH* 595.2–14 = *Bürgschaft*, §51a–c (p. 15).

145. *CIH* 598.16–29 = *Bürgschaft*, §74 (pp. 26–28).

146. *CIH* 599.10–11 = *Bürgschaft*, §76 (pp. 28–29), and compare *gaib fort laim fiuch dam-sa*, "take on your hand this debt to me" (from the binding of the debt), with *aicc macu hi foisam do raithe frisin fiach-so*, "invoke sureties in support of your *ráth*-suretyship with respect to this debt" (from the binding of the *ráth*); and *gaib it laim samlaid cen eluth cen esngabail*, "take in your hand likewise [that you will act] without evasion, without defect" (from the binding of the debt), with *aicc macu do samlaith cen frithaie, cin frithrim*, "invoke sureties likewise [that you will act] without a counter-reckoning, without a countersuit" (from the binding of the *ráth*).

147. *CIH* 595.24–27 = *Bürgschaft*, §53 (p. 17).

148. *CIH* 595.2–14 = *Bürgschaft*, §51a–c (pp. 15–17).

149. *CIH* 595.20–27 = *Bürgschaft*, §52 (p. 17); *CIH* 595.24–27=*Bürgschaft*, §53 (p. 17).

150. *CIH* 595.24–27 = *Bürgschaft*, §53 (p. 17)

151. *CIH* 595.31–33 = *Bürgschaft*, §55 (p. 18).

152. *CIH* 598.31–599.1 = *Bürgschaft*, §76 (pp. 28–29).

153. *CIH* 598.16–26 = *Bürgschaft*, §74 (pp. 26–28). The phrase *(in) huidib 7 airis-nib* appears both in the oath the debtor requires the creditor to swear guaranteeing the propriety of the *ráth*'s having had to pay, and in the oath the *ráth* requires the creditor to swear to guarantee that he has paid the debt fully and at the proper time.

154. *CIH* 595.31–36 = *Bürgschaft*, §§55–56 (p. 18).

155. Kratz, *Affecting Performance*, 17.

156. Turner, "Liminality and the Performative Genres," 19–41 of MacAloon, *Rite, Drama*, 25 especially.

157. A similar linguistic continuum exists among the Chamula, where "Pure Words," usually identified as authentic Chamula oral tradition, are not so far removed from other types of stylized speech as to be considered separate from it: Gossen, "Chamula Genres," in Bauman and Paredes, *Toward New Perspectives*, 151.

158. Gossen points also to children's games as being important in this respect: "Chamula Genres," in Bauman and Paredes, *Toward New Perspectives*, 151–53.

159. Corthals, "Zur Frage des mündlichen oder schriftlichen Ursprungs der Sagenroscada," 201–20 of Tranter and Tristram, *Early Irish Literature*.

160. McCone, "Zur Frage der Register."

161. *EICL*, §11 (pp. 136–37) and §36 (pp. 168–69), which reads *inscib ánaib air-liter*, "in glorious statements that are spoken." McLeod translates *án* in both instances as "honorable"; it is worth noting, however, that its semantic range includes "fiery, brilliant, glorious, splendid, glowing": *DIL* p. 40, cols. 314–15.

162. Text and translation from Watkins, "*In essar dam do á?*," 163. The text can also be found in *CIH* 2112.37–39, and in Dillon, "Stories," §1 (p. 43), with a slightly different translation than Watkins gives (cited on p. 52).

163. Ó Corráin, "Early Irish Hermit Poetry?," in Ó Corráin, Breatnach, and Mc-Cone, *Sages, Saints*, 251–67.

164. Corthals, "Affiliation of Children." In several of the stories incorporated into TCD 1336, both the plea (sometimes done by a pleader, and sometimes by the plaintiff himself) and verdict are in *rosc*: e.g., at *CIH* 2112.29–35, 2113.6–15.

165. Corthals, "Affiliation of Children," 100.

166. See above, Chapter 2, and Dillon, "Stories."

167. Corthals, "Affiliation of Children," 104.

168. Corthals, "Affiliation of Children," §§2–4 (107–8, with translation on 109–10). Michael Richter argues that "the Irish canons in CCH exclusively in Latin are the earliest available texts that make use of the secular Irish law" in Richter, "Dating the Irish Synods," 75. Bart Jaski argues that relationship between *CCH* and secular law was "certainly not a one-way street," and that "direct borrowing from CCH cannot always be taken for granted . . . in certain cases it is more likely that both CCH and vernacular law borrowed from earlier compilations or florilegia": Jaski, "Cú Chuimne," 69.

169. Corthals, "Affiliation of Children," §3 (p. 107, with translation on p. 110).

170. Corthals, "Affiliation of Children," §4 (p. 108, with translation on p. 110).

171. Corthals, "Affiliation of Children," §3 (p. 107, with translation on p. 110).

172. Corthals, "Affiliation of Children," §6 (p. 108, with translation on p. 110).

173. Corthals, "Affiliation of Children," §6 (p. 108, with translation on p. 110).

174. Corthals, "Affiliation of Children," §7 (pp. 108–9, with translation on pp. 110–11).

175. Corthals, "Affiliation of Children," 104.

176. Corthals, "Affiliation of Children," 113.

177. I owe this point to Thomas Charles-Edwards.

Chapter 4

1. The most famous of these missions were those of Palladius and of Patrick, both of which have usually been dated to the fifth century, although the debate over the dating of St. Patrick has been almost unimaginably ferocious. The most recent series of papers on the saint is Dumville, *Saint Patrick*. The most famously vituperative treatment of the dating issue is Binchy's "Patrick and His Biographers." See also Hanson, *St. Patrick*; and Hanson, "Date of St. Patrick." Charles-Edwards accepts a fifth-century date in his *Early Christian Ireland*, 214–40 (and see 202–14 on Palladius, together with Ó Cróinín's "New Light on Palladius").

2. Binchy, "*Bretha Nemed*"; Binchy, "Date and Provenance"; *GEIL*, 47–48; and see also discussion above in Chapters 2 and 3.

3. Charles-Edwards, *Early Christian Ireland*, 199.

4. Charles-Edwards, *Early Christian Ireland*, 197.

5. See discussion above in Chapter 3.

6. "Pseudo-Historical Prologue," §11 (p. 13, with Carey's translation on p. 19).

7. "Alphabet of Cuigne mac Emoin," §1/11 (p. 48), §1/25 (p. 51), and §2/61 (p. 67), respectively.

8. *Old Irish Wisdom*, §1.31 (pp. 64–65), §1.38 (p. 66–67), §1.54 (pp. 68–69), §5.15 (pp. 78–79), §6.16 (pp. 80–81). Ireland comments on the surprisingly nonaristocratic perspective expressed in the text on pp. 13–20.

9. *CG* 277–80, with notes on p. 70.

10. *CG* 417–19 (with notes on p. 72) and *Br. Crólige* §46 (pp. 36–37) both define him as the lord whose testimony is superior to ranks under him.

11. *CIH* 2221.27. *Fer laburta láin* is part of a pair of qualities itemized as desirable in judges.

12. In the latter case, often a judge: *CIH* 2222.7; 2223.4. Both terms appear also in the *rosc* riddle attached to the tract on court procedure edited by Kelly, "Court Procedure," §7k (p. 88, with notes on p. 104) and §7n (p. 89, with notes on p. 105).

13. *CIH* 1253.6–11. Portions of this text, *Ántéchtae*, display similarities to portions of *BNT*, e.g., *CIH* 2222.9–11, and compare 1253.24 with 2222.30. See on this text Breatnach, *Companion*, 166–69.

14. Ahqvist, "Dialects."

15. *GEIL*, 242–46.

16. Charles-Edwards, *Early Christian Ireland*, 583. On the question of the differences between popular and literary speech and their links to status, see McCone, "Zur Frage der Register."

17. *Br. Crólige*, §32 (p. 27).

18. *CIH* 2222.23, and see discussion of some of the difficulties attendant on these terms in Kelly, "Court Procedure," notes to §7k (p. 104).

19. *UR*, BN IV, line 11 (p. 36, with translation cited above on p. 37). For more on the efforts of upper-class *filid* to construct their lower-class rivals as ignorant and unskilled in speech, see discussion below.

20. *CIH* 592.29–30 = *Bürgschaft*, §22 (p. 9). A passage incorporated into *Di Astud Chor* makes reference to this practice using precisely the same metaphor: a person with supervisory duties over others lesser in status loses all opportunity to negate a disadvantageous contract made against one of his dependents if he remains silent (*con-túaisi*) about the deal at the time it was being made: *EICL* §7 (pp. 132–33).

21. Findon, *Woman's Words*, 79.

22. Ó Cathasaigh, "Sírrabad Súaltaim."

23. Binchy, "Text on the Forms of Distraint," §§7–8 (pp. 78–81).

24. Contractual suretyship is not the only type of guarantor arrangement where such patterns are visible. Hostageship seems to have operated through oaths rather than through *naidm*-sureties, but the patterning of speech and silence visible in contractual arrangements is present there as well. The person on whose behalf the hostage surety known as the *aitire* acts also is the one to voice in detail the obligations that that surety is taking on by his agreement: *CIH* 597.6–25 = *Bürgschaft*, §65 (pp. 22–24).

25. *CIH* 595.21–23 = *Bürgschaft*, §51 (pp. 15–16).

26. *CIH* 598.16–26 = *Bürgschaft*, §74 (pp. 26–28).

27. *CIH* 598.31–599.11 = *Bürgschaft*, §76 (pp. 28–29).

28. The two instances in which the text tells us that the *naidm*-sureties recite this shortened formula are at the time the debtor pledges to compensate his paying surety upon default; and at the time the *ráth*-surety himself undertakes an assignment. Given the nature of the defendant's answer—*aicdiu*, "I appoint"—it seems likely that similar formulas were recited after every guarantor appointment.

29. *CIH* 598.27 = *Bürgschaft*, §75 (p. 28).

30. *CIH* 595.15 = *Bürgschaft*, §51 (pp. 15–16). For a reconstruction of the procedure followed here, see Stacey, *Road to Judgment*, 34–38.

31. Several passages in *Di Astud Chor* underscore the importance of not just the mouth, but also the ears, to the success of the contractual ritual: *EICL* §§16, 20, 29–30 (pp. 142–43, 146–47, and 162–63 respectively). On *Di Astud Chor*, see Breatnach, *Companion*, 244–46.

32. Bloch, *Political Language*, 10.

33. Bloch, *Political Language*, 13–25.

34. "Pseudo-Historical Prologue," §6 (p. 12, with translation on p. 18). The biblical quotation is taken from Matthew 10:20.

35. "Pseudo-Historical Prologue," §7 (p. 12, with translation on p. 18).

36. The relationship between the written and the spoken word adds yet another dimension to the story of Dubthach's performance: see Nagy, *Conversing with Angels,* 200–8 and, on the signing of the mouth, 268–69.

37. *C. Adam.* §§16–21 (pp. 8–12). Melia has made an excellent case for this as a shamanic episode: "Law and the Shaman-Saint." Other valuable studies have been done recently by Ní Dhonnchadha: "Guarantor List"; and "*Lex Innocentium.*" A new translation of *Cáin Adamnáin* by Ní Dhonnchadha is now available in O'Loughlin, *Adomnán at Birr.*

38. The appropriation of voice and the ability to perform are major themes in other literary and hagiographical texts as well, as Nagy's impressive study *Conversing with Angels* makes clear. One tale in which speech and silence play a particularly important role is the *Síaburcharpat Con Culainn,* on which see Nagy, *Conversing with Angels,* 265–78.

39. *Bethu Brigte,* §4 (pp. 1–2, with translation on p. 20).

40. Armagh and Kildare were, along with Iona, the three main contenders for ecclesiastical prominence and patronage in the seventh century. Lives of the founder saints of all three houses were produced as a way of promoting their cults, and the rivalry among them is reflected in numerous texts (e.g., the "Book of the Angel"). But while there is no doubt about Columba's historical role in the foundation of Iona, Patrick's connection with Armagh was a myth propagated by that church in an effort to promote its interests and visibility. Downpatrick is a more likely contender as the primary center of Patrick's mission: Sharpe, "St. Patrick"; Ó Cróinín, *Early Medieval Ireland,* 154–68; and Charles-Edwards, *Early Christian Ireland,* 416–40.

41. *Bethu Brigte,* §40 (pp. 14–15, with translation on p. 31).

42. Nagy's term in his discussion of the passage. It should be noted that Patrick does rejoin Brigit for the miracle of the child, and does not remain outside the proceedings entirely, as Nagy implies: *Conversing with Angels,* 232–33.

43. *Bethu Brigte,* §40 (p. 14), lines 464–65.

44. *Bethu Brigte,* §40 (p. 14), lines 476–77 and 479–80.

45. *Bethu Brigte,* §40 (p. 14), line 487.

46. *Bethu Brigte,* §40 (p. 14), lines 485–86.

47. Kelly, "Court Procedure," §5 (pp. 86–87), and see discussion and diagram on pp. 77–80.

48. Brigit's authority in this instance may also reflect the idea that women were best suited for judging other women, a principle represented in law tracts such as, for example, *Din Techtugud,* where the female judge Bríg (a name related to Brigit) corrects the erroneous judgment of Sencha: (*CIH* 209.12–23).

49. Charles-Edwards outlines the principal kinds of law in his *Gaelic Lawyer.*

50. This text clearly regards druids as rivals of the church in matters of law as well as religion. They were certainly still around in the seventh and eighth centuries, and could not have been expected to relinquish their hold on such an important aspect of community life without a fight: "The First Synod of St. Patrick," in *Irish Penitentials,* §14 (pp. 56–57).

51. Stacey, *Road to Judgment,* 126–29 and references there.

52. Binchy, *Celtic and Anglo-Saxon Kingship.*

53. One of the most insidiously enticing expressions of the romantic image of the Irish people is O'Faolain's *The Irish,* which was already in its third printing at the time Binchy published his famous essays on pre-Viking kingship. Arguably, Binchy's essays, though scholarly in nature and profoundly different in tone and perspective from O'Faolain's work, contributed no less significantly to the image of early Irish kings as "priestly vegetables" (Patrick Wormald's words in "Celtic and Anglo-Saxon

Kingship"). The explosive popularity of the most recent addition to this literary genre, Cahill's *How the Irish Saved Civilization*, demonstrates the enduring appeal of this idea. For recent correctives of Binchy's views, see Wormald, "Celtic and Anglo-Saxon Kingship;" and Ó Corráin, "Nationality and Kingship." On the interplay between popular and scholarly notions of "Celticity," see Sims-Williams, "Celtomania."

54. On Irish and European historians and the question of Irish "otherness," see Stacey, *Road to Judgment*, 1–8, 15–21. Recent writings by historians of Ireland have closed the perceived gap between the Irish and continental experiences; key authors here are Charles-Edwards, Ó Cróinín, McCone, Ó Corráin, Richter, and Picard.

55. See discussion in *GEIL*, 18–26.

56. For a discussion of the distinctive characteristics of *cáin*-law, see Breatnach, *Companion*, 191–202 (and 202–4 on *Cáin Adamnáin* specifically).

57. Charles-Edwards, *Early Christian Ireland*, 523. He suggests looking elsewhere—to their role as lords, and to the contractual powers they exercised over those subordinate to them (522–85). A very important article on the subject of rulership is Ó Corráin's "Nationality and Kingship." The debate over the impact of the Vikings rages on unabated: two recent, and conflicting, views are Ó Corráin, "Ireland, Wales, Man"; and Smyth, "Scandinavian Raiders on the English and Irish Churches: A Preliminary Reassessment," in B. Smith, *Britain and Ireland 900–1300*.

58. Ó Corráin, "Nationality and Kingship"; Charles-Edwards, *Early Christian Ireland*. This is a point made also with respect to jurists in Stacey, *Road to Judgment*, 125–40.

59. Wormald points out that not all codes were associated with specific rulers; however, the majority of them either were or came to be. Moreover, as he argues, the fact of royal lawgiving was very much what the issuing of these texts was intended to prove: Wormald, "*Lex Scripta* and *Verbum Regis*"; and, most recently, *The Making of English Law*.

60. *Irish Penitentials; IK; Medieval Handbooks of Penance*.

61. *Cánai* pertaining to strictly secular situations (e.g., invasions, plague) are mentioned in various sources. However, none are known to exist before the seventh century, and all extant *cánai* are distinctly ecclesiastical in character and tone. Recent discussions include *GEIL*, 21–22; and Charles-Edwards, *Early Christian Ireland*, 559–69.

62. Breatnach, *Companion*, 195.

63. Gerriets, "King as Judge"; and see also *GEIL*, 18–25.

64. Much of what follows is reprinted from Stacey, "Speaking in Riddles," in *Ireland and Europe in the Early Middle Ages: Texts and Transmission*, ed. Richter and Ní Chatháin (Dublin, 2002), 243–48. I would like to express my gratitude to Four Courts Press for allowing the reprinting of this material. See, on *Gúbretha Caratniad*, Breatnach, *Companion*, 262.

65. *GC*, §1 (p. 306).

66. *GC*, 306–7.

67. I owe this explanation to Thomas Charles-Edwards, for whose comments on this gloss I am very grateful.

68. Thurneysen translates this as "*der Geschnittene*," in his commentary to the passage: *GC*, 306–7.

69. Or *tescaid*: *DIL* terms the deuterotonic forms "very doubtful." See *DIL D*, s.v. *do-esc*, col. 257, l. 36.

70. *GC*, 307.

71. A meaning of this kind is perhaps implied by *DIL*'s suggestion for *tescthe*, "deserted": see *DIL D*, s.v. *do-esc*, col. 257, l. 36.

72. N. Chadwick, "*Imbas Forasnaí*"; N. Chadwick, *Poetry and Prophecy*, 4–6, 11–14; Le Roux, "La divination," 233–56; Nagy, "Shamanic Aspects"; Nagy, *Wisdom*, 25, 161; Lonigan, "Shamanism"; Melia, "Law and the Shaman Saint"; Ford, "The Blind, the Dumb." More generally on shamanism, see Eliade, *Shamanism.*

73. The phrase is Nagy's: "Shamanic Aspects," 303.

74. Ford, "The Blind, the Dumb"; Nagy, "Shamanic Aspects," 11–12.

75. *C. Adam.*, §11 (p. 6); Ford, "The Blind, the Dumb," 30. The ambiguity of the pronoun in the relevant passage of *Cáin Adamnáin* makes it uncertain whether the initial "attack" on Adamnán comes first from his mother or from the woman they encounter on the battlefield. Whatever the disposition of this initial assault, however, all subsequent indignities visited upon Adamnán are initiated by his mother.

76. I owe this suggestion to Thomas Charles-Edwards.

77. Literally, "blameless, fitting, reasonable, natural."

78. *GC,* §2 (p. 307). Normally exchanges were considered binding after the parties involved had had twenty-four hours in which to reconsider the arrangement. However, in this case, Caratnia decided that the exchange was to be rescinded because the silver exchanged had hidden flaws that lessened its value. The best account of the complex rules governing the recission of contracts is McLeod's discussion in *EICL*, 32–51.

79. *GC,* §7 (p. 311). Whereas normally sons whose fathers were still living were not allowed to make contractual arrangements independently (here symbolized by the suretyship used to confirm them), the law allowed as exceptions to this rule certain arrangements like the ones mentioned above which were deemed to be of clear and obvious benefit to the parties involved. For the rules governing contracts made by dependents, see McLeod's discussion in *EICL*, 58–80; and also Stacey, *Road to Judgment*, 55–81.

80. *GC,* §9 (p. 316). Whereas normally contracts where the considerations exchanged were judged to be uneven or nonexistent would be rescinded or renegotiated, contracts made by a legally competent person that were obviously disadvantageous to that person at the time the contracts was made, but had been agreed to by him anyway, would be held as binding. In such instances, the loss, or "cheating," would be borne by the person who had so unwisely agreed to the uneven exchange. For the regulations governing such situations, see McLeod, *EICL,* 32–46.

81. Kelly has published another more extended, legal riddle in his "Court Procedure," 87–89, and see especially his note to *nodonaisc* on p. 99.

82. For cross-cultural studies of riddling traditions, see: Hamnett, "Ambiguity"; Burns, "Riddling"; Maranda, "Logic of Riddles"; Abrahams, "Introductory Remarks"; Hart, *Riddles in Filipino Folklore;* Cole-Beuchat, "Riddles in Bantu"; Blacking, "Social Value."

83. Radner, "Threefold Death," especially p. 186.

84. E.g., *GC,* §9 (p. 316), *cach sochoinn a saithiud,* on which see McLeod's notes in *EICL* §14, pp. 207–8.

85. Radner, "Threefold Death," 187.

86. Ford, "The Blind, the Dumb."

87. Gerriets, "King as Judge," 51–52.

88. *CG* 535–37. Involvement in judicial matters is clearly imagined in this text as part of the regular routine. In the highly schematized summary of the royal week outlined in that text, the king reserves Mondays *do breithemhnacht,* "for adjudication," and Saturdays *do brethaib,* "for judgments" (*CG* 542–47). Both Binchy and MacNeill were at somewhat of a loss as to what the difference between these two activities might be, although MacNeill concluded that *breithemhnacht* might refer to "matters

of state," and *do brethaib* to domestic litigation: see *CG* note to line 544, p. 37. Another possibility might be the distinction between adjudication itself (*breithemnacht*) on the one hand, and the proclamation of judgments reached by adjudication on the other (*bretha*).

89. *Triads of Ireland*, §248.

90. In other words, a poet.

91. Ó Cathasaigh stresses the importance of the ritual setting to the regulation of social speech within the Ulster Cycle tales: "*Sírrabad Súaltaim*," 86. Presumably we ought to be imagining regulated public speech in the legal texts as pertaining to formal, marked occasions also.

92. *CIH* 2113.6–15; 2217.8–17. It must be remarked, however, that Cormac mac Airt is a king particularly famed in Irish tradition for the sagacity of his legal verdicts: Ó Cathasaigh, *Heroic Biography*, 62–68. This is tale two from Dillon's collection; according to Breatnach, it goes back to an Old Irish original: Breatnach, *Companion*, 349–50.

93. *CIH* 2117.23–35; 1116.29–34. This is tale thirteen, which has a Middle Irish core: Breatnach, *Companion*, 349–50.

94. *CIH* 2113.22–25. This is tale three, which goes back to an Old Irish text: Breatnach, *Companion*, 349–50.

95. *CIH* 2217.25–35.

96. Kelly, "Court Procedure," §§2–3 (p. 85).

97. Breatnach, "Lawyers in Early Ireland," 8.

98. Breatnach," Lawyers in Early Ireland," 9.

99. The "order of speaking" articulated in the *Táin Bó Cúailnge* and other Ulster Cycle tales imagines druids as speaking first in ritually marked situations of warning or challenge, followed next by kings, and then by "the people." In *Mesca Ulad*, the king's role is limited to stating (in response to a formal question posed by his druid) the nature of a petition brought by a supplicant to the court (in this instance, the Irish hero Cú Chulainn). The druid then passes judgment on this petition without further intervention by the king. Insofar as druids are frequently imagined (as here) as having possessed juridical functions in the pre-Christian period, this text also would seem to speak to precisely the same set of questions raised in the legal sources—in this case coming down squarely on the side of the legal specialist: see Ó Cathasaigh, "Rhetoric"; and Ó Cathasaigh, "Sírrabad Súaltaim."

100. Breatnach, "Canon Law," 439–59.

101. See discussion by Breatnach in *UR*, 98–100.

102. Ó Corráin, Breatnach, and Breen, "Laws of the Irish," 400–403.

103. *UR*, 98–100.

104. Clancy, "Women Poets."

105. *Br. Crólige*, §32 (pp. 26–27); "Saga of Fergus mac Léti," §8 (pp. 38–39).

106. Stacey, "Satire and Its Socio-Legal Rôle"; Clancy, "Women Poets"; Randolph, "Female Satirists."

107. See *UR*, 89–94.

108. *CIH* 1592.26–39, and note also *CIH* 1111.28, "spear-points of shame." For discussion and other references, see Breatnach, "Addenda and Corrigenda"; and Breatnach, "On Satire."

109. *UR*, 89–94.

110. *UR*, "BN XIII," p. 50, with translation on p. 51. The best discussion of the relationship between learning, artistry, and noble status is Charles-Edwards, "Context and Uses of Literacy in Early Christian Ireland," 62–82 of Pryce, *Literacy in Medieval Celtic Societies*.

111. Carey, "Three Things," 46–47, and 57–58 and, on the ambivalence some-

times attendant on this later enthusiasm for the magic of the pagan past, Carey's "Uses of Tradition."

112. See references in McCone, *Pagan Past*, 220–26; McCone, "Tale of Two Ditties"; and Sharpe, "Hiberno-Latin *laicus*." See also *GEIL*, 49–51.

113. *UR*, §7–12 (pp. 106–9) spells out the relationship between learning and inheritance. See also Breatnach, "Caldron of Poesy," §3 (pp. 64–65); and *UR*, "BN IX," p. 46; and *UR* discussion, 94–98.

114. See references above in n. 108 and, in Chapter 3, n. 63.

115. Breatnach, "Caldron of Poesy," §12 (pp. 68–69) and see §§15–16 (pp. 72–73).

116. *CIH* 2221.27.

117. *CIH* 2222.9–33 is in part a meditation on the proper balance between *eolus* (or *fis*), "knowledge," *aicned*, "nature" (here standing in for a whole complex of ideas about the melding of the pagan past with the Christian present), and *roscad*, "rhetorical speech."

118. *CIH* 2222.7–8.

119. *UR*, "BN IV," p. 36, with translation on p. 37.

120. *UR*, "BN I," p. 23, with translation on p. 24; and see "BN IV," pp. 37, with translation on p. 38. See also *CIH* 2222.15. Poets are enjoined when attempting such levying to use the most noble meter they know how to compose, and the presumption here is the low status poets cannot produce poetry of sufficient complexity: *CIH* 552.9–11.

121. *UR*, "BN XV," p. 55, with translation on p. 56.

122. *CIH* 2224.27–28: *dith noe dit nagaire i naguib anochtuibh ardrochtuibh i ngraduib mo neire.*

123. *UR*, "BN XIV," p. 52, with translation on p. 53; and see *UR* itself, §21 (pp. 112–13); and "BN IV," p. 36, with translation on p. 37 on the *longbard*.

124. *UR*, "BN III," p. 34, with translation on p. 35. The reference to the *drisiuc* "remaining in the ashes" may speak to the same idea: *UR*, "BN XIV," p. 52, with translation on p. 53.

125. See further discussion below in Chapter 5.

126. *UR*, "BN IV," p. 37, with translation on 37–38.

127. *UR*, §§18 and 20 (pp. 112–13), respectively.

128. *CIH* 2221.22.

129. See discussion below in Chapter 5, and *UR*, §6 (pp. 104–5); *CIH* 591.27–29 = *Bürgschaft*, §7 (p. 7); "Caldron of Poesy," 12 (pp. 68–69); *CIH* 2224.3–28. *BNT* stipulates that judges must not be partial or allow bribes to blind them to the true justice of the situation: *CIH* 2221.12–16.

130. Nagy, *Conversing with Angels*, 154–56 and 169–78. On the historical reality of Druim Cet, see Ryan, "Convention of Druim Ceat"; and, more recently, Bannerman, *Studies in the History of Dalriada*, 157–70.

131. A number of these tales have been made available in English translation by Ford in his *Celtic Poets*.

132. "*Imacallam im dá Thuarad*" was edited by Stokes in *Revue Celtique* 26 (1905): 4–64.

133. "Pseudo-Historical Prologue," §7 (p. 12, with translation on p. 18). On the implications of this text for how the Irish saw themselves fitting into Christian history, see Carey, "Two Laws."

134. "Pseudo-Historical Prologue," §§9–11 (pp. 12–13, with translation on p. 19).

135. *CIH* 1613.38–1614.32.

136. Kelly, "Court Procedure, §2 (p. 85).

137. *CIH* 24.22.

138. *CIH* 349.7–21, and see discussion of this passage in Carey, "Three Things," 54–57.

139. *CIH* 349.22–24.

140. "Pseudo-Historical Prologue," §11.3–6 (pp. 27–28). The compiler also (in §11) makes an explicit reference to a passage in *Bretha Nemed* (which lawbook he calls by name).

141. Another interesting departure from the *Senchas Már* is visible in the image of law to which this passage implicitly speaks. Here justice in Ireland is presented as having originated in the judgments of individuals, some of which judgments then found their way into written form to become texts within the tradition. It is worth keeping in mind that although we can identify today tracts associated only with three of the persons named in the text, there may once have been texts linked to the other names given that are today no longer extant. It is certainly suggestive that all of them are titled in exactly the same way—*Bretha Echach maic Luchta, Bretha Fachtnai maic Senchath, Bretha Déin Chécht,* and the like. According to the "Pseudo-Historical Prologue," then, law originates in the judgments issued by ancestor figures within the tradition. The *Senchas Már* itself, by contrast, generally (though not always) eschews an image of law as originating in the sayings of authoritative individuals, and proffers instead legal treatises authored (at least by implication) by contemporary jurists devoted to the explication of particular topics—clientship, fosterage, distraint, and the like. Two exceptions to this are *Bretha Déin Chécht* and *Bretha Creidini,* a tract on (probably) smithing. The existence of a *Bretha Luchtaini* or a *Bretha Goibnenn* is uncertain: Breatnach, "Original Extent," especially p. 33, and see Breatnach, *Companion,* 268–314 on the lawbook as a whole. Of the other 47 or 48 (Breatnach, "Extent," 20–21; Breatnach, *Companion,* 268–314) tracts incorporated into the *Senchas Már,* none is attributed to an individual jurist or king, although of course sayings attributed to individual jurists do appear throughout the lawbook. See further Chapter 5 on the *Senchas Már* and its relationship to other legal texts.

142. *AM,* §1 (pp. 2–3), with Kelly's notes on 23.

143. *CIH* 209.12–23; 406.26–407.2.

144. Much of *Audacht Morainn* is written in an alliterative meter common in Old Irish legal poetry, but Morann is characterized as a jurist, rather than a poet, in Irish tradition. The alliterative rhetorical passages of *Bretha Déin Chécht* are ascribed in the text to one Laidcenn mac Ercaid, identified in the gloss as an Ulidian judge: *BDC,* §25 (pp. 36–37).

145. *Triads of Ireland,* §248.

146. A point also underscored earlier in the text by King Lóegaire's prostration in submission to Patrick: "Pseudo-Historical Prologue," §4 (p. 11, with translation on p. 18).

147. Binchy, "*Bretha Nemed*"; Binchy, "Date and Provenance."

148. *CIH* 634.12–636.1.

149. My translation here omits the "7" to make the passage parallel to 636.1 (my reading here is consistent with the two other versions of this text, BB [*CIH* 1591.14] and Nat. Libr. Ireland G 3 [*CIH* 2256.26]).

150. Reading "*7 cocorus*" for "*co corus*" in accordance with the other two manuscripts: *CIH* 1591.24 and 2256.35.

151. *DIL* s.v. *fír* pp. 307–8, cols. 146–49.

152. For a discussion of these terms and their possible meanings, see Sharpe, "Dispute Settlement"; and Stacey, *Road to Judgment,* pp. 114–40.

153. These are members of the *saernemed,* or "noble *nemed*" classes; the text also lists persons of considerably lower status (*daernemed*) whose art or profession earns them a privilege they would otherwise not enjoy: *CIH* 636.22ff.

154. This issue of differences among schools is explored in greater detail below in Chapter 5.

155. On which see discussion below in Chapter 5.

Chapter 5

1. Kelly cites some differences between tracts and possible reasons for them, but concludes that "[i]n spite of such divergences and disagreements, our sources display an essential unity": *GEIL*, 1–2.

2. Breatnach, "*Cáin Fhuithirbe*," 52.

3. See *DAC* notes to §§33–34 (pp. 221–23) and discussion there; *DAC* notes to §§39 and 44 (pp. 226, 230–31) and discussion there.

4. Compare *CIH* 596.20–22 with 2218.4–7; and 596.24–25 with 2224.2–28.

5. Compare *Br. Crólige* §17 (pp. 14–15) with *CIH* 466.30–33.

6. Compare *BDC* §23 (pp. 36–37) with *CIH* 1756.18–21. On these "sharings" among tracts, see further Stacey, "Law and Memory."

7. Tracts also often refer to other tracts by name: e.g., *CIH* 229.12; 2213.30.

8. *GEIL*, 2. The relationship between vernacular law and Latin ecclesiastical tradition (especially as represented by the *CCH*), has come in for considerably more attention: see discussion below, and Hughes, *Church in Early Irish Society*, 123–33; Charles-Edwards, "Uses of Literacy"; Charles-Edwards, *Gaelic Lawyer*, Ó Corráin, Breatnach, and Breen, "Laws of the Irish"; Ó Corráin, "Irish Law"; Breatnach, "Canon Law"; and Jaski, "Cú Chuimne."

9. It was largely on the basis of provisions about the *nemed* classes (and its affiliation with Munster) that he argued that the plain prose tract *Uraicecht Becc* should be assigned to the *Bretha Nemed* school: Binchy, "*Bretha Nemed*"; and Binchy, "Date and Provenance."

10. Binchy, "*Bretha Nemed*," 5–6.

11. Charles-Edwards, *Gaelic Lawyer*, 39–42; and Charles-Edwards, "Uses of Literacy."

12. Equally telling in terms of the impact of conversion was the extreme self-consciousness with which the literati began to reflect on questions crucial to the reshaping of traditional notions of law, like the relationship between oral and written. As Nagy has demonstrated, intellectuals of the period took visibly different stances on such issues, even while making use of a common literary pattern—dialogues among saints, angels, and pagan revenants—to stake out their positions: Nagy, *Conversing with Angels*.

13. The promulgation of such *cáin*-laws began in the seventh century and continued up until the resurgence in Viking attacks in the second half of the ninth century, when the practice seems to have come more or less to an end: Charles-Edwards, *Gaelic Lawyer*, 43–62.

14. *GEIL*, 242–50.

15. Charles-Edwards, "The Pastoral Role of the Church in the Early Irish Laws," in Blair and Sharpe, *Pastoral Care*, 65–66; Jaski, "Cú Chuimne," 65; Charles-Edwards, *Gaelic Lawyer*, 6; and see discussion below.

16. Charles-Edwards points to visible differences in the reasoning and foundational principles separating the work of "secular lawyers" from their ecclesiastical counterparts, and argues that many of these differences were consciously recognized and exploited, at least by those on the secular side of the fence: Charles-Edwards, *Gaelic Lawyer*, 24–25. In employing the term "secular lawyers," he of course recognizes that many of these men would have been clerically trained, sometimes

even to a high degree: *Gaelic Lawyer*, "Uses of Literacy." See also the case made by Kelly in *GEIL*, 232–36.

17. Hughes, *Church in Early Irish Society*, 123–33. Jaski has recently suggested, by contrast, that the dispute between the two had "lost its edge" by the time the *CCH* was compiled: "Cú Chuimne," 52. Another recent discussion is Richter, "Dating the Irish Synods."

18. Radding, *Medieval Jurisprudence*; Reynolds, *Kingdoms and Communities*; Brand, *English Legal Profession*; Pryce, "Origins and the Medieval Period"; Pryce, "Lawbooks and Literacy."

19. Many of these developments are discussed in detail by Wormald in his "*Lex Scripta*"; and by Davies and Fouracres in their *Settlement of Disputes*.

20. Wormald, "*Lex Scripta* and *Verbum Regis*," original essay published in 1977, reprinted in Wormald, *Legal Culture*, 1–43 (including "Additional Note").

21. Noble, "Literacy and the Papal Government in Late Antiquity and the Early Middle Ages," in McKitterick, *Uses of Literacy*, 102.

22. Three important volumes edited by Ní Chatháin and Richter speak directly to such contacts: *Ireland and Europe in the Early Middle Ages*; *Ireland and Europe*; and *Ireland and Christendom*. See also Whitelock, McKitterick, and Dumville, *Ireland in Early Mediaeval Europe*; Hillgarth, "Ireland and Spain in the Seventh Century"; and a host of important articles by Ó Cróinín, including "Irish Provenance"; "Pelagianism"; "New Light on Palladius"; and "Irish as Mediators of Antique Culture."

23. Charles-Edwards, *Gaelic Lawyer*, 4.

24. Ó Corráin, "Nationality and Kingship," 7–16, 19, 22–24.

25. Charles-Edwards, "*Corpus Iuris Hibernici*," 154–55; *GEIL*, 225–40; Breatnach, *Companion*, 354–72.

26. Richter, "Dating the Irish Synods," 75. There are some indications that the *CCH* may contain synodal provisions of an even earlier date: L. M. Davies, "Isidorian Texts," 212; Breatnach, "Canon Law."

27. E.g., *CG* and *BA*, on which see discussion below.

28. *GEIL*, 242–63; Breatnach, *Companion*, 268–314 on the *Senchas Már*, and 184–91 on *Bretha Nemed*.

29. L. M. Davies spells out the arguments in her "'Mouth of Gold,'" 249. For the dating of the roughly contemporaneous *Bretha Nemed*, see Breatnach, "Canon Law," and discussion below.

30. L. M. Davies, "Isidorian Texts," 210–16 is the best discussion. Also helpful are Jaski, "Cú Chuimne," 66–67; Breatnach, "Canon Law," 456; Charles-Edwards, *Gaelic Lawyer*, 19; Dumville, "Transmission and Use"; and Howlett, "Prologue."

31. Thurneysen, "Kanonensammlung," 1–5; Breatnach, "Canon Law," 456; L. M. Davies, "Isidorian Texts," 212–15; Dumville, "Transmission and Use," 85–95; Jaski, "Cú Chuimne," 66–67.

32. The evidence for collaboration occurs in a colophon extant only in a single manuscript of one of the two recensions—a fact that might reasonably be taken as suggesting the involvement of those two compilers in that recension only of the text. Moreover, a preface to the work found in three manuscripts is phrased in the first person, as though there had been only one compiler. It is possible to imagine any number of explanations for this constellation of facts. Jaski suggests a variety of possible connections between the two houses, among them a shared adherence to the old Easter, a common interest in *céli Dé* principles, and close connections between Tech Taille (which he identifies as the house of Ruben's father) and the Columban monastery of Durrow: Jaski, "Cú Chuimne," 55–63.

33. O'Loughlin, "Marriage and Sexuality," 190.

34. L. M. Davies, "Mouth of Gold."

35. L. M. Davies, "Isidorian Texts," 242.

36. L. M. Davies, "Gallic Councils," 86.

37. Hughes, *Church in Early Irish Society*, 123–33. Much of the discussion has centered on the question of whether Bede exaggerated the seriousness of the impact of the Easter dispute, on which see "Cummian's Letter." Another contentious issue has been that of early Irish church organization, on which see Sharpe, "Organization of the Church"; Etchingham, "Early Irish Church"; Etchingham, *Church Organisation*.

38. *IK*, XVIII.2 and 3.

39. Jaski, "Cú Chuimne," 60–63, with quotation on p. 62.

40. Wormald, "Origins of the *Gens Anglorum*," 102–4, 120–23; Stacey, "Texts and Society," 254–56.

41. L. M. Davies, "Mouth of Gold," 265–67; Sheehy, "*Collectio Canonum Hibernensis*," 528.

42. O'Loughlin, "Marriage and Sexuality."

43. Jaski, "Cú Chuimne," 65, and references there.

44. Meens, "Oldest Manuscript Witness," 7–8.

45. Sheehy, "*Collectio Canonum Hibernensis*," 527.

46. Jaski, "Cú Chuimne," 64.

47. L. M. Davies, "Isidorian Texts," 208, 210–11.

48. Stacey, *Road to Judgment*, 136–37.

49. Jaski, "Cú Chuimne," 51, 63–69.

50. Stacey, *Road to Judgment*, 136–37.

51. Breatnach, "Original Extent"; and *Companion*, 268–314. The discussion that follows summarizes points made by Breatnach; Kelly in *GEIL*, 242–46; and Thurneysen, "Zu den bisherigen Ausgaben der irischen Rechtstexte," 167–96; Thurneysen, "Nachträgliches," 406–10; and Thurneysen, "Celtic Law," in *CLP*, 54–59.

52. *GEIL*, 245. This is distinct from the later "Pseudo-Historical Prologue to the *Senchas Már*." For reasons of clarity, I will refer throughout to the *Senchas Már* compiler as though there were only one; however, it is of course entirely possible that more than one compiler was involved.

53. Breatnach, "Original Extent," 2; Breatnach, *Companion*, 270–71.

54. See discussion and references in Breatnach, "Original Extent," 38–41; Breatnach, *Companion*, 310–14.

55. Binchy, "*Bretha Nemed*"; Binchy, "Date and Provenance"; *GEIL*, 246; Breatnach, *Companion*, 184–91. For discussions of individual tracts often ascribed to *Bretha Nemed* see *Companion*, 176–82 and 378–464 (*Bretha Éitgid*); 233–34 (*CCF*); 253–57 (*Findsruth Fíthail*); 315–18 (*UB*); and 320–21 (*UR*).

56. See discussion and translation of the title of this text by Breatnach in "First Third," 1–2 and 8–9 respectively.

57. Binchy, "*Bretha Nemed*," 4.

58. Binchy, "*Bretha Nemed*," 4.

59. Breatnach, "Canon Law."

60. Binchy, "*Bretha Nemed*," 6. The legal texts are available in the *CIH*; for the others, see "Alphabet"; and *Audacht Morainn. Findsruth Fíthail* itself survives only in fragments (*CIH* 786.25–789.17; 2131.1–2143.40), and has been discussed by R. Smith in "Fithal and Flann Fína"; and "Further Light on the *Finnsruth Fíthail*"; and by Breatnach in *Companion*, 253–57. Another wisdom text ascribed to Fíthal is the *Senbríathra Fíthail*, for which see R. Smith, "*Senbriathra Fithail* and Related Texts." See also *GEIL*, 284–86 for a listing of the extant wisdom tracts.

61. *UR*, 79–80.

62. *GEIL*, 235–36, 246; *AM*, xviii–xix.

63. Charles-Edwards gave the name *Fénechas* to this style of language in his 1980 review of Binchy's *Corpus Iuris Hibernici*: "*Corpus Iuris Hibernici.*"

64. Binchy, "*Bretha Nemed*"; Binchy, "Date and Provenance."

65. *AM*, xviii–xix; *GEIL*, 235–36.

66. *UR*, 80.

67. *GEIL*, 235–36, 246; *AM*, xviii–xix.

68. *CIH* 250.1–337.36; *CIH* 312.35–37 = 2228.18–20; 336.30 = 2215.29.

69. *CIH* 250.15–18.

70. *Findsruth Fíthail* survives only in fragments. Compare *CIH* 1113.19 (*BND*) with, for example, 786.25, 787.13, 20, 24; 788.3, 12, 30; 789.1, 4, 6.

71. *CIH* 1123.12–14.

72. *UR*, 79–80.

73. *UR*, 79–80.

74. E.g., Smith, "Alphabet," §§13–14 (p. 49) and §§48–50 (pp. 54–55), with note to §48.

75. *Old Irish Wisdom*, 10–12; R. Smith, "*Cach* Formulas."

76. Rhetorical language is not terribly common in the *Senchas Már*, but it does appear in certain tracts, most notably *DT*, *Tosach Bésgnai*, *Bretha Crólige*, *BDC*, and *Di Gnímaib Gíall Gaibter*. There are, of course, tracts that are not (to our knowledge) associated with either the *Senchas Már* or the *Bretha Nemed* schools that contain this type of language as well (*DAC*; *Do Ércib Fola*).

77. *CIH* 596.3–597.3 (*Bürgschaft*, §§58–63).

78. Compare *CIH* 596.3–6 with 597.4–5 (*Bürgschaft* §58 with §64).

79. Compare in *BNT*, *CIH* 2222.5, 2223.8, 10.

80. *CIH* 596.20 = 2218.5; 596.24 = 2224.27 (note how differently the latter phrase particularly is contextualized in the two tracts).

81. *CIH* 1121.38–1122.37 (*BND*).

82. *CIH* 591.27–29 (*Bürgschaft*, §7); 592.10–13 (*Bürgschaft*, §§13–15). Compare also the *macshlabra* passages on *CIH* 591.32–34 (*Bürgschaft*, §9) including *cis lír*, with the commentary in *Findsruth Fíthail* (2139.25–40) and with 1123–25 (*cis lír* phrases).

83. *AM* §§34–45 (pp. 12–13).

84. *CIH* 2221.17–21, and see 2224.1–28, where the issue is clearly one of judges (*brithem*) ranking poets according to their learning, their purity, and their attainments. See discussion below.

85. For example *CIH* 2224.1–28; 2225.31–2226.2; and see discussion below on the related themes of *fís*, "knowledge," *eolus*, "wisdom," and *fogluim*, "learning."

86. *GEIL*, 235–36.

87. *UR*, 80; and see MacNeill, "Ancient Irish Law," 311–13.

88. *CIH* 582.32–589.32. For Cormac, Cenn Faeladh, and Morann, see 584.5ff. and 17ff.; 586.14ff.; and 587.30ff., respectively. The citation from Proverbs occurs on 587.23–24.

89. *CIH* 588.11–25. This section may originally have been an independent text: *CIH* 588.1–589.32; see discussion in *GEIL*, 267.

90. Although, as Ó Corráin, Breatnach, and Breen have shown, there is a great deal of Latin in many of the extant vernacular tracts: "Laws of the Irish," 430–38.

91. Charles-Edwards, "*Corpus Iuris Hibernici*," explains these terms.

92. Charles-Edwards, "*Corpus Iuris Hibernici*," 146–47.

93. Compare *CIH* 488.25ff. with what precedes it. The alliterative and rhetorical aspects of *CB* are similarly enhanced in that section of the tract consisting of a series of maxims on the subject of contract: *CIH* 521.13–522.19 versus what follows it.

94. Binchy, "Linguistic and Historical Value," and "Linguistic and Legal Archaisms"; contrast with this McCone, *Pagan Past*, 1–24.

95. Binchy, *CG*.

96. Thurneysen, *Bürgschaft*; Stacey, "*Berrad Airechta*," respectively.

97. It is on this basis, for example, that Charles-Edwards assigns the name *Fénechas* to any material in the archaic style: Charles-Edwards, "*Corpus Iuris Hibernici*"; Stacey, "Law and Memory," 46–51; and see discussion below.

98. *CG*, p. 88.

99. *GEIL*, 311.

100. *Br. Crólige* §5 (p. 8); *GEIL*, 8, 56–57, 62, 234. In *CIH* 1402.12–15, *Fénechas* is distinguished both from *Críth Gablach* and from the *Senchas Már*.

101. *CIH* 210.25–35.

102. *CG* 21, 272, and cf. 461, where the compiler introduces a poem with the words *amail ar[a]cain*, the subject for which is almost certainly intended to be understood as *Fénechas*.

103. In the rhetorical style typical of this sort of prose, it contrasts *fírflaithi* (those who are truly lords) with the *anflaith*, literally "nonlord"—in this context, those who have not yet ascended into the ranks of the nobility: *CG* 272–76, with note on p. 32.

104. *CG* 21–22, with note on p. 22.

105. Stacey, "Law and Memory," argues for the ongoing composition of "traditional" oral law.

106. Both *Críth Gablach* and *Berrad Airechta* appear to cite *Fénechas* in the same way, date to approximately the same period, and are written largely in the same style. Moreover, both may conceptualize the *ráth* as a form of *aitire* (*CG* 59), and the *Berrad Airechta* compiler appears to refer directly to himself as having been involved in the composition of *Críth Gablach*: "as we have said" (compare *CIH* 594.1–2 = *Bürgschaft* §38 with *CG* 143–44).

107. *CIH* 591.34; 592.6–7; 596.6; 596.19; 599.16–17; 599.31 (*Bürgschaft*, §§9, 12, 59, 60, 79, 83, respectively). The omission occurs at *CIH* 591.34ff. A miscellany contained in H 3. 18 reproduces the *Berrad Airechta* text on *macshlabra* reasonably faithfully up through the *arachan fenechus* introduction—and then cites a passage in *rosc* that it attributes to Sencha: *CIH* 1109.14–21.

108. *CIH* 592.6–7 (*Bürgschaft*, §12), with notes on p. 228 of Stacey, "*Berrad Airechta*." The gloss (*ma fasaith suide no osath*) replicates rather than corrects the archaic spelling of the word it is glossing, which is not the usual pattern of glossing in *BA*. Of course, it is impossible to tell at what point such a gloss might have entered the tradition, although it must have been done sufficiently early as to allow it to have become completely absorbed into the text surrounding it. However, at the very least one written source must have intervened between any original oral phrase and the quotation as extant today. The glossator is here surmising that *fasaith* represents a nonhistorical f added to an original *osath*, a process that would likely not have happened orally: *CIH* 592.5ff. (*Bürgschaft*, §12). Note also that the putatively oral formulas in *CIH* 595.3 and 598.23 also contain what appear to be embedded glosses.

109. The tract begins on *CIH* 596.3 with a standard textbook prose introduction. The part ascribed to *Fénechas*, however, begins when the rhetorical questions themselves begin: *CIH* 596.6ff. and 596.19ff. (*Bürgschaft*, §§58–60). Note that two of the phrases ascribed to *Fénechas* here occur also in the main *Bretha Nemed* tracts: *CIH* 596.20–21, and 596.24 (and see discussion below on *Bretha Nemed*'s concept of *Fénechas*).

110. One could make this case also for the *Uraicecht na Ríar* compiler: see discussion of *Fénechas* in the *Bretha Nemed* tracts below.

111. It is unclear whether all of the maxims cited are to be attributed to *Fénechas* or merely those that follow immediately upon the "as the *Fénechas* sings it" introductory phrase: *CIH* 599.16–38 (*Bürgschaft*, §§79–84).

112. Breatnach, "Canon Law," and Ó Corráin, Breatnach, and Breen, "Laws of the Irish."

113. Charles-Edwards, "*Corpus Iuris Hibernici*," 146, n. 14.

114. Charles-Edwards, "*Corpus Iuris Hibernici*," 146–47, 154–55.

115. *CIH* 2211.1–3 = 2100.11–13; 2213.29–30; the reference to *Fénechas* in 2213.30–31 appears more coincident with *BA* and *CG*'s understanding of the term. See also Charles-Edwards, unpublished essay, "Early Irish Law."

116. *CIH* 2213.29–31. The passage seems most easily read as though *Críth Gablach* was here imagined as itself constituting or conveying *Fénechas*, since the tract is indeed devoted to a discussion of the "lordly grades together with the grades of the *Féni*." However, that particular section of *Críth Gablach* also contains a brief passage in archaic style expressly attributed to *Fénechas: Ara fesser gráda Féne fri mes [n-]airechtae[e] adrímter,* "That thou shouldst know the grades of the *Féni*: according to the estimation of the court are they enumerated" (*CG* 21–22, with note on p. 25). Nothing more is said in the archaic style about the various social ranks—all subsequent discussion of the subject is conducted in the same plain/textbook prose in which the rest of the tract is written. However, the presence of this one sentence in the archaic style makes it impossible to tell which the *Bretha Nemed* compiler had in mind—*Críth Gablach* itself or the quotation contained within it. It is worth noting also that *Bretha Nemed* uses this same expression, "sings it," with a written text as though it were oral, a fact that may suggest either that its compiler does not always distinguish clearly between (supposedly) "oral" and "written" law, or that the essence of the law that the text describes was conceptualized as oral: *Is do suidiu arachain i nAntéchtu Breth* (Breatnach, "First Third," §5 [pp. 10–11]).

117. *UR* §4 (pp. 104–5). Bergin's Law is present, but otherwise the sentence is relatively unornamented. See *UR* note on p. 119, and note that the phrase attributed to Neire comes from *Bretha Nemed Toísech* as well: *CIH* 2220.28–29.

118. *UR* §3 (pp. 102–3, with note on p. 132) = *CIH* 1114.29–31 (*BND* in *Eriu* XIII, 18.4–9); and *UR* §18 (pp. 112–13) = *BNT* in *CIH* 2222.15.

119. Or forty-seven, depending on whether tract 2a is taken as separate: Breatnach, "Original Extent," 37; Breatnach, *Companion*, 287–88.

120. *CIH* 2108.30. The tract is incomplete, and the *Fénechas* quotation itself is either not extant or, if 2108.37ff. is the quotation in question, written in textbook prose rather than *Fénechas* style.

121. The issue of whether *Córus Aithni* ought properly to be considered a *Senchas Már* tract is open to challenge on other grounds as well. Breatnach's reasons for concluding that it did belong to the *Senchas Már* are the following: 1) the tract appears bundled together with other tract-fragments, many (though not all) of which are referred to in a list of texts, many (though not all) of which belong to the *Senchas Már*; and 2) two citations from it appear in O'Davoren in close proximity to citations that can be shown to be from the *Senchas Már*. However, to take these arguments in turn: 1) deposits are not one of the items mentioned in the list of texts referred to by Breatnach, nor can all the texts in this list be shown to have been included in the *Senchas Már* in any case; and 2) although these citations from *Córus Aithni* do appear in proximity to citations from the *Senchas Már*, they are actually distant from them, grouped together on the side furthest away from the *Senchas Már* quotations with a block of citations that cannot be identified as coming from the *Senchas Már*. Breatnach makes his case in "Original Extent," 36–37, and see Breatnach, *Companion*, 308; and Ó Corráin, Breatnach, and Breen, "Laws of the Irish," 415–16.

122. *BDC* §§25–37 (pp. 36–48).

123. *BC* §§58–66 (pp. 46–55).

124. *CIH* 228.14–17 (*Di Astud Chirt 7 Dligid*); 486–89 (*C. Aicillne*); 521.13–14, 28–29; 522.16–18 (*CB*). Compare with these *CIH* 599.16–23 and 599.31–38 (*Bürgschaft*, §§79–80 and 83–84).

125. A point I intend to take up soon in a separate article. See brief discussion by Stacey, "Law and Memory."

126. *DIL, Compact Edition*, p. 299, cols. 76–77, under *fénechas*.

127. In decreasing order of frequency, with the (approximate) number of instances following after the title: *Heptads* 63; *Bretha Crólige* 32; *BFG* 23; *Do Astud Chirt 7 Dligid* 16; *Coibnes Uisci Thairidne* 10; *Di Chetharshlicht Athgabála* 7; *Recholl Breth* 6, *Córus Aithni* 4; *Di Dligiud Raith, De Brethaib Gaire, Díre* 3; *Di Thúaslucud Rudradh, Fuidir, Cáin Lánamna, Tosach Béscnai*, the *Senchas Már* status tract, *Béscnae Ráithe* 2; *Bretha Déin Chécht, CB, DT, Bandíre*, the *Senchas Már* Introduction, *Bretha im Gatta* 1; *Bechbretha, C. Aicillne, Bretha Comaithchesa, CS, Bretha for Techt Medbae, Bretha for Mac-shlechtaib, Bretha for Conshlechtaib, Bretha Creidini, Lestrai, Dúiguin, Slicht Othrusa, Bretha for Catshlechtaib, Bretha Cairdi, Muirbretha*, Tract on Marriage and Divorce, *Fidbretha, Dúilchinni, Bretha Sén Formae, Turbaid* tract 0 (many of the latter are fragmentary).

128. *CIH* 344.24–347.7.

129. *CIH* 348.10–351.19.

130. *DT* and *Tosach Bésgnai: CIH* 205.22–213.37 and 214.1–218.30, and see 910–13 and 1864–66.

131. Breatnach, *Companion*, 361–72.

132. E.g., Sencha and Bríg, Cóicthe, and Cíannacht, Fergus mac Léti: *CIH* 207.22–210.14; 215.15–17; 352.26–354.14; 406.26–407.2, and the like. Many of these are characters in leading case dramas: e.g., Cóicthe, literally "five-day period," who in *Di Chetharshlicht Athgabála* gives her name to a particular form of distraint: *CIH* 406.26–407.2; see also Binchy, "Distraint," 37. Another example is Cíannacht, cited in *DT* in order to illustrate how female *tellach* procedures differ from male *tellach* procedures: *CIH* 207.22–23. In addition to her appearances in these two *Senchas Már* tracts, Bríg is mentioned also in the "Kinship and Women" tract: 215.16. Historians have remarked on how frequently tales of this sort seem to accompany (and validate) relatively recent innovations in legal practice; interestingly, and perhaps significantly as well, both of these tracts contain more than the average amount of poetic or rhetorical language. It is worth noting as well that the other instance in which they tend to appear (in the *Senchas Már* at least) is when legal issues pertaining to women are under consideration—the categories of "pertaining to women" and "innovation in the law" may, of course, overlap with one another.

133. *CIH* 209.22–23. In another gloss, she is identified as Sencha's mother: Binchy, "Distraint," 37, and see Breatnach, *Companion*, 175. On Sencha himself, see Breatnach, *Companion*, 367; and Hollo, "Do My Bidding."

134. Breatnach, "Original Extent," 40–41.

135. To those mentioned by Breatnach, "Original Extent," 40–41, ought to be added as *possible* Patrick references the glosses in *Bretha Creidini* and in *Lestrai: CIH* 1491.15–16 and 1571.28 respectively. Both of these references occur in glosses to now only partially extant texts, so it is difficult to tell whether Patrick was mentioned also in the tract itself.

136. The fullest account of his intervention in the legal tradition outside the later "Pseudo-Historical Prologue to the *Senchas Már*," occurs in *CB* and *Do Astud Chirt 7 Dligid*, tracts of the first and second parts of the *Senchas Már* lawbook respectively.

137. *CIH* 344.24–347.7

138. *CIH* 348.10–351.28.

139. *CIH* 527–29.

140. *CIH* 2103.33; see also Breatnach, "Original Extent," 35 and 41.

141. *CIH* 226.31–33.

142. *CIH* 1977.35.

143. *CIH* 1551.8 corresponding to 1481.22–24; and see also the discussion by Breatnach, "Original Extent," 31, 40–41.

144. *CIH* 2211–32 and 1111.1–1138 (Gwynn, "Old-Irish Tract"), respectively.

145. The term is used also in its "generic" meaning of "native law"—e.g., *CIH* 1114.26–27, where it is one of the elements that exalt a poet, or the gloss on 1137.39.

146. *UR* §§3–4, and 18 (pp. 102–5, 112–13). *BNT* uses *ar-cain* in part 1 and *do-accair,* "tells, relates" in part 2: Breatnach, "First Third," §1 (pp. 8–9), and *CIH* 2213.29–31, respectively.

147. *CIH* 2213.29–31.

148. Which could, of course, have become known to the *Bretha Nemed* compiler in its oral form rather than from the *Senchas Már* directly.

149. *BND*: *CIH* 1111.12–17, with supporting poetic citations on 1111.17–25.

150. Examples of *cánai* include *Cáin Adamnáin, Cáin Domnaig, Cáin Phátraic,* and *Cáin Dar Í*—the latter of which is no longer extant.

151. For more on their sense of the past, see Stacey, "Law and Memory."

152. Athairne: *CIH* 1111.1–11; 1115.3–34; 1115.35ff.; 1117.1–10, for example (the latter has a *dúnad* structure); Neire 1119.28–32; Nin 1122.3–37; Morann 1130–38–1131.8; Senchán Torpéist 1116.11–16; Conchobar 1116.29–34; Cormac 1126.27–32. (These are just a few of the many references: this list is by no means comprehensive.)

153. Amairgen in *CIH* 1119.28, 1125.2, for example; see also Roighin (1112.8; 1113.14); Ferchertne (1113.14); and Áed Sláne (1129.35).

154. E.g., *CIH* 1111.22; 1112.6, 30, etc.

155. *UR* §4 (pp. 104–5) citing Neire, and §23 (pp. 114–15) citing Néide.

156. *CIH* 1122.3–37; 1116.29–34; and 1126.27–32, respectively.

157. This theme is pervasive throughout, but a particularly potent passage (attributed to Athairne) is *CIH* 1119.17–26.

158. *CIH* 1112.9.

159. *CIH* 1112.9–10, 13–23.

160. *CIH* 1130.1–37.

161. Gwynn, "An Old-Irish Tract," 3–4.

162. Breatnach, "Canon Law."

163. Breatnach, "First Third," §8 (pp. 12–13); Breatnach, *Companion,* 368–69. See p. 5 for Breatnach's discussion as to how much of the text is to be attributed to Cenn Fáelad.

164. Mac Cana, "Three Languages"; MacNeill, "Pioneer of Nations."

165. That this author drew on written sources as well is evident from its parallels with the *Hibernensis*: Breatnach, "Canon Law."

166. E.g., *CIH* 2213.34 (*A Aimirgen*); 2215.15, 36; 2216.15, 25; 2218.4; 2219.4, 16; 2220.26, 30; 2221.1 (*A Moraind a maine a mochta*).

167. *CIH* 2221.8–9; and 2221.12, 16, 17; 2222.33, 34, 38, 39; 2223.18; 2224.1, 29; 2225.12, 25, 31; 2226.2, 25; 2227.3, 33; 2228.18, 20, 34, 35; 2229.4, 5, 9–10, 11, 37, 38; 2230.6; 2231.8, 10, 37; 2232.23, 32 (*Mo Nere Nuallgnaith*); 2232.24 (*A Moruind a mainich i mochta*).

168. E.g., *CIH* 2215.15–35 (= *UR* pp. 28–31) in part two; 2222.12–14, 20–21, 28–30 in part three. On memorization within the legal context, see Stacey, "Law and Memory."

169. See Chapter 2 above.

170. *AM* §§33–52 (pp. 12–15).

171. In *UB*: *CIH* 1616.37–1617.3; and 1593.15.

172. *CIH* 2225.7–8 (which then adds on *firbrithem co firbrethuib,* "a true judge with true judgments," as though it ought also to be considered a member of the same group); Breatnach, "First Third," §1 (pp. 8–9). *UB* substitutes *Feine* for *ecnae*: *CIH* 1593.4–6.

173. See references in Breatnach's discussion, "First Third," 25–26, and *CIH* 1123.34–39, and cf. 1118.21.

174. The issue is infinitely complicated in ways that cannot be gone into here. One open question is that of the position of the *éices,* "learned scholar, poet," on which see Charles-Edwards, "Uses of Literacy," 62–86; and *CIH* 2225.22, where *éices* seems to function as the equivalent of *fili.*

175. *UR,* 23, with translation (which I have followed, but not reproduced verbatim here) on p. 24.

176. *CIH* 2221.17–21.

177. Reading a second person subjunctive form to keep consistent with the tone of the passage.

178. Literally, "cases of ignorance." In this passage, I am reading *is* for *us,* and *fogluim* for *fodluim,* as suggested by Binchy's notes.

179. The form *arfoilge* is not clear to me, but may be either a form of a verb *fo-ligi,* literally "lies under, supports," with the conjunction *ar,* or an unattested compound *ar-fuilgi,* meaning approximately the same thing. I have taken *fircerda* as an object here, but it could also be a genitive: "the learning of a true craftsman supports."

180. *DIL,* p. 506, cols. 58–60, and see *CG* 280–82, where the text refers to the *aire coisring* giving a gage on behalf of his kindred (fine) "to king and synod and *óes cherdd* to constrain them to [their] authority." On the *óes cherdd* in this passage, see Breatnach, "On Satire," 29.

181. *CIH* 1614.20 (in reference to a judge whose expertise covers both poetry and the law of the Féni; the judge in 1614.32 is an expert in all three fields.)

182. *CIH* 1613.38–1614.4, and see discussion in Stacey, *Road to Judgment,* 127.

183. *AM* §§32–52 (pp. 10–15). Similarly, in *Uraicecht Becc,* the king's judgment is said to encompass all of the forms of judicial "testimony" associated with the leading groups in the community: church judgments are grounded in Scripture, poetic judgments in *roscada,* judgments among the *Féni* in maxims, but the judgments of rulers are based upon them all: *CIH* 1592.3–20.

184. Ó Corráin, Breatnach, and Breen, "Laws of the Irish," 386–87, n. 3.

185. *IK* XXI.29.

186. *CIH* 2226.3, 23–24, quoted again on 2232.1.

187. Ó Corráin, Breatnach, and Breen, "Laws of the Irish," 398, 393, n. 1.

188. For discussion of the Irish situation specifically, see Ó Corráin, Breatnach, and Breen, "Laws of the Irish," 386–87, n. 3, and 397–98.

189. *CG* 5–9. For a discussion of this system as it pertains to poets, see *UR,* 85–89.

190. *CIH* 530.1–3 includes the phrase *cach cind a cuindrech for a memru,* "to every lord (lit. 'head') his rights of correction over his dependents (lit. 'members')." See discussion by Ó Corráin, Breatnach, and Breen, "Laws of the Irish," 408–9. It may be significant that the phrasing of the one that follows immediately on from it in *CB* suggests a context of familial or political lordship: *CIH* 530.9–12.

191. Ó Corráin, Breatnach, and Breen, "Laws of the Irish," 394–406.

192. *UR* §6 (pp. 104–5); Ó Corráin, Breatnach, and Breen, "Laws of the Irish," 397, 400–1, and 403. The text cited on p. 403 regarding the sexual status of the "materials of a bishop" sought by Patrick from among the pupils of Dubthach seems just as likely to speak to the requirements desirable in a man destined to become a high-ranking

cleric as it is to requirements incumbent on the poetic class in general. As we shall see, there is other evidence to support the argument that this notion of poet as Levite was a common conceit of the *Bretha Nemed* school—the emphasis on purity in poets, for example, on which see discussion below. Indeed, it is noticeable (and likely not coincidental) how many of the vernacular texts cited by Ó Corráin, Breatnach, and Breen in their study of the use by native lawyers of the Old Testament come from *Bretha Nemed* texts: 386–87, 393, n. 1, 396–400, and 403, n. 4.

193. Ó Corráin, Breatnach, and Breen, "Laws of the Irish," 395, esp. n. 1.

194. Breatnach, "First Third," §§6–7 (pp. 10–11); §§12, 14 (12–15); §§20, 22 (pp. 16–19).

195. *CIH* 591.25–27, 30–31 (*Bürgschaft*, §§5–6, 8)

196. *UR* §§3, 6 (pp. 102–5), and see discussion by Ó Corráin, Breatnach, and Breen, "Laws of the Irish," 394–404. *UR* §3 cites *BND*: *CIH* 1114.32–33.

197. *CIH* 1613.17–18.

198. *CIH* 1114.26–27.

199. *CIH* 1131.2–3.

200. *CIH* 1131.33 = *UR* BN XIV, lines 15–17 (pp. 52–53).

201. See also, in part three, *CIH* 2224.6.

202. *CIH* 2221.12–16.

203. *CIH* 2224.3–5, which is part of a larger section on purity and learning: 2224.1–28.

204. *CIH* 2224.20–22.

205. *CIH* 2224.10–11 (see notes and translation by Breatnach in *UR*, 123), and cf. *UR* §6 (pp. 104–5).

206. These references are far too numerous to enumerate, but include the following: *UR* (where detailing the differences between educated and noneducated poets is one of the main goals of the tract), §§2, 6, 8–12, 18 (pp. 102–3, 104–9 and 112–13); *AM* §23 (lines 58–59); *BND* in *CIH* 1112.9, 1114.26–27, 1116.9–10, 1118.24–25; 1123.12–14; 1132.20–21; 1136.11–12; *BNT* in *CIH* 2213.39–40, 2221.12, 17–22, 25; 2222.9, 12–14, 23, 2224.1–28.

207. *UR* §§8–12 (pp. 106–9). Excellent discussions of the emphasis on learning include Breatnach, "Caldron of Poesy," 47–52 and *UR*, 87–100.

208. *CIH* 1615.4–18.

209. Breatnach, "First Third," §24 (pp. 20–21).

210. *UR*, 42–44 (= *CIH* 1117.29–35). Poets who do not learn nor are learned from (*na fogluim nad fogluimter uad*) are not "paid in ranks": *CIH* 2224.20–21.

211. *CIH* 2221.12–30, for example.

212. *UR*, 21–23, lines 15–30, especially the phrase *certaige eolus*, in Breatnach's translation "knowledge is the proper material."

213. *CIH* 2224.3, 9–11.

214. *CIH* 2224.12–15.

215. *CIH* 2224.16–23.

216. *UR*, 98–100.

217. Breatnach, "Canon Law," and Ó Corráin, Breatnach, and Breen, "Laws of the Irish."

218. For example, *UR*, 22–24, lines 62–63.

219. For *ellach/in-loing* in *BND*, see *CIH* 1114.26, 38; 1128.3, etc.

220. *CIH* 2224.4–26.

221. Defined in some contexts as the type of poem associated specifically with the *ánruth*, a poet second in rank only to the highest grade, the *ollam*: *DIL* 474, col. 16. *Uraicecht na Ríar* makes clear that *ánruth* status entails hereditary poetic standing, extensive learning, and considerable artistic merit: *UR* §§11–12 (pp. 108–9).

222. Read *firidna* with Binchy instead of the manuscript's *for idna*.

223. *UR*, 22–24 (*BN* I).

224. *CIH* 2224.10–11; *UR* §6 (pp. 104–5).

225. Breatnach, "On Satire," 31–34 and references there.

226. *CIH* 1118.24–25, with which compare 2221.20–22. In *BNT*, this passage follows immediately on the passage cited above.

227. E.g., a lawsuit is not clarified or illuminated. *Aí* can also mean "poetic inspiration," but seems in this context to have the legal meaning of "lawsuit, legal case." I take *neble* to be *nem-féle*, "nonmodesty."

228. *CIH* 2222.31–2222.8. His presentation is already a *frithbrudh*, "refutation," and therefore by definition secondary speech. Included among the "speech" words in his presentation are: *lonn labhar, atabonnar, as-indet, gobelach, dicanar, ar-tuasi, suitheangaidh, do-can*, and *roscad*.

229. Texts and translations in this paragraph are from Breatnach, "First Third," §24 (pp. 20–21). Pages 14–15 of this same text detail the seven church grades.

230. *GEIL* 196–97 and references there.

231. *CIH* 2221.16; 1592.3–20.

232. *CIH* 2222.9.

233. *CIH* 2222.8.

234. *CIH* 1113.7.

235. For a normalized version of this text (here reproduced in the translation, which is Breatnach's), see *UR* §18 (pp. 112–13) and notes.

236. A very low rank of poet, someone not educated up to a very high standard: *UR*, 88, with n. 27.

237. Text from *CIH* 2222.13–18; the translation is Breatnach's: *UR* §18 (pp. 112–13), and p. 132, with discussion also on p. 133.

238. Binchy, "Pseudo-Historical Prologue," 19; Ó Corráin, Breatnach, and Breen, "Laws of the Irish," 391–94; *GEIL*, 197; McLeod, "Concept of Law"; McCone, "Dubthach maccu Lugair"; Carey, "Two Laws."

239. *UR*, 133, and see Stacey, "Law and Memory" on the subject of memory and composition.

240. *CIH* 2222.36–38 (Irish text cited earlier in Chapter 2).

241. *DIL*, 336, cols. 372–73; *GEIL*, 195–96; Breatnach, *Companion*, 196; Binchy, "*Féchem*," 31–32.

242. E.g. *CIH* 595.2–3 (*Bürgschaft*, §51a): *gaib fort laim fiach dam-sa huait dia laithiu airchiunn isind forus amscogeth, cen indscugud*, "take on your hand [the payment of this] debt to me by you on [such-and-such] a future day, in this place appointed for payment (*forus*) unchanged [and] without alteration." See also 595.9, 598.23, 32, 38. And see also *BNT*, *CIH* 2223.13–17, and the helpful discussion by Charles-Edwards in *Gaelic Lawyer*, 55.

243. *C. Adam.*, §§ 28, 34, 36, 39–41, 48 (pp. 14–32); MacAirt, *Annals of Ulster*, A.D. 782, recte 783 (p. 238); MacAirt, *Annals of Ulster*, A.D. 813, recte 814 (p. 270); *EICL* §43 (p. 176); §57 (p. 194).

244. See *CIH* 422.13–16.

245. *CIH* 1120.5–6.

246. *CIH* 2221.32, with Dub's refutation 2221.34–2222.8.

247. *CIH* 2228.35–36.

248. *CIH* 2221.12, 25–26.

249. *CIH* 2222.35–36.

250. Kelly, "Old-Irish Text," 95 (note to *foros*).

251. *CIH* 2215.37–39 (here *dicedal* instead of *roscada*). See also examples cited above in Chapter 2.

252. *CIH* 1590.1–1592.20.

253. E.g., *Di Chetharshlicht Athgabála, Bretha Crólige, Bretha Déin Chécht, DT.*

254. *CIH* 2223.18ff., 2226.25ff., and 2231.10ff., for example.

255. *CIH* 1122.3ff., especially 1122.27–31, and see Smith, "Advice to Doidín."

256. *IK* XXXIV.4–5 and XL.9–10, respectively.

257. *IK* books XII and XIII, XVI, and XXXV respectively.

258. "Pseudo-Historical Prologue," §11 (pp. 13, 19), with note on pp. 27–28.

259. *BDC*, §§25–37 (pp. 36–47) and *Br. Crólige* §§58–64, 66 (pp. 46–55). *Br. Crólige* §61 (pp. 48–49), is phrased as a jussive instruction and thus reads more like a judgment than does the rest.

260. "Stories from the Law-Tracts."

261. O'Daly, *Cath Maige Mucrama.*

262. Corthals, "Affiliation of Children."

263. *Esnada Tige Buchet,* lines 27–44.

264. *Triads* 12 (Cloyne), 16 (Cork), and 21 (Slane).

265. On the nature of Munster polity and its difference from polity elsewhere in Ireland, see the interesting Ph.D. dissertation done in 2002 for the University of Wales, Lampeter by Dr. David Price: "An Archaeology of Text in the Contested Landscape of Early Medieval Munster, c. 750–1167." I am grateful to the author for making his work available to me in advance of publication. Another valuable resource is Monk and Sheehan, *Early Medieval Munster.*

266. E.g., *CIH* 211.35–212.28; 356.5–9; *Br. Crólige* §§58–66 (pp. 46–55); *BDC* §§25–37 (pp. 36–47). On the difficulties of knowing what role these rhetorical passages might have played, see Charles-Edwards, *Gaelic Lawyer,* 28–37.

267. *GEIL*, 196.

268. Indeed, Corthals may even have found an example of one such instance in the (admittedly stylized) judgment of the *Immathchor.* "Affiliation of Children," §7 (p. 109, with translation 110–11 and discussion on pp. 102 and 122).

269. E.g., *CIH* 400.12–13; 466.32–33; 510.31; 530.1–26; 536.15. *Is de atá* is a phrase that almost always introduces a maxim. [A]*racain Fénechas*, by contrast, usually introduces a phrase in rhetorical language. Only occasionally (e.g., *Bürgschaft*, §§79–80, 83–84) do the two overlap, and when they do, there is often a poetic or rhetorical structure to the maxims that follow.

270. *CIH* 424.21.

271. *CIH* 358.1–4.

272. *Berrad Airechta*'s provenance is uncertain. *Córus Fíadnaise*'s style may link at least that part of the text to Munster and the *Bretha Nemed* school. However, such a connection says nothing necessarily about the rest of the text, and its similarities to *Críth Gablach* (particularly on the issue of *Fénechas*) may suggest that they originated in the same school. *Críth Gablach*'s origins are also uncertain, although as the tract mentions the *rechtge Adamnáin* by name, a northern or midlands origin does not seem improbable.

273. Breatnach, "Canon Law," particularly conclusions on 459.

274. "Pseudo-Historical Prologue," §11 (pp. 13 and 19). Note that the verb in this final clause is the preterite—*gabsat*, with perfective particle *ro.*

275. "Pseudo-Historical Prologue," 1–10.

276. Breatnach, "Canon Law," 445–57, p. 456 particularly.

277. Charles-Edwards, *Gaelic Lawyer,* 17–43.

278. Charles-Edwards, *Gaelic Lawyer,* 20–21.

279. Charles-Edwards, *Gaelic Lawyer,* 36–38.

280. See Charles-Edwards, *Gaelic Lawyer,* 39–43.

281. Ó Corráin, Breatnach, and Breen, "Laws of the Irish," 413–17.

282. Ó Corráin, Breatnach, and Breen, "Laws of the Irish," 412.

283. Charles-Edwards, "Chuch in the Early Irish Laws," 67–75.

284. Charles-Edwards, *Gaelic Lawyer*, 36–43; "Uses of Literacy."

285. Charles-Edwards, *Gaelic Lawyer*, 42.

286. Charles-Edwards, *Gaelic Lawyer*, 41.

287. Charles-Edwards, *Gaelic Lawyer*, 24.

288. On the relative dating of the two texts, see Thurneysen, "Zu den bisherigen Ausgaben." On the *Senchas Már's* relation to the *CCH*, see Charles-Edwards, "Early Irish Law"; Charles-Edwards, *Gaelic Lawyer*, 16–43; Charles-Edwards, "Construction of the *Hibernensis*," 209–37; and Charles-Edwards, "Church in the Early Irish Laws"; Stacey, *Road to Judgment*, 136–37.

289. *IK*, books XXXI-XXXIV; and LIII, respectively.

290. E.G. *IK*, books XXI.12, XXXIV.2b, and so on.

291. *IK*, book XXXIV.3.

292. *IK*, book XXXIV, especially XXXIV.6c.

293. *CIH* 1040.37–40.

294. McLeod, "Concept of Law," explores native concepts of "nature."

295. The redactor of *Bretha Crólige* acknowledges a dispute as to whether polygyny is licit—and cites the Old Testament in favor of his position that it might well be acceptable: *Br. Crólige* §57 (pp. 44–45).

296. *IK*, XLVI.11, 31 and 38.

297. *Br. Crólige* §57 (pp. 44–45).

298. Charles-Edwards, "Church in the Early Irish Laws," 71–73.

299. Hughes, *Church in Early Irish Society*, 129–30.

300. Charles-Edwards, *Gaelic Lawyer*.

Conclusion

1. *C. Adam.*, §§2–3 (pp. 2–3).

2. Wormald cites a memorable Frankish practice in which a person wishing to force his relatives to participate in paying compensation for a homicide gathers dust from the corners of their houses, throws it over his left shoulder onto his kinsmen, and then jumps a fence wearing a shirt and waving a stake in the air: *Making of English Law*, 47.

3. Pertinent studies would include (but are certainly not limited to): Schmidt-Wiegand, "Eid und Gelöbnis"; Magnou-Nortier, "Fidélité et féodalité"; Magnou-Nortier, *Foi et fidélité*; Althoff, *Spielregeln*; Koziol, *Begging Pardon and Favor*; Rosenwein, *Anger's Past*; White, *Custom, Kinship, and Gifts to Saints*; Theuws and Nelson, *Rituals of Power*; Rollo-Koster, *Medieval and Early Modern Rituals*. The literature on the ordeal is voluminous: Bartlett, *Trial by Fire and Water*; Brown, "Society and the Supernatural"; Hyams, "Trial by Ordeal." Particularly suggestive is the wide-ranging essay by Hibbitts: "Coming to Our Senses."

4. Events of this sort have generally not figured prominently in accounts of the origins of "true" drama, on which see Enders, *Origins of Medieval Drama*; and Symes, "Early Vernacular Plays."

5. Theuws and Nelson, *Rituals of Power*; Kosto, *Making Agreements*, 366; Davies, *Settlement of Disputes*, 302; Brown, *Unjust Seizure*, 223; Koziol, *Begging Pardon and Favor*, 456. An exception—and perhaps an indication that perceptions are changing—is Rollo-Koster, *Medieval and Early Modern Ritual*, the introduction to which (written by Catherine Bell) speaks openly of performance. On the other hand, it is ritual, and not performance, which takes center stage in the title of the book.

6. Geertz, *Negara*.

7. Courtemanche, "Medical Expertise," 122, and see discussion 121–23.

8. Geary, "Oblivion," 121, for example: "oral, performative, ritualized statements." See also, in Geary's "Land, Language and Memory," "ritual process" (181), "ritualized performance" (182), and "rituals" (183). Danet and Bogoch are very aware of the significance of the performative environment within which the wills they are examining had meaning; however, they also speak in terms of "ceremony " (101), "magic" (103–4), and "ritual" (105): Danet and Bogoch, "Oral Ceremony to Written Document."

9. Most revealing is the subtitle of the section in which the oath is discussed: "Poetry, Ritual, and Magic": Cheyette, *Ermengard*, 188, and see 192–94 on ritual, and 233–47 on politics and poetry.

10. Buc, *Dangers of Ritual*, 248.

11. Koziol, "Dangers of Polemic," 373–74.

12. Koziol, "Dangers of Polemic," suggests that Buc's book underestimates the historiographical sophistication of the scholars actually working in the field of "ritual studies" today. I would agree.

13. Buc intentionally alludes to the title of Koziol's final chapter, "How Does a Ritual Mean?" in subtitles within his own work: "Why Should a Ritual Mean?" and "What Will a Ritual Mean?" (*Dangers of Ritual* 67, 79).

14. Buc, *Dangers of Ritual*, 257–58.

15. Buc, *Dangers of Ritual*, 255 and 248–61.

16. Buc himself senses this, beginning and ending his book by acknowledging the "destructive" and "lachrymose" tone of what he has written—although he of course maintains the inherent value of overturning a paradigm that he regards as dangerous and misleading: Buc, *Dangers of Ritual*, viii, 248.

17. Buc, *Dangers of Ritual*, 56–87. Theutberga was the wife of the Carolingian Lothar II, who had married her out of political expediency in 855, but who vastly preferred his mistress (and mother of his bastard son Hugh) Waldrada. When the marriage produced no children, Lothar and his advisers tried everything to engineer a divorce so that Lothar could return to Waldrada, including a highly publicized ordeal in which Theutberga was forced to defend herself against charges of scandalous sexual misbehavior. The struggle over the divorce lasted until Lothar's death in 869; Hugh remained illegitimate.

18. Buc, *Dangers of Ritual*, 249–50. Buc is interestingly predisposed to believe that local ordeals would lead more naturally to consensus because of the more intimate circumstances in which they were conducted. One can imagine things working in this way; on the other hand, intimacy breeds contempt and division at least as often as it breeds consensus, so this does not seem a necessary conclusion.

19. A point made also by Koziol, "Dangers of Polemic," 375.

20. I would like to acknowledge the valuable input of University of Washington graduate students Elizabeth Campbell, Dustin Clark, Joe Creamer, and Ethan Spanier on these and other points pertaining to ritual. The example of the nap was suggested by Joe Creamer.

21. Buc underestimates Koziol on this point. The constant reinterpretation of the ritual with which he is concerned—the changes in meaning and application (and even of form) that take place across periods and venues—is one of the main subjects of *Begging Pardon and Favor*. See also Koziol's own defense of the writings of himself and other scholars: "Dangers of Polemic," 370–74.

22. Buc criticizes models like that of Geertz and followers, who use theatre as a metaphor for the static modeling of a state or society (*Repräsentation*) in the context of ritual: *Dangers of Ritual*, 227–37, and especially n. 119, and see Geertz, *Negara*.

23. G. Nagy, *Poetry as Performance*, 7–38, especially pp. 18–19.

24. Crescentius, for example, who falls afoul of Otto III: Koziol, *Begging Pardon and Favor*, 233.

25. Cheyette, *Ermengard*, 188–89, with discussion on pages 187–94 and 204–6.

26. Kosto, *Making Agreements*, 53–59, 64–74, 143–57. I would here like to express my gratitude to Professor Kosto for the helpful assistance he has given me on this chapter. The most important printed sources for these texts are outlined in Kosto, *Making Agreements*, xvi–xvii.

27. Cheyette, *Ermengard*, 190.

28. Débax distinguishes two different types of oath: *des serments féodaux* and *des serments féodo-vassaliques*: Débax, *La féodalité Languedocienne*, chaps. 3 and 4.

29. Although cf. Wright on the nature of the vernacular: references below in note 49.

30. Literally, "the respiration of the text," and "the skeletal structure of the oath." Zimmermann, "Aux origines," 146–47.

31. *Liber feudorum maior*, §713 (p. 228), undated, but assigned by the editor to the period 1102–15.

32. A point made by Kosto: "As integral elements of the ritual that created an agreement, *convenientiae* and written oaths added an additional layer of guarantee. . . . [T]he written word served alongside the spoken word and ritual gestures to make agreements—and to insure that they would be kept": Kosto, *Making Agreements*, 156–57.

33. *Liber feudorum maior*, §671 (p. 181); §720 (p. 231); §697 (pp. 210–11), for example.

34. *Liber feudorum maior*, §671 (p. 181); §684 (p. 194), for example.

35. *Liber feudorum maior*, §826 (p. 313); §827 (pp. 313–14); §713 (p. 228); §725 (p. 235); §727 (p. 237); §742 (p. 248).

36. *Liber feudorum maior*, §671 (p. 181), for example.

37. *Liber feudorum maior*, §720 (p. 231).

38. Cheyette, *Ermengard*, text and translation on p. 188.

39. *Liber feudorum maior*, §713 (p. 228).

40. *Liber feudorum maior*, §713 (p. 228).

41. *Liber feudorum maior*, §720 (p. 231).

42. *Liber feudorum maior*, §671 (p. 181).

43. *Liber feudorum maior*, §720 (p. 231); §697 (pp. 210–11); §698 (pp. 211–12), etc.

44. As is evident from *CIH* 595.2–14 = *Bürgschaft*, §51a–c (p. 15).

45. Cheyette, *Ermengard*, 191.

46. On which see Hexter, *Equivocal Oaths*.

47. Débax, *La féodalité Languedocienne*, 134–35.

48. Schmidt-Wiegand, "Eid und Gelöbnis," 62–68; Magnou-Nortier, "Fidélité et féodalité"; Magnou-Nortier, *Foi et fidélité*.

49. The sources vary in this respect: some are all Latin, some all vernacular, and some mixed. Roger Wright has argued for a very different understanding of the relationship between Latin and the vernacular in these crucial centuries. If he is correct, what we know as Latin was, until the Carolingian period, actually the written form of the spoken vernacular language, which, though originating in Latin, had subsequently evolved away from it. In his view, Latin and Romance did not emerge as languages separate from one another until after the pronunciation reforms initiated by the Carolingians, which necessitated the development of a new way of writing the language as it had evolved. For a variety of reasons, this development came late to Spain: Wright, *Late Latin and Early Romance*; Wright, *Early Ibero-Romance*; Wright, *Latin and the Romance Languages*. If this is correct, the codeswitching visible

in these texts is more apparent than real. On the other hand, Wright's views are controversial, and have been challenged by many recent scholars: Kosto, *Making Agreements*, 152–54; Banniard, *Viva Voce*, 506–7.

50. McKitterick, "Latin and Romance"; Nelson, "Public *Histories*"; Danet and Bogoch, "Oral Ceremony to Written Document," 104; Wright, *Late Latin*, 144; Geary, "Land, Language and Memory"; Geary, "Oblivion." In Ireland, codeswitching between the vernacular and Latin is found not only in the legal sources (on which see Ó Corráin, Breatnach, and Breen, "Laws of the Irish"), but in other texts and genres as well (for example, the saint's life *Bethu Brígte*).

51. Koziol, *Begging Pardon and Favor*, 57–58 and, on the rhetorical structures of the oath, see Débax, *La féodalité Languedocienne*, chapters 2–4.

52. "N'oublions pas que le serment est un acte essentiellement oral et qu'il a laissé comme tel ses traces dans la charte écrite à laquelle il a donné naissance, fait qui rend compte d'une part de la langue hybride en laquelle nous le trouvons rédigé . . ." (Magnou-Nortier, "Fidélité et féodalité," 463). The reference to "le style oral" is to be found on p. 468, and see her discussion of these issues on pp. 463–68.

53. Brunel, "Les premiers exemples," 361–62.

54. Zimmermann, "Aux origines," 145–48.

55. Kosto, *Making Agreements*, 154–57; Zimmermann, "Aux origines," 143–44.

56. E.g., *Liber feudorum maior*, §713 (p. 228); §715 (p. 229); §826 (p. 313); etc., and see Kosto, *Making Agreements*, 155–57.

57. Geary, "Oblivion," 116, 121–22; Geary, "Land, Language and Memory," 173–74.

58. "And indeed, the oaths were formulaic in the extreme, even for an age and region in which all documents seem to be largely constructed from scribal boilerplate . . ." (Cheyette, *Ermengard*, 191); and see Kosto, *Making Agreements*, 155.

59. G. Nagy, *Poetry as Performance*, 28.

60. Cheyette, *Ermengard*, 193.

61. Débax, *La féodalité Languedocienne*, 134–35; Kosto, *Making Agreements*, 150–51.

62. Cheyette, *Ermengard*, 188–89.

63. Carruthers, *Book of Memory*, 8–10, 19–26; and see Stacey, "Law and Memory," 53–55.

64. Aurell, *La vielle et l'épée*.

65. Aurell, *La vielle et l'épée*, 278–84.

66. Aurell, *La vielle et l'épée*, 119–29.

67. Aurell, *La vielle et l'épée*, 65–94.

68. Cheyette, *Ermengard*, 232.

69. Cheyette, *Ermengard*, 242–45.

70. Aurell, *La vielle et l'épée*, 40–58.

71. Aurell, *La vielle et l'épée*, 40–58. See also Kendrick, "Jongleur as Propagandist."

72. Kosto, *Making Agreements*, 65–67, 151–57.

73. See discussion by McKitterick, "Latin and Romance," 138–39.

74. McKitterick, "Latin and Romance," 143. She does concede, however, that "given the familiarity of the Carolingians with oath-taking, it may not have differed all that much in content."

75. McKitterick, "Latin and Romance," 139.

76. Nelson, "Public *Histories*," 208–11.

77. Schmidt-Wiegand, "Eid und Gelöbnis," 62–68.

78. Kosto, *Making Agreements*, 156, especially n. 161

79. *Annales Fuldenses*, year 876.

80. I owe this suggestion to Patrick Geary, whose very kind assistance I wish to acknowledge here.

81. McKitterick, "Latin and Romance," 143.

82. Nelson, "Public *Histories*," 210.

83. Lauer, Nithard's *Histoire des fils de Louis le Pieux*, §3.5 (pp. 102–8).

84. Loyn and Percival, *Reign of Charlemagne*, 36.

85. Scholz, with Rogers, *Carolingian Chronicles*, 162. Note that Scholz's translation omits the mention of Charles's name in Louis's oath that appears in the original, and adds a mention of Louis's name in Charles's oath where it does not appear in the original, in order to make the two oaths look like they are saying exactly the same thing.

86. I am indebted to Professors Stephen Jaeger, Adam Kosto, Patrick Geary, and Eve Sweetser for valuable comments and criticisms on matters pertaining to the translation of these oaths.

87. Two other (though to my mind considerably less likely) possibilities must be acknowledged. If McKitterick is right about this being an account largely constructed by Nithard, then it is conceivable that the deceit could have originated with him and been perpetuated in his own personal interests as a player in Carolingian aristocratic politics. It is even possible that the true referent here is the politics of a later date. The sole manuscript of Nithard's history dates to the late tenth century; technically speaking, the excision of Louis's name (had it ever been included in Nithard's account in the first place) could have happened at any point after Nithard first wrote down his account. See on this dating, Nelson, "Public *Histories*," 195–96, n. 3, which puts forward the case for Lauer's dating the manuscript to the late ninth century being a misprint.

88. Bjork, "Speech as Gift."

89. As Bjork points out, "gift" in the Germanic languages has the ominous dual meaning of "gift" and "poison": Bjork, "Speech as Gift," 995. The Irish too saw things in this way. A prominent etymology for the word *fili*, "poet," links it both to *fí*, "poison, venom" to *lí*, "beauty," because the words poets produce both wound and exalt: *DIL* p. 303, col. 107.

Bibliography

PRIMARY SOURCES (INCLUDING SOURCES IN TRANSLATION)

Adomnan's Life of Columba. Ed. A. O. Anderson and M. O. Anderson. London: Thomas Nelson and Sons, 1961.

"Advice to a Prince." Ed. Tadhg O'Donoghue. *Ériu* 9 (1921–23): 43–54.

"The Advice to Doidin." Ed. Roland M. Smith. *Ériu* 11 (1932): 66–85.

Aibidil Luigne maic Éremóin. See "The Alphabet of Cuigne mac Emoin."

"*Aimirgein Glúngel Tuir Tend*: A Middle-Irish Poem on the Authors and Laws of Ireland." Ed. Peter Smith. *Peritia* 8 (1994): 120–50.

"The Alphabet of Cuigne mac Emoin." Ed. Roland Smith. *ZCP* 17 (1928): 45–72.

Annales Fuldenses. Ed. F. Kurze. *Monumenta Germaniae Historica. Scriptores rerum Germanicarum in usum scholarum separatim editi.* Hannover: Hahnsche Buchhandlung, 1891.

The Annals of Ulster (to A.D. 1131). Ed. Seán MacAirt and Gearóid MacNiocaill. Dublin: DIAS, 1983.

Audacht Morainn. Ed. Fergus Kelly. Dublin: DIAS, 1976.

Auraicept na n-Éces: "The Scholars' Primer." Ed. George Calder. Edinburgh: J. Grant, 1917.

"Aus dem irischen Recht I–V." Ed. R. Thurneysen. *ZCP* 14 (1923): 335–94; *ZCP* 15 (1925): 238–96, 302–76; *ZCP* 16 (1927): 167–230; *ZCP* 18 (1930): 353–408.

Bechbretha: An Old Irish Law-tract on Bee-keeping. Ed. T. M. Charles-Edwards and Fergus Kelly. Early Irish Law Series, vol. I. Dublin: DIAS, 1983.

Berrad Airechta. See *Die Bürgschaft im irischen Recht.*

Bethu Brigte. Ed. Donncha Ó hAodha. Dublin: DIAS, 1978.

Bethu Phátraic: The Tripartite Life of Patrick. Ed. Kathleen Mulchrone. Dublin: Royal Irish Academy, 1939.

Bretha Crólige. Ed. D. A. Binchy. *Ériu* 12 (1934): 1–77.

Bretha Déin Chécht. Ed. D. A. Binchy. *Ériu* 20 (1966): 1–66.

Bretha Nemed. See "An Old-Irish Tract on the Privileges and Responsibilities of Poets"; "The Advice to Doidin"; and "The First Third of *Bretha Nemed Toísech.*"

Bríathra Flainn Fhína maic Ossu. See *Old Irish Wisdom Attributed to Aldfrith of Northumbria.*

Die Bürgschaft im irischen Recht. Ed. Rudolf Thurneysen. *Abhandlungen der preussischen Akademie der Wissenschaften* 2. Phil.-Hist. Klasse. Jahrgang 1928. Berlin: Verlag der preussischen Akademie der Wissenschaften, 1928. *Berrad Airechta* translated by Robin Chapman Stacey in "*Berrad Airechta*: An Old Irish Tract on Suretyship." In *Lawyers and Laymen: Studies in the History of Law Presented to Dafydd Jenkins on His*

Seventy-fifth Birthday, edited by T. M. Charles-Edwards, Morfydd Owen, and Dafydd Walters, 210–33. Cardiff: University of Wales Press, 1986.

Caesar. *Seven Commentaries on The Gallic War with an Eighth Commentary by Aulus Hirtius.* Trans. Carolyn Hammond. Oxford and New York: Oxford University Press, 1996.

Cáin Adamnáin: An Old-Irish Treatise on the Law of Adamnán. Ed. Kuno Meyer. *Anecdota Oxoniensia.* Medieval and Modern Series 12. Oxford: Clarendon Press, 1905. Translated by Gilbert Márkus OP as *Adomnán's "Law of the Innocents."* Glasgow: Blackfriars Books, 1997. Newly translated by Máirín Ní Dhonnchadha in *Adomnán at Birr, AD 697: Essays in Commemoration of the Law of the Innocents.* Ed. Thomas O'Loughlin, 53–68. Dublin: Four Courts, 2001.

Cáin Aicillne. Ed. R. Thurneysen. "Aus dem irischen Recht I. Das Unfrei-Lehen." *ZCP* 14 (1923): 336–94.

Cáin Domnaig. Ed. Vernam Hull. *Ériu* 20 (1966): 151–77.

"*Cáin Domnaig*: I. The Epistle Concerning Sunday." Ed. J. G. O'Keeffe. *Ériu* 2 (1905) 189–214.

Cáin Éimíne Báin. Ed. Erich Poppe. *Celtica* 18 (1986): 35–52.

Cáin Lánamna. Ed. R. Thurneysen. In *Studies in Early Irish Law*, edited by D. A. Binchy, 1–80. Dublin: Royal Irish Academy, 1936.

Cáin Sóerraith. Ed. R. Thurneysen. "Aus dem irischen Recht II. Das Frei-Lehen." *ZCP* 15 (1925): 238–60.

"The Caldron of Poesy." Ed. Liam Breatnach. *Ériu* 32 (1981): 45–93.

Carolingian Chronicles: Royal Frankish Annals and Nithard's Histories. Trans. Bernhard Walter Scholz, with Barbara Rogers. Ann Arbor: University of Michigan Press, 1972.

Cath Maige Mucrama: The Battle of Mag Mucrama. Ed. Máirín Ó Daly. Irish Texts Society, vol. 50. Dublin: Irish Texts Society, 1975.

The Celtic Poets: Songs and Tales from Early Ireland and Wales. Trans. Patrick Ford. Belmont, Mass.: Ford and Bailie, 1999.

Coibnes Uisci Thairidne. Ed. D. A. Binchy. *Ériu* 17 (1955): 52–85.

Collectio Canonum Hibernensis. See *Die irische Kanonensammlung.*

Cóic Conara Fugill: Die fünf Wege zum Urteil. Ed. R. Thurneysen. *Abhandlungen der preussischen Akademie der Wissenschaften* 7. Phil.-Hist. Klasse. Jahrgang 1925. Berlin: Verlag der preussischen Akademie der Wissenschaften, 1926.

Corpus Genealogiarum Hiberniae. Ed. M. A. O'Brien. Vol. I. Dublin: DIAS, 1962; reprinted, 1976.

Corpus Iuris Hibernici. Ed. Daniel A. Binchy. 6 vols. Dublin: DIAS, 1978.

Councils and Ecclesiastical Documents Relating to Great Britain and Ireland. Ed. A. W. Haddan and W. Stubbs. 3 vols. 1869–78. Reprint, Oxford: Clarendon Press, 1965.

Críth Gablach. Ed. Daniel Binchy. Mediaeval and Modern Irish Series, vol. II. 1941. Reprint, Dublin: DIAS, 1979. Translated by Eoin MacNeill in "Ancient Irish Law: the Law of Status or Franchise." *Proceedings of the Royal Irish Academy* 36 C (1923): 265–306.

"Cummian's Letter '*De controversia paschali*' Together with a Related Irish Computistical Tract '*De ratione computandi.*'" Ed. Maura Walsh and Dáibhí Ó Cróinín. Toronto: University of Toronto Press, 1988.

Di Astud Chor. See *Early Irish Contract Law.*

"*Di Ércib Fola.*" Ed. Neil McLeod. *Ériu* 52 (2002): 123–216.

Díre. See *Irisches Recht*, I. Ed. R. Thurneysen, 1–37.

Early Irish Contract Law. Ed. Neil McLeod. Sydney, Australia: Centre for Celtic Studies, University of Sydney, 1992.

Early Irish Myths and Sagas. Trans. Jeffrey Gantz. Harmondsworth: Penguin, 1981.

Early Irish Verse. Trans. R. Lehmann. Austin: University of Texas Press, 1982.

"An Edition of the Pseudo-Historical Prologue to the *Senchas Már.*" Ed. John Carey. *Ériu* 45 (1994): 1–32.

Esnada Tige Buchet. Ed. David Greene. 1955. Reprint, Dublin: DIAS, 1975.

"Das Fest des Bricriu und die Verbannung der Mac Duil Dermait." In *Irische Texte* II, i, edited by E. Windisch, 164–217. Leipzig: S. Hirzel, 1884.

Fingal Rónáin and Other Stories. Ed. David Greene. Medieval and Modern Irish Series XVI. Dublin: DIAS, 1955.

"The First Third of *Bretha Nemed Toísech.*" Ed. Liam Breatnach. *Ériu* 40 (1989): 1–40.

Fled Bricrend. Ed. George Henderson. Dublin: Irish Texts Society, 1899. And see "Das Fest des Bricriu." Trans. Gantz, *Early Irish Myths and Sagas,* 219–55.

Die Gesetze der Langobarden. Ed. Franz Beyerle. Weimar: Hahnsche Buchhandlung, 1947.

Gúbretha Caratniad. Ed. R. Thurneysen. "Aus dem irischen Recht III. Die falschen Urteilssprüche Caratnia's." *ZCP* 15 (1925): 302–70.

Histoire des fils de Louis le Pieux. Ed. Philippe Lauer. Paris: H. Campion, 1926.

"*Imacallam in dá Thuarad.*" Ed. Whitley Stokes. *Revue Celtique* 26 (1905): 4–64.

Immathchor nAilella 7 Airt. In "Affiliation of Children: *Immathchor nAilella 7 Airt.*" Ed. Johan Corthals. *Peritia* 9 (1995): 92–124.

The Instructions of King Cormac mac Airt. Ed. Kuno Meyer. Royal Irish Academy Lecture Series XV. Dublin: Hodges, Figgis, 1909.

An Introduction to Irish Syllabic Poetry of the Period 1200–1600. Ed. Eleanor Knott. Dublin: DIAS, 1974.

Die irische Kanonensammlung. Ed. H. Wasserschleben. Leipzig: Verlag Bernhard Tauchnitz, 1885.

Irisches Recht. Parts I and II. Ed. R. Thurneysen. *Abhandlungen der preussischen Akademie der Wissenschaften* 2. Phil.-Hist. Klasse. Jahrgang 1931. Berlin: Verlag der preussischen Akademie der Wissenschaften, 1931.

Irische Texte. Ed. Ernst Windisch and Whitley Stokes. 4 vols. Leipzig: S. Hirzel, 1880–1909.

"Irish Miscellanies." Ed. C. Plummer. *Revue Celtique* 6 (1883–85): 162–72.

"The Irish Ordeals, Cormac's Adventure in the Land of Promise, and the Decision as to Cormac's Sword." In *Irische Texte,* vol. III, i, edited by Whitley Stokes, 183–229. Leipzig: S. Hirzel, 1891.

The Irish Penitentials. Ed. Ludwig Bieler. *Scriptores Latini Hiberniae,* vol. 5. Dublin: DIAS, 1963; reprinted, 1975.

Lebor na Huidre: Book of the Dun Cow. Ed. R. I. Best and Osborn Bergin. Dublin: Royal Irish Academy, 1929.

Leges Burgundionum. Ed. R. de Salis. *MGH, Legum* Sectio I. *Leges Nationum Germanicarum,* vol. 2, part 1. 1892. Reprint, Hannover: Hahnsche Buchhandlung, 1973. Translated by Katherine Drew in *The Burgundian Code.* 1949. Reprint, Philadelphia: University of Pennsylvania Press, 1972.

Lex Salica. Ed. K. A. Eckhardt. *MGH, Legum* Sectio I. *Leges Nationum Germanicarum,* vol. 4, part 2. Hannover: Hahnsche Buchhandlung, 1969. Translated by T. J. Rivers in *Laws of the Salian and Ripuarian Franks.* New York: AMS Press, 1986.

Liber feudorum maior: Cartulario real que se conserva en el Archivo de la Corona de Aragón. Ed. Francisco Miquel Rosell. 2 vols. Barcelona: Consejo Superior de Investigaciones Cientícas Sección de estudios medievales de Barcelona, 1945–47.

Longes mac n-Uislenn: The Exile of the Sons of Uisliu. Ed. Vernam Hull. New York: Modern Language Association of America, 1949. Translated by Gantz, *Early Irish Myths and Sagas,* 256–67.

Medieval Handbooks of Penance: A Translation of the Principal Libri Poenitentiales and Selections from Related Documents. Ed. J. T. McNeill and Helena Gamer. New York: Columbia University Press, 1938; reprint, Octagon Books, 1979.

Medieval Irish Lyrics Selected and Translated with The Irish Bardic Poet. Ed. James Carney. First published separately Dublin: Dolmen Press, 1967. New edition in one volume, Dublin, 1985.

"*Mellbretha.*" Ed. D. A. Binchy. *Celtica* 8 (1968): 144–54.

Mesca Ulad. Ed. J. Carmichael Watson. Dublin: DIAS, 1967. Trans. Gantz, *Early Irish Myths and Sagas,* 188–218.

"Mittelirische Verslehren." Ed. R. Thurneysen. In *Irische Texte,* ed. Stokes and Windisch, vol. III, i: 1–182.

"An Old-Irish Tract on Court Procedure." Ed. Fergus Kelly. *Peritia* 5 (1986): 74–106.

"An Old-Irish Tract on the Privileges and Responsibilities of Poets." Ed. E. J. Gwynn. *Ériu* 13 (1942): 1–60, 220–36.

Old Irish Wisdom Attributed to Aldfrith of Northumbria: An Edition of Bríathra Flainn Fhína maic Ossu. Ed. Colin Ireland. Medieval and Renaissance Texts and Studies, vol. 205. Tempe: Arizona Center for Medieval and Renaissance Studies, 1999.

The Patrician Texts in the Book of Armagh. Ed. Ludwig Bieler. *Scriptores Latini Hiberniae,* vol. 10. Dublin: DIAS, 1979.

"A Poem on the Airgialla." Ed. Máirín Ó Daly. *Ériu* 16 (1952): 179–88.

The Poems of Blathmac son of Cú Brettan Together with the Irish Gospel of Thomas and a Poem on the Virgin Mary. Ed. James Carney. Irish Texts Society, vol. 47. Dublin: Irish Texts Society by the Educational Company of Ireland, 1964.

The Poetry of Llywarch Hen: Introduction, Text, and Translation. Ed. Patrick Ford. Berkeley and Los Angeles: University of California Press, 1974.

"Pseudo-Historical Prologue to the *Senchas Már.*" See "An Edition of the Pseudo-Historical Prologue to the *Senchas Már.*"

The Reign of Charlemagne: Documents on Carolingian Government and Administration. Ed. J. R. Loyn and J. Percival. London: Edward Arnold, 1975.

Ríagail Phátraic. Ed. J. G. O'Keeffe. "The Rule of Patrick." *Ériu* 1 (1904): 216–24.

"The Saga of Fergus mac Léti." Ed. D. A. Binchy. *Ériu* 16 (1952): 33–48.

Sanas Cormaic: An Old-Irish Glossary. Ed. Kuno Meyer. *Anecdota from Irish Manuscripts* 4 (1912): 1–128.

Scél na Fír Flatha, Echtra Cormaic i Tír Tairngiri ocus Ceart Claidib Cormaic. See "The Irish Ordeals, Cormac's Adventure in the Land of Promise, and the Decision as to Cormac's Sword."

Scéla Mosauluim. See *Cath Maige Mucrama.*

Scéla Mucce Meic Dathó. Ed. Rudolf Thurneysen. Dublin: DIAS, 1975. Trans. Gantz, *Early Irish Myths and Sagas,* 179–87.

"*Slicht Libair Dromma Snechta inso.*" See *Lebor na Huidre: Book of the Dun Cow,* 244–45.

Select English Historical Documents of the Ninth and Tenth Centuries. Ed. F. E. Harmer. Cambridge: Cambridge University Press, 1914.

"The *Senbríathra Fíthail* and Related Texts." Ed. Roland Smith. *Revue Celtique* 45 (1928): 1–92.

Silva Gadelica: A Collection of Tales in Irish. Ed. Standish Hayes O'Grady. 2 vols. London: William and Norgate, 1892.

"Stories from the Law Tracts." Ed. Myles Dillon. *Ériu* 11 (1932): 42–65.

Táin Bó Cúailnge, Recension I. Ed. Cecile O'Rahilly. Dublin: DIAS, 1976.

Táin Bó Cúalnge from the Book of Leinster. Ed. Cecile O'Rahilly. Dublin: DIAS, 1970.

Tales of the Elders of Ireland. Ed. Ann Dooley and Harry Roe. Oxford: Oxford University Press, 1999.

Tecosca Cormaic. See *The Instructions of King Cormac mac Airt.*

"A Text on the Forms of Distraint." Ed. D. A. Binchy. *Celtica* 10 (1973): 72–86.

Togail Bruidne Da Derga. Ed. Eleanor Knott. Mediaeval and Modern Irish Series, vol. VIII. Dublin: DIAS, 1975. Trans. Gantz, *Early Irish Myths and Sagas,* 60–106.

The Triads of Ireland. Ed. Kuno Meyer. Todd Lecture Series 13. Dublin: Hodges, Figgis, 1906.

The Tripartite Life of Patrick, with Other Documents Relating to that Saint. Ed. Whitley Stokes. 2 vols. London: HMSO, 1887. Reprint Kraus Reprints, 1965.

Uraicecht Becc. Translated by Eoin MacNeill in "Ancient Irish Law: The Law of Status or Franchise." *Proceedings of the Royal Irish Academy* 36 C (1923): 272–81.

Uraicecht na Ríar: The Poetic Grades in Early Irish Law. Ed. Liam Breatnach. Early Irish Law Series, vol. 2. Dublin: DIAS, 1987.

SECONDARY SOURCES

Abrahams, Roger. "Introductory Remarks to a Rhetorical Theory of Folklore." *Journal of American Folklore* 81 (1968): 143–58.

Ahqvist, Anders. "Remarks on the Question of Dialects in Old Irish." In *Historical Dialectology, Regional and Social, Trends in Linguistics, Studies and Monographs,* edited by J. Fisiak, 23–38. Berlin: Mouton de Gruyter, 1988.

Aitchison, N. B. *Armagh and the Royal Centres in Early Medieval Ireland: Monuments, Cosmology, and the Past.* Woodbridge, Suffolk and Rochester, N.Y.: Boydell and Brewer for Cruithne Press, 1994.

———. "The Ulster Cycle: Heroic Image and Historical Reality." *Journal of Medieval History* 13 (1987): 87–116.

Althoff, Gerd. *Spielregeln der Politik im Mittelalter: Kommunikation in Frieden und Fehde.* Darmstadt: Primus, 1997.

Anhalt, Emily Katz. *Solon the Singer: Politics and Poetics.* Lanham, Md.: Rowan and Littlefield, 1993.

Ardener, Edwin. *Social Anthropology and Language.* London: Tavistock, 1971.

Aurell, Martin. *La vielle et l'épée: Troubadours et politique en Provence au XIIIe siècle.* Paris: Editions Aubier Montaigne, 1989.

Austin, J. L. *How to Do Things with Words.* 2nd ed. edited by J. O. Urmson and Marina Sbisà. Cambridge, Mass.: Harvard University Press, 1975.

Babcock, Barbara. "The Story in the Story: Metanarration in Folk Narrative." In Bauman, *Verbal Art as Performance,* 61–79.

Bakhtin, Mikhail. *Rabelais and His World.* Trans. Helen Iswolsky. Bloomington: Indiana University Press, 1984.

Bannerman, John. *Studies in the History of Dalriada.* Edinburgh: Scottish Academic Press, 1974.

Banniard, Michel. *Viva Voce: Communication écrite et communication orale du IVe au IXe siècle en Occident latin.* Paris: Institute des Études Augustiniennes, 1992.

Barba, Eugenio, and N. Savarese, eds. *The Dictionary of Theatre Anthropology: The Secret Art of the Performer.* Translated by Richard Fowler. London: Published for the Centre for Performance Research by Routledge, 1991.

Bartlett, Robert. "Mortal Enmities: The Legal Aspect of Hostility in the Middle Ages." Lecture presented to the symposium "Courts, Customs and Canons: Law in the Middle Ages," held at the University of Victoria on February 15–16, 1990.

———. *Trial by Fire and Water: The Medieval Judicial Ordeal.* Oxford: Oxford University Press, 1986.

Bateson, Gregory, ed. *Steps to an Ecology of Mind: Collected Essays in Anthropology, Psychiatry, Evolution, and Epistemology.* Chicago: University of Chicago Press, 2000.

Bauman, R. *Story, Performance, and Event: Contextual Studies in Oral Narrative.* 1986. Reprint, Cambridge: Cambridge University Press, 1992.

———, ed. *Verbal Art as Performance*. 1977. Reprint, Prospect Heights, Ill.: Waveland Press, 1984.

Bauman, R., and Américo Paredes, eds. *Toward New Perspectives in Folklore*. Austin: American Folklore Society by the University of Texas Press, 1972.

Bauman, R., and Charles Briggs. "Poetics and Performance as Critical Perspectives on Language and Social Life." *Annual Review of Anthropology* 19 (1990): 59–88.

Bauman, R., and J. Sherzer, eds. *Explorations in the Ethnography of Speaking*. Cambridge: Cambridge University Press, 1974.

Bell, Catherine. "The Ritual Body." In *The Body as a Medium of Expression*, edited by Jonathan Benthall and Ted Polhemus, 94–117. New York: Penguin, 1975.

———. *Ritual Theory, Ritual Practice*. New York: Oxford University Press, 1992.

Ben-Amos, Dan, and Kenneth Goldstein, eds. *Folklore: Performance and Communication*. Paris: Mouton, 1975.

Bent, Margaret. "The Musical Stanzas in Martin Le Franc's *Le Champion des Dames*." In *Music and Medieval Manuscripts: Paleography and Performance*, edited by John Haines and Randall Rosenfeld, 91–127. Aldershot, Hampshire: Ashgate Publishing, 2004.

Binchy, D. A. *"Bretha Nemed."* *Ériu* 17 (1955): 4–6.

———. "Brewing in Eighth-Century Ireland." In *Studies on Early Ireland: Essays in Honour of M.V. Duignan*, edited by B. G. Scott, 3–6. Belfast: Appletree Press, 1981.

———. *Celtic and Anglo-Saxon Kingship*. Oxford: Clarendon Press, 1970.

———. "The Date and Provenance of *Uraicecht Becc*." *Ériu* 18 (1958): 44–54.

———. "Distraint in Irish Law." *Celtica* 10 (1973): 22–71.

———. *"Féchem, Fethem, Aigne."* *Celtica* 11 (1976): 18–33.

———. "Irish History and Irish Law." *Studia Hibernica* 15 (1975): 7–36; *Studia Hibernica* 16 (1976), 7–45.

———. "The Linguistic and Historical Value of the Irish Law Tracts." *Proceedings of the British Academy* 29 (1943): 195–227. Reprinted in Jenkins, *Celtic Law Papers*, 71–107.

———. "Linguistic and Legal Archaisms in the Celtic Law-Books." *Transactions of the Philological Society* (1959): 14–24. Reprinted in Jenkins, *Celtic Law Papers*, 109–20.

———. *"Mellbretha."* *Celtica* 8 (1968): 144–54.

———. "The Passing of the Old Order." In *Proceedings of the International Congress of Celtic Studies*, 119–32. Dublin, 1962.

———. "Patrick and His Biographers: Ancient and Modern." *Studia Hibernica* 2 (1962): 7–173.

———. "The Pseudo-Historical Prologue to the *Senchas Már*." *Studia Celtica* 10/11 (1975–76): 15–28.

———. "The Saga of Fergus mac Léti." *Ériu* 16 (1952): 33–48.

———. "Sick-Maintenance in Irish Law." *Ériu* 12 (1934): 78–134.

Bitel, Lisa. *Isle of the Saints: Monastic Settlement and Christian Community in Early Ireland*. Ithaca, N.Y.: Cornell University Press, 1990.

Bjork, Robert. "Speech as Gift in *Beowulf*." *Speculum* 69 (1994): 993–1022.

Blacking, John. "The Social Value of Venda Riddles." *African Studies* 20 (1961): 1–32.

Blair, John, and Richard Sharpe, eds. *Pastoral Care Before the Parish*. Leicester: Leicester University Press, 1992.

Bloch, Maurice. *Political Language and Oratory in Traditional Society*. New York: Academic Press, 1975.

Bloomfield, M.W., and Charles W. Dunn. *The Role of the Poet in Early Societies*. Cambridge: D.S. Brewer, 1989.

Boyer, Pascal. *Tradition as Truth and Communication: A Cognitive Description of Traditional Discourse*. Cambridge: Cambridge University Press, 1990.

Bracken, D. "Latin Passages in Irish Vernacular Law: Notes on Sources." *Peritia* 9 (1995): 187–96.

Brand, Paul. *The Origins of the English Legal Profession.* Oxford: Blackwells, 1992.

Breatnach, Liam. "Addenda and Corrigenda to 'The Caldron of Poesy.'" *Ériu* 35 (1984): 189–91.

———. "An Aoir sa Ré Luath." *Léachtaí Cholm Cille* 18 (1988): 11–19.

———. "Canon Law and Secular Law in Early Ireland: The Significance of *Bretha Nemed.*" *Peritia* 3 (1984): 439–59.

———. *A Companion to the Corpus Iuris Hibernici.* Dublin: Dublin Institute for Advanced Studies, 2005.

———. "The Ecclesiastical Element in the Old Irish Legal Tract *Cáin Fhuithirbe.*" *Peritia* 5 (1986): 36–52.

———. "Zur Frage der *roscada* im Irischen." In Tristam, *Metrics and Media,* 179–205.

———. "Law." In McCone and Simms, *Progress in Medieval Irish Studies,* 107–21.

———. "Lawyers in Early Ireland." In *Brehons, Serjeants and Attorneys: Studies in the History of the Irish Legal Profession,* edited by Daire Hogan and W. N. Osborough, 1–13. Blackrock, Co. Dublin: Irish Academic Press, 1990.

———. "On the Original Extent of the *Senchas Már.*" *Ériu* 47 (1996): 1–43.

———. "On Satire and the Poet's Circuit." In *Unity in Diversity: Studies in Irish and Scottish Gaelic Language, Literature and History,* edited by Cathal G. Ó Háinle and Donald E. Meek, 24–35. Dublin: School of Irish, Trinity College Dublin, 2004.

———. "Poets and Poetry." In McCone and Simms, *Progress in Medieval Irish Studies,* 65–77.

Brown, Peter. "Society and the Supernatural: A Medieval Change." In *Society and the Holy in Late Antiquity,* edited by Peter Brown, 302–32. Berkeley and Los Angeles: University of California Press, 1982.

Brown, Warren. *Unjust Seizure: Conflict, Interest, and Authority in an Early Medieval Society.* Ithaca, N.Y.: Cornell University Press, 2001.

Brundage, James. "The Medieval Advocate's Profession." *Law and History Review* 6 (1988): 439–64.

Brunel, Clovis. "Les premiers exemples de l'emploi du Provençal dans les chartes." *Romania* 48 (1922): 361–62.

Buc, Philippe. *The Dangers of Ritual: Between Early Medieval Texts and Social Scientific Theory.* Princeton, N.J.: Princeton University Press, 2001.

Burns, Thomas. "Riddling: Occasion to Act." *Journal of American Folklore* 89 (1976): 139–65.

Bynum, Caroline. "Did the Twelfth Century Discover the Individual?" In *Jesus as Mother: Studies in the Spirituality of the High Middle Ages,* 82–109. Berkeley and Los Angeles: University of California Press, 1982.

———. *Holy Feast and Holy Fast: The Religious Significance of Food to Medieval Women.* Berkeley and Los Angeles: University of California Press, 1987.

Byrne, F. J. *The Rise of the Uí Néill and the High-Kingship of Ireland.* Dublin: National University of Ireland, 1969.

———. "Tribes and Tribalism in Early Ireland." *Ériu* 21 (1971): 128–64.

Byrne, M. E. "On the Punishment of Setting Adrift." *Ériu* 11 (1932): 97–102.

Cahill, Thomas. *How the Irish Saved Civilization: The Untold Story of Ireland's Heroic Role from the Fall of Rome to the Rise of Medieval Europe.* New York: Anchor, 1995.

Carey, John. "Obscure Styles in Medieval Ireland." *Mediaevalia: A Journal of Medieval Studies* 19 (1996): 23–39.

———. "The Rhetoric of *Echtrae Chonlai.*" *CMCS* 30 (1995): 41–65.

———. "The Three Things Required of a Poet." *Ériu* 48 (1997): 41–58.

———. "The Two Laws in Dubthach's Judgment." *CMCS* 19 (Summer 1990): 1–18.

———. "The Uses of Tradition in *Serglige Con Culainn.*" In Mallory and Stockman, *Ulidia,* 77–84.

———. "Vernacular Irish Learning: Three Notes." *Éigse* 24 (1990): 39–41.

Carlson, Marvin. *Performance: A Critical Introduction.* London: Routledge, 1996.

Carney, J. *Medieval Irish Lyrics* with *The Irish Bardic Poet.* Dublin: Dolmen Press, 1985.

Carruthers, Mary. *The Book of Memory: A Study of Memory in Medieval Culture.* Cambridge: Cambridge University Press, 1990.

———. *The Craft of Thought: Meditation, Rhetoric, and the Making of Images, 400–1200.* Cambridge: Cambridge University Press, 1998.

Chadwick, Nora. *"Imbas Forasnai." Scottish Gaelic Studies* 4 (1934): 98–135.

———. *Poetry and Prophecy.* Cambridge: Cambridge University Press, 1942.

Charles-Edwards, T. M. "Boundaries in Irish Law." In *Medieval Settlement: Continuity and Change,* edited by P. H. Sawyer, 83–87. London: Edward Arnold, 1976.

———. "The Construction of the *Hibernensis.*" *Peritia* 12 (1998): 209–37.

———. "The Context and Uses of Literacy in Early Christian Ireland." In Pryce, *Literacy in Medieval Celtic Societies,* 62–86.

———. "A Contract between King and People in Early Medieval Ireland? *Críth Gablach* on Kingship." *Peritia* 8 (1994): 107–19.

———. "*Críth Gablach* and the Law of Status." *Peritia* 5 (1986): 53–73.

———. "Custom in Early Irish Law." *Recueils de la Société Jean Bodin* 52, part 2 (1990): 435–43.

———. *Early Christian Ireland.* Cambridge History of Ireland. Cambridge: Cambridge University Press, 2000.

———. *Early Irish and Welsh Kinship.* Oxford: Clarendon Press, 1993.

———. "Early Irish Law." Unpublished paper made available by courtesy of the author.

———. *The Early Mediaeval Gaelic Lawyer.* Cambridge: Cambridge University Press, 1999.

———. "Honour and Status in Some Irish and Welsh Prose Tales." *Ériu* 29 (1978): 123–41.

———. "Palladius, Prosper, and Leo the Great: Mission and Primatial Authority." In Dumville, *Saint Patrick,* 1–12.

———. "The Pastoral Role of the Church in the Early Irish Laws." In Blair and Sharpe, *Pastoral Care before the Parish,* 63–80.

———. "Review of the *Corpus Iuris Hibernici.*" *Studia Hibernica* 20 (1980): 141–62.

———. "Some Celtic Kinship Terms." *BBCS* 24 (1970–72): 105–22.

Charles-Edwards, T. M., Morfydd E. Owen, and Dafydd Walters, eds. *Lawyers and Laymen: Studies in the History of Law Presented to Professor Dafydd Jenkins.* Cardiff: University of Wales Press, 1986.

Charles-Edwards, T. M., Morfydd E. Owen, and Paul Russell, eds. *The Welsh King and His Court.* Cardiff: University of Wales Press, 2000.

Cheyette, Fredric L. *Ermengard of Narbonne and the World of the Troubadours.* Ithaca, N.Y.: Cornell University Press, 2001.

Classen, Peter. *Recht und Schrift im Mittelalter.* Sigmaringen: Thorbecke, 1977.

Clanchy, Michael. *From Memory to Written Record: England, 1066–1307.* 2nd rev. ed. Oxford: Blackwell, 1993.

Clancy, Thomas Owen. "Women Poets in Early Medieval Ireland: Stating the Case." In *"The Fragility of Her Sex"? Medieval Irish Women in Their European Context,* edited by Catherine E. Meek and M. K. Simms, 43–72. Dublin: Four Courts Press, 1996.

Clarke, H. B., Máire Ní Mhaonaigh and Raghnall Ó Floinn, eds. *Ireland and Scandinavia in the Early Viking Age.* Dublin: Four Courts Press, 1998.

Cole-Beuchat, P.-D. "Riddles in Bantu." *African Studies* 16, no. 3 (1957): 133–49.

Connerton, Paul. *How Societies Remember.* Cambridge: Cambridge University Press, 1989.

Corthals, Johan. "Early Irish *Retoirics* and Their Late Antique Background." *CMCS* 31 (Summer, 1996): 17–36.

———. "Zur Frage des mündlichen oder schriftlichen Ursprungs der Sagenroscada." In Tranter and Tristram, *Early Irish Literature*, 201–20.

———. "The *retoiric* in Aided Chonchobuir." *Ériu* 40 (1989): 41–59.

Courtemanche, A. "The Judge, the Doctor and the Poisoner: Medical Expertise in Manosquin Judicial Rituals at the End of the Fourteenth Century." In Rollo-Koster, *Medieval and Early Modern Ritual*, 105–26.

Danet, Brenda, and Bryna Bogoch. "From Oral Ceremony to Written Document: The Transitional Language of Anglo-Saxon Wills." *Language and Communication* 12, no. 2 (1992): 95–122.

D'Arbois de Jubainville, Honoré. "Études sur le droit celtique." In *Cours de littérature celtique.* Vols. 7 and 8. Paris, 1895.

Davies, Luned Mair. "The Biblical Text of the *Collectio Canonum Hibernensis*." In Ní Chatháin and Richter, *Ireland and Europe in the Early Middle Ages: Learning and Literature*, 17–41.

———. "Isidorian Texts and the *Hibernensis*." *Peritia* 11 (1997): 207–49.

———. "The 'Mouth of Gold': Gregorian Texts in the *Collectio Canonum Hibernensis*." In Ní Chatháin and Richter, *Ireland and Europe in the Early Middle Ages: Texts and Transmission*, 249–67.

———. "*Statuta Ecclesiae Antiqua* and the Gallic Councils in the *Hibernensis*." *Peritia* 14 (2000): 85–110.

Davies, Wendy. "The Latin Charter-Tradition in Western Britain, Brittany and Ireland in the Early Mediaeval Period." In *Ireland in Early Mediaeval Europe: Studies in Memory of Kathleen Hughes*, edited by Dorothy Whitelock, 258–80. Cambridge: Cambridge University Press, 1982.

———. *Small Worlds: The Village Community in Early Medieval Brittany.* Berkeley and Los Angeles: University of California Press, 1988.

Davies, Wendy, and Paul Fouracre, eds. *Property and Power in the Early Middle Ages.* Cambridge: Cambridge University Press, 1995.

———, eds. *The Settlement of Disputes in Early Medieval Europe.* Cambridge: Cambridge University Press, 1986.

Débax, Hélène. *La féodalité Languedocienne—Xieme–XIIeme siècles: Serments, hommages et fiefs dans le Languedoc des Trencavel.* Toulouse: Presses universitaires du Mirail, 2003.

(Contributions to A) Dictionary of the Irish Language. Dublin: Royal Irish Academy, 1913–76. Compact edition, 1983.

Dillon, Myles. "The Archaism of Early Irish Tradition." *Proceedings of the British Academy* 33 (1947): 245–64.

Dooley, Ann, and Harry Roe, eds. *Tales of the Elders of Ireland.* Oxford: Oxford University Press, 1999.

Duden, Barbara. "A Repertory of Body History." In *Fragments for a History of the Human Body*, edited by Michael Feher, 470–578. New York: Zone, 1989.

Dumville, David. "Ireland, Brittany and England: Transmission and Use of the *Collectio Canonum Hibernensis*." In *Irlande et Bretagne, vingt siècles d'histoire: Actes du colloque de Rennes (29–31 mars 1993)*, edited by Catherine Laurent and Helen Davis, 85–95. Rennes, 1994.

———. Review of Dáibhi Ó Cróinín's *Early Medieval Ireland, 400–1200. Times Literary Supplement*, January 3, 1997: 29.

———. "Two Troublesome Abbots." *Celtica* 21 (1990): 146–52.

Dumville, David, et al., ed. *Saint Patrick, A.D. 493–1993*. Woodbridge: Boydell and Brewer, 1993.

Edel, Doris. "Die inselkeltische Erzähltradition zwischen Mündlichkeit und Schriftlichkeit." In Tranter and Tristram, *Early Irish Literature*, 99–124.

———. "Stability and Fluidity in the Transmission of Narrative Texts: The Delineation of Characters in *Táin Bó Cúailnge: Texts and Transmission*." In Ní Chatháin and Richter, *Ireland and Europe in the Early Middle Ages*, 313–25.

Eliade, Mircea. *Shamanism: Archaic Techniques of Ecstasy*. Trans. Willard Trask. Princeton, N.J.: Princeton University Press, 1964.

Elliott, R. *The Power of Satire: Magic, Ritual, Art*. Princeton, N.J.: Princeton University Press, 1960.

Enders, Jody. *Rhetoric and the Origins of Medieval Drama*. Ithaca, N.Y.: Cornell University Press, 1992.

Etchingham, Colmán. *Church Organisation in Ireland, AD 650 to 1000*. 1999. Reprint, Naas, Co. Kildare: Laigin Publications, 2002.

———. "The Early Irish Church: Some Observations on Pastoral Care and Dues." *Ériu* 42 (1991): 99–118.

Feher, Michael, with R. Naddaff and N. Tazi, eds. *Fragments for a History of the Human Body*. New York: Zone, 1989.

Fentress, James, and Chris Wickham. *Social Memory*. Oxford: Blackwells, 1992.

Fichtenau, Heinrich. *Living in the Tenth Century: Mentalities and Social Orders*. Chicago: University of Chicago Press, 1991.

Findon, Joanne. *A Woman's Words: Emer and Female Speech in the Ulster Cycle*. Toronto: University of Toronto Press, 1997.

———. "A Woman's Words: Emer Versus Cú Chulainn in *Aided Óenfir Aífe*." In Mallory, *Ulidia*, 139–48.

Finnegan, Ruth. *Literacy and Orality: Studies in the Technology of Communication*. Oxford: Blackwell, 1988.

———. *Oral Poetry: Its Nature, Significance and Social Context*. Bloomington: Indiana University Press, 1992.

Foley, John Miles. *The Singer of Tales in Performance*. Bloomington: University of Indiana Press, 1995.

———. *The Theory of Oral Composition: History and Methodology*. Bloomington: University of Indiana Press, 1988.

Ford, Patrick. "The Blind, the Dumb, and the Ugly: Aspects of Poets and Their Craft in Early Ireland and Wales." *CMCS* 19 (1990): 27–40.

Geary, Patrick. "Humiliation of Saints." In *Saints and Their Cults: Studies in Religious Sociology, Folklore and History*, edited by Stephen Wilson, 123–40. 1983. Reprint, Cambridge: Cambridge University Press, 1987.

———. "Land, Language and Memory in Europe, 700–1100." *Transactions of the Royal Historical Society*, 6th ser., 9 (1999): 169–84.

———. "Oblivion between Orality and Textuality in the Tenth Century." In *Medieval Concepts of the Past: Ritual, Memory, Historiography*, edited by Gerd Althoff, Johannes Fried, and Patrick Geary, 111–22. Cambridge: Cambridge University Press, 2002.

———. *Phantoms of Remembrance: Memory and Oblivion at the End of the First Millenium*. Princeton, N.J.: Princeton University Press, 1994.

Geertz, Clifford. "Blurred Genres." In *Local Knowledge: Further Essays in Interpretive Anthropology*, edited by Clifford Geertz, 19–35. Stanford, Calif.: Stanford University Press, 1983.

———. *Negara: The Theatre State in Nineteenth-Century Bali*. Princeton, N.J.: Princeton University Press, 1980.

Gerriets, Marilyn. "The King as Judge in Early Ireland." *Celtica* 20 (1988): 29–52.
———. "Theft, Penitentials and the Compilation of the Early Irish Laws." *Celtica* 22 (1991): 18–32.
Gibbons, John. *Code-Mixing and Code Choice: A Hong Kong Case Study.* Clevedon, Avon, England: Multilingual Matters, 1987.
Goffman, Erving. *Frame Analysis: An Essay on the Organization of Experience.* Garden City, N.Y.: Harper and Row, 1974; reprint, Boston: Northeastern University Press, 1986.
———. "On Facework: An Analysis of Ritual Elements in Social Interaction." *Psychiatry* 18 (1955): 213–31.
———. *The Presentation of Self in Everyday Life.* Garden City, N.Y.: Harper and Row, 1959.
Gossen, Gary G. "Chamula Genres of Verbal Behavior." In Bauman and Paredes, *Toward New Perspectives in Folklore,* 151–53.
Green, Richard Firth. *A Crisis of Truth: Literature and Law in Ricardian England.* Philadelphia: University of Pennsylvania Press, 1999.
Gumperz J. J., and Dell Hymes, eds. *Directions in Sociolinguistics: The Ethnography of Communication.* New York: Holt, Rinehart, and Winston, 1972.
Hamnett, I. "Ambiguity, Classification and Change: The Function of Riddles." *Man,* n.s. 2 (1967): 379–92.
Handelman, Don. *Models and Mirrors: Towards an Anthropology of Public Events.* Cambridge: Cambridge University Press, 1990.
Hanson, R. "The Date of St. Patrick." *Bulletin of the John Rylands Library* 61 (1978): 60–77.
———. *St. Patrick: His Origins and Career.* Oxford: Clarendon Press, 1968.
Harris, William. *Ancient Literacy.* Cambridge, Mass.: Harvard University Press, 1989.
Hart, Donn. *Riddles in Filipino Folklore: An Anthropological Analysis.* Syracuse, N.Y.: Syracuse University Press, 1964.
Heller, Monica, ed. *Codeswitching: Anthropological and Sociolinguistic Perspectives.* Berlin: Mouton de Gruyter, 1988.
Hellgardt, Ernst. "Zur Mehrsprachigkeit im Karolingerreich: Bemerkungen aus Anlass von Rosamond McKittericks Buch *The Carolingians and the Written Word.*" *Beiträge zur Geschichte der deutschen Sprache und Literatur* 118 (1996): 1–48.
Hen, Yitzhak, and Matthew Innes, eds. *The Uses of the Past in the Early Middle Ages.* Cambridge: Cambridge University Press, 2000.
Heraughty, Patrick. *Inishmurray: Ancient Monastic Island.* Dublin: O'Brien Press, 1982.
Herbert, Máire. *Iona, Kells, and Derry.* Oxford: Clarendon Press, 1988.
Hexter, Ralph J. *Equivocal Oaths and Ordeals in Medieval Literature.* Cambridge, Mass.: Harvard University Press, 1975.
Hibbitts, Bernard J. "'Coming to Our Senses': Communication and Legal Expression in Performance Cultures." *Emory Law Journal* 41, no. 4 (Fall 1992): 873–960.
Hillgarth, J. N. "Ireland and Spain in the Seventh Century." *Peritia* 3 (1984): 1–16.
Hogan, Edmund. *Onomasticon Goedelicum: Locorum et Tribuum Hiberniae et Scotiae.* 1910. Reprint, Blackrock, Co. Dublin: Four Courts, 1993.
Hollo, Kaarina. "'Do my bidding': Sencha mac Ailella in *Fled Bricrenn* and other Ulster Cycle Tales." In *New Critical Essays on Gaelic Literature,* edited by Michel Byrne and Thomas Owen Clancy. Dublin: Four Courts Press, forthcoming 2006.
Hughes, Kathleen. *The Church in Early Irish Society.* London: Methuen, 1966, reprinted, 1980.
———. *Early Christian Ireland: Introduction to the Sources.* Ithaca, N.Y.: Cornell University Press, 1972.

Humphreys, Sally. "Social Relations on Stage: Witnesses in Classical Athens." *History and Anthropology* 1, part 2 (1985): 313–69.

Hyams, Paul. "Trial by Ordeal: The Key to Proof in the Early Common Law." In *On the Laws and Customs of England: Essays in Honor of Samuel Thorne*, edited by M. Arnold, T. Green, S. Scully, and S. White, 90–126. Chapel Hill: University of North Carolina Press, 1981.

Hymes, Dell. "Breakthrough into Performance." In *Folklore: Performance and Communication*, 13–74.

Hymes, Dell. "The Contribution of Folklore to Sociolinguistic Research." In Bauman and Paredes, *Toward New Perspectives in Folklore*, 42–50.

———. *Ethnography, Linguistics, Narrative Inequality: Toward an Understanding of Voice.* London: Taylor and Francis, 1996.

———. "The Ethnography of Speaking." In *Readings in the Sociology of Language*, edited by J. Fishman, 99–138. The Hague: Mouton, 1968.

———. "Models of the Interaction of Language and Social Life." *Journal of Social Issues* 23, no. 2 (1967): 8–28.

Jaffee, Martin. *Torah in the Mouth: Writing and Oral Tradition in Palestinian Judaism, 200 BCE–400CE.* New York: Oxford University Press, 2001.

Jaski, Bart. "Cú Chuimne, Ruben and the Compilation of the *Collectio Canonum Hibernensis*." *Peritia* 14 (2000): 51–69.

Jenkins, Dafydd, ed. *Celtic Law Papers Introductory to Welsh Medieval Law and Government: Studies Presented to the International Commission for the History of Representative and Parliamentary Institutions* 42. Brussels: Les Éditions de la Librairie Encyclopédique, 1973.

Jones, C., G. Wainwright and E. Yarnold. *The Study of Liturgy.* Oxford: Oxford University Press, 1978.

Jungmann, Josef. *The Mass of the Roman Rite: Its Origins and Development (Missarum Sollemnia).* Trans. Francis Brunner. New York: Benziger, 1951–55.

Kelly, Fergus. *Early Irish Farming.* Early Irish Law Series 4. Dublin: DIAS, 1997.

———. *A Guide to Early Irish Law.* Early Irish Series 3. Dublin: DIAS, 1988.

———. "An Old Irish Tract on Court Procedure." *Peritia* 5 (1986): 74–106.

Kendrick, Laura. "Jongleur as Propagandist: The Ecclesiastical Politics of Marcabru's Poetry." In *Cultures of Power: Lordship, Status, and Process in Twelfth-Century Europe*, edited by Thomas Bisson, 259–86. Philadelphia: University of Pennsylvania Press, 1995.

Kosto, Adam. *Making Agreements in Medieval Catalonia: Power, Order, and the Written Word, 1000–1200.* Cambridge: Cambridge University Press, 2001.

Koziol, Geoffrey. *Begging Pardon and Favor: Ritual and Political Order in Early Medieval France.* Ithaca, N.Y.: Cornell University Press, 1992.

———. "Review Article: The Dangers of Polemic: Is Ritual Still an Interesting Topic of Historical Study?" *Early Medieval Europe* 11 (2002): 367–88.

Kratz, Corinne. *Affecting Performance: Meaning, Movement, and Experience in Okiek Women's Initiation.* Washington, D.C.: Smithsonian, 1994.

Ledwon, Lenora, ed. *Law and Literature: Text and Theory.* New York: Garland, 1995.

Le Roux, Françoise. "La divination chez les Celtes." In *La Divination: Études recueillies par André Caquot et Marcel Leibovici*, edited by André Caquot, vol. I, 233–56. 2 vols. Paris: Presses Universitaires de France, 1968.

Lesses, Rebecca. "The Adjuration of the Sar ha-Panim: 'Performative Utterance' in a Jewish Ritual." In *Ancient Magic and Ritual Power*, edited by M. Meyer and P. Mirecki, 185–206. Leiden: Brill, 1997.

Leyser, Karl. *Rule and Conflict in an Early Medieval Society: Ottonian Saxony.* Oxford: Blackwell, 1979. Paperback ed., 1989.

Little, Lester K. *Benedictine Maledictions: Liturgical Cursing in Romanesque France.* Ithaca, N.Y.: Cornell University Press, 1993.

Lonigan, Paul R. "Shamanism in the Old Irish Tradition." *Éire* 20 (1985): 109–29.

Lord, Albert B. *The Singer of Tales.* Cambridge, Mass.: Harvard University Press, 1960.

Lucas, A. T. "Irish Norse Relations: Time for a Reappraisal." *Journal of the Cork Historical and Archaeological Society* 71 (1966): 62–75.

MacAloon, John J., ed. *Rite, Drama, Festival, Spectacle: Rehearsals toward a Theory of Cultural Performance.* Philadelphia: ISHI, 1984.

Mac Cana, Proinsias. *The Learned Tales of Medieval Ireland.* Dublin: DIAS, 1980.

———. "Notes on the Combination of Prose and Verse in Early Irish Narrative." In Tranter and Tristram, *Early Irish Literature,* 125–47.

———. "On the Use of the Term *retoiric.*" *Celtica* 7 (1966): 65–90.

———. "The Three Languages and the Three Laws." *Studia Celtica* 5 (1970): 62–78.

MacNeill, Eóin. "A Pioneer of Nations." *Studies* 11 (1911): 13–28, 435–46.

Magnou-Nortier, Élisabeth. "Fidélité et féodalité méridionales d'après les serments de fidélité (Xe -début XIIe siècle)." *Annales du Midi* 80 (Oct.–Dec. 1968): 457–84.

———. *Foi et fidélité: Recherches sur l'évolution des liens personnels chez les Francs du VIIe au IXe siècle.* Toulouse: Association des publications de l'Université de Toulouse-Le-Mirail, 1976.

Mallory, J. P., ed. *Aspects of the Táin.* Belfast: December Publications, 1992.

Mallory, J. P., and G. Stockman, eds. *Ulidia: Proceedings of the First International Conference on the Ulster Cycle of Tales, Belfast and Emain Macha, 8–12 April, 1994.* Belfast: December Publications, 1994.

Maranda, E. K. "The Logic of Riddles." In *Structural Analysis of Oral Tradition,* edited by P. Maranda and E. K. Maranda, 189–232. Philadelphia: University of Pennsylvania Press, 1971.

Martin, F. X., and F. J. Byrne, eds. *The Scholar Revolutionary: Eoin MacNeill, 1867–1945 and the Making of the New Ireland.* Shannon: Irish University Press, 1973.

Martin, Richard. The *Language of Heroes: Speech and Performance in the Iliad.* Ithaca, N.Y.: Cornell University Press, 1989.

McCone, Kim. "Dubthach maccu Lugair and A Matter of Life and Death in the Pseudo-Historical Prologue to the *Senchas Már.*" *Peritia* 5 (1986): 1–35.

———. "Zur Frage der Register im frühen Irischen." In Tranter and Tristram, *Early Irish Literature,* 57–97.

———. "Notes on the Text and Authorship of the Early Irish Bee-Laws." *CMCS* 8 (Winter 1984): 45–50.

———. *Pagan Past and Christian Present.* Maynooth Monographs 3. Maynooth: An Sagart, 1990.

———. "A Tale of Two Ditties: Poet and Satirist in *Cath Maige Tuired.*" In *Sages, Saints and Storytellers: Celtic Studies in Honour of Professor James Carney,* edited by D. Ó Corráin, L. Breatnach, and K. McCone, 122–43. Maynooth: An Sagart, 1989.

———. "Werewolves, Cyclops, Díberga, and Fíanna: Juvenile Delinquency in Early Ireland." *CMCS* 12 (1986): 1–22.

McCone, K., and K. Simms. *Progress in Medieval Irish Studies.* Maynooth: An Sagart, 1996.

McKitterick, Rosamond. *The Carolingians and the Written Word.* Cambridge: Cambridge University Press, 1989.

———. "Latin and Romance: An Historian's Perspective." In Wright, *Latin and the Romance Languages,* 130–45.

———. *The Uses of Literacy in Early Mediaeval Europe.* Cambridge: Cambridge University Press, 1990.

McLeod, Neil. "Assault and Attempted Murder in Brehon Law." *Irish Jurist* 33 (1998): 351–91.

———. *Bloodshed and Compensation in Ancient Ireland*. Perth: Centre for Irish Studies, Murdoch University, 1999.

———. "Compensation for Fingers and Teeth in Early Irish Law." *Peritia* 16 (2002): 344–59.

———. "The Concept of Law in Ancient Irish Jurisprudence." *Irish Jurist* 17 (1982): 356–67.

———. "Interpreting Early Irish Law: Status and Currency." Part I: *ZCP* 41 (1986): 46–65; Part II: *ZCP* 42 (1987): 41–115.

———. "Kinship." *Ériu* 52 (2000): 1–22.

———. "The Not-So-Exotic Law of Dian Cécht." In *Origins and Revivals: Proceedings of the First Australian Conference of Celtic Studies*, edited by G. Evans, B. Martin, and J. M. Wooding, 381–99. Sydney: Sydney Series in Celtic Studies 3, 2000.

———. "Property and Honour-Price in the Brehon Law Glosses and Commentaries." *Irish Jurist* 31 (1992): 280–95.

McRae, Shannon. "'A Dream of Purely Burning': Myth, Gender and Modernism." Ph.D. diss. University of Washington, 1999.

Meens, Rob. "The Oldest Manuscript Witness of the *Collectio Canonum Hibernensis*." *Peritia* 14 (2000): 1–19.

Melia, Daniel. "Further Speculation on Marginal .r." *Celtica* 21 (1990): 362–67.

———. "Law and the Shaman Saint." In *Celtic Folklore and Christianity: Studies in Honor of William W. Heist*, edited by Patrick Ford, 113–28. Berkeley and Los Angeles: University of California Press, 1983.

———. "Parallel Versions of 'The Boyhood Deeds of Cuchulainn,'" In *Oral Literature: Seven Essays*, edited by Joseph J. Duggan, 25–40. New York: Barnes and Noble Books, 1975.

———. "Remarks on the Structure and Composition of the Ulster Death Tales." *Studia Hibernica* 17–18 (1977–78): 36–57.

Meroney, Howard. "Studies in Early Irish Satire: I. *"Cis lir fodla áire?"* and II. *Glám Dícind*," *Journal of Celtic Studies* 1 (1950): 199–212 and 212–26.

———. "Studies in Early Irish Satire: III. *Tréfhocal Fócrai*." *Journal of Celtic Studies* 2 (1953): 59–130.

Miller, William Ian. *Bloodtaking and Peacemaking: Feud, Law, and Society in Saga Iceland*. Chicago: University of Chicago Press, 1990.

Monk, Michael A., and John Sheehan. *Early Medieval Munster: Archaeology, History and Society*. Cork: Cork University Press, 1998.

Murphy, William. "Creating the Appearance of Consensus in Mende Political Discourse." *American Anthropologist* 92, no. 1 (1990): 24–41.

Myerhoff, Barbara. *Number Our Days*. New York: Dutton, 1978.

Myers-Scotton, Carol. *Codes and Consequences: Choosing Linguistic Varieties*. New York: Oxford University Press, 1998.

Nagy, Gregory. *Poetry as Performance: Homer and Beyond*. Cambridge: Cambridge University Press, 1996.

Nagy, J. F. *Conversing with Angels and Ancients: Literary Myths of Medieval Ireland*. Ithaca, N.Y.: Cornell University Press, 1997.

———. "Liminality and Knowledge in Irish Tradition." *Studia Celtica* 16–17 (1981–82): 135–43.

———. "Orality in Medieval Irish Literature: An Overview." *Oral Tradition* 1 (1986): 272–301.

———. "Oral Life and Literary Death in Medieval Irish Tradition." *Oral Tradition* 3, no. 3 (1988): 368–80.

———. "Oral Tradition in the *Acallam na Senórach.*" In *Oral Tradition in the Middle Ages*, edited by W. F. H. Nicolaisen, 77–95. Binghamton, N.Y.: Medieval and Renaissance Texts and Studies, 1995.

———. "Representations of Oral Tradition in Medieval Irish Literature." *Language and Communication* 9, no. 2/3 (1989): 143–58.

———. "Shamanic Aspects of the *Bruidhean* Tale." *History of Religions* 20 (1981): 302–22.

———. "Sword as Audacht." In *Celtic Language, Celtic Culture: A Festschrift for Eric P. Hamp*, edited by A. T. E. Matonis and Daniel F. Melia, 131–36. Ford and Bailie, Van Nuys, Calif.: 1990.

———. "The Wisdom of the *Geilt.*" *Éigse* 19 (1982): 44–60.

———. *The Wisdom of the Outlaw: The Boyhood Deeds of Finn in Gaelic Narrative Tradition.* Berkeley and Los Angeles: University of California Press, 1985.

Nelson, Janet L. "Presidential Address: England and the Continent in the Ninth Century: I: Ends and Beginnings." *Transactions of the Royal Historical Society*, 6th ser., XII: 1–21.

Nelson, Janet. "Public *Histories* and Private History in the Work of Nithard." *Speculum* 60 (1985): 251–95.

Ní Chatháin, Próinséas, and Richter, Michael, eds. *Ireland and Christendom: The Bible and the Missions/Irland und die Christenheit: Bibelstudien und Mission.* Stuttgart: Klett-Cotta, 1987.

———, eds. *Ireland and Europe in the Early Middle Ages: Learning and Literature/Irland und Europa im früheren Mittelalter: Bildung und Literatur.* Stuttgart: Klett-Cotta, 1996.

———, eds. *Ireland and Europe in the Early Middle Ages: Texts and Transmission/Irland und Europa im früheren Mittelalter: Texte und Überlieferung.* Dublin: Four Courts, 2002.

———, eds. *Ireland and Europe: The Early Church/Irland und Europa: Die Kirche im Frühmittelalter.* Stuttgart: Klett-Cotta, 1984.

Ní Dhonnchadha, Máirín. "*Caillech* and Other Terms for Veiled Women in Medieval Irish Texts." *Éigse* 28 (1994–95): 71–96.

———. "The Guarantor List of *Cáin Adomnáin*, 697." *Peritia* 1 (1982): 178–215.

———. "The *Lex Innocentium*: Adomnán's Law for Women, Clerics and Youths, 697 A.D." In *Chattel, Servant or Citizen: Women's Status in Church, State and Society*, edited by M. O'Dowd and S. Wichert, 58–69. Belfast: Institute of Irish Studies, The Queen's University of Belfast, 1995.

Noble, Thomas F. X. "Literacy and the Papal Government in Late Antiquity and the Early Middle Ages." In McKitterick, *The Uses of Literacy in Early Mediaeval Europe*, 82–108.

Ó Cathasaigh, Tomás. "Curse and Satire." *Éigse* 21 (1986): 10–15.

———. *The Heroic Biography of Cormac mac Airt.* Dublin: DIAS, 1977.

———. "The Rhetoric of *Fingal Rónáin.*" *Celtica* 17 (1986): 123–44.

———. "*Sírrabad Súaltaim* and the Order of Speaking Among the Ulaid." In *A Companion in Linguistics: A Festschrift for Anders Ahlqvist on the Occasion of His Sixtieth Birthday*, edited by B. Smelik, R. Hofman, C. Hamans, and D. Cram, 80–91. Nijmegen: Stichting Uitgeverij de Keltische Draak, 2005.

Ó Coileáin, Seán. "The Making of *Tromdám Guaire.*" *Ériu* 28 (1977): 32–67.

———. "Oral or Literary? Some Strands of the Argument." *Studia Hibernica* 17/18 (1978): 7–35.

Ó Concheanainn, Tomás. "Notes on *Togail Bruidne Da Derga.*" *Celtica* 17 (1985): 73–90.

Ó Corráin, Donnchadh. "The Early Irish Churches: Some Aspects of Organisation." In *Irish Antiquity*, edited by D. Ó Corráin, 320–41. Cork: Cork University Press, 1981.

———. "Early Irish Hermit Poetry?" In Ó Corráin, Breatnach, and McCone, *Sages, Saints, and Storytellers*, 251–67.

———. "High-kings, Vikings and Other Kings." *Irish Historical Studies* 21 (1979): 283–323.

———. "Historical Need and Literary Narrative." In *Proceedings of the Seventh International Congress of Celtic Studies, Oxford, 1983*, edited by D. Ellis Evans, J. G. Griffith, and E. M. Jope, 141–58. Jesus College, Oxford: Cranham Press, 1986.

———. "Ireland, Wales, Man, and the Hebrides." In *The Oxford Illustrated History of the Vikings*, ed. Peter Sawyer, 83–109. Oxford: Oxford University Press, 1997.

———. "Irish Law and Canon Law." In Ní Chatháin and Richter, *Ireland and Europe: The Church in the Early Middle Ages*, 157–66.

———. "Irish Vernacular Law and the Old Testament." In Ní Chatháin and Richter, *Ireland and Christendom: The Bible and the Missions*, 284–307.

———. "Law and Society—Principles of Classification." In *Geschichte und Kultur der Kelten/History and Culture of the Celts*, edited by Karl Horst Schmidt with Rolf Ködderitzsch, 234–40. Heidelberg: Carl Winter, 1986.

———. "Nationality and Kingship in Pre-Norman Ireland." In *Nationality and the Pursuit of National Independence*, edited by T. W. Moody, 1–35. Belfast: Appletree Press, 1978.

Ó Corráin, Donnchadh, L. Breatnach, and A. Breen. "The Laws of the Irish." *Peritia* 3 (1984): 382–438.

Ó Corráin, Donnchadh, L. Breatnach, and K. McCone, eds. *Sages, Saints, and Storytellers: Celtic Studies in Honour of Professor James Carney*. Maynooth: An Sagart, 1989.

Ó Cróinín, Dáibhí. *Early Medieval Ireland, 400–1200*. London: Longman, 1995.

———. "The Irish as Mediators of Antique Culture on the Continent." In *Science in Western and Eastern Civilization in Carolingian Times*, edited by P. Butzer and D. Lohrmann, 41–52. Basel: Birkhäuser Verlag, 1993.

———. "The Irish Provenance of Bede's Computus." *Peritia* 2 (1983): 229–47.

———. "New Heresy for Old: Pelagianism in Ireland and the Papal Letter of 640." *Speculum* 60 (1985): 505–16.

———. "New Light on Palladius." *Peritia* 5 (1986): 276–83.

O'Faolain, Sean. *The Irish: A Character Study*. Old Greenwich, Conn.: Devin-Adair Publishers, 1949.

O'Leary, Philip. "Jeers and Judgments: Laughter in Early Irish Literature," *CMCS* 22 (Winter 1991): 15–29.

O'Loughlin, Thomas. "Marriage and Sexuality in the *Hibernensis*." *Peritia* 11 (1997): 188–206.

Ong, Walter J. *Orality and Literacy: The Technologizing of the Word*. 1982. Reprint, London: Routledge, 1991.

O'Rahilly, Cecile. "Five Notes: Marginal .r." *Celtica* 10 (1973): 148–50.

Ó Riain, Pádraig. "Boundary Association in Early Irish Society." *Studia Celtica* 7 (1972): 12–29.

———. "The *crech ríg* or "royal prey." *Éigse* 15, no. 1 (1973): 24–30.

O'Sullivan, Anne and William. "A Legal Fragment." *Celtica* 8 (1968): 140–43.

Patterson, Nerys. *Cattle-Lords and Clansmen: Kinship and Rank in Early Ireland*. 2nd ed. South Bend, Ind.: University of Notre Dame Press, 1994.

———. "Honour and Shame in Medieval Welsh Society: A Study of the Role of Burlesque in the Welsh Laws." *Studia Celtica* 16–17 (1981–82): 73–103.

Picard, J. M. *Aquitaine und Ireland in the Middle Ages*. Blackrock, Ireland: Four Courts Press, 1995.

Pierce, Leslie. " 'She Is Trouble . . . and I Will Divorce Her': Orality, Honor, and Representation in the Ottoman Court of 'Aintab.' " In *Women in the Medieval Is-*

lamic World: Power, Patronage, and Piety, edited by Gavin R. G. Hambly, 269–300. New York: Palgrave MacMillan, 1998.

Price, David. "An Archaeology of Text in the Contested Landscape of Early Medieval Munster, c. 750–1167." Doctoral dissertation, University of Wales, Lampeter, 2002.

Pryce, Huw. "Lawbooks and Literacy in Medieval Wales." *Speculum* 75 (2000): 29–67.

———. *Literacy in Medieval Celtic Societies.* Cambridge: Cambridge University Press, 1998.

———. "The Origins and the Medieval Period." In *A Nation and its Books: A History of the Book in Wales,* edited by P. H. Jones and E. Rees, 1–23. Aberystwyth: National Library of Wales, 1998.

Radner, Joan. "'Men Will Die': Poets, Harpers, and Women in Early Irish Literature." In *Celtic Language, Celtic Culture: A Festschrift for Eric P. Hamp,* edited by A. T. E. Matonis and Daniel F. Melia, 172–86. Van Nuys, Calif.: Ford and Bailie Press, 1990.

Radding, C. F. *The Origins of Medieval Jurisprudence: Pavia and Bologna, 850–1150.* New Haven, Conn.: Yale University Press, 1988.

Radner, Joan Newlon. "The Threefold Death in Celtic Tradition." In Ford, *Celtic Folklore and Christianity,* 180–99.

Randolph, Mary Claire. "Female Satirists of Ancient Ireland." *Southern Folklore Quarterly* 6, no. 2 (June, 1942): 75–87.

———. "Rat Satires and the Pied Piper of Hamelin Legend." *Southern Folklore Quarterly* 5, no. 2 (June 1941): 81–100.

Reynolds, Susan. *Kingdoms and Communities in Western Europe, 900–1300.* 2nd ed. Oxford: Clarendon Press, 1996.

Richter, Michael. "Dating the Irish Synods in the *Collectio Canonum Hibernensis.*" *Peritia* 14 (2000): 70–84.

———. *The Formation of the Medieval West: Studies in the Oral Culture of the Barbarians.* Dublin: Four Courts, 1994.

———. *Studies in Medieval Language and Literature.* Dublin: Four Courts, 1995.

Riddles and Riddling. Special issue of the Journal of American Folklore 89 (April–June 1976).

Robinson, F.N. "Notes on the Irish Practice of Fasting as a Means of Distraint." In *Putnam Anniversary Volume: Anthropological Essays Presented to Frederic Ward Putnam in Honor of his Seventieth Birthday, April 16, 1909, by His Friends and Associates,* edited by Franz Boas et al., 567–83. New York: G. E. Stechert, 1909.

Rollo-Koster, Joëlle. *Medieval and Early Modern Ritual: Formalized Behavior in Europe, China and Japan.* Leiden: Brill, 2002.

Rosenwein, Barbara. *Rhinoceros Bound: Cluny in the Tenth Century, 909–1049.* Philadelphia: University of Pennsylvania Press, 1982.

Rosenwein, Barbara. *To Be the Neighbor of Saint Peter: The Social Meaning of Cluny's Property, 909–1049.* Ithaca, N.Y.: Cornell University Press, 1989.

———, ed. *Anger's Past: The Social Uses of an Emotion in the Middle Ages.* Ithaca, N.Y.: Cornell University Press, 1998.

Ryan, John. "The Convention of Druim Ceat." *Journal of the Royal Society of Antiquaries of Ireland* 76 (1946): 35–55.

Sahlins, Marshall. *Islands of History.* Chicago: University of Chicago Press, 1985.

Sayers, William. "Concepts of Eloquence in '*Tochmarc Emire.*'" *Studia Celtica* 26–27 (1991–92): 125–54.

———. "Games, Sport, and Para-Military Exercise in Early Ireland." *Aethlon: Journal of Sport Literature* 10, no. 1 (1992): 105–23.

Schaller, Barry. *A Vision of American Law: Judging Law, Literature, and the Stories We Tell.* Westport, Conn.: Praeger, 1997.

Schechner, Richard. *Between Theater and Anthropology*. Philadelphia: University of Pennsylvania Press, 1985.

———. *Essays on Performance Theory, 1970–1976*. New York: Drama Book Specialists, 1977.

———. "Performance and the Social Sciences." *Drama Review* 17 (1973): 5–36.

Schmidt-Wiegand, Ruth. "Eid und Gelöbnis, Formel und Formular im mittelalterlichen Recht." In Classen, *Recht und Schrift im Mittelalter*, 55–90.

———. "Gebärdensprache im mittelalterlichen Recht." *Frühmittelalterliche Studien* 16 (1982): 363–79.

Schmitt, Jean-Claude. *La raison des gestes dans l'Occident medieval*. Paris: Gallimard, 1990.

Scott, Joan Wallach. "Gender: A Useful Category of Historical Analysis." In *Gender and the Politics of History*, edited by Joan Scott, 28–50. New York: Columbia University Press, 1988.

Scowcroft, R. Mark. "Abstract Narrative in Ireland." *Ériu* 46 (1995): 121–58.

Sharpe, Richard. "Dispute Settlement in Medieval Ireland." In Davies and Fouracre, *Settlement of Disputes*, 169–89.

———. "Hiberno-Latin *laicus*, Irish *láech* and the Devil's Men." *Ériu* 30 (1979): 75–92.

———. "Some Problems Concerning the Organization of the Church in Early Medieval Ireland." *Peritia* 3 (1984): 230–70.

———. "St. Patrick and the See of Armagh." *CMCS* 4 (1982): 33–59.

Sherzer, Joel. *Kuna Ways of Speaking: An Ethnographic Perspective*. Austin: University of Texas Press, 1983.

Sheehy, M. P. "The *Collectio Canonum Hibernensis*: A Celtic Phenomenon." In *Die Iren und Europa im früheren Mittelalter*, edited by H. Löwe, 525–35. Stuttgart: Klett-Cotta, 1982.

———. "Influences of Ancient Irish Law on the *Collectio Canonum Hibernensis*." In *Proceedings of the Third International Congress of Medieval Canon Law, Strasbourg, 3–6 September 1968*, edited by S. Kuttner, 31–41. Monumenta Iuris Canonici, Ser. C, Subsidia 4. Vatican City, 1971.

Simms, K. *From Kings to Warlords: The Changing Political Structure of Gaelic Ireland in the Later Middle Ages*. Woodbridge, Suffolk: Boydell and Brewer, 1987.

Sims-Williams, Patrick. "Celtomania and Celtoscepticism." *CMCS* 36 (Winter 1998): 1–35.

Sjöblom, Tom. "On the Threshold: The Sacredness of Borders in Early Irish Literature." In Mallory and Stockman, *Ulidia*, 159–64.

Smith, Peter. "*Aimirgein Glúngel Tuir Tend*: A Middle-Irish Poem on the Authors and Laws of Ireland." *Peritia* 8 (1994): 120–50.

———. "Early Irish Historical Verse: The Evolution of a Genre." In Ní Chatháin and Richter, *Ireland and Europe in the Early Middle Ages*, 326–41.

Smith, Philip. "Review of *Ritual Theory, Ritual Practice*, by Catherine Bell." *American Journal of Sociology* 98, no. 1 (1992): 420–22.

Smith, R. "The *Cach* Formulas in the Irish Laws." *ZCP* 20 (1936): 262–77.

———. "Fithal and Flann Fína." *Revue Celtique* 47 (1930): 30–38.

———. "Further Light on the *Finnsruth Fithail*." *Revue Celtique* 48 (1931): 325–31.

Smyth, A. P. *Scandinavian York and Dublin*. 2 vols. Dublin: Templekieran, 1975, 1979.

Smyth, Alfred P. "The Effect of Scandinavian Raiders on the English and Irish Churches: A Preliminary Reassessment." In *Britain and Ireland 900–1300: Insular Responses to Medieval European Change*, edited by Brendan Smith, 1–38. Cambridge: Cambridge University Press, 1999.

Somerville, Edith Oenone, and Martin Ross. *Experiences of an Irish R.M. and Further Experiences of an Irish R.M.* London: J. M. Dent and Sons, and New York: E. P. Dutton, 1944.

Stacey, Robin Chapman. "Law and Literature in Medieval Ireland and Wales." In *Medieval Celtic Literature and Society*, edited by Helen Fulton, 65–82. Dublin: Four Courts Press, 2005.

———. "Law and Memory in Early Mediaeval Ireland." *Journal of Celtic Studies* 4 (2004): 43–69.

———. *The Road to Judgment: From Custom to Court in Medieval Ireland and Wales.* Philadelphia: University of Pennsylvania Press, 1994.

———. "Satire and Its Socio-Legal Rôle." In *Celtic Culture: A Historical Encyclopedia*, edited by John T. Koch, vol. 4, 1560–66. 5 vols. Santa Barbara, Calif.: ABC-CLIO, 2006.

———. "Speaking in Riddles." In Ní Chatháin and Richter, *Ireland and Europe in the Early Middle Ages*, 243–48.

———. "Texts and Society." In *After Rome*, edited by T. M. Charles-Edwards, 220–57. Oxford: Oxford University Press, 2003.

———. "Ties That Bind: Immunities in Irish and Welsh Law." *CMCS* 20 (Winter 1990): 39–60.

Stevenson, Jane. "The Beginnings of Literacy in Ireland." *Proceedings of the Royal Irish Academy* 89 C (1989): 127–65.

———. "Literacy and Orality in Early Medieval Ireland." In *Cultural Identity and Cultural Integration: Ireland and Europe in the Early Middle Ages*, edited by D. Edel, 11–22. Blackrock, Co. Dublin: Irish Academic Press, 1995.

———. "Literacy in Ireland: The Evidence of the Patrick Dossier in the Book of Armagh." In *The Uses of Literacy in Early Mediaeval Europe*, edited by Rosamond McKitterick, 11–35. Cambridge: Cambridge University Press, 1990.

Stock, Brian. *The Implications of Literacy: Written Language and Models of Interpretation in the Eleventh and Twelfth Centuries.* Princeton, N.J.: Princeton University Press, 1983.

Sullivan, Richard. "The Carolingian Age: Reflections on Its Place in the History of the Middle Ages." *Speculum* 64 (1989): 267–306.

Symes, Carol. "The Appearance of Early Vernacular Plays: Forms, Functions, and the Future of Medieval Theater." *Speculum* 77, no. 3 (July 2002): 778–831.

Tedlock, D. *The Spoken Word and the Work of Interpretation.* Philadelphia: University of Pennsylvania Press, 1983.

Theuws, Frans, and Janet Nelson. *Rituals of Power from Late Antiquity to the Early Middle Ages.* Leiden: Brill, 2000.

Thurneysen, R. "Allerlei Keltisches." *ZCP* 16 (1927): 267–78.

———. "Allerlei Nachträge." *ZCP* 19 (1933): 125–33.

———. "Aus dem irischen Recht I." [1. Das Unfrei-Lehen.] *ZCP* 14 (1923): 335–94.

———. "Aus dem irischen Recht II." [2. Das Frei-Lehen; 3. Das Fasten beim Pfändungsverfahren.] *ZCP* 15 (1925): 238–96.

———. "Aus dem irischen Recht III." [4. Die Falschen Urteilssprüche Caratnia's; 5. Zur Überlieferung und zur Ausgabe der Texte über das Unfrei-Lehen und das Frei-Lehen.] *ZCP* 15 (1925): 302–76.

———. "Aus dem irischen Recht IV." [6. Zu den bisherigen Ausgaben der irischen Rechtstexte.] *ZCP* 16 (1927): 167–230.

———. "Aus dem irischen Recht V." [7. Zu *Gúbretha Caradniad*; 8. Zum ursprünglichen Umfang das *Senchas Már*; 9. Zu der Etymologie von irisch *ráth* "Bürgschaft" und zu der irischen Kanonensammlung und den Triaden; 10. Nachträge zur *Bürgschaft*.] *ZCP* 18 (1930): 353–408.

———. *Die Bürgschaft im irischen Recht. Abhandlungen der preussischen Akademie der Wissenschaften* 2. Phil.-Hist. Klasse. Jahrgang 1928. Berlin: Verlag der preussischen Akademie der Wissenschaften, 1928.

———. "Celtic Law." In Jenkins, *Celtic Law Papers*, 51–70.

———. *Cóic Conara Fugill: Die fünf Wege zum Urteil. Abhandlungen der preussischen Akademie der Wissenschaften* 2. Phil.-Hist. Klasse. Jahrgang 1925. Berlin: Verlag der preussischen Akademie der Wissenschaften, 1926.

———. "Zur irischen Kanonensammlung." *ZCP* 6 (1907–8): 1–5.

———. *Irisches Recht* [1. *Díre*. Ein altirischer Rechtstext; 2. Zu den unteren Ständen in Irland]. *Abhandlungen der preussischen Akademie der Wissenschaften* 2. Phil.-Hist. Klasse. Jahrgang 1931. Berlin: Verlag der preussischen Akademie der Wissenschaften, 1931.

———. "Nachträge zur Bürgschaft." *ZCP* 18 (1930): 375–408.

———. "Nachträgliches." *ZCP* 16 (1927): 406–10.

Thurneysen, R., D. A. Binchy, et al., eds. *Studies in Early Irish Law.* Dublin: Royal Irish Academy, 1936.

Tranter, S., and H. L. C. Tristram, eds. *Early Irish Literature—Media and Communication/Mündlichkeit und Schriftlichkeit in der frühen irischen Literatur.* Tübingen: Gunter Narr Verlag, 1989.

Tristram, Hildegard. "Zur Frage der roscada im Irischen." In Tristram, *Metrik und Medienwechsel,* 197–206.

———, ed. *Metrik und Medienwechsel/Metrics and Media.* Tübingen: Gunter Narr, 1991.

Turner, Victor. *Drama, Fields and Metaphors.* Ithaca, N.Y.: Cornell University Press, 1974.

———. *From Ritual to Theatre: The Human Seriousness of Play.* New York: Performing Arts Publications, 1982.

———. "Liminality and the Performative Genres." In MacAloon, *Rite, Drama, Festival, Spectacle,* 19–41.

———. *The Ritual Process: Structure and Anti-Structure.* Chicago: University of Chicago Press, 1969.

Tymoczko, Maria. "Inversions, Subversions, Reversions: The Form of Early Irish Narrative." In *Text und Zeittiefe,* edited by Hildegard Tristram, 71–85. Tübingen: Gunter Narr Verlag, 1993.

———. "The Metonymics of Translating Marginalized Texts." *Comparative Literature* 47, no. 1 (Winter 1995): 11–24.

———. "A Poetry of Masks: The Poet's Persona in Early Celtic Poetry." In *A Celtic Florilegium: Studies in Memory of Brendan O Hehir,* edited by Kathryn A. Klar, Eve E. Sweetser, and Claire Thomas, 187–209. Lawrence, Mass.: Celtic Studies Publications, 1996.

Wagner, Heinrich. "A Syntactical Feature of Archaic Old Irish Poetry." *ZCP* 39 (1982): 78–82.

Ward, Ian. *Law and Literature: Possibilities and Perspectives.* Cambridge: Cambridge University Press, 1996.

Warren, F. E. *Liturgy and Ritual of the Celtic Church.* Oxford: Clarendon Press, 1881. Reprinted with introduction by Jane Stevenson, Woodbridge, Suffolk: Boydell Press, 1987.

Watkins, Calvert. "Indo-European Metrics and Archaic Irish Verse." *Celtica* 6 (1963): 194–249.

———. *"In essar dam do á?"* in "Varia III." *Ériu* 29 (1978): 155–65.

———. "Language of Gods and Language of Men: Remarks on Some Indo-European Metalinguistic Traditions." In *Myth and Law among the Indo-Europeans: Studies in Indo-European Comparative Mythology,* edited by Jaan Puhvel. Berkeley and Los Angeles: University of California Press, 1970.

White, Stephen D. *Custom, Kinship, and Gifts to Saints: The* Laudatio Parentum *in Western France, 1050–1150.* Chapel Hill: University of North Carolina Press, 1988.

Whitelock, D., McKitterick, R. and Dumville, D., eds. *Ireland in Early Mediaeval Europe: Studies in Memory of Kathleen Hughes*. Cambridge: Cambridge University Press, 1982.

Wiley, Dan. "The Maledictory Psalms." *Peritia* 15 (2001): 261–79.

Wormald, Patrick. "Bede, *Bretwaldas* and the Origins of the *Gens Anglorum*." In *Ideal and Reality in Frankish and Anglo-Saxon Society*, edited by P. Wormald, D. Bullough and R. Collins, 99–129. Oxford: Blackwell, 1993.

———. "Celtic and Anglo-Saxon Kingship: Some Further Thoughts." In *Sources of Anglo-Saxon Culture*, edited by P. Szarmach with V. Oggins, 151–83. Kalamazoo, Mich.: Medieval Institute Publications, Western Michigan University, 1986.

———. *Legal Culture in the Early Medieval West: Law as Text, Image and Experience*. Rio Grande, Ohio: Hambledon Press, 1999.

———. "*Lex Scripta* and *Verbum Regis*: Legislation and Germanic Kingship, from Euric to Cnut." In *Early Medieval Kingship*, edited P. H. Sawyer and I. N. Wood, 105–38. 1977. Reprint, Leeds: School of History, University of Leeds, 1979.

———. "The Uses of Literacy in Anglo-Saxon England and Its Neighbours." *Transactions of the Royal Historical Society* 5th series, 27 (1977): 95–114.

Wright, Roger. *Early Ibero-Romance: Twenty-one Studies on Language and Texts from the Iberian Peninsula between the Roman Empire and the Thirteenth Century*. Newark, Del.: Juan de la Cuesta, 1994.

———. *Late Latin and Early Romance in Spain and Carolingian France*. Liverpool: Cairns, 1982.

———, ed. *Latin and the Romance Languages in the Early Middle Ages*. London: Routledge, 1991.

Zimmermann, M. "Aux origines de la Catalogne féodale: les serments non datés du règne de Ramon Berenguer 1er." In *La formació i expansió del feudalisme català: Actes del col·loqui organitzat pel Col·legi universitari de Girona (8–11 de gener de 1985): Homenatge a Santiago Sobrequés i Vidal*, edited by Jaume Portella i Comas, 109–51. Girona: Col·legi Universitari de Girona, Universitat Autonoma de Barcelona, 1985.

Index

265 n.218; and prophecy, 82–89, 93,
226–27; in recent scholarship, 2–5, 8–9,
15–16, 20, 48, 191, 228–29; relative emphasis on within different legal schools, 172,
175–76, 214–17; and risk, 2–3, 13, 89,
227–34, 242–54, 248–49, 279 nn. 205, 208;
and ritual, 3–6, 26–27, 90, 228–34, 248–49,
253 n.2, 255 n.3, 258 n.62, 309 n.5, 310 n.8;
and speech and language, 1–6. See also
fásach; forus; language; *roscad*
physicians, 164, 181, 193, 261 n.125. *See also*
doctors
piety (filial), 32, 50, 66, 256 n.38, 259 n.106,
269 n.76. *See also* cold son; *gor*
pigs, 71–73, 81, 88, 154–55, 272 nn.113–14,
277 nn. 176, 179
place-name tales, 6. See also *dindsenchas*
placita, 60, 92, 176
plain prose, 121, 183–84, 187–89, 192–93, 197,
199, 217
pleas, pleading: authority of, 89; in court,
60–61, 64–67, 268 n.67, 274–75 n.134, 275
n.138; language of, 74–75, 131–33, 270–71
n.94, 272 n.108, 273–74 n.129, 289 n.164;
and poets, 207
pledges, 181. *See also* gages
poets, poetry, 6, 18, 93, 249, 256 n.32, 275
n.147, 280 n.8; appointment of, 59–60, 96;
attitudes toward, 106–9, 157–71, 208–13,
228, 284 n.73; and breaths, 76–77; and
Bretha Nemed school, 58, 112, 173, 182–86,
197–217, 305–6 n.192; female, 108, 157–58;
and gages, 263 n.187; and paganism, 82–85,
87, 135, 159–60; and politics in Languedoc,
234, 241–43; and prophecy, 57, 82–89, 159,
226, 269–70 n.82, 277 n.179; ranks of, 58,
108–9, 116–17, 138, 157–62, 205–13, 284
n.73, 295 n.120, 300 n.84, 306 nn. 206, 221,
307 n.236; role in judgment and law, 5, 27,
36–40, 55–60, 63, 67–82, 84–85, 88, 91–93,
102, 107–8, 112–13, 138, 141–42, 146,
153–71, 185, 188, 192–95, 198–203, 216,
226–27, 273 n.123, 274 n.131, 274–75
n.134, 285 n.98, 305 n.183; in *Senchas Már*
lawbook, 195, 214–15; ties with church, 83,
106–7, 116–17, 135, 141, 157–62, 198,
202–13, 216–17, 267 n.34, 274 n.131, 305
n.183, 305–6 n.192; training of, 82–83. *See
also* Dubthach; Patrick; satire
politics, and art, 5–6, 13. *See also* aesthetics
polygyny, 33, 222, 309 n.295
populus Christianus, 245

praise, 75, 100, 106–18, 154, 164, 186, 199,
283 n.65
prescriptive right. See *rudrad*
priests, 27–28, 40, 205. *See also* church; clerics
prophecy: and authority, 57, 82–89, 100, 204,
226–27; and Brigit, 143; and Dubthach,
83–85, 141–42, 163–70, 204; and law,
82–89; and poetry, 82–85; as source of specialist knowledge, 82–89. *See also* Brigit;
Dubthach; Patrick; "Pseudo-Historical Prologue to the *Senchas Már*"
prostitutes, 271 nn.100–102
Provençal, 239
Proverbs, 186, 300 n.88
psalms of malediction, 117. *See also* curses
"Pseudo-Historical Prologue to the *Senchas Már*,"
74, 214–15; and *Bretha Nemed* tradition, 214,
217; and origins of written law, 55, 84–85,
90–91, 141–42, 163–65, 296 n.141; and
reapportioning of speech, 136, 163–71. *See
also* Dubthach; Patrick; *Senchas Már*
puns, 114
purity (*idnae*), 102, 160, 162, 185, 204–9, 217,
305–6 n.192, 306 n.203

queen, 81, 88

Radner, Joan, 152
Rahab the harlot, 218
rank. *See* status
rape, 88, 144
rat rhyming, 111
rata (borrowed into Latin from Irish *ráth*), 221
ráth ("paying surety"): *aitire* as type of, 301
n.106; in contract, 119, 123–24, 126, 140,
260 n.124, 286–87 n.124, 288 nn. 146, 153,
290 n.282; in court, 63; in paternity case,
271 n.99
recht litre. See law, written
rechtaire ("steward"), 66, 76, 269 n.77
rechtge Adamnáin, 308 n.272. See *Cáin Adamnáin*
reflexivity, 128
retoiric, 99. See also *rosc; roscad*
revenge, 273 n.117
ríar ("authority"), 201–3. See also *Uraicecht na
Ríar*
Richard Lionheart, 242
Richter, Michael, 178
riddles, 151–54, 265 n.218, 290 n.12
ritual: authority of, 5, 48–52, 98, 124, 231–31,
264 nn.212–13, 311 n.32; and the body,
40–43; contractual, 120, 122–23; and dis-

Acknowledgments

This book has been on the boil for a long, long time—so long, in fact, that one of my most pressing tasks in revising it was to make sure that references made to "this century" pertained in fact to, well, *this* century. Obviously the rewards of coming finally to the end of such a long-term project are many and great. For me, however, one of the most pleasurable is the opportunity to look back and reflect upon the many good friends I have worked with along the way. I have been most fortunate in the assistance I have received with this book. Thomas Charles-Edwards was my earliest guide through the dense tangled underbrush of early Irish law and has remained my keenest critic ever since; without his wisdom, unstinting hospitality, and unselfish support, this book would never have been completed. He, Patrick Geary, Fergus Kelly, Dennis King, and Adam Kosto read significant portions of this work in draft form and saved me from innumerable errors; I am extremely grateful to them for their patience and insight, and I gladly exculpate them from the blunders that remain. Other scholars also have given generously of their time and expertise: Margaret Bent, Liam Breatnach, Mary Carruthers, Joy Connolly, Patrick Ford, Barbara Fuchs, Ralph Hexter, Stephen Jaeger, Kathryn Klar, John Koch, Geoffrey Koziol, Jeremy Lowe, Charlie MacQuarrie, Catherine McKenna, Daniel Melia, Joseph Falaky Nagy, Donnchadh Ó Corráin, Dáibhí Ó Cróinín, William Rich, Edgar Slotkin, Robert Stacey, Eve Sweetser, Carol Thomas, Eugene Vance, Daniel Waugh, and the late Patrick Wormald. Still others have provided me with copies of their unpublished work or called my attention to resources of which I had previously been unaware: Robert Bartlett, Paul Brand, James Campbell, Kaarina Hollo, Neil McLeod, Shannon McRae, Tomás Ó Cathasaigh, David Price, William Sayers, and Dan Wiley. Graduate students Russell Black, Elizabeth Campbell, Dustin Clark, Tom Cramer, Joe Creamer, Jennifer McKnight Dean, Liz Johnson, Laura Erickson, and Ethan Spanier helped me think through the intricate twists and turns of my arguments. My work is considerably richer for the input of all of these scholars; needless to say, such errors as remain are my own responsibility.

As anyone long in the business will know, research and writing cost money—lots of it—and I have been fortunate to have received financial assistance from a variety of institutions and sources. I am particularly grateful to the John Simon Guggenheim Memorial Foundation and to the American Council of Learned Societies, whose generous support provided me with the most important gift of all: time to read and to think. The Guggenheim Foundation also provided generous financial assistance with the publication of this book, for which again I am very grateful. My time as a Visiting Fellow at All Souls College, Oxford, was exceptionally pleasant and rewarding. Howard and Frances Keller have given generously over the years to the History Department at the University of Washington, and I have drawn many times during the course of this project on the funds they have so kindly provided. The Humanities Center at the University of Washington provided me with financial and intellectual support during an important moment in the life of this book. ABC-CLIO and Four Courts Press allowed me to reprint in this book material from previously published works, for which permission I am very grateful. My interactions with the University of Pennsylvania Press have been unfailingly efficient and productive.

A few personal notes. This past year saw the deaths of two brilliant historians, both at the height of their intellectual powers and both persons whose example and friendship meant a great deal to me. Rees Davies restored Wales, Ireland, and Scotland to their rightful place and, in so doing, redefined "British" history forever. His clarity and wit are greatly missed by this "manuscript S" historian. Patrick Wormald was one of the most imaginative minds of his generation. Five minutes in his company would enlarge and enrich any project and invariably left one thinking that whatever one was working on was really quite the most interesting thing in the world. I am grateful to have known them both, and I acknowledge my debt to them by the dedication.

And finally, to my family and friends: my love and gratitude to you all. I cannot imagine having written this book without Bob's steady love and support; Will's outrageous imitations of Leif, Nam, and the fiberglass banana; Anna's turtle songs, home design shows, and boisterous giggles; Dad's willingness to try anything, even dogsledding and sweetbreads; Wes's sagacity in the face of wooden spoons, chocolate museums, and being only one year younger; Rosemarie's devotion to chocolate-enhanced European travel; Kathy's Sunday morning coffees and downtown Christmas shopping; Pat and Joan's musical laughter and Scotties; and Z's cowgirl cheeses, bodacious red wines, and exquisitely inlaid shower at the "House of Girls." For me, these are the people and things that make it all worthwhile.